A Heron Books Collection

HISTORY OF ENGLAND

LORD MACAULAY

HISTORY OF ENGLAND

To the Death of William III

VOL. I

Introduction by A.G. Dickens

HERON BOOKS

INTRODUCTION

Leslie Stephen observed of Macaulay's historical characters that, when not wholly black or wholly white, they are bundles of violently contrasting qualities. James I is a witty, learned scholar, yet in action "a nervous drivelling idiot"; Boswell the greatest of biographers and the meanest of men; Francis Bacon the "soaring angel" and the "creeping snake"; Dundee a distinguished soldier, but "rapacious and profane, of violent temper and of obdurate heart". In considering Macaulay the historian, one finds it hard to avoid falling into this same infectious idiom. Everywhere he displays a fine precision and vigour of style, an easy flow of thought, sentences which never need to be read twice, an immense range of knowledge, a capacity for arranging complex materials into seemingly inevitable patterns. At the same time he exudes some powerful irritants: the outrageous Whiggism which has resulted in a few real injustices, the cocksure dogmatism, the desire to judge rather than to understand, the complacency which contrasts the poverty of former times with the Utopia of early Victorian England.

No historian can wholly detach himself from his local values, yet Macaulay seldom if ever made the attempt, for in those values he beheld pinnacles of human progress. Most historians of our own day have grown up in a different tradition, one which owes more to that other great master of the nineteenth century, Leopold von Ranke. With Ranke we at least aspire to see every age "as it really was", to see the dead as persons in their own right rather than as stepping-stones to our noble selves. We lack enthusiasm for moral judgments, concentrate warily on the sifting of evidence, and strive to exclude current political passions from our historical thinking. These ideals are doubtless conducive to truth and justice. Yet in practice, divorced from Ranke's own breadth of view, have they not encouraged specialists to write merely for other specialists, to rest content with erudite *little articles on technical problems, to cultivate a spiritual pride which shirks great tasks for fear of making mistakes?*

If we believe the reading of history will educate and entertain all sorts and conditions of men, we shall not ridicule Macaulay's famous hope that this History of England *would "for a few days supersede the last fashionable novel on the tables of young ladies". And while in fact he made history popular throughout literate Victorian society, this was by no means the full measure of his success, for in several respects he was an originator and a trend-setter. The most widely-read British historians of our own country are those who, like G. M. Trevelyan, A. L. Rowse, and Miss Wedgwood, have by no means despised Macaulay's broad, literary approach, but have sought to combine it with the more scientific methods of the rival tradition.*

The History of England *forms the crowning achievement of a life divided between politics and letters. Macaulay began to plan it in 1838, the year before he resigned his lucrative seat on the Supreme Council of India and returned to England. Alongside its early stages he wrote the last of those essays which since 1825 had been making the fortunes of the* Edinburgh Review. *Though he represented Edinburgh in Parliament (1839-1847 and 1852-1856) and even served for a time (1839-1841) as Secretary at War, the* History *remained his major concern until his death in December 1859. While Ranke laboured on to the age of ninety, Macaulay died in his sixtieth year, his original project by no means completed. In 1838 he had intended to traverse the long period from the Restoration to the death of George IV, but as the years passed he became ever more aware of the immensity of the source-materials. He disciplined himself to produce a daily quota, but during the fifties indifferent health began to sap his hitherto amazing energies. When the end came he had just reached the death of William III, the last passages being deciphered from his hieroglyphics by his sister Lady Trevelyan. By then the work had already become a best-seller*, contributing to maintain his Kensington bachelor-household, with its four manservants, smart carriages and magnificent garden.*

The first three chapters of the History *furnish an introduction to the detailed narrative, which covers the history of only two reigns. In every aspect of this momentous period Macaulay steeped his mind. He disdained no source of information, and at a time when the feat was easier than today, he strove to visualise and describe every aspect of human life in late Stuart Britain. Though his Tory predecessor Hume had proclaimed that history should embrace a whole people, not merely its politics, Macaulay was the first British historian to embody this ideal. His command of the literary sources became superb. For social conditions and economic grievances he exploited the plays of Shadwell and Farquhar, the poems of Dryden, the*

---

* Vols. 1 and 2 (ch. 1-10) appeared in 1848 ; vols. 3 and 4 (ch. 11-22) in 1855 ; vol. 5 (ch. 23-25) early in 1861. Many later editions followed.

*popular ballads and broadsides, even the farces performed at
Bartholomew Fair. He visited the main places on which he was
writing: he applied local knowledge to national history in a
manner prophetic of much recent historiography. On the other
hand he did not neglect the more conventional theme of high
politics. He understood the untrustworthy character of memoirs,
including those of the Whig Bishop Burnet, whose undoctored
original manuscript he rightly preferred to the printed edition.
For the reign of James II he was fortunate to have Sir James
Mackintosh's vast collection of transcripts from despatches,
private correspondence and newsletters. The reign of William III
proved a relatively untrodden field, and here Macaulay did his
most valuable pioneering.*

*A historian's achievement lies in the advances he makes upon
his predecessors, and the giants of the nineteenth century are too
often castigated by the ungrateful dwarfs who stand upon their
shoulders. Macaulay's mistakes must be seen alongside the great
scale of his work and of the problems involved in its execution.
Those mistakes sprang less from his prejudices than from his
unavoidable lack of the scholarly aids which we now take as a
matter of course. How dare anyone have tackled an assignment
of this complexity before the Public Record Office came into
being, before the State Papers were calendared, before the*
Dictionary of National Biography *had been conceived, before
the Historical Manuscripts Commission began issuing its
voluminous reports? Fifty years ago, but already enjoying most
of these aids, Sir Charles Firth delivered lectures of unrivalled
learning which were later (1938) published as* A Commentary
on Macaulay's History of England. *This volume lists a good
many errors and misconceptions, yet properly understood it
forms a tribute quite as much as a criticism. How very few
historians have received this flattering degree of attention from
a great successor so long afterwards!*

*Macaulay's habit of overstatement and lurid antithesis has
clear links with his political experience. In the Commons he
was a renowned orator and the seats rapidly filled when word
spread round the lobbies that he had risen to speak. Those
modern readers who find themselves less moved by his printed
oratorical flights should remember that the same politician's
background also made possible a profounder and more durable
brilliance—that with which he analyses historical situations as
if he were personally confronting them. Our author was also a
voracious reader of plays and of Milton's dramatic poetry.
Lacking a great contemporary drama, the Victorians wanted a
strong dramatic as well as a strong didactic element in their
novels and histories. This combination Macaulay gave them,
especially in the clash between William III and James II,
which has been aptly compared with Milton's war between
God and Satan. Yet the facts remain: the real William was a
great leader and the real James a figure calculated to make
Whigs of us all. Macaulay has also been reproved for over-
dramatising Marlborough's treasonable correspondence with*

James, yet since then the episode may have been a trifle white-washed by Churchillian hero-worship. And had Macaulay lived to chronicle Blenheim, he would doubtless have balanced his denunciations by a handsome tribute.

Concerning a few of the less famous people, Macaulay's prejudices seem more likely to mislead. His whole account of the Navy after the Revolution is distorted by his hatred for Torrington, whose administration and conduct at sea have both been vindicated by specialist naval historians. In the case of William Penn, the suggestions of hypocrisy, greed and complicity with James lack even a decent substratum of truth. Almost as soon as uttered they were refuted by W. E. Forster and should have been retracted. Again, the crimes attributed to Dundee are mainly fables invented by Scottish Whigs of the next generation. Of the five specific instances given, it has been shown that Dundee had no share in three, while in the fourth he actually protested against the execution of the victim and tried to save his life. Dundee did not in fact personally shoot the fifth victim John Brown; more important, Brown had been sentenced not for religious nonconformity but for concealing arms and for refusing to take an oath not to rebel. Yet in relation to Scotland and Ireland, Macaulay's mistakes must be judged the more venial, since in his day not a single good history of either country had been written.

The above are by no means the only passages demanding correction and modification. Burnet had claimed that 600 rebels were hanged as a result of the Bloody Assizes. And although Macaulay reduces this figure to 320, the gaol-books (since discovered) yield a probable total of less than 150. The transportations were also far less numerous than here supposed. Again, in the magnificent and justly famous third chapter, he exaggerates the ignorance and servility of the parish clergy, always a heterogeneous body unamenable to such vivid generalisation. He also overstresses the illiterate character of the gentry, many of whom bought books and were well-read. He speaks of their "rude paternal justice", yet in fact their work in the Quarter Sessions formed the basis of a very advanced system of local government. The plain facts are that the rural gentry and clergy were the twin pillars of Toryism, and that Macaulay prefabricated their images without reflecting on the whole of the available evidence.

On the appearance of the later volumes, J. M. Kemble praised their English history but attacked as superficial the presentation of William's foreign policy. In his view Macaulay had disparaged the German members of the coalition in order to glorify William. Macaulay read Kemble's article, and in his diary he grants that continental politics had been too lightly treated. He then adds, "but was this wrong?... I am writing a history of England". Yet even his hero may be somewhat diminished when viewed in this English perspective. As we now see William, he was much less of an adopted Englishman, much more a continental politician, eager to place the resources of Britain

*behind the great international resistance to Louis XIV.
Likewise, if Macaulay's European background has some
unsatisfactory features, the same can be said of his world-
background. Apart from India, to which personal experience
attracted him, he finds extremely little to say of the transoceanic
Empire which was leading Britain into a marvellous phase of
world-power. He could legitimately ignore the internal history
of the West Indian and American colonies, yet he should have
described their trade with England, a topic more important
than the Darien Scheme, to which he devotes nearly thirty pages.*

*Such flaws must be seen in their due proportions against the
grand dimensions of the whole, for it was Macaulay's achievement to write the* grandest *historical work by any British
author since Gibbon. Quite inevitably, amongst its multitude
of truths there lie not a few untruths and half-truths. Good
history is above all true history, yet truth may be reached by
many paths and every path has its own pitfalls. In 1840 the
listing and printing of documents, the compilation of reference-
books, the detailed, painstaking researches were indeed prime
necessities. Yet in relation to many fields of history there was
also need for a summary attack by a major intelligence, for a
painting on the largest canvas which later craftsmen might
retouch or even repaint at leisure. Such a broad picture Macaulay
essayed with enormous energy and confidence. In the process he
inspired—and continues to inspire—thousands of readers with
a new concept and a new love of history. He also left many
authors and scholars with a burning ambition to follow where
he had so fearlessly led. "His great achievements", wrote the
prescient Mr. Gladstone, "may be at once commemorated and
corrected by men of slower pace... and more tranquil, broad-set
and comprehensive judgment."*

A. G. DICKENS

King's College, London.

CONTENTS

OF

THE FIRST VOLUME.

CHAPTER I.

CHAPTER II.

CHAPTER III.

CHAPTER IV.

CHAPTER V.

CHAPTER VI.

LIST OF ILLUSTRATIONS

HISTORY OF ENGLAND.

CHAPTER I.

I PURPOSE to write the history of England from the accession of King James the Second down to a time which is within the memory of men still living. I shall recount the Introduction. errors which, in a few months, alienated a loyal gentry and priesthood from the House of Stuart. I shall trace the course of that revolution which terminated the long struggle between our sovereigns and their parliaments, and bound up together the rights of the people and the title of the reigning dynasty. I shall relate how the new settlement was, during many troubled years, successfully defended against foreign and domestic enemies; how, under that settlement, the authority of law and the security of property were found to be compatible with a liberty of discussion and of individual action never before known; how, from the auspicious union of order and freedom, sprang a prosperity of which the annals of human affairs had furnished no example; how our country, from a state of ignominious vassalage, rapidly rose to the place of umpire among European powers; how her opulence and her martial glory grew together; how, by wise and resolute good faith, was gradually established a public credit fruitful of marvels which to the statesmen of any former age would have seemed incredible; how a gigantic commerce gave birth to a maritime power, compared with which every other maritime power, ancient or modern, sinks into insignificance; how Scotland, after ages of enmity, was at length united to England, not merely by legal bonds, but by indissoluble ties of interest and affection; how, in America, the British colonies rapidly became far mightier and wealthier than the realms which Cortes and Pizarro had added to the dominions of Charles the Fifth; how in Asia, British adventurers founded an empire not less splendid and more durable than that of Alexander.

Nor will it be less my duty faithfully to record disasters mingled with triumphs, and great national crimes and follies far more humiliating than any disaster. It will be seen that even what we justly account our chief blessings were not without alloy. It will be seen that the system which effectually secured our liberties against the encroachments of kingly power gave birth to a new class of abuses from which absolute monarchies are exempt. It will be seen that, in consequence partly of unwise interference, and partly of unwise neglect, the increase of wealth and the extension of trade produced, together with immense good, some evils from which poor and rude societies are free. It will be seen how, in two important dependencies of the crown, wrong was followed by just retribution; how imprudence and obstinacy broke the ties which bound the North American colonies to the parent state; how Ireland, cursed by the domination of race over race, and of religion over religion, remained indeed a member of the empire, but a withered and distorted member, adding no strength to the body politic, and reproachfully pointed at by all who feared or envied the greatness of England.

Yet, unless I greatly deceive myself, the general effect of this chequered narrative will be to excite thankfulness in all religious minds, and hope in the breasts of all patriots. For the history of our country during the last hundred and sixty years is eminently the history of physical, of moral, and of intellectual improvement. Those who compare the age on which their lot has fallen with a golden age which exists only in their imagination may talk of degeneracy and decay: but no man who is correctly informed as to the past will be disposed to take a morose or desponding view of the present.

I should very imperfectly execute the task which I have undertaken if I were merely to treat of battles and sieges, of the rise and fall of administrations, of intrigues in the palace, and of debates in the parliament. It will be my endeavour to relate the history of the people as well as the history of the government, to trace the progress of useful and ornamental arts, to describe the rise of religious sects and the changes of literary taste, to portray the manners of successive generations, and not to pass by with neglect even the revolutions which have taken place in dress, furniture, repasts, and public amusements. I shall cheerfully bear the reproach of having descended below the dignity of history, if I can succeed in placing before the English of the nineteenth century a true picture of the life of their ancestors.

The events which I propose to relate form only a single act of a great and eventful drama extending through ages, and must be very imperfectly understood unless the plot of the preceding acts be well known. I shall therefore introduce my narrative by a slight sketch of the history of our country from the earliest times. I shall pass very rapidly over many centuries : but I shall dwell at some length on the vicissitudes of that contest which the administration of King James the Second brought to a decisive crisis.*

Nothing in the early existence of Britain indicated the greatness which she was destined to attain. Her inhabitants when first they became known to the Tyrian mariners, were little superior to the natives of the Sandwich Islands. She was subjugated by the Roman arms; but she received only a faint tincture of Roman arts and letters. Of the western provinces which obeyed the Cæsars, she was the last that was conquered, and the first that was flung away. No magnificent remains of Latin porches and aqueducts are to be found in Britain. No writer of British birth is reckoned among the masters of Latin poetry and eloquence. It is not probable that the islanders were at any time generally familiar with the tongue of their Italian rulers. From the Atlantic to the vicinity of the Rhine the Latin has, during many centuries, been predominant. It drove out the Celtic; it was not driven out by the Teutonic; and it is at this day the basis of the French, Spanish and Portuguese languages. In our island the Latin appears never to have superseded the old Gaelic speech, and could not stand its ground against the German.

The scanty and superficial civilisation which the Britons had derived from their southern masters was effaced by the calamities of the fifth century. In the continental kingdoms into which the Roman empire was then dissolved, the con-

Britain under the Romans.

---

* In this, and in the next chapter, I have very seldom thought it necessary to cite authorities: for, in these chapters, I have not detailed events minutely, or used recondite materials; and the facts which I mention are for the most part such that a person tolerably well read in English history, if not already apprised of them, will at least know where to look for evidence of them. In the subsequent chapters I shall carefully indicate the sources of my information.

querors learned much from the conquered race. In Britain
the conquered race became as barbarous as the conquerors.

All the chiefs who founded Teutonic dynasties in the continental provinces of the Roman empire, Alaric, Theodoric,
Clovis, Alboin, were zealous Christians. The followers of Ida
and Cerdic, on the other hand, brought to their settlements
in Britain all the superstitions of the Elbe. While the German princes who reigned at Paris, Toledo, Arles, and Ra-
venna listened with reverence to the instructions of bishops,
adored the relics of martyrs, and took part eagerly in disputes touching the Nicene theology, the rulers of Wessex and
Mercia were still performing savage rites in the temples of
Thor and Woden.

The continental kingdoms which had risen on the ruins of
the Western Empire kept up some intercourse with those
eastern provinces where the ancient civilisation, though
slowly fading away under the influence of misgovernment,
might still astonish and instruct barbarians, where the court
still exhibited the splendour of Diocletian and Constantine,
where the public buildings were still adorned with the sculp-
tures of Polycletus and the paintings of Apelles, and where
laborious pedants, themselves destitute of taste, sense, and
spirit, could still read and interpret the masterpieces of
Sophocles, of Demosthenes, and of Plato. From this communion Britain was cut off. Her shores were, to the polished
race which dwelt by the Bosporus, objects of a mysterious
horror, such as that with which the Ionians of the age of
Homer had regarded the Straits of Scylla and the city of the
Læstrygonian cannibals. There was one province of our
island in which, as Procopius had been told, the ground was
covered with serpents, and the air was such that no man
could inhale it and live. To this desolate region the spirits
of the departed were ferried over from the land of the Franks
at midnight. A strange race of fishermen performed the
ghastly office. The speech of the dead was distinctly heard
by the boatmen : their weight made the keel sink deep in the
water ; but their forms were invisible to mortal eye. Such
were the marvels which an able historian, the contemporary
of Belisarius, of Simplicius, and of Tribonian, gravely related
in the rich and polite Constantinople, touching the country
in which the founder of Constantinople had assumed the
imperial purple. Concerning all the other provinces of the
Western Empire we have continuous information. It is only

in Britain that an age of fable completely separates two ages of truth. Odoacer and Totila, Euric and Thrasimund, Clovis, Fredegunda, and Brunechild, are historical men and women. But Hengist and Horsa, Vortigern and Rowena, Arthur and Mordred are mythical persons, whose very existence may be questioned, and whose adventures must be classed with those of Hercules and Romulus.

At length the darkness begins to break; and the country which had been lost to view as Britain reappears as England. The conversion of the Saxon colonists to Christianity was the first of a long series of salutary revolutions. It is true that the Church had been deeply corrupted both by that superstition and by that philosophy against which she had long contended, and over which she had at last triumphed. She had given a too easy admission to doctrines borrowed from the ancient schools, and to rites borrowed from the ancient temples. Roman policy and Gothic ignorance, Grecian ingenuity and Syrian asceticism, had contributed to deprave her. Yet she retained enough of the sublime theology and benevolent morality of her earlier days to elevate many intellects, and to purify many hearts. Some things also which at a later period were justly regarded as among her chief blemishes were, in the seventh century, and long afterwards, among her chief merits. That the sacerdotal order should encroach on the functions of the civil magistrate would, in our time, be a great evil. But that which in an age of good government is an evil may, in an age of grossly bad government, be a blessing. It is better that mankind should be governed by wise laws well administered, and by an enlightened public opinion, than by priestcraft: but it is better that men should be governed by priestcraft than by brute violence, by such a prelate as Dunstan than by such a warrior as Penda. A society sunk in ignorance, and ruled by mere physical force, has great reason to rejoice when a class, of which the influence is intellectual and moral, rises to ascendency. Such a class will doubtless abuse its power: but mental power, even when abused, is still a nobler and better power than that which consists merely in corporeal strength. We read in our Saxon chronicles of tyrants, who, when at the height of greatness, were smitten with remorse, who abhorred the pleasures and dignities which they had purchased by guilt, who abdicated their crowns, and who sought to atone for their offences by cruel penances

Conversion of the Saxons to Christianity.

and incessant prayers. These stories have drawn forth bitter expressions of contempt from some writers who, while they boasted of liberality, were in truth as narrow-minded as any monk of the dark ages, and whose habit was to apply to all events in the history of the world the standard received in the Parisian society of the eighteenth century. Yet surely a system which, however deformed by superstition, introduced strong moral restraints into communities previously governed only by vigour of muscle and by audacity of spirit, a system which taught the fiercest and mightiest ruler that he was, like his meanest bondman, a responsible being, might have seemed to deserve a more respectful mention from philosophers and philanthropists.

The same observations will apply to the contempt with which, in the last century, it was fashionable to speak of the pilgrimages, the sanctuaries, the crusades, and the monastic institutions of the middle ages. In times when men were scarcely ever induced to travel by liberal curiosity, or by the pursuit of gain, it was better that the rude inhabitant of the North should visit Italy and the East as a pilgrim, than that he should never see anything but those squalid cabins and uncleared woods amidst which he was born. In times when life and when female honour were exposed to daily risk from tyrants and marauders, it was better that the precinct of a shrine should be regarded with an irrational awe, than that there should be no refuge inaccessible to cruelty and licentiousness. In times when statesmen were incapable of forming extensive political combinations, it was better that the Christian nations should be roused and united for the recovery of the Holy Sepulchre, than that they should, one by one, be overwhelmed by the Mahometan power. Whatever reproach may, at a later period, have been justly thrown on the indolence and luxury of religious orders, it was surely good that, in an age of ignorance and violence, there should be quiet cloisters and gardens, in which the arts of peace could be safely cultivated, in which gentle and contemplative natures could find an asylum, in which one brother could employ himself in transcribing the Æneid of Virgil, and another in meditating the Analytics of Aristotle, in which he who had a genius for art might illuminate a martyrology or carve a crucifix, and in which he who had a turn for natural philosophy might make experiments on the properties of plants and minerals. Had not such retreats been scattered here and there, among the huts of a miserable peasantry, and the castles of a ferocious aristocracy, European society would have consisted merely of beasts of burden and beasts of prey. The Church has many times been compared by divines to the ark of which we read in the Book of Genesis : but never was the resemblance more perfect than during that evil time when she alone rode, amidst darkness and tempest, on the deluge beneath which all the great works of ancient power and wisdom lay entombed, bearing within her that feeble germ from which a second and more glorious civilisation was to spring.

Even the spiritual supremacy arrogated by the Pope was, in the dark ages, productive of far more good than evil. Its effect was to unite the nations of Western Europe in one great commonwealth. What the Olympian chariot course and the Pythian oracle were to all the Greek cities, from Trebizond to Marseilles, Rome and her Bishop were to all Christians of the Latin communion, from Calabria to the Hebrides. Thus grew up sentiments of enlarged benevolence. Races separated from each other by seas and mountains acknowledged a fraternal tie and a common code of public law. Even in war, the cruelty of the conqueror was not seldom mitigated by the recollection that he and his vanquished enemies were all members of one great federation.

Into this federation our Saxon ancestors were now admitted. A regular communication was opened between our shores and that part of Europe in which the traces of ancient power and policy were yet discernible. Many noble monuments which have since been destroyed or defaced still retained their pristine magnificence ; and travellers, to whom Livy and Sallust were unintelligible, might gain from the Roman aqueducts and temples some faint notion of Roman history. The dome of Agrippa, still glittering with bronze, the mausoleum of Adrian, not yet deprived of its columns and statues, the Flavian amphitheatre, not yet degraded into a quarry, told to the rude English pilgrims some part of the story of that great civilised world which had passed away. The islanders returned, with awe deeply impressed on their half opened minds, and told the wondering inhabitants of the hovels of London and York that, near the grave of Saint Peter, a mighty race, now extinct, had piled up buildings which would never be dissolved till the judgment day. Learning followed in the train of Christianity. The poetry and eloquence of the Augustan age was assiduously studied in Mercian and Nor-

thumbrian monasteries. The names of Bede and Alcuin were
justly celebrated throughout Europe. Such was the state of
our country when, in the ninth century, began the last great
migration of the northern barbarians.

Danish invasions. During many years Denmark and Scandinavia continued
to pour forth innumerable pirates, distinguished by strength,
by valour, by merciless ferocity, and by hatred of the Christian name. No country suffered so much from these invaders
as England. Her coast lay near to the ports whence they
sailed; nor was any shire so far distant from the sea as to
be secure from attack. The same atrocities which had attended the victory of the Saxon over the Celt were now, after
the lapse of ages, suffered by the Saxon at the hand of the
Dane. Civilisation, just as it began to rise, was met by this
blow, and sank down once more. Large colonies of adventurers from the Baltic established themselves on the eastern
shores of our island, spread gradually westward, and, supported by constant reinforcements from beyond the sea,
aspired to the dominion of the whole realm. The struggle
between the two fierce Teutonic breeds lasted through six
generations. Each was alternately paramount. Cruel massacres followed by cruel retribution, provinces wasted, convents plundered, and cities rased to the ground, make up the
greater part of the history of those evil days. At length the
North ceased to send forth a constant stream of fresh depre-
dators; and from that time the mutual aversion of the races
began to subside. Intermarriage became frequent. The
Danes learned the religion of the Saxons; and thus one
cause of deadly animosity was removed. The Danish and
Saxon tongues, both dialects of one widespread language,
were blended together. But the distinction between the two
nations was by no means effaced, when an event took place
which prostrated both, in common slavery and degradation,
at the feet of a third people.

**The Nor-
mans.** The Normans were then the foremost race of Christendom.
Their valour and ferocity had made them conspicuous among
the rovers whom Scandinavia had sent forth to ravage Western Europe. Their sails were long the terror of both coasts
of the Channel. Their arms were repeatedly carried far into
the heart of the Carlovingian empire, and were victorious
under the walls of Maestricht and Paris. At length one of
the feeble heirs of Charlemagne ceded to the strangers a
fertile province, watered by a noble river, and contiguous to

the sea which was their favourite element. In that province they founded a mighty state, which gradually extended its influence over the neighbouring principalities of Britanny and Maine. Without laying aside that dauntless valour which had been the terror of every land from the Elbe to the Pyrenees, the Normans rapidly acquired all, and more than all, the knowledge and refinement which they found in the country where they settled. Their courage secured their territory against foreign invasion. They established internal order, such as had long been unknown in the Frank empire. They embraced Christianity; and with Christianity they learned a great part of what the clergy had to teach. They abandoned their native speech, and adopted the French tongue, in which the Latin was the predominant element. They speedily raised their new language to a dignity and importance which it had never before possessed. They found it a barbarous jargon; they fixed it in writing; and they employed it in legislation, in poetry, and in romance. They renounced that brutal intemperance to which all the other branches of the great German family were too much inclined. The polite luxury of the Norman presented a striking contrast to the coarse voracity and drunkenness of his Saxon and Danish neighbours. He loved to display his magnificence, not in huge piles of food and hogsheads of strong drink, but in large and stately edifices, rich armour, gallant horses, choice falcons, well ordered tournaments, banquets delicate rather than abundant, and wines remarkable rather for their exquisite flavour than for their intoxicating power. That chivalrous spirit, which has exercised so powerful an influence on the politics, morals, and manners of all the European nations, was found in the highest exaltation among the Norman nobles. Those nobles were distinguished by their graceful bearing and insinuating address. They were distinguished also by their skill in negotiation, and by a natural eloquence which they assiduously cultivated. It was the boast of one of their historians that the Norman gentlemen were orators from the cradle. But their chief fame was derived from their military exploits. Every country, from the Atlantic Ocean to the Dead Sea, witnessed the prodigies of their discipline and valour. One Norman knight, at the head of a handful of warriors, scattered the Celts of Connaught. Another founded the monarchy of the Two Sicilies, and saw the emperors both of the East and of the West fly before his arms. A third, the Ulysses of the first crusade, was invested by his fellow soldiers with the sovereignty of Antioch ; and a fourth, the Tancred whose name lives in the great poem of Tasso, was celebrated through Christendom as the bravest and most generous of the deliverers of the Holy Sepulchre.

The vicinity of so remarkable a people early began to produce an effect on the public mind of England. Before the Conquest, English princes received their education in Normandy. English sees and English estates were bestowed on Normans. The French of Normandy was familiarly spoken in the palace of Westminster. The court of Rouen seems to have been to the court of Edward the Confessor what the court of Versailles long afterwards was to the court of Charles the Second.

The Norman Conquest.

The battle of Hastings, and the events which followed it, not only placed a Duke of Normandy on the English throne, but gave up the whole population of England to the tyranny of the Norman race. The subjugation of a nation by a nation has seldom, even in Asia, been more complete. The country was portioned out among the captains of the invaders. Strong military institutions, closely connected with the institution of property, enabled the foreign conquerors to oppress the children of the soil. A cruel penal code, cruelly enforced, guarded the privileges, and even the sports, of the alien tyrants. Yet the subject race, though beaten down and trodden under foot, still made its sting felt. Some bold men, the favourite heroes of our oldest ballads, betook themselves to the woods, and there, in defiance of curfew laws and forest laws, waged a predatory war against their oppressors. Assassination was an event of daily occurrence. Many Normans suddenly disappeared leaving no trace. The corpses of many were found bearing the marks of violence. Death by torture was denounced against the murderers, and strict search was made for them, but generally in vain ; for the whole nation was in a conspiracy to screen them. It was at length thought necessary to lay a heavy fine on every Hundred in which a person of French extraction should be found slain ; and this regulation was followed up by another regulation, providing that every person who was found slain should be supposed to be a Frenchman, unless he was proved to be a Saxon.

During the century and a half which followed the Conquest, there is, to speak strictly, no English history. The

Fitz-Arthur forbidding the Burial of William

French Kings of England rose, indeed, to an eminence which was the wonder and dread of all neighbouring nations. They conquered Ireland. They received the homage of Scotland. By their valour, by their policy, by their fortunate matrimonial alliances, they became far more powerful on the Continent than their liege lords the Kings of France. Asia, as well as Europe, was dazzled by the power and glory of our tyrants. Arabian chroniclers recorded with unwilling admiration the fall of Acre, the defence of Joppa, and the victorious march to Ascalon ; and Arabian mothers long awed their infants to silence with the name of the lionhearted Plantagenet. At one time it seemed that the line of Hugh Capet was about to end as the Merovingian and Carlovingian lines had ended, and that a single great monarchy would spread from the Orkneys to the Pyrenees. So strong an association is established in most minds between the greatness of a sovereign and the greatness of the nation which he rules, that almost every historian of England has expatiated with a sentiment of exultation on the power and splendour of her foreign masters, and has lamented the decay of that power and splendour as a calamity to our country. This is, in truth, as absurd as it would be in a Haytian negro of our time to dwell with national pride on the greatness of Lewis the Fourteenth, and to speak of Blenheim and Ramilies with patriotic regret and shame. The Conqueror and his descendants to the fourth generation were not Englishmen: most of them were born in France : they spent the greater part of their lives in France : their ordinary speech was French: almost every high office in their gift was filled by a Frenchman : every acquisition which they made on the Continent estranged them more and more from the population of our island. One of the ablest among them indeed attempted to win the hearts of his English subjects by espousing an English princess. But, by many of his barons, this marriage was regarded as a marriage between a white planter and a quadroon girl would now be regarded in Virginia. In history he is known by the honourable surname of Beauclerc; but, in his own time, his own countrymen called him by a Saxon nickname, in contemptuous allusion to his Saxon connection.

Had the Plantagenets, as at one time seemed likely, succeeded in uniting all France under their government, it is probable that England would never have had an independent existence. Her princes, her lords, her prelates, would have

been men differing in race and language from the artisans
and the tillers of the earth.   The revenues of her great proprietors would have been spent in festivities and diversions on
the banks of the Seine.   The noble language of Milton and
Burke would have remained a rustic dialect, without a literature, a fixed grammar, or a fixed orthography, and would
have been contemptuously abandoned to the use of boors.
No man of English extraction would have risen to eminence,
except by becoming in speech and habits a Frenchman.

Separation of England and Normandy.   England owes her escape from such calamities to an event
which her historians have generally represented as disas-
trous.   Her interest was so directly opposed to the interest of
her rulers that she had no hope but in their errors and misfortunes.   The talents and even the virtues of her first six
French Kings were a curse to her.   The follies and vices of
the seventh were her salvation.   Had John inherited the
great qualities of his father, of Henry Beauclerc, or of the
Conqueror, nay, had he even possessed the martial courage
of Stephen or of Richard, and had the King of France at the
same time been as incapable as all the other successors of
Hugh Capet had been, the House of Plantagenet must have
risen to unrivalled ascendency in Europe.   But, just at this
conjuncture, France, for the first time since the death of
Charlemagne, was governed by a prince of great firmness and
ability.   On the other hand England, which, since the battle
of Hastings, had been ruled generally by wise statesmen, always by brave soldiers, fell under the dominion of a trifler
and a coward.   From that moment her prospects brightened.
John was driven from Normandy.   The Norman nobles were
compelled to make their election between the island and the
continent.   Shut up by the sea with the people whom they
had hitherto oppressed and despised, they gradually came to
regard England as their country, and the English as their
countrymen.   The two races, so long hostile, soon found that
they had common interests and common enemies.   Both
were alike aggrieved by the tyranny of a bad king.   Both
were alike indignant at the favour shown by the court to the
natives of Poitou and Aquitaine.   The greatgrandsons of
those who had fought under William and the greatgrandsons
of those who had fought under Harold began to draw near to
each other in friendship ; and the first pledge of their reconciliation was the Great Charter, won by their united
exertions, and framed for their common benefit.

Here commences the history of the English nation. The history of the preceding events is the history of wrongs inflicted and sustained by various tribes, which indeed all dwelt on English ground, but which regarded each other with aversion such as has scarcely ever existed between communities separated by physical barriers. For even the mutual animosity of countries at war with each other is languid when compared with the animosity of nations which, morally separated, are yet locally intermingled. In no country has the enmity of race been carried farther than in England. In no country has that enmity been more completely effaced. The stages of the process by which the hostile elements were melted down into one homogeneous mass are not accurately known to us. But it is certain that, when John became King, the distinction between Saxons and Normans was strongly marked, and that before the end of the reign of his grandson it had almost disappeared. In the time of Richard the First, the ordinary imprecation of a Norman gentleman was " May I become an Englishman ! " His ordinary form of indignant denial was " Do you take me for an Englishman ? " The descendant of such a gentleman a hundred years later was proud of the English name.

Amalgamation of races.

The sources of the noblest rivers which spread fertility over continents, and bear richly laden fleets to the sea, are to be sought in wild and barren mountain tracts, incorrectly laid down in maps, and rarely explored by travellers. To such a tract the history of our country during the thirteenth century may not unaptly be compared. Sterile and obscure as is that portion of our annals, it is there that we must seek for the origin of our freedom, our prosperity, and our glory. Then it was that the great English people was formed, that the national character began to exhibit those peculiarities which it has ever since retained, and that our fathers became emphatically islanders, islanders not merely in geographical position, but in their politics, their feelings, and their manners. Then first appeared with distinctness that constitution which has ever since, through all changes, preserved its identity ; that constitution of which all the other free constitutions in the world are copies, and which, in spite of some defects, deserves to be regarded as the best under which any great society has ever yet existed during many ages. Then it was that the House of Commons, the archetype of all the representative assemblies which now meet, either in the old or in the new world, held its first sittings. Then it was that the common law rose to the dignity of a science, and rapidly became a not unworthy rival of the imperial jurisprudence. Then it was that the courage of those sailors who manned the rude barks of the Cinque Ports first made the flag of England terrible on the seas. Then it was that the most ancient colleges which still exist at both the great national seats of learning were founded. Then was formed that language, less musical indeed than the languages of the south, but in force, in richness, in aptitude for all the highest purposes of the poet, the philosopher, and the orator, inferior to the tongue of Greece alone. Then too appeared the first faint dawn of that noble literature, the most splendid and the most durable of the many glories of England.

Early in the fourteenth century the amalgamation of the races was all but complete ; and it was soon made manifest, by signs not to be mistaken, that a people inferior to none existing in the world had been formed by the mixture of three branches of the great Teutonic family with each other, and with the aboriginal Britons. There was, indeed, scarcely any thing in common between the England to which John had been chased by Philip Augustus, and the England from which the armies of Edward the Third went forth to conquer France.

English Conquests on the Continent. A period of more than a hundred years followed, during which the chief object of the English was to establish, by force of arms, a great empire on the Continent. The claim of Edward to the inheritance occupied by the House of Valois was a claim in which it might seem that his subjects were little interested. But the passion for conquest spread fast from the prince to the people. The war differed widely from the wars which the Plantagenets of the twelfth century had waged against the descendants of Hugh Capet. For the success of Henry the Second, or of Richard the First, would have made England a province of France. The effect of the successes of Edward the Third and Henry the Fifth was to make France, for a time, a province of England. The disdain with which, in the twelfth century, the conquerors from the Continent had regarded the islanders, was now retorted by the islanders on the people of the Continent. Every yeoman from Kent to Northumberland valued himself as one of a race born for victory and dominion, and looked down with scorn on the nation before which his ancestors had trembled. Even those knights of Gascony and Guienne who had fought gallantly under the Black Prince were regarded by the English as men of an inferior breed, and were contemptuously excluded from honourable and lucrative commands. In no long time our ancestors altogether lost sight of the original ground of quarrel. They began to consider the crown of France as a mere appendage to the crown of England; and when, in violation of the ordinary law of succession, they transferred the crown of England to the House of Lancaster, they seem to have thought that the right of Richard the Second to the crown of France passed, as of course, to that house. The zeal and vigour which they displayed present a remarkable contrast to the torpor of the French, who were far more deeply interested in the event of the struggle. The most splendid victories recorded in the history of the middle ages were gained at this time, against great odds, by the English armies. Victories indeed they were of which a nation may justly be proud; for they are to be attributed to the moral superiority of the victors, a superiority which was most striking in the lowest ranks. The knights of England found worthy rivals in the knights of France. Chandos encountered an equal foe in Du Guesclin. But France had no infantry that dared to face the English bows and bills. A French King was brought prisoner to London. An English King was crowned at Paris. The banner of Saint George was carried far beyond the Pyrenees and the Alps. On the south of the Ebro the English won a great battle, which for a time decided the fate of Leon and Castile; and the English Companies obtained a terrible preeminence among the bands of warriors who let out their weapons for hire to the princes and commonwealths of Italy.

Nor were the arts of peace neglected by our fathers during that stirring period. While France was wasted by war, till she at length found in her own desolation a miserable defence against invaders, the English gathered in their harvests, adorned their cities, pleaded, traded, and studied in security. Many of our noblest architectural monuments belong to that age. Then rose the fair chapels of New College and of Saint George, the nave of Winchester and the choir of York, the spire of Salisbury and the majestic towers of Lincoln. A copious and forcible language, formed by an infusion of French into German, was now the common property of the aristocracy and of the people. Nor was it long before genius began to apply that admirable machine to worthy purposes. While

English warriors, leaving behind them the devastated provinces of France, entered Valladolid in triumph, and spread terror to the gates of Florence, English poets depicted in vivid tints all the wide variety of human manners and fortunes, and English thinkers aspired to know, or dared to doubt, where bigots had been content to wonder and to believe. The same age which produced the Black Prince and Derby, Chandos and Hawkwood, produced also Geoffrey Chaucer and John Wycliffe.

In so splendid and imperial a manner did the English people, properly so called, first take place among the nations of the world. Yet while we contemplate with pleasure the high and commanding qualities which our forefathers displayed, we cannot but admit that the end which they pursued was an end condemned both by humanity and by enlightened policy, and that the reverses which compelled them, after a long and bloody struggle, to relinquish the hope of establishing a great continental empire, were really blessings in the guise of disasters. The spirit of the French was at last aroused: they began to oppose a vigorous national resistance to the foreign conquerors; and from that time the skill of the English captains and the courage of the English soldiers were, happily for mankind, exerted in vain. After many desperate struggles, and with many bitter regrets, our ancestors gave up the contest. Since that age no British government has ever seriously and steadily pursued the design of making great conquests on the Continent. The people, indeed, continued to cherish with pride the recollection of Cressy, of Poitiers, and of Agincourt. Even after the lapse of many years it was easy to fire their blood and to draw forth their subsidies by promising them an expedition for the conquest of France. But happily the energies of our country have been directed to better objects; and she now occupies in the history of mankind a place far more glorious than if she had, as at one time seemed not improbable, acquired by the sword an ascendency similar to that which formerly belonged to the Roman republic.

Wars of the Roses.
Cooped up once more within the limits of the island, the warlike people employed in civil strife those arms which had been the terror of Europe. The means of profuse expenditure had long been drawn by the English barons from the oppressed provinces of France. That source of supply was gone: but the ostentatious and luxurious habits which prosperity had

engendered still remained; and the great lords, unable to gratify their tastes by plundering the French, were eager to plunder each other. The realm to which they were now confined would not, in the phrase of Comines, the most judicious observer of that time, suffice for them all. Two aristocratical factions, headed by two branches of the royal family, engaged in a long and fierce struggle for supremacy. As the animosity of those factions did not really arise from the dispute about the succession, it lasted long after all ground of dispute about the succession was removed. The party of the Red Rose survived the last prince who claimed the crown in right of Henry the Fourth. The party of the White Rose survived the marriage of Richmond and Elizabeth. Left without chiefs who had any decent show of right, the adherents of Lancaster rallied round a line of bastards, and the adherents of York set up a succession of impostors. When, at length, many aspiring nobles had perished on the field of battle or by the hands of the executioner, when many illustrious houses had disappeared for ever from history, when those great families which remained had been exhausted and sobered by calamities, it was universally acknowledged that the claims of all the contending Plantagenets were united in the house of Tudor.

Meanwhile a change was proceeding infinitely more momentous than the acquisition or loss of any province, than the rise or fall of any dynasty. Slavery and the evils by which slavery is everywhere accompanied were fast disappearing.

Extinction of villenage.

It is remarkable that the two greatest and most salutary social revolutions which have taken place in England, that revolution which, in the thirteenth century, put an end to the tyranny of nation over nation, and that revolution which, a few generations later, put an end to the property of man in man, were silently and imperceptibly effected. They struck contemporary observers with no surprise, and have received from historians a very scanty measure of attention. They were brought about neither by legislative regulation nor by physical force. Moral causes noiselessly effaced first the distinction between Norman and Saxon, and then the distinction between master and slave. None can venture to fix the precise moment at which either distinction ceased. Some faint traces of the old Norman feeling might perhaps have been found late in the fourteenth century. Some faint traces of the institution of villenage were detected by the curious so late as the days of the Stuarts; nor has that institution ever, to this hour, been abolished by statute.

Beneficial operation of the Roman Catholic religion.

It would be most unjust not to acknowledge that the chief agent in these two great deliverances was religion; and it may perhaps be doubted whether a purer religion might not have been found a less efficient agent. The benevolent spirit of the Christian morality is undoubtedly adverse to distinctions of caste. But to the Church of Rome such distinctions are peculiarly odious; for they are incompatible with other distinctions which are essential to her system. She ascribes to every priest a mysterious dignity which entitles him to the reverence of every layman; and she does not consider any man as disqualified, by reason of his nation or of his family, for the priesthood. Her doctrines respecting the sacerdotal character, however erroneous they may be, have repeatedly mitigated some of the worst evils which can afflict society. That superstition cannot be regarded as unmixedly noxious which, in regions cursed by the tyranny of race over race, creates an aristocracy altogether independent of race, inverts the relation between the oppressor and the oppressed, and compels the hereditary master to kneel before the spiritual tribunal of the hereditary bondman. To this day, in some countries where negro slavery exists. Popery appears in advantageous contrast to other forms of Christianity. It is notorious that the antipathy between the European and African races is by no means so strong at Rio Janeiro as at Washington. In our own country this peculiarity of the Roman Catholic system produced, during the middle ages, many salutary effects. It is true that, shortly after the battle of Hastings, Saxon prelates and abbots were violently deposed, and that ecclesiastical adventurers from the Continent were intruded by hundreds into lucrative benefices. Yet even then pious divines of Norman blood raised their voices against such a violation of the constitution of the Church, refused to accept mitres from the hands of William, and charged him, on the peril of his soul, not to forget that the vanquished islanders were his fellow Christians. The first protector whom the English found among the dominant caste was Archbishop Anselm. At a time when the English name was a reproach, and when all the civil and military dignities of the kingdom were supposed to belong exclusively to the countrymen of the Conqueror, the despised race learned, with transports of delight, that one of themselves, Nicholas Breakspear, had been elevated to the papal throne, and had held out his foot to be kissed by ambassadors sprung from the noblest houses of Normandy. It was a national as well as a religious feeling that drew great multitudes to the shrine of Becket, whom they regarded as the enemy of their enemies. Whether he was a Norman or a Saxon may be doubted: but there is no doubt that he perished by Norman hands, and that the Saxons cherished his memory with peculiar tenderness and veneration, and, in their popular poetry, represented him as one of their own race. A successor of Becket was foremost among the refractory magnates who obtained that charter which secured the privileges both of the Norman barons and of the Saxon yeomanry. How great a part the Roman Catholic ecclesiastics subsequently had in the abolition of villenage we learn from the unexceptionable testimony of Sir Thomas Smith, one of the ablest Protestant counsellors of Elizabeth. When the dying slaveholder asked for the last sacraments, his spiritual attendants regularly adjured him, as he loved his soul, to emancipate his brethren for whom Christ had died. So successfully had the Church used her formidable machinery that, before the Reformation came, she had enfranchised almost all the bondmen in the kingdom except her own, who, to do her justice, seem to have been very tenderly treated.

There can be no doubt that, when these two great revolutions had been effected, our forefathers were by far the best governed people in Europe. During three hundred years the social system had been in a constant course of improvement. Under the first Plantagenets there had been barons able to bid defiance to the sovereign, and peasants degraded to the level of the swine and oxen which they tended. The exorbitant power of the baron had been gradually reduced. The condition of the peasant had been gradually elevated. Between the aristocracy and the working people had sprung up a middle class, agricultural and commercial. There was still, it may be, more inequality than is favourable to the happiness and virtue of our species : but no man was altogether above the restraints of law; and no man was altogether below its protection.

That the political institutions of England were, at this early period, regarded by the English with pride and affection, and by the most enlightened men of neighbouring nations with admiration and envy, is proved by the clearest evidence. But touching the nature of those institutions there has been much dishonest and acrimonious controversy.

The early English polity often mis-represen-ted, and why ? The historical literature of England has indeed suffered grievously from a circumstance which has not a little contributed to her prosperity. The change, great as it is, which her polity has undergone during the last six centuries, has been the effect of gradual development, not of demolition and reconstruction. The present constitution of our country is, to the constitution under which she flourished five hundred years ago, what the tree is to the sapling, what the man is to the boy. The alteration has been great. Yet there never was a moment at which the chief part of what existed was not old. A polity thus formed must abound in anomalies. But for the evils arising from mere anomalies we have ample compensation. Other societies possess written constitutions more symmetrical. But no other society has yet succeeded in uniting revolution with prescription, progress with stability, the energy of youth with the majesty of immemorial antiquity.

This great blessing, however, has its drawbacks : and one of those drawbacks is that every source of information as to our early history has been poisoned by party spirit. As there is no country where statesmen have been so much under the influence of the past, so there is no country where historians have been so much under the influence of the present. Between these two things, indeed, there is a natural connection. Where history is regarded merely as a picture of life and manners, or as a collection of experiments from which general maxims of civil wisdom may be drawn, a writer lies under no very pressing temptation to misrepresent transactions of ancient date. But where history is regarded as a repository of titledeeds, on which the rights of governments and nations depend, the motive to falsification becomes almost irresistible. A Frenchman is not now impelled by any strong interest either to exaggerate or to underrate the power of the Kings of the house of Valois. The privileges of the States General, of the States of Britanny, of the States of Burgundy, are to him matters of as little practical importance as the constitution of the Jewish Sanhedrim or of the Amphictyonic Council. The gulph of a great revolution completely separates the new from the old system. No such chasm divides the existence of the English nation into two distinct parts. Our laws and customs have never been lost in general and irreparable ruin. With us the precedents of the middle ages are still valid precedents, and are still cited, on the gravest occasions, by the most eminent statesmen. For example, when King George the Third was attacked by the malady which made him incapable of performing his regal functions, and when the most distinguished lawyers and politicians differed widely as to the course which ought, in such circumstances, to be pursued, the Houses of Parliament would not proceed to discuss any plan of regency till all the precedents which were to be found in our annals, from the earliest times, had been collected and arranged. Committees were appointed to examine the ancient records of the realm. The first case reported was that of the year 1217: much importance was attached to the cases of 1326, of 1377, and of 1422: but the case which was justly considered as most in point was that of 1455. Thus in our country the dearest interests of parties have frequently been staked on the results of the researches of antiquaries. The inevitable consequence was that our antiquaries conducted their researches in the spirit of partisans.

It is therefore not surprising that those who have written concerning the limits of prerogative and liberty in the old polity of England should generally have shown the temper, not of judges, but of angry and uncandid advocates. For they were discussing, not a speculative matter, but a matter which had a direct and practical connection with the most momentous and exciting disputes of their own day. From the commencement of the long contest between the Parliament and the Stuarts down to the time when the pretensions of the Stuarts ceased to be formidable, few questions were practically more important than the question whether the administration of that family had or had not been in accordance with the ancient constitution of the kingdom. This question could be decided only by reference to the records of preceding reigns. Bracton and Fleta, the Mirror of Justice and the Rolls of Parliament, were ransacked to find pretexts for the excesses of the Star Chamber on one side, and of the High Court of Justice on the other. During a long course of years every Whig historian was anxious to prove that the old English government was all but republican, every Tory historian to prove that it was all but despotic.

With such feelings, both parties looked into the chronicles of the middle ages. Both readily found what they sought;

and both obstinately refused to see anything but what they sought. The champions of the Stuarts could easily point out instances of oppression exercised on the subject. The defenders of the Roundheads could as easily produce instances of determined and successful resistance offered to the Crown. The Tories quoted, from ancient writings, expressions almost as servile as were heard from the pulpit of Mainwaring. The Whigs discovered expressions as bold and severe as any that resounded from the judgment seat of Bradshaw. One set of writers adduced numerous instances in which Kings had extorted money without the authority of Parliament. Another set cited cases in which the Parliament had assumed to itself the power of inflicting punishment on Kings. Those who saw only one half of the evidence would have concluded that the Plantagenets were as absolute as the Sultans of Turkey : those who saw only the other half would have concluded that the Plantagenets had as little real power as the Doges of Venice ; and both conclusions would have been equally remote from the truth.

Nature of the limited monarchies of the middle ages.

The old English government was one of a class of limited monarchies which sprang up in Western Europe during the middle ages, and which, notwithstanding many diversities, bore to one another a strong family likeness. That there should have been such a likeness is not strange. The countries in which those monarchies arose had been provinces of the same great civilised empire, and had been overrun and conquered, about the same time, by tribes of the same rude and warlike nation. They were members of the same great coalition against Islam. They were in communion with the same superb and ambitious Church. Their polity naturally took the same form. They had institutions derived partly from imperial Rome, partly from papal Rome, partly from the old Germany. All had Kings ; and in all the kingly office became by degrees strictly hereditary. All had nobles bearing titles which had originally indicated military rank. The dignity of knighthood, the rules of heraldry, were common to all. All had richly endowed ecclesiastical establishments, municipal corporations enjoying large franchises, and senates whose consent was necessary to the validity of some public acts.

Prerogatives of the early English Kings.

Of these kindred constitutions the English was, from an early period, justly reputed the best. The prerogatives of the sovereign were undoubtedly extensive. The spirit of re-

ligion and the spirit of chivalry concurred to exalt his dignity.
The sacred oil had been poured on his head. It was no disparagement to the bravest and noblest knights to kneel at his
feet. His person was inviolable. He alone was entitled to
convoke the Estates of the realm: he could at his pleasure
dismiss them; and his assent was necessary to all their legislative acts. He was the chief of the executive administration, the sole organ of communication with foreign powers,
the captain of the military and naval forces of the state, the
fountain of justice, of mercy, and of honour. He had large
powers for the regulation of trade. It was by him that
money was coined, that weights and measures were fixed,
that marts and havens were appointed. His ecclesiastical
patronage was immense. His hereditary revenues, econo-
mically administered, sufficed to meet the ordinary charges
of government. His own domains were of vast extent. He
was also feudal lord paramount of the whole soil of his kingdom, and, in that capacity, possessed many lucrative and
many formidable rights, which enabled him to annoy and depress those who thwarted him, and to enrich and aggrandise,
without any cost to himself, those who enjoyed his favour.

But his power, though ample, was limited by three great   Limita-
constitutional principles, so ancient that none can say when   tions of
they began to exist, so potent that their natural develop-   the prero-
ment, continued through many generations, has produced   gative
the order of things under which we now live.

First, the King could not legislate without the consent of
his Parliament. Secondly, he could impose no tax without
the consent of his Parliament. Thirdly, he was bound to
conduct the executive administration according to the laws
of the land, and, if he broke those laws, his advisers and his
agents were responsible.

No candid Tory will deny that these principles had, five
hundred years ago, acquired the authority of fundamental
rules. On the other hand, no candid Whig will affirm that
they were, till a later period, cleared from all ambiguity, or
followed out to all their consequences. A constitution of
the middle ages was not, like a constitution of the eighteenth
or nineteenth century, created entire by a single act, and fully
set forth in a single document. It is only in a refined and
speculative age that a polity is constructed on system. In
rude societies the progress of government resembles the progress of language and of versification. Rude societies have

language, and often copious and energetic language: but
they have no scientific grammar, no definitions of nouns and
verbs, no names for declensions, moods, tenses, and voices.
Rude societies have versification, and often versification of
great power and sweetness: but they have no metrical canons; and the minstrel whose numbers, regulated solely by
his ear, are the delight of his audience, would himself be unable to say of how many dactyls and trochees each of his
lines consists. As eloquence exists before syntax, and song
before prosody, so government may exist in a high degree of
excellence long before the limits of legislative, executive, and
judicial power have been traced with precision.

It was thus in our country. The line which bounded the
royal prerogative, though in general sufficiently clear, had
not everywhere been drawn with accuracy and distinctness.
There was, therefore, near the border some debatable ground
on which incursions and reprisals continued to take place,
till, after ages of strife, plain and durable landmarks were at
length set up. It may be instructive to note in what way,
and to what extent, our ancient sovereigns were in the habit
of violating the three great principles by which the liberties
of the nation were protected.

No English King has ever laid claim to the general legislative power. The most violent and imperious Plantagenet
never fancied himself competent to enact, without the con
sent of his great council, that a jury should consist of ten
persons instead of twelve, that a widow's dower should be a
fourth part instead of a third, that perjury should be a felony,
or that the custom of gavelkind should be introduced into
Yorkshire.* But the King had the power of pardoning
offenders; and there is one point at which the power of pardoning and the power of legislating seem to fade into each
other, and may easily, at least in a simple age, be confounded.
A penal statute is virtually annulled if the penalties which it
imposes are regularly remitted as often as they are incurred.
The sovereign was undoubtedly competent to remit penalties
without limit. He was therefore competent to annul virtually a penal statute. It might seem that there could be no
serious objection to his doing formally what he might do virtually. Thus, with the help of subtle and courtly lawyers,
grew up, on the doubtful frontier which separates executive

* This is excellently put by Mr. Hallam in the first chapter of his Constitutional History.

from legislative functions, that great anomaly known as the dispensing power.

That the King could not impose taxes without the consent of Parliament is admitted to have been, from time immemorial, a fundamental law of England. It was among the articles which John was compelled by the Barons to sign. Edward the First ventured to break through the rule: but, able, powerful, and popular as he was, he encountered an opposition to which he found it expedient to yield. He covenanted accordingly in express terms, for himself and his heirs, that they would never again levy any aid without the assent and goodwill of the Estates of the realm. His powerful and victorious grandson attempted to violate this solemn compact: but the attempt was strenuously withstood. At length the Plantagenets gave up the point in despair: but, though they ceased to infringe the law openly, they occasionally contrived, by evading it, to procure an extraordinary supply for a temporary purpose. They were interdicted from taxing; but they claimed the right of begging and borrowing. They therefore sometimes begged in a tone not easily to be distinguished from that of command, and sometimes borrowed with small thought of repaying. But the fact that they thought it necessary to disguise their exactions under the names of benevolences and loans sufficiently proves that the authority of the great constitutional rule was universally recognised.

The principle that the King of England was bound to conduct the administration according to law, and that, if he did anything against law, his advisers and agents were answerable, was established at a very early period, as the severe judgments pronounced and executed on many royal favourites sufficiently prove. It is, however, certain that the rights of individuals were often violated by the Plantagenets, and that the injured parties were often unable to obtain redress. According to law no Englishman could be arrested or detained in confinement merely by the mandate of the sovereign. In fact, persons obnoxious to the government were frequently imprisoned without any other authority than a royal order. According to law, torture, the disgrace of the Roman jurisprudence, could not, in any circumstances, be inflicted on an English subject. Nevertheless, during the troubles of the fifteenth century, a rack was introduced into the Tower, and was occasionally used under the plea of political necessity. But it would be a great error to infer from such irregularities that the English monarchs were, either in theory or in practice, absolute. We live in a highly civilised society, through which intelligence is so rapidly diffused by means of the press and of the post office that any gross act of oppression committed in any part of our island is, in a few hours, discussed by millions. If the sovereign were now to immure a subject in defiance of the writ of Habeas Corpus, or to put a conspirator to the torture, the whole nation would be instantly electrified by the news. In the middle ages the state of society was widely different. Rarely and with great difficulty did the wrongs of individuals come to the knowledge of the public. A man might be illegally confined during many months in the castle of Carlisle or Norwich ; and no whisper of the transaction might reach London. It is highly probable that the rack had been many years in use before the great majority of the nation had the least suspicion that it was ever employed. Nor were our ancestors by any means so much alive as we are to the importance of maintaining great general rules. We have been taught by long experience that we cannot without danger suffer any breach of the constitution to pass unnoticed. It is therefore now universally held that a government which unnecessarily exceeds its powers ought to be visited with severe parliamentary censure, and that a government which, under the pressure of a great exigency, and with pure intentions, has exceeded its powers, ought without delay to apply to Parliament for an act of indemnity. But such were not the feelings of the Englishmen of the fourteenth and fifteenth centuries. They were little disposed to contend for a principle merely as a principle, or to cry out against an irregularity which was not also felt to be a grievance. As long as the general spirit of the administration was mild and popular, they were willing to allow some latitude to their sovereign. If, for ends generally acknowledged to be good, he exerted a vigour beyond the law, they not only forgave, but applauded him, and while they enjoyed security and prosperity under his rule, were but too ready to believe that whoever had incurred his displeasure had deserved it. But to this indulgence there was a limit; nor was that King wise who presumed far on the forbearance of the English people. They might sometimes allow him to overstep the constitutional line : but they also claimed the privilege of overstepping that line themselves, whenever his encroachments were so serious as to excite alarm. If, not content with occasionally oppressing individuals, he dared to oppress great masses, his subjects promptly appealed to the laws, and, that appeal failing, appealed as promptly to the God of battles.

Our forefathers might indeed safely tolerate a king in a few excesses; for they had in reserve a check which soon brought the fiercest and proudest king to reason, the check of physical force. It is difficult for an Englishman of the nineteenth century to imagine to himself the facility and rapidity with which, four hundred years ago, this check was applied. The people have long unlearned the use of arms. The art of war has been carried to a perfection unknown to former ages; and the knowledge of that art is confined to a particular class. A hundred thousand soldiers, well disciplined and commanded, will keep down ten millions of ploughmen and artisans. A few regiments of household troops are sufficient to overawe all the discontented spirits of a large capital. In the meantime the effect of the constant progress of wealth has been to make insurrection far more terrible to thinking men than maladministration. Immense sums have been expended on works which, if a rebellion broke out, might perish in a few hours. The mass of movable wealth collected in the shops and warehouses of London alone exceeds five hundredfold that which the whole island contained in the days of the Plantagenets; and, if the government were subverted by physical force, all this movable wealth would be exposed to imminent risk of spoliation and destruction. Still greater would be the risk to public credit, on which thousands of families directly depend for subsistence, and with which the credit of the whole commercial world is inseparably connected. It is no exaggeration to say that a civil war of a week on English ground would now produce disasters which would be felt from the Hoangho to the Missouri, and of which the traces would be discernible at the distance of a century. In such a state of society resistance must be regarded as a cure more desperate than almost any malady which can afflict the state. In the middle ages, on the contrary, resistance was an ordinary remedy for political distempers, a remedy which was always at hand, and which, though doubtless sharp at the moment, produced no deep or lasting ill effects.

Resistance an ordinary check on tyranny in the middle ages.

If a popular chief raised his standard in a popular cause, an irregular army could be assembled in a day. Regular army tnere was none. Every man had a slight tincture of soldiership, and scarcely any man more than a slight tincture. The national wealth consisted chiefly in flocks and herds, in the harvest of the year, and in the simple buildings inhabited by the people. All the furniture, the stock of shops, the machinery which could be found in the realm was of less value than the property which some single parishes now contain. Manufactures were rude; credit was almost unknown. Society, therefore, recovered from the shock as soon as the actual conflict was over. The calamities of civil war were confined to the slaughter on the field of battle, and to a few subsequent executions and confiscations. In a week the peasant was driving his team and the esquire flying his hawks over the field of Towton or of Bosworth, as if no extraordinary event had interrupted the regular course of human life.

More than a hundred and sixty years have now elapsed since the English people have by force subverted a government. During the hundred and sixty years which preceded the union of the Roses, nine Kings reigned in England. Six of these nine Kings were deposed. Five lost their lives as well as their crowns. It is evident, therefore, that any comparison between our ancient and our modern polity must lead to most erroneous conclusions, unless large allowance be made for the effect of that restraint which resistance and the fear of resistance constantly imposed on the Plantagenets. As our ancestors had against tyranny a most important security which we want, they might safely dispense with some securities to which we justly attach the highest importance. As we cannot, without the risk of evils from which the imagination recoils, employ physical force as a check on misgovernment, it is evidently our wisdom to keep all the constitutional checks on misgovernment in the highest state of efficiency, to watch with jealousy the first beginnings of encroachment, and never to suffer irregularities, even when harmless in themselves, to pass unchallenged, lest they acquire the force of precedents. Four hundred years ago such minute vigilance might well seem unnecessary. A nation of hardy archers and spearmen might, with small risk to its liberties, connive at some illegal acts on the part of a prince whose general administration was good, and whose throne was not defended by a single company of regular soldiers.

Under this system, rude as it may appear when compared with those elaborate constitutions of which the last seventy years have been fruitful, the English long enjoyed a large measure of freedom and happiness. Though, during the feeble reign of Henry the Sixth, the state was torn, first by factions, and at length by civil war; though Edward the Fourth was a prince of dissolute and imperious character; though Richard the Third has generally been represented as a monster of depravity; though the exactions of Henry the Seventh caused great repining; it is certain that our ancestors, under those Kings, were far better governed than the Belgians under Philip, surnamed the Good, or the French under that Lewis who was styled the Father of his people. Even while the wars of the Roses were actually raging, our country appears to have been in a happier condition than the neighbouring realms during years of profound peace. Comines was one of the most enlightened statesmen of his time. He had seen all the richest and most highly civilised parts of the Continent. He had lived in the opulent towns of Flanders, the Manchesters and Liverpools of the fifteenth century. He had visited Florence, recently adorned by the magnificence of Lorenzo, and Venice, not yet humbled by the Confederates of Cambray. This eminent man deliberately pronounced England to be the best governed country of which he had any knowledge. Her constitution he emphatically designated as a just and holy thing, which, while it protected the people, really strengthened the hands of a prince who respected it. In no other country, he said, were men so effectually secured from wrong. The calamities produced by our intestine wars seemed to him to be confined to the nobles and the fighting men, and to leave no traces such as he had been accustomed to see elsewhere, no ruined dwellings, no depopulated cities.

It was not only by the efficiency of the restraints imposed on the royal prerogative that England was advantageously distinguished from most of the neighbouring countries. A peculiarity equally important, though less noticed, was the relation in which the nobility stood here to the commonalty. There was a strong hereditary aristocracy: but it was of all hereditary aristocracies the least insolent and exclusive. It had none of the invidious cha-

Peculiar character of the English aristocracy.

racter of a caste. It was constantly receiving members from the people, and constantly sending down members to mingle with the people. Any gentleman might become a peer. The younger son of a peer was but a gentleman. Grandsons of peers yielded precedence to newly made knights. The dignity of knighthood was not beyond the reach of any man who could by diligence and thrift realise a good estate, or who could attract notice by his valour in a battle or a siege. It was regarded as no disparagement for the daughter of a Duke, nay of a royal Duke, to espouse a distinguished commoner. Thus, Sir John Howard married the daughter of Thomas Mowbray Duke of Norfolk. Sir Richard Pole married the Countess of Salisbury, daughter of George Duke of Clarence. Good blood was indeed held in high respect: but between good blood and the privileges of peerage there was, most fortunately for our country, no necessary connection. Pedigrees as long, and scutcheons as old, were to be found out of the House of Lords as in it. There were new men who bore the highest titles. There were untitled men well known to be descended from knights who had broken the Saxon ranks at Hastings, and scaled the walls of Jerusalem. There were Bohuns, Mowbrays, De Veres, nay, kinsmen of the House of Plantagenet, with no higher addition than that of Esquire, and with no civil privileges beyond those enjoyed by every farmer and shopkeeper. There was therefore here no line like that which in some other countries divided the patrician from the plebeian. The yeoman was not inclined to murmur at dignities to which his own children might rise. The grandee was not inclined to insult a class into which his own children must descend.

After the wars of York and Lancaster, the links which connected the nobility and the commonalty became closer and more numerous than ever. The extent of the destruction which had fallen on the old aristocracy may be inferred from a single circumstance. In the year 1451 Henry the Sixth summoned fifty-three temporal Lords to parliament. The temporal Lords summoned by Henry the Seventh to the parliament of 1485 were only twenty-nine, and of these several had recently been elevated to the peerage. During the following century the ranks of the nobility were largely recruited from among the gentry. The constitution of the House of Commons tended greatly to promote the salutary intermixture of classes. The knight of the shire was the connecting link between the baron and the shopkeeper. On the same benches on which sate the goldsmiths, drapers, and grocers, who had been returned to parliament by the commercial towns, sate also members who, in any other country, would have been called noblemen, hereditary lords of manors, entitled to hold courts and to bear coat armour, and able to trace back an honourable descent through many generations. Some of them were younger sons and brothers of lords. Others could boast of even royal blood. At length the eldest son of an Earl of Bedford, called in courtesy by the second title of his father, offered himself as candidate for a seat in the House of Commons, and his example was followed by others. Seated in that house, the heirs of the great peers naturally became as zealous for its privileges as any of the humble burgesses with whom they were mingled. Thus our democracy was, from an early period, the most aristocratic, and our aristocracy the most democratic in the world; a peculiarity which has lasted down to the present day, and which has produced many important moral and political effects.

The government of Henry the Seventh, of his son, and of his grandchildren was, on the whole, more arbitrary than that of the Plantagenets. Personal character may in some degree explain the difference; for courage and force of will were common to all the men and women of the House of Tudor. They exercised their power during a period of a hundred and twenty years, always with vigour, often with violence, sometimes with cruelty. They, in imitation of the dynasty which had preceded them, occasionally invaded the rights of the subject, occasionally exacted taxes under the name of loans and gifts, and occasionally dispensed with penal statutes: nay, though they never presumed to enact any permanent law by their own authority, they occasionally took upon themselves, when Parliament was not sitting, to meet temporary exigencies by temporary edicts. It was, however, impossible for the Tudors to carry oppression beyond a certain point: for they had no armed force, and they were surrounded by an armed people. Their palace was guarded by a few domestics, whom the array of a single shire, or of a single ward of London, could with ease have overpowered. These haughty princes were therefore under a restraint stronger than any which mere law can impose, under a restraint which did not, indeed, prevent them from sometimes treating an individual in an arbitrary and even in

Government of the Tudors.

a barbarous manner, but which effectually secured the nation against general and long continued oppression. They might safely be tyrants within the precinct of the court: but it was necessary for them to watch with constant anxiety the temper of the country. Henry the Eighth, for example, encountered no opposition when he wished to send Buckingham and Surrey, Anne Boleyn and Lady Salisbury, to the scaffold. But when, without the consent of Parliament, he demanded of his subjects a contribution amounting to one sixth of their goods, he soon found it necessary to retract. The cry of hundreds of thousands was that they were English and not French, freemen and not slaves. In Kent the royal commissioners fled for their lives. In Suffolk four thousand men appeared in arms. The King's lieutenants in that county vainly exerted themselves to raise an army. Those who did not join in the insurrection declared that they would not fight against their brethren in such a quarrel. Henry, proud and selfwilled as he was, shrank, not without reason, from a conflict with the roused spirit of the nation. He had before his eyes the fate of his predecessors who had perished at Berkeley and Pomfret. He not only cancelled his illegal commissions; he not only granted a general pardon to all the malecontents; but he publicly and solemnly apologised for his infraction of the laws.

His conduct, on this occasion, well illustrates the whole policy of his house. The temper of the princes of that line was hot, and their spirit high : but they understood the character of the nation which they governed, and never once, like some of their predecessors, and some of their successors, carried obstinacy to a fatal point. The discretion of the Tudors was such, that their power, though it was often resisted, was never subverted. The reign of every one of them was disturbed by formidable discontents : but the government was always able either to soothe the mutineers, or to conquer and punish them. Sometimes, by timely concessions, it succeeded in averting civil hostilities ; but in general it stood firm, and called for help on the nation. The nation obeyed the call, rallied round the sovereign, and enabled him to quell the disaffected minority.

Thus, from the age of Henry the Third to the age of Elizabeth, England grew and flourished under a polity which contained the germ of our present institutions, and which, though not very exactly defined, or very exactly observed, was yet effectually prevented from degenerating into despotism, by the awe in which the governors stood of the spirit and strength of the governed.

But such a polity is suited only to a particular stage in the progress of society. The same causes which produce a division of labour in the peaceful arts must at length make war a distinct science and a distinct trade. A time arrives when the use of arms begins to occupy the entire attention of a separate class. It soon appears that peasants and burghers, however brave, are unable to stand their ground against veteran soldiers, whose whole life is a preparation for the day of battle, whose nerves have been braced by long familiarity with danger, and whose movements have all the precision of clockwork. It is found that the defence of nations can no longer be safely entrusted to warriors taken from the plough or the loom for a campaign of forty days. If any state forms a great regular army, the bordering states must imitate the example, or must submit to a foreign yoke. But, where a great regular army exists, limited monarchy, such as it was in the middle ages, can exist no longer. The sovereign is at once emancipated from what had been the chief restraint on his power; and he inevitably becomes absolute, unless he is subjected to checks such as would be superfluous in a society where all are soldiers occasionally, and none permanently.

With the danger came also the means of escape. In the monarchies of the middle ages the power of the sword belonged to the prince; but the power of the purse belonged to the nation; and the progress of civilisation, as it made the sword of the prince more and more formidable to the nation, made the purse of the nation more and more necessary to the prince. His hereditary revenues would no longer suffice, even for the expenses of civil government. It was utterly impossible that, without a regular and extensive system of taxation, he could keep in constant efficiency a great body of disciplined troops. The policy which the parliamentary assemblies of Europe ought to have adopted was to take their stand firmly on their constitutional right to give or withhold money, and resolutely to refuse funds for the support of armies, till ample securities had been provided against despotism.

This wise policy was followed in our country alone. In the neighbouring kingdoms great military establishments

Limited monarchies of the middle ages generally turned into absolute monarchies.

were formed; no new safeguards for public liberty were devised; and the consequence was, that the old parliamentary institutions everywhere ceased to exist. In France, where they had always been feeble, they languished, and at length died of mere weakness. In Spain, where they had been as strong as in any part of Europe, they struggled fiercely for life, but struggled too late. The mechanics of Toledo and Valladolid vainly defended the privileges of the Castilian Cortes against the veteran battalions of Charles the Fifth. As vainly, in the next generation, did the citizens of Saragossa stand up against Philip the Second, for the old constitution of Aragon. One after another, the great national councils of the continental monarchies, councils once scarcely less proud and powerful than those which sate at Westminster, sank into utter insignificance. If they met, they met merely as our Convocation now meets, to go through some venerable forms.

The English monarchy a singular exception.

In England events took a different course. This singular felicity she owed chiefly to her insular situation. Before the end of the fifteenth century great military establishments were indispensable to the dignity, and even to the safety, of the French and Castilian monarchies. If either of those two powers had disarmed, it would soon have been compelled to submit to the dictation of the other. But England, protected by the sea against invasion, and rarely engaged in warlike operations on the Continent, was not, as yet, under the necessity of employing regular troops. The sixteenth century, the seventeenth century, found her still without a standing army. At the commencement of the seventeenth century political science had made considerable progress. The fate of the Spanish Cortes and of the French States General had given solemn warning to our Parliaments; and our Parliaments, fully aware of the nature and magnitude of the danger, adopted, in good time, a system of tactics which, after a contest protracted through three generations, was at length successful.

Almost every writer who has treated of that contest has been desirous to show that his own party was the party which was struggling to preserve the old constitution unaltered. The truth however is that the old constitution could not be preserved unaltered. A law, beyond the control of human wisdom, had decreed that there should no longer be governments of that peculiar class which, in the fourteenth and fifteenth centuries, had been common throughout Europe.

The question, therefore, was not whether our polity should undergo a change, but what the nature of the change should be. The introduction of a new and mighty force had disturbed the old equilibrium, and had turned one limited monarchy after another into an absolute monarchy. What had happened elsewhere would assuredly have happened here, unless the balance had been redressed by a great transfer of power from the crown to the parliament. Our princes were about to have at their command means of coercion such as no Plantagenet or Tudor had ever possessed. They must inevitably have become despots, unless they had been, at the same time, placed under restraints to which no Plantagenet or Tudor had ever been subject.

It seems certain, therefore, that, had none but political causes been at work, the seventeenth century would not have passed away without a fierce conflict between our Kings and their Parliaments. But other causes of perhaps greater potency contributed to produce the same effect. While the government of the Tudors was in its highest vigour an event took place which has coloured the destinies of all Christian nations, and in an especial manner the destinies of England. Twice during the middle ages the mind of Europe had risen up against the domination of Rome. The first insurrection broke out in the south of France. The energy of Innocent the Third, the zeal of the young orders of Francis and Dominic, and the ferocity of the Crusaders whom the priesthood let loose on an unwarlike population, crushed the Albigensian churches. The second reformation had its origin in England, and spread to Bohemia. The Council of Constance, by removing some ecclesiastical disorders which had given scandal to Christendom, and the princes of Europe, by unsparingly using fire and sword against the heretics, succeeded in arresting and turning back the movement. Nor is this much to be lamented. The sympathies of a Protestant, it is true, will naturally be on the side of the Albigensians and of the Lollards. Yet an enlightened and temperate Protestant will perhaps be disposed to doubt whether the success, either of the Albigensians or of the Lollards, would, on the whole, have promoted the happiness and virtue of mankind. Corrupt as the Church of Rome was, there is reason to believe that, if that Church had been overthrown in the twelfth or even in the fourteenth century, the vacant space would have been occupied by some system more corrupt

still. There was then, through the greater part of Europe,
very little knowledge; and that little was confined to the
clergy. Not one man in five hundred could have spelled his
way through a psalm. Books were few and costly. The art
of printing was unknown. Copies of the Bible, inferior in
beauty and clearness to those which every cottager may now
command, sold for prices which many priests could not afford
to give. It was obviously impossible that the laity should
search the Scriptures for themselves. It is probable therefore, that, as soon as they had put off one spiritual yoke, they
would have put on another, and that the power lately exercised
by the clergy of the Church of Rome would have passed to a
far worse class of teachers. The sixteenth century was comparatively a time of light. Yet even in the sixteenth century
a considerable number of those who quitted the old religion
followed the first confident and plausible guide who offered
himself, and were soon led into errors far more serious than
those which they had renounced. Thus Matthias and Kniper-
doling, apostles of lust, robbery, and murder, were able for a
time to rule great cities. In a darker age such false prophets
might have founded empires; and Christianity might have
been distorted into a cruel and licentious superstition, more
noxious, not only than Popery, but even than Islamism.

About a hundred years after the rising of the Council of
Constance, that great change emphatically called the Reformation began. The fulness of time was now come. The
clergy were no longer the sole or the chief depositories of
knowledge. The invention of printing had furnished the
assailants of the Church with a mighty weapon which had
been wanting to their predecessors. The study of the ancient
writers, the rapid development of the powers of the modern
languages, the unprecedented activity which was displayed in
every department of literature, the political state of Europe,
the vices of the Roman court, the exactions of the Roman
chancery, the jealousy with which the wealth and privileges
of the clergy were naturally regarded by laymen, the jealousy
with which the Italian ascendency was naturally regarded by
men born on our side of the Alps, all these things gave to the
teachers of the new theology an advantage which they perfectly understood how to use.

Those who hold that the influence of the Church of Rome
in the dark ages was, on the whole, beneficial to mankind
may yet with perfect consistency regard the Reformation as

an inestimable blessing. The leading strings, which preserve and uphold the infant, would impede the fullgrown man. And so the very means by which the human mind is, in one stage of its progress, supported and propelled, may, in another stage, be mere hindrances. There is a season in the life both of an individual and of a society, at which submission and faith, such as at a later period would be justly called servility and credulity, are useful qualities. The child who teachably and undoubtingly listens to the instructions of his elders is likely to improve rapidly. But the man who should receive with childlike docility every assertion and dogma uttered by another man no wiser than himself would become contemptible. It is the same with communities. The childhood of the European nations was passed under the tutelage of the clergy. The ascendency of the sacerdotal order was long the ascendency which naturally and properly belongs to intellectual superiority. The priests, with all their faults, were by far the wisest portion of society. It was, therefore, on the whole, good that they should be respected and obeyed. The encroachments of the ecclesiastical power on the province of the civil power produced much more happiness than misery, while the ecclesiastical power was in the hands of the only class that had studied history, philosophy, and public law, and while the civil power was in the hands of savage chiefs, who could not read their own grants and edicts. But a change took place. Knowledge gradually spread among laymen. At the commencement of the sixteenth century many of them were in every intellectual attainment fully equal to the most enlightened of their spiritual pastors. Thenceforward that dominion, which, during the dark ages, had been, in spite of many abuses, a legitimate and salutary guardianship, became an unjust and noxious tyranny.

From the time when the barbarians overran the Western Empire to the time of the revival of letters, the influence of the Church of Rome had been generally favourable to science, to civilisation, and to good government. But, during the last three centuries, to stunt the growth of the human mind has been her chief object. Throughout Christendom, whatever advance has been made in knowledge, in freedom, in wealth, and in the arts of life, has been made in spite of her, and has everywhere been in inverse proportion to her power. The loveliest and most fertile provinces of Europe have, under her rule, been sunk in poverty, in political servitude, and in

intellectual torpor, while Protestant countries, once proverbial
for sterility and barbarism, have been turned by skill and
industry into gardens, and can boast of a long list of heroes
and statesmen, philosophers and poets.   Whoever, knowing what Italy and Scotland naturally are, and what, four
hundred years ago, they actually were, shall now compare
the country round Rome with the country round Edinburgh,
will be able to form some judgment as to the tendency of
Papal domination.   The descent of Spain, once the first
among monarchies, to the lowest depths of degradation, the
elevation of Holland, in spite of many natural disadvantages,
to a position such as no commonwealth so small has ever
reached, teach the same lesson. Whoever passes in Germany
from a Roman Catholic to a Protestant principality, in Switzerland from a Roman Catholic to a Protestant canton, in
Ireland from a Roman Catholic to a Protestant county, finds
that he has passed from a lower to a higher grade of civilisation.   On the other side of the Atlantic the same law prevails.
The Protestants of the United States have left far behind
them the Roman Catholics of Mexico, Peru, and Brazil. The
Roman Catholics of Lower Canada remain inert, while the
whole continent round them is in a ferment with Protestant
activity and enterprise.   The French have doubtless shown
an energy and an intelligence which, even when misdirected,
have justly entitled them to be called a great people.   But
this apparent exception, when examined, will be found to
confirm the rule; for in no country that is called Roman
Catholic, has the Roman Catholic Church, during several
generations, possessed so little authority as in France.   The
literature of France is justly held in high esteem throughout
the world.   But if we deduct from that literature all that
belongs to four parties which have been, on different grounds,
in rebellion against the Papal domination, all that belongs to
the Protestants, all that belongs to the assertors of the
Gallican liberties, all that belongs to the Jansenists, and all
that belongs to the philosophers, how much will be left?

It is difficult to say whether England owes more to the
Roman Catholic religion or to the Reformation.   For the
amalgamation of races and for the abolition of villenage, she
is chiefly indebted to the influence which the priesthood in
the middle ages exercised over the laity.   For political and
intellectual freedom, and for all the blessings which political
and intellectual freedom have brought in their train, she is

hiefly indebted to the great rebellion of the laity against the priesthood.

The struggle between the old and the new theology in our country was long, and the event sometimes seemed doubtful. There were two extreme parties, prepared to act with violence or to suffer with stubborn resolution. Between them lay, during a considerable time, a middle party, which blended, very illogically, but by no means unnaturally, lessons learned in the nursery with the sermons of the modern evangelists, and, while clinging with fondness to old observances, yet detested abuses with which those observances were closely connected. Men in such a frame of mind were willing to obey, almost with thankfulness, the dictation of an able ruler who spared them the trouble of judging for themselves, and, raising a firm and commanding voice above the uproar of controversy, told them how to worship and what to believe. It is not strange, therefore, that the Tudors should have been able to exercise a great influence on ecclesiastical affairs; nor is it strange that their influence should, for the most part, have been exercised with a view to their own interest.

Henry the Eighth attempted to constitute an Anglican Church differing from the Roman Catholic Church on the point of the supremacy, and on that point alone. His success in this attempt was extraordinary. The force of his character, the singularly favourable situation in which he stood with respect to foreign powers, the immense wealth which the spoliation of the abbeys placed at his disposal, and the support of that class which still halted between two opinions, enabled him to bid defiance to both the extreme parties, to burn as heretics those who avowed the tenets of the Reformers, and to hang as traitors those who owned the authority of the Pope. But Henry's system died with him. Had his life been prolonged, he would have found it difficult to maintain a position assailed with equal fury by all who were zealous either for the new or for the old opinions. The ministers who held the royal prerogatives in trust for his infant son could not venture to persist in so hazardous a policy; nor could Elizabeth venture to return to it. It was necessary to make a choice. The government must either submit to Rome, or must obtain the aid of the Protestants. The government and the Protestants had only one thing in common, hatred of the Papal power. The English Reformers were eager to go as far as their brethren on the Continent. They unanimously

condemned as Antichristian numerous dogmas and practices
to which Henry had stubbornly adhered, and which Elizabeth
reluctantly abandoned.   Many felt a strong repugnance even
to things indifferent which had formed part of the polity or
ritual of the mystical Babylon.   Thus Bishop Hooper, who
died manfully at Gloucester for his religion, long refused to
wear the episcopal vestments.   Bishop Ridley, a martyr of
still greater renown, pulled down the ancient altars of his
diocese, and ordered the Eucharist to be administered in the
middle of churches, at tables which the Papists irreverently
termed oyster boards.   Bishop Jewel pronounced the clerical
garb to be a stage dress, a fool's coat, a relique of the Amorites,
and promised that he would spare no labour to extirpate such
degrading absurdities.   Archbishop Grindal long hesitated
about accepting a mitre from dislike of what he regarded as
the mummery of consecration.   Bishop Parkhurst uttered a
fervent prayer that the Church of England would propose to
herself the Church of Zurich as the absolute pattern of a
Christian community.   Bishop Ponet was of opinion that the
word Bishop should be abandoned to the Papists, and that
the chief officers of the purified church should be called
Superintendents.   When it is considered that none of these
prelates belonged to the extreme section of the Protestant
party, it cannot be doubted that, if the general sense of that
party had been followed,the work of reform would have been
carried on as unsparingly in England as in Scotland.

Origin of   But, as the government needed the support of the Protes-
the Church tants, so the Protestants needed the protection of the govern-
of Eng-
land.   ment.   Much was therefore given up on both sides : an union
was effected ; and the fruit of that union was the Church of
England.

To the peculiarities of this great institution, and to the
strong passions which it has called forth in the minds both
of friends and of enemies, are to be attributed many of the
most important events which have, since the Reformation,
taken place in our country ; nor can the secular history of
England be at all understood by us, unless we study it in constant connection with the history of her ecclesiastical polity.

The man who took the chief part in settling the conditions
of the alliance which produced the Anglican Church was
Archbishop Cranmer.   He was the representative of both the
parties which, at that time, needed each other's assistance.
He was at once a divine and a courtier.   In his character of

divine he was perfectly ready to go as far in the way of change as any Swiss or Scottish Reformer. In his character of courtier he was desirous to preserve that organisation which had, during many ages, admirably served the purposes of the Bishops of Rome, and might be expected now to serve equally well the purposes of the English Kings and of their ministers. His temper and his understanding eminently fitted him to act as mediator. Saintly in his professions, unscrupulous in his dealings, zealous for nothing, bold in speculation, a coward and a timeserver in action, a placable enemy and a lukewarm friend, he was in every way qualified to arrange the terms of the coalition between the religious and the worldly enemies of Popery.

To this day the constitution, the doctrines, and the services of the Church, retain the visible marks of the compromise from which she sprang. She occupies a middle position between the Churches of Rome and Geneva. Her doctrinal confessions and discourses, composed by Protestants, set forth principles of theology in which Calvin or Knox would have found scarcely a word to disapprove. Her prayers and thanksgivings, derived from the ancient Breviaries, are very generally such that Cardinal Fisher or Cardinal Pole might have heartily joined in them. A controversialist who puts an Arminian sense on her Articles and Homilies will be pronounced by candid men to be as unreasonable as a controversialist who denies that the doctrine of baptismal regeneration can be discovered in her Liturgy.

The Church of Rome held that episcopacy was of divine institution, and that certain supernatural graces of a high order had been transmitted by the imposition of hands through fifty generations, from the Eleven who received their commission on the Galilean mount, to the bishops who met at Trent. A large body of Protestants, on the other hand, regarded prelacy as positively unlawful, and persuaded themselves that they found a very different form of ecclesiastical government prescribed in Scripture. The founders of the Anglican Church took a middle course. They retained episcopacy; but they did not declare it to be an institution essential to the welfare of a Christian society, or to the efficacy of the sacraments. Cranmer, indeed, on one important occasion, plainly avowed his conviction that, in the primitive times, there was no distinction between bishops and priests, and that the laying on of hands was altogether superfluous.

Her peculiar character

Among the Presbyterians the conduct of public worship is, to a great extent, left to the minister. Their prayers, therefore, are not exactly the same in any two assemblies on the same day, or on any two days in the same assembly. In one parish they are fervent, eloquent, and full of meaning. In the next parish they may be languid or absurd. The priests of the Roman Catholic Church, on the other hand, have, during many generations, daily chaunted the same ancient confessions, supplications, and thanksgivings, in India and Lithuania, in Ireland and Peru. The service, being in a dead language, is intelligible only to the learned; and the great majority of the congregation may be said to assist as spectators rather than as auditors. Here, again, the Church of England took a middle course. She copied the Roman Catholic forms of prayer, but translated them into the vulgar tongue, and invited the illiterate multitude to join its voice to that of the minister.

In every part of her system the same policy may be traced. Utterly rejecting the doctrine of transubstantiation, and condemning as idolatrous all adoration paid to the sacramental bread and wine, she yet, to the disgust of the Puritan, required her children to receive the memorials of divine love, meekly kneeling upon their knees. Discarding many rich vestments which surrounded the altars of the ancient faith, she yet retained, to the horror of weak minds, a robe of white linen, typical of the purity which belonged to her as the mystical spouse of Christ. Discarding a crowd of pantomimic gestures which, in the Roman Catholic worship, are substituted for intelligible words, she yet shocked many rigid Protestants by marking the infant just sprinkled from the font with the sign of the cross. The Roman Catholic addressed his prayers to a multitude of Saints, among whom were numbered many men of doubtful, and some of hateful, character. The Puritan refused the addition of Saint even to the apostle of the Gentiles, and to the disciple whom Jesus loved. The Church of England, though she asked for the intercession of no created being, still set apart days for the commemoration of some who had done and suffered great things for the faith. She retained confirmation and ordination as edifying rites; but she degraded them from the rank of sacraments. Shrift was no part of her system. Yet she gently invited the dying penitent to confess his sins to a divine, and empowered her ministers to soothe the departing soul by an absolution which breathes the very spirit of the old religion. In general it may be said that she appeals more to the understanding, and less to the senses and the imagination, than the Church of Rome, and that she appeals less to the understanding, and more to the senses and imagination, than the Protestant Churches of Scotland, France, and Switzerland.

Nothing, however, so strongly distinguished the Church of England from other Churches as the relation in which she stood to the monarchy. The King was her head. The limits of the authority which he possessed, as such, were not traced, and indeed have never yet been traced, with precision. The laws which declared him supreme in ecclesiastical matters were drawn rudely and in general terms. If, for the purpose of ascertaining the sense of those laws, we examine the books and lives of those who founded the English Church, our perplexity will be increased. For the founders of the English Church wrote and acted in an age of violent intellectual fermentation, and of constant action and reaction. They therefore often contradicted each other, and sometimes contradicted themselves. That the King was, under Christ, sole head of the Church, was a doctrine which they all with one voice affirmed: but those words had very different significations in different mouths, and in the same mouth at different conjunctures. Sometimes an authority which would have satisfied Hildebrand was ascribed to the sovereign: then it dwindled down to an authority little more than that which had been claimed by many ancient English princes who had been in constant communion with the Church of Rome. What Henry and his favourite counsellors meant, at one time, by the supremacy, was certainly nothing less than the whole power of the keys. The King was to be the Pope of his kingdom, the vicar of God, the expositor of Catholic verity, the channel of sacramental graces. He arrogated to himself the right of deciding dogmatically what was orthodox doctrine and what was heresy, of drawing up and imposing confessions of faith, and of giving religious instruction to his people. He proclaimed that all jurisdiction, spiritual as well as temporal, was derived from him alone, and that it was in his power to confer episcopal authority, and to take it away. He actually ordered his seal to be put to commissions by which bishops were appointed, who were to exercise their functions as his deputies, and during his pleasure. According to this system, as expounded by Cranmer, the King was the spiritual as well

Relation in which she stood to the crown

as the temporal chief of the nation. In both capacities His Highness must have lieutenants. As he appointed civil officers to keep his seal, to collect his revenues, and to dispense justice in his name, so he appointed divines of various ranks to preach the gospel, and to administer the sacraments. It was unnecessary that there should be any imposition of hands. The King,—such was the opinion of Cranmer given in the plainest words,—might, in virtue of authority derived from God, make a priest; and the priest so made needed no ordination whatever. These opinions the Archbishop, in spite of the opposition of less courtly divines, followed out to every legitimate consequence. He held that his own spiritual functions, like the secular functions of the Chancellor and Treasurer, were at once determined by a demise of the crown. When Henry died, therefore, the Primate and his suffragans took out fresh commissions, empowering them to ordain and to govern the Church till the new sovereign should think fit to order otherwise. When it was objected that a power to bind and to loose, altogether distinct from temporal power, had been given by our Lord to his apostles, some theologians of this school replied that the power to bind and to loose had descended, not to the clergy, but to the whole body of Christian men, and ought to be exercised by the chief magistrate as the representative of the society. When it was objected that Saint Paul had spoken of certain persons whom the Holy Ghost had made overseers and shepherds of the faithful, it was answered that King Henry was the very overseer, the very shepherd, whom the Holy Ghost had appointed, and to whom the expressions of Saint Paul applied.*

These high pretensions gave scandal to Protestants as well as to Catholics; and the scandal was greatly increased when the supremacy, which Mary had resigned back to the Pope, was again annexed to the crown, on the accession of Elizabeth. It seemed monstrous that a woman should be the chief bishop of a Church in which an apostle had forbidden her even to let her voice be heard. The Queen, therefore, found it necessary expressly to disclaim that sacerdotal character which her father had assumed, and which, according to Cranmer, had been inseparably joined, by divine ordinance, to the regal function. When the Anglican confession of faith was revised in her reign, the supremacy was explained in a manner somewhat

* See ·a very curious paper which handwriting. Ecclesiastical Memorials Strype believed to be in Gardiner's Book I. Chap. xvii.

different from that which had been fashionable at the court of Henry. Cranmer had declared, in emphatic terms, that God had immediately committed to Christian princes the whole cure of all their subjects, as well concerning the administration of God's word for the cure of souls, as concerning the administration of things political.* The thirty-seventh article of religion, framed under Elizabeth, declares, in terms as emphatic, that the ministering of God's word does not belong to princes. The Queen, however, still had over the Church a visitatorial power of vast and undefined extent. She was entrusted by Parliament with the office of restraining and punishing heresy and every sort of ecclesiastical abuse, and was permitted to delegate her authority to commissioners. The Bishops were little more than her ministers. Rather than grant to the civil magistrate the absolute power of nominating spiritual pastors, the Church of Rome, in the eleventh century, set all Europe on fire. Rather than grant to the civil magistrate the absolute power of nominating spiritual pastors, the ministers of the Church of Scotland, in our our time, resigned their livings by hundreds. The Church of England had no such scruples. By the royal authority alone her prelates were appointed. By the royal authority alone her Convocations were summoned, regulated, prorogued, and dissolved. Without the royal sanction her canons had no force. One of the articles of her faith was that without the royal consent no ecclesiastical council could lawfully assemble. From all her judicatures an appeal lay, in the last resort, to the sovereign, even when the question was whether an opinion ought to be accounted heretical, or whether the administration of a sacrament had been valid. Nor did the Church grudge this extensive power to our princes. By them she had been called into existence, nursed through a feeble infancy, guarded from Papists on one side and from Puritans on the other, protected against Parliaments which bore her no good will, and avenged on literary assailants whom she found it hard to answer. Thus gratitude, hope, fear, common attachments, common enmities, bound her to the throne. All her traditions, all her tastes, were monarchical. Loyalty became a point of professional honour among her clergy, the peculiar badge which distinguished them at once from Calvinists and from Papists. Both the Calvinists and the Papists,

* These are Cranmer's own words. See the Appendix to Burnet's History of the Reformation, Part I. Book III. No. 21. Question 9

widely as they differed in other respects, regarded with extreme jealousy all encroachments of the temporal power on the domain of the spiritual power. Both Calvinists and Papists maintained that subjects might justifiably draw the sword against ungodly rulers. In France Calvinists resisted Charles the Ninth: Papists resisted Henry the Fourth: both Papists and Calvinists resisted Henry the Third. In Scotland Calvinists led Mary captive. On the north of the Trent Papists took arms against the English throne. The Church of England meantime condemned both Calvinists and Papists, and loudly boasted that no duty was more constantly or earnestly inculcated by her than that of submission to princes.

The advantages which the crown derived from this close alliance with the Established Church were great; but they were not without serious drawbacks. The compromise arranged by Cranmer had from the first been considered by a large body of Protestants as a scheme for serving two masters, as an attempt to unite the worship of the Lord with the worship of Baal. In the days of Edward the Sixth the scruples of this party had repeatedly thrown great difficulties in the way of the government. When Elizabeth came to the throne, those difficulties were much increased. Violence naturally engenders violence. The spirit of Protestantism was therefore far fiercer and more intolerant after the cruelties of Mary than before them. Many persons who were warmly attached to the new opinions had, during the evil days, taken refuge in Switzerland and Germany. They had been hospitably received by their brethren in the faith, had sate at the feet of the great doctors of Strasburg, Zurich, and Geneva, and had been, during some years, accustomed to a more simple worship, and to a more democratical form of church government, than England had yet seen. These men returned to their country, convinced that the reform which had been effected under King Edward had been far less searching and extensive than the interests of pure religion required. But it was in vain that they attempted to obtain any concession from Elizabeth. Indeed her system, whereever it differed from her brother's, seemed to them to differ for the worse. They were little disposed to submit, in matters of faith, to any human authority. They had recently, in reliance on their own interpretation of Scripture, risen up against a Church strong in immemorial antiquity and catholic consent. It was by no common exertion of intellectual

The Puritans.

energy that they had thrown off the yoke of that gorgeous and imperial superstition; and it was vain to expect that, immediately after such an emancipation, they would patiently submit to a new spiritual tyranny. Long accustomed, when the priest lifted up the host, to bow down with their faces to the earth, as before a present God, they had learned to treat the mass as an idolatrous mummery. Long accustomed to regard the Pope as the successor of the chief of the apostles, as the bearer of the keys of earth and heaven, they had learned to regard him as the Beast, the Antichrist, the Man of Sin. It was not to be expected that they would immediately transfer to an upstart authority the homage which they had withdrawn from the Vatican; that they would submit their private judgment to the authority of a Church founded on private judgment alone; that they would be afraid to dissent from teachers who themselves dissented from what had lately been the universal faith of western Christendom. It is easy to conceive the indignation which must have been felt by bold and inquisitive spirits, glorying in newly acquired freedom, when an institution younger by many years than themselves, an institution which had, under their own eyes, gradually received its form from the passions and interests of a court, began to mimic the lofty style of Rome.

Since these men could not be convinced, it was determined that they should be persecuted. Persecution produced its natural effect on them. It found them a sect: it made them a faction. To their hatred of the Church was now added *Their re-* hatred of the Crown. The two sentiments were inter- *publican* mingled; and each embittered the other. The opinions of *spirit.* the Puritan concerning the relation of ruler and subject were widely different from those which were inculcated in the Homilies. His favourite divines had, both by precept and by example, encouraged resistance to tyrants and persecutors. His fellow Calvinists in France, in Holland, and in Scotland, were in arms against idolatrous and cruel princes. His notions, too, respecting the government of the state took a tinge from his notions respecting the government of the Church. Some of the sarcasms which were popularly thrown on episcopacy might, without much difficulty, be turned against royalty; and many of the arguments which were used to prove that spiritual power was best lodged in a synod seemed to lead to the conclusion that temporal power was best lodged in a parliament.

Thus, as the priest of the Established Church was, from interest, from principle, and from passion, zealous for the royal prerogatives, the Puritan was, from interest, from principle, and from passion, hostile to them. The power of the discontented sectaries was great. They were found in every rank; but they were strongest among the mercantile classes in the towns, and among the small proprietors in the country. Early in the reign of Elizabeth they began to

No systematic parliamentary opposition offered to the government of Elizabeth.

return a majority of the House of Commons. And doubtless, had our ancestors been then at liberty to fix their attention entirely on domestic questions, the strife between the Crown and the Parliament would instantly have commenced. But that was no season for internal dissensions. It might, indeed, well be doubted whether the firmest union among all the orders of the state could avert the common danger by which all were threatened. Roman Catholic Europe and reformed Europe were struggling for death or life. France, divided against herself, had, for a time, ceased to be of any account in Christendom. The English Government was at the head of the Protestant interest, and, while persecuting Presbyterians at home, extended a powerful protection to Presbyterian Churches abroad. At the head of the opposite party was the mightiest prince of the age, a prince who ruled Spain, Portugal, Italy, the Netherlands, the East and the West Indies, whose armies repeatedly marched to Paris, and whose fleets kept the coasts of Devonshire and Sussex in alarm. It long seemed probable that Englishmen would have to fight desperately on English ground for their religion and independence. Nor were they ever for a moment free from apprehensions of some great treason at home. For in that age it had become a point of conscience and of honour with many men of generous natures to sacrifice their country to their religion. A succession of dark plots, formed by Roman Catholics against the life of the Queen and the existence of the nation, kept society in constant alarm. Whatever might be the faults of Elizabeth, it was plain that, to speak humanly, the fate of the realm and of all reformed Churches was staked on the security of her person and on the success of her administration. To strengthen her hands was, therefore, the first duty of a patriot and a Protestant; and that duty was well performed. The Puritans, even in the depths of the prisons to which she had sent them, prayed, and with no simulated fervour, that she might be kept from the dagger of the assassin, that rebellion might be put down under her feet, and that her arms might be victorious by sea and land. One of the most stubborn of the stubborn sect, immediately after his hand had been lopped off for an offence into which he had been hurried by his intemperate zeal, waved his hat with the hand which was still left him, and shouted "God save the Queen!" The sentiment with which these men regarded her has descended to their posterity. The Nonconformists, rigorously as she treated them, have, as a body, always venerated her memory.*

During the greater part of her reign, therefore, the Puritans in the House of Commons, though sometimes mutinous, felt no disposition to array themselves in systematic opposition to the government. But, when the defeat of the Armada, the successful resistance of the United Provinces to the Spanish power, the firm establishment of Henry the Fourth on the throne of France, and the death of Philip the Second, had secured the State and the Church against all danger from abroad, an obstinate struggle, destined to last during several generations, instantly began at home.

It was in the Parliament of 1601 that the opposition which had, during forty years, been silently gathering and husbanding strength, fought its first great battle and won its first victory. The ground was well chosen. The English sovereigns had always been entrusted with the supreme direction of commercial police. It was their undoubted prerogative to regulate coin, weights, and measures, and to appoint fairs, markets, and ports. The line which bounded their authority over trade had, as usual, been but loosely drawn. They therefore, as usual, encroached on the province which rightfully belonged to the legislature. The encroachment was, as usual, patiently borne, till it became serious. But at length the Queen took upon herself to grant patents of monopoly by scores. There was scarcely a family in the realm which did not feel itself aggrieved by the oppression and extortion which this abuse naturally caused. Iron, oil, vinegar, coal,

Marginal note: Question of the monopolies.

---

* The Puritan historian, Neal, after censuring the cruelty with which she treated the sect to which he belonged, concludes thus: "However, notwithstanding all these blemishes, Queen Elizabeth stands upon record as a wise and politic princess, for delivering her kingdom from the difficulties in which it was involved at her accession, for preserving the Protestant reformation against the potent attempts of the Pope, the Emperor, and King of Spain abroad, and the Queen of Scots and her Popish subjects at home. . . . She was the glory of the age in which she lived, and will be the admiration of posterity."—History of the Puritans, Part I. Chap. viii.

saltpetre, lead, starch, yarn, skins, leather, glass, could be bought only at exorbitant prices. The House of Commons met in an angry and determined mood. It was in vain that a courtly minority blamed the Speaker for suffering the acts of the Queen's Highness to be called in question. The language of the discontented party was high and menacing, and was echoed by the voice of the whole nation. The coach of the chief minister of the crown was surrounded by an indignant populace, who cursed the monopolies, and exclaimed that the prerogative should not be suffered to touch the old liberties of England. There seemed for a moment to be some danger that the long and glorious reign of Elizabeth would have a shameful and disastrous end. She, however, with admirable judgment and temper, declined the contest, put herself at the head of the reforming party, redressed the grievance, thanked the Commons, in touching and dignified language, for their tender care of the general weal, brought back to herself the hearts of the people, and left to her successors a memorable example of the way in which it behoves a ruler to deal with public movements which he has not the means of resisting.

Scotland and Ireland become parts of the same empire with England.

In the year 1603 the great Queen died. That year is, on many accounts, one of the most important epochs in our history. It was then that both Scotland and Ireland became parts of the same empire with England. Both Scotland and Ireland, indeed, had been subjugated by the Plantagenets ; but neither country had been patient under the yoke. Scotland had, with heroic energy, vindicated her independence, had, from the time of Robert Bruce, been a separate kingdom, and was now joined to the southern part of the island in a manner which rather gratified than wounded her national pride.   Ireland had never, since the days of Henry the Second, been able to expel the foreign invaders ; but she had struggled against them long and fiercely. During the fourteenth and fifteenth centuries the English power in that island was constantly declining, and, in the days of Henry the Seventh, sank to the lowest point. The Irish dominions of that prince consisted only of the counties of Dublin and Louth, of some parts of Meath and Kildare, and of a few seaports scattered along the coast. A large portion even of Leinster was not yet divided into counties. Munster, Ulster, and Connaught were ruled by petty sovereigns, partly Celts, and partly degenerate Normans, who had forgotten their origin and had adopted the Celtic language and manners. But, during the sixteenth century, the English power had made great progress. The half savage chieftains who reigned beyond the pale had submitted one after another to the lieutenants of the Tudors. At length, a few weeks before the death of Elizabeth, the conquest, which had been begun more than four hundred years before by Strongbow, was completed by Mountjoy. Scarcely had James the First mounted the English throne when the last O'Donnel and O'Neil who have held the rank of independent princes kissed his hand at Whitehall. Thenceforward his writs ran and his judges held assizes in every part of Ireland; and the English law superseded the customs which had prevailed among the aboriginal tribes.

In extent Scotland and Ireland were nearly equal to each other, and were together nearly equal to England, but were much less thickly peopled than England, and were very far behind England in wealth and civilisation. Scotland had been kept back by the sterility of her soil; and, in the midst of light, the thick darkness of the middle ages still rested on Ireland.

The population of Scotland, with the exception of the Celtic tribes which were thinly scattered over the Hebrides and over the mountainous parts of the northern shires, was of the same blood with the population of England, and spoke a tongue which did not differ from the purest English more than the dialects of Somersetshire and Lancashire differed from each other. In Ireland, on the contrary, the population, with the exception of the small English colony near the coast, was Celtic, and still kept the Celtic speech and manners.

In natural courage and intelligence both the nations which now became connected with England ranked high. In perseverance, in selfcommand, in forethought, in all the virtues which conduce to success in life, the Scots have never been surpassed. The Irish, on the other hand, were distinguished by qualities which tend to make men interesting rather than prosperous. They were an ardent and impetuous race, easily moved to tears or to laughter, to fury or to love. Alone among the nations of northern Europe they had the susceptibility, the vivacity, the natural turn for acting and rhetoric, which are indigenous on the shores of the Mediterranean Sea. In mental cultivation Scotland had an indisputable superiority. Though that kingdom was then the poorest in

Christendom, it already vied in every branch of learning with the most favoured countries. Scotsmen, whose dwellings and whose food were as wretched as those of the Icelanders of our time, wrote Latin verse with more than the delicacy of Vida, and made discoveries in science which would have added to the renown of Galileo. Ireland could boast of no Buchanan or Napier. The genius, with which her aboriginal inhabitants were largely endowed, showed itself as yet only in ballads which, wild and rugged as they were, seemed to the judging eye of Spenser to contain a portion of the pure gold of poetry.

Scotland, in becoming part of the British monarchy, preserved her dignity. Having, during many generations, courageously withstood the English arms, she was now joined to her stronger neighbour on the most honourable terms. She gave a King instead of receiving one. She retained her own constitution and laws. Her tribunals and parliaments remained entirely independent of the tribunals and parliaments which sate at Westminster. The administration of Scotland was in Scottish hands; for no Englishman had any motive to emigrate northward, and to contend with the shrewdest and most pertinacious of all races for what was to be scraped together in the poorest of all treasuries. Nevertheless Scotland by no means escaped the fate ordained for every country which is connected, but not incorporated, with another country of greater resources. Though in name an independent kingdom, she was, during more than a century, really treated, in many respects, as a subject province.

Ireland was undisguisedly governed as a dependency won by the sword. Her rude national institutions had perished. The English colonists submitted to the dictation of the mother country, without whose support they could not exist, and indemnified themselves by trampling on the people among whom they had settled. The parliaments which met at Dublin could pass no law which had not been previously approved by the English Privy Council. The authority of the English legislature extended over Ireland. The executive administration was entrusted to men taken either from England or from the English pale, and, in either case, regarded as foreigners, and even as enemies, by the Celtic population.

But the circumstance which, more than any other, has made Ireland to differ from Scotland remains to be noticed. Scotland was Protestant. In no part of Europe had the movement of the popular mind against the Roman Catholic Church been so rapid and violent. The Reformers had vanquished, deposed, and imprisoned their idolatrous sovereign. They would not endure even such a compromise as had been effected in England. They had established the Calvinistic doctrine, discipline, and worship; and they made little distinction between Popery and Prelacy, between the Mass and the Book of Common Prayer. Unfortunately for Scotland, the prince whom she sent to govern a fairer inheritance had been so much annoyed by the pertinacity with which her theologians had asserted against him the privileges of the synod and the pulpit that he hated the ecclesiastical polity to which she was fondly attached as much as it was in his effeminate nature to hate anything, and had no sooner mounted the English throne than he began to show an intolerant zeal for the government and ritual of the English Church.

The Irish were the only people of northern Europe who had remained true to the old religion. This is to be partly ascribed to the circumstance that they were some centuries behind their neighbours in knowledge. But other causes had cooperated. The Reformation had been a national as well as a moral revolt. It had been, not only an insurrection of the laity against the clergy, but also an insurrection of all the branches of the great German race against an alien domination. It is a most significant circumstance that no large society of which the tongue is not Teutonic has ever turned Protestant, and that, wherever a language derived from that of ancient Rome is spoken, the religion of modern Rome to this day prevails. The patriotism of the Irish had taken a peculiar direction. The object of their animosity was not Rome, but England; and they had especial reason to abhor those English sovereigns who had been the chiefs of the great schism, Henry the Eighth and Elizabeth. During the vain struggle which two generations of Milesian princes maintained against the Tudors, religious enthusiasm and national enthusiasm became inseparably blended in the minds of the vanquished race. The new feud of Protestant and Papist inflamed the old feud of Saxon and Celt. The English conquerors, meanwhile, neglected all legitimate means of conversion. No care was taken to provide the vanquished nation with instructors capable of making themselves understood. No translation of the Bible was put forth in the Irish language. The government contented itself with setting up a vast hierarchy of Protestant archbishops, bishops, and rectors, who did nothing, and who, for doing nothing, were paid out of the spoils of a Church loved and revered by the great body of the people.

There was much in the state both of Scotland and of Ireland which might well excite the painful apprehensions of a farsighted statesman. As yet, however, there was the appearance of tranquillity. For the first time all the British isles were peaceably united under one sceptre.

It should seem that the weight of England among European nations ought, from this epoch, to have greatly increased. The territory which her new King governed was, in extent, nearly double that which Elizabeth had inherited. His empire was the most complete within itself and the most secure from attack that was to be found in the world. The Plantagenets and Tudors had been repeatedly under the necessity of defending themselves against Scotland while they were engaged in continental war. The long conflict in Ireland had been a severe and perpetual drain on their resources. Yet even under such disadvantages those sovereigns had been highly considered throughout Christendom. It might, therefore, not unreasonably be expected that England, Scotland, and Ireland combined would form a state second to none that then existed.

Diminution of the importance of England after the accession of James I. All such expectations were strangely disappointed. On the day of the accession of James the First England descended from the rank which she had hitherto held, and began to be regarded as a power hardly of the second order. During many years the great British monarchy, under four successive princes of the House of Stuart, was scarcely a more important member of the European system than the little kingdom of Scotland had previously been. This, however, is little to be regretted. Of James the First, as of John, it may be said that, if his administration had been able and splendid, it would probably have been fatal to our country, and that we owe more to his weakness and meanness than to the wisdom and courage of much better sovereigns. He came to the throne at a critical moment. The time was fast approaching when either the King must become absolute, or the Parliament must control the whole executive administration. Had James been, like Henry the Fourth, like Maurice of Nassau, or like Gustavus Adolphus, a valiant, active, and politic ruler, had he put himself at the head of the Protestants of Europe, had he gained great victories over Tilly and Spinola, had he adorned Westminster with the spoils of Bavarian monasteries and Flemish cathedrals, had he hung Austrian and Castilian banners in Saint Paul's, and had he found himself, after great achievements, at the head of fifty thousand troops, brave, well disciplined, and devotedly attached to his person, the English Parliament would soon have been nothing more than a name. Happily he was not a man to play such a part. He began his administration by putting an end to the war which had raged during many years between England and Spain; and from that time he shunned hostilities with a caution which was proof against the insults of his neighbours and the clamours of his subjects. Not till the last year of his life could the influence of his son, his favourite, his Parliament, and his people combined, induce him to strike one feeble blow in defence of his family and of his religion. It was well for those whom he governed that he in this matter disregarded their wishes. The effect of his pacific policy was that, in his time, no regular troops were needed, and that, while France, Spain, Italy, Belgium, and Germany swarmed with mercenary soldiers, the defence of our island was still confided to the militia.

As the King had no standing army, and did not even attempt to form one, it would have been wise in him to avoid any conflict with his people. But such was his indiscretion that, while he altogether neglected the means which alone could make him really absolute, he constantly put forward, in the most offensive form, claims of which none of his predecessors had ever dreamed. It was at this time that those strange theories which Filmer afterwards formed into a system, and which became the badge of the most violent class of Tories and high churchmen, first emerged into notice. It was gravely maintained that the Supreme Being regarded hereditary monarchy, as opposed to other forms of government, with peculiar favour; that the rule of succession in order of primogeniture was a divine institution, anterior to the Christian, and even to the Mosaic dispensation; that no human power, not even that of the whole legislature, no length of adverse possession, though it extended to ten centuries, could deprive a legitimate prince of his rights; that the authority of such a prince was necessarily always despotic; that the laws, by which, in England and in other countries, the prerogative was limited, were to be regarded merely

Doctrine of divine right.

as concessions which the sovereign had freely made and might at his pleasure resume; and that any treaty which a king might conclude with his people was merely a declaration of his present intentions, and not a contract of which the performance could be demanded. It is evident that this theory, though intended to strengthen the foundations of government, altogether unsettles them. Does the divine and immutable law of primogeniture admit females, or exclude them? On either supposition half the sovereigns of Europe must be usurpers, reigning in defiance of the law of God, and liable to be dispossessed by the rightful heirs. The doctrine that kingly government is peculiarly favoured by Heaven receives no countenance from the Old Testament; for in the Old Testament we read that the chosen people were blamed and punished for desiring a king, and that they were afterwards commanded to withdraw their allegiance from him. Their whole history, far from countenancing the notion that succession in order of primogeniture is of divine institution, would rather seem to indicate that younger brothers are under the especial protection of heaven. Isaac was not the eldest son of Abraham, nor Jacob of Isaac, nor Judah of Jacob, nor David of Jesse, nor Solomon of David. Nor does the system of Filmer receive any countenance from those passages of the New Testament which describe government as an ordinance of God: for the government under which the writers of the New Testament lived was not a hereditary monarchy. The Roman Emperors were republican magistrates, named by the senate. None of them pretended to rule by right of birth; and, in fact, both Tiberius, to whom Christ commanded that tribute should be given, and Nero, whom Paul directed the Romans to obey, were, according to the patriarchal theory of government, usurpers. In the middle ages the doctrine of indefeasible hereditary right would have been regarded as heretical: for it was altogether incompatible with the high pretensions of the Church of Rome. It was a doctrine unknown to the founders of the Church of England. The Homily on Wilful Rebellion had strongly, and indeed too strongly, inculcated submission to constituted authority, but had made no distinction between hereditary and elective monarchies, or between monarchies and republics. Indeed most of the predecessors of James would, from personal motives, have regarded the patriarchal theory of government with aversion. William Rufus, Henry the First, Stephen,

John, Henry the Fourth, Henry the Fifth, Henry the Sixth, Richard the Third, and Henry the Seventh, had all reigned in defiance of the strict rule of descent. A grave doubt hung over the legitimacy both of Mary and of Elizabeth. It was impossible that both Catharine of Aragon and Anne Boleyn could have been lawfully married to Henry the Eighth; and the highest authority in the realm had pronounced that neither was so. The Tudors, far from considering the law of succession as a divine and unchangeable institution, were constantly tampering with it. Henry the Eighth obtained an act of parliament, giving him power to leave the crown by will, and actually made a will to the prejudice of the royal family of Scotland. Edward the Sixth, unauthorised by Parliament, assumed a similar power, with the full approbation of the most eminent Reformers. Elizabeth, conscious that her own title was open to grave objection, and unwilling to admit even a reversionary right in her rival and enemy the Queen of Scots, induced the Parliament to pass a law, enacting that whoever should deny the competency of the reigning sovereign, with the assent of the Estates of the realm, to alter the succession, should suffer death as a traitor. But the situation of James was widely different from that of Elizabeth. Far inferior to her in abilities and in popularity, regarded by the English as an alien, and excluded from the throne by the testament of Henry the Eighth, the King of Scots was yet the undoubted heir of William the Conqueror and of Egbert. He had, therefore, an obvious interest in inculcating the superstitious notion that birth confers rights anterior to law, and unalterable by law. It was a notion, moreover, well suited to his intellect and temper. It soon found many advocates among those who aspired to his favour, and made rapid progress among the clergy of the Established Church.

Thus, at the very moment at which a republican spirit began to manifest itself strongly in the Parliament and in the country, the claims of the monarch took a monstrous form which would have disgusted the proudest and most arbitrary of those who had preceded him on the throne.

James was always boasting of his skill in what he called kingcraft; and yet it is hardly possible even to imagine a course more directly opposed to all the rules of kingcraft than that which he followed. The policy of wise rulers has always been to disguise strong acts under popular forms. It was thus that Augustus and Napoleon established absolute monarchies, while the public regarded them merely as eminent citizens invested with temporary magistracies. The policy of James was the direct reverse of theirs. He enraged and alarmed his Parliament by constantly telling them that they held their privileges merely during his pleasure, and that they had no more business to inquire what he might lawfully do than what the Deity might lawfully do Yet he quailed before them, abandoned minister after minister to their vengeance, and suffered them to tease him into acts directly opposed to his strongest inclinations. Thus the indignation excited by his claims and the scorn excited by his concessions went on growing together. By his fondness for worthless minions, and by the sanction which he gave to their tyranny and rapacity, he kept discontent constantly alive. His cowardice, his childishness, his pedantry, his ungainly person and manners, his provincial accent, made him an object of derision. Even in his virtues and accomplishments there was something eminently unkingly. Throughout the whole course of his reign, all the venerable associations by which the throne had long been fenced were gradually losing their strength. During two hundred years all the sovereigns who had ruled England, with the single exception of the unfortunate Henry the Sixth, had been strongminded, highspirited, courageous, and of princely bearing. Almost all had possessed abilities above the ordinary level. It was no light thing that, on the very eve of the decisive struggle between our Kings and their Parliaments, royalty should be exhibited to the world stammering, slobbering, shedding unmanly tears, trembling at a drawn sword, and talking in the style alternately of a buffoon and of a pedagogue.

The separation between the Church and the Puritans becomes wider.

In the meantime the religious dissensions, by which, from the days of Edward the Sixth, the Protestant body had been distracted, had become more formidable than ever. The interval which had separated the first generation of Puritans from Cranmer and Jewel was small indeed when compared with the interval which separated the third generation of Puritans from Laud and Hammond. While the recollection of Mary's cruelties was still fresh, while the powers of the Roman Catholic party still inspired apprehension, while Spain still retained ascendency and aspired to universal dominion, all the reformed sects knew that they had a strong common interest and a deadly common enemy. The animosity which they felt towards each other was languid when compared with the animosity which they all felt towards Rome. Conformists and Nonconformists had heartily joined in enacting penal laws of extreme severity against the Papists. But when more than half a century of undisturbed possession had given confidence to the Established Church, when nine tenths of the nation had become heartily Protestant, when England was at peace with all the world, when there was no danger that Popery would be forced by foreign arms on the nation, when the last confessors who had stood before Bonner had passed away, a change took place in the feeling of the Anglican clergy. Their hostility to the Roman Catholic doctrine and discipline was considerably mitigated. Their dislike of the Puritans, on the other hand, increased daily. The controversies which had from the beginning divided the Protestant party took such a form as made reconciliation hopeless; and new controversies of still greater importance were added to the old subjects of dispute.

The founders of the Anglican Church had retained episcopacy as an ancient, a decent, and a convenient ecclesiastical polity, but had not declared that form of church government to be of divine institution. We have already seen how low an estimate Cranmer had formed of the office of a Bishop. In the reign of Elizabeth, Jewel, Cooper, Whitgift, and other eminent doctors defended prelacy, as innocent, as useful, as what the state might lawfully establish, as what, when established by the state, was entitled to the respect of every citizen. But they never denied that a Christian community without a Bishop might be a pure Church.* On the contrary, they

* On this subject, Bishop Cooper's language is remarkably clear and strong. He maintains, in his Answer to Martin Marprelate, printed in 1589, that no form of church government is divinely ordained; that Protestant communities, in establishing different forms, have only made a legitimate use of their Christian liberty; and that episcopacy is peculiarly suited to England, because the English constitution is monarchical. "All those Churches," says the Bishop, "in which the Gospell, in these daies, after great darknesse, was first renewed, and the learned men whom God sent to instruct them, I doubt not but have been directed by the Spirite of God to retaine this liberty, that, in external government and other outward orders, they might choose such as they thought in wisedome and godlinesse to be most convenient for the state of their countrey and disposition of their people. Why then should this liberty that other countreys have used under anie colour be wrested from us? I think it therefore great presumption and boldnesse that some of our nation, and those, whatever they may think of themselves, not of the greatest wisedome and skill, should take upon them to controlle the whole realme, and to binde both prince and people in respect of conscience to alter the present state, and tie themselves to a certain platforme devised by some of our neighbours, which, in the judgment of many wise and godly persons, is most unfit for the state of a Kingdome."

regarded the Protestants of the Continent as of the same household of faith with themselves. Englishmen in England were indeed bound to acknowledge the authority of the Bishop, as they were bound to acknowledge the authority of the Sheriff and of the Coroner: but the obligation was purely local. An English churchman, nay even an English prelate, if he went to Holland, conformed without scruple to the established religion of Holland. Abroad the ambassadors of Elizabeth and James went in state to the very worship which Elizabeth and James persecuted at home, and carefully abstained from decorating their private chapels after the Anglican fashion, lest scandal should be given to weaker brethren. An instrument is still extant by which the Primate of all England, in the year 1582, authorised a Scotch minister, ordained, according to the laudable forms of the Scotch Church, by the Synod of East Lothian, to preach and administer the sacraments in any part of the province of Canterbury.* In the year 1603, the Convocation solemnly recognised the Church of Scotland, a Church in which episcopal control and episcopal ordination were then unknown, as a branch of the Holy Catholic Church of Christ.† It was even held that Presbyterian ministers were entitled to place and voice in œcumenical councils. When the States General of the United Provinces convoked at Dort a synod of doctors not episcopally ordained, an English Bishop and an English Dean, commissioned by the head of the English Church, sate with those doctors, preached to them, and voted with them on the gravest questions of theology.‡ Nay, many English benefices were held by divines who had been admitted to the ministry in the Calvinistic form used on the Continent; nor was reordination by a Bishop in such cases then thought necessary, or even lawful.§

* Strype's Life of Grindal, Appendix to Book II. No. xvii.

† Canon 55. of 1603.

‡ Joseph Hall, then dean of Worcester, and afterwards bishop of Norwich, was one of the commissioners. In his life of himself, he says: " My unworthiness was named for one of the assistants of that honourable, grave, and reverend meeting." To high churchmen this humility will seem not a little out of place.

§ It was by the Act of Uniformity, passed after the Restoration, that persons not episcopally ordained were, for the first time, made incapable of holding benefices. No man was more zealous for this law than Clarendon. Yet he says: " This was new; for there had been many, and at present there were some, who possessed benefices with cure of souls and other ecclesiastical promotions, who had never received orders but in France or Holland; and these men must now receive new ordination, which had been always held unlawful in the Church, or by this act of parliament must be deprived of their livelihood which they enjoyed in the most flourishing and peaceable time of the Church."

But a new race of divines was already rising in the Church of England. In their view the episcopal office was essential to the welfare of a Christian society and to the efficacy of the most solemn ordinances of religion. To that office belonged certain high and sacred privileges, which no human power could give or take away. A Church might as well be without the doctrine of the Trinity, or the doctrine of the Incarnation, as without the apostolical orders; and the Church of Rome, which, in the midst of all her corruptions, had retained the apostolical orders, was nearer to primitive purity than those reformed societies which had rashly set up, in opposition to the divine model, a system invented by men.

In the days of Edward the Sixth and of Elizabeth, the defenders of the Anglican ritual had generally contented themselves with saying that it might be used without sin, and that, therefore, none but a perverse and undutiful subject would refuse to use it when enjoined to do so by the magistrate. Now, however, that rising party which claimed for the polity of the Church a celestial origin began to ascribe to her services a new dignity and importance. It was hinted that, if the established worship had any fault, that fault was extreme simplicity, and that the Reformers had, in the heat of their quarrel with Rome, abolished many ancient ceremonies which might with advantage have been retained. Days and places were again held in mysterious veneration. Some practices which had long been disused, and which were commonly regarded as superstitious mummeries, were revived. Paintings and carvings, which had escaped the fury of the first generation of Protestants, became the objects of a respect such as to many seemed idolatrous.

No part of the system of the old Church had been more detested by the Reformers than the honour paid to celibacy. They held that the doctrine of Rome on this subject had been prophetically condemned by the apostle Paul, as a doctrine of devils; and they dwelt much on the crimes and scandals which seemed to prove the justice of this awful denunciation. Luther had evinced his own opinion in the clearest manner, by espousing a nun. Some of the most illustrious bishops and priests who had died by fire during the reign of Mary had left wives and children. Now, however, it began to be rumoured that the old monastic spirit had reappeared in the Church of England; that there was in high quarters a prejudice against married priests; that even laymen, who called

themselves Protestants, had made resolutions of celibacy
which almost amounted to vows; nay, that a minister of the
established religion had set up a nunnery, in which the
psalms were chaunted at midnight, by a company of virgins
dedicated to God.*

Nor was this all. A class of questions, as to which the
founders of the Anglican Church and the first generation
of Puritans had differed little or not at all, began to furnish
matter for fierce disputes. The controversies which had
divided the Protestant body in its infancy had related almost
exclusively to Church government and to ceremonies. There
had been no serious quarrel between the contending parties
on points of metaphysical theology. The doctrines held by
the chiefs of the hierarchy touching original sin, faith, grace,
predestination, and election, were those which are popularly
called Calvinistic. Towards the close of Elizabeth's reign her
favourite prelate, Archbishop Whitgift, drew up, in concert
with the Bishop of London and other theologians, the celebrated instrument known by the name of the Lambeth Articles.
In that instrument the most startling of the Calvinistic doctrines are affirmed with a distinctness which would shock
many who, in our age, are reputed Calvinists. One clergyman, who took the opposite side, and spoke harshly of Calvin, was arraigned for his presumption by the University of
Cambridge, and escaped punishment only by expressing his
firm belief in the tenets of reprobation and final perseverance,
and his sorrow for the offence which he had given to pious
men by reflecting on the great French reformer. The school
of divinity of which Hooker was the chief occupies a middle
place between the school of Cranmer and the school of
Laud; and Hooker has, in modern times, been claimed by
the Arminians as an ally. Yet Hooker pronounced Calvin
to have been a man superior in wisdom to any other divine
that France had produced, a man to whom thousands were
indebted for the knowledge of divine truth, but who was himself indebted to God alone. When the Arminian controversy
arose in Holland, the English government and the English
Church lent strong support to the Calvinistic party; nor is
the English name altogether free from the stain which has
been left on that party by the imprisonment of Grotius and
the judicial murder of Barneveldt.

* Peckard's Life of Ferrar; The Arminian Nunnery, or a Brief Description
of the late erected monastical Place
called the Arminian Nunnery, at Little
Gidding in Huntingdonshire, 1641.

But, even before the meeting of the Dutch synod, that part of the Anglican clergy which was peculiarly hostile to the Calvinistic Church government and to the Calvinistic worship had begun to regard with dislike the Calvinistic metaphysics; and this feeling was very naturally strengthened by the gross injustice, insolence, and cruelty of the party which was prevalent at Dort. The Arminian doctrine, a doctrine less austerely logical than that of the early Reformers, but more agreeable to the popular notions of the divine justice and benevolence, spread fast and wide. The infection soon reached the court. Opinions which, at the time of the accession of James, no clergyman could have avowed without imminent risk of being stripped of his gown, were now the best title to preferment. A divine of that age, who was asked by a simple country gentleman what the Arminians held, answered, with as much truth as wit, that they held all the best bishoprics and deaneries in England.

While the majority of the Anglican clergy quitted, in one direction, the position which they had originally occupied, the majority of the Puritan body departed, in a direction diametrically opposite, from the principles and practices of their fathers. The persecution which the separatists had undergone had been severe enough to irritate, but not severe enough to destroy. They had been, not tamed into submission, but baited into savageness and stubbornness. After the fashion of oppressed sects, they mistook their own vindictive feelings for emotions of piety, encouraged in themselves by reading and meditation a disposition to brood over their wrongs, and, when they had worked themselves up into hating their enemies, imagined that they were only hating the enemies of heaven. In the New Testament there was little indeed which, even when perverted by the most disingenuous exposition, could seem to countenance the indulgence of malevolent passions. But the Old Testament contained the history of a race selected by God to be witnesses of his unity and ministers of his vengeance, and specially commanded by him to do many things which, if done without his special command, would have been atrocious crimes. In such a history it was not difficult for fierce and gloomy spirits to find much that might be distorted to suit their wishes. The extreme Puritans therefore began to feel for the Old Testament a preference, which, perhaps, they did not distinctly avow even to themselves; but which showed itself in all their sentiments and habits. They paid to the Hebrew language a respect which they refused to that tongue in which the discourses of Jesus and the epistles of Paul have come down to us. They baptized their children by the names, not of Christian saints, but of Hebrew patriarchs and warriors. In defiance of the express and reiterated declarations of Luthei and Calvin, they turned the weekly festival by which the Church had, from the primitive times, commemorated the resurrection of her Lord, into a Jewish Sabbath. They sought for principles of jurisprudence in the Mosaic law, and for precedents to guide their ordinary conduct in the books of Judges and Kings. Their thoughts and discourse ran much on acts which were assuredly not recorded as examples for our imitation. The prophet who hewed in pieces a captive king, the rebel general who gave the blood of a queen to the dogs, the matron who, in defiance of plighted faith, and of the laws of eastern hospitality, drove the nail into the brain of the fugitive ally who had just fed at her board, and who was sleeping under the shadow of her tent, were proposed as models to Christians suffering under the tyranny of princes and prelates. Morals and manners were subjected to a code resembling that of the synagogue, when the synagogue was in its worst state. The dress, the deportment, the language, the studies, the amusements of the rigid sect were regulated on principles not unlike those of the Pharisees who, proud of their washed hands and broad phylacteries, taunted the Redeemer as a sabbathbreaker and a winebibber. It was a sin to hang garlands on a Maypole, to drink a friend's health, to fly a hawk, to hunt a stag, to play at chess, to wear lovelocks, to put starch into a ruff, to touch the virginals, to read the Fairy Queen. Rules such as these, rules which would have appeared insupportable to the free and joyous spirit of Luther, and contemptible to the serene and philosophical intellect of Zwingle, threw over all life a more than monastic gloom. The learning and eloquence by which the great Reformers had been eminently distinguished, and to which they had been, in no small measure, indebted for their success, were regarded by the new school of Protestants with suspicion, if not with aversion. Some precisians had scruples about teaching the Latin grammar, because the names of Mars, Bacchus, and Apollo occurred in it. The fine arts were all but proscribed. The solemn peal of the organ was superstitious. The light music of Ben Jonson's masques was dissolute. Half the fine paintings in England were idolatrous, and the other half indecent. The extreme Puritan was at once known from other men by his gait, his garb, his lank hair, the sour solemnity of his face, the upturned white of his eyes, the nasal twang with which he spoke, and above all, by his peculiar dialect. He employed, on every occasion, the imagery and style of Scripture. Hebraisms violently introduced into the English language, and metaphors borrowed from the boldest lyric poetry of a remote age and country, and applied to the common concerns of English life, were the most striking peculiarities of this cant, which moved, not without cause, the derision both of Prelatists and libertines.

Thus the political and religious schism which had originated in the sixteenth century was, during the first quarter of the seventeenth century, constantly widening. Theories tending to Turkish despotism were in fashion at Whitehall. Theories tending to republicanism were in favour with a large portion of the House of Commons. The violent Prelatists who were, to a man, zealous for prerogative, and the violent Puritans who were, to a man, zealous for the privileges of Parliament, regarded each other with animosity more intense than that which, in the preceding generation, had existed between Catholics and Protestants.

While the minds of men were in this state, the country, after a peace of many years, at length engaged in a war which required strenuous exertions. This war hastened the approach of the great constitutional crisis. It was necessary that the King should have a large military force. He could not have such a force without money. He could not legally raise money without the consent of Parliament. It followed, therefore, that he either must administer the government in conformity with the sense of the House of Commons, or must venture on such a violation of the fundamental laws of the land as had been unknown during several centuries. The Plantagenets and the Tudors had, it is true, occasionally supplied a deficiency in their revenue by a benevolence or a forced loan: but these expedients were always of a temporary nature. To meet the regular charge of a long war by regular taxation, imposed without the consent of the Estates of the realm, was a course which Henry the Eighth himself would not have dared to take. It seemed, therefore, that the decisive hour was approaching, and that the English

Parliament would soon either share the fate of the senates of the Continent, or obtain supreme ascendency in the state.

Accession and character of Charles I.

Just at this conjuncture James died. Charles the First succeeded to the throne. He had received from nature a far better understanding, a far stronger will, and a far keener and firmer temper than his father's. He had inherited his father's political theories, and was much more disposed than his father to carry them into practice. He was, like his father, a zealous Episcopalian. He was, moreover, what his father had never been, a zealous Arminian, and, though no Papist, liked a Papist much better than a Puritan. It would be unjust to deny that Charles had some of the qualities of a good, and even of a great prince. He wrote and spoke, not, like his father, with the exactness of a professor, but after the fashion of intelligent and well educated gentlemen. His taste in literature and art was excellent, his manner dignified, though not gracious, his domestic life without blemish. Faithlessness was the chief cause of his disasters, and is the chief stain on his memory. He was, in truth, impelled by an incurable propensity to dark and crooked ways. It may seem strange that his conscience, which, on occasions of little moment, was sufficiently sensitive, should never have reproached him with this great vice. But there is reason to believe that he was perfidious, not only from constitution and from habit, but also on principle. He seems to have learned from the theologians whom he most esteemed that between him and his subjects there could be nothing of the nature of mutual contract; that he could not, even if he would, divest himself of his despotic authority; and that, in every promise which he made, there was an implied reservation that such promise might be broken in case of necessity, and that of the necessity he was the sole judge.

Tactics of the opposition in the House of Commons.

And now began that hazardous game on which were staked the destinies of the English people. It was played on the side of the House of Commons with keenness, but with admirable dexterity, coolness, and perseverance. Great statesmen who looked far behind them and far before them were at the head of that assembly. They were resolved to place the King in such a situation that he must either conduct the administration in conformity with the wishes of his Parliament, or make outrageous attacks on the most sacred principles of the constitution. They accordingly doled out supplies to him very sparingly. He found that he must govern either in harmony with the House of Commons, or in defiance of all law. His choice was soon made. He dissolved his first Parliament, and levied taxes by his own authority. He convoked a second Parliament, and found it more intractable than the first. He again resorted to the expedient of dissolution, raised fresh taxes without any show of legal right, and threw the chiefs of the opposition into prison. At the same time a new grievance, which the peculiar feelings and habits of the English nation made insupportably painful, and which seemed to all discerning men to be of fearful augury, excited general discontent and alarm. Companies of soldiers were billeted on the people; and martial law was, in some places, substituted for the ancient jurisprudence of the realm.

The King called a third Parliament, and soon perceived that the opposition was stronger and fiercer than ever. He now determined on a change of tactics. Instead of opposing an inflexible resistance to the demands of the Commons, he, after much altercation and many evasions, agreed to a compromise which, if he had faithfully adhered to it, would have averted a long series of calamities. The Parliament granted an ample supply. The King ratified, in the most solemn manner, that celebrated law, which is known by the name of the Petition of Right, and which is the second Great Charter of the liberties of England. By ratifying that law he bound himself never again to raise money without the consent of the Houses, never again to imprison any person, except in due course of law, and never again to subject his people to the jurisdiction of courts martial.

Petition of Right.

The day on which the royal sanction was, after many delays, solemnly given to this great Act, was a day of joy and hope. The Commons, who crowded the bar of the House of Lords, broke forth into loud acclamations as soon as the clerk had pronounced the ancient form of words by which our princes have, during many ages, signified their assent to the wishes of the Estates of the realm. Those acclamations were reechoed by the voice of the capital and of the nation; but within three weeks it became manifest that Charles had no intention of observing the compact into which he had entered. The supply given by the representatives of the nation was collected. The promise by which that supply had been obtained was broken. A violent contest followed. The Parliament was dissolved with every mark of royal displeasure. Some of the most distinguished members were imprisoned:

and one of them, Sir John Eliot, after years of suffering, died in confinement.

Charles, however, could not venture to raise, by his own authority, taxes sufficient for carrying on war. He accordingly hastened to make peace with his neighbours, and thenceforth gave his whole mind to British politics.

Now commenced a new era. Many English Kings had occasionally committed unconstitutional acts : but none had ever systematically attempted to make himself a despot, and to reduce the Parliament to a nullity. Such was the end which Charles distinctly proposed to himself. From March 1629 to April 1640, the Houses were not convoked. Never in our history had there been an interval of eleven years between Parliament and Parliament. Only once had there been an interval of even half that length. This fact alone is sufficient to refute those who represent Charles as having merely trodden in the footsteps of the Plantagenets and Tudors.

Petition of Right violated.

It is proved, by the testimony of the King's most strenuous supporters, that, during this part of his reign, the provisions of the Petition of Right were violated by him, not occasionally, but constantly, and on system ; that a large part of the revenue was raised without any legal authority ; and that persons obnoxious to the government languished for years in prison, without being ever called upon to plead before any tribunal.

For these things history must hold the King himself chiefly responsible. From the time of his third Parliament he was his own prime minister. Several persons, however, whose temper and talents were suited to his purposes, were at the head of different departments of the administration.

Character and designs of Wentworth.

Thomas Wentworth, successively created Lord Wentworth and Earl of Strafford, a man of great abilities, eloquence, and courage, but of a cruel and imperious nature, was the counsellor most trusted in political and military affairs. He had been one of the most distinguished members of the opposition, and felt towards those whom he had deserted that peculiar malignity which has, in all ages, been characteristic of apostates. He perfectly understood the feelings, the resources, and the policy of the party to which he had lately belonged, and had formed a vast and deeply meditated scheme which very nearly confounded even the able tactics of the statesmen by whom the House of Commons had been directed. To this scheme, in his confidential correspondence, he gave the expressive name of Thorough. His object was to do in England all, and more than all, that Richelieu was doing in France; to make Charles a monarch as absolute as any on the Continent; to put the estates and the personal liberty of the whole people at the disposal of the crown; to deprive the courts of law of all independent authority, even in ordinary questions of civil right between man and man; and to punish with merciless rigour all who murmured at the acts of the government, or who applied, even in the most decent and regular manner, to any tribunal for relief against those acts.*

This was his end; and he distinctly saw in what manner alone this end could be attained. There was, in truth, about all his notions a clearness, a coherence, a precision, which, if he had not been pursuing an object pernicious to his country and to his kind, would have justly entitled him to high admiration. He saw that there was one instrument, and only one, by which his vast and daring projects could be carried into execution. That instrument was a standing army. To the forming of such an army, therefore, he directed all the energy of his strong mind. In Ireland, where he was viceroy, he actually succeeded in establishing a military despotism, not only over the aboriginal population, but also over the English colonists, and was able to boast that, in that island, the King was as absolute as any prince in the whole world could be.†

The ecclesiastical administration was, in the meantime, principally directed by William Laud, Archbishop of Canterbury. Of all the prelates of the Anglican Church, Laud had departed farthest from the principles of the Reformation, and had drawn nearest to Rome. His theology was more remote than even that of the Dutch Arminians from the theology of the Calvinists. His passion for ceremonies, his reverence for holidays, vigils, and sacred places, his ill concealed dislike of the marriage of ecclesiastics, the ardent and not altogether disinterested zeal with which he asserted the claims of the clergy to the reverence of the laity, would have made him an object of aversion to the Puritans, even if he had used only

Character of Laud.

---

* The correspondence of Wentworth seems to me fully to bear out what I have said in the text. To transcribe all the passages which have led me to the conclusion at which I have arrived, would be impossible; nor would it be easy to make a better selection than has already been made by Mr. Hallam. I may, however, direct the attention of the reader particularly to the very able paper which Wentworth drew up respecting the affairs of the Palatinate. The date is March 31, 1637.

† These are Wentworth's own words. See his letter to Laud, dated Dec. 16, 1634.

legal and gentle means for the attainment of his ends. But his understanding was narrow; and his commerce with the world had been small. He was by nature rash, irritable, quick to feel for his own dignity, slow to sympathise with the sufferings of others, and prone to the error, common in superstitious men, of mistaking his own peevish and malignant moods for emotions of pious zeal. Under his direction every corner of the realm was subjected to a constant and minute inspection. Every little congregation of separatists was tracked out and broken up. Even the devotions of private families could not escape the vigilance of his spies. Such fear did his rigour inspire that the deadly hatred of the Church, which festered in innumerable bosoms, was generally disguised under an outward show of conformity. On the very eve of troubles, fatal to himself and to his order, the Bishops of several extensive dioceses were able to report to him that not a single dissenter was to be found within their jurisdiction.*

The tribunals afforded no protection to the subject against the civil and ecclesiastical tyranny of that period. The judges of the common law, holding their situations during the pleasure of the King, were scandalously obsequious. Yet, obsequious as they were, they were less ready and less efficient instruments of arbitrary power than a class of courts, the memory of which is still, after the lapse of more than two centuries, held in deep abhorrence by the nation. Foremost among these courts in power and in infamy were the Star Chamber and the High Commission, the former a political, the latter a religious inquisition. Neither was a part of the old constitution of England. The Star Chamber had been remodelled, and the High Commission created, by the Tudors. The power which these boards had possessed before the accession of Charles had been extensive and formidable, but had been small indeed when compared with that which they now usurped. Guided chiefly by the violent spirit of the primate, and freed from the control of Parliament, they displayed a rapacity, a violence, a malignant energy, which had been unknown to any former age. The government was able through their instrumentality, to fine, imprison, pillory, and mutilate without restraint. A separate council which sate at York, under the presidency of Wentworth, was armed, in defiance of law, by a pure act of prerogative, with almost

Star Chamber and High Commission.

* See his report to Charles for the year 1639.

boundless power over the northern counties. All these tribunals insulted and defied the authority of Westminster Hall, and daily committed excesses which the most distinguished Royalists have warmly condemned. We are informed by Clarendon that there was hardly a man of note in the realm who had not personal experience of the harshness and greediness of the Star Chamber, that the High Commission had so conducted itself that it had scarce a friend left in the kingdom, and that the tyranny of the Council of York had made the Great Charter a dead letter on the north of the Trent.

The government of England was now, in all points but one, as despotic as that of France. But that one point was all important. There was still no standing army. There was, therefore, no security that the whole fabric of tyranny might not be subverted in a single day; and, if taxes were imposed by the royal authority for the support of an army, it was probable that there would be an immediate and irresistible explosion. This was the difficulty which more than any other perplexed Wentworth. The Lord Keeper Finch, in concert with other lawyers who were employed by the government, recommended an expedient, which was eagerly adopted. The ancient princes of England, as they called on the inhabitants of the counties near Scotland to arm and array themselves for the defence of the border, had sometimes called on the maritime counties to furnish ships for the defence of the coast. In the room of ships money had sometimes been accepted. This old practice it was now determined, after a long interval, not only to revive but to extend. Former princes had raised shipmoney only in time of war: it was now exacted in a time of profound peace. Former princes, even in the most perilous wars, had raised shipmoney only along the coasts: it was now exacted from the inland shires. Former princes had raised shipmoney only for the maritime defence of the country: it was now exacted, by the admission of the Royalists themselves, with the object, not of maintaining a navy, but of furnishing the King with supplies which might be increased at his discretion to any amount, and expended at his discretion for any purpose.

The whole nation was alarmed and incensed. John Hampden, an opulent and well born gentleman of Buckinghamshire, highly considered in his own neighbourhood, but as yet little known to the kingdom generally, had the

Shipmoney.

courage to step forward, to confront the whole power of the government, and take on himself the cost and the risk of disputing the prerogative to which the King laid claim. The case was argued before the judges in the Exchequer Chamber. So strong were the arguments against the pretensions of the crown that, dependent and servile as the judges were, the majority against Hampden was the smallest possible. Still there was a majority. The interpreters of the law had pronounced that one great and productive tax might be imposed by the royal authority. Wentworth justly observed that it was impossible to vindicate their judgment except by reasons directly leading to a conclusion which they had not ventured to draw. If money might legally be raised without the consent of Parliament for the support of a fleet, it was not easy to deny that money might, without consent of Parliament, be legally raised for the support of an army.

The decision of the judges increased the irritation of the people. A century earlier, irritation less serious would have produced a general rising. But discontent did not now so readily as in an earlier age take the form of rebellion. The nation had been long steadily advancing in wealth and in civilisation. Since the great northern Earls took up arms against Elizabeth seventy years had elapsed; and during those seventy years there had been no civil war. Never, during the whole existence of the English nation, had so long a period passed without intestine hostilities. Men had become accustomed to the pursuits of peaceful industry, and, exasperated as they were, hesitated long before they drew the sword.

This was the conjuncture at which the liberties of the nation were in the greatest peril. The opponents of the government began to despair of the destiny of their country; and many looked to the American wilderness as the only asylum in which they could enjoy civil and spiritual freedom. There a few resolute Puritans, who, in the cause of their religion, feared neither the rage of the ocean nor the hardships of uncivilised life, neither the fangs of savage beasts nor the tomahawks of more savage men, had built, amidst the primeval forests, villages which are now great and opulent cities, but which have, through every change, retained some trace of the character derived from their founders. The government regarded these infant colonies with aversion, and attempted violently to stop the stream of emigration, but could not prevent the population of New England from being largely recruited by stouthearted and Godfearing men from every part of the old England. And now Wentworth exulted in the near prospect of Thorough. A few years might probably suffice for the execution of his great design. If strict economy were observed, if all collision with foreign powers were carefully avoided, the debts of the crown would be cleared off: there would be funds available for the support of a large military force; and that force would soon break the refractory spirit of the nation.

At this crisis an act of insane bigotry suddenly changed the whole face of public affairs. Had the King been wise, he would have pursued a cautious and soothing policy towards Scotland till he was master in the South. For Scotland was of all his kingdoms that in which there was the greatest risk that a spark might produce a flame, and that a flame might become a conflagration. Constitutional opposition, indeed, such as he had encountered at Westminster, he had not to apprehend at Edinburgh. The Parliament of his northern kingdom was a very different body from that which bore the same name in England. It was ill constituted: it was little considered; and it had never imposed any serious restraint on any of his predecessors. The three Estates sate in one house. The commissioners of the burghs were considered merely as retainers of the great nobles. No act could be introduced till it had been approved by the Lords of Articles, a committee which was really, though not in form, nominated by the crown. But, though the Scottish Parliament was obsequious, the Scottish people had always been singularly turbulent and ungovernable. They had butchered their first James in his bedchamber: they had repeatedly arrayed themselves in arms against James the Second: they had slain James the Third on the field of battle: their disobedience had broken the heart of James the Fifth: they had deposed and imprisoned Mary: they had led her son captive; and their temper was still as intractable as ever. Their habits were rude and martial. All along the southern border, and all along the line between the highlands and the lowlands, raged an incessant predatory war. In every part of the country men were accustomed to redress their wrongs by the strong hand. Whatever loyalty the nation had anciently felt to the Stuarts had cooled during their long absence. The supreme influence over the

Resistance to the Liturgy in Scotland.

public mind was divided between two classes of malecontents, the lords of the soil and the preachers; lords animated by the same spirit which had often impelled the old Douglasses to withstand the royal house, and preachers who had inherited the republican opinions and the unconquerable spirit of Knox. Both the national and religious feelings of the population had been wounded. All orders of men complained that their country, that country which had, with so much glory, defended her independence against the ablest and bravest Plantagenets, had, through the instrumentality of her native princes, become in effect, though not in name, a province of England. In no part of Europe had the Calvinistic doctrine and discipline taken so strong a hold on the public mind. The Church of Rome was regarded by the great body of the people with a hatred which might justly be called ferocious; and the Church of England, which seemed to be every day becoming more and more like the Church of Rome, was an object of scarcely less aversion.

The government had long wished to extend the Anglican system over the whole island, and had already, with this view, made several changes highly distasteful to every Presbyterian. One innovation, however, the most hazardous of all, because it was directly cognisable by the senses of the common people, had not yet been attempted. The public worship of God was still conducted in the manner acceptable to the nation. Now, however, Charles and Laud determined to force on the Scots the English liturgy, or rather a liturgy which, wherever it differed from that of England, differed, in the judgment of all rigid Protestants, for the worse.

To this step, taken in the mere wantonness of tyranny, and in criminal ignorance or more criminal contempt of public feeling, our country owes her freedom. The first performance of the foreign ceremonies produced a riot. The riot rapidly became a revolution. Ambition, patriotism, fanaticism, were mingled in one headlong torrent. The whole nation was in arms. The power of England was indeed, as appeared some years later, sufficient to coerce Scotland: but a large part of the English people sympathised with the religious feelings of the insurgents; and many Englishmen who had no scruple about antiphonies and genuflexions, altars and surplices, saw with pleasure the progress of a rebellion which seemed likely to confound the arbitrary projects of the court, and to make the calling of a Parliament necessary.

For the senseless freak which had produced these effects Wentworth is not responsible.* It had, in fact, thrown all his plans into confusion. To counsel submission, however, was not in his nature. An attempt was made to put down the insurrection by the sword : but the King's military means and military talents were unequal to the task. To impose fresh taxes on England in defiance of law, would, at this conjuncture, have been madness. No resource was left but a Parliament ; and in the spring of 1640 a Parliament was convoked.

A Parliament called and dissolved.

The nation had been put into good humour by the prospect of seeing constitutional government restored, and grievances redressed. The new House of Commons was more temperate and more respectful to the throne than any which had sate since the death of Elizabeth. The moderation of this assembly has been highly extolled by the most distinguished Royalists, and seems to have caused no small vexation and disappointment to the chiefs of the opposition : but it was the uniform practice of Charles, a practice equally impolitic and ungenerous, to refuse all compliance with the desires of his people, till those desires were expressed in a menacing tone. As soon as the Commons showed a disposition to take into consideration the grievances under which the country had suffered during eleven years, the King dissolved the Parliament with every mark of displeasure.

Between the dissolution of this shortlived assembly and the meeting of that ever memorable body known by the name of the Long Parliament, intervened a few months, during which the yoke was pressed down more severely than ever on the nation, while the spirit of the nation rose up more angrily than ever against the yoke. Members of the House of Commons were questioned by the Privy Council touching their parliamentary conduct, and thrown into prison for refusing to reply. Shipmoney was levied with increased rigour. The Lord Mayor and the Sheriffs of London were threatened with imprisonment for remissness in collecting the payments. Soldiers were enlisted by force. Money for their support was exacted from their counties. Torture, which had always been illegal, and which had recently been declared illegal even by the servile judges of that age, was inflicted for the last time in England in the month of May 1640.

* See his letter to the Earl of Northumberland, dated July 30. 1638.

Everything now depended on the event of the King's military operations against the Scots. Among his troops there was little of that feeling which separates professional soldiers from the mass of a nation, and attaches them to their leaders. His army, composed for the most part of recruits, who regretted the plough from which they had been violently taken, and who were imbued with the religious and political sentiments then prevalent throughout the country, was more formidable to himself than to the enemy. The Scots, encouraged by the heads of the English opposition, and feebly resisted by the English forces, marched across the Tweed and the Tyne, and encamped on the borders of Yorkshire. And now the murmurs of discontent swelled into an uproar by which all spirits save one were overawed. But the voice of Strafford was still for Thorough; and he even, in this extremity, showed a nature so cruel and despotic, that his own pikemen were ready to tear him in pieces.

There was yet one last expedient which, as the King flattered himself, might save him from the misery of facing another House of Commons. To the House of Lords he was less averse. The Bishops were devoted to him; and, though the temporal peers were generally dissatisfied with his administration, they were, as a class, so deeply interested in the maintenance of order, and in the stability of ancient institutions, that they were not likely to call for extensive reforms. Departing from the uninterrupted practice of centuries, he called a Great Council consisting of Lords alone. But the Lords were too prudent to assume the unconstitutional functions with which he wished to invest them. Without money, without credit, without authority even in his own camp, he yielded to the pressure of necessity. The Houses were convoked; and the elections proved that, since the spring, the distrust and hatred with which the government was regarded had made fearful progress.

The Long Parliament. In November 1640 met that renowned Parliament which, in spite of many errors and disasters, is justly entitled to the reverence and gratitude of all who, in any part of the world, enjoy the blessings of constitutional government.

During the year which followed, no very important division of opinion appeared in the Houses. The civil and ecclesiastical administration had, through a period of near twelve years, been so oppressive and so unconstitutional that even those classes of which the inclinations are generally on the side of order and authority were eager to promote popular reforms, and to bring the instruments of tyranny to justice. It was enacted that no interval of more than three years should ever elapse between Parliament and Parliament, and that, if writs under the Great Seal were not issued at the proper time, the returning officers should, without such writs, call the constituent bodies together for the choice of representatives. The Star Chamber, the High Commission, the Council of York were swept away. Men who, after suffering cruel mutilations, had been confined in remote dungeons, regained their liberty. On the chief ministers of the crown the vengeance of the nation was unsparingly wreaked. The Lord Keeper, the Primate, the Lord Lieutenant were impeached. Finch saved himself by flight. Laud was flung into the Tower. Strafford was put to death by act of attainder. On the day on which this act passed, the King gave his assent to a law by which he bound himself not to adjourn, prorogue, or dissolve the existing Parliament without its own consent.

After ten months of assiduous toil, the Houses, in September 1641, adjourned for a short vacation; and the King visited Scotland. He with difficulty pacified that kingdom by consenting, not only to relinquish his plans of ecclesiastical reform, but even to pass, with a very bad grace, an act declaring that episcopacy was contrary to the word of God.

The recess of the English Parliament lasted six weeks. The day on which the Houses met again is one of the most remarkable epochs in our history. From that day dates the corporate existence of the two great parties which have ever since alternately governed the country. In one sense, indeed, the distinction which then became obvious had always existed, and always must exist. For it has its origin in diversities of temper, of understanding, and of interest, which are found in all societies, and which will be found till the human mind ceases to be drawn in opposite directions by the charm of habit and by the charm of novelty. Not only in politics but in literature, in art, in science, in surgery and mechanics, in navigation and agriculture, nay, even in mathematics, we find this distinction. Everywhere there is a class of men who cling with fondness to whatever is ancient, and who, even when convinced by overpowering reasons that innovation would be beneficial, consent to it with many misgivings and forebodings. We find also everywhere another class of men, sanguine in hope, bold in

First appearance of the two great English parties.

speculation, always pressing forward, quick to discern the imperfections of whatever exists, disposed to think lightly of the risks and inconveniences which attend improvements, and disposed to give every change credit for being an improvement. In the sentiments of both classes there is something to approve. But of both the best specimens will be found not far from the common frontier. The extreme section of one class consists of bigoted dotards : the extreme section of the other consists of shallow and reckless empirics.

There can be no doubt that in our very first Parliaments might have been discerned a body of members anxious to preserve, and a body eager to reform. But, while the sessions of the legislature were short, these bodies did not take definite and permanent forms, array themselves under recognised leaders, or assume distinguishing names, badges, and war cries. During the first months of the Long Parliament, the indignation excited by many years of lawless oppression was so strong and general that the House of Commons acted as one man. Abuse after abuse disappeared without a struggle. If a small minority of the representative body wished to retain the Star Chamber and the High Commission, that minority, overawed by the enthusiasm and by the numerical superiority of the reformers, contented itself with secretly regretting institutions which could not, with any hope of success, be openly defended. At a later period the Royalists found it convenient to antedate the separation between themselves and their opponents, and to attribute the Act which restrained the King from dissolving or proroguing the Parliament, the Triennial Act, the impeachment of the ministers, and the attainder of Strafford, to the faction which afterwards made war on the King. But no artifice could be more disingenuous. Every one of those strong measures was actively promoted by the men who were afterwards foremost among the Cavaliers. No republican spoke of the long misgovernment of Charles more severely than Colepepper. The most remarkable speech in favour of the Triennial Bill was made by Digby. The impeachment of the Lord Keeper was moved by Falkland. The demand that the Lord Lieutenant should be kept close prisoner was made at the bar of the Lords by Hyde. Not till the law attainting Strafford was proposed did the signs of serious disunion become visible. Even against that law, a law which nothing but extreme necessity could justify, only about sixty members of the House of Commons voted. It is certain that Hyde was not in the minority, and that Falkland not only voted with the majority, but spoke strongly for the bill. Even the few who entertained a scruple about inflicting death by a retrospective enactment thought it necessary to express the utmost abhorrence of Strafford's character and administration.

But under this apparent concord a great schism was latent; and when, in October 1641, the Parliament reassembled after a short recess, two hostile parties, essentially the same with those which, under different names, have ever since contended, and are still contending, for the direction of public affairs, appeared confronting each other. During some years they were designated as Cavaliers and Roundheads. They were subsequently called Tories and Whigs; nor does it seem that these appellations are likely soon to become obsolete.

It would not be difficult to compose a lampoon or a panegyric on either of these renowned factions. For no man not utterly destitute of judgment and candour will deny that there are many deep stains on the fame of the party to which he belongs, or that the party to which he is opposed may justly boast of many illustrious names, of many heroic actions, and of many great services rendered to the state. The truth is that, though both parties have often seriously erred, England could have spared neither. If, in her institutions, freedom and order, the advantages arising from innovation and the advantages arising from prescription, have been combined to an extent elsewhere unknown, we may attribute this happy peculiarity to the strenuous conflicts and alternate victories of two rival confederacies of statesmen, a confederacy zealous for authority and antiquity, and a confederacy zealous for liberty and progress.

It ought to be remembered that the difference between the two great sections of English politicians has always been a difference rather of degree than of principle. There were certain limits on the right and on the left, which were very rarely overstepped. A few enthusiasts on one side were ready to lay all our laws and franchises at the feet of our Kings. A few enthusiasts on the other side were bent on pursuing, through endless civil troubles, their darling phantom of a republic. But the great majority of those who fought for the crown were averse to despotism; and the great majority of the champions of popular rights were averse to anarchy. Twice, in the course of the seventeenth century, the two parties suspended their dissensions, and united their strength in a common cause. Their first coalition restored hereditary monarchy. Their second coalition rescued constitutional freedom.

It is also to be noted that these two parties have never been the whole nation, nay, that they have never, taken together, made up a majority of the nation. Between them has always been a great mass, which has not steadfastly adhered to either, which has sometimes remained inertly neutral, and which has sometimes oscillated to and fro. That mass has more than once passed in a few years from one extreme to the other, and back again. Sometimes it has changed sides, merely because it was tired of supporting the same men, sometimes because it was dismayed by its own excesses, sometimes because it had expected impossibilities, and had been disappointed. But, whenever it has leaned with its whole weight in either direction, that weight has, for the time, been irresistible.

When the rival parties first appeared in a distinct form, they seemed to be not unequally matched. On the side of the government was a large majority of the nobles, and of those opulent and well descended gentlemen to whom nothing was wanting of nobility but the name. These, with the dependents whose support they could command, were no small power in the state. On the same side were the great body of the clergy, both the Universities, and all those laymen who were strongly attached to episcopal government and to the Anglican ritual. These respectable classes found themselves in the company of some allies much less decorous than themselves. The Puritan austerity drove to the King's faction all who made pleasure their business, who affected gallantry, splendour of dress, or taste in the lighter arts. With these went all who live by amusing the leisure of others, from the painter and the comic poet, down to the ropedancer and the Merry Andrew. For these artists well knew that they might thrive under a superb and luxurious despotism, but must starve under the rigid rule of the precisians. In the same interest were the Roman Catholics to a man. The Queen, a daughter of France, was of their own faith. Her husband was known to be strongly attached to her, and not a little in awe of her. Though undoubtedly a

Protestant on conviction, he regarded the professors of the old religion with no ill-will, and would gladly have granted them a much larger toleration than he was disposed to concede to the Presbyterians. If the opposition obtained the mastery, it was probable that the sanguinary laws enacted against Papists, in the reign of Elizabeth, would be severely enforced. The Roman Catholics were therefore induced by the strongest motives to espouse the cause of the court. They in general acted with a caution which brought on them the reproach of cowardice and lukewarmness: but it is probable that, in maintaining great reserve, they consulted the King's interest as well as their own. It was not for his service that they should be conspicuous among his friends.

The main strength of the opposition lay among the small freeholders in the country, and among the merchants and shopkeepers of the towns. But these were headed by a formidable minority of the aristocracy, a minority which included the rich and powerful Earls of Northumberland, Bedford, Warwick, Stamford, and Essex, and several other Lords of great wealth and influence. In the same ranks was found the whole body of Protestant Nonconformists, and most of those members of the Established Church who still adhered to the Calvinistic opinions which, forty years before, had been generally held by the prelates and clergy. The municipal corporations took, with few exceptions, the same side. In the House of Commons the opposition preponderated, but not very decidedly.

Neither party wanted strong arguments for the course which it was disposed to take. The reasonings of the most enlightened Royalists may be summed up thus :—" It is true that great abuses have existed; but they have been redressed. It is true that precious rights have been invaded; but they have been vindicated and surrounded with new securities. The sittings of the Estates of the realm have been, in defiance of all precedent and of the spirit of the constitution, intermitted during eleven years; but it has now been provided that henceforth three years shall never elapse without a Parliament. The Star Chamber, the High Commission, the Council of York, oppressed and plundered us; but those hateful courts have now ceased to exist. The Lord Lieutenant aimed at establishing military despotism; but he has answered for his treason with his head. The Primate tainted our worship with Popish rites, and punished our scruples with Popish cruelty; but he is awaiting in the Tower the judgment of his peers. The Lord Keeper sanctioned a plan by which the property of every man in England was placed at the mercy of the Crown; but he has been disgraced, ruined, and compelled to take refuge in a foreign land. The ministers of tyranny have expiated their crimes. The victims of tyranny have been compensated for their sufferings. It would therefore be most unwir to persevere further in that course which was justifiable and necessary when we first met, after a long interval, and found the whole administration one mass of abuses. It is time to take heed that we do not so pursue our victory over despotism as to run into anarchy. It was not in our power to overturn the bad institutions which lately afflicted our country, without shocks which have loosened the foundations of government. Now that those institutions have fallen, we must hasten to prop the edifice which it was lately our duty to batter. Henceforth it will be our wisdom to look with jealousy on schemes of innovation, and to guard from encroachment all the prerogatives with which the law has, for the public good, armed the sovereign."

Such were the views of those men of whom the excellent Falkland may be regarded as the leader. It was contended on the other side with not less force, by men of not less ability and virtue, that the safety which the liberties of the English people enjoyed was rather apparent than real, and that the arbitrary projects of the court would be resumed as soon as the vigilance of the Commons was relaxed. True it was,—such was the reasoning of Pym, of Hollis, and of Hampden,—that many good laws had been passed: but, it good laws had been sufficient to restrain the King, his subjects would have had little reason ever to complain of his administration. The recent statutes were surely not of more authority than the Great Charter or the Petition of Right. Yet neither the Great Charter, hallowed by the veneration of four centuries, nor the Petition of Right, sanctioned, after mature reflection, and for valuable consideration, by Charles himself, had been found effectual for the protection of the people. If once the check of fear were withdrawn, if once the spirit of opposition were suffered to slumber, all the securities for English freedom resolved themselves into a single one, the royal word; and it had been proved by a long and severe experience that the royal word could not be trusted.

The two parties were still regarding each other with cautious hostility, and had not yet measured their strength, when news arrived which inflamed the passions and confirmed the opinions of both. The great chieftains of Ulster, who, at the time of the accession of James, had, after a long struggle, submitted to the royal authority, had not long brooked the humiliation of dependence. They had conspired against the English government, and had been attainted of treason. Their immense domains had been forfeited to the crown, and had soon been peopled by thousands of English and Scotch emigrants. The new settlers were, in civilisation and intelligence, far superior to the native population, and sometimes abused their superiority. The animosity produced by difference of race was increased by difference of religion. Under the iron rule of Wentworth, scarcely a murmur was heard: but, when that strong pressure was withdrawn, when Scotland had set the example of successful resistance, when England was distracted by internal quarrels, the smothered rage of the Irish broke forth into acts of fearful violence. On a sudden, the aboriginal population rose on the colonists. A war, to which national and theological hatred gave a character of peculiar ferocity, desolated Ulster, and spread to the neighbouring provinces. The castle of Dublin was scarcely thought secure. Every post brought to London exaggerated accounts of outrages which, without any exaggeration, were sufficient to move pity and horror. These evil tidings roused to the height the zeal of both the great parties which were marshalled against each other at Westminster. The Royalists maintained that it was the first duty of every good Englishman and Protestant, at such a crisis, to strengthen the hands of the sovereign. To the opposition it seemed that there were now stronger reasons than ever for thwarting and restraining him. That the commonwealth was in danger was undoubtedly a good reason for giving large powers to a trustworthy magistrate: but it was a good reason for taking away powers from a magistrate who was at heart a public enemy. To raise a great army had always been the King's first object. A great army must now be raised. It was to be feared that, unless some new securities were devised, the forces levied for the reduction of Ireland would be employed against the liberties of England. Nor was this all. A horrible suspicion, unjust indeed, but not altogether unnatural, had arisen in many minds. The Queen

The Irish Rebellion.

was an avowed Roman Catholic: the King was not regarded by the Puritans, whom he had mercilessly persecuted, as a sincere Protestant; and so notorious was his duplicity, that there was no treachery of which his subjects might not, with some show of reason, believe him capable. It was soon whispered that the rebellion of the Roman Catholics of Ulster was part of a vast work of darkness which had been planned at Whitehall.

The remonstrance.

After some weeks of prelude, the first great parliamentary conflict between the parties, which have ever since contended, and are still contending, for the government of the nation, took place on the twenty-second of November 1641. It was moved by the opposition, that the House of Commons should present to the King a remonstrance, enumerating the faults of his administration from the time of his accession, and expressing the distrust with which his policy was still regarded by his people. That assembly, which a few months before had been unanimous in calling for the reform of abuses, was now divided into two fierce and eager factions of nearly equal strength. After a hot debate of many hours, the remonstrance was carried by only eleven votes.

The result of this struggle was highly favourable to the conservative party. It could not be doubted that only some great indiscretion could prevent them from shortly obtaining the predominance in the Lower House. The Upper House was already their own. Nothing was wanting to insure their success, but that the King should, in all his conduct, show respect for the laws and scrupulous good faith towards his subjects.

His first measures promised well. He had, it seemed, at last discovered that an entire change of system was necessary, and had wisely made up his mind to what could no longer be avoided. He declared his determination to govern in harmony with the Commons, and, for that end, to call to his councils men in whose talents and character the Commons might place confidence. Nor was the selection ill made. Falkland, Hyde, and Colepepper, all three distinguished by the part which they had taken in reforming abuses and in punishing evil ministers, were invited to become the confidential advisers of the Crown, and were solemnly assured by Charles that he would take no step in any way affecting the Lower House of Parliament without their privity.

Had he kept this promise, it cannot be doubted that the

reaction which was already in progress would very soon have become quite as strong as the most respectable Royalists would have desired. Already the violent members of the opposition had begun to despair of the fortunes of their party, to tremble for their own safety, and to talk of selling their estates and emigrating to America. That the fair prospects which had begun to open before the King were suddenly overcast, that his life was darkened by adversity, and at length shortened by violence, is to be attributed to his own faithlessness and contempt of law.

The truth seems to be that he detested both the parties into which the House of Commons was divided : nor is this strange ; for in both those parties the love of liberty and the love of order were mingled, though in different proportions. The advisers whom necessity had compelled him to call round him were by no means men after his own heart. They had joined in condemning his tyranny, in abridging his power, and in punishing his instruments. They were now indeed prepared to defend in a strictly legal way his strictly legal prerogative ; but they would have recoiled with horror from the thought of reviving Wentworth's projects of Thorough. They were, therefore, in the King's opinion, traitors, who differed only in the degree of their seditious malignity from Pym and Hampden.

He accordingly, a few days after he had promised the chiefs of the constitutional Royalists that no step of importance should be taken without their knowledge, formed a resolution the most momentous of his whole life, carefully concealed that resolution from them, and executed it in a manner which overwhelmed them with shame and dismay. He sent the Attorney General to impeach Pym, Hollis, Hampden, and other members of the House of Commons of high treason at the bar of the House of Lords. Not content with this flagrant violation of the Great Charter and of the uninterrupted practice of centuries, he went in person, accompanied by armed men, to seize the leaders of the opposition within the walls of Parliament. *Impeachment of the five members.*

The attempt failed. The accused members had left the House a short time before Charles entered it. A sudden and violent revulsion of feeling, both in the Parliament and in the country, followed. The most favourable view that has ever been taken of the King's conduct on this occasion by his most partial advocates is that he had weakly suffered himself to be hurried into a gross indiscretion by the evil counsels of his wife and of his courtiers. But the general voice loudly charged him with far deeper guilt. At the very moment at which his subjects, after a long estrangement produced by his maladministration, were returning to him with feelings of confidence and affection, he had aimed a deadly blow at all their dearest rights, at the privileges of Parliament, at the very principle of trial by jury. He had shown that he considered opposition to his arbitrary designs as a crime to be expiated only by blood. He had broken faith, not only with his Great Council and with his people, but with his own adherents. He had done what, but for an unforeseen accident, would probably have produced a bloody conflict round the Speaker's chair. Those who had the chief sway in the Lower House now felt that not only their power and popularity, but their lands and their necks, were staked on the event of the struggle in which they were engaged. The flagging zeal of the party opposed to the court revived in an instant. During the night which followed the outrage the whole city of London was in arms. In a few hours the roads leading to the capital were covered with multitudes of yeomen spurring hard to Westminster with the badges of the parliamentary cause in their hats. In the House of Commons the opposition became at once irresistible, and carried, by more than two votes to one, resolutions of unprecedented violence. Strong bodies of the trainbands, regularly relieved, mounted guard round Westminster Hall. The gates of the King's palace were daily besieged by a furious multitude whose taunts and execrations were heard even in the presence chamber, and who could scarcely be kept out of the royal apartments by the gentlemen of the household. Had Charles remained much longer in his stormy capital, it is probable that the Commons would have found a plea for making him, under outward forms of respect, a state prisoner.

Departure of Charles from London.

He quitted London, never to return till the day of a terrible and memorable reckoning had arrived. A negotiation began which occupied many months. Accusations and recriminations passed backward and forward between the contending parties. All accommodation had become impossible. The sure punishment which waits on habitual perfidy had at length overtaken the King. It was to no purpose that he now pawned his royal word, and invoked heaven to witness the sincerity of his professions. The distrust with which his adversaries regarded him was not to be removed by oaths or treaties. They were convinced that they could be safe only when he was utterly helpless. Their demand, therefore, was, that he should surrender, not only those prerogatives which he had usurped in violation of ancient laws and of his own recent promises, but also other prerogatives which the English Kings had always possessed, and continue to possess at the present day. No minister must be appointed, no peer created, without the consent of the Houses. Above all, the sovereign must resign that supreme military authority which, from time beyond all memory, had appertained to the regal office.

That Charles would comply with such demands while he had any means of resistance, was not to be expected. Yet it will be difficult to show that the Houses could safely have exacted less. They were truly in a most embarrassing position. The great majority of the nation was firmly attached to hereditary monarchy. Those who held republican opinions were as yet few, and did not venture to speak out. It was therefore impossible to abolish kingly government. Yet it was plain that no confidence could be placed in the King. It would have been absurd in those who knew, by recent proof, that he was bent on destroying them, to content themselves with presenting to him another Petition of Right, and receiving from him fresh promises similar to those which he had repeatedly made and broken. Nothing but the want of an army had prevented him from entirely subverting the old constitution of the realm. It was now necessary to levy a great regular army for the conquest of Ireland; and it would therefore have been mere insanity to leave him in possession of that plenitude of military authority which his ancestors had enjoyed.

When a country is in the situation in which England then was, when the kingly office is regarded with love and veneration, but the person who fills that office is hated and distrusted, it should seem that the course which ought to be taken is obvious. The dignity of the office should be preserved: the person should be discarded. Thus our ancestors acted in 1399 and in 1689. Had there been, in 1642, any man occupying a position similar to that which Henry of Lancaster occupied at the time of the deposition of Richard the Second, and which William of Orange occupied at the

time of the deposition of James the Second, it is probable
that the Houses would have changed the dynasty, and would
have made no formal change in the constitution.   The new
King, called to the throne by their choice, and dependent on
their support, would have been under the necessity of governing in conformity with their wishes and opinions.   But there
was no prince of the blood royal in the parliamentary party;
and, though that party contained many men of high rank
and many men of eminent ability, there was none who
towered so conspicuously above the rest that he could be proposed as a candidate for the crown.   As there was to be a
King, and as no new King could be found, it was necessary
to leave the regal title to Charles.   Only one course, therefore, was left: and that was to disjoin the regal title from the
regal prerogatives.

The change which the Houses proposed to make in our institutions, though it seems exorbitant, when distinctly set
forth and digested into articles of capitulation, really amounts
to little more than the change which, in the next generation,
was effected by the Revolution.   It is true that, at the Revolution, the sovereign was not deprived by law of the power of
naming his ministers: but it is equally true that, since the
Revolution, no minister has been able to retain office six
months in opposition to the sense of the House of Commons.
It is true that the sovereign still possesses the power of
creating peers, and the more important power of the sword:
but it is equally true that in the exercise of these powers the
sovereign has, ever since the Revolution, been guided by advisers who possess the confidence of the representatives of the
nation.   In fact, the leaders of the Roundhead party in 1642,
and the statesmen who, about half a century later, effected
the Revolution, had exactly the same object in view.   That
object was to terminate the contest between the Crown and
the Parliament, by giving to the Parliament a supreme control over the executive administration.   The statesmen of the
Revolution effected this indirectly by changing the dynasty.
The Roundheads of 1642, being unable to change the dynasty, were compelled to take a direct course towards their
end.

We cannot, however, wonder that the demands of the
opposition, importing as they did a complete and formal
transfer to the Parliament of powers which had always
belonged to the Crown, should have shocked that great party

of which the characteristics are respect for constitutional
authority and dread of violent innovation. That party had
recently been in hopes of obtaining by peaceable means the
ascendency in the House of Commons; but every such hope
had been blighted. The duplicity of Charles had made his
old enemies irreconcileable, had driven back into the ranks of
the disaffected a crowd of moderate men who were in the
very act of coming over to his side, and had so cruelly mortified his best friends that they had for a time stood aloof in
silent shame and resentment. Now, however, the constitutional Royalists were forced to make their choice between
two dangers; and they thought it their duty rather to rally
round a prince whose past conduct they condemned, and
whose word inspired them with little confidence, than to
suffer the regal office to be degraded, and the polity of the
realm to be entirely remodelled. With such feelings, many
men whose virtues and abilities would have done honour to
any cause, ranged themselves on the side of the King.

In August 1642 the sword was at length drawn; and soon, Com-
in almost every shire of the kingdom, two hostile factions mence-
appeared in arms against each other. It is not easy to say the civil
which of the contending parties was at first the more formid- war.
able. The Houses commanded London and the counties
round London, the fleet, the navigation of the Thames, and
most of the large towns and seaports. They had at their
disposal almost all the military stores of the kingdom, and
were able to raise duties, both on goods imported from
foreign countries, and on some important products of domestic industry. The King was ill provided with artillery
and ammunition. The taxes which he laid on the rural districts occupied by his troops produced, it is probable, a sum
far less than that which the Parliament drew from the city
of London alone. He relied, indeed, chiefly, for pecuniary
aid, on the munificence of his opulent adherents. Many of
these mortgaged their land, pawned their jewels, and broke
up their silver chargers and christening bowls, in order
to assist him. But experience has fully proved that the
voluntary liberality of individuals, even in times of the
greatest excitement, is a poor financial resource when compared with severe and methodical taxation, which presses on
the willing and unwilling alike.

Charles, however, had one advantage, which, if he had
used it well, would have more than compensated for the want

of stores and money, and which, notwithstanding his mismanagement, gave him, during some months, a superiority
in the war. His troops at first fought much better than
those of the Parliament. Both armies, it is true, were
almost entirely composed of men who had never seen a field
of battle. Nevertheless, the difference was great. The par
liamentary ranks were filled with hirelings whom want and
idleness had induced to enlist. Hampden's regiment was regarded as one of the best; and even Hampden's regiment
was described by Cromwell as a mere rabble of tapsters and
serving men out of place. The royal army, on the other
hand, consisted in great part of gentlemen, high spirited,
ardent, accustomed to consider dishonour as more terrible
than death, accustomed to fencing, to the use of fire arms, to
bold riding, and to manly and perilous sport, which has been
well called the image of war. Such gentlemen, mounted on
their favourite horses, and commanding little bands, composed of their younger brothers, grooms, gamekeepers, and
huntsmen, were, from the very first day on which they took
the field, qualified to play their part with credit in a skirmish. The steadiness, the prompt obedience, the mechanical
precision of movement, which are characteristic of the regular soldier, these gallant volunteers never attained. But they
were at first opposed to enemies as undisciplined as themselves, and far less active, athletic, and daring. For a time,
therefore, the Cavaliers were successful in almost every encounter.

The Houses had also been unfortunate in the choice of a
general. The rank and wealth of the Earl of Essex made
him one of the most important members of the parliamentary
party. He had borne arms on the Continent with credit,
and, when the war began, had as high a military reputation as
any man in the country. But it soon appeared that he was
unfit for the post of Commander in Chief. He had little
energy and no originality. The methodical tactics which he
had learned in the war of the Palatinate did not save him
from the disgrace of being surprised and baffled by such a
Captain as Rupert, who could claim no higher fame than
that of an enterprising partisan.

Nor were the officers who held the chief commissions under
Essex qualified to supply what was wanting in him. For
this, indeed, the Houses are scarcely to be blamed. In a
country which had not, within the memory of the oldest

person living, made war on a great scale by land, generals of tried skill and valour were not to be found. It was necessary, therefore, in the first instance, to trust untried men; and the preference was naturally given to men distinguished either by their station, or by the abilities which they had displayed in Parliament. In scarcely a single instance, however, was the selection fortunate. Neither the grandees nor the orators proved good soldiers. The Earl of Stamford, one of the greatest nobles of England, was routed by the Royalists at Stratton. Nathaniel Fiennes, inferior to none of his contemporaries in talents for civil business, disgraced himself by the pusillanimous surrender of Bristol. Indeed, of all the statesmen who at this juncture accepted high military commands, Hampden alone appears to have carried into the camp the capacity and strength of mind which had made him eminent in politics.

When the war had lasted a year, the advantage was decidedly with the Royalists. They were victorious, both in the western and in the northern counties. They had wrested Bristol, the second city in the kingdom, from the Parliament. They had won several battles, and had not sustained a single serious or ignominious defeat. Among the Roundheads adversity had begun to produce dissension and discontent. The Parliament was kept in alarm, sometimes by plots, and sometimes by riots. It was thought necessary to fortify London against the royal army, and to hang some disaffected citizens at their own doors. Several of the most distinguished peers who had hitherto remained at Westminster fled to the court at Oxford; nor can it be doubted that, if the operations of the Cavaliers had, at this season, been directed by a sagacious and powerful mind, Charles would soon have marched in triumph to Whitehall. *Successes of the Royalists.*

But the King suffered the auspicious moment to pass away; and it never returned. In August 1643 he sate down before the city of Gloucester. That city was defended by the inhabitants and by the garrison, with a determination such as had not, since the commencement of the war, been shown by the adherents of the Parliament. The emulation of London was excited. The trainbands of the City volunteered to march wherever their services might be required. A great force was speedily collected, and began to move westward. The siege of Gloucester was raised: the Royalists in every part of the kingdom were disheartened: the spirit of the

parliamentary party revived: and the apostate Lords, who
had lately fled from Westminster to Oxford, hastened back
from Oxford to Westminster.

Rise of the Indepen- dents.
And now a new and alarming class of symptoms began to
appear in the distempered body politic. There had been,
from the first, in the parliamentary party, some men whose
minds were set on objects from which the majority of that
party would have shrunk with horror. These men were, in
religion, Independents. They conceived that every Christian
congregation had, under Christ, supreme jurisdiction in things
spiritual; that appeals to provincial and national synods were
scarcely less unscriptural than appeals to the Court of Arches,
or to the Vatican; and that Popery, Prelacy, and Presbyterianism were merely three forms of one great apostasy.
In politics, the Independents were, to use the phrase of their
time, root and branch men, or, to use the kindred phrase
of our own time, radicals. Not content with limiting the
power of the monarch, they were desirous to erect a commonwealth on the ruins of the old English polity. At first they
had been inconsiderable, both in numbers and in weight;
but before the war had lasted two years they became, not
indeed the largest, but the most powerful faction in the
country. Some of the old parliamentary leaders had been
removed by death; and others had forfeited the public confidence. Pym had been borne, with princely honours, to a
grave among the Plantagenets. Hampden had fallen, as became him, while vainly endeavouring, by his heroic example,
to inspire his followers with courage to face the fiery cavalry
of Rupert. Bedford had been untrue to the cause. Northumberland was known to be lukewarm. Essex and his
lieutenants had shown little vigour and ability in the conduct
of military operations. At such a conjuncture it was that
the Independent party, ardent, resolute, and uncompromising,
began to raise its head, both in the camp and in the House
of Commons.

Oliver Cromwell.
The soul of that party was Oliver Cromwell. Bred to
peaceful occupations, he had, at more than forty years of age,
accepted a commission in the parliamentary army. No sooner
had he become a soldier than he discerned, with the keen
glance of genius, what Essex, and men like Essex, with all
their experience, were unable to perceive. He saw precisely
where the strength of the Royalists lay, and by what means
alone that strength could be overpowered. He saw that it

was necessary to reconstruct the army of the Parliament. He saw also that there were abundant and excellent materials for the purpose, materials less showy, indeed, but more solid, than those of which the gallant squadrons of the King were composed. It was necessary to look for recruits who were not mere mercenaries, for recruits of decent station and grave character, fearing God and zealous for public liberty. With such men he filled his own regiment, and, while he subjected them to a discipline more rigid than had ever before been known in England, he administered to their intellectual and moral nature stimulants of fearful potency.

The events of the year 1644 fully proved the superiority of his abilities. In the south, where Essex held the command, the parliamentary forces underwent a succession of shameful disasters; but in the north the victory of Marston Moor fully compensated for all that had been lost elsewhere. That victory was not a more serious blow to the Royalists than to the party which had hitherto been dominant at Westminster; for it was notorious that the day, disgracefully lost by the Presbyterians, had been retrieved by the energy of Cromwell, and by the steady valour of the warriors whom he had trained.

These events produced the Selfdenying Ordinance and the new model of the army. Under decorous pretexts, and with every mark of respect, Essex and most of those who had held high posts under him were removed; and the conduct of the war was intrusted to very different hands. Fairfax, a brave soldier, but of mean understanding and irresolute temper, was the nominal Lord General of the forces; but Cromwell was their real head. *Selfdenying Ordinance.*

Cromwell made haste to organise the whole army on the same principles on which he had organised his own regiment. As soon as this process was complete, the event of the war was decided. The Cavaliers had now to encounter natural courage equal to their own, enthusiasm stronger than their own, and discipline such as was utterly wanting to them. It soon became a proverb that the soldiers of Fairfax and Cromwell were men of a different breed from the soldiers of Essex. At Naseby took place the first great encounter between the Royalists and the remodelled army of the Houses. The victory of the Roundheads was complete and decisive. It was followed by other triumphs in rapid succession. In a few months the authority of the Parliament was fully established over the whole kingdom. Charles fled to the Scots, and was by them, *Victory of the Parliament.*

in a manner which did not much exalt their national character, delivered up to his English subjects.

While the event of the war was still doubtful, the Houses had put the Primate to death, had interdicted, within the sphere of their authority, the use of the Liturgy, and had required all men to subscribe that renowned instrument known by the name of the Solemn League and Covenant. Covenanting work, as it was called, went on fast. Hundreds of thousands affixed their names to the rolls, and, with hands lifted up towards heaven, swore to endeavour, without respect of persons, the extirpation of Popery and Prelacy, heresy and schism, and to bring to public trial and condign punishment all who should hinder the reformation of religion. When the struggle was over, the work of innovation and revenge was pushed on with increased ardour. The ecclesiastical polity of the kingdom was remodelled. Most of the old clergy were ejected from their benefices. Fines, often of ruinous amount, were laid on the Royalists, already impoverished by large aids furnished to the King. Many estates were confiscated. Many proscribed Cavaliers found it expedient to purchase, at an enormous cost, the protection of eminent members of the victorious party. Large domains, belonging to the crown, to the bishops, and to the chapters, were seized, and either granted away or put up to auction. In consequence of these spoliations, a great part of the soil of England was at once offered for sale. As money was scarce, as the market was glutted, as the title was insecure, and as the awe inspired by powerful bidders prevented free competition, the prices were often merely nominal. Thus many old and honourable families disappeared and were heard of no more ; and many new men rose rapidly to affluence.

But, while the Houses were employing their authority thus, it suddenly passed out of their hands. It had been obtained by calling into existence a power which could not be controlled. In the summer of 1647, about twelve months after the last fortress of the Cavaliers had submitted to the Parliament, the Parliament was compelled to submit to its own soldiers.

Domination and character of the army.

Thirteen years followed, during which England was, under various names and forms, really governed by the sword. Never before that time, or since that time, was the civil power in our country subjected to military dictation.

The army which now became supreme in the state was an

army very different from any that has since been seen among us. At present the pay of the common soldier is not such as can seduce any but the humblest class of English labourers from their calling. A barrier almost impassable separates him from the commissioned officer. The great majority of those who rise high in the service rise by purchase. So numerous and extensive are the remote dependencies of England, that every man who enlists in the line must expect to pass many years in exile, and some years in climates unfavourable to the health and vigour of the European race. The army of the Long Parliament was raised for home service. The pay of the private soldier was much above the wages earned by the great body of the people; and, if he distinguished himself by intelligence and courage, he might hope to attain high commands. The ranks were accordingly composed of persons superior in station and education to the multitude. These persons, sober, moral, diligent, and accustomed to reflect, had been induced to take up arms, not by the pressure of want, not by the love of novelty and license, not by the arts of recruiting officers, but by religious and political zeal, mingled with the desire of distinction and promotion. The boast of the soldiers, as we find it recorded in their solemn resolutions, was that they had not been forced into the service, nor had enlisted chiefly for the sake of lucre, that they were no janissaries, but freeborn Englishmen, who had, of their own accord, put their lives in jeopardy for the liberties and religion of England, and whose right and duty it was to watch over the welfare of the nation which they had saved.

A force thus composed might, without injury to its efficiency, be indulged in some liberties which, if allowed to any other troops, would have proved subversive of all discipline. In general, soldiers who should form themselves into political clubs, elect delegates, and pass resolutions on high questions of state, would soon break loose from all control, would cease to form an army, and would become the worst and most dangerous of mobs. Nor would it be safe, in our time, to tolerate in any regiment religious meetings, at which a corporal versed in Scripture should lead the devotions of his less gifted colonel, and admonish a backsliding major. But such was the intelligence, the gravity, and the selfcommand of the warriors whom Cromwell had trained, that in their camp a political organisation and a religious organisation could exist without destroying military organisation. The same men, who, off duty, were noted as demagogues and field preachers, were distinguished by steadiness, by the spirit of order, and by prompt obedience on watch, on drill, and on the field of battle.

In war this strange force was irresistible. The stubborn courage characteristic of the English people was, by the system of Cromwell, at once regulated and stimulated. Other leaders have maintained order as strict. Other leaders have inspired their followers with zeal as ardent. But in his camp alone the most rigid discipline was found in company with the fiercest enthusiasm. His troops moved to victory with the precision of machines, while burning with the wildest fanaticism of Crusaders. From the time when the army was remodelled to the time when it was disbanded, it never found, either in the British islands or on the Continent, an enemy who could stand its onset. In England, Scotland, Ireland, Flanders, the Puritan warriors, often surrounded by difficulties, sometimes contending against threefold odds, not only never failed to conquer, but never failed to destroy and break in pieces whatever force was opposed to them. They at length came to regard the day of battle as a day of certain triumph, and marched against the most renowned battalions of Europe with disdainful confidence. Turenne was startled by the shout of stern exultation with which his English allies advanced to the combat, and expressed the delight of a true soldier, when he learned that it was ever the fashion of Cromwell's pikemen to rejoice greatly when they beheld the enemy ; and the banished Cavaliers felt an emotion of national pride, when they saw a brigade of their countrymen, outnumbered by foes and abandoned by friends, drive before it in headlong rout the finest infantry of Spain, and force a passage into a counterscarp which had just been pronounced impregnable by the ablest of the Marshals of France.

But that which chiefly distinguished the army of Cromwell from other armies was the austere morality and the fear of God which pervaded all ranks. It is acknowledged by the most zealous Royalists that, in that singular camp, no oath was heard, no drunkenness or gambling was seen, and that, during the long dominion of the soldiery, the property of the peaceable citizen and the honour of woman were held sacred. If outrages were committed, they were outrages of a very different kind from those of which a victorious army is generally guilty. No servant girl complained of the rough gallantry of the redcoats. Not an ounce of plate was taken from the shops of the goldsmiths. But a Pelagian sermon, or a window on which the Virgin and Child were painted, produced in the Puritan ranks an excitement which it required the utmost exertions of the officers to quell. One of Cromwell's chief difficulties was to restrain his musketeers and dragoons from invading by main force the pulpits of ministers whose discourses, to use the language of that time, were not savoury ; and too many of our cathedrals still bear the marks of the hatred with which those stern spirits regarded every vestige of Popery.

To keep down the English people was no light task even for that army. No sooner was the first pressure of military tyranny felt, than the nation, unbroken to such servitude, began to struggle fiercely. Insurrections broke out even in those counties which, during the recent war, had been the most submissive to the Parliament. Indeed, the Parliament itself abhorred its old defenders more than its old enemies, and was desirous to come to terms of accommodation with Charles at the expense of the troops. In Scotland at the same time, a coalition was formed between the Royalists and a large body of Presbyterians who regarded the doctrines of the Independents with detestation. At length the storm burst. There were risings in Norfolk, Suffolk, Essex, Kent, Wales. The fleet in the Thames suddenly hoisted the royal colours, stood out to sea, and menaced the southern coast. A great Scottish force crossed the frontier and advanced into Lancashire. It might well be suspected that these movements were contemplated with secret complacency by a majority both of the Lords and of the Commons.

Risings against the military government suppressed.

But the yoke of the army was not to be so shaken off. While Fairfax suppressed the risings in the neighbourhood of the capital, Oliver routed the Welsh insurgents, and, leaving their castles in ruins, marched against the Scots. His troops were few, when compared with the invaders ; but he was little in the habit of counting his enemies. The Scottish army was utterly destroyed. A change in the Scottish government followed. An administration, hostile to the King, was formed at Edinburgh ; and Cromwell, more than ever the darling of his soldiers, returned in triumph to London.

And now a design, to which, at the commencement of the civil war, no man would have dared to allude, and which was not less inconsistent with the Solemn League and Covenant than with the old law of England, began to take a distinct

form. The austere warriors who ruled the nation had, during some months, meditated a fearful vengeance on the captive King. When and how the scheme originated; whether it spread from the general to the ranks, or from the ranks to the general; whether it is to be ascribed to policy using fanaticism as a tool, or to fanaticism bearing down policy with headlong impulse, are questions which, even at this day, cannot be answered with perfect confidence. It seems, however, on the whole, probable that he who seemed to lead was really forced to follow, and that, on this occasion, as on another great occasion a few years later, he sacrificed his own judgment and his own inclinations to the wishes of the army. For the power which he had called into existence was a power which even he could not always control; and, that he might ordinarily command, it was necessary that he should sometimes obey. He publicly protested that he was no mover in the matter, that the first steps had been taken without his privity, that he could not advise the Parliament to strike the blow, but that he submitted his own feelings to the force of circumstances which seemed to him to indicate the purposes of Providence. It has been the fashion to consider these professions as instances of the hypocrisy which is vulgarly imputed to him. But even those who pronounce him a hypocrite will scarcely venture to call him a fool. They are therefore bound to show that he had some purpose to serve by secretly stimulating the army to take that course which he did not venture openly to recommend. It would be absurd to suppose that he, who was never by his respectable enemies represented as wantonly cruel or implacably vindictive, would have taken the most important step of his life under the influence of mere malevolence. He was far too wise a man not to know, when he consented to shed that august blood, that he was doing a deed which was inexpiable, and which would move the grief and horror, not only of the Royalists, but of nine tenths of those who had stood by the Parliament. Whatever visions may have deluded others, he was assuredly dreaming neither of a republic on the antique pattern, nor of the millennial reign of the Saints. If he already aspired to be himself the founder of a new dynasty, it was plain that Charles the First was a less formidable competitor than Charles the Second would be. At the moment of the death of Charles the

First the loyalty of every Cavalier would be transferred, unimpaired, to Charles the Second. Charles the First was a captive: Charles the Second would be at liberty, Charles the First was an object of suspicion and dislike to a large proportion of those who yet shuddered at the thought of slaying him: Charles the Second would excite all the interest which belongs to distressed youth and innocence. It is impossible to believe that considerations so obvious, and so important, es caped the most profound politician of that age. The truth is that Cromwell had, at one time, meant to mediate between the throne and the Parliament, and to reorganise the distracted State by the power of the sword, under the sanction of the royal name. In this design he persisted till he was compelled to abandon it by the refractory temper of the soldiers, and by the incurable duplicity of the King. A party in the camp began to clamour for the head of the traitor, who was for treating with Agag. Conspiracies were formed. Threats of impeachment were loudly uttered. A mutiny broke out, which all the vigour and resolution of Oliver could hardly quell. And though, by a judicious mixture of severity and kindness, he succeeded in restoring order, he saw that it would be in the highest degree difficult and perilous to contend against the rage of warriors, who regarded the fallen tyrant as their foe, and as the foe of their God. At the same time it became more evident than ever that the King could not be trusted. The vices of Charles had grown upon him. They were, indeed, vices which difficulties and perplexities generally bring out in the strongest light. Cunning is the natural defence of the weak. A prince therefore, who is habitually a deceiver when at the height of power, is not likely to learn frankness in the midst of embarrassments and distresses. Charles was not only a most unscrupulous but a most unlucky dissembler. There never was a politician to whom so many frauds and falsehoods were brought home by undeniable evidence. He publicly recognised the Houses at Westminster as a legal Parliament, and at the same time, made a private minute in council declaring the recognition null. He publicly disclaimed all thought of calling in foreign aid against his people: he privately solicited aid from France, from Denmark, and from Lorraine. He publicly denied that he employed Papists: at the same time he privately sent to his generals directions to employ every Papist that would serve. He publicly took the sacrament at Oxford, as a pledge that he never would even connive at Popery. He privately assured his wife, that he intended to tolerate Popery in England; and he authorised Lord Glamorgan to promise that Popery should be established in Ireland. Then he attempted to clear himself at his agent's expense. Glamorgan received, in the Royal handwriting, reprimands intended to be read by others, and eulogies which were to be seen only by himself. To such an extent, indeed, had insincerity now tainted the King's whole nature, that his most devoted friends could not refrain from complaining to each other, with bitter grief and shame, of his crooked politics. His defeats, they said, gave them less pain than his intrigues. Since he had been a prisoner, there was no section of the victorious party which had not been the object both of his flatteries and of his machinations : but never was he more unfortunate than when he attempted at once to cajole and to undermine Cromwell.

Cromwell had to determine whether he would put to hazard the attachment of his party, the attachment of his army, his own greatness, nay his own life, in an attempt which would probably have been vain, to save a prince whom no engagement could bind. With many struggles and misgivings, and probably not without many prayers, the decision was made. Charles was left to his fate. The military saints resolved that, in defiance of the old laws of the realm, and of the almost universal sentiment of the nation, the King should expiate his crimes with his blood. He for a time expected a death like that of his unhappy predecessors, Edward the Second and Richard the Second. But he was in no danger of such treason. Those who had him in their gripe were not midnight stabbers. What they did they did in order that it might be a spectacle to heaven and earth, and that it might be held in everlasting remembrance. They enjoyed keenly the very scandal which they gave. That the ancient constitution and the public opinion of England were directly opposed to regicide made regicide seem strangely fascinating to a party bent on effecting a complete political and social revolution. In order to accomplish their purpose, it was necessary that they should first break in pieces every part of the machinery of the government; and this necessity was rather agreeable than painful to them. The Commons passed a vote tending to accommodation with the King. The soldiers excluded the majority by force. The Lords unanimously rejected the proposition that the King should be brought to trial. Their house was instantly closed. No court, known to the law, would take on itself the office of judging the fountain of justice. A revolutionary tribunal was created. That tribunal pronounced Charles a tyrant, a traitor, a murderer, and a public enemy; and his head was severed from his shoulders, before thousands of spectators, in front of the banqueting hall of his own palace.

His execution.

In no long time it became manifest that those political and religious zealots, to whom this deed is to be ascribed, had committed, not only a crime, but an error. They had given to a prince, hitherto known to his people chiefly by his faults, an opportunity of displaying, on a great theatre, before the eyes of all nations and all ages, some qualities which irresistibly call forth the admiration and love of mankind, the high spirit of a gallant gentleman, the patience and meekness of a penitent Christian. Nay, they had so contrived their revenge that the very man whose life had been a series of attacks on the liberties of England now seemed to die a martyr in the cause of those liberties. No demagogue ever produced such an impression on the public mind as the captive King, who, retaining in that extremity all his regal dignity, and confronting death with dauntless courage, gave utterance to the feelings of his oppressed people, manfully refused to plead before a court unknown to the law, appealed from military violence to the principles of the constitution, asked by what right the House of Commons had been purged of its most respectable members and the House of Lords deprived of its legislative functions, and told his weeping hearers that he was defending, not only his own cause, but theirs. His long misgovernment, his innumerable perfidies, were forgotten. His memory was, in the minds of the great majority of his subjects, associated with those free institutions which he had, during many years, laboured to destroy: for those free institutions had perished with him, and, amidst the mournful silence of a community kept down by arms, had been defended by his voice alone. From that day began a reaction in favour of monarchy and of the exiled house, a reaction which never ceased till the throne had again been set up in all its old dignity.

At first, however, the slayers of the King seemed to have derived new energy from that sacrament of blood by which they had bound themselves closely together, and separated themselves for ever from the great body of their countrymen.

England was declared a commonwealth. The House of Commons, reduced to a small number of members, was nominally the supreme power in the state. In fact, the army and its great chief governed everything. Oliver had made his choice. He had kept the hearts of his soldiers, and had broken with almost every other class of his fellow citizens. Beyond the limits of his camps and fortresses he could scarcely be said to have a party. Those elements of force which, when the civil war broke out, had appeared arrayed against each other, were combined against him; all the Cavaliers, the great majority of the Roundheads, the Anglican Church, the Presbyterian Church, the Roman Catholic Church, England, Scotland, Ireland. Yet such was his genius and resolution that he was able to overpower and crush everything that crossed his path, to make himself more absolute master of his country than any of her legitimate Kings had been, and to make his country more dreaded and respected than she had been during many generations under the rule of her legitimate Kings.

England had already ceased to struggle. But the two other kingdoms which had been governed by the Stuarts were hostile to the new republic. The Independent party was equally odious to the Roman Catholics of Ireland and to the Presbyterians of Scotland. Both those countries, lately in rebellion against Charles the First, now acknowledged the authority of Charles the Second.

Subjugation of Ireland and Scotland. But everything yielded to the vigour and ability of Cromwell. In a few months he subjugated Ireland, as Ireland had never been subjugated during the five centuries of slaughter which had elapsed since the landing of the first Norman settlers. He resolved to put an end to that conflict of races and religions which had so long distracted the island, by making the English and Protestant population decidedly predominant. For this end he gave the rein to the fierce enthusiasm of his followers, waged war resembling that which Israel waged on the Canaanites, smote the idolaters with the edge of the sword, so that great cities were left without inhabitants, drove many thousands to the Continent, shipped off many thousands to the West Indies, and supplied the void thus made by pouring in numerous colonists, of Saxon blood, and of Calvinistic faith. Strange to say, under that iron rule, the conquered country began to wear an outward face of prosperity. Districts, which had recently been as wild as

those where the first white settlers of Connecticut were contending with the red men, were in a few years transformed
into the likeness of Kent and Norfolk. New buildings, roads,
and plantations were everywhere seen. The rent of estates
rose fast; and soon the English landowners began to complain that they were met in every market by the products of
Ireland, and to clamour for protecting laws.

From Ireland the victorious chief, who was now in name,
as he had long been in reality, Lord General of the armies
of the Commonwealth, turned to Scotland. The young King
was there. He had consented to profess himself a Presbyterian, and to subscribe the Covenant; and, in return for
these concessions, the austere Puritans who bore sway at
Edinburgh had permitted him to assume the crown, and to
hold, under their inspection and control, a solemn and
melancholy court. This mock royalty was of short duration.
In two great battles Cromwell annihilated the military force
of Scotland. Charles fled for his life, and, with extreme
difficulty, escaped the fate of his father. The ancient kingdom of the Stuarts was reduced, for the first time, to profound submission. Of that independence, so manfully defended against the mightiest and ablest of the Plantagenets,
no vestige was left. The English Parliament made laws for
Scotland. English judges held assizes in Scotland. Even
that stubborn Church, which has held its own against so
many governments, scarce dared to utter an audible murmur.

Thus far there had been at least the semblance of harmony
between the warriors who had subjugated Ireland and Scotland and the politicians who sate at Westminster: but the
alliance which had been cemented by danger was dissolved
by victory. The Parliament forgot that it was but the creature of the army. The army was less disposed than ever to
submit to the dictation of the Parliament. Indeed the few
members who made up what was contemptuously called the
Rump of the House of Commons had no more claim than the
military chiefs to be esteemed the representatives of the
nation. The dispute was soon brought to a decisive issue.
Cromwell filled the House with armed men. The Speaker
was pulled out of his chair, the mace taken from the table,
the room cleared, and the door locked. The nation, which
loved neither of the contending parties, but which was forced,
in its own despite, to respect the capacity and resolution of
the General, looked on with patience, if not with complacency.

Expulsion
of the Long
Parlia-
ment.

King, Lords, and Commons, had now in turn been vanquished and destroyed; and Cromwell seemed to be left the
sole heir of the powers of all three.   Yet were certain limita-
tions still imposed on him by the very army to which he owed
his immense authority.   That singular body of men was, for
the most part, composed of zealous republicans.   In the act
of enslaving their country, they had deceived themselves into
the belief that they were emancipating her.   The book which
they most venerated furnished them with a precedent which
was frequently in their mouths.   It was true that the ignorant
and ungrateful nation murmured against its deliverers.   Even
so had another chosen nation murmured against the leader
who brought it, by painful and dreary paths, from the house
of bondage to the land flowing with milk and honey.   Yet
had that leader rescued his brethren in spite of themselves;
nor had he shrunk from making terrible examples of those
who contemned the proffered freedom, and pined for the
fleshpots, the taskmasters, and the idolatries of Egypt.   The
object of the warlike saints who surrounded Cromwell was
the settlement of a free and pious commonwealth.   For that
end they were ready to employ, without scruple, any means,
however violent and lawless.   It was not impossible, therefore, to establish by their aid a dictatorship such as no King
had ever exercised : but it was probable that their aid would
be at once withdrawn from a ruler who, even under strict
constitutional restraints, should venture to assume the kingly
name and dignity.

The sentiments of Cromwell were widely different.   He was
not what he had been ; nor would it be just to consider the
change which his views had undergone as the effect merely
of selfish ambition.   He had, when he came up to the Long
Parliament, brought with him from his rural retreat little
knowledge of books, no experience of great affairs, and a temper galled by the long tyranny of the government and of the
hierarchy.   He had, during the thirteen years which followed,
gone through a political education of no common kind.   He
had been a chief actor in a succession of revolutions.   He
had been long the soul, and at last the head, of a party.   He
had commanded armies, won battles, negotiated treaties,
subdued, pacified, and regulated kingdoms.   It would have
been strange indeed if his notions had been still the same as
in the days when his mind was principally occupied by his
fields and his religion, and when the greatest events which

diversified the course of his life were a cattle fair or a prayer meeting at Huntingdon. He saw that some schemes of innovation for which he had once been zealous, whether good or bad in themselves, were opposed to the general feeling of the country, and that, if he persevered in those schemes, he had nothing before him but constant troubles, which must be suppressed by the constant use of the sword. He therefore wished to restore, in all essentials, that ancient constitution which the majority of the people had always loved, and for which they now pined. The course afterwards taken by Monk was not open to Cromwell. The memory of one terrible day separated the great regicide for ever from the House of Stuart. What remained was that he should mount the ancient English throne, and reign according to the ancient English polity. If he could effect this, he might hope that the wounds of the lacerated State would heal fast. Great numbers of honest and quiet men would speedily rally round him. Those Royalists whose attachment was rather to institutions than to persons, to the kingly office than to King Charles the First or King Charles the Second, would soon kiss the hand of King Oliver. The peers, who now remained sullenly at their country houses, and refused to take any part in public affairs, would, when summoned to their House by the writ of a King in possession, gladly resume their ancient functions. Northumberland and Bedford, Manchester and Pembroke, would be proud to bear the crown and the spurs, the sceptre and the globe, before the restorer of aristocracy. A sentiment of loyalty would gradually bind the people to the new dynasty; and, on the decease of the founder of that dynasty, the royal dignity might descend with general acquiescence to his posterity.

The ablest Royalists were of opinion that these views were correct, and that, if Cromwell had been permitted to follow his own judgment, the exiled line would never have been restored. But his plan was directly opposed to the feelings of the only class which he dared not offend. The name of King was hateful to the soldiers. Some of them were indeed unwilling to see the administration in the hands of any single person. The great majority, however, were disposed to support their general, as elective first magistrate of a commonwealth, against all factions which might resist his authority: but they would not consent that he should assume the regal title, or that the dignity, which was the just reward of his personal merit, should be declared hereditary in his family. All that was left to him was to give to the new republic a constitution as like the constitution of the old monarchy as the army would bear. That his elevation to power might not seem to be merely his own act, he convoked a council, composed partly of persons on whose support he could depend, and partly of persons whose opposition he might safely defy. This assembly, which he called a Parliament, ·and which the populace nicknamed, from one of the most conspicuous members, Barebone's Parliament, after exposing itself during a short time to the public contempt, surrendered back to the General the powers which it had received from him, and left him at liberty to frame a plan of government.

The Protectorate of Oliver Cromwell.

His plan bore, from the first, a considerable resemblance to the old English constitution : but, in a few years, he thought it safe to proceed further, and to restore almost every part of the ancient system under new names and forms. The title of King was not revived : but the kingly prerogatives were intrusted to a Lord High Protector. The sovereign was called not His Majesty, but His Highness. He was not crowned and anointed in Westminster Abbey, but was solemnly enthroned, girt with a sword of state, clad in a robe of purple, and presented with a rich Bible, in Westminster Hall. His office was not declared hereditary : but he was permitted to name his successor; and none could doubt that he would name his son.

A House of Commons was a necessary part of the new polity. In constituting this body, the Protector showed a wisdom and a public spirit which were not duly appreciated by his contemporaries. The vices of the old representative system, though by no means so serious as they afterwards became, had already been remarked by farsighted men. Cromwell reformed that system on the same principles on which Mr. Pitt, a hundred and thirty years later, attempted to reform it, and on which it was at length reformed in our own times. Small boroughs were disfranchised even more unsparingly than in 1832 ; and the number of county members was greatly increased. Very few unrepresented towns had yet grown into importance. Of those towns the most considerable were Manchester, Leeds, and Halifax. Representatives were given to all three. An addition was made to the number of the members for the capital. The elective franchise was placed on such a footing that every man of sub-

Oliver Cromwell

stance, whether possessed of freehold estates in land or not, had a vote for the county in which he resided. A few Scotchmen and a few of the English colonists settled in Ireland were summoned to the assembly which was to legislate, at Westminster, for every part of the British isles.

To create a House of Lords was a less easy task. Democracy does not require the support of prescription. Monarchy has often stood without that support. But a patrician order is the work of time. Oliver found already existing a nobility, opulent, highly considered, and as popular with the commonalty as any nobility has ever been. Had he, as King of England, commanded the peers to meet him in Parliament according to the old usage of the realm, many of them would undoubtedly have obeyed the call. This he could not do; and it was to no purpose that he offered to the chiefs of illustrious families seats in his new senate. They conceived that they could not accept a nomination to an upstart assembly without renouncing their birthright and betraying their order. The Protector was, therefore, under the necessity of filling his Upper House with new men who, during the late stirring times, had made themselves conspicuous. This was the least happy of his contrivances, and displeased all parties. The Levellers were angry with him for instituting a privileged class. The multitude, which felt respect and fondness for the great historical names of the land, laughed without restraint at a House of Lords, in which lucky draymen and shoemakers were seated, to which few of the old nobles were invited, and from which almost all those old nobles who were invited turned disdainfully away.

How Oliver's Parliaments were constituted, however, was practically of little moment : for he possessed the means of conducting the administration without their support, and in defiance of their opposition. His wish seems to have been to govern constitutionally, and to substitute the empire of the laws for that of the sword. But he soon found that, hated as he was, both by Royalists and Presbyterians, he could be safe only by being absolute. The first House of Commons which the people elected by his command, questioned his authority, and was dissolved without having passed a single act. His second House of Commons, though it recognised him as Protector, and would gladly have made him King, obstinately refused to acknowledge his new Lords. He had

no course left but to dissolve the Parliament.   " God," he
exclaimed, at parting, " be judge between you and me ! "

Yet was the energy of the Protector's administration in
nowise relaxed by these dissensions.   Those soldiers who
would not suffer him to assume the kingly title stood by him
when he ventured on acts of power, as high as any English
King has ever attempted.   The government, therefore, though
in form a republic, was in truth a despotism, moderated only
by the wisdom, the sobriety, and the magnanimity of the despot.   The country was divided into military districts.   Those
districts were placed under the command of Major Generals.
Every insurrectionary movement was promptly put down and
punished.   The fear inspired by the power of the sword, in so
strong, steady, and expert a hand, quelled the spirit both of
Cavaliers and Levellers.   The loyal gentry declared that they
were still as ready as ever to risk their lives for the old government and the old dynasty, if there were the slightest
hope of success : but to rush, at the head of their serving
men and tenants, on the pikes of brigades victorious in a
hundred battles and sieges, would be a frantic waste of innocent and honourable blood.   Both Royalists and Republicans, having no hope in open resistance, began to revolve
dark schemes of assassination : but the Protector's intelligence was good : his vigilance was unremitting ; and, whenever he moved beyond the walls of his palace, the drawn
swords and cuirasses of his trusty bodyguards encompassed
him thick on every side.

Had he been a cruel, licentious, and rapacious prince, the
nation might have found courage in despair, and might have
made a convulsive effort to free itself from military domination.   But the grievances which the country suffered, though
such as excited serious discontent, were by no means such
as impel great masses of men to stake their lives, their fortunes, and the welfare of their families against fearful odds.
The taxation, though heavier than it had been under the
Stuarts, was not heavy when compared with that of the
neighbouring states and with the resources of England.
Property was secure.   Even the Cavalier, who refrained from
giving disturbance to the new settlement, enjoyed in peace
whatever the civil troubles had left him.   The laws were
violated only in cases where the safety of the Protector's
person and government was concerned.   Justice was administered between man and man with an exactness and purity

not before known. Under no English government since the Reformation, had there been so little religious persecution. The unfortunate Roman Catholics, indeed, were held to be scarcely within the pale of Christian charity. But the clergy of the fallen Anglican Church were suffered to celebrate their worship on condition that they would abstain from preaching about politics. Even the Jews, whose public worship had, ever since the thirteenth century, been interdicted, were, in spite of the strong opposition of jealous traders and fanatical theologians, permitted to build a synagogue in London.

The Protector's foreign policy at the same time extorted the ungracious approbation of those who most detested him. The Cavaliers could scarcely refrain from wishing that one who had done so much to raise the fame of the nation had been a legitimate King; and the Republicans were forced to own that the tyrant suffered none but himself to wrong his country, and that, if he had robbed her of liberty, he had at least given her glory in exchange. After half a century during which England had been of scarcely more weight in European politics than Venice or Saxony, she at once became the most formidable power in the world, dictated terms of peace to the United Provinces, avenged the common injuries of Christendom on the pirates of Barbary, vanquished the Spaniards by land and sea, seized one of the finest West Indian islands, and acquired on the Flemish coast a fortress which consoled the national pride for the loss of Calais. She was supreme on the ocean. She was the head of the Protestant interest. All the reformed Churches scattered over Roman Catholic kingdoms acknowledged Cromwell as their guardian. The Huguenots of Languedoc, the shepherds who, in the hamlets of the Alps, professed a Protestantism older than that of Augsburg, were secured from oppression by the mere terror of his great name. The Pope himself was forced to preach humanity and moderation to Popish princes. For a voice which seldom threatened in vain had declared that, unless favour were shown to the people of God, the English guns should be heard in the Castle of Saint Angelo. In truth, there was nothing which Cromwell had, for his own sake and that of his family, so much reason to desire as a general religious war in Europe. In such a war he must have been the captain of the Protestant armies. The heart of England would have been with him. His vic-

tories would have been hailed with an unanimous enthusiasm
unknown in the country since the rout of the Armada, and
would have effaced the stain which one act, condemned by
the general voice of the nation, has left on his splendid fame.
Unhappily for him he had no opportunity of displaying his
admirable military talents, except against the inhabitants of
the British isles.

While he lived his power stood firm, an object of mingled
aversion, admiration, and dread to his subjects. Few indeed
loved his government; but those who hated it most hated
it less than they feared it. Had it been a worse government,
it might perhaps have been overthrown in spite of all its
strength. Had it been a weaker government, it would
certainly have been overthrown in spite of all its merits.
But it had moderation enough to abstain from those op-
pressions which drive men mad ; and it had a force and
energy which none but men driven mad by oppression would
venture to encounter.

Oliver suc-
ceeded by
Richard.

It has often been affirmed, but with little reason, that
Oliver died at a time fortunate for his renown, and that, if
his life had been prolonged, it would probably have closed
amidst disgraces and disasters. It is certain that he was,
to the last, honoured by his soldiers, obeyed by the whole
population of the British islands, and dreaded by all foreign
powers, that he was laid among the ancient sovereigns of
England with funeral pomp such as London had never before
seen, and that he was succeeded by his son Richard as
quietly as any King had ever been succeeded by any Prince
of Wales.

During five months, the administration of Richard Cromwell went on so tranquilly and regularly that all Europe
believed him to be firmly established on the chair of state.
In truth his situation was in some respects much more advantageous than that of his father. The young man had
made no enemy. His hands were unstained by civil blood.
The Cavaliers themselves allowed him to be an honest, good-
natured gentleman. The Presbyterian party, powerful both
in numbers and in wealth, had been at deadly feud with the
late Protector, but was disposed to regard the present
Protector with favour. That party had always been desirous
to see the old civil polity of the realm restored with some
clearer definitions and some stronger safeguards for public
liberty, but had many reasons for dreading the restoration

of the old family. Richard was the very man for politicians of this description. His humanity, ingenuousness, and modesty, the mediocrity of his abilities, and the docility with which he submitted to the guidance of persons wiser than himself, admirably qualified him to be the head of a limited monarchy.

For a time it seemed highly probable that he would, under the direction of able advisers, effect what his father had attempted in vain. A Parliament was called, and the writs were directed after the old fashion. The small boroughs which had recently been disfranchised regained their lost privilege: Manchester, Leeds, and Halifax ceased to return members; and the county of York was again limited to two knights. It may seem strange to a generation which has been excited almost to madness by the question of parliamentary reform that great shires and towns should have submitted with patience, and even with complacency, to this change: but though speculative men might, even in that age, discern the vices of the old representative system, and predict that those vices would, sooner or later, produce serious practical evil, the practical evil had not yet been felt. Oliver's representative system, on the other hand, though constructed on sound principles, was not popular. Both the events in which it originated, and the effects which it had produced, prejudiced men against it. It had sprung from military violence. It had been fruitful of nothing but disputes. The whole nation was sick of government by the sword, and pined for government by the law. The restoration, therefore, even of anomalies and abuses, which were in strict conformity with the law, and which had been destroyed by the sword, gave general satisfaction.

Among the Commons there was a strong opposition, consisting partly of avowed Republicans, and partly of concealed Royalists: but a large and steady majority appeared to be favourable to the plan of reviving the old civil constitution under a new dynasty. Richard was solemnly recognised as first magistrate. The Commons not only consented to transact business with Oliver's Lords, but passed a vote acknowledging the right of those nobles who had, in the late troubles, taken the side of public liberty, to sit in the Upper House of Parliament without any new creation.

Thus far the statesmen by whose advice Richard acted had been successful. Almost all the parts of the government

were now constituted as they had been constituted at the
commencement of the civil war. Had the Protector and the
Parliament been suffered to proceed undisturbed, there can
be little doubt that an order of things similar to that which
was afterwards established under the House of Hanover
would have been established under the House of Cromwell.
But there was in the state a power more than sufficient to
deal with Protector and Parliament together. Over the
soldiers Richard had no authority except that which he
derived from the great name which he had inherited. He
had never led them to victory. He had never even borne
arms. All his tastes and habits were pacific. Nor were his
opinions and feelings on religious subjects approved by the
military saints. That he was a good man he evinced by
proofs more satisfactory than deep groans or long sermons,
by humility and suavity when he was at the height of human
greatness, and by cheerful resignation under cruel wrongs
and misfortunes : but the cant then common in every
guardroom gave him a disgust which he had not always the
prudence to conceal. The officers who had the principal
influence among the troops stationed near London were not
his friends. They were men distinguished by valour and
conduct in the field, but destitute of the wisdom and civil
courage which had been conspicuous in their deceased leader.
Some of them were honest, but fanatical, Independents and
Republicans. Of this class Fleetwood was the representative.
Others were impatient to be what Oliver had been. His
rapid elevation, his prosperity and glory, his inauguration in
the Hall, and his gorgeous obsequies in the Abbey, had
inflamed their imagination. They were as well born as he,
and as well educated: they could not understand why they
were not as worthy to wear the purple robe, and to wield the
sword of state ; and they pursued the objects of their wild
ambition, not, like him, with patience, vigilance, sagacity,
and determination, but with the restlessness and irresolution
characteristic of aspiring mediocrity. Among these feeble
copies of a great original the most conspicuous was Lambert.

Fall of
Richard
and revival
of the
Long Par-
liament.

On the very day of Richard's accession the officers began
to conspire against their new master. The good understanding which existed between him and his Parliament
hastened the crisis. Alarm and resentment spread through
the camp. Both the religious and the professional feelings
of the army were deeply wounded. It seemed that the

Independents were to be subjected to the Presbyterians, and that the men of the sword were to be subjected to the men of the gown. A coalition was formed between the military malecontents and the republican minority of the House of Commons. It may well be doubted whether Richard could have triumphed over that coalition, even if he had inherited his father's clear judgment and iron courage. It is certain that simplicity and meekness like his were not the qualities which the conjuncture required. He fell ingloriously, and without a struggle. He was used by the army as an instrument for the purpose of dissolving the Parliament, and was then contemptuously thrown aside. The officers gratified their republican allies by declaring that the expulsion of the Rump had been illegal, and by inviting that assembly to resume its functions. The old Speaker and a quorum of the old members came together, and were proclaimed, amidst the scarcely stifled derision and execration of the whole nation, the supreme power in the commonwealth. It was at the same time expressly declared that there should be no first magistrate, and no House of Lords.

But this state of things could not last. On the day on which the long Parliament revived, revived also its old quarrel with the army. Again the Rump forgot that it owed its existence to the pleasure of the soldiers, and began to treat them as subjects. Again the doors of the House of Commons were closed by military violence; and a provisional government, named by the officers, assumed the direction of affairs. *Second expulsion of the Long Parliament.*

Meanwhile the sense of great evils, and the strong apprehension of still greater evils close at hand, had at length produced an alliance between the Cavaliers and the Presbyterians. Some Presbyterians had, indeed, been disposed to such an alliance even before the death of Charles the First: but it was not till after the fall of Richard Cromwell that the whole party became eager for the restoration of the royal house. There was no longer any reasonable hope that the old constitution could be reestablished under a new dynasty. One choice only was left, the Stuarts or the army. The banished family had committed great faults; but it had dearly expiated those faults, and had undergone a long, and, it might be hoped, a salutary training in the school of adversity. It was probable that Charles the Second would take warning by the fate of Charles the First. But, be this as it might, the dangers which threatened the country were such that, in order to avert them, some opinions might well be compromised, and some risks might well be incurred. It seemed but too likely that England would fall under the most odious and degrading of all kinds of government, under a government uniting all the evils of despotism to all the evils of anarchy. Anything was preferable to the yoke of a succession of incapable and inglorious tyrants, raised to power, like the Deys of Barbary, by military revolutions recurring at short intervals. Lambert seemed likely to be the first of these rulers; but within a year Lambert might give place to Desborough, and Desborough to Harrison. As often as the truncheon was transferred from one feeble hand to another, the nation would be pillaged for the purpose of bestowing a fresh donative on the troops. If the Presbyterians obstinately stood aloof from the Royalists, the state was lost; and men might well doubt whether, by the combined exertions of Presbyterians and Royalists, it could be saved. For the dread of that invincible army was on all the inhabitants of the island; and the Cavaliers, taught by a hundred disastrous fields how little numbers can effect against discipline, were even more completely cowed than the Roundheads.

The army of Scotland marches into England. While the soldiers remained united, all the plots and risings of the malecontents were ineffectual. But a few days after the second expulsion of the Rump, came tidings which gladdened the hearts of all who were attached either to monarchy or to liberty. That mighty force which had, during many years, acted as one man, and which, while so acting, had been found irresistible, was at length divided against itself. The army of Scotland had done good service to the Commonwealth, and was in the highest state of efficiency. It had borne no part in the late revolutions, and had seen them with indignation resembling the indignation which the Roman legions posted on the Danube and the Euphrates felt, when they learned that the empire had been put up to sale by the Prætorian Guards. It was intolerable that certain regiments should, merely because they happened to be quartered near Westminster, take on themselves to make and unmake several governments in the course of half a year. If it were fit that the state should be regulated by the soldiers, those soldiers who upheld the English ascendency on the north of the Tweed were as well entitled to a voice as those who garrisoned the Tower of London. There appears to have been less fanaticism among the troops stationed in Scotland than in any other part of the army; and their general, George Monk, was himself the very opposite of a zealot. He had, at the commencement of the civil war, borne arms for the King, had been made prisoner by the Roundheads, had then accepted a commission from the Parliament, and, with very slender pretensions to saintship, had raised himself to high commands by his courage and professional skill. He had been an useful servant to both the Protectors, had quietly acquiesced when the officers at Westminster pulled down Richard and restored the Long Parliament, and would perhaps have acquiesced as quietly in the second expulsion of the Long Parliament, if the provisional government had abstained from giving him cause of offence and apprehension. For his nature was cautious and somewhat sluggish; nor was he at all disposed to hazard sure and moderate advantages for the chance of obtaining even the most splendid success. He seems to have been impelled to attack the new rulers of the Commonwealth less by the hope that, if he overthrew them, he should become great, than by the fear that, if he submitted to them, he should not even be secure. Whatever were his motives, he declared himself the champion of the oppressed civil power, refused to acknowledge the usurped authority of the provisional government, and, at the head of seven thousand veterans, marched into England.

This step was the signal for a general explosion. The people everywhere refused to pay taxes. The apprentices of the City assembled by thousands and clamoured for a free Parliament. The fleet sailed up the Thames, and declared against the tyranny of the soldiers. The soldiers, no longer under the control of one commanding mind, separated into factions. Every regiment, afraid lest it should be left alone a mark for the vengeance of the oppressed nation, hastened to make a separate peace. Lambert, who had hastened northward to encounter the army of Scotland, was abandoned by his troops, and became a prisoner. During thirteen years the civil power had, in every conflict, been compelled to yield to the military power. The military power now humbled itself before the civil power. The Rump, generally hated and despised, but still the only body in the country which had any show of legal authority, returned again to the house from which it had been twice ignominiously expelled.

In the mean time Monk was advancing towards London. Wherever he came, the gentry flocked round him, imploring him to use his power for the purpose of restoring peace and liberty to the distracted nation. The General, coldblooded, taciturn, zealous for no polity and for no religion, maintained an impenetrable reserve. What were at this time his plans, and whether he had any plan, may well be doubted. His great object, apparently, was to keep himself, as long as possible, free to choose between several lines of action. Such, indeed, is commonly the policy of men who are, like him, distinguished rather by wariness than by farsightedness. It was probably not till he had been some days in the capital that he had made up his mind. The cry of the whole people was for a free Parliament; and there could be no doubt that a Parliament really free would instantly restore the exiled family. The Rump and the soldiers were still hostile to the House of Stuart. But the Rump was universally detested and despised. The power of the soldiers was indeed still formidable, but had been greatly diminished by discord. They had no head. They had recently been, in many parts of the country, arrayed against each other. On the very day before Monk reached London, there was a fight in the Strand between the cavalry and the infantry. An united army had long kept down a divided nation; but the nation was now united, and the army was divided.

Monk declares for a free Parliament. During a short time the dissimulation or irresolution of Monk kept all parties in a state of painful suspense. At length he broke silence, and declared for a free Parliament.

As soon as his declaration was known, the whole nation was wild with delight. Wherever he appeared thousands thronged round him, shouting and blessing his name. The bells of all England rang joyously: the gutters ran with ale; and, night after night, the sky five miles round London was reddened by innumerable bonfires. Those Presbyterian members of the House of Commons who had many years before been expelled by the army, returned to their seats, and were hailed with acclamations by great multitudes, which filled Westminster Hall and Palace Yard. The Independent leaders no longer dared to show their faces in the streets, and were scarcely safe within their own dwellings. Temporary provision was made for the government: writs were issued for a general election; and then that memorable Parliament, which had, in the course of twenty eventful years, experienced every variety of fortune, which had triumphed over its sovereign, which had been enslaved and degraded by its servants, which had been twice ejected and twice restored, solemnly decreed its own dissolution.

The result of the elections was such as might have been expected from the temper of the nation. The new House of Commons consisted, with few exceptions, of persons friendly to the royal family. The Presbyterians formed the majority.

That there would be a restoration now seemed almost certain; but whether there would be a peaceable restoration was matter of painful doubt. The soldiers were in a gloomy and savage mood. They hated the title of King. They hated the name of Stuart. They hated Presbyterianism much, and Prelacy more. They saw with bitter indignation that the close of their long domination was approaching, and that a life of inglorious toil and penury was before them. They attributed their ill fortune to the weakness of some generals, and to the treason of others. One hour of their beloved Oliver might even now restore the glory which had departed. Betrayed, disunited, and left without any chief in whom they could confide, they were yet to be dreaded. It was no light thing to encounter the rage and despair of fifty thousand fighting men, whose backs no enemy had ever seen. Monk, and those with whom he acted, were well aware that the crisis was most perilous. They employed every art to soothe and to divide the discontented warriors. At the same time vigorous preparation was made for a conflict. The army of Scotland, now quartered in London, was kept in good humour by bribes, praises, and promises. The wealthy citizens grudged nothing to a red coat, and were indeed so liberal of their best wine, that warlike saints were sometimes seen in a condition not very honourable either to their religious or to their military character. Some refractory regiments Monk ventured to disband. In the meantime the greatest exertions were made by the provisional government, with the strenuous aid of the whole body of the gentry and magistracy, to organise the militia. In every county the trainbands were held ready to march; and this force cannot be estimated at less than a hundred and twenty thousand men. In Hyde Park twenty thousand citizens, well armed and accoutred, passed in review, and showed a spirit which justified the hope that, in case of need, they would fight manfully for their shops and firesides. The fleet was heartily with the nation. It was a stirring time, a time of anxiety, yet of hope. The prevailing opinion

General election of 1660.

was that England would be delivered, but not without a desperate and bloody struggle, and that the class which had so long ruled by the sword would perish by the sword.

Happily the dangers of a conflict were averted. There was indeed one moment of extreme peril. Lambert escaped from his confinement, and called his comrades to arms. The flame of civil war was actually rekindled ; but by prompt and vigorous exertion it was trodden out before it had time to spread. The luckless imitator of Cromwell was again a prisoner. The failure of his enterprise damped the spirit of the soldiers ; and they sullenly resigned themselves to their fate

The Restoration. The new Parliament, which, having been called without the royal writ, is more accurately described as a Convention, met at Westminster. The Lords repaired to the hall, from which they had, during more than eleven years, been excluded by force. Both Houses instantly invited the King to return to his country. He was proclaimed with pomp never before known. A gallant fleet convoyed him from Holland to the coast of Kent. When he landed, the cliffs of Dover were covered by thousands of gazers, among whom scarcely one could be found who was not weeping with delight. The journey to London was a continued triumph. The whole road from Rochester was bordered by booths and tents, and looked like an interminable fair. Everywhere flags were flying, bells and music sounding, wine and ale flowing in rivers to the health of him whose return was the return of peace, of law, and of freedom. But in the midst of the general joy, one spot presented a dark and threatening aspect. On Blackheath the army was drawn up to welcome the sovereign. He smiled, bowed, and extended his hand graciously to the lips of the colonels and majors. But all his courtesy was vain. The countenances of the soldiers were sad and lowering ; and had they given way to their feelings, the festive pageant of which they reluctantly made a part would have had a mournful and bloody end. But there was no concert among them. Discord and defection had left them no confidence in their chiefs or in each other. The whole array of the City of London was under arms. Numerous companies of militia had assembled from various parts of the realm, under the command of loyal noblemen and gentlemen, to welcome the King. That great day closed in peace ; and the restored wanderer reposed safe in the palace of his ancestors.

CHAPTER II.

THE history of England, during the seventeenth century, is the history of the transformation of a limited monarchy, constituted after the fashion of the middle ages, into a limited monarchy suited to that more advanced state of society in which the public charges can no longer be borne by the estates of the crown, and in which the public defence can no longer be entrusted to a feudal militia. We have seen that the politicians who were at the head of the Long Parliament made, in 1642, a great effort to accomplish this change by transferring, directly and formally, to the estates of the realm the choice of ministers, the command of the army, and the superintendence of the whole executive administration. This scheme was, perhaps, the best that could then be contrived : but it was completely disconcerted by the course which the civil war took. The Houses triumphed, it is true ; but not till after such a struggle as made it necessary for them to call into existence a power which they could not control, and which soon began to domineer over all orders and all parties. During a few years, the evils inseparable from military government were, in some degree, mitigated by the wisdom and magnanimity of the great man who held the supreme command. But, when the sword, which he had wielded, with energy indeed, but with energy always guided by good sense and generally tempered by good nature, had passed to captains who possessed neither his abilities nor his virtues, it seemed too probable that order and liberty would perish in one ignominious ruin.

That ruin was happily averted. It has been too much the practice of writers zealous for freedom to represent the Restoration as a disastrous event, and to condemn the folly or baseness of that Convention which recalled the royal family without exacting new securities against maladministration. Those who hold this language do not comprehend the real nature of the crisis which followed the deposition of Richard

Conduct of those who restored the House of Stuart unjustly censured.

Cromwell. England was in imminent danger of falling under the tyranny of a succession of small men raised up and pulled down by military caprice. To deliver the country from the domination of the soldiers was the first object of every enlightened patriot : but it was an object which, while the soldiers were united, the most sanguine could scarcely expect to attain. On a sudden a gleam of hope appeared. General was opposed to general, army to army. On the use which might be made of one auspicious moment depended the future destiny of the nation. Our ancestors used that moment well. They forgot old injuries, waved petty scruples, adjourned to a more convenient season all dispute about the reforms which our institutions needed, and stood together, Cavaliers and Roundheads, Episcopalians and Presbyterians, in firm union, for the old laws of the land against military despotism. The exact partition of power among King, Lords, and Commons might well be postponed till it had been decided whether England should be governed by King, Lords, and Commons, or by cuirassiers and pikemen. Had the statesmen of the Convention taken a different course, had they held long debates on the principles of government, had they drawn up a new constitution and sent it to Charles, had conferences been opened, had couriers been passing and repassing during some weeks between Westminster and the Netherlands, with projects and counterprojects, replies by Hyde and rejoinders by Prynne, the coalition on which the public safety depended would have been dissolved : the Presbyterians and Royalists would certainly have quarrelled : the military factions might possibly have been reconciled ; and the misjudging friends of liberty might long have regretted, under a rule worse than that of the worst Stuart, the golden opportunity which had been suffered to escape.

Abolition of tenures by knight service.

The old civil polity was, therefore, by the general consent of both the great parties, reestablished. It was again exactly what it had been when Charles the First, eighteen years before, withdrew from his capital. All those acts of the Long Parliament which had received the royal assent were admitted to be still in full force. One fresh concession, a concession in which the Cavaliers were even more deeply interested than the Roundheads, was easily obtained from the restored King. The military tenure of land had been originally created as a means of national defence. But in the course of ages whatever was useful in the institution had disappeared : and nothing was left but ceremonies and grievances. A landed proprietor who held an estate under the crown by knight service,—and it was thus that most of the soil of England was held,—had to pay a large fine on coming to his property. He could not alienate one acre without purchasing a license. When he died, if his domains descended to an infant, the sovereign was guardian, and was not only entitled to great part of the rents during the minority, but could require the ward, under heavy penalties, to marry any person of suitable rank. The chief bait which attracted a needy sycophant to the court was the hope of obtaining, as the reward of servility and flattery, a royal letter to an heiress. These abuses had perished with the monarchy. That they should not revive with it was the wish of every landed gentleman in the kingdom. They were, therefore, solemnly abolished by statute; and no relic of the ancient tenures in chivalry was suffered to remain, except those honorary services which are still, at a coronation, rendered to the person of the sovereign by some lords of manors.

The troops were now to be disbanded. Fifty thousand men, accustomed to the profession of arms, were at once thrown on the world: and experience seemed to warrant the belief that this change would produce much misery and crime, that the discharged veterans would be seen begging in every street, or that they would be driven by hunger to pillage. But no such result followed. In a few months there remained not a trace indicating that the most formidable army in the world had just been absorbed into the mass of the community. The Royalists themselves confessed that, in every department of honest industry, the discarded warriors prospered beyond other men, that none was charged with any theft or robbery, that none was heard to ask an alms, and that, if a baker, a mason, or a waggoner attracted notice by his diligence and sobriety, he was in all probability one of Oliver's old soldiers.

The military tyranny had passed away; but it had left deep and enduring traces in the public mind. The name of standing army was long held in abhorrence: and it is remarkable that this feeling was even stronger among the Cavaliers than among the Roundheads. It ought to be considered as a most fortunate circumstance that, when our country was, for the first and last time, ruled by the sword, the sword was in the hands, not of her legitimate princes, but of those rebels who slew the King and demolished the Church. Had a prince, with a title as good as that of Charles, commanded an army

Disbandment of the army.

as good as that of Cromwell, there would have been little hope indeed for the liberties of England. Happily that instrument by which alone the monarchy could be made absolute became an object of peculiar horror and disgust to the monarchical party, and long continued to be inseparably associated in the imagination of Royalists and Prelatists with regicide and field preaching. A century after the death of Cromwell, the Tories still continued to clamour against every augmentation of the regular soldiery, and to sound the praise of a national militia. So late as the year 1786, a minister who enjoyed no common measure of their confidence found it impossible to overcome their aversion to his scheme of fortifying the coast : nor did they ever look with entire complacency on the standing army, till the French Revolution gave a new direction to their apprehensions.

Disputes between the Roundheads and Cavaliers renewed.

　　The coalition which had restored the King terminated with the danger from which it had sprung ; and two hostile parties again appeared ready for conflict. Both, indeed, were agreed as to the propriety of inflicting punishment on some unhappy men who were, at that moment, objects of almost universal hatred. Cromwell was no more ; and those who had fled before him were forced to content themselves with the miserable satisfaction of digging up, hanging, quartering, and burning the remains of the greatest prince that has ever ruled England. Other objects of vengeance, few indeed, yet too many, were found among the republican chiefs. Soon, however, the conquerors, glutted with the blood of the regicides, turned against each other. The Roundheads, while admitting the virtues of the late King, and while condemning the sentence passed upon him by an illegal tribunal, yet maintained that his administration had been, in many things, unconstitutional, and that the Houses had taken arms against him from good motives and on strong grounds. The monarchy, these politicians conceived, had no worse enemy than the flatterer who exalted the prerogative above the law, who condemned all opposition to regal encroachments, and who reviled, not only Cromwell and Harrison, but Pym and Hampden, as traitors. If the King wished for a quiet and prosperous reign, he must confide in those who, though they had drawn the sword in defence of the invaded privileges of Parliament, had yet exposed themselves to the rage of the soldiers in order to save his father, and had taken the chief part in bringing back the royal family.

The feeling of the Cavaliers was widely different. During eighteen years they had, through all vicissitudes, been faithful to the Crown. Having shared the distress of their prince, were they not to share his triumph? Was no distinction to be made between them and the disloyal subject who had fought against his rightful sovereign, who had adhered to Richard Cromwell, and who had never concurred in the restoration of the Stuarts, till it appeared that nothing else could save the nation from the tyranny of the army? Grant that such a man had, by his recent services, fairly earned his pardon. Yet were his services, rendered at the eleventh hour, to be put in comparison with the toils and sufferings of those who had borne the burden and heat of the day? Was he to be ranked with men who had no need of the royal clemency, with men who had, in every part of their lives, merited the royal gratitude? Above all, was he to be suffered to retain a fortune raised out of the substance of the ruined defenders of the throne? Was it not enough that his head and his patrimonial estate, a hundred times forfeited to justice, were secure, and that he shared, with the rest of the nation, in the blessings of that mild government of which he had long been the foe? Was it necessary that he should be rewarded for his treason at the expense of men whose only crime was the fidelity with which they had observed their oath of allegiance. And what interest had the King in gorging his old enemies with prey torn from his old friends? What confidence could be placed in men who had opposed their sovereign, made war on him, imprisoned him, and who, even now, instead of hanging down their heads in shame and contrition, vindicated all that they had done, and seemed to think that they had given an illustrious proof of loyalty by just stopping short of regicide? It was true they had lately assisted to set up the throne : but it was not less true that they had previously pulled it down, and that they still avowed principles which might impel them to pull it down again. Undoubtedly it might be fit that marks of royal approbation should be bestowed on some converts who had been eminently useful : but policy, as well as justice and gratitude, enjoined the King to give the highest place in his regard to those who, from first to last, through good and evil, had stood by his house. On these grounds the Cavaliers very naturally demanded indemnity for all that they had suffered, and preference in the distribution of the favours of the

Crown. Some violent members of the party went further, and clamoured for large categories of proscription.

The political feud was, as usual, exasperated by a religious feud. The King found the Church in a singular state. A short time before the commencement of the civil war, his father had given a reluctant assent to a bill, strongly supported by Falkland, which deprived the Bishops of their seats in the House of Lords : but Episcopacy and the Liturgy had never been abolished by law. The Long Parliament, however, had passed ordinances which had made a complete revolution in Church government and in public worship. The new system was, in principle, scarcely less Erastian than that which it displaced. The Houses, guided chiefly by the counsels of the accomplished Selden, had determined to keep the spiritual power strictly subordinate to the temporal power. They had refused to declare that any form of ecclesiastical polity was of divine origin ; and they had provided that, from all the Church courts, an appeal should lie in the last resort to Parliament. With this highly important reservation, it had been resolved to set up in England a hierarchy closely resembling that which now exists in Scotland. The authority of councils, rising one above another in regular gradation, was substituted for the authority of Bishops and Archbishops. The Liturgy gave place to the Presbyterian Directory. But scarcely had the new regulations been framed, when the Independents rose to supreme influence in the state. The Independents had no disposition to enforce the ordinances touching classical, provincial, and national synods. Those ordinances, therefore, were never carried into full execution. The Presbyterian system was fully established nowhere but in Middlesex and Lancashire. In the other fifty counties almost every parish seems to have been unconnected with the neighbouring parishes. In some districts, indeed, the ministers formed themselves into voluntary associations, for the purpose of mutual help and counsel ; but these associations had no coercive power. The patrons of livings, being now checked by neither Bishop nor Presbytery, would have been at liberty to confide the cure of souls to the most scandalous of mankind, but for the arbitrary intervention of Oliver. He established, by his own authority, a board of commissioners, called Triers. Most of these persons were Independent divines ; but a few Presbyterian ministers and a few laymen had seats. The certificate of the

Triers stood in the place both of institution and of induction; and without such a certificate no person could hold a benefice. This was undoubtedly one of the most despotic acts ever done by any English ruler. Yet, as it was generally felt that, without some such precaution, the country would be overrun by ignorant and drunken reprobates, bearing the name and receiving the pay of ministers, some highly respectable persons, who were not in general friendly to Cromwell, allowed that, on this occasion, he had been a public benefactor. The presentees whom the Triers had approved took possession of the rectories, cultivated the glebe lands, collected the tithes, prayed without book or surplice, and administered the Eucharist to communicants seated at long tables.

Thus the ecclesiastical polity of the realm was in inextricable confusion. Episcopacy was the form of government prescribed by the old law which was still unrepealed. The form of government prescribed by parliamentary ordinance was Presbyterian. But neither the old law nor the parliamentary ordinance was practically in force. The Church actually established may be described as an irregular body made up of a few Presbyteries and many Independent congregations, which were all held down and held together by the authority of the government.

Of those who had been active in bringing back the King, many were zealous for Synods and for the Directory, and many were desirous to terminate by a compromise the religious dissensions which had long agitated England. Between the bigoted followers of Laud and the bigoted followers of Knox there could be neither peace nor truce: but it did not seem impossible to effect an accommodation between the moderate Episcopalians of the school of Usher and the moderate Presbyterians of the school of Baxter. The moderate Episcopalians would admit that a Bishop might lawfully be assisted by a council. The moderate Presbyterians would not deny that each provincial assembly might lawfully have a permanent president, and that this president might lawfully be called a Bishop. There might be a revised Liturgy which should not exclude extemporaneous prayer, a baptismal service in which the sign of the cross might be used or omitted at discretion, a communion service at which the faithful might sit if their consciences forbade them to kneel. But to no such plan could the great body of the Cavaliers listen with patience. The religious members of that party were conscientiously attached to the whole system of their Church. She had been dear to their murdered King. She had consoled them in defeat and penury. Her service, so often whispered in an inner chamber during the season of trial, had such a charm for them that they were unwilling to part with a single response. Other Royalists, who made little pretence to piety, yet loved the episcopal church because she was the foe of their foes. They valued a prayer or a ceremony, not on account of the comfort which it conveyed to themselves, but on account of the vexation which it gave to the Roundheads, and were so far from being disposed to purchase union by concession that they objected to concession chiefly because it tended to produce union.

Unpopularity of the Puritans. Such feelings, though blamable, were natural, and not wholly inexcusable. The Puritans had undoubtedly, in the day of their power, given cruel provocation. They ought to have learned, if from nothing else, yet from their own discontents, from their own struggles, from their own victory, from the fall of that proud hierarchy by which they had been so heavily oppressed, that, in England, and in the seventeenth century, it was not in the power of the civil magistrate to drill the minds of men into conformity with his own system of theology. They proved, however, as intolerant and as meddling as ever Laud had been. They interdicted under heavy penalties the use of the Book of Common Prayer, not only in churches, but even in private houses. It was a crime in a child to read by the bedside of a sick parent one of those beautiful collects which had soothed the griefs of forty generations of Christians. Severe punishments were denounced against such as should presume to blame the Calvinistic mode of worship. Clergymen of respectable character were not only ejected from their benefices by thousands, but were frequently exposed to the outrages of a fanatical rabble. Churches and sepulchres, fine works of art and curious remains of antiquity, were brutally defaced. The Parliament resolved that all pictures in the royal collection which contained representations of Jesus or of the Virgin Mother should be burned. Sculpture fared as ill as painting. Nymphs and Graces, the work of Ionian chisels, were delivered over to Puritan stonemasons to be made decent. Against the lighter vices the ruling faction waged war with a zeal little tempered by humanity or by common sense. Sharp laws were passed against betting. It was enacted that adultery should be punished with death. The illicit intercourse of the sexes, even where neither violence nor seduction was imputed, where no public scandal was given, where no conjugal right was violated, was made a misdemeanour. Public amusements, from the masques which were exhibited at the mansions of the great down to the wrestling matches and grinning matches on village greens, were vigorously attacked. One ordinance directed that all the Maypoles in England should forthwith be hewn down. Another proscribed all theatrical diversions. The playhouses were to be dismantled, the spectators fined, the actors whipped at the cart's tail. Ropedancing, puppet-shows, bowls, horseracing, were regarded with no friendly eye. But bearbaiting, then a favourite diversion of high and low, was the abomination which most strongly stirred the wrath of the austere sectaries. It is to be remarked that their antipathy to this sport had nothing in common with the feeling which has, in our own time, induced the legislature to interfere for the purpose of protecting beasts against the wanton cruelty of men. The Puritan hated bearbaiting, not because it gave pain to the bear, but because it gave pleasure to the spectators. Indeed, he generally contrived to enjoy the double pleasure of tormenting both spectators and bear.*

Perhaps no single circumstance more strongly illustrates the temper of the precisians than their conduct respecting Christmas day. Christmas had been, from time immemorial, the season of joy and domestic affection, the season when families assembled, when children came home from school,

---

* How little compassion for the bear had to do with the matter is sufficiently proved by the following extract from a paper entitled A perfect Diurnal of some Passages of Parliament, and from other Parts of the Kingdom, from Monday July 24th, to Monday July 31st, 1643. "Upon the Queen's coming from Holland, she brought with her, besides a company of savage-like ruffians, a company of savage bears, to what purpose you may judge by the sequel. Those bears were left about Newark, and were brought into country towns constantly on the Lord's day to be baited, such is the religion those here related would settle amongst us; and, if any went about to hinder or but speak against their damnable profanations, they were presently noted as Roundheads and Puritans, and sure to be plundered for it. But some of Colonel Cromwell's forces coming by accident into Uppingham town, in Rutland, on the Lord's day, found these bears playing there in the usual manner, and, in the height of their sport, caused them to be seized upon, tied to a tree and shot." This was by no means a solitary instance. Colonel Pride, when Sheriff of Surrey, ordered the beasts in the bear garden of Southwark to be killed. He is represented by a loyal satirist as defending the act thus:—"The first thing that is upon my spirits is the killing of the bears, for which the people hate me, and call me all the names in the rainbow. But did not David kill a bear? Did not the Lord Deputy Ireton kill a bear? Did not another lord of ours kill five bears?"—Last Speech and Dying Words of Thomas Pride.

when quarrels were made up, when carols were heard in every
street, when every house was decorated with evergreens, and
every table was loaded with good cheer.   At that season all
hearts not utterly destitute of kindness were enlarged and
softened.   At that season the poor were admitted to partake
largely of the overflowings of the wealth of the rich, whose
bounty was peculiarly acceptable on account of the shortness
of the days and of the severity of the weather.   At that season, the interval between landlord and tenant, master and
servant, was less marked than through the rest of the year.
Where there is much enjoyment there will be some excess:
yet, on the whole, the spirit in which the holiday was kept
was not unworthy of a Christian festival.   The long Parliament gave orders, in 1644, that the twenty-fifth of December
should be strictly observed as a fast, and that all men should
pass it in humbly bemoaning the great national sin which
they and their fathers had so often committed on that day by
romping under the misletoe, eating boar's head, and drinking
ale flavoured with roasted apples.   No public act of that time
seems to have irritated the common people more.   On the
next anniversary of the festival formidable riots broke out in
many places.   The constables were resisted, the magistrates
insulted, the houses of noted zealots attacked, and the proscribed service of the day openly read in the churches.

Such was the spirit of the extreme Puritans, both Presbyterian and Independent.   Oliver, indeed, was little disposed
to be either a persecutor or a meddler.   But Oliver, the head
of a party, and consequently, to a great extent, the slave of a
party, could not govern altogether according to his own inclinations.   Even under his administration many magistrates,
within their own jurisdiction, made themselves as odious as
Sir Hudibras, interfered with all the pleasures of the neighbourhood, dispersed festive meetings, and put fiddlers in the
stocks.   Still more formidable was the zeal of the soldiers.
In every village where they appeared there was an end of
dancing, bellringing, and hockey.   In London they several
times interrupted theatrical performances at which the Protector had the judgment and good nature to connive.

With the fear and hatred inspired by such a tyranny contempt was largely mingled.   The peculiarities of the Puritan,
his look, his dress, his dialect, his strange scruples, had been,
ever since the time of Elizabeth, favourite subjects with
mockers.   But these peculiarities appeared far more grotesque

in a faction which ruled a great empire than in obscure and persecuted congregations. The cant, which had moved laughter when it was heard on the stage from Tribulation Wholesome and Zeal-of-the-Land Busy, was still more laughable when it proceeded from the lips of Generals and Councillors of State. It is also to be noticed that during the civil troubles several sects had sprung into existence, whose eccentricities surpassed anything that had before been seen in England. A mad tailor, named Lodowick Muggleton, wandered from pothouse to pothouse, tippling ale, and denouncing eternal torments against those who refused to believe, on his testimony, that the Supreme Being was only six feet high, and that the sun was just four miles from the earth.* George Fox had raised a tempest of derision by proclaiming that it was a violation of Christian sincerity to designate a single person by a plural pronoun, and that it was an idolatrous homage to Janus and Woden to talk about January and Wednesday. His doctrine, a few years later, was embraced by some eminent men, and rose greatly in the public estimation. But at the time of the Restoration the Quakers were popularly regarded as the most despicable of fanatics. By the Puritans they were treated with severity here, and were persecuted to the death in New England. Nevertheless the public, which seldom makes nice distinctions, often confounded the Puritan with the Quaker. Both were schismatics. Both hated episcopacy and the Liturgy. Both had what seemed extravagant whimsies about dress, diversions, and postures. Widely as the two differed in opinion, they were popularly classed together as canting schismatics; and whatever was ridiculous or odious in either increased the scorn and aversion which the multitude felt for both.

Before the civil wars, even those who most disliked the opinions and manners of the Puritan were forced to admit that his moral conduct was generally, in essentials, blameless; but this praise was now no longer bestowed, and, unfortunately, was no longer deserved. The general fate of sects is to obtain a high reputation for sanctity while they are oppressed, and to lose it as soon as they become powerful: and the reason is obvious. It is seldom that a man enrolls himself in a proscribed body from any but conscientious motives. Such a body, therefore, is composed, with scarcely an exception, of sincere persons. The most rigid discipline

* See Penn's New Witnesses proved Old Heretics, and Muggleton's works, *passim*.

that can be enforced within a religious society is a very feeble instrument of purification, when compared with a little sharp persecution from without. We may be certain that very few persons, not seriously impressed by religious convictions, applied for baptism while Diocletian was vexing the Church, or joined themselves to Protestant congregations at the risk of being burned by Bonner. But, when a sect becomes powerful, when its favour is the road to riches and dignities, worldly and ambitious men crowd into it, talk its language, conform strictly to its ritual, mimic its peculiarities, and frequently go beyond its honest members in all the outward indications of zeal. No discernment, no watchfulness, on the part of ecclesiastical rulers, can prevent the intrusion of such false brethren. The tares and the wheat must grow together. Soon the world begins to find out that the godly are not better than other men, and argues, with some justice, that, if not better, they must be much worse. In no long time all those signs which were formerly regarded as characteristic of a saint are regarded as characteristic of a knave.

Thus it was with the English Nonconformists. They had been oppressed; and oppression had kept them a pure body. They then became supreme in the state. No man could hope to rise to eminence and command but by their favour. Their favour was to be gained only by exchanging with them the signs and passwords of spiritual fraternity. One of the first resolutions adopted by Barebone's Parliament, the most intensely Puritanical of all our political assemblies, was that no person should be admitted into the public service till the House should be satisfied of his real godliness. What were then considered as the signs of real godliness, the sadcoloured dress, the sour look, the straight hair, the nasal whine, the speech interspersed with quaint texts, the Sunday, gloomy as a Pharisaical Sabbath, were easily imitated by men to whom all religions were the same. The sincere Puritans soon found themselves lost in a multitude, not merely of men of the world, but of the very worst sort of men of the world. For the most notorious libertine who had fought under the royal standard might justly be thought virtuous when compared with some of those who, while they talked about sweet experiences and comfortable scriptures, lived in the constant practice of fraud, rapacity, and secret debauchery. The people, with a rashness which we may justly lament, but at which we cannot wonder, formed their estimate of the whole body from these hypocrites. The theology, the manners, the dialect of the Puritan were thus associated in the public mind with the darkest and meanest vices. As soon as the Restoration had made it safe to avow enmity to the party which had so long been predominant, a general outcry against Puritanism rose from every corner of the kingdom, and was often swollen by the voices of those very dissemblers whose villany had brought disgrace on the Puritan name.

Thus the two great parties, which, after a long contest, had for a moment concurred in restoring monarchy, were, both in politics and in religion, again opposed to each other. The great body of the nation leaned to the Royalists. The crimes of Strafford and Laud, the excesses of the Star Chamber and of the High Commission, the great services which the Long Parliament had, during the first year of its existence, rendered to the state, had faded from the minds of men. The execution of Charles the First, the sullen tyranny of the Rump, the violence of the army, were remembered with loathing; and the multitude was inclined to hold all who had withstood the late King responsible for his death and for the subsequent disasters.

The House of Commons, having been elected while the Presbyterians were dominant, by no means represented the general sense of the people. Most of the members, while execrating Cromwell and Bradshaw, reverenced the memory of Essex and of Pym. One sturdy Cavalier, who ventured to declare that all who had drawn the sword against Charles the First were as much traitors as those who had cut off his head, was called to order, placed at the bar, and reprimanded by the Speaker. The general wish of the House undoubtedly was to settle the ecclesiastical disputes in a manner satisfactory to the moderate Puritans. But to such a settlement both the court and the nation were averse.

The restored King was at this time more loved by the people than any of his predecessors had ever been. The calamities of his house, the heroic death of his father, his own long sufferings and romantic adventures, made him an object of tender interest. His return had delivered the country from an intolerable bondage. Recalled by the voice of both the contending factions, he was in a position which enabled him to arbitrate between them; and in some respects he was well qualified for the task. He had received from nature excellent parts and a happy temper. His education

Character of Charles II.

had been such as might have been expected to develope his understanding, and to form him to the practice of every pub- lic and private virtue. He had passed through all varieties of fortune, and had seen both sides of human nature. He had, while very young, been driven forth from a palace to a life of exile, penury, and danger. He had, at the age when the mind and body are in their highest perfection, and when the first effervescence of boyish passions should have subsided, been recalled from his wanderings to wear a crown. He had been taught by bitter experience how much baseness, perfidy, and ingratitude may lie hid under the obsequious demeanour of courtiers. He had found, on the other hand, in the huts of the poorest, true nobility of soul. When wealth was offered to any who would betray him, when death was denounced against all who should shelter him, cottagers and serving men had kept his secret truly, and had kissed his hand under his mean disguises with as much reverence as if he had been seated on his ancestral throne. From such a school it might have been expected that a young man who wanted neither abilities nor amiable qualities would have come forth a great and good King. Charles came forth from that school with social habits, with polite and engaging manners, and with some talent for lively conversation, addicted beyond measure to sensual indulgence, fond of sauntering and of frivolous amusements, incapable of selfdenial and of exertion, without faith in human virtue or in human attachment, without desire of renown, and without sensibility to reproach. According to him, every person was to be bought: but some people haggled more about their price than others; and when this haggling was very obstinate and very skilful it was called by some fine name. The chief trick by which clever men kept up the price of their abilities was called integrity. The chief trick by which handsome women kept up the price of their beauty was called modesty. The love of God, the love of country, the love of family, the love of friends, were phrases of the same sort, delicate and convenient synonymes for the love of self. Thinking thus of mankind, Charles naturally cared very little what they thought of him. Honour and shame were scarcely more to him than light and darkness to the blind. His contempt of flattery has been highly com- mended, but seems, when viewed in connection with the rest of his character, to deserve no commendation. It is possible to be below flattery as well as above it. One who trusts nobody will not trust sycophants. One who does not value real glory will not value its counterfeit.

It is creditable to Charles's temper that, ill as he thought of his species, he never became a misanthrope. He saw little in men but what was hateful. Yet he did not hate them. Nay, he was so far humane that it was highly disagreeable to him to see their sufferings or to hear their complaints. This, however, is a sort of humanity which, though amiable and laudable in a private man whose power to help or hurt is bounded by a narrow circle, has in princes often been rather a vice than a virtue. More than one well disposed ruler has given up whole provinces to rapine and oppression, merely from a wish to see none but happy faces round his own board and in his own walks. No man is fit to govern great societies who hesitates about disobliging the few who have access to him, for the sake of the many whom he will never see. The facility of Charles was such as has perhaps never been found in any man of equal sense. He was a slave without being a dupe. Worthless men and women, to the very bottom of whose hearts he saw, and whom he knew to be destitute of affection for him and undeserving of his confidence, could easily wheedle him out of titles, places, domains, state secrets and pardons. He bestowed much; yet he neither enjoyed the pleasure nor acquired the fame of beneficence. He never gave spontaneously; but it was painful to him to refuse. The consequence was that his bounty generally went, not to those who deserved it best, nor even to those whom he liked best, but to the most shameless and importunate suitor who could obtain an audience.

The motives which governed the political conduct of Charles the Second differed widely from those by which his predecessor and his successor were actuated. He was not a man to be imposed upon by the patriarchal theory of government and the doctrine of divine right. He was utterly without ambition. He detested business, and would sooner have abdicated his crown than have undergone the trouble of really directing the administration. Such was his aversion to toil, and such his ignorance of affairs, that the very clerks who attended him when he sate in council could not refrain from sneering at his frivolous remarks, and at his childish impatience. Neither gratitude nor revenge had any share in determining his course; for never was there a mind on which both services and injuries left such faint and transitory impressions. He wished merely to be a King such as Lewis the Fifteenth of France afterwards was; a King who could draw without limit on the treasury for the gratification of his private tastes, who could hire with wealth and honours persons capable of assisting him to kill the time, and who, even when the state was brought by maladministration to the depths of humiliation and to the brink of ruin, could still exclude unwelcome truth from the purlieus of his own seraglio, and refuse to see and hear whatever might disturb his luxurious repose. For these ends, and for these ends alone, he wished to obtain arbitrary power, if it could be obtained without risk or trouble. In the religious disputes which divided his Protestant subjects his conscience was not at all interested. For his opinions oscillated in contented suspense between infidelity and Popery. But, though his conscience was neutral in the quarrel between the Episcopalians and the Presbyterians, his taste was by no means so. His favourite vices were precisely those to which the Puritans were least indulgent. He could not get through one day without the help of diversions which the Puritans regarded as sinful. As a man eminently well bred, and keenly sensible of the ridiculous, he was moved to contemptuous mirth by the Puritan oddities. He had indeed some reason to dislike the rigid sect. He had, at the age when the passions are most impetuous and when levity is most pardonable, spent some months in Scotland, a King in name, but in fact a state prisoner in the hands of austere Presbyterians. Not content with requiring him to conform to their worship and to subscribe their Covenant, they had watched all his motions, and lectured him on all his youthful follies. He had been compelled to give reluctant attendance at endless prayers and sermons, and might think himself fortunate when he was not insolently reminded from the pulpit of his own frailties, of his father's tyranny, and of his mother's idolatry. Indeed he had been so miserable during this part of his life that the defeat which made him again a wanderer might be regarded as a deliverance rather than as a calamity. Under the influence of such feelings as these Charles was desirous to depress the party which had resisted his father.

Characters of the Duke of The King's brother, James Duke of York, took the same side. Though a libertine, James was diligent, methodical, and fond of authority and business. His understanding was singularly slow and narrow, and his temper obstinate, harsh, and unforgiving. That such a prince should have looked with no good will on the free institutions of England, and on the party which was peculiarly zealous for those institutions, can excite no surprise. As yet the Duke professed himself a member of the Anglican Church : but he had already shown inclinations which had seriously alarmed good Protestants.

York and Earl of Clarendon.

The person on whom devolved at this time the greatest part of the labour of governing was Edward Hyde, Chancellor of the realm, who was soon created Earl of Clarendon. The respect which we justly feel for Clarendon as a writer must not blind us to the faults which he committed as a statesman. Some of those faults, however, are explained and excused by the unfortunate position in which he stood. He had, during the first year of the Long Parliament, been honourably distinguished among the senators who laboured to redress the grievances of the nation. One of the most odious of those grievances, the Council of York, had been removed in consequence chiefly of his exertions. When the great schism took place, when the reforming party and the conservative party first appeared marshalled against each other, he, with many wise and good men, took the conservative side. He thenceforward followed the fortunes of the court, enjoyed as large a share of the confidence of Charles the First as the reserved nature and tortuous policy of that prince allowed to any minister, and subsequently shared the exile and directed the political conduct of Charles the Second. At the Restoration Hyde became chief minister. In a few months it was announced that he was closely related by affinity to the royal house. His daughter had become, by a secret marriage, Duchess of York. His grandchildren might perhaps wear the crown. He was raised by this illustrious connection over the heads of the old nobility of the land, and was for a time supposed to be allpowerful. In some respects he was well fitted for his great place. No man wrote abler state papers. No man spoke with more weight and dignity in Council and in Parliament. No man was better acquainted with general maxims of statecraft. No man observed the varieties of character with a more discriminating eye. It must be added that he had a strong sense of moral and religious obligation, a sincere reverence for the laws of his country, and a conscientious regard for the honour and interest of the Crown.

But his temper was sour, arrogant, and impatient of opposition. Above all, he had been long an exile; and this circumstance alone would have completely disqualified him for the supreme direction of affairs. It is scarcely possible that a politician, who has been compelled by civil troubles to go into banishment, and to pass many of the best years of his life abroad, can be fit, on the day on which he returns to his native land, to be at the head of the government. Clarendon was no exception to this rule. He had left England with a mind heated by a fierce conflict which had ended in the downfall of his party and of his own fortunes. From 1646 to 1660 he had lived beyond sea, looking on all that passed at home from a great distance, and through a false medium. His notions of public affairs were necessarily derived from the reports of plotters, many of whom were ruined and desperate men. Events naturally seemed to him auspicious, not in proportion as they increased the prosperity and glory of the nation, but in proportion as they tended to hasten the hour of his own return. His wish, a wish which he has not disguised, was that, till his countrymen brought back the old line, they might never enjoy quiet or freedom. At length he returned; and, without having a single week to look about him, to mix with society, to note the changes which fourteen eventful years had produced in the national character and feelings, he was at once set to rule the state. In such circumstances, a minister of the greatest tact and docility would probably have fallen into serious errors. But tact and docility made no part of the character of Clarendon. To him England was still the England of his youth; and he sternly frowned down every theory and every practice which had sprung up during his own exile. Though he was far from meditating any attack on the ancient and undoubted power of the House of Commons, he saw with extreme uneasiness the growth of that power. The royal prerogative, for which he had long suffered, and by which he had at length been raised to wealth and dignity, was sacred in his eyes. The Roundheads he regarded both with political and with personal aversion. To the Anglican Church he had always been strongly attached, and had repeatedly, where her interests were concerned, separated himself with regret from his dearest friends. His zeal for Episcopacy and for the Book of Common Prayer was now more ardent than ever, and was mingled with a vindictive hatred of the Puritans, which did him little honour either as a statesman or as a Christian.

While the House of Commons which had recalled the royal family was sitting, it was impossible to effect the reestablishment of the old ecclesiastical system. Not only were the intentions of the court strictly concealed, but assurances which quieted the minds of the moderate Presbyterians were given by the King in the most solemn manner. He had promised, before his restoration, that he would grant liberty of conscience to his subjects. He now repeated that promise, and added a promise to use his best endeavours for the purpose of effecting a compromise between the contending sects. He wished, he said, to see the spiritual jurisdiction divided between bishops and synods. The Liturgy should be revised by a body of learned divines, one half of whom should be Presbyterians. The questions respecting the surplice, the posture at the Eucharist, and the sign of the cross in baptism, should be settled in a way which would set tender consciences at ease. When the King had thus laid asleep the vigilance of those whom he most feared, he dissolved the Parliament. He had already given his assent to an act by which an amnesty was granted, with few exceptions, to all who, during the late troubles, had been guilty of political offences. He had also obtained from the Commons a grant for life of taxes, the annual produce of which was estimated at twelve hundred thousand pounds. The actual income, indeed, during some years, amounted to little more than a million : but this sum, together with the hereditary revenue of the crown, was then sufficient to defray the expenses of the government in time of peace. Nothing was allowed for a standing army. The nation was sick of the very name; and the least mention of such a force would have incensed and alarmed all parties.

Early in 1661 took place a general election. The people were mad with loyal enthusiasm. The capital was excited by preparations for the most splendid coronation that had ever been known. The result was that a body of representatives was returned, such as England had never yet seen. A large proportion of the successful candidates were men who had fought for the Crown and the Church, and whose minds had been exasperated by many injuries and insults suffered at the hands of the Roundheads. When the members met, the passions which animated each individually

General election of 1661.

acquired new strength from sympathy. The House of Commons was, during some years, more zealous for royalty than the King, more zealous for episcopacy than the Bishops. Charles and Clarendon were almost terrified at the completeness of their own success. They found themselves in a situation not unlike that in which Lewis the Eighteenth and the Duke of Richelieu were placed while the Chamber of 1815 was sitting. Even if the King had been desirous to fulfil the promises which he had made to the Presbyterians, it would have been out of his power to do so. It was indeed only by the strong exertion of his influence that he could prevent the victorious Cavaliers from rescinding the act of indemnity, and retaliating without mercy all that they had suffered.

Violence of the Cavaliers in the new Parliament.

The Commons began by resolving that every member should, on pain of expulsion, take the sacrament according to the form prescribed by the old Liturgy, and that the Covenant should be burned by the hangman in Palace Yard. An act was passed, which not only acknowledged the power of the sword to be solely in the King, but declared that in no extremity whatever could the two Houses be justified in withstanding him by force. Another act was passed which required every officer of a corporation to receive the Eucharist according to the rites of the Church of England, and to swear that he held resistance to the King's authority to be in all cases unlawful. A few hotheaded men wished to bring in a bill, which should at once annul all the statutes passed by the Long Parliament, and should restore the Star Chamber and the High Commission; but the reaction, violent as it was, did not proceed quite to this length. It still continued to be the law that a Parliament should be held every three years: but the stringent clauses which directed the returning officers to proceed to election at the proper time, even without the royal writ, were repealed. The Bishops were restored to their seats in the Upper House. The old ecclesiastical polity and the old Liturgy were revived without any modification which had any tendency to conciliate even the most reasonable Presbyterians. Episcopal ordination was now, for the first time, made an indispensable qualification for church preferment. About two thousand ministers of religion, whose conscience did not suffer them to conform, were driven from their benefices in one day. The dominant party exultingly reminded the sufferers that the

Long Parliament, when at the height of power, had turned out a still greater number of Royalist divines. The reproach was but too well founded : but the Long Parliament had at least allowed to the divines whom it ejected a provision sufficient to keep them from starving; and this example the Cavaliers, intoxicated with animosity, had not the justice and humanity to follow.

Then came penal statutes against Nonconformists, statutes for which precedents might too easily be found in the Puritan legislation, but to which the King could not give his assent without a breach of promises publicly made, in the most important crisis of his life, to those on whom his fate depended. The Presbyterians, in extreme distress and terror, fled to the foot of the throne, and pleaded their recent services and the royal faith solemnly and repeatedly plighted. The King wavered. He could not deny his own hand and seal. He could not but be conscious that he owed much to the petitioners. He was little in the habit of resisting importunate solicitation. His temper was not that of a persecutor. He disliked the Puritans indeed; but in him dislike was a languid feeling, very little resembling the energetic hatred which had burned in the heart of Laud. He was, moreover, partial to the Roman Catholic religion; and he knew that it would be impossible to grant liberty of worship to the professors of that religion without extending the same indulgence to Protestant dissenters. He therefore made a feeble attempt to restrain the intolerant zeal of the House of Commons; but that House was under the influence of far deeper convictions and far stronger passions than his own. After a faint struggle he yielded, and passed, with the show of alacrity, a series of odious acts against the separatists. It was made a crime to attend a dissenting place of worship. A single justice of the peace might convict without a jury, and might, for the third offence, pass sentence of transportation beyond sea for seven years. With refined cruelty it was provided that the offender should not be transported to New England, where he was likely to find sympathising friends. If he returned to his own country before the expiration of his term of exile, he was liable to capital punishment. A new and most unreasonable test was imposed on divines who had been deprived of their benefices for nonconformity; and all who refused to take that test were prohibited from coming within five miles of any town which was

Persecution of the Puritans.

governed by a corporation, of any town which was represented
in Parliament, or of any town where they had themselves
resided as ministers. The magistrates, by whom these
rigorous statutes were to be enforced, were in general men
inflamed by party spirit and by the remembrance of wrongs
suffered in the time of the Commonwealth. The gaols were
therefore soon crowded with dissenters; and, among the
sufferers, were some of whose genius and virtue any Christian
society might well be proud.

Zeal of the Church for hereditary monarchy.
The Church of England was not ungrateful for the protection which she received from the government. From the
first day of her existence, she had been attached to monarchy.
But, during the quarter of a century which followed the Restoration, her zeal for royal authority and hereditary right
passed all bounds. She had suffered with the House of
Stuart. She had been restored with that House. She was
connected with it by common interests, friendships, and enmities. It seemed impossible that a day could ever come when
the ties which bound her to the children of her august martyr would be sundered, and when the loyalty in which she
gloried would cease to be a pleasing and profitable duty.
She accordingly magnified in fulsome phrase that prerogative
which was constantly employed to defend and to aggrandise
her, and reprobated, much at her ease, the depravity of those
whom oppression, from which she was exempt, had goaded
to rebellion. Her favourite theme was the doctrine of nonresistance. That doctrine she taught without any qualification, and followed out to all its extreme consequences. Her
disciples were never weary of repeating that in no conceivable
case, not even if England were cursed with a King resembling Busiris or Phalaris, with a King who, in defiance
of law, and without the pretence of justice, should daily doom
hundreds of innocent victims to torture and death, would all
the Estates of the realm united be justified in withstanding
his tyranny by physical force. Happily the principles of
human nature afford abundant security that such theories
will never be more than theories. The day of trial came;
and the very men who had most loudly and most sincerely
professed this extravagant loyalty were, in every county of
England, arrayed in arms against the throne.

Property all over the kingdom was now again changing
hands. The national sales, not having been confirmed by
Act of Parliament, were regarded by the tribunals as nul-

lities. The bishops, the deans, the chapters, the Royalist nobility and gentry, reentered on their confiscated estates, and ejected even purchasers who had given fair prices. The losses which the Cavaliers had sustained during the ascendency of their opponents were thus in part repaired; but in part only. All actions for mesne profits were effectually barred by the general amnesty; and the numerous Royalists, who, in order to discharge fines imposed by the Long Parliament, or in order to purchase the favour of powerful Roundheads, had sold lands for much less than the real value, were not relieved from the legal consequences of their own acts.

While these changes were in progress, a change still more important took place in the morals and manners of the community. Those passions and tastes which, under the rule of the Puritans, had been sternly repressed, and, if gratified at all, had been gratified by stealth, broke forth with ungovernable violence as soon as the check was withdrawn. Men flew to frivolous amusements and to criminal pleasures with the greediness which long and enforced abstinence naturally produces. Little restraint was imposed by public opinion. For the nation, nauseated with cant, suspicious of all pretensions to sanctity, and still smarting from the recent tyranny of rulers austere in life and powerful in prayer, looked for a time with complacency on the softer and gayer vices. Still less restraint was imposed by the government. Indeed there was no excess which was not encouraged by the ostentatious profligacy of the King and of his favourite courtiers. A few counsellors of Charles the First, who were now no longer young, retained the decorous gravity which had been thirty years before in fashion at Whitehall. Such were Clarendon himself, and his friends, Thomas Wriothesley, Earl of Southampton, Lord Treasurer, and James Butler, Duke of Ormond, who, having through many vicissitudes struggled gallantly for the royal cause in Ireland, now governed that kingdom as Lord Lieutenant. But neither the memory of the services of these men, nor their great power in the state, could protect them from the sarcasms which modish vice loves to dart at obsolete virtue. The praise of politeness and vivacity could now scarcely be obtained except by some violation of decorum. Talents great and various assisted to spread the contagion. Ethical philosophy had recently taken a form well suited to please a generation equally devoted to monarchy and to vice. Thomas Hobbes had, in language more

Change in the morals of the community.

precise and luminous than has ever been employed by any
other metaphysical writer, maintained that the will of the
prince was the standard of right and wrong, and that every
subject ought to be ready to profess Popery, Mahometanism,
or Paganism, at the royal command.   Thousands who were
incompetent to appreciate what was really valuable in his
speculations, eagerly welcomed a theory which, while it exalted the kingly office, relaxed the obligations of morality,
and degraded religion into a mere affair of state.   Hobbism
soon became an almost essential part of the character of the
fine gentleman.   All the lighter kinds of literature were
deeply tainted by the prevailing licentiousness.   Poetry
stooped to be the pandar of every low desire.   Ridicule, instead of putting guilt and error to the blush, turned her formidable shafts against innocence and truth.   The restored
Church contended indeed against the prevailing immorality,
but contended feebly, and with half a heart.   It was necessary to the decorum of her character that she should admonish her erring children : but her admonitions were given in
a somewhat perfunctory manner.   Her attention was elsewhere engaged.   Her whole soul was in the work of crushing
the Puritans, and of teaching her disciples to give unto Cæsar
the things which were Cæsar's.   She had been pillaged and
oppressed by the party which preached an austere morality.
She had been restored to opulence and honour by libertines.
Little as the men of mirth and fashion were disposed to shape
their lives according to her precepts, they were yet ready to
fight knee deep in blood for her cathedrals and palaces, for
every line of her rubric and every thread of her vestments.
If the debauched Cavalier haunted brothels and gambling
houses, he at least avoided conventicles.   If he never spoke
without uttering ribaldry and blasphemy, he made some
amends by his eagerness to send Baxter and Howe to gaol
for preaching and praying.   Thus the clergy, for a time,
made war on schism with so much vigour that they had
little leisure to make war on vice.   The ribaldry of Etherege
and Wycherley was, in the presence and under the special
sanction of the head of the Church, publicly recited by female
lips in female ears, while the author of the Pilgrim's Progress
languished in a dungeon for the crime of proclaiming the
gospel to the poor.   It is an unquestionable and a most instructive fact that the years during which the political power
of the Anglican hierarchy was in the zenith were precisely

the years during which national virtue was at the lowest point.

Scarcely any rank or profession escaped the infection of the prevailing immorality; but those persons who made politics their business were perhaps the most corrupt part of the corrupt society. For they were exposed, not only to the same noxious influences which affected the nation generally, but also to a taint of a peculiar and of a most malignant kind. Their character had been formed amidst frequent and violent revolutions and counterrevolutions. In the course of a few years they had seen the ecclesiastical and civil polity of their country repeatedly changed. They had seen an Episcopal Church persecuting Puritans, a Puritan Church persecuting Episcopalians, and an Episcopal Church persecuting Puritans again. They had seen hereditary monarchy abolished and restored. They had seen the Long Parliament thrice supreme in the state, and thrice dissolved amidst the curses and laughter of millions. They had seen a new dynasty rapidly rising to the height of power and glory, and then on a sudden hurled down from the chair of state without a struggle. They had seen a new representative system devised, tried, and abandoned. They had seen a new House of Lords created and scattered. They had seen great masses of property violently transferred from Cavaliers to Roundheads, and from Roundheads back to Cavaliers. During these events no man could be a stirring and thriving politician who was not prepared to change with every change of fortune. It was only in retirement that any person could long keep the character either of a steady Royalist or of a steady Republican. One who, in such an age, is determined to attain civil greatness must renounce all thought of consistency. Instead of affecting immutability in the midst of endless mutation, he must be always on the watch for the indications of a coming reaction. He must seize the exact moment for deserting a falling cause. Having gone all lengths with a faction while it was uppermost, he must suddenly extricate himself from it when its difficulties begin, must assail it, must persecute it, must enter on a new career of power and prosperity in company with new associates. His situation naturally developes in him to the highest degree a peculiar class of abilities and a peculiar class of vices. He becomes quick of observation and fertile of resource. He catches without effort the tone of any sect or party with

Profligacy of politicians.

which he chances to mingle. He discerns the signs of the times with a sagacity which to the multitude appears miraculous, with a sagacity resembling that with which a veteran police officer pursues the faintest indications of crime, or with which a Mohawk warrior follows a track through the woods. But we shall seldom find, in a statesman so trained, integrity, constancy, any of the virtues of the noble family of Truth. He has no faith in any doctrine, no zeal for any cause. He has seen so many old institutions swept away, that he has no reverence for prescription. He has seen so many new institutions, from which much had been expected, produce mere disappointment, that he has no hope of improvement. He sneers alike at those who are anxious to preserve and at those who are eager to reform. There is nothing in the state which he could not, without a scruple or a blush, join in defending or in destroying. Fidelity to opinions and to friends seems to him mere dulness and wrongheadedness. Politics he regards, not as a science of which the object is the happiness of mankind, but as an exciting game of mixed chance and skill, at which a dexterous and lucky player may win an estate, a coronet, perhaps a crown, and at which one rash move may lead to the loss of fortune and of life. Ambition, which, in good times, and in good minds, is half a virtue, now, disjoined from every elevated and philanthropic sentiment, becomes a selfish cupidity scarcely less ignoble than avarice. Among those politicians who, from the Restoration to the accession of the House of Hanover, were at the head of the great parties in the state, very few can be named whose reputation is not stained by what, in our age, would be called gross perfidy and corruption. It is scarcely an exaggeration to say that the most unprincipled public men who have taken part in affairs within our memory would, if tried by the standard which was in fashion during the latter part of the seventeenth century, deserve to be regarded as scrupulous and disinterested.

State of Scotland.

While these political, religious, and moral changes were taking place in England, the Royal authority had been without difficulty reestablished in every other part of the British islands. In Scotland the restoration of the Stuarts had been hailed with delight; for it was regarded as the restoration of national independence. And true it was that the yoke which Cromwell had imposed was, in appearance, taken away, that the Scottish Estates again met in their old hall at Edinburgh, and that the Senators of the College of Justice again administered the Scottish law according to the old forms. Yet was the independence of the little kingdom necessarily rather nominal than real: for, as long as the King had England on his side, he had nothing to apprehend from disaffection in his other dominions. He was now in such a situation that he could renew the attempt which had proved destructive to his father without any danger of his father's fate. Charles the First had tried to force his own religion by his regal power on the Scots at a moment when both his religion and his regal power were unpopular in England; and he had not only failed, but had raised troubles which had ultimately cost him his crown and his head. Times had now changed: England was zealous for monarchy and prelacy: and therefore the scheme which had formerly been in the highest degree imprudent might be resumed with little risk to the throne. The government resolved to set up a prelatical church in Scotland. The design was disapproved by every Scotchman whose judgment was entitled to respect. Some Scottish statesmen who were zealous for the King's prerogative had been bred Presbyterians. Though little troubled with scruples, they retained a preference for the religion of their childhood; and they well knew how strong a hold that religion had on the hearts of their countrymen. They remonstrated strongly: but, when they found that they remonstrated in vain, they had not virtue enough to persist in an opposition which would have given offence to their master; and several of them stooped to the wickedness and baseness of persecuting what in their consciences they believed to be the purest form of Christianity. The Scottish Parliament was so constituted that it had scarcely ever offered any serious opposition even to Kings much weaker than Charles then was. Episcopacy, therefore, was established by law. As to the form of worship, a large discretion was left to the clergy. In some churches the English Liturgy was used. In others, the ministers selected from that Liturgy such prayers and thanksgivings as were likely to be least offensive to the people. But in general the doxology was sung at the close of public worship; and the Apostles' Creed was recited when baptism was administered. By the great body of the Scottish nation the new Church was detested both as superstitious and as foreign; as tainted with the corruptions of Rome, and as a mark of the predominance of England. There was, however, no general insurrection. The country was not what it had been twenty-two years before. Disastrous war and alien domination had tamed the spirit of the people. The aristocracy, which was held in great honour by the middle class and by the populace, had put itself at the head of the movement against Charles the First, but proved obsequious to Charles the Second. From the English Puritans no aid was now to be expected. They were a feeble party, proscribed both by law and by public opinion. The bulk of the Scottish nation, therefore, sullenly submitted, and, with many misgivings of conscience, attended the ministrations of the Episcopal clergy, or of Presbyterian divines who had consented to accept from the government a half toleration, known by the name of the Indulgence. But there were, particularly in the western lowlands, many fierce and resolute men who held that the obligation to observe the Covenant was paramount to the obligation to obey the magistrate. These people, in defiance of the law, persisted in meeting to worship God after their own fashion. The Indulgence they regarded, not as a partial reparation of the wrongs inflicted by the State on the Church, but as a new wrong, the more odious because it was disguised under the appearance of a benefit. Persecution, they said, could only kill the body; but the black Indulgence was deadly to the soul. Driven from the towns, they assembled on heaths and mountains. Attacked by the civil power, they without scruple repelled force by force. At every conventicle they mustered in arms. They repeatedly broke out into open rebellion. They were easily defeated, and mercilessly punished : but neither defeat nor punishment could subdue their spirit. Hunted down like wild beasts, tortured till their bones were beaten flat, imprisoned by hundreds, hanged by scores, exposed at one time to the license of soldiers from England, abandoned at another time to the mercy of troops of marauders from the Highlands, they still stood at bay in a mood so savage that the boldest and mightiest oppressor could not but dread the audacity of their despair.

State of Ireland.

Such was, during the reign of Charles the Second, the state of Scotland. Ireland was not less distracted. In that island existed feuds, compared with which the hottest animosities of English politicians were lukewarm. The enmity between the Irish Cavaliers and the Irish Roundheads was almost forgotten in the fiercer enmity which raged between the English and the Celtic races. The interval between the Episcopalian and the Presbyterian seemed to vanish, when compared with the interval which separated both from the Papist. During the late civil troubles the greater part of the Irish soil had been transferred from the vanquished nation to the victors. To the favour of the Crown few either of the old or of the new occupants had any pretensions. The despoilers and the despoiled had, for the most part, been rebels alike. The government was soon perplexed and wearied by the conflicting claims and mutual accusations of the two incensed factions. Those colonists among whom Cromwell had portioned out the conquered territory, and whose descendants are still called Cromwellians, asserted that the aboriginal inhabitants were deadly enemies of the English nation under every dynasty, and of the Protestant religion in every form. They described and exaggerated the atrocities which had disgraced the insurrection of Ulster: they urged the King to follow up with resolution the policy of the Protector; and they were not ashamed to hint that there would never be peace in Ireland till the old Irish race should be extirpated. The Roman Catholics extenuated their offence as they best might, and expatiated in piteous language on the severity of their punishment, which, in truth, had not been lenient. They implored Charles not to confound the innocent with the guilty, and reminded him that many of the guilty had atoned for their fault by returning to their allegiance, and by defending his rights against the murderers of his father. The court, sick of the importunities of two parties, neither of which it had any reason to love, at length relieved itself from trouble by dictating a compromise. That system, cruel, but most complete and energetic, by which Oliver had proposed to make the island thoroughly English, was abandoned. The Cromwellians were induced to relinquish a third part of their acquisitions. The land thus surrendered was capriciously divided among claimants whom the government chose to favour. But great numbers who protested that they were innocent of all disloyalty, and some persons who boasted that their loyalty had been signally displayed, obtained neither restitution nor compensation, and filled France and Spain with outcries against the injustice and ingratitude of the House of Stuart.

Meantime the government had, even in England, ceased to be popular. The Royalists had begun to quarrel with the court and with each other; and the party which had been vanquished, trampled down, and, as it seemed, annihilated, but which had still retained a strong principle of life, again raised its head, and renewed the interminable war.

The government become unpopular in England.

Had the administration been faultless, the enthusiasm with which the return of the King and the termination of the military tyranny had been hailed could not have been permanent. For it is the law of our nature that such fits of excitement shall always be followed by remissions. The manner in which the court abused its victory made the remission speedy and complete. Every moderate man was shocked by the insolence, cruelty, and perfidy with which the Nonconformists were treated. The penal laws had effectually purged the oppressed party of those insincere members whose vices had disgraced it, and had made it again an honest and pious body of men. The Puritan, a conqueror, a ruler, a persecutor, a sequestrator, had been detested. The Puritan, betrayed and evil entreated, deserted by all the timeservers who, in his prosperity, had claimed brotherhood with him, hunted from his home, forbidden under severe penalties to pray or receive the sacrament according to his conscience, yet still firm in his resolution to obey God rather than man, was, in spite of some unpleasing recollections, an object of pity and respect to well constituted minds. These feelings became stronger when it was noised abroad that the court was not disposed to treat Papists with the same rigour which had been shown to Presbyterians. A vague suspicion that the King and the Duke were not sincere Protestants sprang up and gathered strength. Many persons too who had been disgusted by the austerity and hypocrisy of the Saints of the Commonwealth began to be still more disgusted by the open profligacy of the court and of the Cavaliers, and were disposed to doubt whether the sullen preciseness of Praise God Barebone might not be preferable to the outrageous profaneness and licentiousness of the Buckinghams and Sedleys. Even immoral men, who were not utterly destitute of sense and public spirit, complained that the government treated the most serious matters as trifles, and made trifles its serious business. A King might be pardoned for amusing his leisure with wine, wit, and beauty. But it was intolerable that he should sink into a mere lounger and voluptuary, that the gravest affairs of state should be neglected, and that the public service should be starved and the finances deranged in order that harlots and parasites might grow rich.

A large body of Royalists joined in these complaints, and added many sharp reflections on the King's ingratitude. His whole revenue, indeed, would not have sufficed to reward

them all in proportion to their own consciousness of desert.
For to every distressed gentleman who had fought under
Rupert or Derby his own services seemed eminently meritorious, and his own sufferings eminently severe. Every one
had flattered himself that, whatever became of the rest, he
should be largely recompensed for all that he had lost during
the civil troubles, and that the restoration of the monarchy
would be followed by the restoration of his own dilapidated
fortunes. None of these expectants could restrain his indignation, when he found that he was as poor under the King
as he had been under the Rump or the Protector. The negligence and extravagance of the court excited the bitter
indignation of these loyal veterans. They justly said that
one half of what His Majesty squandered on concubines and
buffoons would gladden the hearts of hundreds of old Cavaliers who, after cutting down their oaks and melting their
plate to help his father, now wandered about in threadbare
suits, and did not know where to turn for a meal.

At the same time a sudden fall of rents took place. The
income of every landed proprietor was diminished by five
shillings in the pound. The cry of agricultural distress rose
from every shire in the kingdom; and for that distress the
government was, as usual, held accountable. The gentry, compelled to retrench their expenses for a period, saw with indignation the increasing splendour and profusion of Whitehall, and were immovably fixed in the belief that the money
which ought to have supported their households had, by some
inexplicable process, gone to the favourites of the King.

The minds of men were now in such a temper that every
public act excited discontent. Charles had taken to wife
Catharine Princess of Portugal. The marriage was generally
disliked; and the murmurs became loud when it appeared
that the King was not likely to have any legitimate posterity. Dunkirk, won by Oliver from Spain, was sold to Lewis
the Fourteenth, King of France. This bargain excited general indignation. Englishmen were already beginning to
observe with uneasiness the progress of the French power,
and to regard the House of Bourbon with the same feeling
with which their grandfathers had regarded the House of
Austria. Was it wise, men asked, at such a time, to make
any addition to the strength of a monarchy already too formidable? Dunkirk was, moreover, prized by the people, not
merely as a place of arms, and as a key to the Low Coun-

tries, but also as a trophy of English valour. It was to the subjects of Charles what Calais had been to an earlier generation, and what the rock of Gibraltar, so manfully defended, through disastrous and perilous years, against the fleets and armies of a mighty coalition, is to ourselves. The plea of economy might have had some weight, if it had been urged by an economical government. But it was notorious that the charges of Dunkirk fell far short of the sums which were wasted at court in vice and folly. It seemed insupportable that a sovereign, profuse beyond example in all that regarded his own pleasures, should be niggardly in all that regarded the safety and honour of the state.

The public discontent was heightened, when it was found that, while Dunkirk was abandoned on the plea of economy, the fortress of Tangier, which was part of the dower of Queen Catharine, was repaired and kept up at an enormous charge. That place was associated with no recollections gratifying to the national pride : it could in no way promote the national interests : it involved us in inglorious, unprofitable, and interminable wars with tribes of half savage Mussulmans ; and it was situated in a climate singularly unfavourable to the health and vigour of the English race.

War with the Dutch.

But the murmurs excited by these errors were faint, when compared with the clamours which soon broke forth. The government engaged in war with the United Provinces. The House of Commons readily voted sums unexampled in our history, sums exceeding those which had supported the fleets and armies of Cromwell at the time when his power was the terror of all the world. But such was the extravagance, dishonesty, and incapacity of those who had succeeded to his authority, that this liberality proved worse than useless. The sycophants of the court, ill qualified to contend against the great men who then directed the arms of Holland, against such a statesman as De Witt, and such a commander as De Ruyter, made fortunes rapidly, while the sailors mutinied from very hunger, while the dockyards were unguarded, while the ships were leaky and without rigging. It was at length determined to abandon all schemes of offensive war ; and it soon appeared that even a defensive war was a task too hard for that administration. The Dutch fleet sailed up the Thames, and burned the ships of war which lay at Chatham. It was said that, on the very day of that great humiliation, the King feasted with the ladies of his seraglio, and amused himself with hunting a moth about the supper room. Then, at length, tardy justice was done to the memory of Oliver. Everywhere men magnified his valour, genius, and patriotism. Everywhere it was remembered how, when he ruled, all foreign powers had trembled at the name of England, how the States General, now so haughty, had crouched at his feet, and how, when it was known that he was no more, Amsterdam was lighted up as for a great deliverance, and children ran along the canals, shouting for joy that the Devil was dead. Even Royalists exclaimed that the state could be saved only by calling the old soldiers of the Commonwealth to arms. Soon the capital began to feel the miseries of a blockade. Fuel was scarcely to be procured. Tilbury Fort, the place where Elizabeth had, with manly spirit, hurled foul scorn at Parma and Spain, was insulted by the invaders. The roar of foreign guns was heard, for the first and last time, by the citizens of London. In the Council it was seriously proposed that, if the enemy advanced, the Tower should be abandoned. Great multitudes of people assembled in the streets crying out that England was bought and sold. The houses and carriages of the ministers were attacked by the populace; and it seemed likely that the government would have to deal at once with an invasion and with an insurrection. The extreme danger, it is true, soon passed by. A treaty was concluded, very different from the treaties which Oliver had been in the habit of signing; and the nation was once more at peace, but was in a mood scarcely less fierce and sullen than in the days of shipmoney.

The discontent engendered by maladministration was heightened by calamities which the best administration could not have averted. While the ignominious war with Holland was raging, London suffered two great disasters, such as never, in so short a space of time, befel one city. A pestilence, surpassing in horror any that during three centuries had visited the island, swept away, in six months, more than a hundred thousand human beings. And scarcely had the dead cart ceased to go its rounds, when a fire, such as had not been known in Europe since the conflagration of Rome under Nero, laid in ruins the whole city, from the Tower to the Temple, and from the river to the purlieus of Smithfield.

Had there been a general election while the nation was smarting under so many disgraces and misfortunes, it is probable that the Roundheads would have regained ascen-

Opposition in the House of Commons.

dency in the state.   But the Parliament was still the Cavalier
Parliament, chosen in the transport of loyalty which had followed the Restoration.   Nevertheless it soon became evident
that no English legislature, however loyal, would now consent
to be merely what the legislature had been under the Tudors.
From the death of Elizabeth to the eve of the civil war, the
Puritans, who predominated in the representative body, had
been constantly, by a dexterous use of the power of the purse,
encroaching on the province of the executive government.
The gentlemen who, after the Restoration, filled the Lower
House, though they abhorred the Puritan name, were well
pleased to inherit the fruit of the Puritan policy.   They were
indeed most willing to employ the power which they possessed
in the state for the purpose of making their King mighty and
honoured, both at home and abroad : but with the power
itself they were resolved not to part.   The great English
revolution of the seventeenth century, that is to say, the
transfer of the supreme control of the executive administration from the crown to the House of Commons, was, through
the whole long existence of this Parliament, proceeding noiselessly, but rapidly and steadily.   Charles, kept poor by his
follies and vices, wanted money.   The Commons alone could
legally grant him money.   They could not be prevented from
putting their own price on their grants.   The price which
they put on their grants was this, that they should be allowed
to interfere with every one of the King's prerogatives, to
wring from him his consent to laws which he disliked, to
break up cabinets, to dictate the course of foreign policy, and
even to direct the administration of war.   To the royal office,
and the royal person, they loudly and sincerely professed the
Fall of strongest attachment.   But to Clarendon they owed no alle-
Clarendon. giance ; and they fell on him as furiously as their predecessors
had fallen on Strafford.   The minister's virtues and vices alike
contributed to his ruin.   He was the ostensible head of the
administration, and was therefore held responsible even for
those acts which he had strongly, but vainly, opposed in
Council.   He was regarded by the Puritans, and by all who
pitied them, as an implacable bigot, a second Laud, with
much more than Laud's understanding.   He had on all occasions maintained that the Act of Indemnity ought to be strictly
observed ; and this part of his conduct, though highly honourable to him, made him hateful to all those Royalists who
wished to repair their ruined fortunes by suing the Round-

Lord Clarendon

heads for damages and mesne profits. The Presbyterians of
Scotland attributed to him the downfall of their Church.
The Papists of Ireland attributed to him the loss of their
lands. As father of the Duchess of York, he had an obvious
motive for wishing that there might be a barren Queen; and
he was therefore suspected of having purposely recommended
one. The sale of Dunkirk was justly imputed to him. For the
war with Holland, he was, with less justice, held accountable.
His hot temper, his arrogant deportment, the indelicate
eagerness with which he grasped at riches, the ostentation
with which he squandered them, his picture gallery, filled
with masterpieces of Vandyke which had once been the property of ruined Cavaliers, his palace, which reared its long
and stately front right opposite to the humbler residence of
our Kings, drew on him much deserved, and some undeserved,
censure. When the Dutch fleet was in the Thames, it was
against the Chancellor that the rage of the populace was
chiefly directed. His windows were broken; the trees of his
garden were cut down; and a gibbet was set up before his
door. But nowhere was he more detested than in the House
of Commons. He was unable to perceive that the time was
fast approaching when that House, if it continued to exist at
all, must be supreme in the state, when the management of
that House would be the most important department of politics,
and when, without the help of men possessing the ear of that
House, it would be impossible to carry on the government.
He obstinately persisted in considering the Parliament as a
body in no respect differing from the Parliament which had
been sitting when, forty years before, he first began to study
law at the Temple. He did not wish to deprive the legislature
of those powers which were inherent in it by the old constitution of the realm: but the new development of those powers,
though a development natural, inevitable, and to be prevented
only by utterly destroying the powers themselves, disgusted
and alarmed him. Nothing would have induced him to put
the great seal to a writ for raising shipmoney, or to give his
voice in Council for committing a member of Parliament to
the Tower, on account of words spoken in debate: but, when
the Commons began to inquire in what manner the money
voted for the war had been wasted, and to examine into the
maladministration of the navy, he flamed with indignation.
Such inquiry, according to him, was out of their province.
He admitted that the House was a most loyal assembly, that

it had done good service to the crown, and that its intentions
were excellent. But, both in public and in the closet, he,
on every occasion, expressed his concern that gentlemen
so sincerely attached to monarchy should unadvisedly encroach on the prerogative of the monarch. Widely as they
differed in spirit from the members of the Long Parliament,
they yet, he said, imitated that Parliament in meddling with
matters which lay beyond the sphere of the Estates of the
realm, and which were subject to the authority of the crown
alone. The country, he maintained, would never be well
governed till the knights of shires and the burgesses were
content to be what their predecessors had been in the days of
Elizabeth. All the plans which men more observant than
himself of the signs of that time proposed, for the purpose of
maintaining a good understanding between the Court and
the Commons, he disdainfully rejected as crude projects, inconsistent with the old polity of England. Towards the young
orators, who were rising to distinction and authority in the
Lower House, his deportment was ungracious : and he succeeded in making them, with scarcely an exception, his deadly
enemies. Indeed one of his most serious faults was an inordinate contempt for youth : and this contempt was the more
unjustifiable, because his own experience in English politics
was by no means proportioned to his age. For so great a
part of his life had been passed abroad that he knew less of
that world in which he found himself on his return than many
who might have been his sons.

For these reasons he was disliked by the Commons. For
very different reasons he was equally disliked by the Court.
His morals as well as his politics were those of an earlier
generation. Even when he was a young law student, living
much with men of wit and pleasure, his natural gravity and
his religious principles had to a great extent preserved him
from the contagion of fashionable debauchery ; and he was by
no means likely, in advanced years and in declining health, to
turn libertine. On the vices of the young and gay he looked
with an aversion almost as bitter and contemptuous as that
which he felt for the theological errors of the sectaries. He
missed no opportunity of showing his scorn of the mimics,
revellers, and courtesans who crowded the palace ; and the
admonitions which he addressed to the King himself were
very sharp, and, what Charles disliked still more, very long.
Scarcely any voice was raised in favour of a minister loaded

with the double odium of faults which roused the fury of the people, and of virtues which annoyed and importuned the sovereign. Southampton was no more. Ormond performed the duties of friendship manfully and faithfully, but in vain. The Chancellor fell with a great ruin. The seal was taken from him: the Commons impeached him: his head was not safe: he fled from the country: an act was passed which doomed him to perpetual exile; and those who had assailed and undermined him began to struggle for the fragments of his power.

The sacrifice of Clarendon in some degree took off the edge of the public appetite for revenge. Yet was the anger excited by the profusion and negligence of the government, and by the miscarriages of the late war, by no means extinguished. The counsellors of Charles, with the fate of the Chancellor before their eyes, were anxious for their own safety. They accordingly advised their master to soothe the irritation which prevailed both in the Parliament and throughout the country, and for that end, to take a step which has no parallel in the history of the House of Stuart, and which was worthy of the prudence and magnanimity of Oliver.

We have now reached a point at which the history of the great English revolution begins to be complicated with the history of foreign politics. The power of Spain had, during many years, been declining. She still, it is true, held in Europe the Milanese and the two Sicilies, Belgium, and Franche Comté. In America her dominions still spread, on both sides of the equator, far beyond the limits of the torrid zone. But this great body had been smitten with palsy, and was not only incapable of giving molestation to other states, but could not, without assistance, repel aggression. France was now, beyond all doubt, the greatest power in Europe. Her resources have, since those days, absolutely increased, but have not increased so fast as the resources of England. It must also be remembered that, a hundred and eighty years ago, the empire of Russia, now a monarchy of the first class, was as entirely out of the system of European politics as Abyssinia or Siam, that the House of Brandenburg was then hardly more powerful than the House of Saxony, and that the republic of the United States had not then begun to exist. The weight of France, therefore, though still very considerable, has relatively diminished. Her territory was not in the days of Lewis the Fourteenth quite so extensive as at present: but it was large, compact, fertile, well placed both for attack

State of European politics, and ascendency of France

and for defence, situated in a happy climate, and inhabited by a brave, active, and ingenious people. The state implicitly obeyed the direction of a single mind. The great fiefs which, three hundred years before, had been, in all but name, independent principalities, had been annexed to the crown. Only a few old men could remember the last meeting of the States General. The resistance which the Huguenots, the nobles, and the parliaments had offered to the kingly power, had been put down by the two great Cardinals who had ruled the nation during forty years. The government was now a despotism, but, at least in its dealings with the upper classes, a mild and generous despotism, tempered by courteous manners and chivalrous sentiments. The means at the disposal of the sovereign were, for that age, truly formidable. His revenue, raised, it is true, by a severe and unequal taxation which pressed heavily on the cultivators of the soil, far exceeded that of any other potentate. His army, excellently disciplined, and commanded by the greatest generals then living, already consisted of more than a hundred and twenty thousand men. Such an array of regular troops had not been seen in Europe since the downfall of the Roman empire. Of maritime powers France was not the first. But, though she had rivals on the sea, she had not yet a superior. Such was her strength during the last forty years of the seventeenth century, that no enemy could singly withstand her, and that two great coalitions, in which half Christendom was united against her, failed of success.

Character of Lewis XIV.

The personal qualities of the French King added to the respect inspired by the power and importance of his kingdom. No sovereign has ever represented the majesty of a great state with more dignity and grace. He was his own prime minister, and performed the duties of a prime minister with an ability and industry which could not be reasonably expected from one who had in infancy succeeded to a crown, and who had been surrounded by flatterers before he could speak. He had shown, in an eminent degree, two talents invaluable to a prince, the talent of choosing his servants well, and the talent of appropriating to himself the chief part of the credit of their acts. In his dealings with foreign powers he had some generosity, but no justice. To unhappy allies who threw themselves at his feet, and had no hope but in his compassion, he extended his protection with a romantic disinterestedness, which seemed better suited to a knight errant than to a statesman. But he broke through the most sacred ties of public faith without scruple or shame, whenever they interfered with his interest, or with what he called his glory. His perfidy and violence, however, excited less enmity than the insolence with which he constantly reminded his neighbours of his own greatness and of their littleness. He did not at this time profess the austere devotion which, at a later period, gave to his court the aspect of a monastery. On the contrary, he was as licentious, though by no means as frivolous and indolent, as his brother of England. But he was a sincere Roman Catholic; and both his conscience and his vanity impelled him to use his power for the defence and propagation of the true faith, after the example of his renowned predecessors, Clovis, Charlemagne, and Saint Lewis.

Our ancestors naturally looked with serious alarm on the growing power of France. This feeling, in itself perfectly reasonable, was mingled with other feelings less praiseworthy. France was our old enemy. It was against France that the most glorious battles recorded in our annals had been fought. The conquest of France had been twice effected by the Plantagenets. The loss of France had been long remembered as a great national disaster. The title of King of France was still borne by our sovereigns. The lilies of France still appeared, mingled with our own lions, on the shield of the House of Stuart. In the sixteenth century the dread inspired by Spain had suspended the animosity of which France had anciently been the object. But the dread inspired by Spain had given place to contemptuous compassion; and France was again regarded as our national foe. The sale of Dunkirk to France had been the most generally unpopular act of the restored King. Attachment to France had been prominent among the crimes imputed by the Commons to Clarendon. Even in trifles the public feeling showed itself. When a brawl took place in the streets of Westminster between the retinues of the French and Spanish embassies, the populace, though forcibly prevented from interfering, had given unequivocal proofs that the old antipathy to France was not extinct.

France and Spain were now engaged in a more serious contest. One of the chief objects of the policy of Lewis throughout his life was to extend his dominions towards the Rhine. For this end he had engaged in war with Spain, and he was now in the full career of conquest. The United Provinces saw with anxiety the progress of his arms. That renowned federation had reached the height of power, prosperity, and glory. The Batavian territory, conquered from the waves and defended against them by human art, was in extent little superior to the principality of Wales. But all that narrow space was a busy and populous hive, in which new wealth was every day created, and in which vast masses of old wealth were hoarded. The aspect of Holland, the rich cultivation, the innumerable canals, the ever whirling mills, the endless fleets of barges, the quick succession of great towns, the ports bristling with thousands of masts, the large and stately mansions, the trim villas, the richly furnished apartments, the picture galleries, the summer houses, the tulip beds, produced on English travellers in that age an effect similar to the effect which the first sight of England now produces on a Norwegian or a Canadian. The States General had been compelled to humble themselves before Cromwell. But after the Restoration they had taken their revenge, had waged war with success against Charles, and had concluded peace on honourable terms. Rich, however, as the Republic was, and highly considered in Europe, she was no match for the power of Lewis. She apprehended, not without good cause, that his kingdom might soon be extended to her frontiers; and she might well dread the immediate vicinity of a monarch so great, so ambitious, and so unscrupulous. Yet it was not easy to devise any expedient which might avert the danger. The Dutch alone could not turn the scale against France. On the side of the Rhine no help was to be expected. Several German princes had been gained by Lewis; and the Emperor himself was embarrassed by the discontents of Hungary. England was separated from the United Provinces by the recollection of cruel injuries recently inflicted and endured; and her policy had, since the Restoration, been so devoid of wisdom and spirit, that it was scarcely possible to expect from her any valuable assistance.

But the fate of Clarendon and the growing ill humour of the Parliament determined the advisers of Charles to adopt on a sudden a policy which amazed and delighted the nation. The Triple Alliance. The English resident at Brussels, Sir William Temple, one of the most expert diplomatists and most pleasing writers of that age, had already represented to his court that it was both desirable and practicable to enter into engagements with the States General for the purpose of checking the progress of France. For a time his suggestions had been slighted; but it was now thought expedient to act on them. He was commissioned to negotiate with the States General. He proceeded to the Hague, and soon came to an understanding with John De Witt, then the chief minister of Holland. Sweden, small as her resources were, had, forty years before, been raised by the genius of Gustavus Adolphus to a high rank among European powers, and had not yet descended to her natural position. She was induced to join on this occasion with England and the States. Thus was formed that coalition known as the Triple Alliance. Lewis showed signs of vexation and resentment, but did not think it politic to draw on himself the hostility of such a confederacy in addition to that of Spain. He consented, therefore to relinquish a large part of the territory which his armies had occupied. Peace was restored to Europe; and the English government, lately an object of general contempt, was, during a few months, regarded by foreign powers with respect scarcely less than that which the Protector had inspired.

At home the Triple Alliance was popular in the highest degree. It gratified alike national animosity and national pride. It put a limit to the encroachments of a powerful and ambitious neighbour. It bound the leading Protestant states together in close union. Cavaliers and Roundheads rejoiced in common: but the joy of the Roundhead was even greater than that of the Cavalier. For England had now allied herself strictly with a country republican in government and Presbyterian in religion, against a country ruled by an arbitrary prince and attached to the Roman Catholic Church. The House of Commons loudly applauded the treaty; and some uncourtly grumblers described it as the only good thing that had been done since the King came in.

The King, however, cared little for the approbation of his Parliament or of his people. The Triple Alliance he regarded merely as a temporary expedient for quieting discontents which had seemed likely to become serious. The independence, the safety, the dignity of the nation over which he presided were nothing to him. He had begun to find constitutional restraints galling. Already had been formed in the Parliament a strong connection known by the name of the Country

The Country Party.

Party. That party included all the public men who leaned towards Puritanism and Republicanism, and many who, though attached to the Church and to hereditary monarchy, had been driven into opposition by dread of Popery, by dread of France, and by disgust at the extravagance, dissoluteness, and faithlessness of the court. The power of this band of politicians was constantly growing. Every year some of those members who had been returned to Parliament during the loyal excitement of 1661 had dropped off; and the vacant seats had generally been filled by persons less tractable. Charles did not think himself a King while an assembly of subjects could call for his accounts before paying his debts, and could insist on knowing which of his mistresses or boon companions had intercepted the money destined for the equipping and manning of the fleet. Though not very studious of fame, he was galled by the taunts which were sometimes uttered in the discussions of the Commons, and on one occasion attempted to restrain the freedom of speech by disgraceful means. Sir John Coventry, a country gentleman, had, in debate, sneered at the profligacy of the court. In any former reign he would probably have been called before the Privy Council and committed to the Tower. A different course was now taken. A gang of bullies was secretly sent to slit the nose of the offender. This ignoble revenge, instead of quelling the spirit of opposition, raised such a tempest that the King was compelled to submit to the cruel humiliation of passing an act which attainted the instruments of his revenge, and which took from him the power of pardoning them.

But, impatient as he was of constitutional restraints, how was he to emancipate himself from them? He could make himself despotic only by the help of a great standing army; and such an army was not in existence. His revenues did indeed enable him to keep up some regular troops: but those troops, though numerous enough to excite great jealousy and apprehension in the House of Commons and in the country, were scarcely numerous enough to protect Whitehall and the Tower against a rising of the mob of London. Such risings were, indeed, to be dreaded; for it was calculated that in the capital and its suburbs dwelt not less than twenty thousand of Oliver's old soldiers.

Connection between Charles II. and France.

Since the King was bent on emancipating himself from the control of Parliament, and since, in such an enterprise, he could not hope for effectual aid at home, it followed that he must look for aid abroad. The power and wealth of the King of France might be equal to the arduous task of establishing absolute monarchy in England. Such an ally would undoubtedly expect substantial proofs of gratitude for such a service. Charles must descend to the rank of a great vassal, and must make peace and war according to the directions of the government which protected him. His relation to Lewis would closely resemble that in which the Rajah of Nagpore and the King of Oude now stand to the British Government. Those princes are bound to aid the East India Company in all hostilities, defensive and offensive, and to have no diplomatic relations but such as the East India Company shall sanction. The Company in return guarantees them against insurrection. As long as they faithfully discharge their obligations to the paramount power, they are permitted to dispose of large revenues, to fill their palaces with beautiful women, to besot themselves in the company of their favourite revellers, and to oppress with impunity any subject who may incur their displeasure.* Such a life would be insupportable to a man of high spirit and of powerful understanding. But to Charles, sensual, indolent, unequal to any strong intellectual exertion, and destitute alike of all patriotism and of all sense of personal dignity, the prospect had nothing unpleasing.

That the Duke of York should have concurred in the design of degrading that crown which it was probable that he would himself one day wear may seem more extraordinary. For his nature was haughty and imperious; and, indeed, he continued to the very last to show, by occasional starts and struggles, his impatience of the French yoke. But he was almost as much debased by superstition as his brother by indolence and vice. James was now a Roman Catholic. Religious bigotry had become the dominant sentiment of his narrow and stubborn mind, and had so mingled itself with his love of rule, that the two passions could hardly be distinguished from each other. It seemed highly improbable that, without foreign aid, he would be able to obtain ascendency, or even toleration, for his own faith: and he was in a temper to see nothing humiliating in any step which might promote the interests of the true Church.

* I am happy to say, that, since this passage was written, the territories both of the Rajah of Nagpore and of the King of Oude have been added to the British dominions. (1857.)

A negotiation was opened which lasted during several months. The chief agent between the English and French courts was the beautiful, graceful, and intelligent Henrietta, Duchess of Orleans, sister of Charles, sister in law of Lewis, and a favourite with both. The King of England offered to declare himself a Roman Catholic, to dissolve the Triple Alliance, and to join with France against Holland, if France would engage to lend him such military and pecuniary aid as might make him independent of his Parliament. Lewis at first affected to receive these propositions coolly, and at length agreed to them with the air of a man who is conferring a great favour : but in truth, the course which he had resolved to take was one by which he might gain and could not lose.

Views of Lewis with respect to England.

It seems certain that he never seriously thought of establishing despotism and Popery in England by force of arms. He must have been aware that such an enterprise would be in the highest degree arduous and hazardous, that it would task to the utmost all the energies of France during many years, and that it would be altogether incompatible with more promising schemes of aggrandisement, which were dear to his heart. He would indeed willingly have acquired the merit and the glory of doing a great service on reasonable terms to the Church of which he was a member. But he was little disposed to imitate his ancestors who, in the twelfth and thirteenth centuries, had led the flower of French chivalry to die in Syria and Egypt: and he well knew that a crusade against Protestantism in Great Britain would not be less perilous than the expeditions in which the armies of Lewis the Seventh and of Lewis the Ninth had perished. He had no motive for wishing the Stuarts to be absolute. He did not regard the English constitution with feelings at all resembling those which have in later times induced princes to make war on the free institutions of neighbouring nations. At present a great party zealous for popular government has ramifications in every civilised country. Any important advantage gained anywhere by that party is almost certain to be the signal for general commotion. It is not wonderful that governments threatened by a common danger should combine for the purpose of mutual insurance. But in the seventeenth century no such danger existed. Between the public mind of England and the public mind of France, there was a great gulph. Our institutions and our factions were as little understood at Paris as at Constantinople. It may be doubted whether any one of the forty members of the French Academy had an English volume in his library, or knew Shakspeare, Jonson, or Spenser, even by name. A few Huguenots, who had inherited the mutinous spirit of their ancestors, might perhaps have a fellow feeling with their brethren in the faith, the English Roundheads : but the Huguenots had ceased to be formidable. The French, as a people, attached to the Church of Rome, and proud of the greatness of their King and of their own loyalty, looked on our struggles against Popery and arbitrary power, not only without admiration or sympathy, but with strong disapprobation and disgust. It would therefore be a great error to ascribe the conduct of Lewis to apprehensions at all resembling those which, in our age, induced the Holy Alliance to interfere in the internal troubles of Naples and Spain.

Nevertheless, the propositions made by the court of Whitehall were most welcome to him. He already meditated gigantic designs, which were destined to keep Europe in constant fermentation during more than forty years. He wished to humble the United Provinces, and to annex Belgium, Franche Comté, and Loraine to his dominions. Nor was this all. The King of Spain was a sickly child. It was likely that he would die without issue. His eldest sister was Queen of France. A day would almost certainly come, and might come very soon, when the House of Bourbon might lay claim to that vast empire on which the sun never set. The union of two great monarchies under one head would doubtless be opposed by a continental coalition. But for any continental coalition France singlehanded was a match. England could turn the scale. On the course which, in such a crisis, England might pursue, the destinies of the world would depend; and it was notorious that the English Parliament and nation were strongly attached to the policy which had dictated the Triple Alliance. Nothing, therefore, could be more gratifying to Lewis than to learn that the princes of the House of Stuart needed his help, and were willing to purchase that help by unbounded subserviency. He determined to profit by the opportunity, and laid down for himself a plan to which, without deviation, he adhered, till the Revolution of 1688 disconcerted all his politics. He professed himself desirous to promote the designs of the English court. He promised large aid. He from time to time doled out such aid as might serve to keep hope alive, and as he could without risk or inconvenience spare. In this way, at an expense very much less than that which he incurred in building and decorating Versailles or Marli, he succeeded in making England, during nearly twenty years, almost as insignificant a member of the political system of Europe as the republic of San Marino.

His object was not to destroy our constitution, but to keep the various elements of which it was composed in a perpetual state of conflict, and to set irreconcilable enmity between those who had the power of the purse and those who had the power of the sword. With this view he bribed and stimulated both parties in turn, pensioned at once the ministers of the crown and the chiefs of the opposition, encouraged the court to withstand the seditious encroachments of the Parliament, and conveyed to the Parliament intimations of the arbitrary designs of the court.

One of the devices to which he resorted for the purpose of obtaining an ascendency in the English counsels deserves especial notice. Charles, though incapable of love in the highest sense of the word, was the slave of any woman whose person excited his desires, and whose airs and prattle amused his leisure. Indeed a husband would be justly derided who should bear from a wife of exalted rank and spotless virtue half the insolence which the King of England bore from concubines who, while they owed everything to his bounty, caressed his courtiers almost before his face. He had patiently endured the termagant passions of Barbara Palmer and the pert vivacity of Eleanor Gwynn. Lewis thought that the most useful envoy who could be sent to London, would be a handsome, licentious, and crafty Frenchwoman. Such a woman was Louisa, a lady of the House of Querouaille, whom our rude ancestors called Madam Carwell. She was soon triumphant over all her rivals, was created Duchess of Portsmouth, was loaded with wealth, and obtained a dominion which ended only with the life of Charles.

Treaty of Dover.

The most important conditions of the alliance between the crowns were digested into a secret treaty which was signed at Dover in May 1670, just ten years after the day on which Charles had landed at that very port amidst the acclamations and joyful tears of a too confiding people.

By this treaty Charles bound himself to make public profession of the Roman Catholic religion, to join his arms to those of Lewis for the purpose of destroying the power of the

United Provinces, and to employ the whole strength of England, by land and sea, in support of the rights of the House of Bourbon to the vast monarchy of Spain. Lewis, on the other hand, engaged to pay a large subsidy, and promised that, if any insurrection should break out in England, he would send an army at his own charge to support his ally.

This compact was made with gloomy auspices. Six weeks after it had been signed and sealed, the charming princess, whose influence over her brother and brother in law had been so pernicious to her country, was no more. Her death gave rise to horrible suspicions which, for a moment, seemed likely to interrupt the newly formed friendship between the Houses of Stuart and Bourbon : but in a short time fresh assurances of undiminished good will were exchanged betwen the confederates.

The Duke of York, too dull to apprehend danger, or too fanatical to care about it, was impatient to see the article touching the Roman Catholic religion carried into immediate execution : but Lewis had the wisdom to perceive that, if this course were taken, there would be such an explosion in England as would probably frustrate those parts of the plan which he had most at heart. It was therefore determined that Charles should still call himself a Protestant, and should still, at high festivals, receive the sacrament according to the ritual of the Church of England. His more scrupulous brother ceased to appear in the royal chapel.

About this time died the Duchess of York, daughter of the banished Earl of Clarendon. She had been, during some years, a concealed Roman Catholic. She left two daughters, Mary and Anne, afterwards successively Queens of Great Britain. They were bred Protestants by the positive command of the King, who knew that it would be vain for him to profess himself a member of the Church of England, if children who seemed likely to inherit his throne were, by his permission, brought up as members of the Church of Rome.

The principal servants of the crown at this time were men whose names have justly acquired an unenviable notoriety. We must take heed, however, that we do not load their memory with infamy which of right belongs to their master. For the treaty of Dover the King himself is chiefly answerable. He held conferences on it with the French agents : he wrote many letters concerning it with his own hand : he was the person who first suggested the most disgraceful articles which it contained; and he carefully concealed some of those articles from the majority of his Cabinet.

Nature of the English Cabinet. Few things in our history are more curious than the origin and growth of the power now possessed by the Cabinet. From an early period the Kings of England had been assisted by a Privy Council to which the law assigned many important functions and duties. During several centuries this body deliberated on the gravest and most delicate affairs. But by degrees its character changed. It became too large for despatch and secrecy. The rank of Privy Councillor was often bestowed as an honorary distinction on persons to whom nothing was confided, and whose opinion was never asked. The sovereign, on the most important occasions, resorted for advice to a small knot of leading ministers. The advantages and disadvantages of this course were early pointed out by Bacon, with his usual judgment and sagacity: but it was not till after the Restoration that the interior council began to attract general notice. During many years old fashioned politicians continued to regard the Cabinet as an unconstitutional and dangerous board. Nevertheless, it constantly became more and more important. It at length drew to itself the chief executive power, and has now been regarded, during several generations, as an essential part of our polity. Yet, strange to say, it still continues to be altogether unknown to the law: the names of the noblemen and gentlemen who compose it are never officially announced to the public: no record is kept of its meetings and resolutions; nor has its existence ever been recognised by any Act of Parliament.

The Cabal. During some years the word Cabal was popularly used as synonymous with Cabinet. But it happened by a whimsical coincidence that, in 1671, the Cabinet consisted of five persons the initial letters of whose names made up the word Cabal; Clifford, Arlington, Buckingham, Ashley, and Lauderdale. These ministers were therefore emphatically called the Cabal; and they soon made that appellation so infamous that it has never since their time been used except as a term of reproach.

Sir Thomas Clifford was a Commissioner of the Treasury, and had greatly distinguished himself in the House of Commons. Of the members of the Cabal he was the most respectable. For, with a fiery and imperious temper, he had a strong though a lamentably perverted sense of duty and honour.

Henry Bennet, Lord Arlington, then Secretary of State, had, since he came to manhood, resided principally on the Continent, and had learned that cosmopolitan indifference to constitutions and religions which is often observable in persons whose life has been passed in vagrant diplomacy. If there was any form of government which he liked, it was that of France. If there was any Church for which he felt a preference, it was that of Rome. He had some talent for conversation, and some talent also for transacting the ordinary business of office. He had learned, during a life passed in travelling and negotiating, the art of accommodating his language and deportment to the society in which he found himself. His vivacity in the closet amused the King: his gravity in debates and conferences imposed on the public; and he had succeeded in attaching to himself, partly by services and partly by hopes, a considerable number of personal retainers.

Buckingham, Ashley, and Lauderdale were men in whom the immorality which was epidemic among the politicians of that age appeared in its most malignant type, but variously modified by great diversities of temper and understanding. Buckingham was a sated man of pleasure, who had turned to ambition as to a pastime. As he had tried to amuse himself with architecture and music, with writing farces and with seeking for the philosopher's stone, so he now tried to amuse himself with a secret negotiation and a Dutch war. He had already, rather from fickleness and love of novelty than from any deep design, been faithless to every party. At one time he had ranked among the Cavaliers. At another time warrants had been out against him for maintaining a treasonable correspondence with the remains of the Republican party in the city. He was now again a courtier, and was eager to win the favour of the King by services from which the most illustrious of those who had fought and suffered for the royal house would have recoiled with horror.

Ashley, with a far stronger head, and with a far fiercer and more earnest ambition, had been equally versatile. But Ashley's versatility was the effect, not of levity, but of deliberate selfishness. He had served and betrayed a succession of governments. But he had timed all his treacheries so well that, through all revolutions, his fortunes had constantly been rising. The multitude, struck with admiration by a prosperity which, while everything else was constantly changing, remained unchangeable, attributed to him a prescience almost miraculous, and likened him to the Hebrew statesman of whom it is written that his counsel was as if a man had inquired of the oracle of God.

Lauderdale, loud and coarse both in mirth and anger, was perhaps, under the outward show of boisterous frankness, the most dishonest man in the whole Cabal. He had made himself conspicuous among the Scotch insurgents of 1638 by his zeal for the Covenant. He was accused of having been deeply concerned in the sale of Charles the First to the English Parliament, and was therefore, in the estimation of good Cavaliers, a traitor, if possible, of a worse description than those who had sate in the High Court of Justice. He often talked with noisy jocularity of the days when he was a canter and a rebel. He was now the chief instrument employed by the court in the work of forcing episcopacy on his reluctant countrymen; nor did he in that cause shrink from the unsparing use of the sword, the halter, and the boot. Yet those who knew him knew that thirty years had made no change in his real sentiments, that he still hated the memory of Charles the First, and that he still preferred the Presbyterian form of church government to every other.

Unscrupulous as Buckingham, Ashley, and Lauderdale were, it was not thought safe to intrust to them the King's intention of declaring himself a Roman Catholic. A false treaty, in which the article concerning religion was omitted, was shown to them. The names and seals of Clifford and Arlington are affixed to the genuine treaty. Both these statesmen had a partiality for the old Church, a partiality which the brave and vehement Clifford in no long time manfully avowed, but which the colder and meaner Arlington concealed, till the near approach of death scared him into sincerity. The three other cabinet ministers, however, were not men to be easily kept in the dark, and probably suspected more than was distinctly avowed to them. They were certainly privy to all the political engagements contracted with France, and were not ashamed to receive large gratifications from Lewis.

The first object of Charles was to obtain from the Commons supplies which might be employed in executing the secret treaty. The Cabal, holding power at a time when our government was in a state of transition, united in itself

two different kinds of vices belonging to two different ages
and to two different systems.   As those five evil counsellors
were among the last English statesmen who seriously
thought of destroying the Parliament, so they were the
first English statesmen who attempted extensively to corrupt it.   We find in their policy at once the latest trace
of the Thorough of Strafford, and the earliest trace of
that methodical bribery which was afterwards practised by
Walpole.   They soon perceived, however, that, though the
House of Commons was chiefly composed of Cavaliers, and
though places and French gold had been lavished on the
members, there was no chance that even the least odious
parts of the scheme arranged at Dover would be supported
by a majority.   It was necessary to have recourse to fraud.
The King accordingly professed great zeal for the principles
of the Triple Alliance, and pretended that, in order to hold
the ambition of France in check, it would be necessary to
augment the fleet.   The Commons fell into the snare, and
voted a grant of eight hundred thousand pounds.   The
Parliament was instantly prorogued; and the court, thus
emancipated from control, proceeded to the execution of the
great design.

The financial difficulties however were serious.   A war
with Holland could be carried on only at enormous cost.
The ordinary revenue was not more than sufficient to support the government in time of peace.   The eight hundred
thousand pounds out of which the Commons had just been
tricked would not defray the naval and military charge of a
single year of hostilities.   After the terrible lesson given by
the Long Parliament, even the Cabal did not venture to
recommend benevolences or shipmoney.   In this perplexity
Ashley and Clifford proposed a flagitious breach of public
faith.   The goldsmiths of London were then not only dealers
in the precious metals, but also bankers, and were in the
habit of advancing large sums of money to the government.
In return for these advances they received assignments on
the revenue, and were repaid with interest as the taxes came
in.   About thirteen hundred thousand pounds had been in
this way intrusted to the honour of the state.   On a sudden it was announced that it was not convenient to pay
the principal, and that the lenders must content themselves
with interest.   They were consequently unable to meet their
own engagements.   The Exchange was in an uproar : several

[margin: Shutting of the Ex-chequer.]

great mercantile houses broke; and dismay and distress spread through all society. Meanwhile rapid strides were made towards despotism. Proclamations, dispensing with Acts of Parliament, or enjoining what only Parliament could lawfully enjoin, appeared in rapid succession. Of these edicts the most important was the Declaration of Indulgence. By this instrument the penal laws against Roman Catholics were set aside; and, that the real object of the measure might not be perceived, the laws against Protestant Nonconformists were also suspended.

War with the United Provinces, and their extreme danger.

A few days after the appearance of the Declaration of Indulgence, war was proclaimed against the United Provinces. By sea the Dutch maintained the struggle with honour; but on land they were at first borne down by irresistible force. A great French army passed the Rhine. Fortress after fortress opened its gates. Three of the seven provinces of the federation were occupied by the invaders. The fires of the hostile camp were seen from the top of the Stadthouse of Amsterdam. The Republic, thus fiercely assailed from without, was torn at the same time by internal dissensions. The government was in the hands of a close oligarchy of powerful burghers. There were numerous selfelected Town Councils, each of which exercised, within its own sphere, many of the rights of sovereignty. These councils sent delegates to the Provincial States, and the Provincial States again sent delegates to the States General. A hereditary first magistrate was no essential part of this polity. Nevertheless one family, singularly fertile of great men, had gradually obtained a large and somewhat indefinite authority. William, first of the name, Prince of Orange Nassau, and Stadtholder of Holland, had headed the memorable insurrection against Spain. His son Maurice had been Captain General and first minister of the States, had, by eminent abilities and public services, and by some treacherous and cruel actions, raised himself to almost kingly power, and had bequeathed a great part of that power to his family. The influence of the Stadtholders was an object of extreme jealousy to the municipal oligarchy. But the army, and that great body of citizens which was excluded from all share in the government, looked on the Burgomasters and Deputies with a dislike resembling the dislike with which the legions and the common people of Rome regarded the Senate, and were as zealous for the House of Orange as the legions and the common people of

Rome for the House of Cæsar. The Stadtholder commanded the forces of the commonwealth, disposed of all military commands, had a large share of the civil patronage, and was surrounded by pomp almost regal.

Prince William the Second had been strongly opposed by the oligarchical party. His life had terminated in the year 1650, amidst great civil troubles. He died childless: the adherents of his house were left for a short time without a head; and the powers which he had exercised were divided among the Town Councils, the Provincial States, and the States General.

But, a few days after William's death, his widow, Mary, daughter of Charles the first, King of Great Britain, gave birth to a son, destined to raise the glory and authority of the House of Nassau to the highest point, to save the United Provinces from slavery, to curb the power of France, and to establish the English constitution on a lasting foundation.

This Prince, named William Henry, was from his birth an object of serious apprehension to the party now supreme in Holland, and of loyal attachment to the old friends of his line. He enjoyed high consideration as the possessor of a splendid fortune, as the chief of one of the most illustrious houses in Europe, as a Magnate of the German empire, as a prince of the blood royal of England, and, above all, as the descendant of the founders of Batavian liberty. But the high office which had once been considered as hereditary in his family remained in abeyance; and the intention of the aristocratical party was that there should never be another Stadtholder. The want of a first magistrate was, to a great extent, supplied by the Grand Pensionary of the Province of Holland, John de Witt, whose abilities, firmness, and integrity had raised him to unrivalled authority in the councils of the municipal oligarchy. *William, Prince of Orange.*

The French invasion produced a complete change. The suffering and terrified people raged fiercely against the government. In their madness they attacked the bravest captains and the ablest statesmen of the distressed commonwealth. De Ruyter was insulted by the rabble. De Witt was torn in pieces before the gate of the palace of the States General at the Hague. The Prince of Orange, who had no share in the guilt of the murder, but who, on this occasion, as on another lamentable occasion twenty years later, extended to crimes perpetrated in his cause an indulgence which has left a stain on his glory, became chief of the government without a rival. Young as he was, his ardent and unconquerable spirit, though disguised by a cold and sullen manner, soon roused the courage of his dismayed countrymen. It was in vain that both his uncle and the French King attempted by splendid offers to seduce him from the cause of the Republic. To the States General he spoke a high and inspiriting language. He even ventured to suggest a scheme which has an aspect of antique heroism, and which, if it had been accomplished, would have been the noblest subject for epic song that is to be found in the whole compass of modern history. He told the deputies that, even if their natal soil and the marvels with which human industry had covered it were buried under the ocean, all was not lost. The Hollanders might survive Holland. Liberty and pure religion, driven by tyrants and bigots from Europe, might take refuge in the farthest isles of Asia. The shipping in the ports of the republic would suffice to carry two hundred thousand emigrants to the Indian Archipelago. There the Dutch commonwealth might commence a new and more glorious existence, and might rear, under the Southern Cross, amidst the sugar canes and nutmeg trees, the Exchange of a wealthier Amsterdam, and the schools of a more learned Leyden. The national spirit swelled and rose high. The terms offered by the allies were firmly rejected. The dykes were opened. The whole country was turned into one great lake, from which the cities, with their ramparts and steeples, rose like islands. The invaders were forced to save themselves from destruction by a precipitate retreat. Lewis, who, though he sometimes thought it necessary to appear at the head of his troops, greatly preferred a palace to a camp, had already returned to enjoy the adulation of poets and the smiles of ladies in the newly planted alleys of Versailles.

And now the tide turned fast. The event of the maritime war had been doubtful; by land the United Provinces had obtained a respite; and a respite, though short, was of infinite importance. Alarmed by the vast designs of Lewis, both the branches of the great House of Austria sprang to arms. Spain and Holland, divided by the memory of ancient wrongs and humiliations, were reconciled by the nearness of the common danger. From every part of Germany troops poured towards the Rhine. The English government had already expended all the funds which had been obtained by pillaging the public creditor. No loan could be expected from the City. An attempt to raise taxes by the royal authority would have at once produced a rebellion; and Lewis, who had now to maintain a contest against half Europe, was in no condition to furnish the means of coercing the people of England. It was necessary to convoke the Parliament.

In the spring of 1673, therefore, the Houses reassembled after a recess of near two years. Clifford, now a peer and Lord Treasurer, and Ashley, now Earl of Shaftesbury and Lord Chancellor, were the persons on whom the King principally relied as Parliamentary managers. The Country Party instantly began to attack the policy of the Cabal. The attack was made, not in the way of storm, but by slow and scientific approaches. The Commons at first held out hopes that they would give support to the king's foreign policy, but insisted that he should purchase that support by abandoning his whole system of domestic policy. Their chief object was to obtain the revocation of the Declaration of Indulgence. Of all the many unpopular steps taken by the government the most unpopular was the publishing of this Declaration. The most opposite sentiments had been shocked by an act so liberal, done in a manner so despotic. All the enemies of religious freedom, and all the friends of civil freedom, found themselves on the same side; and these two classes made up nineteen twentieths of the nation. The zealous churchman exclaimed against the favour which had been shown both to the Papist and to the Puritan. The Puritan, though he might rejoice in the suspension of the persecution by which he had been harassed, felt little gratitude for a toleration which he was to share with Antichrist. And all Englishmen who valued liberty and law, saw with uneasiness the deep inroad which the prerogative had made into the province of the legislature.

It must in candour be admitted that the constitutional question was then not quite free from obscurity. Our ancient Kings had undoubtedly claimed and exercised the right of suspending the operation of penal laws. The tribunals had recognised that right. Parliaments had suffered it to pass unchallenged. That some such right was inherent in the crown, few even of the Country Party ventured, in the face of precedent and authority, to deny. Yet it was clear that, if this prerogative were without limit, the English government could scarcely be distinguished from a pure despotism.

That there was a limit was fully admitted by the King and
his ministers.   Whether the Declaration of Indulgence lay
within or without the limit was the question ; and neither
party could succeed in tracing any line which would bear
examination.   Some opponents of the government complained
that the Declaration suspended not less than forty statutes.
But why not forty as well as one ?   There was an orator who
gave it as his opinion that the King might constitutionally
dispense with bad laws, but not with good laws.   The absurdity of such a distinction it is needless to expose.   The doctrine
which seems to have been generally received in the House of
Commons was, that the dispensing power was confined to
secular matters, and did not extend to laws enacted for the
security of the established religion.   Yet, as the King was
supreme head of the Church, it should seem that, if he possessed the dispensing power at all, he might well possess that
power where the Church was concerned.   When the courtiers
on the other side attempted to point out the bounds of this
prerogative, they were not more successful than the opposition had been.

The truth is that the dispensing power was a great anomaly
in politics.   It was utterly inconsistent in theory with the
principles of mixed government : but it had grown up in
times when people troubled themselves little about theories.*
It had not been very grossly abused in practice.   It had
therefore been tolerated, and had gradually acquired a kind
of prescription.   At length it was employed, after a long
interval, in an enlightened age, and at an important conjuncture, to an extent never before known, and for a purpose
generally abhorred.   It was instantly subjected to a severe
scrutiny.   Men did not, indeed, at first, venture to pronounce
it altogether unconstitutional.   But they began to perceive
that it was at direct variance with the spirit of the constitution, and would, if left unchecked, turn the English government from a limited into an absolute monarchy.

It is can-   Under the influence of such apprehensions, the Commons
celled, and
the Test   denied the King's right to dispense, not indeed with all
Act passed.   penal statutes, but with penal statutes in matters ecclesiastical, and gave him plainly to understand that, unless he
renounced that right, they would grant no supply for the

* The most sensible thing said in the   ancestors never did draw a line to cir-
House of Commons, on this subject,   cumscribe prerogative and liberty."
came from Sir William Coventry :—" Our

Dutch war. He, for a moment, showed some inclination to put everything to hazard: but he was strongly advised by Lewis to submit to necessity, and to wait for better times, when the French armies, now employed in an arduous struggle on the Continent, might be available for the purpose of suppressing discontent in England. In the Cabal itself the signs of disunion and treachery began to appear. Shaftesbury, with his proverbial sagacity, saw that a violent reaction was at hand, and that all things were tending towards a crisis resembling that of 1640. He was determined that such a crisis should not find him in the situation of Strafford. He therefore turned suddenly round, and acknowledged, in the House of Lords, that the Declaration was illegal. The King, thus deserted by his ally and by his Chancellor, yielded, cancelled the Declaration, and solemnly promised that it should never be drawn into precedent.

Even this concession was insufficient. The Commons, not content with having forced their sovereign to annul the Indulgence, next extorted his unwilling assent to a celebrated law, which continued in force down to the reign of George the Fourth. This law, known as the Test Act, provided that all persons holding any office, civil or military, should take the oath of supremacy, should subscribe a declaration against transubstantiation, and should publicly receive the sacrament according to the rites of the Church of England. The preamble expressed hostility only to the Papists: but the enacting clauses were scarcely more unfavourable to the Papists than to the rigid Puritans. The Puritans, however, terrified at the evident leaning of the court towards Popery, and encouraged by some churchmen to hope that, as soon as the Roman Catholics should have been effectually disarmed, relief would be extended to Protestant Nonconformists, made little opposition; nor could the King, who was in extreme want of money, venture to withhold his sanction. The act was passed; and the Duke of York was consequently under the necessity of resigning the great place of Lord High Admiral.

Hitherto the Commons had not declared against the Dutch war. But, when the King had, in return for money cautiously doled out, relinquished his whole plan of domestic policy, they fell impetuously on his foreign policy. They requested him to dismiss Buckingham and Lauderdale from his councils for ever, and appointed a committee to consider the propriety

The Cabal dissolved.

of impeaching Arlington. In a short time the Cabal was no more. Clifford, who, alone of the five, had any claim to be regarded as an honest man, refused to take the new test, laid down his white staff, and retired to his country seat. Arlington quitted the post of Secretary of State for a quiet and dignified employment in the Royal household. Shaftesbury and Buckingham made their peace with the opposition, and appeared at the head of the stormy democracy of the city. Lauderdale, however, still continued to be minister for Scotch affairs, with which the English Parliament could not interfere.

And now the Commons urged the King to make peace with Holland, and expressly declared that no more supplies should be granted for the war, unless it should appear that the enemy obstinately refused to consent to reasonable terms. Charles found it necessary to postpone to a more convenient season all thought of executing the treaty of Dover, and to cajole the nation by pretending to return to the policy of the Triple Alliance. Temple, who, during the ascendency of the Cabal, had lived in seclusion among his books and flower beds, was called forth from his hermitage. By his instrumentality a separate peace was concluded with the United Provinces ; and he again became ambassador at the Hague, where his presence was regarded as a sure pledge for the sincerity of his court.

Peace with the United Provinces.

The chief direction of affairs was now intrusted to Sir Thomas Osborne, a Yorkshire baronet, who had, in the House of Commons, shown eminent talents for business and debate. Osborne became Lord Treasurer, and was soon created Earl of Danby. He was not a man whose character, if tried by any high standard of morality, would appear to merit approbation. He was greedy of wealth and honours, corrupt himself, and a corrupter of others. The Cabal had bequeathed to him the art of bribing Parliaments, an art still rude, and giving little promise of the rare perfection to which it was brought in the following century. He improved greatly on the plan of the first inventors. They had merely purchased orators : but every man who had a vote, might sell himself to Danby. Yet the new minister must not be confounded with the negotiators of Dover. He was not without the feelings of an Englishman and a Protestant ; nor did he, in his solicitude for his own interests, ever wholly forget the interests of his country and of his religion. He was desirous,

Administration of Danby.

indeed, to exalt the prerogative: but the means by which he proposed to exalt it were widely different from those which had been contemplated by Arlington and Clifford. The thought of establishing arbitrary power, by calling in the aid of foreign arms, and by reducing the kingdom to the rank of a dependent principality, never entered into his mind. His plan was to rally round the monarchy those classes which had been the firm allies of the monarchy during the troubles of the preceding generation, and which had been disgusted by the recent crimes and errors of the court. With the help of the old Cavalier interest, of the nobles, of the country gentlemen, of the clergy, and of the Universities, it might, he conceived, be possible to make Charles, not indeed an absolute sovereign, but a sovereign scarcely less powerful than Elizabeth had been.

Prompted by these feelings, Danby formed the design of securing to the Cavalier party the exclusive possession of all political power, both executive and legislative. In the year 1675, accordingly, a bill was offered to the Lords which provided that no person should hold any office, or should sit in either House of Parliament, without first declaring on oath that he considered resistance to the kingly power as in all cases criminal, and that he would never endeavour to alter the government either in Church or State. During several weeks the debates, divisions, and protests caused by this proposition kept the country in a state of excitement. The opposition in the House of Lords, headed by two members of the Cabal who were desirous to make their peace with the nation, Buckingham and Shaftesbury, was beyond all precedent vehement and pertinacious, and at length proved successful. The bill was not indeed rejected, but was retarded, mutilated, and at length suffered to drop.

So arbitrary and so exclusive was Danby's scheme of domestic policy. His opinions touching foreign policy did him more honour. They were in truth directly opposed to those of the Cabal, and differed little from those of the Country Party. He bitterly lamented the degraded situation to which England was reduced, and declared, with more energy than politeness, that his dearest wish was to cudgel the French into a proper respect for her. So little did he disguise his feelings that, at a great banquet where the most illustrious dignitaries of the State and of the Church were assembled, he not very decorously filled his glass to the confusion of all who were against a war with France. He would indeed most gladly have seen his country united with the powers which were then combined against Lewis, and was for that end bent on placing Temple, the author of the Triple Alliance, at the head of the department which directed foreign affairs. But the power of the prime minister was limited. In his most confidential letters he complained that the infatuation of his master prevented England from taking her proper place among European nations. Charles was insatiably greedy of French gold: he had by no means relinquished the hope that he might, at some future day, be able to establish absolute monarchy by the help of the French arms; and for both reasons he wished to maintain a good understanding with the court of Versailles.

Thus the sovereign leaned towards one system of foreign politics, and the minister towards a system diametrically opposite. Neither the sovereign nor the minister, indeed, was of a temper to pursue any object with undeviating constancy. Each occasionally yielded to the importunity of the other; and their jarring inclinations and mutual concessions gave to the whole administration a strangely capricious character. Charles sometimes, from levity and indolence, suffered Danby to take steps which Lewis resented as mortal injuries. Danby, on the other hand, rather than relinquish his great place, sometimes stooped to compliances which caused him bitter pain and shame. The King was brought to consent to a marriage between the Lady Mary, eldest daughter and presumptive heiress of the Duke of York, and William of Orange, the deadly enemy of France, and the hereditary champion of the Reformation. Nay, the brave Earl of Ossory, son of Ormond, was sent to assist the Dutch with some British troops, who, on the most bloody day of the whole war, signally vindicated the national reputation for stubborn courage. The Treasurer, on the other hand, was induced, not only to connive at some scandalous pecuniary transactions which took place between his master and the court of Versailles, but to become, unwillingly indeed and ungraciously, an agent in those transactions.

Embarrassing situation of the Country Party.

Meanwhile, the Country Party was driven by two strong feelings in two opposite directions. The popular leaders were afraid of the greatness of Lewis, who was not only making head against the whole strength of the continental alliance, but was even gaining ground. Yet they were afraid to entrust their own King with the means of curbing France, lest those means should be used to destroy the liberties of England. The conflict between these apprehensions, both of which were perfectly legitimate, made the policy of the Opposition seem as eccentric and fickle as that of the Court. The Commons called for a war with France, till the King, pressed by Danby to comply with their wish, seemed disposed to yield, and began to raise an army. But, as soon as they saw that the recruiting had commenced, their dread of Lewis gave place to a nearer dread. They began to fear that the new levies might be employed on a service in which Charles took much more interest than in the defence of Flanders. They therefore refused supplies, and clamoured for disbanding as loudly as they had just before clamoured for arming. Those historians who have severely reprehended this inconsistency do not appear to have made sufficient allowance for the embarrassing situation of subjects who have reason to believe that their prince is conspiring with a foreign and hostile power against their liberties. To refuse him military resources is to leave the state defenceless. Yet to give him military resources may be only to arm him against the state. In such circumstances vacillation cannot be considered as a proof of dishonesty or even of weakness.

These jealousies were studiously fomented by the French King. He had long kept England passive by promising to support the throne against the Parliament. He now, alarmed at finding that the patriotic counsels of Danby seemed likely to prevail in the closet, began to inflame the Parliament against the throne. Between Lewis and the Country Party there was one thing, and one only in common, profound distrust of Charles. Could the Country Party have been certain that their sovereign meant only to make war on France, they would have been eager to support him. Could Lewis have been certain that the new levies were intended only to make war on the constitution of England, he would have made no attempt to stop them. But the unsteadiness and faithlessness of Charles were such that the French Government and the English opposition, agreeing in nothing else, agreed in disbelieving his protestations, and were equally desirous to keep him poor and without an army. Communications were opened between Barillon, the Ambassador of Lewis, and those English politicians who had always professed, and who indeed sincerely felt, the greatest dread and dislike of the French ascendency. The most up-

Dealings of that party with the French embassy.

right of the Country Party, William Lord Russell, son of the Earl of Bedford, did not scruple to concert with a foreign mission schemes for embarrassing his own sovereign. This was the whole extent of Russell's offence. His principles and his fortune alike raised him above all temptations of a sordid kind: but there is too much reason to believe that some of his associates were less scrupulous. It would be unjust to impute to them the extreme wickedness of taking bribes to injure their country. On the contrary, they meant to serve her: but it is impossible to deny that they were mean and indelicate enough to let a foreign prince pay them for serving her. Among those who cannot be acquitted of this degrading charge was one man who is popularly considered as the personification of public spirit, and who, in spite of some great moral and intellectual faults, has a just claim to be called a hero, a philosopher, and a patriot. It is impossible to see without pain such a name in the list of the pensioners of France. Yet it is some consolation to reflect that, in our time, a public man would be thought lost to all sense of duty and of shame, who should not spurn from him a temptation which conquered the virtue and the pride of Algernon Sydney.

Peace of Nimeguen.

The effect of these intrigues was that England, though she occasionally took a menacing attitude, remained inactive till the continental war, having lasted near seven years, was terminated by the treaty of Nimeguen. The United Provinces, which in 1672 had seemed to be on the verge of utter ruin, obtained honourable and advantageous terms. This narrow escape was generally ascribed to the ability and courage of the young Stadtholder. His fame was great throughout Europe, and especially among the English, who regarded him as one of their own princes, and rejoiced to see him the husband of their future Queen. France retained many important towns in the Low Countries and the great province of Franche Comté. Almost the whole loss was borne by the decaying monarchy of Spain.

Violent discontents in England.

A few months after the termination of hostilities on the Continent came a great crisis in English politics. Towards such a crisis things had been tending during eighteen years. The whole stock of popularity, great as it was, with which the King had commenced his administration, had long been expended. To loyal enthusiasm had succeeded profound disaffection. The public mind had now measured back again the space over which it had passed between 1640 and 1660, and was once more in the state in which it had been when the Long Parliament met.

The prevailing discontent was compounded of many feelings. One of these was wounded national pride. That generation had seen England, during a few years, allied on equal terms with France, victorious over Holland and Spain, the mistress of the sea, the terror of Rome, the head of the Protestant interest. Her resources had not diminished; and it might have been expected that she would have been at least as highly considered in Europe under a legitimate King, strong in the affection and willing obedience of his subjects, as she had been under an usurper whose utmost vigilance and energy were required to keep down a mutinous people. Yet she had, in consequence of the imbecility and meanness of her rulers, sunk so low that any German or Italian principality which brought five thousand men into the field was a more important member of the commonwealth of nations.

With the sense of national humiliation was mingled anxiety for civil liberty. Rumours, indistinct indeed, but perhaps the more alarming by reason of their indistinctness, imputed to the court a deliberate design against all the constitutional rights of Englishmen. It had even been whispered that this design was to be carried into effect by the intervention of foreign arms. The thought of such intervention made the blood, even of the Cavaliers, boil in their veins. Some who had always professed the doctrine of nonresistance in its full extent were now heard to mutter that there was one limitation to that doctrine. If a foreign force were brought over to coerce the nation, they would not answer for their own patience.

But neither national pride nor anxiety for public liberty had so great an influence on the popular mind as hatred of the Roman Catholic religion. That hatred had become one of the ruling passions of the community, and was as strong in the ignorant and profane as in those who were Protestants from conviction. The cruelties of Mary's reign, cruelties which even in the most accurate and sober narrative excite just detestation, and which were neither accurately nor soberly related in the popular martyrologies, the conspiracies against Elizabeth, and above all the Gunpowder Plot, had left in the minds of the vulgar a deep and bitter feeling which was kept up by annual commemorations, prayers, bonfires, and processions. It should be added that those classes which were peculiarly distinguished by attachment to the throne, the clergy and the landed gentry, had peculiar reasons for regarding the Church of Rome with aversion. The clergy trembled for their benefices; the landed gentry for their abbeys and great tithes. While the memory of the reign of the Saints was still recent, hatred of Popery had in some degree given place to hatred of Puritanism: but, during the eighteen years which had elapsed since the Restoration, the hatred of Puritanism had abated, and the hatred of Popery had increased. The stipulations of the treaty of Dover were accurately known to very few: but some hints had got abroad. The general impression was that a great blow was about to be aimed at the Protestant religion. The King was suspected by many of a leaning towards Rome. His brother and heir presumptive was known to be a bigoted Roman Catholic. The first Duchess of York had died a Roman Catholic. James had then, in defiance of the remonstrances of the House of Commons, taken to wife the Princess Mary of Modena, another Roman Catholic. If there should be sons by this marriage, there was reason to fear that they might be bred Roman Catholics, and that a long succession of princes, hostile to the established faith, might sit on the English throne. The constitution had recently been violated for the purpose of protecting the Roman Catholics from the penal laws. The ally by whom the policy of England had, during many years, been chiefly governed, was not only a Roman Catholic, but a persecutor of the reformed Churches. Under such circumstances it is not strange that the common people should have been inclined to apprehend a return of the times of her whom they called Bloody Mary.

Thus the nation was in such a temper that the smallest spark might raise a flame. At this conjuncture fire was set in two places at once to the vast mass of combustible matter; and in a moment the whole was in a blaze.

Fall of Danby. The French court, which knew Danby to be its mortal enemy, artfully contrived to ruin him by making him pass for its friend. Lewis, by the instrumentality of Ralph Montague, a faithless and shameless man who had resided in France as minister from England, laid before the House of Commons proofs that the Treasurer had been concerned in an application made by the Court of Whitehall to the court of Versailles for a sum of money. This discovery produced its natural effect. The Treasurer was, in truth, exposed to the vengeance of Parliament, not on account of his delinquencies, but on account of his merits; not because he had been an accomplice in a criminal transaction, but because he had been a most unwilling and unserviceable accomplice. But of the circumstances, which have, in the judgment of posterity, greatly extenuated his fault, his contemporaries were ignorant. In their view he was the broker who had sold England to France. It seemed clear that his greatness was at an end, and doubtful whether his head could be saved.

Yet was the ferment excited by this discovery slight, when compared with the commotion which arose when it was noised abroad that a great Popish plot had been detected. One Titus Oates, a clergyman of the Church of England, had, by his disorderly life and heterodox doctrine, drawn on himself the censure of his spiritual superiors, had been compelled to quit his benefice, and had ever since led an infamous and vagrant life. He had once professed himself a Roman Catholic, and had passed some time on the Continent in English colleges of the order of Jesus. In those seminaries he had heard much wild talk about the best means of bringing England back to the true Church. From hints thus furnished he constructed a hideous romance, resembling rather the dream of a sick man than any transaction which ever took place in the real world. The Pope, he said, had entrusted the government of England to the Jesuits. The Jesuits had, by commissions under the seal of their society, appointed Roman Catholic clergymen, noblemen, and gentlemen, to all the highest offices in Church and State. The Papists had burned down London once. They had tried to burn it down again. They were at that moment planning a scheme for setting fire to all the shipping in the Thames. They were to rise at a signal and massacre all their Protestant neighbours. A French army was at the same time to land in Ireland. All the leading statesmen and divines of England were to be murdered. Three or four schemes had been formed for assassinating the King. He was to be stabbed. He was to be poisoned in his medicine. He was to be shot with silver bullets. The public mind was so sore and excitable that these lies readily found credit with the vulgar; and two events which speedily took place led even some reflecting men to suspect that the tale, though evidently distorted and exaggerated, might have some foundation.

Edward Coleman, a very busy, and not very honest, Roman

The Popish plot.

Catholic intriguer, had been among the persons accused. Search was made for his papers. It was found that he had just destroyed the greater part of them. But a few which had escaped contained some passages such as, to minds strongly prepossessed, might seem to confirm the evidence of Oates. Those passages indeed, when candidly construed, appear to express little more than the hopes which the posture of affairs, the predilections of Charles, the still stronger predilections of James, and the relations existing between the French and English courts, might naturally excite in the mind of a Roman Catholic strongly attached to the interests of his Church. But the country was not then inclined to construe the letters of Papists candidly; and it was urged, with some show of reason, that, if papers which had been passed over as unimportant were filled with matter so suspicious, some great mystery of iniquity must have been contained in those documents which had been carefully committed to the flames.

A few days later it was known that Sir Edmondsbury Godfrey, an eminent justice of the peace who had taken the depositions of Oates against Coleman, had disappeared. Search was made; and Godfrey's corpse was found in a field near London. It was clear that he had died by violence. It was equally clear that he had not been set upon by robbers. His fate is to this day a secret. Some think that he perished by his own hand; some, that he was slain by a private enemy. The most improbable supposition is that he was murdered by the party hostile to the court, in order to give colour to the story of the plot. The most probable supposition seems, on the whole, to be that some hotheaded Roman Catholic, driven to frenzy by the lies of Oates and by the insults of the multitude, and not nicely distinguishing between the perjured accuser and the innocent magistrate, had taken a revenge of which the history of persecuted sects furnishes but too many examples. If this were so, the assassin must have afterwards bitterly execrated his own wickedness and folly. The capital and the whole nation went mad with hatred and fear. The penal laws, which had begun to lose something of their edge, were sharpened anew. Everywhere justices were busied in searching houses and seizing papers. All the gaols were filled with Papists. London had the aspect of a city in a state of siege. The trainbands were under arms all night. Preparations were made for barricading the great thoroughfares. Patrols marched up and down the streets. Cannon were planted round Whitehall. No citizen thought himself safe unless he carried under his coat a small flail loaded with lead to brain the Popish assassins. The corpse of the murdered magistrate was exhibited during several days to the gaze of great multitudes, and was then committed to the grave with strange and terrible ceremonies, which indicated rather fear and the thirst of vengeance than sorrow or religious hope. The Houses insisted that a guard should be placed in the vaults over which they sate, in order to secure them against a second Gunpowder Plot. All their proceedings were of a piece with this demand. Ever since the reign of Elizabeth the oath of supremacy had been exacted from members of the House of Commons. Some Roman Catholics, however, had contrived so to interpret this oath that they could take it without scruple. A more stringent test was now added: every member of Parliament was required to make the Declaration against Transubstantiation; and thus the Roman Catholic Lords were for the first time excluded from their seats. Strong resolutions were adopted against the Queen. The Commons threw one of the Secretaries of State into prison for having countersigned commissions directed to gentlemen who were not good Protestants. They impeached the Lord Treasurer of high treason. Nay, they so far forgot the doctrine which, while the memory of the civil war was still recent, they had loudly professed, that they even attempted to wrest the command of the militia out of the King's hands. To such a temper had eighteen years of misgovernment brought the most loyal Parliament that had ever met in England.

Yet it may seem strange that, even in that extremity, the King should have ventured to appeal to the people; for the people were more excited than their representatives. The Lower House, discontented as it was, contained a larger number of Cavaliers than were likely to find seats again. But it was thought that a dissolution would put a stop to the prosecution of the Lord Treasurer, a prosecution which might probably bring to light all the guilty mysteries of the French alliance, and might thus cause extreme personal annoyance and embarrassment to Charles. Accordingly, in January 1679, the Parliament, which had been in existence ever since the beginning of the year 1661, was dissolved; and writs were issued for a general election.

During some weeks the contention over the whole country was fierce and obstinate beyond example. Unprecedented sums were expended. New tactics were employed. It was remarked by the pamphleteers of that time as something extraordinary that horses were hired at a great charge for the conveyance of electors. The practice of splitting freeholds for the purpose of multiplying votes dates from this memorable struggle. Dissenting preachers, who had long hidden themselves in quiet nooks from persecution, now emerged from their retreats, and rode from village to village, for the purpose of rekindling the zeal of the scattered people of God. The tide ran strong against the government. Most of the new members came up to Westminster in a mood little differing from that of their predecessors who had sent Strafford and Laud to the Tower.

First general election of 1679.

Meanwhile the courts of justice, which ought to be, in the midst of political commotions, sure places of refuge for the innocent of every party, were disgraced by wilder passions and fouler corruptions than were to be found even on the hustings. The tale of Oates, though it had sufficed to convulse the whole realm, would not, unless confirmed by other evidence, suffice to destroy the humblest of those whom he had accused. For, by the old law of England, two witnesses are necessary to establish a charge of treason. But the success of the first impostor produced its natural consequences. In a few weeks he had been raised from penury and obscurity to opulence, to power which made him the dread of princes and nobles, and to notoriety such as has for low and bad minds all the attractions of glory. He was not long without coadjutors and rivals. A wretch named Carstairs, who had earned a livelihood in Scotland by going disguised to conventicles and then informing against the preachers, led the way. Bedloe, a noted swindler, followed; and soon, from all the brothels, gambling houses, and spunging houses of London, false witnesses poured forth to swear away the lives of Roman Catholics. One came with a story about an army of thirty thousand men who were to muster in the disguise of pilgrims at Corunna, and to sail thence to Wales. Another had been promised canonisation and five hundred pounds to murder the King. A third had stepped into an eating house in Covent Garden, and had there heard a great Roman Catholic banker vow, in the hearing of all the guests and drawers, to kill the heretical tyrant. Oates, that he might not be eclipsed by his imitators, soon added a large supplement to his original narrative. He had the portentous impudence to affirm, among other things, that he had once stood behind a door which was ajar, and had there overheard the Queen declare that she had resolved to give her consent to the assassination of her husband. The vulgar believed, and the highest magistrates pretended to believe, even such fictions as these. The chief judges of the realm were corrupt, cruel, and timid. The leaders of the Country Party encouraged the prevailing delusion. The most respectable among them, indeed, were themselves so far deluded as to believe the greater part of the evidence of the plot to be true. Such men as Shaftesbury and Buckingham doubtless perceived that the whole was a romance. But it was a romance which served their turn; and to their seared consciences the death of an innocent man gave no more uneasiness than the death of a partridge. The juries partook of the feelings then common throughout the nation, and were encouraged by the bench to indulge those feelings without restraint. The multitude applauded Oates and his confederates, hooted and pelted the witnesses who appeared on behalf of the accused, and shouted with joy when the verdict of Guilty was pronounced. It was in vain that the sufferers appealed to the respectability of their past lives : for the public mind was possessed with a belief that the more conscientious a Papist was, the more likely he must be to plot against a Protestant government. It was in vain that, just before the cart passed from under their feet, they resolutely affirmed their innocence : for the general opinion was that a good Papist considered all lies which were serviceable to his Church as not only excusable but meritorious.

While innocent blood was shedding under the forms of justice, the new Parliament met; and such was the violence of the predominant party that even men whose youth had been passed amidst revolutions, men who remembered the attainder of Strafford, the attempt on the five members, the abolition of the House of Lords, the execution of the King, stood aghast at the aspect of public affairs. The impeachment of Danby was resumed. He pleaded the royal pardon. But the Commons treated the plea with contempt, and insisted that the trial should proceed. Danby, however, was not their chief object. They were convinced that the only effectual way of securing the liberties and religion of the nation was to exclude the Duke of York from the throne.

Violence of the new House of Commons.

The King was in great perplexity. He had insisted that his brother, the sight of whom inflamed the populace to madness, should retire for a time to Brussels: but this concession did not seem to have produced any favourable effect. The Roundhead party was now decidedly preponderant. Towards that party leaned millions who had, at the time of the Restoration, leaned towards the side of prerogative. Of the old Cavaliers many participated in the prevailing fear of Popery, and many, bitterly resenting the ingratitude of the prince for whom they had sacrificed so much, looked on his distress as carelessly as he had looked on theirs. Even the Anglican clergy, mortified and alarmed by the apostasy of the Duke of York, so far countenanced the opposition as to join cordially in the outcry against the Roman Catholics.

Temple's plan of government.

The King in this extremity had recourse to Sir William Temple. Of all the official men of that age Temple had preserved the fairest character. The Triple Alliance had been his work. He had refused to take any part in the politics of the Cabal, and had, while that administration directed affairs, lived in strict privacy. He had quitted his retreat at the call of Danby, had made peace between England and Holland, and had borne a chief part in bringing about the marriage of the Lady Mary to her cousin the Prince of Orange. Thus he had the credit of every one of the few good things which had been done by the government since the Restoration. Of the numerous crimes and blunders of the last eighteen years none could be imputed to him. His private life, though not austere, was decorous: his manners were popular; and he was not to be corrupted either by titles or by money. Something, however, was wanting to the character of this respectable statesman. The temperature of his patriotism was lukewarm. He prized his ease and his personal dignity too much, and shrank from responsibility with a pusillanimous fear. Nor indeed had his habits fitted him to bear a part in the conflicts of our domestic factions. He had reached his fiftieth year without having sate in the English Parliament; and his official experience had been almost entirely acquired at foreign courts. He was justly esteemed one of the first diplomatists in Europe: but the talents and accomplishments of a diplomatist are widely different from those which qualify a politician to lead the House of Commons in agitated times.

The scheme which he proposed showed considerable ingenuity. Though not a profound philosopher, he had thought more than most busy men of the world on the general principles of government; and his mind had been enlarged by historical studies and foreign travel. He seems to have discerned more clearly than most of his contemporaries one cause of the difficulties by which the government was beset. The character of the English polity was gradually changing. The Parliament was slowly, but constantly, gaining ground on the prerogative. The line between the legislative and executive powers was in theory as strongly marked as ever, but in practice was daily becoming fainter and fainter. The theory of the constitution was that the King might name his own ministers. But the House of Commons had driven Clarendon, the Cabal, and Danby successively from the direction of affairs. The theory of the constitution was that the King alone had the power of making peace and war. But the House of Commons had forced him to make peace with Holland, and had all but forced him to make war with France. The theory of the constitution was that the King was the sole judge of the cases in which it might be proper to pardon offenders. Yet he was so much in dread of the House of Commons that, at that moment, he could not venture to rescue from the gallows men whom he well knew to be the innocent victims of perjury.

Temple, it should seem, was desirous to secure to the legislature its undoubted constitutional powers, and yet to prevent it, if possible, from encroaching further on the province of the executive administration. With this view he determined to interpose between the sovereign and the Parliament a body which might break the shock of their collision. There was a body, ancient, highly honourable, and recognised by the law, which, he thought, might be so remodelled as to serve this purpose. He determined to give to the Privy Council a new character and office in the government. The number of Councillors he fixed at thirty. Fifteen of them were to be the chief ministers of state, of law, and of religion. The other fifteen were to be unplaced noblemen and gentlemen of ample fortune and high character. There was to be no interior cabinet. All the thirty were to be entrusted with every political secret, and summoned to every meeting; and the King was to declare that he would, on every occasion, be guided by their advice.

Temple seems to have thought that, by this contrivance, he could at once secure the nation against the tyranny of the

Crown, and the Crown against the encroachments of the Parliament. It was, on one hand, highly improbable that schemes such as had been formed by the Cabal would be even propounded for discussion in an assembly consisting of thirty eminent men, fifteen of whom were bound by no tie of interest to the court. On the other hand, it might be hoped that the Commons, content with the guarantee against misgovernment which such a Privy Council furnished, would confine themselves more than they had of late done to their strictly legislative functions, and would no longer think it necessary to pry into every part of the executive administration.

This plan, though in some respects not unworthy of the abilities of its author, was in principle vicious. The new board was half a cabinet and half a Parliament, and, like almost every other contrivance, whether mechanical or political, which is meant to serve two purposes altogether different, failed of accomplishing either. It was too large and too divided to be a good administrative body. It was too closely connected with the Crown to be a good checking body. It contained just enough of popular ingredients to make it a bad council of state, unfit for the keeping of secrets, for the conducting of delicate negotiations, and for the administration of war. Yet were these popular ingredients by no means sufficient to secure the nation against misgovernment. The plan, therefore, even if it had been fairly tried, could scarcely have succeeded; and it was not fairly tried. The King was fickle and perfidious: the Parliament was excited and unreasonable; and the materials out of which the new Council was made, though perhaps the best which that age afforded, were still bad.

The commencement of the new system was, however, hailed with general delight; for the people were in a temper to think any change an improvement. They were also pleased by some of the new nominations. Shaftesbury, now their favourite, was appointed Lord President. Russell and some other distinguished members of the Country Party were sworn of the Council. But a few days later all was again in confusion. The inconveniences of having so numerous a cabinet were such that Temple himself consented to infringe one of the fundamental rules which he had laid down, and to become one of a small knot which really directed everything. With him were joined three other ministers, Arthur Capel, Earl of

Essex, George Savile, Viscount Halifax, and Robert Spencer, Earl of Sunderland.

Of the Earl of Essex, then First Commissioner of the Treasury, it is sufficient to say that he was a man of solid, though not brilliant parts, and of grave and melancholy character, that he had been connected with the Country Party, and that he was at this time honestly desirous to effect, on terms beneficial to the state, a reconciliation between that party and the throne.

Among the statesmen of those times Halifax was, in genius, the first. His intellect was fertile, subtle, and capacious. His polished, luminous, and animated eloquence, set off by the silver tones of his voice, was the delight of the House of Lords. His conversation overflowed with thought, fancy, and wit. His political tracts well deserve to be studied for their literary merit, and fully entitle him to a place among English classics. To the weight derived from talents so great and various he united all the influence which belongs to rank and ample possessions. Yet he was less successful in politics than many who enjoyed smaller advantages. Indeed, those intellectual peculiarities which make his writings valuable frequently impeded him in the contests of active life. For he always saw passing events, not in the point of view in which they commonly appear to one who bears a part in them, but in the point of view in which, after the lapse of many years, they appear to the philosophic historian. With such a turn of mind, he could not long continue to act cordially with any body of men. All the prejudices, all the exaggerations, of both the great parties in the state moved his scorn. He despised the mean arts and unreasonable clamours of demagogues. He despised still more the doctrines of divine right and passive obedience. He sneered impartially at the bigotry of the Churchman and at the bigotry of the Puritan. He was equally unable to comprehend how any man should object to Saints' days and surplices, and how any man should persecute any other man for objecting to them. In temper he was what, in our time, is called a Conservative : in theory he was a Republican. Even when his dread of anarchy and his disdain for vulgar delusions led him to side for a time with the defenders of arbitrary power, his intellect was always with Locke and Milton. Indeed, his jests upon hereditary monarchy were sometimes such as would have better become a member of the Calf's Head Club than a Privy Councillor of the Stuarts.

Character of Halifax.

In religion he was so far from being a zealot that he was called by the uncharitable an atheist : but this imputation he vehemently repelled ; and in truth, though he sometimes gave scandal by the way in which he exerted his rare powers both of reasoning and of ridicule on serious subjects, he seems to have been by no means unsusceptible of religious impressions.

He was the chief of those politicians whom the two great parties contemptuously called Trimmers. Instead of quarrelling with this nickname, he assumed it as a title of honour, and vindicated, with great vivacity, the dignity of the appellation. Everything good, he said, trims between extremes. The temperate zone trims between the climate in which men are roasted and the climate in which they are frozen. The English Church trims between the Anabaptist madness and the Papist lethargy. The English constitution trims between Turkish despotism and Polish anarchy. Virtue is nothing but a just temper between propensities any one of which, if indulged to excess, becomes vice. Nay, the perfection of the Supreme Being himself consists in the exact equilibrium of attributes, none of which could preponderate without disturbing the whole moral and physical order of the world.* Thus Halifax was a Trimmer on principle. He was also a Trimmer by the constitution both of his head and of his heart. His understanding was keen, sceptical, inexhaustibly fertile in distinctions and objections ; his taste refined ; his sense of the ludicrous exquisite ; his temper placid and forgiving, but fastidious, and by no means prone either to malevolence or to enthusiastic admiration. Such a man could not long be constant to any band of political allies. He must not, however, be confounded with the vulgar crowd of renegades. For though, like them, he passed from side to side, his transition was always in the direction opposite to theirs. He had nothing in common with those who fly from extreme to extreme, and who regard the party which they have deserted with an animosity far exceeding that of consistent enemies. His place was on the debatable ground between the hostile divisions of the community, and he never wandered far beyond the frontier of either. The party to which he at any moment belonged was the party which, at that moment, he liked least, because it was the party of which at that moment he had the nearest view. He was

* Halifax was undoubtedly the real author of the Character of a Trimmer, which, for a time, went under the name of his kinsman, Sir William Coventry.

therefore always severe upon his violent associates, and was always in friendly relations with his moderate opponents. Every faction in the day of its insolent and vindictive triumph incurred his censure; and every faction, when vanquished and persecuted, found in him a protector. To his lasting honour it must be mentioned that he attempted to save those victims whose fate has left the deepest stain both on the Whig and on the Tory name.

He had greatly distinguished himself in opposition, and had thus drawn on himself the royal displeasure, which was indeed so strong that he was not admitted into the Council of Thirty without much difficulty and long altercation. As soon, however, as he had obtained a footing at court, the charms of his manner and of his conversation made him a favourite. He was seriously alarmed by the violence of the public discontent. He thought that liberty was for the present safe, and that order and legitimate authority were in danger. He therefore, as was his fashion, joined himself to the weaker side. Perhaps his conversion was not wholly disinterested. For study and reflection, though they had emancipated him from many vulgar prejudices, had left him a slave to vulgar desires. Money he did not want; and there is no evidence that he ever obtained it by any means which, in that age, even severe censors considered as dishonourable; but rank and power had strong attractions for him. He pretended, indeed, that he considered titles and great offices as baits which could allure none but fools, that he hated business, pomp, and pageantry, and that his dearest wish was to escape from the bustle and glitter of Whitehall to the quiet woods which surrounded his ancient mansion in Nottinghamshire: but his conduct was not a little at variance with his professions. In truth he wished to command the respect at once of courtiers and of philosophers, to be admired for attaining high dignities, and to be at the same time admired for despising them.

Sunderland was Secretary of State. In this man the political immorality of his age was personified in the most lively manner. Nature had given him a keen understanding, a restless and mischievous temper, a cold heart, and an abject spirit. His mind had undergone a training by which all his vices had been nursed up to the rankest maturity. At his entrance into public life, he had passed several years in diplomatic posts abroad, and had been, during some time,

Character of Sunderland.

minister in France. Every calling has its peculiar temptations. There is no injustice in saying that diplomatists, as a class, have always been more distinguished by their address, by the art with which they win the confidence of those with whom they have to deal, and by the ease with which they catch the tone of every society into which they are admitted, than by generous enthusiasm or austere rectitude; and the relations between Charles and Lewis were such that no English nobleman could long reside in France as envoy, and retain any patriotic or honourable sentiment. Sunderland came forth from the bad school in which he had been brought up, cunning, supple, shameless, free from all prejudices, and destitute of all principles. He was, by hereditary connection, a Cavalier: but with the Cavaliers he had nothing in common. They were zealous for monarchy, and condemned in theory all resistance. Yet they had sturdy English hearts which would never have endured real despotism. He, on the contrary, had a languid speculative liking for republican institutions, which was compatible with perfect readiness to be in practice the most servile instrument of arbitrary power. Like many other accomplished flatterers and negotiators, he was far more skilful in the art of reading the characters and practising on the weaknesses of individuals, than in the art of discerning the feelings of great masses, and of foreseeing the approach of great revolutions. He was adroit in intrigue; and it was difficult even for shrewd and experienced men who had been amply forewarned of his perfidy to withstand the fascination of his manner, and to refuse credit to his professions of attachment. But he was so intent on observing and courting particular persons, that he often forgot to study the temper of the nation. He therefore miscalculated grossly with respect to some of the most momentous events of his time. More than one important movement and rebound of the public mind took him by surprise; and the world, unable to understand how so clever a man could be blind to what was clearly discerned by the politicians of the coffee houses, sometimes attributed to deep design what were in truth mere blunders.

It was only in private conference that his eminent abilities displayed themselves. In the royal closet, or in a very small circle, he exercised great influence. But at the Council board he was taciturn; and in the House of Lords he never opened his lips.

The four confidential advisers of the crown soon found that their position was embarrassing and invidious. The other members of the Council murmured at a distinction inconsistent with the King's promises; and some of them, with Shaftesbury at their head, again betook themselves to strenuous opposition in Parliament. The agitation, which had been suspended by the late changes, speedily become more violent than ever. It was in vain that Charles offered to grant to the Commons any security for the Protestant religion which they could devise, provided only that they would not touch the order of succession. They would hear of no compromise. They would have the Exclusion Bill, and nothing but the Exclusion Bill. The King, therefore, a few weeks after he had publicly promised to take no step without the advice of his new Council, went down to the House of Lords without mentioning his intention in Council, and prorogued the Parliament.

The day of that prorogation, the twenty-sixth of May 1679, is a great era in our history. For on that day the Habeas Corpus Act received the royal assent. From the time of the Great Charter the substantive law respecting the personal liberty of Englishmen had been nearly the same as at present: but it had been inefficacious for want of a stringent system of procedure. What was needed was not a new right, but a prompt and searching remedy; and such a remedy the Habeas Corpus Act supplied. The King would gladly have refused his consent to that measure : but he was about to appeal from his Parliament to his people on the question of the succession, and he could not venture, at so critical a moment, to reject a bill which was in the highest degree popular.

Prorogation of the Parliament.

Habeas Corpus Act.

On the same day, the press of England became for a short time free. In old times printers had been strictly controlled by the Court of Star Chamber. The Long Parliament had abolished the Star Chamber, but had, in spite of the philosophical and eloquent expostulation of Milton, established and maintained a censorship. Soon after the Restoration, an Act had been passed which prohibited the printing of unlicensed books; and it had been provided that this Act should continue in force till the end of the first session of the next Parliament. That moment had now arrived; and the King, in the very act of dismissing the Houses, emancipated the Press.

Shortly after the prorogation came a dissolution and another general election. The zeal and strength of the

Second general election of 1679.

opposition were at the height.   The cry for the Exclusion Bill
was louder than ever; and with this cry was mingled another
cry, which fired the blood of the multitude, but which was
heard with regret and alarm by all judicious friends of freedom.   Not only the rights of the Duke of York, an avowed
Papist, but those of his two daughters, sincere and zealous
Protestants, were assailed.   It was confidently affirmed that
the eldest natural son of the King had been born in wedlock,
and was lawful heir to the crown.

Popularity of Monmouth.

Charles, while a wanderer on the Continent, had fallen in
at the Hague with Lucy Walters, a Welsh girl of great
beauty, but of weak understanding and dissolute manners.
She became his mistress, and presented him with a son.   A
suspicious lover might have had his doubts; for the lady had
several admirers, and was not supposed to be cruel to any.
Charles, however, readily took her word, and poured forth
on little James Crofts, as the boy was then called, an overflowing fondness, such as seemed hardly to belong to that
cool and careless nature.   Soon after the Restoration, the
young favourite, who had learned in France the exercises
then considered necessary to a fine gentleman, made his
appearance at Whitehall.   He was lodged in the palace,
attended by pages, and permitted to enjoy several distinctions
which had till then been confined to princes of the blood
royal.   He was married, while still in tender youth, to Anne
Scott, heiress of the noble house of Buccleuch.   He took her
name, and received with her hand possession of her ample
domains.   The estate which he had acquired by this match
was popularly estimated at not less than ten thousand pounds
a year.   Titles, and favours more substantial than titles, were
lavished on him.   He was made Duke of Monmouth in England, Duke of Buccleuch in Scotland, a Knight of the Garter,
Master of the Horse, Commander of the first troop of Life
Guards, Chief Justice of Eyre south of Trent, and Chancellor
of the University of Cambridge.   Nor did he appear to the
public unworthy of his high fortunes.   His countenance was
eminently handsome and engaging, his temper sweet, his manners polite and affable.   Though a libertine, he won the hearts
of the Puritans.   Though he was known to have been privy to
the shameful attack on Sir John Coventry, he easily obtained
the forgiveness of the Country Party.   Even austere moralists owned that, in such a court, strict conjugal fidelity was
scarcely to be expected from one who, while a child, had been

married to another child. Even patriots were willing to excuse a headstrong boy for visiting with immoderate vengeance
an insult offered to his father. And soon the stain left
by loose amours and midnight brawls was effaced by
honourable exploits. When Charles and Lewis united their
forces against Holland, Monmouth commanded the English
auxiliaries who were sent to the Continent, and approved
himself a gallant soldier and a not unintelligent officer. On
his return he found himself the most popular man in the
kingdom. Nothing was withheld from him but the crown;
nor did even the crown seem to be absolutely beyond his
reach. The distinction which had most injudiciously been
made between him and the highest nobles had produced evil
consequences. When a boy he had been invited to put on
his hat in the presence chamber, while Howards and Sey-
mours stood uncovered round him. When foreign princes
died, he had mourned for them in the long purple cloak,
which no other subject, except the Duke of York and Prince
Rupert, was permitted to wear. It was natural that these
things should lead him to regard himself as a legitimate
prince of the House of Stuart. Charles, even at a ripe age,
was devoted to his pleasures and regardless of his dignity.
It could hardly be thought incredible that he should at twenty
have secretly gone through the form of espousing a lady
whose beauty had fascinated him. While Monmouth was still
a child, and while the Duke of York still passed for a Protestant, it was rumoured throughout the country, and even
in circles which ought to have been well informed, that the
King had made Lucy Walters his wife, and that, if every
one had his right, her son would be Prince of Wales. Much
was said of a certain black box which, according to the vulgar
belief, contained the contract of marriage. When Monmouth
had returned from the Low Countries with a high character
for valour and conduct, and when the Duke of York was
known to be a member of a church detested by the great
majority of the nation, this idle story became important. For
it there was not the slightest evidence. Against it there was
the solemn asseveration of the King, made before his Council,
and by his order communicated to his people. But the multitude, always fond of romantic adventures, drank in eagerly
the tale of the secret espousals and the black box. Some
chiefs of the opposition acted on this occasion as they acted
with respect to the more odious fable of Oates, and counte-

nanced a story which they must have despised. The interest
which the populace took in him whom they regarded as the
champion of the true religion, and the rightful heir of the
British throne, was kept up by every artifice. When Monmouth arrived in London at midnight, the watchmen were
ordered by the magistrates to proclaim the joyful event
through the streets of the City : the people left their beds :
bonfires were lighted : the windows were illuminated : the
churches were opened ; and a merry peal rose from all the
steeples. When he travelled, he was everywhere received
with not less pomp, and with far more enthusiasm, than had
been displayed when Kings had made progresses through the
realm. He was escorted from mansion to mansion by long
cavalcades of armed gentlemen and yeomen. Cities poured
forth their whole population to receive him. Electors thronged
round him, to assure him that their votes were at his disposal. To such a height were his pretensions carried, that
he not only exhibited on his escutcheon the lions of England
and the lilies of France without the baton sinister under
which, according to the law of heraldry, they should have
been debruised in token of his illegitimate birth, but ventured
to touch for the king's evil. At the same time he neglected
no art of condescension by which the love of the multitude
could be conciliated. He stood godfather to the children of
the peasantry, mingled in every rustic sport, wrestled, played
at quarterstaff, and won footraces in his boots against fleet
runners in shoes.

It is a curious circumstance that, at two of the greatest
conjunctures in our history, the chiefs of the Protestant
party should have committed the same error, and should by
that error have greatly endangered their country and their
religion. At the death of Edward the Sixth they set up the
Lady Jane, without any show of birthright, in opposition, not
only to their enemy Mary, but also to Elizabeth, the true
hope of England and of the Reformation. Thus the most
respectable Protestants, with Elizabeth at their head, were
forced to make common cause with the Papists. In the same
manner, a hundred and thirty years later, a part of the opposition, by setting up Monmouth as a claimant of the crown,
attacked the rights, not only of James, whom they justly regarded as an implacable foe of their faith and their liberties,
but also of the Prince and Princess of Orange, who were
eminently marked out, both by situation and by personal

qualities, as the defenders of all free governments and of all reformed churches.

The folly of this course speedily became manifest. At present the popularity of Monmouth constituted a great part of the strength of the opposition. The elections went against the court: the day fixed for the meeting of the Houses drew near; and it was necessary that the King should determine on some line of conduct. Those who advised him discerned the first faint signs of a change of public feeling, and hoped that, by merely postponing the conflict, he would be able to secure the victory. He therefore, without even asking the opinion of the Council of the Thirty, resolved to prorogue the new Parliament before it entered on business. At the same time the Duke of York, who had returned from Brussels, was ordered to retire to Scotland, and was placed at the head of the administration of that kingdom.

Temple's plan of government was now avowedly abandoned and very soon forgotten. The Privy Council again became what it had been. Shaftesbury, and those who were connected with him in politics resigned their seats. Temple himself, as was his wont in unquiet times, retired to his garden and his library. Essex quitted the board of Treasury, and cast in his lot with the opposition. But Halifax, disgusted and alarmed by the violence of his old associates, and Sunderland, who never quitted place while he could hold it, remained in the King's service.

In consequence of the resignations which took place at this conjuncture, the way to greatness was left clear to a new set of aspirants. Two statesmen, who subsequently rose to the highest eminence which a British subject can reach, soon began to attract a large share of the public attention. These were Lawrence Hyde and Sidney Godolphin.

Lawrence Hyde was the second son of the Chancellor Clarendon, and was brother of the first Duchess of York. He had excellent parts, which had been improved by parliamentary and diplomatic experience; but the infirmities of his temper detracted much from the effective strength of his abilities. Negotiator and courtier as he was, he never learned the art of governing or of concealing his emotions. When prosperous, he was insolent and boastful: when he sustained a check, his undisguised mortification doubled the triumph of his enemies: very slight provocations sufficed to kindle his anger; and when he was angry he said bitter things

Lawrence Hyde.

which he forgot as soon as he was pacified, but which others remembered many years. His quickness and penetration would have made him a consummate man of business but for his selfsufficiency and impatience. His writings proved that he had many of the qualities of an orator: but his irritability prevented him from doing himself justice in debate: for nothing was easier than to goad him into a passion; and, from the moment when he went into a passion, he was at the mercy of opponents far inferior to him in capacity.

Unlike most of the leading politicians of that generation he was a consistent, dogged, and rancorous party man, a Cavalier of the old school, a zealous champion of the Crown and of the Church, and a hater of Republicans and Nonconformists. He had consequently a great body of personal adherents. The clergy especially looked on him as their own man, and extended to his foibles an indulgence of which, to say the truth, he stood in some need: for he drank deep; and when he was in a rage,—and he very often was in a rage,—he swore like a porter.

He now succeeded Essex at the treasury. It is to be observed that the place of First Lord of the Treasury had not then the importance and dignity which now belong to it. When there was a Lord Treasurer, that great officer was generally prime minister: but, when the white staff was in commission, the chief commissioner hardly ranked so high as a Secretary of State. It was not till the time of Walpole that the First Lord of the Treasury became, under a humbler name, all that the Lord High Treasurer had been.

Sidney Godolphin. Godolphin had been bred a page at Whitehall, and had early acquired all the flexibility and the selfpossession of a veteran courtier. He was laborious, clearheaded, and profoundly versed in the details of finance. Every government, therefore, found him an useful servant; and there was nothing in his opinions or in his character which could prevent him from serving any government. "Sidney Godolphin," said Charles, "is never in the way, and never out of the way." This pointed remark goes far to explain Godolphin's extraordinary success in life.

He acted at different times with both the great political parties: but he never shared in the passions of either. Like most men of cautious tempers and prosperous fortunes, he had a strong disposition to support whatever existed. He disliked revolutions; and, for the same reason for which he disliked revolutions, he disliked counterrevolutions. His deportment was remarkably grave and reserved: but his personal tastes were low and frivolous; and most of the time which he could save from public business was spent in racing, cardplaying, and cockfighting. He now sate below Rochester at the Board of Treasury, and distinguished himself there by assiduity and intelligence.

Before the new Parliament was suffered to meet for the despatch of business a whole year elapsed, an eventful year, which has left lasting traces in our manners and language. Never before had political controversy been carried on with so much freedom. Never before had political clubs existed with so elaborate an organisation or so formidable an influence. The one question of the Exclusion occupied the public mind. All the presses and pulpits of the realm took part in the conflict. On one side it was maintained that the constitution and religion of the state could never be secure under a Popish King; on the other, that the right of James to wear the crown in his turn was derived from God, and could not be annulled, even by the consent of all the branches of the legislature. Every county, every town, every family, was in agitation. The civilities and hospitalities of neighbourhood were interrupted. The dearest ties of friendship and of blood were sundered. Even schoolboys were divided into angry parties; and the Duke of York and the Earl of Shaftesbury had zealous adherents on all the forms of Westminster and Eton. The theatres shook with the roar of the contending factions. Pope Joan was brought on the stage by the zealous Protestants. Pensioned poets filled their prologues and epilogues with eulogies on the King and the Duke. The malecontents besieged the throne with petitions, demanding that Parliament might be forthwith convened. The loyalists sent up addresses, expressing the utmost abhorrence of all who presumed to dictate to the sovereign. The citizens of London assembled by tens of thousands to burn the Pope in effigy. The government posted cavalry at Temple Bar, and placed ordnance round Whitehall. In that year our tongue was enriched with two words, Mob and Sham, remarkable memorials of a season of tumult and imposture.* Opponents of the court were called Birminghams, Petitioners, and Exclusionists. Those who took the King's side were Antibirminghams, Abhorrers, and Tantivies. These appellations soon become

Marginal note: Violence of factions on the subject of the Exclusion Bill

* North's Examen, 231. 574.

obsolete: but at this time were first heard two nicknames which, though originally given in insult, were soon assumed with pride, which are still in daily use, which have spread as widely as the English race, and which will last as long as the English literature. It is a curious circumstance that one of these nicknames was of Scotch, and the other of Irish, origin. Both in Scotland and in Ireland, misgovernment had called into existence bands of desperate men whose ferocity was heightened by religious enthusiasm. In Scotland some of the persecuted Covenanters, driven mad by oppression, had lately murdered the Primate, had taken arms against the government, had obtained some advantages against the King's forces, and had not been put down till Monmouth, at the head of some troops from England, had routed them at Bothwell Bridge. These zealots were most numerous among the rustics of the western lowlands, who were vulgarly called Whigs. Thus the appellation of Whig was fastened on the Presbyterian zealots of Scotland, and was transferred to those English politicians who showed a disposition to oppose the court, and to treat Protestant Nonconformists with indulgence. The bogs of Ireland, at the same time, afforded a refuge to Popish outlaws, much resembling those who were afterwards known as Whiteboys. These men were then called Tories. The name of Tory was therefore given to Englishmen who refused to concur in excluding a Roman Catholic prince from the throne.

The rage of the hostile factions would have been sufficiently violent, if it had been left to itself. But it was studiously exasperated by the common enemy of both. Lewis still continued to bribe and flatter both the court and the opposition. He exhorted Charles to be firm: he exhorted James to raise a civil war in Scotland: he exhorted the Whigs not to flinch, and to rely with confidence on the protection of France.

Through all this agitation a discerning eye might have perceived that the public opinion was gradually changing. The persecution of the Roman Catholics went on; but convictions were no longer matters of course. A new brood of false witnesses, among whom a villain named Dangerfield was the most conspicuous, infested the courts: but the stories of these men, though better constructed than that of Oates, found less credit. Juries were no longer so easy of belief as during the panic which had followed the murder of Godfrey; and Judges, who, while the popular frenzy was at the height, had been its most obsequious instruments, now ventured to express some part of what they had from the first thought.

At length, in October 1680, the Parliament met. The Whigs had so great a majority in the Commons that the Exclusion Bill went through all its stages there without difficulty. The King scarcely knew on what members of his own cabinet he could reckon. Hyde had been true to his Tory opinions, and had steadily supported the cause of hereditary monarchy. But Godolphin, anxious for quiet, and believing that quiet could be restored only by concession, wished the bill to pass. Sunderland, ever false, and ever shortsighted, unable to discern the signs of approaching reaction, and anxious to conciliate the party which he believed to be irresistible, determined to vote against the court. The Duchess of Portsmouth implored her royal lover not to rush headlong to destruction. If there were any point on which he had a scruple of conscience or of honour, it was the question of the succession; but during some days it seemed that he would submit. He wavered, asked what sum the Commons would give him if he yielded, and suffered a negotiation to be opened with the leading Whigs. But a deep mutual distrust which had been many years growing, and which had been carefully nursed by the arts of France, made a treaty impossible. Neither side would place confidence in the other. The whole nation now looked with breathless anxiety to the House of Lords. The assemblage of peers was large. The King himself was present. The debate was long, earnest, and occasionally furious. Some hands were laid on the pommels of swords, in a manner which revived the recollection of the stormy Parliaments of Edward the Third and Richard the Second. Shaftesbury and Essex were joined by the treacherous Sunderland. But the genius of Halifax bore down all opposition. Deserted by his most important colleagues, and opposed to a crowd of able antagonists, he defended the cause of the Duke of York, in a succession of speeches which, many years later, were remembered as masterpieces of reasoning, of wit, and of eloquence. It is seldom that oratory changes votes. Yet the attestation of contemporaries leaves no doubt that, on this occasion, votes were changed by the oratory of Halifax. The Bishops, true to their doctrines, supported the principle

Meeting of Parliament; the Exclusion Bill passes the Commons.

Exclusion Bill rejected by the Lords.

of hereditary right, and the bill was rejected by a great majority.*

The party which preponderated in the House of Commons, bitterly mortified by this defeat, found some consolation in shedding the blood of Roman Catholics. William Howard, Viscount Stafford, one of the unhappy men who had been accused of a share in the plot, was impeached; and on the testimony of Oates and of two other false witnesses, Dugdale and Turberville, was found guilty of high treason, and suffered death. But the circumstances of his trial and execution ought to have given an useful warning to the Whig leaders. A large and respectable minority of the House of Lords pronounced the prisoner not guilty. The multitude, which a few months before had received the dying declarations of Oates's victims with mockery and execrations, now loudly expressed a belief that Stafford was a murdered man. When he with his last breath protested his innocence, the cry was, "God bless you, my Lord! We believe you, my Lord." A judicious observer might easily have predicted that the blood then shed would shortly have blood.

General election of 1681.

The King determined to try once more the experiment of a dissolution. A new Parliament was summoned to meet at Oxford, in March 1681. Since the days of the Plantagenets the Houses had constantly sat at Westminster, except when the plague was raging in the capital: but so extraordinary a conjuncture seemed to require extraordinary precautions. If the Parliament were held in its usual place of assembling, the House of Commons might declare itself permanent, and might call for aid on the magistrates and citizens of London. The trainbands might rise to defend Shaftesbury as they had risen forty years before to defend Pym and Hampden. The

* A peer who was present has described the effect of Halifax's oratory in words which I will quote, because, though they have been long in print, they are probably known to few even of the most curious and diligent readers of history.

"Of powerful eloquence and great parts were the Duke's enemies who did assert the Bill; but a noble Lord appeared against it who, that day, in all the force of speech, in reason, in arguments of what could concern the public or the private interests of men, in honour, in conscience, in estate, did outdo himself and every other man; and in fine his conduct and his parts were both victorious, and by him all the wit and malice of that party was overthrown."

This passage is taken from a memoir of Henry Earl of Peterborough, in a volume entitled "Succinct Genealogies, by Robert Halstead," fol. 1685. The name of Halstead is fictitious. The real authors were the Earl of Peterborough himself and his chaplain. The book is extremely rare. Only twenty-four copies were printed, two of which are now in the British Museum. Of these two one belonged to George the Fourth, and the other to Mr. Grenville.

The Duke of Monmouth

Guards might be overpowered, the palace forced, the King a prisoner in the hands of his mutinous subjects. At Oxford there was no such danger. The University was devoted to the crown; and the gentry of the neighbourhood were generally Tories. Here, therefore, the opposition had more reason than the King to apprehend violence.

The elections were sharply contested. The Whigs still composed a majority of the House of Commons: but it was plain that the Tory spirit was fast rising throughout the country. It should seem that the sagacious and versatile Shaftesbury ought to have foreseen the coming change, and to have consented to the compromise which the court offered: but he appears to have forgotten his old tactics. Instead of making dispositions which, in the worst event, would have secured his retreat, he took up a position in which it was necessary that he should either conquer or perish. Perhaps his head, strong as it was, had been turned by popularity, by success, and by the excitement of conflict. Perhaps he had spurred his party till he could no longer curb it, and was really hurried on headlong by those whom he seemed to guide.

The eventful day arrived. The meeting at Oxford resembled rather that of a Polish Diet than that of an English Parliament. The Whig members were escorted by great numbers of their armed and mounted tenants and serving men, who exchanged looks of defiance with the royal Guards. The slightest provocation might, under such circumstances, have produced a civil war; but neither side dared to strike the first blow. The King again offered to consent to anything but the Exclusion Bill. The Commons were determined to accept nothing but the Exclusion Bill. In a few days the Parliament was again dissolved. *Parliament held at Oxford, and dissolved.*

The King had triumphed. The reaction, which had begun some months before the meeting of the Houses at Oxford, now went rapidly on. The nation, indeed, was still hostile to Popery: but, when men reviewed the whole history of the plot, they felt that their Protestant zeal had hurried them into folly and crime, and could scarcely believe that they had been induced by nursery tales to clamour for the blood of fellow subjects and fellow Christians. The most loyal, indeed, could not deny that the administration of Charles had often been highly blamable. But men who had not the full information which we possess touching his dealings with *Tory reaction.*

France, and who were disgusted by the violence of the
Whigs, enumerated the large concessions which, during the
last few years, he had made to his Parliaments, and the still
larger concessions which he had declared himself willing to
make. He had consented to the laws which excluded Roman
Catholics from the House of Lords, from the Privy Council,
and from all civil and military offices. He had passed the
Habeas Corpus Act. If securities yet stronger had not been
provided against the dangers to which the constitution and
the Church might be exposed under a Roman Catholic
sovereign, the fault lay, not with Charles who had invited
the Parliament to propose such securities, but with those
Whigs who had refused to hear of any substitute for the
Exclusion Bill. One thing only had the King denied to his
people. He had refused to take away his brother's birthright. And was there not good reason to believe that this
refusal was prompted by laudable feelings? What selfish
motive could faction itself impute to the royal mind? The
Exclusion Bill did not curtail the reigning King's prerogatives, or diminish his income. Indeed, by passing it, he
might easily have obtained an ample addition to his own
revenue. And what was it to him who ruled after him?
Nay, if he had personal predilections, they were known to be
rather in favour of the Duke of Monmouth than of the
Duke of York. The most natural explanation of the King's
conduct seemed to be that, careless as was his temper and
loose as were his morals, he had, on this occasion, acted from
a sense of duty and honour. And, if so, would the nation
compel him to do what he thought criminal and disgraceful?
To apply, even by strictly constitutional means, a violent
pressure to his conscience, seemed to zealous royalists ungenerous and undutiful. But strictly constitutional means
were not the only means which the Whigs were disposed to
employ. Signs were already discernible which portended
the approach of great troubles. Men, who, in the time of
the civil war and of the Commonwealth, had acquired an
odious notoriety, had emerged from the obscurity in which,
after the Restoration, they had hidden themselves from the
general hatred, showed their confident and busy faces everywhere, and appeared to anticipate a second reign of the
Saints. Another Naseby, another High Court of Justice,
another usurper on the throne, the Lords again ejected from
their hall by violence, the Universities again purged, the

Church again robbed and persecuted, the Puritans again dominant, to such results did the desperate policy of the opposition seem to tend.

Strongly moved by these apprehensions, the majority of the upper and middle classes hastened to rally round the throne. The situation of the King bore, at this time, a great resemblance to that in which his father stood just after the Remonstrance had been voted. But the reaction of 1641 had not been suffered to run its course. Charles the First, at the very moment when his people, long estranged, were returning to him with hearts disposed to reconciliation, had, by a perfidious violation of the fundamental laws of the realm, forfeited their confidence for ever. Had Charles the Second taken a similar course, had he arrested the Whig leaders in an irregular manner, had he impeached them of high treason before a tribunal which had no legal jurisdiction over them, it is highly probable that they would speedily have regained the ascendency which they had lost. Fortunately for himself, he was induced, at this crisis, to adopt a policy singularly judicious. He determined to conform to the law, but at the same time to make vigorous and unsparing use of the law against his adversaries. He was not bound to convoke a Parliament till three years should have elapsed. He was not much distressed for money. The produce of the taxes which had been settled on him for life exceeded the estimate. He was at peace with all the world. He could retrench his expenses by giving up the costly and useless settlement of Tangier; and he might hope for pecuniary aid from France. He had, therefore, ample time and means for a systematic attack on the opposition under the forms of the constitution. The Judges were removable at his pleasure: the juries were nominated by the Sheriffs; and, in almost all the counties of England, the Sheriffs were nominated by himself. Witnesses, of the same class with those who had recently sworn away the lives of Papists, were ready to swear away the lives of Whigs.

The first victim was College, a noisy and violent demagogue of mean birth and education. He was by trade a joiner, and was celebrated as the inventor of the Protestant flail.* He had been at Oxford when the Parliament sate there, and was

Persecution of the Whigs.

---

* This is mentioned in the curious work entitled "Ragguaglio della solenne Comparsa fatta in Roma gli otto di Gennaio, 1687, dall' illustrissimo et eccellentissimo signor Conte di Castlemaine."

accused of having planned a rising and an attack on the King's guards. Evidence was given against him by Dugdale and Turberville, the same infamous men who had, a few months earlier, borne false witness against Stafford. In the sight of a jury of country squires no Exclusionist was likely to find favour. College was convicted. The crowd which filled the court house of Oxford received the verdict with a roar of exultation, as barbarous as that which he and his friends had been in the habit of raising when innocent Papists were doomed to the gallows. His execution was the beginning of a new judicial massacre, not less atrocious than that in which he had himself borne a share.

The government, emboldened by this first victory, now aimed a blow at an enemy of a very different class. It was resolved that Shaftesbury should be brought to trial for his life. Evidence was collected which, it was thought, would support a charge of treason. But the facts which it was necessary to prove were alleged to have been committed in London. The Sheriffs of London, chosen by the citizens, were zealous Whigs. They named a Whig grand jury, which threw out the bill. This defeat, far from discouraging those who advised the King, suggested to them a new and daring scheme. Since the charter of the capital was in their way, that charter must be annulled. It was pretended, therefore, that the City had by some irregularities forfeited its municipal privileges; and proceedings were instituted against the corporation in the Court of King's Bench. At the same time those laws which had, soon after the Restoration, been enacted against Nonconformists, and which had remained dormant during the ascendency of the Whigs, were enforced all over the kingdom with extreme rigour.

Yet the spirit of the Whigs was not subdued. Though in evil plight, they were still a numerous and powerful party; and, as they mustered strong in the large towns, and especially in the capital, they made a noise and a show more than proportioned to their real force. Animated by the recollection of past triumphs, and by the sense of present oppression, they overrated both their strength and their wrongs. It was not in their power to make out that clear and overwhelming case which can alone justify so violent a remedy as resistance to an established government. Whatever they might suspect, they could not prove that their sovereign had entered into a treaty with France against the religion and liberties of

Charter of the City confiscated.

Whig conspiracies.

England. What was apparent was not sufficient to warrant an appeal to the sword. If the Lords had thrown out the Exclusion Bill, they had thrown it out in the exercise of a right coeval with the constitution. If the King had dissolved the Oxford Parliament, he had done so by virtue of a prerogative which had never been questioned. If he had, since the dissolution, done some harsh things, still those things were in strict conformity with the letter of the law, and with the recent practice of the malecontents themselves. If he had prosecuted his opponents, he had prosecuted them according to the proper forms, and before the proper tribunals. The evidence now produced for the crown was at least as worthy of credit as the evidence on which the noblest blood of England had lately been shed by the opposition. The treatment which an accused Whig had now to expect from judges, advocates, sheriffs, juries, and spectators, was no worse than the treatment which had lately been thought by the Whigs good enough for an accused Papist. If the privileges of the City of London were attacked, they were attacked, not by military violence or by any disputable exercise of prerogative, but according to the regular practice of Westminster Hall. No tax was imposed by royal authority. No law was suspended. The Habeas Corpus Act was respected. Even the Test Act was enforced. The opposition therefore could not bring home to the King that species of misgovernment which alone could justify insurrection. And, even had his misgovernment been more flagrant than it was, insurrection would still have been criminal, because it was almost certain to be unsuccessful. The situation of the Whigs in 1682 differed widely from that of the Roundheads forty years before. Those who took up arms against Charles the First acted under the authority of a Parliament which had been legally assembled, and which could not, without its own consent, be legally dissolved. The opponents of Charles the Second were private men. Almost all the military and naval resources of the kingdom had been at the disposal of those who resisted Charles the First. All the military and naval resources of the kingdom were at the disposal of Charles the Second. The House of Commons had been supported by at least half the nation against Charles the First. But those who were disposed to levy war against Charles the Second were certainly a minority. It could hardly be doubted, therefore, that, if they attempted a rising, they would fail. Still less could it be doubted that their failure would aggravate every evil of which they complained. The true policy of the Whigs was to submit with patience to adversity which was the natural consequence and the just punishment of their errors, to wait patiently for that turn of public feeling which must inevitably come, to observe the law, and to avail themselves of the protection, imperfect indeed, but by no means nugatory, which the law afforded to innocence. Unhappily they took a very different course. Unscrupulous and hotheaded chiefs of the party formed and discussed schemes of resistance, and were heard, if not with approbation, yet with the show of acquiescence, by much better men than themselves. It was proposed that there should be simultaneous insurrections in London, in Cheshire, at Bristol, and at Newcastle. Communications were opened with the discontented Presbyterians of Scotland, who were suffering under a tyranny such as England, in the worst times, had never known. While the leaders of the opposition thus revolved plans of open rebellion, but were still restrained by fears or scruples from taking any decisive step, a design of a very different kind was meditated by some of their accomplices. To fierce spirits, unrestrained by principle, or maddened by fanaticism, it seemed that to waylay and murder the King and his brother was the shortest and surest way of vindicating the Protestant religion and the liberties of England. A place and a time were named; and the details of the butchery were frequently discussed, if not definitely arranged. This scheme was known but to few, and was concealed with especial care from the upright and humane Russell, and from Monmouth, who, though not a man of delicate conscience, would have recoiled with horror from the guilt of parricide. Thus there were two plots, one within the other. The object of the great Whig plot was to raise the nation in arms against the government. The lesser plot, commonly called the Rye House Plot, in which only a few desperate men were concerned, had for its object the assassination of the King and of the heir presumptive.

Detection of the Whig conspiracies.

Both plots were soon discovered. Cowardly traitors hastened to save themselves, by divulging all, and more than all, that had passed in the deliberations of the party. That only a small minority of those who meditated resistance had admitted into their minds the thought of assassination is fully established: but, as the two conspiracies ran into each other, it was not difficult for the government to confound them together. The just indignation excited by the Rye House Plot was extended for a time to the whole Whig body. The King was now at liberty to exact full vengeance for years of restraint and humiliation. Shaftesbury, indeed, had escaped the fate which his manifold perfidy had well deserved. He had seen that the ruin of his party was at hand, had in vain endeavoured to make his peace with the royal brothers, had fled to Holland, and had died there, under the generous protection of a government which he had cruelly wronged. Monmouth threw himself at his father's feet and found mercy, but soon gave new offence, and thought it prudent to go into voluntary exile. Essex perished by his own hand in the Tower. Russell, who appears to have been guilty of no offence falling within the definition of high treason, and Sidney, of whose guilt no legal evidence could be produced, were beheaded in defiance of law and justice. Russell died with the fortitude of a Christian, Sidney with the fortitude of a Stoic. Some active politicians of meaner rank were sent to the gallows. Many quitted the country. Numerous prosecutions for misprision of treason, for libel, and for conspiracy were instituted. Convictions were obtained without difficulty from Tory juries, and rigorous punishments were inflicted by courtly judges. With these criminal proceedings were joined civil proceedings scarcely less formidable. Actions were brought against persons who had defamed the Duke of York; and damages tantamount to a sentence of perpetual imprisonment were demanded by the plaintiff, and without difficulty obtained. The Court of King's Bench pronounced that the franchises of the City of London were forfeited to the Crown. Flushed with this great victory, the government proceeded to attack the constitutions of other corporations which were governed by Whig officers, and which had been in the habit of returning Whig members to Parliament. Borough after borough was compelled to surrender its privileges; and new charters were granted which gave the ascendency everywhere to the Tories. Seizure of charters.

These proceedings, however reprehensible, had yet the semblance of legality. They were also accompanied by an act intended to quiet the uneasiness with which many loyal men looked forward to the accession of a Popish sovereign. The Lady Anne, younger daughter of the Duke of York by his first wife, was married to George, a prince of the orthodox

House of Denmark. The Tory gentry and clergy might now flatter themselves that the Church of England had been effectually secured without any violation of the order of succession. The King and the heir presumptive were nearly of the same age. Both were approaching the decline of life. The King's health was good. It was therefore probable that James, if he ever came to the throne, would have but a short reign. Beyond his reign there was the gratifying prospect of a long series of Protestant sovereigns.

The liberty of unlicensed printing was of little or no use to the vanquished party; for the temper of judges and juries was such that no writer whom the government prosecuted for a libel had any chance of escaping. The dread of punishment therefore did all that a censorship could have done. Meanwhile, the pulpits resounded with harangues against the sin of rebellion. The treatises in which Filmer maintained that hereditary despotism was the form of government ordained by God, and that limited monarchy was a pernicious absurdity, had recently appeared, and had been favourably received by a large section of the Tory party. The University of Oxford, on the very day on which Russell was put to death, adopted by a solemn public act these strange doctrines, and ordered the political works of Buchanan, Milton, and Baxter to be publicly burned in the court of the Schools.

Thus emboldened, the King at length ventured to overstep the bounds which he had during some years observed, and to violate the plain letter of the law. The law was that not more than three years should pass between the dissolving of one Parliament and the convoking of another. But, when three years had elapsed after the dissolution of the Parliament which sate at Oxford, no writs were issued for an election. This infraction of the constitution was the more reprehensible, because the King had little reason to fear a meeting with a new House of Commons. The counties were generally on his side; and many boroughs in which the Whigs had lately held sway had been so remodelled that they were certain to return none but courtiers.

Influence of the Duke of York.

In a short time the law was again violated in order to gratify the Duke of York. That prince was, partly on account of his religion, and partly on account of the sternness and harshness of his nature, so unpopular that it had been thought necessary to keep him out of sight while the Exclusion Bill was before Parliament, lest his appearance should give an advantage to the party which was struggling to deprive him of his birthright. He had therefore been sent to govern Scotland, where the savage old tyrant Lauderdale was sinking into the grave. Even Lauderdale was now outdone. The administration of James was marked by odious laws, by barbarous punishments, and by judgments to the iniquity of which even that age furnished no parallel. The Scottish Privy Council had power to put state prisoners to the question. But the sight was so dreadful that, as soon as the boots appeared, even the most servile and hard-hearted courtiers hastened out of the chamber. The board was sometimes quite deserted: and it was at length found necessary to make an order that the members should keep their seats on such occasions. The Duke of York, it was remarked, seemed to take pleasure in the spectacle which some of the worst men then living were unable to contemplate without pity and horror. He not only came to Council when the torture was to be inflicted, but watched the agonies of the sufferers with that sort of interest and complacency with which men observe a curious experiment in science. Thus he employed himself at Edinburgh, till the event of the conflict between the court and the Whigs was no longer doubtful. He then returned to England: but he was still excluded by the Test Act from all public employment; nor did the King at first think it safe to violate a statute which the great majority of his most loyal subjects regarded as one of the chief securities of their religion and of their civil rights. When, however, it appeared, from a succession of trials, that the nation had patience to endure almost anything that the government had courage to do, Charles ventured to dispense with the law in his brother's favour. The Duke again took his seat in the Council, and resumed the direction of naval affairs.

These breaches of the constitution excited, it is true, some murmurs among the moderate Tories, and were not unanimously approved even by the King's ministers. Halifax in particular, now a Marquess and Lord Privy Seal, had, from the very day on which the Tories had by his help gained the ascendant, begun to turn Whig. As soon as the Exclusion Bill had been thrown out, he had pressed the House of Lords to make provision against the danger to which, in the next reign, the liberties and religion of the nation might be exposed. He now saw with alarm the violence of that reaction

He is opposed by Halifax.

which was, in no small measure, his own work. He did not try to conceal the scorn which he felt for the servile doctrines of the University of Oxford. He detested the French alliance. He disapproved of the long intermission of Parliaments. He regretted the severity with which the vanquished party was treated. He who, when the Whigs were predominant, had ventured to pronounce Stafford not guilty, ventured, when they were vanquished and helpless, to intercede for Russell. At one of the last Councils which Charles held a remarkable scene took place. The charter of Massachusetts had been forfeited. A question arose how, for the future, the colony should be governed. The general opinion of the board was that the whole power, legislative as well as executive, should abide in the crown. Halifax took the opposite side, and argued with great energy against absolute monarchy, and in favour of representative government. It was vain, he said, to think that a population, sprung from the English stock, and animated by English feelings, would long bear to be deprived of English institutions. Life, he exclaimed, would not be worth having in a country where liberty and property were at the mercy of one despotic master. The Duke of York was greatly incensed by this language, and represented to his brother the danger of retaining in office a man who appeared to be infected with all the worst notions of Marvell and Sidney.

Some modern writers have blamed Halifax for continuing in the ministry while he disapproved of the manner in which both domestic and foreign affairs were conducted. But this censure is unjust. Indeed it is to be remarked that the word ministry, in the sense in which we use it, was then unknown.* The thing itself did not exist; for it belongs to an age in which parliamentry government is fully established. At present the chief servants of the crown form one body. They are understood to be on terms of friendly confidence with each other, and to agree as to the main principles on which the executive administration ought to be conducted. If a slight difference of opinion arises among them, it is easily compromised : but, if one of them differs from the rest on a vital point, it is his duty to resign. While he retains his office, he is held responsible even for steps which he has tried to dissuade his colleagues from taking. In the seventeenth century, the heads of the

* North's Examen, 69.

various branches of the administration were bound together in no such partnership. Each of them was accountable for his own acts, for the use which he made of his own official seal, for the documents which he signed, for the counsel which he gave to the King. No statesman was held answerable for what he had not himself done, or induced others to do. If he took care not to be the agent in what was wrong, and if, when consulted, he recommended what was right, he was blameless. It would have been thought strange scrupulosity in him to quit his post, because his advice as to matters not strictly within his own department was not taken by his master; to leave the Board of Admiralty, for example, because the finances were in disorder, or the Board of Treasury because the foreign relations of the kingdom were in an unsatisfactory state. It was, therefore, by no means unusual to see in high office, at the same time, men who avowedly differed from one another as widely as ever Pulteney differed from Walpole, or Fox from Pitt.

The moderate and constitutional counsels of Halifax were Lord timidly and feebly seconded by Francis North, Lord Guild- Guildford. ford, who had lately been made Keeper of the Great Seal. The character of Guildford has been drawn at full length by his brother Roger North, a most intolerant Tory, a most affected and pedantic writer, but a vigilant observer of all those minute circumstances which throw light on the dispositions of men. It is remarkable that the biographer, though he was under the influence of the strongest fraternal partiality, and though he was evidently anxious to produce a flattering likeness, was unable to portray the Lord Keeper otherwise than as the most ignoble of mankind. Yet the intellect of Guildford was clear, his industry great, his proficiency in letters and science respectable, and his legal learning more than respectable. His faults were selfishness, cowardice, and meanness. He was not insensible to the power of female beauty, nor averse from excess in wine. Yet neither wine nor beauty could ever seduce the cautious and frugal libertine, even in his earliest youth, into one fit of indiscreet generosity. Though of noble descent, he rose in his profession by paying ignominious homage to all who possessed influence in the courts. He became Chief Justice of the Common Pleas, and as such was party to some of the foulest judicial murders recorded in our history. He had sense enough to perceive from the first that Oates and

Bedloe were impostors : but the Parliament and the country were greatly excited : the government had yielded to the pressure ; and North was not a man to risk a good place for the sake of justice and humanity. Accordingly, while he was in secret drawing up a refutation of the whole romance of the Popish plot, he declared in public that the truth of the story was as plain as the sun in heaven, and was not ashamed to browbeat, from the seat of judgment, the unfortunate Roman Catholics who were arraigned before him for their lives. He had at length reached the highest post in the law. But a lawyer, who, after many years devoted to professional labour, engages in politics for the first time at an advanced period of life, seldom distinguishes himself as a statesman ; and Guildford was no exception to the general rule. He was indeed so sensible of his deficiencies that he never attended the meetings of his colleagues on foreign affairs. Even on questions relating to his own profession his opinion had less weight at the Council board than that of any man who has ever held the Great Seal. Such as his influence was, however, he used it, as far as he dared, on the side of the laws.

The chief opponent of Halifax was Lawrence Hyde, who had recently been created Earl of Rochester. Of all Tories, Rochester was the most intolerant and uncompromising. The moderate members of his party complained that the whole patronage of the Treasury, while he was First Commissioner there, went to noisy zealots, whose only claim to promotion was that they were always drinking confusion to Whiggery, and lighting bonfires to burn the Exclusion Bill. The Duke of York, pleased with a spirit which so much resembled his own, supported his brother in law passionately and obstinately.

The attempts of the rival ministers to surmount and supplant each other kept the court in incessant agitation. Halifax pressed the King to summon a Parliament, to grant a general amnesty, to deprive the Duke of York of all share in the government, to recall Monmouth from banishment, to break with Lewis, and to form a close union with Holland on the principles of the Triple Alliance. The Duke of York, on the other hand, dreaded the meeting of a Parliament, regarded the vanquished Whigs with undiminished hatred, still flattered himself that the design formed fourteen years before at Dover might be accomplished, daily represented to his brother the impropriety of suffering one who was at heart a Republican to hold the Privy Seal, and strongly recommended Rochester for the great place of Lord Treasurer.

While the two factions were struggling, Godolphin, cautious, silent, and laborious, observed a neutrality between them. Sunderland, with his usual restless perfidy, intrigued against them both. He had been turned out of office in disgrace for having voted in favour of the Exclusion Bill, but had made his peace by employing the good offices of the Duchess of Portsmouth and by cringing to the Duke of York, and was once more Secretary of State.

Nor was Lewis negligent or inactive. Everything at that moment favoured his designs. He had nothing to apprehend from the German empire, which was then contending against the Turks on the Danube. Holland could not, unsupported, venture to oppose him. He was therefore at liberty to indulge his ambition and insolence without restraint. He seized Strasburg, Courtray, Luxemburg. He exacted from the republic of Genoa the most humiliating submissions. The power of France at that time reached a higher point than it ever before or ever after attained, during the ten centuries which separated the reign of Charlemagne from the reign of Napoleon. It was not easy to say where her acquisitions would stop, if only England could be kept in a state of vassalage. The first object of the court of Versailles was therefore to prevent the calling of a Parliament and the reconciliation of English parties. For this end bribes, promises, and menaces were unsparingly employed. Charles was sometimes allured by the hope of a subsidy, and sometimes frightened by being told that, if he convoked the Houses, the secret articles of the treaty of Dover should be published. Several Privy Councillors were bought; and attempts were made to buy Halifax, but in vain. When he had been found incorruptible, all the art and influence of the French embassy were employed to drive him from office: but his polished wit and his various accomplishments had made him so agreeable to his master, that the design failed.*

Policy of Lewis.

* Lord Preston, who was envoy at Paris, wrote thence to Halifax as follows :—" I find that your lordship lies still under the same misfortune of being no favourite to this court; and Monsieur Barillon dare not do you the honour to shine upon you, since his master frowneth. They know very well your lordship's qualifications, which make them fear and consequently hate you; and be assured, my lord, if all their strength can send you to Rufford, it shall be employed for

Halifax was not content with standing on the defensive. He openly accused Rochester of malversation. An inquiry took place. It appeared that forty thousand pounds had been lost to the public by the mismanagement of the First Lord of the Treasury. In consequence of this discovery he was not only forced to relinquish his hopes of the white staff, but was removed from the direction of the finances to the more dignified but less lucrative and important post of Lord President. "I have seen people kicked down stairs," said Halifax; "but my Lord Rochester is the first person that I ever saw kicked up stairs." Godolphin, now a peer, became First Commissioner of the Treasury.

State of factions in the court of Charles at the time of his death.

Still, however, the contest continued. The event depended wholly on the will of Charles; and Charles could not come to a decision. In his perplexity he promised everything to everybody. He would stand by France: he would break with France: he would never meet another Parliament: he would order writs for a Parliament to be issued without delay. He assured the Duke of York that Halifax should be dismissed from office, and Halifax that the Duke should be sent to Scotland. In public he affected implacable resentment against Monmouth, and in private conveyed to Monmouth assurances of unalterable affection. How long, if the King's life had been protracted, his hesitation would have lasted, and what would have been his resolve, can only be conjectured. Early in the year 1685, while hostile parties were anxiously awaiting his determination, he died, and a new scene opened. In a few months the excesses of the government obliterated the impression which had been made on the public mind by the excesses of the opposition. The violent reaction which had laid the Whig party prostrate was followed by a still more violent reaction in the opposite direction; and signs not to be mistaken indicated that the great conflict between the prerogatives of the Crown and the privileges of the Parliament, was about to be brought to a final issue.

that end. Two things, I hear, they particularly object against you, your secrecy, and your being incapable of being cor- rupted. Against these two things I know they have declared." The date of the letter is October 5. N. S. 1683.

CHAPTER III.

I INTEND, in this chapter, to give a description of the state in which England was at the time when the crown passed from Charles the Second to his brother. Such a description, composed from scanty and dispersed materials, must necessarily be very imperfect. Yet it may perhaps correct some false notions which would make the subsequent narrative unintelligible or uninstructive.

If we would study with profit the history of our ancestors, we must be constantly on our guard against that delusion which the well known names of families, places, and offices naturally produce, and must never forget that the country of which we read was a very different country from that in which we live. In every experimental science there is a tendency towards perfection. In every human being there is a wish to ameliorate his own condition. These two principles have often sufficed, even when counteracted by great public calamities and by bad institutions, to carry civilisation rapidly forward. No ordinary misfortune, no ordinary misgovernment, will do so much to make a nation wretched, as the constant progress of physical knowledge and the constant effort of every man to better himself will do to make a nation prosperous. It has often been found that profuse expenditure, heavy taxation, absurd commercial restrictions, corrupt tribunals, disastrous wars, seditions, persecutions, conflagrations, inundations, have not been able to destroy capital so fast as the exertions of private citizens have been able to create it. It can easily be proved that, in our own land, the national wealth has, during at least six centuries, been almost uninterruptedly increasing; that it was greater under the Tudors than under the Plantagenets; that it was greater under the Stuarts than under the Tudors; that, in spite of battles, sieges, and confiscations, it was greater on the day of the Restoration than on the day when the Long Parliament met; that, in spite of maladministration, of extravagance, of public bankruptcy, of two costly and unsuccessful wars, of the pestilence and of the fire, it was greater on the day of the death of Charles the Second than on the day of his Restoration. This progress, having continued during many ages, became at length, about the middle of the eighteenth century, portentously rapid, and has proceeded, during the nineteenth, with accelerated velocity. In consequence partly of our geographical and partly of our moral position, we have, during several generations, been exempt from evils which have elsewhere impeded the efforts and destroyed the fruits of industry. While every part of the Continent, from Moscow to Lisbon, has been the theatre of bloody and devastating wars, no hostile standard has been seen here but as a trophy. While revolutions have taken place all around us, our government has never once been subverted by violence. During more than a hundred years there has been in our island no tumult of sufficient importance to be called an insurrection; nor has the law been once borne down either by popular fury or by regal tyranny: public credit has been held sacred: the administration of justice has been pure: even in times which might by Englishmen be justly called evil times, we have enjoyed what almost every other nation in the world would have considered as an ample measure of civil and religious freedom. Every man has felt entire confidence that the state would protect him in the possession of what had been earned by his diligence and hoarded by his selfdenial. Under the benignant influence of peace and liberty, science has flourished, and has been applied to practical purposes on a scale never before known. The consequence is that a change to which the history of the old world furnishes no parallel has taken place in our country. Could the England of 1685 be, by some magical process, set before our eyes, we should not know one landscape in a hundred or one building in ten thousand. The country gentleman would not recognise his own fields. The inhabitant of the town would not recognise his own street. Everything has been changed, but the great features of nature, and a few massive and durable works of human art. We might find out Snowdon and Windermere, the Cheddar Cliffs and Beachy Head. We might find out here and there a Norman minster, or a castle which witnessed the wars of the Roses. But, with such rare exceptions, everything would be strange to us. Many thousands of square miles which are now rich corn land and meadow, intersected by green hedgerows, and dotted with villages and pleasant country seats,

Great change in the state of England since 1685.

would appear as moors overgrown with furze, or fens abandoned to wild ducks. We should see straggling huts built of wood and covered with thatch, where we now see manufacturing towns and seaports renowned to the farthest ends of the world. The capital itself would shrink to dimensions not much exceeding those of its present suburb on the south of the Thames. Not less strange to us would be the garb and manners of the people, the furniture and the equipages, the interior of the shops and dwellings. Such a change in the state of a nation seems to be at least as well entitled to the notice of a historian as any change of the dynasty or of the ministry.*

One of the first objects of an inquirer, who wishes to form a correct notion of the state of a community at a given time, must be to ascertain of how many persons that community then consisted. Unfortunately the population of England in 1685 cannot be ascertained with perfect accuracy. For no great state had then adopted the wise course of periodically numbering the people. All men were left to conjecture for themselves ; and, as they generally conjectured without examining facts, and under the influence of strong passions and prejudices, their guesses were often ludicrously absurd. Even intelligent Londoners ordinarily talked of London as containing several millions of souls. It was confidently asserted by many that, during the thirty-five years which had elapsed between the accession of Charles the First and the Restoration, the population of the City had increased by two millions.† Even while the ravages of the plague and fire were recent, it was the fashion to say that the capital still had a million and a half of inhabitants.‡ Some persons, disgusted by these exaggerations, ran violently into the opposite extreme. Thus Isaac Vossius, a man of undoubted parts and learning, strenuously maintained that there were only two millions of human beings in England, Scotland, and Ireland taken together.§

Population of England in 1685.

---

* During the interval which has elapsed since this chapter was written, England has continued to advance rapidly in material prosperity. I have left my text nearly as it originally scood; but I have added a few notes which may enable the reader to form some notion of the progress which has been made during the last nine years; and, in general, I would desire him to remember that there is scarcely a district which is not more populous, or a source of wealth which is not more pro-

ductive, at present than in 1848. (1857.)

† Observations on the Bills of Mortality, by Captain John Graunt (Sir William Petty), chap. xi.

‡   "She doth comprehend Full fifteen hundred thousand which do spend Their days within."

Great Britain's Beauty, 1671.

§ Isaac Vossius, De Magnitudine Urbium Sinarum, 1685. Vossius, as we learn from Saint Evremond, talked on this subject oftener and longer than fashionable circles cared to listen.

We are not, however, left without the means of correcting the wild blunders into which some minds were hurried by national vanity and others by a morbid love of paradox. There are extant three computations which seem to be entitled to peculiar attention. They are entirely independent of each other : they proceed on different principles ; and yet there is little difference in the results.

One of these computations was made in the year 1696 by Gregory King, Lancaster herald, a political arithmetician of great acuteness and judgment. The basis of his calculations was the number of houses returned in 1690 by the officers who made the last collection of the hearth money. The conclusion at which he arrived was that the population of England was nearly five millions and a half.*

About the same time King William the Third was desirous to ascertain the comparative strength of the religious sects into which the community was divided. An inquiry was instituted ; and reports were laid before him from all the dioceses of the realm. According to these reports the number of his English subjects must have been about five million two hundred thousand.†

Lastly, in our own days, Mr. Finlaison, an actuary of eminent skill, subjected the ancient parochial registers of baptisms, marriages, and burials, to all the tests which the modern improvements in statistical science enabled him to apply. His opinion was, that, at the close of the seventeenth century, the population of England was a little under five million two hundred thousand souls.‡

Of these three estimates, framed without concert by different persons from different sets of materials, the highest, which is that of King, does not exceed the lowest, which is that of Finlaison, by one twelfth. We may, therefore, with confidence pronounce that, when James the Second reigned, England contained between five million and five million five hundred thousand inhabitants. On the very highest supposition she then had less than one third of her present popu-

* King's Natural and Political Observations, 1696. This valuable treatise, which ought to be read as the author wrote it, and not as garbled by Davenant, will be found in some editions of Chalmers's Estimate.

† Dalrymple's Appendix to Part II. Book I. The practice of reckoning the population by sects was long fashion-

able. Gulliver says of the King of Brobdignag ; "He laughed at my odd arithmetic, as he was pleased to call it, in reckoning the numbers of our people by a computation drawn from the several sects among us in religion and politics."

‡ Preface to the Population Returns of 1831.

lation, and less than three times the population which is now collected in her gigantic capital.

The increase of the people has been great in every part of the kingdom, but generally much greater in the northern than in the southern shires. In truth a large part of the country beyond Trent was, down to the eighteenth century, in a state of barbarism. Physical and moral causes had concurred to prevent civilisation from spreading to that region. The air was inclement; the soil was generally such as required skilful and industrious cultivation; and there could be little skill or industry in a tract which was often the theatre of war, and which, even when there was nominal peace, was constantly desolated by bands of Scottish marauders. Before the union of the two British crowns, and long after that union, there was as great a difference between Middlesex and Northumberland as there now is between Massachusetts and the settlements of those squatters who, far to the west of the Mississippi, administer a rude justice with the rifle and the dagger. In the reign of Charles the Second, the traces left by ages of slaughter and pillage were distinctly perceptible, many miles south of the Tweed, in the face of the country and in the lawless manners of the people. There was still a large class of mosstroopers, whose calling was to plunder dwellings and to drive away whole herds of cattle. It was found necessary, soon after the Restoration, to enact laws of great severity for the prevention of these outrages. The magistrates of Northumberland and Cumberland were authorised to raise bands of armed men for the defence of property and order; and provision was made for meeting the expense of these levies by local taxation.* The parishes were required to keep bloodhounds for the purpose of hunting the freebooters. Many old men who were living in the middle of the eighteenth century could well remember the time when those ferocious dogs were common.† Yet, even with such auxiliaries, it was often found impossible to track the robbers to their retreats among the hills and morasses. For the geography of that wild country was very imperfectly known. Even after the accession of George the Third, the path over the fells from Borrowdale to Ravenglas was still a secret carefully kept by the dalesmen, some of whom had probably in

---

* Statutes 14 Car. II. c. 22.; 18 & 19 Car. II. c. 3.; 29 & 30 Car. II. c. 2.   † Nicholson and Bourne, Discourse on the Ancient State of the Border, 1777.

their youth escaped from the pursuit of justice by that road.[*]
The seats of the gentry and the larger farmhouses were for-
tified. Oxen were penned at night beneath the overhanging
battlements of the residence, which was known by the name
of the Peel. The inmates slept with arms at their sides.
Huge stones and boiling water were in readiness to crush and
scald the plunderer who might venture to assail the little
garrison. No traveller ventured into that country without
making his will. The Judges on circuit, with the whole body
of barristers, attorneys, clerks, and serving men, rode on
horseback from Newcastle to Carlisle, armed and escorted by
a strong guard under the command of the Sheriffs. It was
necessary to carry provisions ; for the country was a wilderness which afforded no supplies. The spot where the cavalcade
halted to dine, under an immense oak, is not yet forgotten.
The irregular vigour with which criminal justice was administered shocked observers whose lives had been passed in more
tranquil districts. Juries, animated by hatred and by a sense
of common danger, convicted housebreakers and cattle stealers
with the promptitude of a court martial in a mutiny ; and
the convicts were hurried by scores to the gallows.[†] Within
the memory of some whom this generation has seen, the
sportsman who wandered in pursuit of game to the sources
of the Tyne found the heaths round Keeldar Castle peopled
by a race scarcely less savage than the Indians of California,
and heard with surprise the half naked women chaunting a
wild measure, while the men with brandished dirks danced a
war dance.[‡]

Slowly and with difficulty peace was established on the
border. In the train of peace came industry and all the arts
of life. Meanwhile it was discovered that the regions north
of the Trent possessed in their coal beds a source of wealth
far more precious than the gold mines of Peru. It was found
that, in the neighbourhood of these beds, almost every manufacture might be most profitably carried on. A constant
stream of emigrants began to roll northward. It appeared
by the returns of 1841 that the ancient archiepiscopal province of York contained two-sevenths of the population of
England. At the time of the Revolution that province was

<hr />

* Gray's Journal of a Tour in the
Lakes, Oct. 3. 1769.

† North's Life of Guildford ; Hutchinson's History of Cumberland, Parish

of Brampton.

‡ See Sir Walter Scott's Journal, Oct.
7. 1827, in his Life by Mr. Lockhart.

believed to contain only one seventh of the population.* In Lancashire the number of inhabitants appears to have increased ninefold, while in Norfolk, Suffolk, and Northamptonshire it has hardly doubled.†

Of the taxation we can speak with more confidence and precision than of the population. The revenue of England, when Charles the Second died, was small, when compared with the resources which she even then possessed, or with the sums which were raised by the governments of the neighbouring countries. It had, from the time of the Restoration, been almost constantly increasing: yet it was little more than three fourths of the revenue of the United Provinces, and was hardly one fifth of the revenue of France.

Revenue in 1685.

The most important head of receipt was the excise, which, in the last year of the reign of Charles, produced five hundred and eighty-five thousand pounds, clear of all deductions. The net proceeds of the customs amounted in the same year to five hundred and thirty thousand pounds. These burdens did not lie very heavy on the nation. The tax on chimneys, though less productive, called forth far louder murmurs. The discontent excited by direct imposts is, indeed, almost always out of proportion to the quantity of money which they bring into the Exchequer; and the tax on chimneys was, even among direct imposts, peculiarly odious: for it could be levied only by means of domiciliary visits; and of such visits the English have alwayz been impatient to a degree which the people of other countries can but faintly conceive. The poorer householders were frequently unable to pay their hearth money to the day. When this happened, their furniture was distrained without mercy: for the tax was farmed; and a farmer of taxes is, of all creditors, proverbially the most rapacious. The collectors were loudly accused of performing their unpopular duty with harshness and insolence. It was said that, as soon as they appeared at the threshold of a cottage, the children began to wail, and the old women ran to hide their earthenware. Nay, the single bed of a poor family had sometimes been carried away

---

* Dalrymple, Appendix to Part II. Book I. The returns of the hearth money lead to nearly the same conclusion. The hearths in the province of York were not a sixth of the hearths of England.

† I do not, of course, pretend to strict accuracy here; but I believe that whoever will take the trouble to compare the last returns of hearth money in the reign of William the Third with the census of 1841, will come to a conclusion not very different from mine.

and sold. The net annual receipt from this tax was two hundred thousand pounds.*

When to the three great sources of income which have been mentioned we add the royal domains, then far more extensive than at present, the first fruits and tenths, which had not yet been surrendered to the Church, the Duchies of Cornwall and Lancaster, the forfeitures, and the fines, we shall find that the whole annual revenue of the crown may be fairly estimated at about fourteen hundred thousand pounds. Of this revenue part was hereditary: the rest had been granted to Charles for life ; and he was at liberty to lay out the whole exactly as he thought fit. Whatever he could save by retrenching from the expenditure of the public departments was an addition to his privy purse. Of the Post Office more will hereafter be said. The profits of that establishment had been appropriated by Parliament to the Duke of York.

The King's revenue was, or rather ought to have been, charged with the payment of about eighty thousand pounds a year, the interest of the sum fraudulently detained in the Exchequer by the Cabal. While Danby was at the head of the finances, the creditors had received dividends, though not with the strict punctuality of modern times : but those who had succeeded him at the Treasury had been less expert, or less solicitous to maintain public faith. Since the victory won by the court over the Whigs, not a farthing had been paid ; and no redress was granted to the sufferers, till a new dynasty had been many years on the throne. There can be no greater error than to imagine that the device of meeting the exigencies of the state by loans was imported into our island by William the Third. What really dates from his reign is not the system of borrowing, but the system of fund-

---

* There are in the Pepysian Library some ballads of that age on the chimney money. I will give a specimen or two:—

"The good old dames, whenever they the chimney man espied,
Unto their nooks they haste away, their pots and pipkins hide.
There is not one old dame in ten, and search the nation through,
But, if you talk of chimney men, will spare a curse or two."

Again :

"Like plundering soldiers they'd enter the door,
And make a distress on the goods of the poor,
While frighted poor children distractedly cried ;
This nothing abated their insolent pride."

In the British Museum there are doggrel verses composed on the same subject and in the same spirit :

"Or, if through poverty it be not paid,
For cruelty to tear away the single bed,
On which the poor man rests his weary head,
At once deprives him of his rest and bread."

I take this opportunity, the first which occurs, of acknowledging most gratefully the kind and liberal manner in which the Master and Vicemaster of Magdalene College, Cambridge, gave me access to the valuable collections of Pepys.

ing. From a period of immemorial antiquity it had been the practice of every English government to contract debts. What the Revolution introduced was the practice of honestly paying them.*

By plundering the public creditor, it was possible to make an income of about fourteen hundred thousand pounds, with some occasional help from Versailles, support the necessary charges of the government and the wasteful expenditure of the court. For that load which pressed most heavily on the finances of the great continental states was here scarcely felt. In France, Germany, and the Netherlands, armies, such as Henry the Fourth and Philip the Second had never employed in time of war, were kept up in the midst of peace. Bastions and ravelins were everywhere rising, constructed on principles unknown to Parma and Spinola. Stores of artillery and ammunition were accumulated, such as even Richelieu, whom the preceding generation had regarded as a worker of prodigies, would have pronounced fabulous. No man could journey many leagues in those countries without hearing the drums of a regiment on march, or being challenged by the sentinels on the drawbridge of a fortress. In our island, on the contrary, it was possible to live long and to travel far, without being once reminded, by any martial sight or sound, that the defence of nations had become a science and a calling. The majority of Englishmen who were under twenty-five years of age had probably never seen a company of regular soldiers. Of the cities which, in the civil war, had valiantly repelled hostile armies, scarcely one was now capable of sustaining a siege. The gates stood open night and day. The ditches were dry. The ramparts had been suffered to fall into decay, or were repaired only that the townsfolk might have a pleasant walk on summer evenings. Of the old baronial keeps many had been shattered by the cannon of Fairfax and Cromwell, and lay in heaps of ruin, overgrown with ivy. Those which remained had lost their martial character, and were now rural palaces of the aristocracy. The moats were turned into preserves of carp and pike. The mounds were planted with fragrant shrubs, through which spiral walks ran up to summer houses adorned with mirrors and paintings.† On the capes of the sea coast, and on many

Military system.

---

* My chief authorities for this financial statement will be found in the Commons' Journal, March 1. and March 20. 168⁸⁄₉.

† See for example the picture of the mound at Marlborough, in Stukeley's Itinerarium Curiosum.

inland hills, were still seen tall posts, surmounted by barrels.
Once those barrels had been filled with pitch. Watchmen
had been set round them in seasons of danger; and, within
a few hours after a Spanish sail had been discovered in the
Channel, or after a thousand Scottish mosstroopers had
crossed the Tweed, the signal fires were blazing fifty miles
off, and whole counties were rising in arms. But many years
had now elapsed since the beacons had been lighted; and
they were regarded rather as curious relics of ancient manners than as parts of a machinery necessary to the safety of
the state.*

The only army which the law recognised was the militia.
That force had been remodelled by two Acts of Parliament
passed shortly after the Restoration. Every man who possessed five hundred pounds a year derived from land, or six
thousand pounds of personal estate, was bound to provide,
equip, and pay, at his own charge, one horseman. Every
man who had fifty pounds a year derived from land, or six
hundred pounds of personal estate, was charged in like manner with one pikeman or musketeer. Smaller proprietors
were joined together in a kind of society, for which our language does not afford a special name, but which an Athenian
would have called a Synteleia; and each society was required
to furnish, according to its means, a horse soldier or a foot
soldier. The whole number of cavalry and infantry thus
maintained was popularly estimated at a hundred and thirty
thousand men.†

The King was, by the ancient constitution of the realm,
and by the recent and solemn acknowledgment of both
Houses of Parliament, the sole Captain General of this large
force. The Lords Lieutenants and their Deputies held the
command under him, and appointed meetings for drilling
and inspection. The time occupied by such meetings, however, was not to exceed fourteen days in one year. The Justices of the Peace were authorised to inflict slight penalties
for breaches of discipline. Of the ordinary cost no part was
paid by the crown: but when the trainbands were called out
against an enemy, their subsistence became a charge on the
general revenue of the state, and they were subject to the
utmost rigour of martial law.

---

* Chamberlayne's State of England, c. 4. Chamberlayne's State of England,
1684.   1684.
† 13 & 14 Car. II. c. 3.; 15 Car. II.

There were those who looked on the militia with no friendly eye. Men who had travelled much on the Continent, who had marvelled at the stern precision with which every sentinel moved and spoke in the citadels built by Vauban, who had seen the mighty armies which poured along all the roads of Germany to chase the Ottoman from the Gates of Vienna, and who had been dazzled by the well ordered pomp of the household troops of Lewis, sneered much at the way in which the peasants of Devonshire and Yorkshire marched and wheeled, shouldered muskets and ported pikes. The enemies of the liberties and religion of England looked with aversion on a force which could not, without extreme risk, be employed against those liberties and that religion, and missed no opportunity of throwing ridicule on the rustic soldiery.* Enlightened patriots, when they contrasted these rude levies with the battalions which, in time of war, a few hours might bring to the coast of Kent or Sussex, were forced to acknowledge that, dangerous as it might be to keep up a permanent military establishment, it might be more dangerous still to stake the honour and independence of the country on the result of a contest between ploughmen officered by Justices of the Peace, and veteran warriors led by Marshals of France. In Parliament, however, it was necessary to express such opinions with some reserve; for the militia was an institution eminently popular. Every reflection thrown on it excited the indignation of both the great parties in the state, and especially of that party which was distinguished by peculiar zeal for monarchy and for the Anglican Church. The array of the counties was commanded almost exclusively by Tory noblemen and gentlemen. They were proud of their military rank, and considered an insult offered to the service to which they belonged as offered to themselves. They were also perfectly aware that whatever was said against a militia was said in favour of a standing army; and the name of standing army was hateful to them. One such army had held dominion in England; and under that dominion the King had been murdered, the nobility degraded, the landed gentry plundered,

---

* Dryden, in his Cymon and Iphigenia, expressed, with his usual keenness and energy, the sentiments which had been fashionable among the sycophants of James the Second:—

" The country rings around with loud alarms,
And raw in fields the rude militia swarms;

Mouths without hands, maintained at vast expense,
In peace a charge, in war a weak defence.
Stout once a month they march, a blustering band,
And ever, but in time of need, at hand.
This was the morn when, issuing on the guard,
Drawn up in rank and file, they stood prepared
Of seeming arms to make a short essay, [day."
Then hasten to be drunk, the business of the

the Church persecuted.   There was scarcely a rural grandee
who could not tell a story of wrongs and insults suffered by
himself, or by his father, at the hands of the parliamentary
soldiers.   One old Cavalier had seen half his manor house
blown up.   The hereditary elms of another had been hewn
down.   A third could never go into his parish church without being reminded by the defaced scutcheons and headless
statues of his ancestry, that Oliver's redcoats had once
stabled their horses there.   The consequence was that those
very Royalists, who were most ready to fight for the King
themselves, were the last persons whom he could venture to
ask for the means of hiring regular troops.

Charles, however, had, a few months after his restoration,
begun to form a small standing army.   He felt that, without
some better protection than that of the trainbands and beefeaters, his palace and person would hardly be secure, in the
vicinity of a great city swarming with warlike Fifth Monarchy
men who had just been disbanded.   He therefore, careless and
profuse as he was, contrived to spare from his pleasures a
sum sufficient to keep up a body of guards.   With the increase
of trade and of public wealth his revenues increased; and he
was thus enabled, in spite of the occasional murmurs of the
Commons, to make gradual additions to his regular forces.
One considerable addition was made a few months before the
close of his reign.   The costly, useless, and pestilential settlement of Tangier was abandoned to the barbarians who dwelt
around it; and the garrison, consisting of one regiment of
horse and two regiments of foot, was brought to England.

The little army formed by Charles the Second was the germ
of that great and renowned army which has, in the present
century, marched triumphant into Madrid and Paris, into
Canton and Candahar.   The Life Guards, who now form two
regiments, were then distributed into three troops, each of
which consisted of two hundred carabineers, exclusive of
officers.   This corps, to which the safety of the King and
royal family was confided, had a very peculiar character.
Even the privates were designated as gentlemen of the Guard.
Many of them were of good families, and had held commissions in the civil war.   Their pay was far higher than that
of the most favoured regiment of our time, and would in that
age have been thought a respectable provision for the younger
son of a country squire.   Their fine horses, their rich hous-
ings, their cuirasses, and their buff coats adorned with ribands,

velvet, and gold lace, made a splendid appearance in Saint James's Park. A small body of grenadier dragoons, who came from a lower class and received lower pay, was attached to each troop. Another body of household cavalry distinguished by blue coats and cloaks, and still called the Blues, was generally quartered in the neighbourhood of the capital. Near the capital lay also the corps which is now designated as the first regiment of dragoons, but which was then the only regiment of dragoons on the English establishment. It had recently been formed out of the cavalry which had returned from Tangier. A single troop of dragoons, which did not form part of any regiment, was stationed near Berwick, for the purpose of keeping the peace among the mosstroopers of the border. For this species of service the dragoon was then thought to be peculiarly qualified. He has since become a mere horse soldier. But in the seventeenth century he was accurately described by Montecuculi as a foot soldier who used a horse only in order to arrive with more speed at the place where military service was to be performed.

The household infantry consisted of two regiments, which were then, as now, called the first regiment of Foot Guards, and the Coldstream Guards. They generally did duty near Whitehall and Saint James's Palace. As there were then no barracks, and as, by the Petition of Right, it had been declared unlawful to quarter soldiers on private families, the redcoats filled all the alehouses of Westminster and the Strand.

There were five other regiments of foot. One of these, called the Admiral's Regiment, was especially destined to service on board of the fleet. The remaining four still rank as the first four regiments of the line. Two of these represented two brigades which had long sustained on the Continent the fame of British valour. The first, or Royal regiment, had, under the great Gustavus, borne a conspicuous part in the deliverance of Germany. The third regiment, distinguished by fleshcoloured facings, from which it had derived the well known name of the Buffs, had, under Maurice of Nassau, fought not less bravely for the deliverance of the Netherlands. Both these gallant bands had at length, after many vicissitudes, been recalled from foreign service by Charles the Second, and had been placed on the English establishment.

The regiments which now rank as the second and fourth

of the line had, in 1685, just returned from Tangier, bringing
with them cruel and licentious habits contracted in a long
course of warfare with the Moors. A few companies of
infantry which had not been regimented lay in garrison at
Tilbury Fort, at Portsmouth, at Plymouth, and at some
other important stations on or near the coast.

Since the beginning of the seventeenth century a great
change had taken place in the arms of the infantry. The
pike had been gradually giving place to the musket; and, at
the close of the reign of Charles the Second, most of his foot
were musketeers. Still, however, there was a large intermixture of pikemen. Each class of troops was occasionally
instructed in the use of the weapon which peculiarly belonged
to the other class. Every foot soldier had at his side a sword
for close fight. The musketeer was generally provided with
a weapon which had, during many years, been gradually
coming into use, and which the English then called a dagger,
but which, from the time of William the Third, has been
known among us by the French name of bayonet. The bayonet
seems not to have been then so formidable an instrument of
destruction as it has since become; for it was inserted in the
muzzle of the gun; and in action much time was lost while
the soldier unfixed his bayonet in order to fire, and fixed it
again in order to charge. The dragoon, when dismounted,
fought as a musketeer.

The regular army which was kept up in England at the beginning of the year 1685 consisted, all ranks included, of about
seven thousand foot, and about seventeen hundred cavalry
and dragoons. The whole charge amounted to about two
hundred and ninety thousand pounds a year, less than a tenth
part of what the military establishment of France then cost
in time of peace. The daily pay of a private in the Life
Guards was four shillings, in the Blues two shillings and
sixpence, in the Dragoons eighteen pence, in the Foot Guards
tenpence, and in the line eightpence. The discipline was lax,
and indeed could not be otherwise. The common law of
England knew nothing of courts martial, and made no distinction, in time of peace, between a soldier and any other
subject; nor could the government then venture to ask even
the most loyal Parliament for a Mutiny Bill. A soldier,
therefore, by knocking down his colonel, incurred only the
ordinary penalties of assault and battery, and by refusing to
obey orders, by sleeping on guard, or by deserting his colours,

incurred no legal penalty at all.   Military punishments were doubtless inflicted during the reign of Charles the Second; but they were inflicted very sparingly, and in such a manner as not to attract public notice, or to produce an appeal to the courts of Westminster Hall.

Such an army as has been described was not very likely to enslave five millions of Englishmen.   It would indeed have been unable to suppress an insurrection in London, if the trainbands of the City had joined the insurgents.   Nor could the King expect that, if a rising took place in England, he would obtain effectual help from his other dominions.   For, though both Scotland and Ireland supported separate military establishments, those establishments were not more than sufficient to keep down the Puritan malecontents of the former kingdom and the Popish malecontents of the latter. The government had, however, an important military resource which must not be left unnoticed.   There were in the pay of the United Provinces six fine regiments, of which three had been raised in England and three in Scotland.   Their native prince had reserved to himself the power of recalling them, if he needed their help against a foreign or domestic enemy. In the meantime they were maintained without any charge to him, and were kept under an excellent discipline, to which he could not have ventured to subject them.*

If the jealousy of the Parliament and of the nation made The navy it impossible for the King to maintain a formidable standing army, no similar impediment prevented him from making England the first of maritime powers.   Both Whigs and Tories were ready to applaud every step tending to increase the efficiency of that force which, while it was the best protection of the island against foreign enemies, was powerless against civil liberty.   All the greatest exploits achieved within the memory of that generation by English soldiers had been achieved in war against English princes.   The victories of our sailors had been won over foreign foes, and had averted havoc and rapine from our own soil.   By at least half the nation the battle of Naseby was remembered with horror, and the battle of Dunbar with pride chequered by

* Most of the materials which I have used for this account of the regular army will be found in the Historical Records of Regiments, published by command of King William the Fourth, and under the direction of the Adjutant General. See also Chamberlayne's State of England, 1684; Abridgment of the English Military Discipline, printed by especial command, 1685; Exercise of Foot, by their Majesties' command, 1690.

many painful feelings : but the defeat of the Armada, and the
encounters of Blake with the Hollanders and Spaniards were
recollected with unmixed exultation by all parties.   Ever
since the Restoration, the Commons, even when most discontented and most parsimonious, had always been bountiful to
profusion where the interest of the navy was concerned.   It
had been represented to them, while Danby was minister,
that many of the vessels in the royal fleet were old and unfit
for sea ; and, although the House was, at that time, in no
giving mood, an aid of near six hundred thousand pounds had
been granted for the building of thirty new men of war.

But the liberality of the nation had been made fruitless by
the vices of the government.   The list of the King's ships, it
is true, looked well.   There were nine first rates, fourteen
second rates, thirty-nine third rates, and many smaller vessels.
The first rates, indeed, were less than the third rates of our
time ; and the third rates would not now rank as very large
frigates.   This force, however, if it had been efficient, would
in those days have been regarded by the greatest potentate
as formidable.   But it existed only on paper.   When the
reign of Charles terminated, his navy had sunk into degradation and decay, such as would be almost incredible if it
were not certified to us by the independent and concurring
evidence of witnesses whose authority is beyond exception.
Pepys, the ablest man in the English Admiralty, drew up, in
the year 1684, a memorial on the state of his department,
for the information of Charles.   A few months later Bonrepaux, the ablest man in the French Admiralty, having visited
England for the especial purpose of ascertaining her maritime
strength, laid the result of his inquiries before Lewis.   The
two reports are to the same effect.   Bonrepaux declared that
he found everything in disorder and in miserable condition,
that the superiority of the French marine was acknowledged
with shame and envy at Whitehall, and that the state of our
shipping and dockyards was of itself a sufficient guarantee
that we should not meddle in the disputes of Europe.*

* I refer to a despatch of Bonrepaux
to Seignelay, dated Feb. ${}^{8}_{18}$. 1686.   It
was transcribed for Mr. Fox from the
French archives, during the peace of
Amiens, and, with the other materials
brought together by that great man, was
entrusted to me by the kindness of the
late Lady Holland, and of the present
Lord Holland.   I ought to add that, even
in the midst of the troubles which have
lately agitated Paris, I found no difficulty in obtaining, from the liberality
of the functionaries there, extracts supplying some chasms in Mr. Fox's collection.   (1848.)

Pepys informed his master that the naval administration was a prodigy of wastefulness, corruption, ignorance, and indolence, that no estimate could be trusted, that no contract was performed, that no check was enforced. The vessels which the recent liberality of Parliament had enabled the government to build, and which had never been out of harbour, had been made of such wretched timber that they were more unfit to go to sea than the old hulls which had been battered thirty years before by Dutch and Spanish broadsides. Some of the new men of war, indeed, were so rotten that, unless speedily repaired, they would go down at their moorings. The sailors were paid with so little punctuality that they were glad to find some usurer who would purchase their tickets at forty per cent. discount. The commanders who had not powerful friends at court were even worse treated. Some officers, to whom large arrears were due, after vainly importuning the government during many years, had died for want of a morsel of bread.

Most of the ships which were afloat were commanded by men who had not been bred to the sea. This, it is true, was not an abuse introduced by the government of Charles. No state, ancient or modern, had, before that time, made a complete separation between the naval and military services. In the great civilised nations of antiquity, Cimon and Lysander, Pompey and Agrippa, had fought battles by sea as well as by land. Nor had the impulse which nautical science received at the close of the fifteenth century produced any new division of labour. At Flodden the right wing of the victorious army was led by the Admiral of England. At Jarnac and Moncontour the Huguenot ranks were marshalled by the Admiral of France.. Neither John of Austria, the conqueror of Lepanto, nor Lord Howard of Effingham, to whose direction the marine of England was confided when the Spanish invaders were approaching our shores, had received the education of a sailor. Raleigh, highly celebrated as a naval commander, had served during many years as a soldier in France, the Netherlands, and Ireland. Blake had distinguished himself by his skilful and valiant defence of an inland town before he humbled the pride of Holland and of Castile on the ocean. Since the Restoration the same system had been followed. Great fleets had been entrusted to the direction of Rupert and Monk; Rupert, who was renowned chiefly as a hot and daring cavalry officer, and Monk, who, when he wished his ship to change her course, moved the mirth of his crew by calling out, "Wheel to the left!"

But about this time wise men began to perceive that the rapid improvement, both of the art of war and of the art of navigation, made it necessary to draw a line between two professions which had hitherto been confounded. Either the command of a regiment or the command of a ship was now a matter quite sufficient to occupy the attention of a single mind. In the year 1672 the French government determined to educate young men of good family from a very early age especially for the sea service. But the English government, instead of following this excellent example, not only continued to distribute high naval commands among landsmen, but selected for such commands landsmen who, even on land, could not safely have been put in any important trust. Any lad of noble birth, any dissolute courtier for whom one of the King's mistresses would speak a word, might hope that a ship of the line, and with it the honour of the country and the lives of hundreds of brave men, would be committed to his care. It mattered not that he had never in his life taken a voyage except on the Thames, that he could not keep his feet in a breeze, that he did not know the difference between latitude and longitude. No previous training was thought necessary; or, at most, he was sent to make a short trip in a man of war, where he was subjected to no discipline, where he was treated with marked respect, and where he lived in a round of revels and amusements. If, in the intervals of feasting, drinking, and gambling, he succeeded in learning the meaning of a few technical phrases and the names of the points of the compass, he was thought fully qualified to take charge of a three-decker. This is no imaginary description. In 1666, John Sheffield, Earl of Mulgrave, at seventeen years of age, volunteered to serve at sea against the Dutch. He passed six weeks on board, diverting himself, as well as he could, in the society of some young libertines of rank, and then returned home to take the command of a troop of horse. After this he was never on the water till the year 1672, when he again joined the fleet, and was almost immediately appointed Captain of a ship of eighty-four guns, reputed the finest in the navy. He was then twenty-three years old, and had not, in the whole course of his life, been three months afloat. As soon as he came back from sea he was made Colonel of a regiment of foot. This is a specimen of the manner in which naval commands of the highest importance were then given; and a very favourable specimen; for Mulgrave, though he wanted experience, wanted neither parts nor courage. Others were promoted in the same way who not only were not good officers, but who were intellectually and morally incapable of ever becoming good officers, and whose only recommendation was that they had been ruined by folly and vice. The chief bait which allured these men into the service was the profit of conveying bullion and other valuable commodities from port to port; for both the Atlantic and the Mediterranean were then so much infested by pirates from Barbary that merchants were not willing to trust precious cargoes to any custody but that of a man of war. A Captain might thus clear several thousands of pounds by a short voyage; and for this lucrative business he too often neglected the interests of his country and the honour of his flag, made mean submissions to foreign powers, disobeyed the most direct injunctions of his superiors, lay in port when he was ordered to chase a Sallee rover, or ran with dollars to Leghorn when his instructions directed him to repair to Lisbon. And all this he did with impunity. The same interest which had placed him in a post for which he was unfit maintained him there. No Admiral, bearded by these corrupt and dissolute minions of the palace, dared to do more than mutter something about a court martial. If any officer showed a higher sense of duty than his fellows, he soon found that he lost money without acquiring honour. One Captain, who, by strictly obeying the orders of the Admiralty, missed a cargo which would have been worth four thousand pounds to him, was told by Charles, with ignoble levity, that he was a great fool for his pains.

The discipline of the navy was of a piece throughout. As the courtly Captain despised the Admiralty, he was in turn despised by his crew. It could not be concealed that he was inferior in seamanship to every foremast man on board. It was idle to expect that old sailors, familiar with the hurricanes of the tropics and with the icebergs of the Arctic Circle, would pay prompt and respectful obedience to a chief who knew no more of winds and waves than could be learned in a gilded barge between Whitehall stairs and Hampton Court. To trust such a novice with the working of a ship was evidently impossible. The direction of the navigation was therefore taken from the Captain and given to the Master: but this partition of authority produced innumerable inconveniences.

The line of demarcation was not, and perhaps could not be, drawn with precision. There was therefore constant wrangling. The Captain, confident in proportion to his ignorance, treated the Master with lordly contempt. The Master, well aware of the danger of disobliging the powerful, too often, after a struggle, yielded against his better judgment; and it was well if the loss of ship and crew was not the consequence. In general the least mischievous of the aristocratical Captains were those who completely abandoned to others the direction of the vessels, and thought only of making money and spending it. The way in which these men lived was so ostentatious and voluptuous that, greedy as they were of gain, they seldom became rich. They dressed as if for a gala at Versailles, ate off plate, drank the richest wines, and kept harems on board, while hunger and scurvy raged among the crews, and while corpses were daily flung out of the portholes.

Such was the ordinary character of those who were then called gentlemen Captains. Mingled with them were to be found, happily for our country, naval commanders of a very different description, men whose whole life had been passed on the deep, and who had worked and fought their way from the lowest offices of the forecastle to rank and distinction. One of the most eminent of these officers was Sir Christopher Mings, who entered the service as a cabin boy, who fell fighting bravely against the Dutch, and whom his crew, weeping and vowing vengeance, carried to the grave. From him sprang, by a singular kind of descent, a line of valiant and expert sailors. His cabin boy was Sir John Narborough; and the cabin boy of Sir John Narborough was Sir Cloudesley Shovel. To the strong natural sense and dauntless courage of this class of men England owes a debt never to be forgotten. It was by such resolute hearts that, in spite of much maladministration, and in spite of the blunders and treasons of more courtly admirals, our coasts were protected and the reputation of our flag upheld during many gloomy and perilous years. But to a landsman these tarpaulins, as they were called, seemed a strange and half savage race. All their knowledge was professional; and their professional knowledge was practical rather than scientific. Off their own element they were as simple as children. Their deportment was uncouth. There was roughness in their very good nature; and their talk, where it was not made up of nautical phrases, was too commonly made up of oaths and curses. Such were the chiefs in whose rude school were formed those sturdy warriors from whom Smollet, in the next age, drew Lieutenant Bowling and Commodore Trunnion.   But it does not appear that there was in the service of any of the Stuarts a single naval officer such as, according to the notions of our times, a naval officer ought to be, that is to say, a man versed in the theory and practice of his calling, and steeled against all the dangers of battle and tempest, yet of cultivated mind and polished manners.   There were gentlemen and there were seamen in the navy of Charles the Second.   But the seamen were not gentlemen; and the gentlemen were not seamen.

The English navy at that time might, according to the most exact estimates which have come down to us, have been kept in an efficient state for three hundred and eighty thousand pounds a year.   Four hundred thousand pounds a year was the sum actually expended, but expended, as we have seen, to very little purpose.   The cost of the French marine was nearly the same; the cost of the Dutch marine considerably more.*

The charge of the English ordnance in the seventeenth century was, as compared with other military and naval charges, much smaller than at present.   At most of the garrisons there were gunners; and here and there, at an important post, an engineer was to be found.   But there was no regiment of artillery, no brigade of sappers and miners, no college in which young soldiers could learn the scientific part of the art of war.   The difficulty of moving field pieces was extreme. When, a few years later, William marched from Devonshire to London, the apparatus which he brought with him, though such as had long been in constant use on the Continent, and such as would now be regarded at Woolwich as rude and cumbrous, excited in our ancestors an admiration resembling that which the Indians of America felt for the Castilian harquebusses.   The stock of gunpowder kept in the English forts and arsenals was boastfully mentioned by patriotic writers as

The ordnance.

* My information respecting the condition of the navy, at this time, is chiefly derived from Pepys. His report, presented to Charles the Second in May 1684, has never, I believe, been printed. The manuscript is at Magdalene College, Cambridge.   At Magdalene College is also a valuable manuscript containing a detailed account of the maritime establishments of the country in December 1684. Pepys's "Memoirs relating to the State of the Royal Navy for Ten Years, determined December 1688," and his diary and correspondence during his mission to Tangier, are in print. I have made large use of them.   See also Sheffield's Memoirs, Teonge's Diary, Aubrey's Life of Monk, the Life of Sir Cloudesley Shovel, 1708, Commons' Journals, March 1. and March 20. 168⅝.

something which might well impress neighbouring nations with awe. It amounted to fourteen or fifteen thousand barrels, about a twelfth of the quantity which it is now thought necessary to have in store. The expenditure under the head of ordnance was on an average a little above sixty thousand pounds a year.*

Noneffective charge. The whole effective charge of the army, navy, and ordnance, was about seven hundred and fifty thousand pounds. The noneffective charge, which is now a heavy part of our public burdens, can hardly be said to have existed. A very small number of naval officers, who were not employed in the public service, drew half pay. No Lieutenant was on the list, nor any Captain who had not commanded a ship of the first or second rate. As the country then possessed only seventeen ships of the first and second rate that had ever been at sea, and as a large proportion of the persons who had commanded such ships had good posts on shore, the expenditure under this head must have been small indeed.† In the army, half pay was given merely as a special and temporary allowance to a small number of officers belonging to two regiments, which were peculiarly situated.‡ Greenwich Hospital had not been founded. Chelsea Hospital was building : but the cost of that institution was defrayed partly by a deduction from the pay of the troops, and partly by private subscription. The King promised to contribute only twenty thousand pounds for architectural expenses, and five thousand a year for the maintenance of the invalids.§ It was no part of the plan that there should be outpensioners. The whole noneffective charge, military and naval, can scarcely have exceeded ten thousands pounds a year. It now exceeds ten thousand pounds a day.

Charge of civil government. Of the expense of civil government only a small portion was defrayed by the crown. The great majority of the functionaries whose business was to administer justice and preserve order either gave their services to the public gratuitously, or were remunerated in a manner which caused no drain on the revenue of the state. The sheriffs, mayors, and aldermen of

---

* Chamberlayne's State of England, 1684 ; Commons 'Journals, March 1. and March 20. 168⅘. In 1833, it was determined, after full enquiry, that a hundred and seventy thousand barrels of gunpowder should constantly be kept in store.

† It appears from the records of the Admiralty, that Flag officers were allowed half pay in 1668, Captains of first and second rates not till 1674.

‡ Warrant in the War Office Records, dated March 26. 1678.

§ Evelyn's Diary, Jan. 27. 1682. I have seen a privy seal, dated May 17. 1683, which confirms Evelyn's testimony.

the towns, the country gentlemen who were in the commission of the peace, the headboroughs, bailiffs, and petty constables, cost the King nothing. The superior courts of law were chiefly supported by fees.

Our relations with foreign courts had been put on the most economical footing. The only diplomatic agent who had the title of Ambassador resided at Constantinople, and was partly supported by the Turkey Company. Even at the court of Versailles England had only an Envoy; and she had not even an Envoy at the Spanish, Swedish, and Danish courts. The whole expense under this head cannot, in the last year of the reign of Charles the Second, have much exceeded twenty thousand pounds.*

In this frugality there was nothing laudable. Charles was, as usual, niggardly in the wrong place, and munificent in the wrong place. The public service was starved that courtiers might be pampered. The expense of the navy, of the ordnance, of pensions to needy old officers, of missions to foreign courts, must seem small indeed to the present generation. But the personal favourites of the sovereign, his ministers, and the creatures of those ministers, were gorged with public money. Their salaries and pensions, when compared with the incomes of the nobility, the gentry, the commercial and professional men of that age, will appear enormous. The greatest estates in the kingdom then very little exceeded twenty thousand a year. The Duke of Ormond had twenty-two thousand a year.† The Duke of Buckingham, before his extravagance had impaired his great property, had nineteen thousand six hundred a year.‡ George Monk, Duke of Albemarle, who had been rewarded for his eminent services with immense grants of crown land, and who had been notorious both for covetousness and for parsimony, left fifteen thousand a year of real estate, and sixty thousand pounds in money which probably yielded seven per cent.§ These three Dukes were supposed to be three of the very richest subjects in England. The Archbishop of Canterbury can hardly have had five thousand a year.‖ The average income of a temporal peer

(margin note:) Great gains of ministers and courtiers.

---

* James the Second sent Envoys to Spain, Sweden, and Denmark; yet in his reign the diplomatic expenditure was little more than 30,000l. a year. See the Commons' Journals, March 20. 168⅔. Chamberlayne's State of England, 1684, 1687.

† Carte's Life of Ormond.

‡ Pepys's Diary, Feb. 14. 166⅝.

§ See the Report of the Bath and Montague case, which was decided by Lord Keeper Somers, in December 1693.

‖ During three quarters of a year, beginning from Christmas 1689, the revenues of the see of Canterbury were received by an officer appointed by the

was estimated, by the best informed persons, at about three
thousand a year, the average income of a baronet at nine
hundred a year, the average income of a member of the House
of Commons at less than eight hundred a year.* A thousand
a year was thought a large revenue for a barrister. Two
thousand a year was hardly to be made in the Court of King's
Bench, except by the crown lawyers.† It is evident, therefore, that an official man would have been well paid if he had
received a fourth or fifth part of what would now be an ade-
quate stipend. In fact, however, the stipends of the higher
class of official men were as large as at present, and not seldom
larger. The Lord Treasurer, for example, had eight thousand
a year, and, when the Treasury was in commission, the junior
Lords had sixteen hundred a year each. The Paymaster of
the Forces had a poundage, amounting, in time of peace, to
about five thousand a year, on all the money which passed
through his hands. The Groom of the Stole had five thousand
a year, the Commissioners of the Customs twelve hundred a
year each, the Lords of the Bedchamber a thousand a year
each.‡ The regular salary, however, was the smallest part
of the gains of an official man of that age. From the noblemen who held the white staff and the great seal, down to the
humblest tidewaiter and gauger, what would now be called
gross corruption was practised without disguise and without
reproach. Titles, places, commissions, pardons, were daily
sold in market overt by the great dignitaries of the realm ;
and every clerk in every department imitated, to the best of
his power, the evil example.

During the last century no prime minister, however powerful, has become rich in office ; and several prime ministers have
impaired their private fortune in sustaining their public character. In the seventeenth century, a statesman who was at
the head of affairs might easily, and without giving scandal,
accumulate in no long time an estate amply sufficient to support a dukedom. It is probable that the income of the prime
minister, during his tenure of power, far exceeded that of any

crown. That officer's accounts are now
in the British Museum. (Lansdowne
MSS. 885.) The gross revenue for the
three quarters was not quite four thousand pounds; and the difference between
the gross and the net revenue was evidently something considerable.

* King's Natural and Political Conclusions. Davenant on the Balance of
Trade. Sir W. Temple says, "The revenues of a House of Commons have
seldom exceeded four hundred thousand
pounds." Memoirs, Third Part.

† Langton's Conversations with Chief
Justice Hale, 1672.

‡ Commons' Journals, April 27. 1689;
Chamberlayne's State of England, 1684.

other subject. The place of Lord Lieutenant of Ireland was popularly reported to be worth forty thousand pounds a year.* The gains of the Chancellor Clarendon, of Arlington, of Lauderdale, and of Danby, were certainly enormous. The sumptuous palace to which the populace of London gave the name of Dunkirk House, the stately pavilions, the fishponds, the deer park and the orangery of Euston, the more than Italian luxury of Ham, with its busts, fountains, and aviaries, were among the many signs which indicated what was the shortest road to boundless wealth. This is the true explanation of the unscrupulous violence with which the statesmen of that day struggled for office, of the tenacity with which, in spite of vexations, humiliations and dangers, they clung to it, and of the scandalous compliances to which they stooped in order to retain it. Even in our own age, formidable as is the power of opinion, and high as is the standard of integrity, there would be great risk of a lamentable change in the character of our public men, if the place of First Lord of the Treasury or Secretary of State were worth a hundred thousand pounds a year. Happily for our country the emoluments of the highest class of functionaries have not only not grown in proportion to the general growth of our opulence, but have positively diminished.

The fact that the sum raised in England by taxation has, *State of agriculture.* in a time not exceeding two long lives, been multiplied fortyfold, is strange, and may at first sight seem appalling. But those who are alarmed by the increase of the public burdens may perhaps be reassured when they have considered the increase of the public resources. In the year 1685, the value of the produce of the soil far exceeded the value of all the other fruits of human industry. Yet agriculture was in what would now be considered as a very rude and imperfect state. The arable land and pasture land were not supposed by the best political arithmeticians of that age to amount to much more than half the area of the kingdom.† The remainder was believed to consist of moor, forest, and fen. These computations are strongly confirmed by the road books and maps of the seventeenth century. From those books and maps it is clear that many routes which now pass through an endless succession of orchards, cornfields, hayfields, and beanfields,

* See the Travels of the Grand Duke Cosmo.

† King's Natural and Political Conclusions. Davenant on the Balance of Trade.

then ran through nothing but heath, swamp, and warren.*
In the drawings of English landscapes made in that age for
the Grand Duke Cosmo, scarce a hedgerow is to be seen, and
numerous tracts, now rich with cultivation, appear as bare as
Salisbury Plain.† At Enfield, hardly out of sight of the smoke
of the capital, was a region of five and twenty miles in circumference, which contained only three houses and scarcely
any enclosed fields. Deer, as free as in an American forest,
wandered there by thousands.‡ It is to be remarked, that
wild animals of large size were then far more numerous than
at present. The last wild boars, indeed, which had been preserved for the royal diversion, and had been allowed to ravage
the cultivated land with their tusks, had been slaughtered by
the exasperated rustics during the license of the civil war.
The last wolf that has roamed our island had been slain in
Scotland a short time before the close of the reign of Charles
the Second. But many breeds, now extinct, or rare, both of
quadrupeds and birds, were still common. The fox, whose
life is now, in many counties, held almost as sacred as that
of a human being, was then considered as a mere nuisance.
Oliver Saint John told the Long Parliament that Strafford
was to be regarded, not as a stag or a hare, to whom some
law was to be given, but as a fox, who was to be snared by
any means, and knocked on the head without pity. This
illustration would be by no means a happy one, if addressed to
country gentlemen of our time : but in Saint John's days there
were not seldom great massacres of foxes to which the peasantry thronged with all the dogs that could be mustered :
traps were set : nets were spread : no quarter was given ; and
to shoot a female with cub was considered as a feat which
merited the warmest gratitude of the neighbourhood. The
red deer were then as common in Gloucestershire and Hampshire, as they now are among the Grampian Hills. On one
occasion Queen Anne, travelling to Portsmouth, saw a herd
of no less than five hundred. The wild bull with his white

---

* See the Itinerarium Angliæ, 1675,
by John Ogilby, Cosmographer Royal.
He describes great part of the land as
wood, fen, heath on both sides, marsh
on both sides. In some of his maps
the roads through enclosed country are
marked by lines, and the roads through
unenclosed country by dots. The proportion of unenclosed country, which, if
cultivated, must have been wretchedly
cultivated, seems to have been very

great. From Abingdon to Gloucester,
for example, a distance of forty or fifty
miles, there was not a single enclosure,
and scarcely one enclosure between Big-
gleswade and Lincoln.

† Large copies of these highly interesting drawings are in the noble collection bequeathed by Mr. Grenville to the
British Museum. See particularly the
drawings of Exeter and Northampton.

‡ Evelyn's Diary, June 2. 1675.

mane was still to be found wandering in a few of the southern forests. The badger made his dark and tortuous hole on the side of every hill where the copsewood grew thick. The wild cats were frequently heard by night wailing round the lodges of the rangers of Whittlebury and Needwood. The yellow-breasted martin was still pursued in Cranbourne Chase for his fur, reputed inferior only to that of the sable. Fen eagles, measuring more than nine feet between the extremities of the wings, preyed on fish along the coast of Norfolk. On all the downs, from the British Channel to Yorkshire, huge bustards strayed in troops of fifty or sixty, and were often hunted with greyhounds. The marshes of Cambridgeshire and Lincolnshire were covered during some months of every year by immense clouds of cranes. Some of these races the progress of cultivation has extirpated. Of others the numbers are so much diminished that men crowd to gaze at a specimen as at a Bengal tiger, or a Polar bear.*

The progress of this great change can nowhere be more clearly traced than in the Statute Book. The number of enclosure acts passed since King George the Second came to the throne exceeds four thousand. The area enclosed under the authority of those acts exceeds, on a moderate calculation, ten thousand square miles. How many square miles, which were formerly uncultivated or ill cultivated, have, during the same period, been fenced and carefully tilled by the proprietors without any application to the legislature, can only be conjectured. But it seems highly probable that a fourth part of England has been, in the course of little more than a century, turned from a wild into a garden.

Even in those parts of the kingdom which at the close of the reign of Charles the Second were the best cultivated, the farming, though greatly improved since the civil war, was not such as would now be thought skilful. To this day no effectual steps have been taken by public authority for the purpose of obtaining accurate accounts of the produce of the English soil. The historian must therefore follow, with some misgivings, the guidance of those writers on statistics whose reputation for diligence and fidelity stands highest. At present an average crop of wheat, rye, barley, oats, and beans,

---

* See White's Selborne; Bell's History of British Quadrupeds; Gentleman's Recreation, 1686; Aubrey's Natural History of Wiltshire, 1685 ; Morton's History of Northamptonshire, 1712; Willoughby's Ornithology, by Ray, 1678 ; Latham's General Synopsis of Birds ; and Sir Thomas Browne's Account of Birds found in Norfolk.

is supposed considerably to exceed thirty millions of quarters. The crop of wheat would be thought wretched if it did not exceed twelve millions of quarters. According to the computation made in the year 1696 by Gregory King, the whole quantity of wheat, rye, barley, oats, and beans, then annually grown in the kingdom, was somewhat less than ten millions of quarters. The wheat, which was then cultivated only on the strongest clay, and consumed only by those who were in easy circumstances, he estimated at less than two millions of quarters. Charles Davenant, an acute and well informed though most unprincipled and rancorous politician, differed from King as to some of the items of the account, but came to nearly the same general conclusions.*

The rotation of crops was very imperfectly understood. It was known, indeed, that some vegetables lately introduced into our island, particularly the turnip, afforded excellent nutriment in winter to sheep and oxen : but it was not yet the practice to feed cattle in this manner. It was therefore by no means easy to keep them alive during the season when the grass is scanty. They were killed and salted in great numbers at the beginning of the cold weather ; and, during several months, even the gentry tasted scarcely any fresh animal food, except game and river fish, which were consequently much more important articles in housekeeping than at present. It appears from the Northumberland Household Book that, in the reign of Henry the Seventh, fresh meat was never eaten even by the gentlemen attendant on a great Earl, except during the short interval between Midsummer and Michaelmas. But in the course of two centuries an improvement had taken place ; and under Charles the Second it was not till the beginning of November that families laid in their stock of salt provisions, then called Martinmas beef.†

The sheep and the ox of that time were diminutive when compared with the sheep and oxen which are now driven to our markets.‡ Our native horses, though serviceable, were held in small esteem, and fetched low prices. They were valued, one with another, by the ablest of those who computed the national wealth, at not more than fifty shillings each. Foreign breeds were greatly preferred. Spanish jennets were regarded as the finest chargers, and were imported for purposes of pageantry and war. The coaches of the

* King's Natural and Political Conclu-   ‡ See Mr. M'Culloch's Statistical Ac-
sions. Davenant on the Balance of Trade.   count of the British Empire, Part III.
† See the Almanacks of 1684 and 1685.   chap. i. sec. 6.

aristocracy were drawn by grey Flemish mares, which trotted, as it was thought, with a peculiar grace, and endured better than any cattle reared in our island the work of dragging a ponderous equipage over the rugged pavement of London. Neither the modern dray horse nor the modern race horse was then known. At a much later period the ancestors of the gigantic quadrupeds, which all foreigners now class among the chief wonders of London, were brought from the marshes of Walcheren; the ancestors of Childers and Eclipse from the sands of Arabia. Already, however, there was among our nobility and gentry a passion for the amusements of the turf. The importance of improving our studs by an infusion of new blood was strongly felt; and with this view a considerable number of barbs had lately been brought into the country. Two men whose authority on such subjects was held in great esteem, the Duke of Newcastle and Sir John Fenwick, pronounced that the meanest hack ever imported from Tangier would produce a finer progeny than could be expected from the best sire of our native breed. They would not readily have believed that a time would come when the princes and nobles of neighbouring lands would be as eager to obtain horses from England as ever the English had been to obtain horses from Barbary.*

The increase of vegetable and animal produce, though great, seems small when compared with the increase of our mineral wealth. In 1685 the tin of Cornwall, which had, more than two thousand years before, attracted the Tyrian sails beyond the pillars of Hercules, was still one of the most valuable subterranean productions of the island. The quantity annually extracted from the earth was found to be, some years later, sixteen hundred tons, probably about a third of what it now is.† But the veins of copper which lie in the same region were, in the time of Charles the Second, altogether neglected, nor did any landowner take them into the account in estimating the value of his property. Cornwall and Wales at present yield annually near fifteen thousand tons of copper, worth near a million and a half sterling; that is to say, worth about twice as much as the annual produce

Mineral wealth of the country.

---

* King and Davenant as before; The Duke of Newcastle on Horsemanship; Gentleman's Recreation, 1686. The "dappled Flanders mares" were marks of greatness in the time of Pope, and even later.

The vulgar proverb, that the grey mare is the better horse, originated, I suspect, in the preference generally given to the grey mares of Flanders over the finest coach horses of England.

† See a curious note by Tonkin, in Lord De Dunstanville's edition of Carew's Survey of Cornwall.

of all English mines of all descriptions in the seventeeth century.* The first bed of rock salt had been discovered in
Cheshire not long after the Restoration, but does not appear
to have been worked till much later. The salt which was
obtained by a rude process from brine pits was held in no
high estimation. The pans in which the manufacture was
carried on exhaled a sulphurous stench; and, when the
evaporation was complete, the substance which was left was
scarcely fit to be used with food. Physicians attributed
the scorbutic and pulmonary complaints which were common
among the English to this unwholesome condiment. It was
therefore seldom used by the upper and middle classes; and
there was a regular and considerable importation from France.
At present our springs and mines not only supply our own
immense demand, but send annually more than seven hundred
millions of pounds of excellent salt to foreign countries.†

Far more important has been the improvement of our iron
works. Such works had long existed in our island, but had
not prospered, and had been regarded with no favourable eye
by the government and by the public. It was not then the
practice to employ coal for smelting the ore; and the rapid
consumption of wood excited the alarm of politicians. As early
as the reign of Elizabeth there had been loud complaints that
whole forests were cut down for the purpose of feeding the
furnaces; and the Parliament had interfered to prohibit the
manufacturers from burning timber. The manufacture consequently languished. At the close of the reign of Charles
the Second, great part of the iron which was used in this
country was imported from abroad; and the whole quantity
cast here annually seems not to have exceeded ten thousand
tons. At present the trade is thought to be in a depressed
state if less than a million of tons are produced in a year.‡

One mineral, perhaps more important than iron itself, remains to be mentioned. Coal, though very little used in any
species of manufacture, was already the ordinary fuel in
some districts which were fortunate enough to possess large

---

* Borlase's Natural History of Cornwall, 1758. The quantity of copper
now produced, I have taken from parliamentary returns. Davenant, in 1700,
estimated the annual produce of all the
mines of England at between seven and
eight hundred thousand pounds.

† Philosophical Transactions, No. 53.
Nov. 1669, No. 66. Dec. 1670, No. 103.

May 1674, No. 156. Feb. 168¾.
‡ Yarranton, England's Improvement
by Sea and Land, 1677; Porter's Progress of the Nation. See also a remarkably perspicuous history, in small
compass, of the English iron works, in
Mr. M'Culloch's Statistical Account of
the British Empire.

beds, and in the capital, which could easily be supplied by water carriage. It seems reasonable to believe that at least one half of the quantity then extracted from the pits was consumed in London. The consumption of London seemed to the writers of that age enormous, and was often mentioned by them as a proof of the greatness of the imperial city. They scarcely hoped to be believed when they affirmed that two hundred and eighty thousand chaldrons, that is to say, about three hundred and fifty thousand tons, were, in the last year of the reign of Charles the Second, brought to the Thames. At present three millions and a half of tons are required yearly by the metropolis; and the whole annual produce cannot, on the most moderate computation, be estimated at less than thirty millions of tons.*

While these great changes have been in progress, the rent of land has, as might be expected, been almost constantly rising. In some districts it has multiplied more than tenfold. In some it has not more than doubled. It has probably, on the average, quadrupled. *Increase of rent.*

Of the rent, a large proportion was divided among the country gentlemen, a class of persons whose position and character it is most important that we should clearly understand; for by their influence and by their passions the fate of the nation was, at several important conjunctures, determined.

We should be much mistaken if we pictured to ourselves the squires of the seventeenth century as men bearing a close resemblance to their descendants, the county members and chairmen of quarter sessions with whom we are familiar. The modern country gentleman generally receives a liberal education, passes from a distinguished school to a distinguished college, and has ample opportunity to become an excellent scholar. He has generally seen something of foreign countries. A considerable part of his life has generally been passed in the capital; and the refinements of the capital follow him into the country. There is perhaps no class of dwellings so pleasing as the rural seats of the English gentry. In the parks and pleasure grounds, nature, dressed yet not disguised by art, wears her most *The country gentlemen.*

* See Chamberlayne's State of England, 1684, 1687; Angliæ Metropolis, 1691; M'Culloch's Statistical Account of the British Empire, Part III. chap. ii. (edition of 1847). In 1845 the quantity of coal brought into London appeared, by the Parliamentary returns, to be 3,460,000 tons. (1848.) In 1854 the quantity of coal brought into London amounted to 4,378,000 tons. (1857.)

alluring form. In the buildings, good sense and good taste combine to produce a happy union of the comfortable and the graceful. The pictures, the musical instruments, the library, would in any other country be considered as proving the owner to be an eminently polished and accomplished man. A country gentleman who witnessed the Revolution was probably in receipt of about a fourth part of the rent which his acres now yield to his posterity. He was, therefore, as compared with his posterity, a poor man, and was generally under the necessity of residing, with little interruption, on his estate. To travel on the Continent, to maintain an establishment in London, or even to visit London frequently, were pleasures in which only the great proprietors could indulge. It may be confidently affirmed that of the squires whose names were then in the Commissions of Peace and Lieutenancy not one in twenty went to town once in five years, or had ever in his life wandered so far as Paris. Many lords of manors had received an education differing little from that of their menial servants. The heir of an estate often passed his boyhood and youth at the seat of his family with no better tutors than grooms and gamekeepers, and scarce attained learning enough to sign his name to a Mittimus. If he went to school and to college, he generally returned before he was twenty to the seclusion of the old hall, and there, unless his mind were very happily constituted by nature, soon forgot his academical pursuits ·in rural business and pleasures. His chief serious employment was the care of his property. He examined samples of grain, handled pigs, and, on market days, made bargains over a tankard with drovers and hop merchants. His chief pleasures were commonly derived from field sports and from an unrefined sensuality. His language and pronunciation were such as we should now expect to hear only from the most ignorant clowns. His oaths, coarse jests, and scurrilous terms of abuse, were uttered with the broadest accent of his province. It was easy to discern, from the first words which he spoke, whether he came from Somersetshire or Yorkshire. He troubled himself little about decorating his abode, and, if he attempted decoration, seldom produced anything but deformity. The litter of a farmyard gathered under the windows of his bedchamber, and the cabbages and gooseberry bushes grew close to his hall door. His table was loaded with coarse plenty; and guests were cordially welcomed to it. But, as the habit of drinking to excess was general in the class to which he belonged, and as his fortune did not enable him to intoxicate large assemblies daily with claret or canary, strong beer was the ordinary beverage. The quantity of beer consumed in those days was indeed enormous. For beer then was to the middle and lower classes, not only all that beer now is, but all that wine, tea, and ardent spirits now are. It was only at great houses, or on great occasions, that foreign drink was placed on the board. The ladies of the house, whose business it had commonly been to cook the repast, retired as soon as the dishes had been devoured, and left the gentlemen to their ale and tobacco. The coarse jollity of the afternoon was often prolonged till the revellers were laid under the table.

It was very seldom that the country gentleman caught glimpses of the great world; and what he saw of it tended rather to confuse than to enlighten his understanding. His opinions respecting religion, government, foreign countries and former times, having been derived, not from study, from observation, or from conversation with enlightened companions, but from such traditions as were current in his own small circle, were the opinions of a child. He adhered to them, however, with the obstinacy which is generally found in ignorant men accustomed to be fed with flattery. His animosities were numerous and bitter. He hated Frenchmen and Italians, Scotchmen and Irishmen, Papists and Presbyterians, Independents and Baptists, Quakers and Jews. Towards London and Londoners he felt an aversion which more than once produced important political effects. His wife and daughter were in tastes and acquirements below a housekeeper or a stillroom maid of the present day. They stitched and spun, brewed gooseberry wine, cured marigolds, and made the crust for the venison pasty.

From this description it might be supposed that the English esquire of the seventeenth century did not materially differ from a rustic miller or alehouse keeper of our time. There are, however, some important parts of his character still to be noted, which will greatly modify this estimate. Unlettered as he was and unpolished, he was still in some most important points a gentleman. He was a member of a proud and powerful aristocracy, and was distinguished by many both of the good and of the bad qualities which belong to aristocrats. His family pride was beyond that of a Talbot or a Howard. He knew the genealogies and coats of arms of all his neighbours, and could tell which of them had assumed supporters without any right, and which of them were so unfortunate as to be greatgrandsons of aldermen. He was a magistrate, and, as such, administered gratuitously to those who dwelt around him a rude patriarchal justice, which, in spite of innumerable blunders and of occasional acts of tyranny, was yet better than no justice at all. He was an officer of the trainbands ; and his military dignity, though it might move the mirth of gallants who had served a campaign in Flanders, raised his character in his own eyes and in the eyes of his neighbours. Nor indeed was his soldiership justly a subject of derision. In every county there were elderly gentlemen who had seen service which was no child's play. One had been knighted by Charles the First, after the battle of Edgehill. Another still wore a patch over the scar which he had received at Naseby. A third had defended his old house till Fairfax had blown in the door with a petard. The presence of these old Cavaliers, with their old swords and holsters, and with their old stories about Goring and Lunsford, gave to the musters of militia an earnest and warlike aspect which would otherwise have been wanting. Even those country gentlemen who were too young to have themselves exchanged blows with the cuirassiers of the Parliament had, from childhood, been surrounded by the traces of recent war, and fed with stories of the martial exploits of their fathers and uncles. Thus the character of the English esquire of the seventeenth century was compounded of two elements which we seldom or never find united. His ignorance and uncouthness, his low tastes and gross phrases, would, in our time, be considered as indicating a nature and a breeding thoroughly plebeian. Yet he was essentially a patrician, and had, in large measure, both the virtues and the vices which flourish among men set from their birth in high place, and used to respect themselves and to be respected by others. It is not easy for a generation accustomed to find chivalrous sentiments only in company with liberal studies and polished manners to image to itself a man with the deportment, the vocabulary, and the accent of a carter, yet punctilious on matters of genealogy and precedence, and ready to risk his life rather than see a stain cast on the honour of his house. It is however only by thus joining together things seldom or never found together in our own experience, that we can form a just idea of that rustic aristocracy which constituted the main strength of the armies of Charles the First, and which long supported, with strange fidelity, the interest of his descendants.

The gross, uneducated, untravelled country gentleman was commonly a Tory; but, though devotedly attached to hereditary monarchy, he had no partiality for courtiers and ministers. He thought, not without reason, that Whitehall was filled with the most corrupt of mankind, and that of the great sums which the House of Commons had voted to the crown since the Restoration part had been embezzled by cunning politicians, and part squandered on buffoons and foreign courtesans. His stout English heart swelled with indignation at the thought that the government of his country should be subject to French dictation. Being himself generally an old Cavalier, or the son of an old Cavalier, he reflected with bitter resentment on the ingratitude with which the Stuarts had requited their best friends. Those who heard him grumble at the neglect with which he was treated, and at the profusion with which wealth was lavished on the bastards of Nell Gwynn and Madam Carwell, would have supposed him ripe for rebellion. But all this ill humour lasted only till the throne was really in danger. It was precisely when those whom the sovereign had loaded with wealth and honours shrank from his side that the country gentlemen, so surly and mutinous in the season of his prosperity, rallied round him in a body. Thus, after murmuring twenty years at the misgovernment of Charles the Second, they came to his rescue in his extremity, when his own Secretaries of State and the Lords of his own Treasury had deserted him, and enabled him to gain a complete victory over the opposition; nor can there be any doubt that they would have shown equal loyalty to his brother James, if James would, even at the last moment, have refrained from outraging their strongest feeling. For there was one institution, and one only, which they prized even more than hereditary monarchy; and that institution was the Church of England. Their love of the Church was not, indeed, the effect of study or meditation. Few among them could have given any reason, drawn from Scripture or ecclesiastical history, for adhering to her doctrines, her ritual, and her polity; nor were they, as a class, by any means strict observers of that code of morality which is common to all Christian sects. But the experience of many ages proves that men may be ready to fight to the death, and to persecute without pity, for a religion whose creed they do not understand, and whose precepts they habitually disobey.*

The
clergy. The rural clergy were even more vehement in Toryism than the rural gentry, and were a class scarcely less important. It is to be observed, however, that the individual clergyman, as compared with the individual gentleman, then ranked much lower than in our days. The main support of the Church was derived from the tithe; and the tithe bore to the rent a much smaller ratio than at present. King estimated the whole income of the parochial and collegiate clergy at only four hundred and eighty thousand pounds a year; Davenant at only five hundred and forty-four thousand a year. It is certainly now more than seven times as great as the larger of these two sums. The average rent of the land has not, according to any estimate, increased proportionally. It follows that the rectors and vicars must have been, as compared with the neighbouring knights and squires, much poorer in the seventeenth than in the nineteenth century.

The place of the clergyman in society had been completely changed by the Reformation. Before that event, ecclesiastics had formed the majority of the House of Lords, had, in wealth and splendour, equalled, and sometimes outshone, the greatest of the temporal barons, and had generally held the highest civil offices. Many of the Treasurers, and almost all the Chancellors of the Plantagenets were Bishops. The Lord Keeper of the Privy Seal and the Master of the Rolls were ordinarily churchmen. Churchmen transacted the most important diplomatic business. Indeed, all that large portion of the administration which rude and warlike nobles were incompetent to conduct was considered as especially belonging to divines. Men, therefore, who were averse to the life of camps, and who were, at the same time, desirous to rise in the state, commonly received the tonsure. Among them were sons of all the most illustrious families, and near kinsmen of the throne, Scroops and Nevilles, Bourchiers, Staffords, and Poles. To the religious houses belonged the rents of immense domains, and all that large portion of the tithe which is now in the hands of laymen. Down to the middle of the

* My notion of the country gentleman of the seventeenth century has been derived from sources too numerous to be recapitulated. I must leave my description to the judgment of those who have studied the history and the lighter literature of that age.

reign of Henry the Eighth, therefore, no line of life was so attractive to ambitious and covetous natures as the priesthood. Then came a violent revolution. The abolition of the monasteries deprived the Church at once of the greater part of her wealth, and of her predominance in the Upper House of Parliament. There was no longer an Abbot of Glastonbury or an Abbot of Reading seated among the peers, and possessed of revenues equal to those of a powerful Earl. The princely splendour of William of Wykeham and of William of Waynflete had disappeared. The scarlet hat of the Cardinal, the silver cross of the Legate, were no more. The clergy had also lost the ascendency which is the natural reward of superior mental cultivation. Once the circumstance that a man could read had raised a presumption that he was in orders. But, in an age which produced such laymen as William Cecil and Nicholas Bacon, Roger Ascham and Thomas Smith, Walter Mildmay and Francis Walsingham, there was no reason for calling away prelates from their dioceses to negotiate treaties, to superintend the finances, or to administer justice. The spiritual character not only ceased to be a qualification for high civil office, but began to be regarded as a disqualification. Those worldly motives, therefore, which had formerly induced so many able, aspiring, and high born youths to assume the ecclesiastical habit, ceased to operate. Not one parish in two hundred then afforded what a man of family considered as a maintenance. There were still indeed prizes in the Church: but they were few; and even the highest were mean, when compared with the glory which had once surrounded the princes of the hierarchy. The state kept by Parker and Grindal seemed beggarly to those who remembered the imperial pomp of Wolsey, his palaces, which had become the favourite abodes of royalty, Whitehall and Hampton Court, the three sumptuous tables daily spread in his refectory, the forty-four gorgeous copes in his chapel, his running footmen in rich liveries, and his body guards with gilded poleaxes. Thus the sacerdotal office lost its attraction for the higher classes. During the century which followed the accession of Elizabeth, scarce a single person of noble descent took orders. At the close of the reign of Charles the Second, two sons of peers were Bishops; four or five sons of peers were priests, and held valuable preferment: but these rare exceptions did not take away the reproach which lay on the body. The clergy were regarded

as, on the whole, a plebeian class.* And, indeed, for one
who made the figure of a gentleman, ten were mere menial
servants. A large proportion of those divines who had no
benefices, or whose benefices were too small to afford a comfortable revenue, lived in the houses of laymen. It had long
been evident that this practice tended to degrade the priestly
character. Laud had exerted himself to effect a change;
and Charles the First had repeatedly issued positive orders
that none but men of high rank should presume to keep domestic chaplains.† But these injunctions had become obsolete. Indeed, during the domination of the Puritans, many
of the ejected ministers of the Church of England could
obtain bread and shelter only by attaching themselves to the
households of royalist gentlemen; and the habits which had
been formed in those times of trouble continued long after
the reestablishment of monarchy and episcopacy. In the
mansions of men of liberal sentiments and cultivated understandings, the chaplain was doubtless treated with urbanity
and kindness. His conversation, his literary assistance, his
spiritual advice, were considered as an ample return for his
food, his lodging, and his stipend. But this was not the
general feeling of the country gentlemen. The coarse and
ignorant squire, who thought that it belonged to his dignity
to have grace said every day at his table by an ecclesiastic
in full canonicals, found means to reconcile dignity with
economy. A young Levite—such was the phrase then in
use—might be had for his board, a small garret, and ten
pounds a year, and might not only perform his own professional functions, might not only be the most patient of butts
and of listeners, might not only be always ready in fine weather for bowls, and in rainy weather for shovelboard, but
might also save the expense of a gardener, or of a groom.
Sometimes the reverend man nailed up the apricots; and
sometimes he curried the coach horses. He cast up the
farrier's bills. He walked ten miles with a message or a
parcel. He was permitted to dine with the family; but he
was expected to content himself with the plainest fare. He

* In the eighteenth century the great
increase in the value of benefices produced a change. The younger sons of
the nobility were allured back to the
clerical profession. Warburton in a letter
to Hurd, dated the 5th of July 1752,
mentions this change, which was then
recent. " Our grandees have at last

found their way back into the Church.
I only wonder they have been so long
about it. But be assured that nothing
but a new religious revolution, to sweep
away the fragments that Henry the
Eighth left after banqueting his courtiers, will drive them out again."

† See Heylin's Cyprianus Anglicus

might fill himself with the corned beef and the carrots: but, as soon as the tarts and cheesecakes made their appearance, he quitted his seat, and stood aloof till he was summoned to return thanks for the repast, from a great part of which he had been excluded.*

Perhaps, after some years of service, he was presented to a living sufficient to support him: but he often found it necessary to purchase his preferment by a species of Simony, which furnished an inexhaustible subject of pleasantry to three or four generations of scoffers. With his cure he was expected to take a wife. The wife had ordinarily been in the patron's service; and it was well if she was not suspected of standing too high in the patron's favour. Indeed, the nature of the matrimonial connections which the clergymen of that age were in the habit of forming is the most certain indication of the place which the order held in the social system. An Oxonian, writing a few months after the death of Charles the Second, complained bitterly, not only that the country attorney and the country apothecary looked down with disdain on the country clergyman, but that one of the lessons most earnestly inculcated on every girl of honourable family was to give no encouragement to a lover in orders, and that, if any young lady forgot this precept, she was almost as much disgraced as by an illicit amour.† Clarendon, who assuredly bore no ill will to the priesthood, mentions it as a sign of the confusion of ranks which the great rebellion had produced, that some damsels of noble families had bestowed themselves on divines.‡ A waiting woman was generally considered as the most suitable helpmate for a parson. Queen Elizabeth, as head of the Church, had given what seemed to be a formal sanction to this prejudice, by issuing special orders that no clergyman should presume to espouse a servant girl, without the consent of the master or mistress.§

---

* Eachard, Causes of the Contempt of the Clergy; Oldham, Satire addressed to a Friend about to leave the University; Tatler, 255. 258. That the English clergy were a lowborn class, is remarked in the Travels of the Grand Duke Cosmo, Appendix A.

† "A causidico, medicastro, ipsaque artificum farragine, ecclesiæ rector aut vicarius contemnitur et fit ludibrio. Gentis et familiæ nitor sacris ordinibus pollutus censetur: fœminisque natalitio insignibus unicum inculcatur sæpius

præceptum, ne modestiæ naufragium faciant, aut, (quod idem auribus tam delicatulis sonat,) ne clerico se nuptas dari patiantur."—Angliæ Notitia, by T. Wood, of New College, Oxford, 1686.

‡ Clarendon's Life, ii. 21.

§ See the Injunctions of 1559, in Bishop Sparrow's Collection. Jeremy Collier, in his Essay on Pride, speaks of this injunction with a bitterness which proves that his own pride had not been effectually tamed.

During several generations accordingly the relation between divines and handmaidens was a theme for endless jest; nor would it be easy to find, in the comedy of the seventeenth century, a single instance of a clergyman who wins a spouse above the rank of a cook.* Even so late as the time of George the Second, the keenest of all observers of life and manners, himself a priest, remarked that, in a great household, the chaplain was the resource of a lady's maid whose character had been blown upon, and who was therefore forced to give up hopes of catching the steward.†

In general the divine who quitted his chaplainship for a benefice and a wife found that he had only exchanged one class of vexations for another. Hardly one living in fifty enabled the incumbent to bring up a family comfortably. As children multiplied and grew, the household of the priest became more and more beggarly. Holes appeared more and more plainly in the thatch of his parsonage and in his single cassock. Often it was only by toiling on his glebe, by feeding swine, and by loading dungcarts, that he could obtain daily bread; nor did his utmost exertions always prevent the bailiffs from taking his concordance and his inkstand in execution. It was a white day on which he was admitted into the kitchen of a great house, and regaled by the servants with cold meat and ale. His children were brought up like the children of the neighbouring peasantry. His boys followed the plough; and his girls went out to service.‡ Study he found impossible: for the advowson of his living would hardly have sold for a sum sufficient to purchase a good theological library; and he might be considered as unusually lucky if he had ten or twelve dogeared volumes among the pots and pans on his shelves. Even a keen and strong intellect might be expected to rust in so unfavourable a situation.

Assuredly there was at that time no lack in the English Church of ministers distinguished by abilities and learning.

* Roger and Abigail in Fletcher's Scornful Lady, Bull and the Nurse in Vanbrugh's Relapse, Smirk and Susan in Shadwell's Lancashire Witches, are instances.

† Swift's Directions to Servants. In Swift's Remarks on the Clerical Residence Bill, he describes the family of an English vicar thus: —" His wife is little better than a Goody, in her birth, education, or dress. . . . . His daughters shall go to service, or be sent apprentice to the sempstress of the next town."

‡ Even in Tom Jones, published two generations later, Mrs. Seagrim, the wife of a gamekeeper, and Mrs. Honour, a waitingwoman, boast of their descent from clergymen. "It is to be hoped," says Fielding, "such instances will in future ages, when some provision is made for the families of the inferior clergy, appear stranger than they can be thought at present."

But it is to be observed that these ministers were not scattered among the rural population. They were brought together at a few places where the means of acquiring knowledge were abundant, and where the opportunities of vigorous intellectual exercise were frequent.* At such places were to be found divines qualified by parts, by eloquence, by wide knowledge of literature, of science, and of life, to defend their Church victoriously against heretics and sceptics, to command the attention of frivolous and worldly congregations, to guide the deliberations of senates, and to make religion respectable, even in the most dissolute of courts. Some laboured to fathom the abysses of metaphysical theology : some were deeply versed in biblical criticism ; and some threw light on the darkest parts of ecclesiastical history. Some proved themselves consummate masters of logic. Some cultivated rhetoric with such assiduity and success that their discourses are still justly valued as models of style. These eminent men were to be found, with scarcely a single exception, at the Universities, at the great Cathedrals, or in the capital. Barrow had lately died at Cambridge ; and Pearson had gone thence to the episcopal bench. Cudworth and Henry More were still living there. South and Pococke, Jane and Aldrich, were at Oxford, Prideaux was in the close of Norwich, and Whitby in the close of Salisbury. But it was chiefly by the London clergy, who were always spoken of as a class apart, that the fame of their profession for learning and eloquence was upheld. The principal pulpits of the metropolis were occupied about this time by a crowd of distinguished men, from among whom was selected a large proportion of the rulers of the Church. Sherlock preached at the Temple, Tillotson at Lincoln's Inn, Wake and Jeremy Collier at Gray's Inn, Burnet at the Rolls, Stillingfleet at Saint Paul's Cathedral, Patrick at Saint Paul's in Covent Garden, Fowler at Saint Giles's, Cripplegate, Sharp at Saint Giles's in the Fields, Tenison at Saint Martin's, Sprat at Saint Margaret's, Beveridge at Saint Peter's in Cornhill. Of these twelve men, all of high note in ecclesiastical history, ten became Bishops, and four Archbishops. Meanwhile almost the only important theological works which came forth from a rural parsonage were those of George Bull, afterwards Bishop of Saint David's ; and Bull never would

---

* This distinction between country clergy and town clergy is strongly marked by Eachard, and cannot but be observed by every person who has studied the ecclesiastical history of that age.

have produced those works, had he not inherited an estate, by the sale of which he was enabled to collect a library, such as probably no other country clergyman in England possessed.*

Thus the Anglican priesthood was divided into two sections, which, in acquirements, in manners, and in social position, differed widely from each other. One section, trained for cities and courts, comprised men familiar with all ancient and modern learning; men able to encounter Hobbes or Bossuet at all the weapons of controversy; men who could, in their sermons, set forth the majesty and beauty of Christianity with such justness of thought, and such energy of language, that the indolent Charles roused himself to listen, and the fastidious Buckingham forgot to sneer; men whose address, politeness, and knowledge of the world qualified them to manage the consciences of the wealthy and noble; men with whom Halifax loved to discuss the interests of empires, and from whom Dryden was not ashamed to own that he had learned to write.† The other section was destined to ruder and humbler service. It was dispersed over the country, and consisted chiefly of persons not at all wealthier, and not much more refined, than small farmers or upper servants. Yet it was in these rustic priests, who derived but a scanty subsistence from their tithe sheaves and tithe pigs, and who had not the smallest chance of ever attaining high professional honours, that the professional spirit was strongest. Among those divines who were the boast of the Universities and the delight of the capital, and who had attained, or might reasonably expect to attain, opulence and lordly rank, a party, respectable in numbers, and more respectable in character, leaned towards constitutional principles of government, lived on friendly terms with Presbyterians, Independents, and Baptists, would gladly have seen a full toleration granted to all Protestant sects, and would even have consented to make alterations in the Liturgy, for the purpose of conciliating honest and candid Nonconformists. But such latitudinarianism was held in horror by the country parson. He took, indeed, more pride in his ragged gown than his superiors in their lawn and their scarlet hoods. The very consciousness

---

* Nelson's Life of Bull. As to the extreme difficulty which the country clergy found in procuring books, see the Life of Thomas Bray, the founder of the Society for the Propagation of the Gospel.

† " I have frequently heard him (Dryden) own with pleasure, that if he had any talent for English prose it was owing to his having often read the writings of the great Archbishop Tillotson." —Congreve's Dedication of Dryden's Plays.

that there was little in his worldly circumstances to distinguish him from the villagers to whom he preached led him to hold immoderately high the dignity of that sacerdotal office which was his single title to reverence. Having lived in seclusion, and having had little opportunity of correcting his opinions by reading or conversation, he held and taught the doctrines of indefeasible hereditary right, of passive obedience, and of non-resistance, in all their crude absurdity. Having been long engaged in a petty war against the neighbouring dissenters, he too often hated them for the wrong which he had done them, and found no fault with the Five Mile Act and the Conventicle Act, except that those odious laws had not a sharper edge. Whatever influence his office gave him was exerted with passionate zeal on the Tory side ; and that influence was immense. It would be a great error to imagine, because the country rector was in general not regarded as a gentleman, because he could not dare to aspire to the hand of one of the young ladies at the manor house, because he was not asked into the parlours of the great, but was left to drink and smoke with grooms and butlers, that the power of the clerical body was smaller than at present. The influence of a class is by no means proportioned to the consideration which the members of that class enjoy in their individual capacity. A Cardinal is a much more exalted personage than a begging friar : but it would be a grievous mistake to suppose that the College of Cardinals has exercised a greater dominion over the public mind of Europe than the Order of Saint Francis. In Ireland, at present, a peer holds a far higher station in society than a Roman Catholic priest : yet there are in Munster and Connaught few counties where a combination of priests would not carry an election against a combination of peers. In the seventeenth century the pulpit was to a large portion of the population what the periodical press now is. Scarce any of the clowns who came to the parish church ever saw a Gazette or a political pamphlet. Ill informed as their spiritual pastor might be, he was yet better informed than themselves : he had every week an opportunity of haranguing them ; and his harangues were never answered. At every important conjuncture, invectives against the Whigs and exhortations to obey the Lord's anointed resounded at once from many thousands of pulpits ; and the effect was formidable indeed. Of all the causes which, after the dissolution of the Oxford Parliament, produced the violent

reaction against the Exclusionists, the most potent seems
to have been the oratory of the country clergy.

The yeo-
manry.

The power which the country gentleman and the country
clergyman exercised in the rural districts was in some
measure counterbalanced by the power of the yeomanry, an
eminently manly and truehearted race. The petty proprietors
who cultivated their own fields with their own hands, and
enjoyed a modest competence, without affecting to have
scutcheons and crests, or aspiring to sit on the bench of
justice, then formed a much more important part of the
nation than at present. If we may trust the best statistical
writers of that age, not less than a hundred and sixty thousand proprietors, who with their families must have made up
more than a seventh of the whole population, derived their
subsistence from little freehold estates. The average income
of these small landholders, an income made up of rent, profit,
and wages, was estimated at between sixty and seventy
pounds a year. It was computed that the number of persons who tilled their own land was greater than the number
of those who farmed the land of others.* A large portion of
the yeomanry had, from the time of the Reformation, leaned
towards Puritanism, had, in the civil war, taken the side of
the Parliament, had, after the Restoration, persisted in hearing Presbyterian and Independent preachers, had, at elections,
strenuously supported the Exclusionists, and had continued,
even after the discovery of the Rye House plot and the proscription of the Whig leaders, to regard Popery and arbitrary
power with unmitigated hostility.

Growth of
the towns.

Great as has been the change in the rural life of England
since the Revolution, the change which has come to pass in
the cities is still more amazing. At present above a sixth
part of the nation is crowded into provincial towns of more
than thirty thousand inhabitants. In the reign of Charles
the Second no provincial town in the kingdom contained
thirty thousand inhabitants; and only four provincial towns
contained so many as ten thousand inhabitants.

Bristol.

Next to the capital, but next at an immense distance,
stood Bristol, then the first English seaport, and Norwich,
then the first English manufacturing town. Both have since
that time been far outstripped by younger rivals; yet both
have made great positive advances. The population of Bris-

* I have taken Davenant's estimate, which is a little lower than King's.

tol has quadrupled. The population of Norwich has more than doubled.

Pepys, who visited Bristol eight years after the Restoration, was struck by the splendour of the city. But his standard was not high; for he noted down as a wonder the circumstance that, in Bristol, a man might look round him and see nothing but houses. It seems that, in no other place with which he was acquainted, except London, did the buildings completely shut out the woods and fields. Large as Bristol might then appear, it occupied but a very small portion of the area on which it now stands. A few churches of eminent beauty rose out of a labyrinth of narrow lanes built upon vaults of no great solidity. If a coach or a cart entered those alleys, there was danger that it would be wedged between the houses, and danger also that it would break in the cellars. Goods were therefore conveyed about the town almost exclusively in trucks drawn by dogs; and the richest inhabitants exhibited their wealth, not by riding in gilded carriages, but by walking the streets with trains of servants in rich liveries, and by keeping tables loaded with good cheer. The pomp of the christenings and burials far exceeded what was seen at any other place in England. The hospitality of the city was widely renowned, and especially the collations with which the sugar refiners regaled their visitors. The repast was dressed in the furnace, and was accompanied by a rich beverage made of the best Spanish wine, and celebrated over the whole kingdom as Bristol milk. This luxury was supported by a thriving trade with the North American plantations and with the West Indies. The passion for colonial traffic was so strong that there was scarcely a small shopkeeper in Bristol who had not a venture on board of some ship bound for Virginia or the Antilles. Some of these ventures indeed were not of the most honourable kind. There was, in the Transatlantic possessions of the crown, a great demand for labour; and this demand was partly supplied by a system of crimping and kidnapping at the principal English seaports. Nowhere was this system in such active and extensive operation as at Bristol. Even the first magistrates of that city were not ashamed to enrich themselves by so odious a commerce. The number of houses appears, from the returns of the hearth money, to have been in the year 1685, just five thousand three hundred. We can hardly suppose the number of persons in a house to have been greater than in the city of London; and in the city of London we learn from the best authority that there were then fifty-five persons to ten houses. The population of Bristol must therefore have been about twenty-nine thousand souls.*

Norwich.
Norwich was the capital of a large and fruitful province. It was the residence of a Bishop and of a Chapter. It was the chief seat of the chief manufacture of the realm. Some men distinguished by learning and science had recently dwelt there; and no place in the kingdom, except the capital and the Universities, had more attractions for the curious. The library, the museum, the aviary, and the botanical garden of Sir Thomas Browne, were thought by Fellows of the Royal Society well worthy of a long pilgrimage. Norwich had also a court in miniature. In the heart of the city stood an old palace of the Dukes of Norfolk, said to be the largest town house in the kingdom out of London. In this mansion, to which were annexed a tennis court, a bowling green, and a wilderness stretching along the banks of the Wansum, the noble family of Howard frequently resided, and kept a state resembling that of petty sovereigns. Drink was served to guests in goblets of pure gold. The very tongs and shovels were of silver. Pictures by Italian masters adorned the walls. The cabinets were filled with a fine collection of gems purchased by that Earl of Arundel whose marbles are now among the ornaments of Oxford. Here, in the year 1671, Charles and his court were sumptuously entertained. Here, too, all comers were annually welcomed, from Christmas to Twelfth Night. Ale flowed in oceans for the populace. Three coaches, one of which had been built at a cost of five hundred pounds to contain fourteen persons, were sent every afternoon round the city to bring ladies to the festivities; and the dances were always followed by a luxurious banquet. When the Duke of Norfolk came to Norwich, he was greeted like a King returning to his capital. The bells of the Cathedral and of St. Peter Mancroft were rung: the

* Evelyn's Diary, June 27. 1654; Pepys's Diary, June 13. 1668; Roger North's Lives of Lord Keeper Guildford, and of Sir Dudley North; Petty's Political Arithmetic. I have taken Petty's facts, but, in drawing inferences from them, I have been guided by King and Davenant, who, though not abler men than he, had the advantage of coming after him. As to the kidnapping for which Bristol was infamous, see North's Life of Guildford, 121. 216., and the harangue of Jeffreys on the subject, in the Impartial History of his Life and Death, printed with the Bloody Assizes. His style was, as usual, coarse; but I cannot reckon the reprimand which he gave to the magistrates of Bristol among his crimes.

guns of the castle were fired; and the Mayor and Aldermen waited on their illustrious fellow citizen with complimentary addresses. In the year 1693 the population of Norwich was found by actual enumeration, to be between twenty-eight and twenty-nine thousand souls.*

Far below Norwich, but still high in dignity and importance, were some other ancient capitals of shires. In that age it was seldom that a country gentleman went up with his family to London. The county town was his metropolis. He sometimes made it his residence during part of the year. At all events, he was often attracted thither by business and pleasure, by assizes, quarter sessions, elections, musters of militia, festivals, and races. There were the halls where the judges, robed in scarlet and escorted by javelins and trumpets, opened the King's commission twice a year. There were the markets at which the corn, the cattle, the wool, and the hops of the surrounding country were exposed to sale. There were the great fairs to which merchants came down from London, and where the rural dealer laid in his annual stores of sugar, stationery, cutlery, and muslin. There were the shops at which the best families of the neighbourhood bought grocery and millinery. Some of these places derived dignity from interesting historical recollections, from cathedrals decorated by all the art and magnificence of the middle ages, from palaces where a long succession of prelates had dwelt, from closes surrounded by the venerable abodes of deans and canons, and from castles which had in the old time repelled the Nevilles or de Veres, and which bore more recent traces of the vengeance of Rupert or of Cromwell.

Conspicuous amongst these interesting cities were York, the capital of the north, and Exeter, the capital of the west. Neither can have contained much more than ten thousand inhabitants. Worcester, the queen of the cider land, had but eight thousand; Nottingham probably as many. Gloucester, renowned for that resolute defence which had been fatal to Charles the First, had certainly between four and five thousand; Derby not quite four thousand. Shrewsbury was the chief place of an extensive and fertile district. The Court of the Marches of Wales was held there. In the language of the gentry many miles round the Wrekin, to go to

Other country towns.

* Fuller's Worthies; Evelyn's Diary, Oct. 17. 1671; Journal of T. Browne, son of Sir Thomas Browne, Jan. 166¾; Blomefield's History of Norfolk; History of the City and County of Norwich, 2 vols. 1768.

Shrewsbury was to go to town. The provincial wits and beauties imitated, as well as they could, the fashions of Saint James's Park, in the walks along the side of the Severn. The inhabitants were about seven thousand.*

The population of every one of these places has, since the Revolution, much more than doubled. The population of some has multiplied sevenfold. The streets have been almost entirely rebuilt. Slate has succeeded to thatch, and brick to timber. The pavements and the lamps, the display of wealth in the principal shops, and the luxurious neatness of the dwellings occupied by the gentry would, in the seventeenth century, have seemed miraculous. Yet is the relative importance of the old capitals of counties by no means what it was. Younger towns, towns which are rarely or never mentioned in our early history and which sent no representatives to our early Parliaments, have, within the memory of persons still living, grown to a greatness which this generation contemplates with wonder and pride, not unaccompanied by awe and anxiety.

The most eminent of these towns were indeed known in the seventeenth century as respectable seats of industry. Nay, their rapid progress and their vast opulence were then sometimes described in language which seems ludicrous to a man who has seen their present grandeur. One of the most populous and prosperous among them was Manchester. Manchester had been required by the Protector to send one representative to his Parliament, and was mentioned by writers of the time of Charles the Second as a busy and opulent place. Cotton had, during half a century, been brought thither from Cyprus and Smyrna; but the manufacture was in its infancy. Whitney had not yet taught how the raw material might be furnished in quantities almost fabulous. Arkwright had not yet taught how it might be worked up with a speed and precision which

Man-
chester.

---

* The population of York appears, from the return of baptisms and burials, in Drake's History, to have been about 13,000 in 1730. Exeter had only 17,000 inhabitants in 1801. The population of Worcester was numbered just before the siege in 1646. See Nash's History of Worcestershire. I have made allowance for the increase which must be supposed to have taken place in forty years. In 1740, the population of Nottingham was found, by enumeration, to be just 10,000. See Dering's History. The population of Gloucester may readily be inferred from the number of houses which King found in the returns of hearth money, and from the number of births and burials which is given in Atkyns's History. The population of Derby was 4000 in 1712. See Wolley's MS. History, quoted in Lyson's Magna Britannia. The population of Shrewsbury was ascertained, in 1695, by actual enumeration. As to the gaieties of Shrewsbury, see Farquhar's Recruiting Officer. Farquhar's description is borne out by a ballad in the Pepysian Library, of which the burden is "Shrewsbury for me."

seem magical. The whole annual import did not, at the end
of the seventeenth century, amount to two millions of pounds,
a quantity which would now hardly supply the demand of
forty-eight hours. That wonderful emporium, which in population and wealth far surpasses capitals so much renowned as
Berlin, Madrid, and Lisbon, was then a mean and ill built
market town, containing under six thousand people. It then
had not a single press. It now supports a hundred printing
establishments. It then had not a single coach. It now supports twenty coachmakers.*

Leeds was already the chief seat of the woollen manufac- Leeds.
tures of Yorkshire: but the elderly inhabitants could still
remember the time when the first brick house, then and long
after called the Red House, was built. They boasted loudly
of their increasing wealth, and of the immense sales of cloth
which took place in the open air on the bridge. Hundreds,
nay thousands of pounds, had been paid down in the course
of one busy market day. The rising importance of Leeds had
attracted the notice of successive governments. Charles the
First had granted municipal privileges to the town. Oliver
had invited it to send one member to the House of Commons.
But from the returns of the hearth money it seems certain
that the whole population of the borough, an extensive district which contains many hamlets, did not, in the reign of
Charles the Second, exceed seven thousand souls. In 1841
there were more than a hundred and fifty thousand.†

About a day's journey south of Leeds, on the verge of a Sheffield.
wild moorland tract, lay an ancient manor, now rich with
cultivation, then barren and unenclosed, which was known
by the name of Hallamshire. Iron abounded there; and, from
a very early period, the rude whittles fabricated there had
been sold all over the kingdom. They had indeed been mentioned by Geoffrey Chaucer in one of his Canterbury Tales.
But the manufacture appears to have made little progress
during the three centuries which followed his time. This
languor may perhaps be explained by the fact that the trade
was, during almost the whole of this long period, subject to

* Blome's Britannia, 1673; Aikin's
Country round Manchester; Manchester
Directory, 1845; Baines, History of the
Cotton Manufacture. The best information which I have been able to find,
touching the population of Manchester
in the seventeenth century, is contained
in a paper drawn up by the Reverend

R. Parkinson, and published in the
Journal of the Statistical Society for
October 1842.

† Thoresby's Ducatus Leodensis;
Whitaker's Loidis and Elmete; War-
dell's Municipal History of the Borough
of Leeds. (1848.) In 1851 Leeds had
172,000 inhabitants. (1857.)

such regulations as the lord and his court leet thought fit to impose. The more delicate kinds of cutlery were either made in the capital, or brought from the Continent. Indeed it was not till the reign of George the First that the English surgeons ceased to import from France those exquisitely fine blades which are required for operations on the human frame. Most of the Hallamshire forges were collected in a market town which had sprung up near the castle of the proprietor, and which, in the reign of James the First, had been a singularly miserable place, containing about two thousand inhabitants, of whom a third were half starved and half naked beggars. It seems certain from the parochial registers that the population did not amount to four thousand at the end of the reign of Charles the Second. The effects of a species of toil singularly unfavourable to the health and vigour of the human frame were at once discerned by every traveller. A large proportion of the people had distorted limbs. This is that Sheffield which now, with its dependencies, contains a hundred and twenty thousand souls, and which sends forth its admirable knives, razors, and lancets to the farthest ends of the world.*

Birmingham.

Birmingham had not been thought of sufficient importance to return a member to Oliver's Parliament. Yet the manufacturers of Birmingham were already a busy and thriving race. They boasted that their hardware was highly esteemed, not indeed as now, at Pekin and Lima, at Bokhara and Timbuctoo, but in London, and even as far off as Ireland. They had acquired a less honourable renown as coiners of bad money. In allusion to their spurious groats, some Tory wit had fixed on demagogues, who hypocritically affected zeal against Popery, the nickname of Birminghams. Yet in 1685 the population, which is now little less than two hundred thousand, did not amount to four thousand. Birmingham buttons were just beginning to be known: of Birmingham guns nobody had yet heard; and the place whence, two generations later, the magnificent editions of Baskerville went forth to astonish all the librarians of Europe, did not contain a single regular shop where a Bible or an almanack could be bought. On Market days a bookseller named Michael Johnson, the father of the great Samuel Johnson, came over from Lich-

* Hunter's History of Hallamshire. (1848.) In 1851 the population of Sheffield had increased to 135,000. (1857.)

field, and opened a stall during a few hours. This supply of literature was long found equal to the demand.*

These four chief seats of our great manufactures deserve especial mention. It would be tedious to enumerate all the populous and opulent hives of industry which, a hundred and fifty years ago, were hamlets without parish churches, or desolate moors, inhabited only by grouse and wild deer. Nor has the change been less signal in those outlets by which the products of the English looms and forges are poured forth over the whole world. At present Liverpool contains more **Liverpool.** than three hundred thousand inhabitants. The shipping registered at her port amounts to between four and five hundred thousand tons. Into her custom house has been repeatedly paid in one year a sum more than thrice as great as the whole income of the English crown in 1685. The receipts of her post office, even since the great reduction of the duty, exceed the sum which the postage of the whole kingdom yielded to the Duke of York. Her endless docks, quays, and warehouses are among the wonders of the world. Yet even those docks and quays and warehouses seem hardly to suffice for the gigantic trade of the Mersey; and already a rival city is growing fast on the opposite shore. In the days of Charles the Second Liverpool was described as a rising town which had recently made great advances, and which maintained a profitable intercourse with Ireland and with the sugar colonies. The customs had multiplied eight-fold within sixteen years, and amounted to what was then considered as the immense sum of fifteen thousand pounds annually. But the population can hardly have exceeded four thousand: the shipping was about fourteen hundred tons, less than the tonnage of a single modern Indiaman of the first class; and the whole number of seamen belonging to the port cannot be estimated at more than two hundred.†

* Blome's Britannia, 1673; Dugdale's Warwickshire; North's Examen, 321.; Preface to Absalom and Achitophel; Hutton's History of Birmingham; Boswell's Life of Johnson. In 1690 the burials at Birmingham were 150, the baptisms 125. I think it probable that the annual mortality was little less than one in twenty-five. In London it was considerably greater. A historian of Nottingham, half a century later, boasted of the extraordinary salubrity of his town, where the annual mortality was one in thirty. See Dering's History of Nottingham. (1848.) In 1851 the population of Birmingham had increased to 232,000. (1857.)

† Blome's Britannia; Gregson's Antiquities of the County Palatine and Duchy of Lancaster, Part II.; Petition from Liverpool in the Privy Council Book, May 10. 1686. In 1690 the burials at Liverpool were 151, the baptisms 120. In 1844 the net receipt of the customs at Liverpool was 4,365,526l. 1s. 8d. (1848.) In 1851 Liverpool contained 375,000 inhabitants, (1857.)

Such has been the progress of those towns where wealth is created and accumulated. Not less rapid has been the progress of towns of a very different kind, towns in which wealth, created and accumulated elsewhere, is expended for purposes of health and recreation. Some of the most remarkable of these gay places have sprung into existence since the time of the Stuarts. Cheltenham is now a greater city than any which the kingdom contained in the seventeenth century, London alone excepted. But in the seventeenth century, and at the beginning of the eighteenth, Cheltenham was mentioned by local historians merely as a rural parish lying under the Cotswold Hills, and affording good ground both for tillage and pasture. Corn grew and cattle browsed over the space now covered by that long succession of streets and villas.*

Brighton. Brighton was described as a place which had once been thriving, which had possessed many small fishing barks, and which had, when at the height of prosperity, contained above two thousand inhabitants, but which was sinking fast into decay. The sea was gradually gaining on the buildings, which at length almost entirely disappeared. Ninety years ago the ruins of an old fort were to be seen lying among the pebbles and seaweed on the beach; and ancient men could still point out the traces of foundations on a spot where a street of more than a hundred huts had been swallowed up by the waves. So desolate was the place after this calamity, that the vicarage was thought scarcely worth having. A few poor fishermen, however, still continued to dry their nets on those cliffs, on which now a town, more than twice as large and populous as the Bristol of the Stuarts, presents, mile after mile, its gay and fantastic front to the sea.†

Buxton. England, however, was not, in the seventeenth century, destitute of watering places. The gentry of Derbyshire and of the neighbouring counties repaired to Buxton, where they were lodged in low rooms under bare rafters, and regaled with oatcake, and with a viand which the hosts called mutton, but which the guests suspected to be dog. A single good house stood near the spring.‡ Tunbridge Wells, lying within a day's journey of the capital, and in one of the richest and most highly civilised parts of the kingdom, had much greater attractions. At present we see there a town which would, a

Watering places.

Cheltenham.

Tunbridge Wells.

---

* Atkyns's Gloucestershire.
† Magna Britannia; Grose's Antiquities; New Brighthelmstone Directory, 1770.
‡ Tour in Derbyshire, by Thomas Browne, son of Sir Thomas.

hundred and sixty years ago, have ranked, in population, fourth or fifth among the towns of England. The brilliancy of the shops and the luxury of the private dwellings far surpasses anything that England could then show. When the court, soon after the Restoration, visited Tunbridge Wells, there was no town : but, within a mile of the spring, rustic cottages, somewhat cleaner and neater than the ordinary cottages of that time, were scattered over the heath. Some of these cabins were movable, and were carried on sledges from one part of the common to another. To these huts men of fashion, wearied with the din and smoke of London, sometimes came in the summer to breathe fresh air, and to catch a glimpse of rural life. During the season a kind of fair was daily held near the fountain. The wives and daughters of the Kentish farmers came from the neighbouring villages with cream, cherries, wheatears, and quails. To chaffer with them, to flirt with them, to praise their straw hats and tight heels, was a refreshing pastime to voluptuaries sick of the airs of actresses and maids of honour. Milliners, toymen, and jewellers came down from London, and opened a bazaar under the trees. In one booth the politician might find his coffee and the London Gazette ; in another were gamblers playing deep at basset ; and, on fine evenings, the fiddles were in attendance, and there were morris dances on the elastic turf of the bowling green. In 1685 a subscription had just been raised among those who frequented the wells for building a church, which the Tories, who then domineered everywhere, insisted on dedicating to Saint Charles the Martyr.*

But at the head of the English watering places, without a Bath. rival, was Bath. The springs of that city had been renowned from the days of the Romans. It had been, during many centuries, the seat of a Bishop. The sick repaired thither from every part of the realm. The King sometimes held his court there. Nevertheless, Bath was then a maze of only four or five hundred houses, crowded within an old wall in the vicinity of the Avon. Pictures of what were considered as the finest of those houses are still extant, and greatly resemble the lowest rag shops and pothouses of Ratcliffe Highway. Travellers indeed complained loudly of the nar-

* Mémoires de Grammont; Hasted's History of Kent; Tunbridge Wells, a Comedy, 1678; Causton's Tunbridgialia, 1688; Metellus, a poem on Tunbridge Wells, 1693.

rowness and meanness of the streets. That beautiful city which charms even eyes familiar with the masterpieces of Bramante and Palladio, and which the genius of Anstey and of Smollett, of Frances Burney and of Jane Austen, has made classic ground, had not begun to exist. Milsom Street itself was an open field lying far beyond the walls ; and hedgerows intersected the space which is now covered by the Crescent and the Circus. The poor patients to whom the waters had been recommended lay on straw in a place which, to use the language of a contemporary physician, was a covert rather than a lodging. As to the comforts and luxuries which were to be found in the interior of the houses of Bath by the fashionable visitors who resorted thither in search of health or amusement, we possess information more complete and minute than can generally be obtained on such subjects. A writer who published an account of that city about sixty years after the Revolution has accurately described the changes which had taken place within his own recollection. He assures us that, in his younger days, the gentlemen who visited the springs slept in rooms hardly as good as the garrets which he lived to see occupied by footmen. The floors of the dining rooms were uncarpeted, and were coloured brown with a wash made of soot and small beer, in order to hide the dirt. Not a wainscot was painted. Not a hearth or a chimneypiece was of marble. A slab of common free-stone and fire irons which had cost from three to four shillings were thought sufficient for any fireplace. The best apartments were hung with coarse woollen stuff, and were furnished with rushbottomed chairs. Readers who take an interest in the progress of civilisation and of the useful arts will be grateful to the humble topographer who has recorded these facts, and will perhaps wish that historians of far higher pretensions had sometimes spared a few pages from military evolutions and political intrigues, for the purpose of letting us know how the parlours and bedchambers of our ancestors looked.*

London.   The position of London, relatively to the other towns of the empire, was, in the time of Charles the Second, far

---

* See Wood's History of Bath, 1749 ; Evelyn's Diary, June 27. 1654 ; Pepys's Diary, June 12. 1668 ; Stukeley's Itinerarium Curiosum ; Collinson's Somersetshire ; Dr. Peirce's History and Memoirs of the Bath, 1713, Book I. chap. viii. obs. 2. 1684. I have consulted several old maps and pictures of Bath, particularly one curious map which is surrounded by views of the principal buildings. It bears the date of 1717.

higher than at present. For at present the population of London is little more than six times the population of Manchester or of Liverpool. In the days of Charles the Second the population of London was more than seventeen times the population of Bristol or of Norwich. It may be doubted whether any other instance can be mentioned of a great kingdom in which the first city was more than seventeen times as large as the second. There is reason to believe that, in 1685, London had been, during about half a century, the most populous capital in Europe. The inhabitants, who are now at least nineteen hundred thousand, were then probably little more than half a million.* London had in the world only one commercial rival, now long ago outstripped, the mighty and opulent Amsterdam. English writers boasted of the forest of masts and yardarms which covered the river from the Bridge to the Tower, and of the stupendous sums which were collected at the Custom House in Thames Street. There is, indeed, no doubt that the trade of the metropolis then bore a far greater proportion than at present to the whole trade of the country; yet to our generation the honest vaunting of our ancestors must appear almost ludicrous. The shipping which they thought incredibly great appears not to have exceeded seventy thousand tons. This was, indeed, then more than a third of the whole tonnage of the kingdom, but is now less than a fourth of the tonnage of Newcastle, and is nearly equalled by the tonnage of the steam vessels of the Thames. The customs of London amounted, in 1685, to about three hundred and thirty thousand pounds a year. In our time the net duty paid annually, at the same place, exceeds ten millions.†

Whoever examines the maps of London which were published towards the close of the reign of Charles the Second will see that only the nucleus of the present capital then existed. The town did not, as now, fade by imperceptible degrees into the country. No long avenues of villas, embowered in lilacs and laburnums, extended from the great centre of wealth and civilisation almost to the boundaries of

---

* According to King 530,000. (1848.) In 1851 the population of London exceeded 2,300,000. (1857.)

† Macpherson's History of Commerce; Chalmers's Estimate; Chamberlayne's State of England, 1684. The tonnage of the steamers belonging to the port of London was, at the end of 1847, about 60,000 tons. The customs of the port, from 1842 to 1845, very nearly averaged 11,000,000l. (1848.) In 1854 the tonnage of the steamers of the port of London amounted to 138,000 tons, without reckoning vessels of less than fifty tons. (1857.)

Middlesex and far into the heart of Kent and Surrey. In the east, no part of the immense line of warehouses and artificial lakes which now stretches from the Tower to Blackwall had even been projected. On the west, scarcely one of those stately piles of building which are inhabited by the noble and wealthy was in existence; and Chelsea, which is now peopled by more than forty thousand human beings, was a quiet country village with about a thousand inhabitants.* On the north, cattle fed, and sportsmen wandered with dogs and guns, over the site of the borough of Marylebone, and over far the greater part of the space now covered by the boroughs of Finsbury and of the Tower Hamlets. Islington was almost a solitude; and poets loved to contrast its silence and repose with the din and turmoil of the monster London.† On the south the capital is now connected with its suburb by several bridges, not inferior in magnificence and solidity to the noblest works of the Cæsars. In 1685, a single line of irregular arches, overhung by piles of mean and crazy houses, and garnished, after a fashion worthy of the naked barbarians of Dahomy, with scores of mouldering heads, impeded the navigation of the river.

The City. Of the metropolis, the City, properly so called, was the most important division. At the time of the Restoration it had been built, for the most part, of wood and plaster; the few bricks that were used were ill baked; the booths where goods were exposed to sale projected far into the streets, and were overhung by the upper stories. A few specimens of this architecture may still be seen in those districts which were not reached by the great fire. That fire had, in a few days, covered a space of little less than a square mile with the ruins of eighty-nine churches and of thirteen thousand houses. But the City had risen again with a celerity which had excited the admiration of neighbouring countries. Unfortunately, the old lines of the streets had been to a great extent preserved; and those lines, originally traced in an age when even princesses performed their journeys on horseback, were often too narrow to allow wheeled carriages to pass each other with ease, and were therefore ill adapted for the residence of wealthy persons in an age when a coach and six was a fashionable luxury. The style of building was, however, far

---

* Lyson's Environs of London. The 1690, were only 42 a year.
baptisms at Chelsea, between 1680 and † Cowley, Discourse of Solitude.

Windsor Castle, from the Brocas

superior to that of the City which had perished. The ordinary material was brick, of much better quality than had formerly been used. On the sites of the ancient parish churches had arisen a multitude of new domes, towers, and spires which bore the mark of the fertile genius of Wren. In every place save one the traces of the great devastation had been completely effaced. But the crowds of workmen, the scaffolds, and the masses of hewn stone were still to be seen where the noblest of Protestant temples was slowly rising on the ruins of the old Cathedral of Saint Paul.*

The whole character of the City has, since that time, undergone a complete change. At present the bankers, the merchants, and the chief shopkeepers repair thither on six mornings of every week for the transaction of business : but they reside in other quarters of the metropolis, or at suburban country seats surrounded by shrubberies and flower gardens. This revolution in private habits has produced a political revolution of no small importance. The City is no longer regarded by the wealthiest traders with that attachment which every man naturally feels for his home. It is no longer associated in their minds with domestic affections and endearments. The fireside, the nursery, the social table, the quiet bed are not there. Lombard Street and Threadneedle Street are merely places where men toil and accumulate. They go elsewhere to enjoy and to expend. On a Sunday, or in an evening after the hours of business, some courts and alleys, which a few hours before had been alive with hurrying feet and anxious faces, are as silent as the glades of a forest. The chiefs of the mercantile interest are no longer citizens. They avoid, they almost contemn, municipal honours and duties. Those honours and duties are abandoned to men who, though useful and highly respectable, seldom belong to the princely commercial houses of which the names are renowned throughout the world.

In the seventeenth century the City was the merchant's residence. Those mansions of the great old burghers which still exist have been turned into counting houses and ware-

* The fullest and most trustworthy information about the state of the buildings of London at this time is to be derived from the maps and drawings in the British Museum and in the Pepysian Library. The badness of the bricks in the old buildings of London is particularly mentioned in the Travels of the Grand Duke Cosmo. There is an account of the works at Saint Paul's in Ward's London Spy. I am almost ashamed to quote such nauseous balderdash; but I have been forced to descend even lower, if possible, in search of materials.

houses: but it is evident that they were originally not inferior in magnificence to the dwellings which were then inhabited by the nobility. They sometimes stand in retired and gloomy courts, and are accessible only by inconvenient passages: but their dimensions are ample, and their aspect stately. The entrances are decorated with richly carved pillars and canopies. The staircases and landing places are not wanting in grandeur. The floors are sometimes of wood, tessellated after the fashion of France. The palace of Sir Robert Clayton, in the Old Jewry, contained a superb banqueting room wainscoted with cedar, and adorned with battles of gods and giants in fresco.* Sir Dudley North expended four thousand pounds, a sum which would then have been important to a Duke, on the rich furniture of his reception rooms in Basinghall Street.† In such abodes, under the last Stuarts, the heads of the great firms lived splendidly and hospitably. To their dwelling place they were bound by the strongest ties of interest and affection. There they had passed their youth, had made their friendships, had courted their wives, had seen their children grow up, had laid the remains of their parents in the earth, and expected that their own remains would be laid. That intense patriotism which is peculiar to the members of societies congregated within a narrow space was, in such circumstances, strongly developed. London was, to the Londoner, what Athens was to the Athenian of the age of Pericles, what Florence was to the Florentine of the fifteenth century. The citizen was proud of the grandeur of his city, punctilious about her claims to respect, ambitious of her offices, and zealous for her franchises.

At the close of the reign of Charles the Second the pride of the Londoners was smarting from a cruel mortification. The old charter had been taken away; and the magistracy had been remodelled. All the civic functionaries were Tories: and the Whigs, though in numbers and in wealth superior to their opponents, found themselves excluded from every local dignity. Nevertheless, the external splendour of the municipal government was not diminished, nay, was rather increased by this change. For, under the administration of some Puritans who had lately borne rule, the ancient fame of the City for good cheer had declined: but under the

* Evelyn's Diary, Sept. 20. 1672.   † Roger North's Life of Sir Dudley North.

new magistrates, who belonged to a more festive party, and at whose boards guests of rank and fashion from beyond Temple Bar were often seen, the Guildhall and the halls of the great companies were enlivened by many sumptuous banquets. During these repasts, odes composed by the poet laureate of the corporation, in praise of the King, the Duke, and the Mayor, were sung to music. The drinking was deep, the shouting loud. An observant Tory, who had often shared in these revels, has remarked that the practice of huzzaing after drinking healths dates from this joyous period.*

The magnificence displayed by the first civic magistrate was almost regal. The gilded coach, indeed, which is now annually admired by the crowd, was not yet a part of his state. On great occasions he appeared on horseback, attended by a long cavalcade inferior in magnificence only to that which, before a coronation, escorted the sovereign from the Tower to Westminster. The Lord Mayor was never seen in public without his rich robe, his hood of black velvet, his gold chain, his jewel, and a great attendance of harbingers and guards.† Nor did the world find anything ludicrous in the pomp which constantly surrounded him. For it was not more than became the place which, as wielding the strength and representing the dignity of the City of London, he was entitled to occupy in the State. That City, being then not only without equal in the country, but without second, had, during five and forty years, exercised almost as great an influence on the politics of England as Paris has, in our own time, exercised on the politics of France. In intelligence London was greatly in advance of every other part of the kingdom. A government, supported and trusted by London, could in a day obtain such pecuniary means as it would have taken months to collect from the rest of the island. Nor were the military resources of the capital to be despised. The power which the Lord Lieutenants exercised in other parts of the kingdom was in London entrusted to a Commission of eminent citizens. Under the order of this Commission were twelve regiments of foot and two regiments of horse. An army of drapers' apprentices and journeymen tailors, with common councilmen for captains and aldermen for colonels, might not

---

* North's Examen. This amusing writer has preserved a specimen of the sublime raptures in which the Pindar of the City indulged:—

"The worshipful Sir John Moor! After age that name adore!"

† Chamberlayne's State of England, 1684; Angliæ Metropolis, 1690; Seymour's London, 1734.

indeed have been able to stand its ground against regular
troops; but there were then very few regular troops in the
kingdom. A town, therefore, which could send forth, at an
hour's notice, thousands of men, abounding in natural courage,
provided with tolerable weapons, and not altogether untinc-
tured with martial discipline, could not but be a valuable ally
and a formidable enemy. It was not forgotten that Hampden and Pym had been protected from lawless tyranny by
the London trainbands; that, in the great crisis of the civil
war, the London trainbands had marched to raise the siege
of Gloucester; or that, in the movement against the military
tyrants which followed the downfall of Richard Cromwell,
the London trainbands had borne a signal part. In truth,
it is no exaggeration to say that, but for the hostility
of the City, Charles the First would never have been vanquished, and that, without the help of the City, Charles the
Second could scarcely have been restored.

These considerations may serve to explain why, in spite
of that attraction which had, during a long course of years,
gradually drawn the aristocracy westward, a few men of high
rank had continued, till a very recent period, to dwell in the
vicinity of the Exchange and of the Guildhall. Shaftesbury
and Buckingham, while engaged in bitter and unscrupulous
opposition to the government, had thought that they could
nowhere carry on their intrigues so conveniently or so securely
as under the protection of the City magistrates and the City
militia. Shaftesbury had therefore lived in Aldersgate Street,
at a house which may still be easily known by pilasters and
wreaths, the graceful work of Inigo. Buckingham had ordered
his mansion near Charing Cross, once the abode of the Archbishops of York, to be pulled down; and, while streets and
alleys which are still named after him were rising on that
site, chose to reside in Dowgate.*

Fashion-
able part
of the
capital.

These, however, were rare exceptions. Almost all the
noble families of England had long migrated beyond the
walls. The district where most of their town houses stood
lies between the city and the regions which are now considered as fashionable. A few great men still retained their
hereditary hotels in the Strand. The stately dwellings on
the south and west of Lincoln's Inn Fields, the Piazza of
Covent Garden, Southampton Square, which is now called

* North's Examen, 116.; Wood, Ath. Ox. Shaftesbury; The Duke of B.'s
Litany.

Bloomsbury Square, and King's Square in Soho Fields, which is now called Soho Square, were among the favourite spots. Foreign princes were carried to see Bloomsbury Square, as one of the wonders of England.* Soho Square, which had just been built, was to our ancestors a subject of pride with which their posterity will hardly sympathise. Monmouth Square had been the name while the fortunes of the Duke of Monmouth flourished; and on the southern side towered his mansion. The front, though ungraceful, was lofty and richly adorned. The walls of the principal apartments were finely sculptured with fruit, foliage, and armorial bearings, and were hung with embroidered satin.† Every trace of this magnificence has long disappeared; and no aristocratical mansion is to be found in that once aristocratical quarter. A little way north from Holborn, and on the verge of the pastures and corn-fields, rose two celebrated palaces, each with an ample garden. One of them, then called Southampton House, and subsequently Bedford House, was removed about fifty years ago to make room for a new city, which now covers with its squares, streets, and churches, a vast area, renowned in the seventeenth century for peaches and snipes. The other, Montague House, celebrated for its frescoes and furniture, was, a few months after the death of Charles the Second, burned to the ground, and was speedily succeeded by a more magnificent Montague House, which, having been long the repository of such various and precious treasures of art, science, and learning as were scarcely ever before assembled under a single roof, has now given place to an edifice more magnificent still.‡

Nearer to the Court, on a space called St. James's Fields, had just been built St. James's Square and Jermyn Street. St. James's Church had recently been opened for the accommodation of the inhabitants of this new quarter.§ Golden Square, which was in the next generation inhabited by lords and ministers of state, had not yet been begun. Indeed the only dwellings to be seen on the north of Piccadilly were three or four isolated and almost rural mansions, of which the most celebrated was the costly pile erected by Clarendon, and nicknamed Dunkirk House. It had been purchased

---

* Travels of the Grand Duke Cosmo.
† Chamberlayne's State of England, 1684; Pennant's London; Smith's Life of Nollekens.

‡ Evelyn's Diary, Oct. 10. 1683, Jan. 19. 168⅘.
§ Stat. 1 Jac. II. c. 22.; Evelyn's Diary, Dec. 7. 1684.

after its founder's downfall by the Duke of Albemarle. The Clarendon Hotel and Albemarle Street still preserve the memory of the site.

He who then rambled to what is now the gayest and most crowded part of Regent Street found himself in a solitude, and was sometimes so fortunate as to have a shot at a woodcock.* On the north the Oxford road ran between hedges. Three or four hundred yards to the south were the garden walls of a few great houses which were considered as quite out of town. On the west was a meadow renowned for a spring from which, long afterwards, Conduit Street was named. On the east was a field not to be passed without a shudder by any Londoner of that age. There, as in a place far from the haunts of men, had been dug, twenty years before, when the great plague was raging, a pit into which the dead carts had nightly shot corpses by scores. It was popularly believed that the earth was deeply tainted with infection, and could not be disturbed without imminent risk to human life. No foundations were laid there till two generations had passed without any return of the pestilence, and till the ghastly spot had long been surrounded by buildings.†

We should greatly err if we were to suppose that any of the streets and squares then bore the same aspect as at present. The great majority of the houses, indeed, have, since that time, been wholly, or in great part, rebuilt. If the most fashionable parts of the capital could be placed before us such as they then were, we should be disgusted by their squalid appearance, and poisoned by their noisome atmosphere.

In Covent Garden a filthy and noisy market was held close to the dwellings of the great. Fruit women screamed, carters fought, cabbage stalks and rotten apples accumulated in heaps at the thresholds of the Countess of Berkshire and of the Bishop of Durham.‡

The centre of Lincoln's Inn Fields was an open space where the rabble congregated every evening, within a few yards of Cardigan House and Winchester House, to hear mountebanks harangue, to see bears dance, and to set dogs at oxen. Rub-

---

* Old General Oglethorpe, who died in 1785, used to boast that he had shot birds here in Anne's reign. See Pennant's London, and the Gentleman's Magazine for July 1785.

† The pest field will be seen in maps of London as late as the end of George

the First's reign.

‡ See a very curious plan of Covent Garden made about 1690, and engraved for Smith's History of Westminster. See also Hogarth's Morning, painted while some of the houses in the Piazza were still occupied by people of fashion.

bish was shot in every part of the area. Horses were exercised there. The beggars were as noisy and importunate as in the worst governed cities of the Continent. A Lincoln's Inn mumper was a proverb. The whole fraternity knew the arms and liveries of every charitably disposed grandee in the neighbourhood, and, as soon as his lordship's coach and six appeared, came hopping and crawling in crowds to persecute him. These disorders lasted, in spite of many accidents, and of some legal proceedings, till, in the reign of George the Second, Sir Joseph Jekyll, Master of the Rolls, was knocked down and nearly killed in the middle of the square. Then at length palisades were set up, and a pleasant garden laid out.*

Saint James's Square was a receptacle for all the offal and cinders, for all the dead cats and dead dogs of Westminster. At one time a cudgel player kept the ring there. At another time an impudent squatter settled himself there, and built a shed for rubbish under the windows of the gilded saloons in which the first magnates of the realm, Norfolk, Ormond, Kent, and Pembroke, gave banquets and balls. It was not till these nuisances had lasted through a whole generation, and till much had been written about them, that the inhabitants applied to Parliament for permission to put up rails, and to plant trees.†

When such was the state of the region inhabited by the most luxurious portion of society, we may easily believe that the great body of the population suffered what would now be considered as insupportable grievances. The pavement was detestable: all foreigners cried shame upon it. The drainage was so bad that in rainy weather the gutters soon became torrents. Several facetious poets have commemorated the fury with which these black rivulets roared down Snow Hill and Ludgate Hill, bearing to Fleet Ditch a vast tribute of animal and vegetable filth from the stalls of butchers and

* London Spy; Tom Brown's comical View of London and Westminster; Turner's Propositions for the employing of the Poor, 1678; Daily Courant and Daily Journal of June 7. 1733; Case of Michael v. Allestree, in 1676, 2 Levinz, p. 172. Michael had been run over by two horses which Allestree was breaking in Lincoln's Inn Fields. The declaration set forth that the defendant "porta deux chivals ungovernable en un coach, et improvide, incaute, et absque debita consideratione ineptitudinis loci la eux drive pur eux faire tractable et apt pur un coach, quels chivals, pur ceo que, per leur ferocite, ne poient estre rule, curre sur le plaintiff et le noie."

† Stat. 12 Geo. I. c. 25.; Commons' Journals, Feb. 25. March 2. 1722⅚; London Gardener, 1712; Evening Post, March 23. 1731. I have not been able to find this number of the Evening Post; I therefore quote it on the faith of Mr. Malcolm, who mentions it in his History of London.

greengrocers. This flood was profusely thrown to right and left by coaches and carts. To keep as far from the carriage road as possible was therefore the wish of every pedestrian. The mild and timid gave the wall. The bold and athletic took it. If two roisterers met, they cocked their hats in each other's faces, and pushed each other about till the weaker was shoved towards the kennel. If he was a mere bully he sneaked off, muttering that he should find a time. If he was pugnacious, the encounter probably ended in a duel behind Montague House.*

The houses were not numbered. There would indeed have been little advantage in numbering them; for of the coachmen, chairmen, porters, and errand boys of London, a very small proportion could read. It was necessary to use marks which the most ignorant could understand. The shops were therefore distinguished by painted or sculptured signs, which gave a gay and grotesque aspect to the streets. The walk from Charing Cross to Whitechapel lay through an endless succession of Saracens' Heads, Royal Oaks, Blue Bears, and Golden Lambs, which disappeared when they were no longer required for the direction of the common people.

When the evening closed in, the difficulty and danger of walking about London became serious indeed. The garret windows were opened, and pails were emptied, with little regard to those who were passing below. Falls, bruises, and broken bones were of constant occurrence. For, till the last year of the reign of Charles the Second, most of the streets were left in profound darkness. Thieves and robbers plied their trade with impunity: yet they were hardly so terrible to peaceable citizens as another class of ruffians. It was a favourite amusement of dissolute young gentlemen to swagger by night about the town, breaking windows, upsetting sedans, beating quiet men, and offering rude caresses to pretty women. Several dynasties of these tyrants had, since the Restoration, domineered over the streets. The Muns and Tityre Tus had given place to the Hectors, and the Hectors had been recently succeeded by the Scourers. At a later period arose the Nicker, the Hawcubite, and the yet more dreaded name of Mohawk.† The machinery for keeping the

Police of London.

---

* Lettres sur les Anglois, written early in the reign of William the Third; Swift's City Shower; Gay's Trivia. Johnson used to relate a curious conversation which he had with his mother about giving and taking the wall.

† Oldham's Imitation of the 3d Satire of Juvenal, 1682; Shadwell's Scourers

peace was utterly contemptible. There was an Act of Common Council which provided that more than a thousand watchmen should be constantly on the alert in the city, from sunset to sunrise, and that every inhabitant should take his turn of duty. But this Act was negligently executed. Few of those who were summoned left their homes; and those few generally found it more agreeable to tipple in alehouses than to pace the streets.*

It ought to be noticed that, in the last year of the reign of Charles the Second, began a great change in the police of London, a change which has perhaps added as much to the happiness of the body of the people as revolutions of much greater fame. An ingenious projector, named Edward Heming, obtained letters patent conveying to him, for a term of years, the exclusive right of lighting up London. He undertook, for a moderate consideration, to place a light before every tenth door, on moonless nights, from Michaelmas to Lady Day, and from six to twelve of the clock. Those who now see the capital all the year round, from dusk to dawn, blazing with a splendour beside which the illuminations for La Hogue and Blenheim would have looked pale, may perhaps smile to think of Heming's lanterns, which glimmered feebly before one house in ten during a small part of one night in three. But such was not the feeling of his contemporaries. His scheme was enthusiastically applauded, and furiously attacked. The friends of improvement extolled him as the greatest of all the benefactors of his city. What, they asked, were the boasted inventions of Archimedes, when compared with the achievement of the man who had turned the nocturnal shades into noon day? In spite of these eloquent eulogies the cause of darkness was not left undefended. There were fools in that age who opposed the introduction of what was called the new light as strenuously as fools in our age have opposed the introduction of vaccination and railroads, as strenuously as the fools of an age anterior to the dawn of history doubtless opposed the introduction of the plough and of alphabetical writing. Many

Lighting of London.

1690. Many other authorities will readily occur to all who are acquainted with the popular literature of that and the succeeding generation. It may be suspected that some of the Tityre Tus, like good Cavaliers, broke Milton's windows shortly after the Restoration. I am confident that he was thinking of those pests of London when he dictated the noble lines:—

" And in luxurious cities, when the noise
Of riot ascends above their loftiest towers,
And injury and outrage, and when night
Darkens the streets, then wander forth the sons
Of Belial, flown with insolence and wine."

* Seymour's London.

years after the date of Heming's patent there were extensive districts in which no lamp was seen.*

White-
friars.

We may easily imagine what, in such times, must have been the state of the quarters of London which were peopled by the outcasts of society. Among those quarters one had attained a scandalous preeminence. On the confines of the City and the Temple had been founded, in the thirteenth century, a House of Carmelite Friars, distinguished by their white hoods. The precinct of this house had, before the Reformation, been a sanctuary for criminals, and still retained the privilege of protecting debtors from arrest. Insolvents consequently were to be found in every dwelling, from cellar to garret. Of these a large proportion were knaves and libertines, and were followed to their asylum by women more abandoned than themselves. The civil power was unable to keep order in a district swarming with such inhabitants ; and thus Whitefriars became the favourite resort of all who wished to be emancipated from the restraints of the law. Though the immunities legally belonging to the place extended only to cases of debt, cheats, false witnesses, forgers, and highwaymen found refuge there. For amidst a rabble so desperate no peace officer's life was in safety. At the cry of "Rescue," bullies with swords and cudgels, and termagant hags with spits and broomsticks, poured forth by hundreds ; and the intruder was fortunate if he escaped back into Fleet Street, hustled, stripped, and pumped upon. Even the warrant of the Chief Justice of England could not be executed without the help of a company of musketeers. Such relics of the barbarism of the darkest ages were to be found within a short walk of the chambers where Somers was studying history and law, of the chapel where Tillotson was preaching, of the coffee house where Dryden was passing judgment on poems and plays, and of the hall where the Royal Society was examining the astronomical system of Isaac Newton.†

The Court.

Each of the two cities which made up the capital of England had its own centre of attraction. In the metropolis of commerce the point of convergence was the Exchange ; in the metropolis of fashion the Palace. But the Palace did not retain its influence so long as the Exchange. The Re-

<hr>

* Angliæ Metropolis, 1690, Sect. 17. entitled, "Of the new lights"; Seymour's London.

† Stowe's Survey of London ; Shadwell's Squire of Alsatia ; Ward's London Spy ; Stat. 8 & 9 Gul. III. cap. 27.

volution completely altered the relations between the Court and the higher classes of society. It was by degrees discovered that the King, in his individual capacity, had very little to give; that coronets and garters, bishoprics and embassies, lordships of the Treasury and tellerships of the Exchequer, nay, even charges in the royal stud and bedchamber, were really bestowed, not by him, but by his advisers. Every ambitious and covetous man perceived that he would consult his own interest far better by acquiring the dominion of a Cornish borough, and by rendering good service to the ministry during a critical session, than by becoming the companion, or even the minion, of his prince. It was therefore in the antechambers, not of George the First and of George the Second, but of Walpole and of Pelham, that the daily crowd of courtiers was to be found. It is also to be remarked that the same Revolution, which made it impossible that our Kings should use the patronage of the state merely for the purpose of gratifying their personal predilections, gave us several Kings unfitted by their education and habits to be gracious and affable hosts. They had been born and bred on the Continent. They never felt themselves at home in our island. If they spoke our language, they spoke it inelegantly and with effort. Our national character they never fully understood. Our national manners they hardly attempted to acquire. The most important part of their duty they performed better than any ruler who had preceded them: for they governed strictly according to law: but they could not be the first gentlemen of the realm, the heads of polite society. If ever they unbent, it was in a very small circle where hardly an English face was to be seen; and they were never so happy as when they could escape for a summer to their native land. They had indeed their days of reception for our nobility and gentry; but the reception was mere matter of form, and became at last as solemn a ceremony as a funeral.

Not such was the court of Charles the Second. Whitehall, when he dwelt there, was the focus of political intrigue and of fashionable gaiety. Half the jobbing and half the flirting of the metropolis went on under his roof. Whoever could make himself agreeable to the prince, or could secure the good offices of the mistress, might hope to rise in the world without rendering any service to the government, without being even known by sight to any minister of state. This courtier got a frigate, and that a company; a third, the pardon of a rich offender; a fourth, a lease of crown land on easy terms. If the King notified his pleasure that a briefless lawyer should be made a judge, or that a libertine baronet should be made a peer, the gravest counsellors, after a little murmuring, submitted.* Interest, therefore, drew a constant press of suitors to the gates of the palace; and those gates always stood wide. The King kept open house every day, and all day long, for the good society of London, the extreme Whigs only excepted. Hardly any gentleman had any difficulty in making his way to the royal presence. The levee was exactly what the word imports. Some men of quality came every morning to stand round their master, to chat with him while his wig was combed and his cravat tied, and to accompany him in his early walk through the Park. All persons who had been properly introduced might, without any special invitation, go to see him dine, sup, dance, and play at hazard, and might have the pleasure of hearing him tell stories, which indeed he told remarkably well, about his flight from Worcester, and about the misery which he had endured when he was a state prisoner in the hands of the canting meddling preachers of Scotland. Bystanders whom His Majesty recognised often came in for a courteous word. This proved a far more successful kingcraft than any that his father or grandfather had practised. It was not easy for the most austere republican of the school of Marvel to resist the fascination of so much good humour and affability: and many a veteran Cavalier, in whose heart the remembrance of unrequited sacrifices and services had been festering during twenty years, was compensated in one moment for wounds and sequestrations by his sovereign's kind nod, and "God bless you, my old friend!"

Whitehall naturally became the chief staple of news. Whenever there was a rumour that anything important had happened or was about to happen, people hastened thither to obtain intelligence from the fountain head. The galleries presented the appearance of a modern club room at an anxious time. They were full of people enquiring whether the Dutch mail was in, what tidings the express from France had brought, whether John Sobiesky had beaten the Turks,

* See Sir Roger North's account of the way in which Wright was made a judge, and Clarendon's account of the way in which Sir George Savile was made a peer.

whether the Doge of Genoa was really at Paris. These were matters about which it was safe to talk aloud. But there were subjects concerning which information was asked and given in whispers. Had Halifax got the better of Rochester? Was there to be a Parliament? Was the Duke of York really going to Scotland? Had Monmouth really been summoned from the Hague? Men tried to read the countenance of every minister as he went through the throng to and from the royal closet. All sorts of auguries were drawn from the tone in which His Majesty spoke to the Lord President, or from the laugh with which His Majesty honoured a jest of the Lord Privy Seal; and in a few hours the hopes and fears inspired by such slight indications had spread to all the coffee houses from Saint James's to the Tower.*

The coffee house must not be dismissed with a cursory mention. It might indeed at that time have been not improperly called a most important political institution. No Parliament had sat for years. The municipal council of the City had ceased to speak the sense of the citizens. Public meetings, harangues, resolutions, and the rest of the modern machinery of agitation had not yet come into fashion. Nothing resembling the modern newspaper existed. In such circumstances the coffee houses were the chief organs through which the public opinion of the metropolis vented itself.

The first of these establishments had been set up, in the time of the Commonwealth, by a Turkey merchant, who had acquired among the Mahometans a taste for their favourite beverage. The convenience of being able to make appointments in any part of the town, and of being able to pass evenings socially at a very small charge, was so great that the fashion spread fast. Every man of the upper or middle class went daily to his coffee house to learn the news and to discuss it. Every coffee house had one or more orators to whose eloquence the crowd listened with admiration, and who soon became, what the journalists of our time have been called, a fourth Estate of the realm. The Court had long seen with uneasiness the growth of this new power in the

The coffee houses

---

* The sources from which I have drawn my information about the state of the Court are too numerous to recapitulate. Among them are the Despatches of Barillon, Van Citters, Ronquillo, and Adda, the Travels of the Grand Duke Cosmo, the works of Roger North, the Diaries of Pepys, Evelyn, and Teonge, and the Memoirs of Grammont and Reresby.

state. An attempt had been made, during Danby's administration, to close the coffee houses. But men of all parties
missed their usual places of resort so much that there was
an universal outcry. The government did not venture, in
opposition to a feeling so strong and general, to enforce a
regulation of which the legality might well be questioned.
Since that time ten years had elapsed, and during those
years the number and influence of the coffee houses had been
constantly increasing. Foreigners remarked that the coffee
house was that which especially distinguished London from
all other cities ; that the coffee house was the Londoner's
home, and that those who wished to find a gentleman commonly asked, not whether he lived in Fleet Street or Chancery Lane, but whether he frequented the Grecian or the
Rainbow. Nobody was excluded from these places who laid
down his penny at the bar. Yet every rank and profession,
and every shade of religious and political opinion, had its
own head quarters. There were houses near Saint James's
Park where fops congregated, their heads and shoulders
covered with black or flaxen wigs, not less ample than those
which are now worn by the Chancellor and by the Speaker
of the House of Commons. The wig came from Paris ; and
so did the rest of the fine gentleman's ornaments, his embroidered coat, his fringed gloves, and the tassel which
upheld his pantaloons. The conversation was in that dialect
which, long after it had ceased to be spoken in fashionable
circles, continued, in the mouth of Lord Foppington, to
excite the mirth of theatres.* The atmosphere was like that
of a perfumer's shop. Tobacco in any other form than that
of richly scented snuff was held in abomination. If any
clown, ignorant of the usages of the house, called for a pipe,
the sneers of the whole assembly and the short answers of
the waiters soon convinced him that he had better go some-
where else. Nor, indeed, would he have had far to go. For,
in general, the coffee rooms reeked with tobacco like a
guardroom ; and strangers sometimes expressed their surprise that so many people should leave their own firesides to
sit in the midst of eternal fog and stench. Nowhere was the
smoking more constant than at Will's. That celebrated

* The chief peculiarity of this dialect
was that, in a large class of words, the O
was pronounced like A. Thus Lord was
pronounced Lard. See Vanbrugh's Relapse. Lord Sunderland was a great
master of this court tune, as Roger
North calls it ; and Titus Oates affected
it in the hope of passing for a fine gentleman. Examen, 77. 254.

house, situated between Covent Garden and Bow Street, was sacred to polite letters. There the talk was about poetical justice and the unities of place and time. There was a faction for Perrault and the moderns, a faction for Boileau and the ancients. One group debated whether Paradise Lost ought not to have been in rhyme. To another an envious poetaster demonstrated that Venice Preserved ought to have been hooted from the stage. Under no roof was a greater variety of figures to be seen. There were Earls ir stars and garters, clergymen in cassocks and bands, pert Templars, sheepish lads from the Universities, translators and indexmakers in ragged coats of frieze. The great press was to get near the chair where John Dryden sate. In winter that chair was always in the warmest nook by the fire; in summer it stood in the balcony. To bow to the Laureate, and to hear his opinion of Racine's last tragedy or of Bossu's treatise on epic poetry, was thought a privilege. A pinch from his snuff box was an honour sufficient to turn the head of a young enthusiast. There were coffee houses where the first medical men might be consulted. Doctor John Radcliffe, who, in the year 1685, rose to the largest practice in London, came daily, at the hour when the Exchange was full, from his house in Bow Street, then a fashionable part of the capital, to Garraway's, and was to be found, surrounded by surgeons and apothecaries, at a particular table. There were Puritan coffee houses where no oath was heard, and where lankhaired men discussed election and reprobation through their noses; Jew coffee houses where darkeyed money changers from Venice and from Amsterdam greeted each other; and Popish coffee houses where, as good Protestants believed, Jesuits planned, over their cups, another great fire, and cast silver bullets to shoot the King.*

These gregarious habits had no small share in forming the character of the Londoner of that age. He was, indeed, a different being from the rustic Englishman. There was not then the intercourse which now exists between the two classes. Only very great men were in the habit of dividing

* Lettres sur les Anglois; Tom Brown's Tour; Ward's London Spy; The Character of a Coffee House, 1673; Rules and Orders of the Coffee House, 1674; Coffee Houses vindicated, 1675; A Satyr against Coffee; North's Examen, 138.; Life of Guildford, 152.; Life of Sir Dudley North, 149.; Life of Dr. Radcliffe, published by Curll in 1715. The liveliest description of Will's is in the City and Country Mouse. There is a remarkable passage about the influence of the coffee house orators in Halstead's Succinct Genealogies, printed in 1685.

the year between town and country. Few esquires came to the capital thrice in their lives. Nor was it yet the practice of all citizens in easy circumstances to breathe the fresh air of the fields and woods during some weeks of every summer. A cockney, in a rural village, was stared at as much as if he had intruded into a Kraal of Hottentots. On the other hand, when the lord of a Lincolnshire or Shropshire manor appeared in Fleet Street, he was as easily distinguished from the resident population as a Turk or a Lascar. His dress, his gait, his accent, the manner in which he gazed at the shops, stumbled into the gutters, ran against the porters, and stood under the waterspouts, marked him out as an excellent subject for the operations of swindlers and banterers. Bullies jostled him into the kennel. Hackney coachmen splashed him from head to foot. Thieves explored with perfect security the huge pockets of his horseman's coat, while he stood entranced by the splendour of the Lord Mayor's show. Moneydroppers, sore from the cart's tail, introduced themselves to him. and appeared to him the most honest friendly gentlemen that he had ever seen. Painted women, the refuse of Lewkner Lane and Whetstone Park, passed themselves on him for countesses and maids of honour. If he asked his way to Saint James's, his informants sent him to Mile End. If he went into a shop, he was instantly discerned to be a fit purchaser of everything that nobody else would buy, of secondhand embroidery, copper rings, and watches that would not go. If he rambled into any fashionable coffee house, he became a mark for the insolent derision of fops and the grave waggery of Templars. Enraged and mortified, he soon returned to his mansion, and there, in the homage of his tenants and the conversation of his boon companions, found consolation for the vexations and humiliations which he had undergone. There he was once more a great man, and saw nothing above himself except when at the assizes he took his seat on the bench near the Judge, or when at the muster of the militia he saluted the Lord Lieutenant.

Difficulty of travelling.

The chief cause which made the fusion of the different elements of society so imperfect was the extreme difficulty which our ancestors found in passing from place to place. Of all inventions, the alphabet and the printing press alone excepted, those inventions which abridge distance have done most for the civilisation of our species. Every improvement of the means of locomotion benefits mankind morally and intellectually as well as materially, and not only facilitates the interchange of the various productions of nature and art, but tends to remove national and provincial antipathies, and to bind together all the branches of the great human family. In the seventeenth century the inhabitants of London were, for almost every practical purpose, farther from Reading than they now are from Edinburgh, and farther from Edinburgh than they now are from Vienna.

The subjects of Charles the Second were not, it is true, quite unacquainted with that principle which has, in our own time, produced an unprecedented revolution in human affairs, which has enabled navies to advance in face of wind and tide, and brigades of troops, attended by all their baggage and artillery, to traverse kingdoms at a pace equal to that of the fleetest race horse. The Marquess of Worcester had recently observed the expansive power of moisture rarefied by heat. After many experiments he had succeeded in constructing a rude steam engine, which he called a fire water work, and which he pronounced to be an admirable and most forcible instrument of propulsion.* But the Marquess was suspected to be a madman, and known to be a Papist. His inventions, therefore, found no favourable reception. His fire water work might, perhaps, furnish matter for conversation at a meeting of the Royal Society, but was not applied to any practical purpose. There were no railways, except a few made of timber, on which coals were carried from the mouths of the Northumbrian pits to the banks of the Tyne.† There was very little internal communication by water. A few attempts had been made to deepen and embank the natural streams, but with slender success. Hardly a single navigable canal had been even projected. The English of that day were in the habit of talking with mingled admiration and despair of the immense trench by which Lewis the Fourteenth had made a junction between the Atlantic and the Mediterranean. They little thought that their country would, in the course of a few generations, be intersected, at the cost of private adventurers, by artificial rivers making up more than four times the length of the Thames, the Severn, and the Trent together.

It was by the highways that both travellers and goods generally passed from place to place; and those highways Badness of the roads.

---

* Century of Inventions, 1663, No. 68.   † North's Life of Guildford, 136.

appear to have been far worse than might have been expected
from the degree of wealth and civilisation which the nation
had even then attained. On the best lines of communication
the ruts were deep, the descents precipitous, and the way
often such as it was hardly possible to distinguish, in the
dusk, from the unenclosed heath and fen which lay on both
sides. Ralph Thoresby, the antiquary, was in danger of
losing his way on the great North road, between Barnby Moor
and Tuxford, and actually lost his way between Doncaster
and York.[*] Pepys and his wife, travelling in their own
coach, lost their way between Newbury and Reading. In the
course of the same tour they lost their way near Salisbury,
and were in danger of having to pass the night on the plain.[†]
It was only in fine weather that the whole breadth of the
road was available for wheeled vehicles. Often the mud lay
deep on the right and the left; and only a narrow track of
firm ground rose above the quagmire.[‡] At such times ob-
structions and quarrels were frequent, and the path was sometimes blocked up during a long time by carriers, neither of
whom would break the way. It happened, almost every day,
that coaches stuck fast, until a team of cattle could be procured from some neighbouring farm, to tug them out of the
slough. But in bad seasons the traveller had to encounter
inconveniences still more serious. Thoresby, who was in the
habit of travelling between Leeds and the capital, has
recorded, in his Diary, such a series of perils and disasters as
might suffice for a journey to the Frozen Ocean or to the
Desert of Sahara. On one occasion he learned that the floods
were out between Ware and London, that passengers had to
swim for their lives, and that a higgler had perished in the
attempt to cross. In consequence of these tidings he turned
out of the high road, and was conducted across some meadows,
where it was necessary for him to ride to the saddle skirts in
water.[§] In the course of another journey he narrowly
escaped being swept away by an inundation of the Trent. He
was afterwards detained at Stamford four days, on account of
the state of the roads, and then ventured to proceed only
because fourteen members of the House of Commons, who
were going up in a body to Parliament with guides and nu-
merous attendants, took him into their company.[||] On the

roads of Derbyshire, travellers were in constant fear for their necks, and were frequently compelled to alight and lead their beasts.* The great route through Wales to Holyhead was in such a state that, in 1685, a viceroy, going to Ireland, was five hours in travelling fourteen miles, from Saint Asaph to Conway. Between Conway and Beaumaris he was forced to walk great part of the way; and his lady was carried in a litter. His coach was, with much difficulty, and by the help of many hands, brought after him entire. In general, carriages were taken to pieces at Conway, and borne, on the shoulders of stout Welsh peasants, to the Menai Straits.† In some parts of Kent and Sussex, none but the strongest horses could, in winter, get through the bog, in which, at every step, they sank deep. The markets were often inaccessible during several months. It is said that the fruits of the earth were sometimes suffered to rot in one place, while in another place, distant only a few miles, the supply fell far short of the demand. The wheeled carriages were, in this district, generally pulled by oxen.‡ When Prince George of Denmark visited the stately mansion of Petworth in wet weather, he was six hours in going nine miles; and it was necessary that a body of sturdy hinds should be on each side of his coach, in order to prop it. Of the carriages which conveyed his retinue several were upset and injured. A letter from one of the party has been preserved, in which the unfortunate courtier complains that, during fourteen hours, he never once alighted, except when his coach was overturned or stuck fast in the mud.§

One chief cause of the badness of the roads seems to have been the defective state of the law. Every parish was bound to repair the highways which passed through it. The peasantry were forced to give their gratuitous labour six days in the year. If this was not sufficient, hired labour was employed, and the expense was met by a parochial rate. That a route connecting two great towns, which have a large and thriving trade with each other, should be maintained at the cost of the rural population scattered between them is obviously unjust; and this injustice was peculiarly glaring in the case of the great North road, which traversed very poor and thinly inhabited districts, and joined very rich and

* Tour in Derbyshire, by J. Browne, son of Sir Thomas Browne, 1662; Cotton's Angler, 1676.

† Correspondence of Henry Earl of Clarendon, Dec. 30. 1685, Jan. 1. 1686.

‡ Postlethwaite's Dictionary, Roads; History of Hawkhurst, in the Bibliotheca Topographica Britannica.

§ Annals of Queen Anne, 1703, Appendix, No. 3.

populous districts. Indeed it was not in the power of the parishes of Huntingdonshire to mend a highway worn by the constant traffic between the West Riding of Yorkshire and London. Soon after the Restoration this grievance attracted the notice of Parliament ; and an act, the first of our many turnpike acts, was passed, imposing a small toll on travellers and goods, for the purpose of keeping some parts of this important line of communication in good repair.*   This innovation, however, excited many murmurs ; and the other great avenues to the capital were long left under the old system. A change was at length effected, but not without much difficulty.   For unjust and absurd taxation to which men are accustomed is often borne far more willingly than the most reasonable impost which is new.   It was not till many toll bars had been violently pulled down, till the troops had in many districts been forced to act against the people, and till much blood had been shed, that a good system was introduced.†   By slow degrees reason triumphed over prejudice ; and our island is now crossed in every direction by near thirty thousand miles of turnpike road.

On the best highways heavy articles were, in the time of Charles the Second, generally conveyed from place to place by stage waggons.   In the straw of these vehicles nestled a crowd of passengers, who could not afford to travel by coach or on horseback, and who were prevented by infirmity, or by the weight of their luggage, from going on foot.   The expense of transmitting heavy goods in this way was enormous. From London to Birmingham the charge was seven pounds a ton ; from London to Exeter twelve pounds a ton.‡   This was about fifteen pence a ton for every mile, more by a third than was afterwards charged on turnpike roads, and fifteen times what is now demanded by railway companies. The cost of conveyance amounted to a prohibitory tax on many useful articles.   Coal in particular was never seen except in the districts where it was produced, or in the districts to which it could be carried by sea, and was indeed always known in the south of England by the name of sea coal.

On byroads, and generally throughout the country north of York and west of Exeter, goods were carried by long trains

---

* 15 Car. II. c. 1.
† The evils of the old system are strikingly set forth in many petitions which appear in the Commons' Journal of 172⅝.   How fierce an opposition was offered to the new system may be learned from the Gentleman's Magazine of 1749.
‡ Postlethwaite's Dict., Roads.

of packhorses. These strong and patient beasts, the breed of which is now extinct, were attended by a class of men who seem to have borne much resemblance to the Spanish muleteers. A traveller of humble condition often found it convenient to perform a journey mounted on a packsaddle between two baskets, under the care of these hardy guides. The expense of this mode of conveyance was small. But the caravan moved at a foot's pace; and in winter the cold was often insupportable.*

The rich commonly travelled in their own carriages, with at least four horses. Cotton, the facetious poet, attempted to go from London to the Peak with a single pair, but found at Saint Albans that the journey would be insupportably tedious, and altered his plan.† A coach and six is in our time never seen, except as part of some pageant. The frequent mention therefore of such equipages in old books is likely to mislead us. We attribute to magnificence what was really the effect of a very disagreeable necessity. People, in the time of Charles the Second, travelled with six horses, because with a smaller number there was great danger of sticking fast in the mire. Nor were even six horses always sufficient. Vanbrugh, in the succeeding generation, described with great humour the way in which a country gentleman, newly chosen a member of Parliament, went up to London. On that occasion all the exertions of six beasts, two of which had been taken from the plough, could not save the family coach from being embedded in a quagmire.

Public carriages had recently been much improved. During the years which immediately followed the Restoration, a diligence ran between London and Oxford in two days. The passengers slept at Beaconsfield. At length, in the spring of 1669, a great and daring innovation was attempted. It was announced that a vehicle, described as the Flying Coach, would perform the whole journey between sunrise and sunset. This spirited undertaking was solemnly considered and sanctioned by the Heads of the University, and appears to have excited the same sort of interest which is excited in our own time by the opening of a new railway. The Vicechancellor, by a notice affixed in all public places, prescribed the hour and place of departure. The success of the experiment was

Stage coaches.

* Loidis and Elmete; Marshall's Rural Economy of England. In 1739 Roderic Random came from Scotland to Newcastle on a packhorse.
† Cotton's Epistle to J. Bradshaw.

complete. At six in the morning the carriage began to move
from before the ancient front of All Souls College; and at
seven in the evening the adventurous gentlemen who had run
the first risk were safely deposited at their inn in London.*
The emulation of the sister University was moved; and soon
a diligence was set up which in one day carried passengers
from Cambridge to the capital. At the close of the reign of
Charles the Second, flying carriages ran thrice a week from
London to the chief towns.   But no stage coach, indeed no
stage waggon, appears to have proceeded further north than
York, or further west than Exeter. The ordinary day's journey of a flying coach was about fifty miles in the summer;
but in winter, when the ways were bad and the nights long,
little more than thirty.   The Chester coach, the York coach,
and the Exeter coach generally reached London in four days
during the fine season, but at Christmas not till the sixth
day.   The passengers, six in number, were all seated in the
carriage.   For accidents were so frequent that it would have
been most perilous to mount the roof.   The ordinary fare
was about twopence halfpenny a mile in summer, and somewhat more in winter.†

   This mode of travelling, which by Englishmen of the present day would be regarded as insufferably slow, seemed to
our ancestors wonderfully and indeed alarmingly rapid. In
a work published a few months before the death of Charles
the Second, the flying coaches are extolled as far superior to
any similar vehicles ever known in the world. Their velocity
is the subject of special commendation, and is triumphantly
contrasted with the sluggish pace of the continental posts.
But with boasts like these was mingled the sound of complaint and invective.   The interests of large classes had been
unfavourably affected by the establishment of the new dili-
gences; and, as usual, many persons were, from mere stupidity and obstinacy, disposed to clamour against the innovation, simply because it was an innovation.   It was vehemently argued that this mode of conveyance would be fatal
to the breed of horses and to the noble art of horsemanship;
that the Thames, which had long been an important nursery
of seamen, would cease to be the chief thoroughfare from
London up to Windsor and down to Gravesend; that saddlers

---

* Anthony à Wood's Life of himself.   and waggons at the end of the book, en-
† Chamberlayne's State of England,   titled Angliæ Metropolis, 1690.
1684.   See also the list of stage coaches

and spurriers would be ruined by hundreds; that numerous inns, at which mounted travellers had been in the habit of stopping, would be deserted, and would no longer pay any rent; that the new carriages were too hot in summer and too cold in winter; that the passengers were grievously annoyed by invalids and crying children; that the coach sometimes reached the inn so late that it was impossible to get supper, and sometimes started so early that it was impossible to get breakfast. On these grounds it was gravely recommended that no public coach should be permitted to have more than four horses, to start oftener than once a week, or to go more than thirty miles a day. It was hoped that, if this regulation were adopted, all except the sick and the lame would return to the old mode of travelling. Petitions embodying such opinions as these were presented to the King in council from several companies of the City of London, from several provincial towns, and from the justices of several counties. We smile at these things. It is not impossible that our descendants, when they read the history of the opposition offered by cupidity and prejudice to the improvements of the nineteenth century, may smile in their turn.*

In spite of the attractions of the flying coaches, it was still usual for men who enjoyed health and vigour, and who were not encumbered by much baggage, to perform long journeys on horseback. If the traveller wished to move expeditiously he rode post. Fresh saddle horses and guides were to be procured at convenient distances along all the great lines of road. The charge was threepence a mile for each horse, and fourpence a stage for the guide. In this manner, when the ways were good, it was possible to travel, for a considerable time, as rapidly as by any conveyance known in England, till vehicles were propelled by steam. There were as yet no post chaises; nor could those who rode in their own coaches ordinarily procure a change of horses. The King, however, and the great officers of state were able to command relays. Thus Charles commonly went in one day from Whitehall to Newmarket, a distance of about fifty-five miles through a level country; and this was thought by his subjects a proof of great activity. Evelyn performed the same journey in company with the Lord Treasurer Clifford. The coach was drawn

* John Cresset's Reasons for suppressing Stage Coaches, 1672. These reasons were afterwards inserted in a tract, entitled "The Grand Concern of England explained, 1673." Cresset's attack on stage coaches called forth some answers which I have consulted.

by six horses, which were changed at Bishop Stortford and again at Chesterford. The travellers reached Newmarket at night. Such a mode of conveyance seems to have been considered as a rare luxury confined to princes and ministers.*

Highway-
men.
Whatever might be the way in which a journey was performed, the travellers, unless they were numerous and well armed, ran considerable risk of being stopped and plundered. The mounted highwayman, a marauder known to our generation only from books, was to be found on every main road. The waste tracts which lay on the great routes near London were especially haunted by plunderers of this class. Hounslow Heath, on the Great Western Road, and Finchley Common, on the Great Northern Road, were perhaps the most celebrated of these spots. The Cambridge scholars trembled when they approached Epping Forest, even in broad daylight. Seamen who had just been paid off at Chatham were often compelled to deliver their purses on Gadshill, celebrated near a hundred years earlier by the greatest of poets as the scene of the depredations of Falstaff. The public authorities seem to have been often at a loss how to deal with the plunderers. At one time it was announced in the Gazette, that several persons, who were strongly suspected of being highwaymen, but against whom there was not sufficient evidence, would be paraded at Newgate in riding dresses : their horses would also be shown ; and all gentlemen who had been robbed were invited to inspect this singular exhibition. On another occasion a pardon was publicly offered to a robber if he would give up some rough diamonds, of immense value, which he had taken when he stopped the Harwich mail. A short time after appeared another proclamation, warning the innkeepers that the eye of the government was upon them. Their criminal connivance, it was affirmed, enabled banditti to infest the roads with impunity. That these suspicions were not without foundation, is proved by the dying speeches of some penitent robbers of that age, who appear to have received from the innkeepers services much resembling those which Farquhar's Boniface rendered to Gibbet.†

It was necessary to the success and even to the safety of the highwayman that he should be a bold and skilful rider,

---

* Chamberlayne's State of England, 1684. ; North's Examen, 105. ; Evelyn's Diary, Oct. 9, 10. 1671.

† See the London Gazette, May 14. 1677, August 4. 1687. Dec. 5. 1687.

The last confession of Augustin King, who was the son of an eminent divine, and had been educated at Cambridge but was hanged at Colchester in March 1688, is highly curious.

and that his manners and appearance should be such as suited the master of a fine horse. He therefore held an aristocratical position in the community of thieves, appeared at fashionable coffee houses and gaming houses, and betted with men of quality on the race ground.* Sometimes, indeed, he was a man of good family and education. A romantic interest therefore attached, and perhaps still attaches, to the names of freebooters of this class. The vulgar eagerly drank in tales of their ferocity and audacity, of their occasional acts of generosity and good nature, of their amours, of their miraculous escapes, of their desperate struggles, and of their manly bearing at the bar and in the cart. Thus it was related of William Nevison, the great robber of Yorkshire, that he levied a quarterly tribute on all the northern drovers, and, in return, not only spared them himself, but protected them against all other thieves; that he demanded purses in the most courteous manner; that he gave largely to the poor what he had taken from the rich; that his life was once spared by the royal clemency, but that he again tempted his fate, and at length died, in 1685, on the gallows of York.† It was related how Claude Duval, the French page of the Duke of Richmond, took to the road, became captain of a formidable gang, and had the honour to be named first in a royal proclamation against notorious offenders; how at the head of his troop he stopped a lady's coach, in which there was a booty of four hundred pounds; how he took only one hundred, and suffered the fair owner to ransom the rest by dancing a coranto with him on the heath; how his vivacious gallantry stole away the hearts of all women; how his dexterity at sword and pistol made him a terror to all men; how, at length, in the year 1670, he was seized when overcome by wine; how dames of high rank visited him in prison, and with tears interceded for his life; how the King would have granted a pardon, but for the interference of Judge Morton, the terror of highwaymen, who threatened to resign his office unless the law were carried into full effect; and how, after the execution, the corpse lay in state with all the

* *Aimwell.* Pray sir, han't I seen your face at Will's coffeehouse?
  Gibbet. Yes, sir, and at White's too.—Beaux' Stratagem.

  † Gent's History of York. Another marauder of the same description, named Biss, was hanged at Salisbury in 1695.

In a ballad which is in the Pepysian Library, he is represented as defending himself thus before the Judge:

  " What say you now, my honoured Lord,
     What harm was there in this?
   Rich, wealthy misers were abhorred
     By brave, freehearted Biss."

pomp of scutcheons, wax lights, black hangings and mutes, till the same cruel Judge, who had intercepted the mercy of the crown, sent officers to disturb the obsequies.* In these anecdotes there is doubtless a large mixture of fable; but they are not on that account unworthy of being recorded; for it is both an authentic and an important fact that such tales, whether false or true, were heard by our ancestors with eagerness and faith.

Inns.

All the various dangers by which the traveller was beset were greatly increased by darkness. He was therefore commonly desirous of having the shelter of a roof during the night; and such shelter it was not difficult to obtain. From a very early period the inns of England had been renowned. Our first great poet had described the excellent accommodation which they afforded to the pilgrims of the fourteenth century. Nine and twenty persons, with their horses, found room in the wide chambers and stables of the Tabard in Southwark. The food was of the best, and the wines such as drew the company on to drink largely. Two hundred years later, under the reign of Elizabeth, William Harrison gave a lively description of the plenty and comfort of the great hostelries. The Continent of Europe, he said, could show nothing like them. There were some in which two or three hundred people, with their horses, could without difficulty be lodged and fed. The bedding, the tapestry, above all, the abundance of clean and fine linen was matter of wonder. Valuable plate was often set on the tables. Nay, there were signs which had cost thirty or forty pounds. In the seventeenth century England abounded with excellent inns of every rank. The traveller sometimes, in a small village, lighted on a public house such as Walton has described, where the brick floor was swept clean, where the walls were stuck round with ballads, where the sheets smelt of lavender, and where a blazing fire, a cup of good ale, and a dish of trouts fresh from the neighbouring brook, were to be procured at small charge. At the larger houses of entertainment were to be found beds hung with silk, choice cookery, and claret equal to the best which was drunk in London.† The innkeepers too, it was said, were not like other innkeepers.

* Pope's Memoirs of Duval, published immediately after the execution. Oates's Εἰκὼν βασιλική, Part I.

† See the prologue to the Canterbury Tales, Harrison's Historical Description of the Island of Great Britain, and Pepys's account of his tour in the summer of 1668. The excellence of the English inns is noticed in the Travels of the Grand Duke Cosmo.

On the Continent the landlord was the tyrant of those who crossed the threshold. In England he was a servant. Never was an Englishman more at home than when he took his ease in his inn. Even men of fortune, who might in their own mansions have enjoyed every luxury, were often in the habit of passing their evenings in the parlour of some neighbouring house of public entertainment. They seem to have thought that comfort and freedom could in no other place be enjoyed with equal perfection. This feeling continued during many generations to be a national peculiarity. The liberty and jollity of inns long furnished matter to our novelists and dramatists. Johnson declared that a tavern chair was the throne of human felicity; and Shenstone gently complained that no private roof, however friendly, gave the wanderer so warm a welcome as that which was to be found at an inn.

Many conveniences, which were unknown at Hampton Court and Whitehall in the seventeenth century, are in all modern hotels. Yet on the whole it is certain that the improvement of our houses of public entertainment has by no means kept pace with the improvement of our roads and of our conveyances. Nor is this strange ; for it is evident that, all other circumstances being supposed equal, the inns will be best where the means of locomotion are worst. The quicker the rate of travelling, the less important is it that there should be numerous agreeable resting places for the traveller. A hundred and sixty years ago a person who came up to the capital from a remote county generally required, by the way, twelve or fifteen meals, and lodging for five or six nights. If he were a great man, he expected the meals and lodging to be comfortable, and even luxurious. At present we fly from York or Exeter to London by the light of a single winter's day. At present, therefore, a traveller seldom interrupts his journey merely for the sake of rest and refreshment. The consequence is that hundreds of excellent inns have fallen into utter decay. In a short time no good houses of that description will be found, except at places where strangers are likely to be detained by business or pleasure.

The mode in which correspondence was carried on between distant places may excite the scorn of the present generation ; yet it was such as might have moved the admiration and envy of the polished nations of antiquity, or of the contemporaries of Raleigh and Cecil. A rude and imperfect establishment of posts for the conveyance of letters had been set

Post office.

up by Charles the First, and had been swept away by the
civil war. Under the Commonwealth the design was resumed.
At the Restoration the proceeds of the Post Office, after all
expenses had been paid, were settled on the Duke of York.
On most lines of road the mails went out and came in only
on the alternate days. In Cornwall, in the fens of Lincolnshire, and among the hills and lakes of Cumberland, letters
were received only once a week. During a royal progress a
daily post was despatched from the capital to the place where
the court sojourned. There was also daily communication
between London and the Downs; and the same privilege was
sometimes extended to Tunbridge Wells and Bath at the
seasons when those places were crowded by the great. The
bags were carried on horseback day and night at the rate of
about five miles an hour.*

The revenue of this establishment was not derived solely
from the charge for the transmission of letters. The Post
Office alone was entitled to furnish post horses; and, from
the care with which this monopoly was guarded, we may infer
that it was found profitable.† If, indeed, a traveller had
waited half an hour without being supplied, he might hire a
horse wherever he could.

To facilitate correspondence between one part of London
and another was not originally one of the objects of the Post
Office. But, in the reign of Charles the Second, an enterprising citizen of London, William Dockwray, set up, at great
expense, a penny post, which delivered letters and parcels six
or eight times a day in the busy and crowded streets near the
Exchange, and four times a day in the outskirts of the capital.
This improvement was, as usual, strenuously resisted. The
porters complained that their interests were attacked, and
tore down the placards in which the scheme was announced
to the public. The excitement caused by Godfrey's death,
and by the discovery of Coleman's papers, was then at the
height. A cry was therefore raised that the penny post was a
Popish contrivance. The great Doctor Oates, it was affirmed,
had hinted a suspicion that the Jesuits were at the bottom of
the scheme, and that the bags, if examined, would be found
full of treason.‡ The utility of the enterprise was, however,
so great and obvious that all opposition proved fruitless. As

* Stat. 12 Car. II. c. 35; Chamberlayne's State of England, 1684; Angliæ
Metropolis, 1690; London Gazette, June
22. 1685, August 15. 1687.

† Lond. Gaz. Sept. 14. 1685.
‡ Smith's Current Intelligence, March
30. and April 3. 1680.

soon as it became clear that the speculation would be lucrative, the Duke of York complained of it as an infraction of his monopoly; and the courts of law decided in his favour.*

The revenue of the Post Office was from the first constantly increasing. In the year of the Restoration a committee of the House of Commons, after strict enquiry, had estimated the net receipt at about twenty thousand pounds. At the close of the reign of Charles the Second, the net receipt was little short of fifty thousand pounds; and this was then thought a stupendous sum. The gross receipt was about seventy thousand pounds. The charge for conveying a single letter was twopence for eighty miles, and threepence for a longer distance. The postage increased in proportion to the weight of the packet.† At present a single letter is carried to the extremity of Scotland or of Ireland for a penny; and the monopoly of post horses has long ceased to exist. Yet the gross annual receipts of the department amount to more than eighteen hundred thousand pounds, and the net receipts to more than seven hundred thousand pounds. It is, therefore, scarcely possible to doubt that the number of letters now conveyed by mail is seventy times the number which was so conveyed at the time of the accession of James the Second.‡

No part of the load which the old mails carried out was more important than the newsletters. In 1685 nothing like the London daily paper of our time existed, or could exist. Neither the necessary capital nor the necessary skill was to be found. Freedom too was wanting, a want as fatal as that of either capital or skill. The press was not indeed at that moment under a general censorship. The licensing act, which had been passed soon after the Restoration, had expired in 1679. Any person might therefore print, at his own risk, a history, a sermon, or a poem, without the previous approbation of any officer; but the Judges were unanimously of opinion that this liberty did not extend to Gazettes, and that, by the common law of England, no man, not authorised by the crown, had a right to publish political news.§ While the Whig party was still formidable, the government thought it expedient occasionally to connive at the violation of this rule.

Newspapers.

* Angliæ Metropolis, 1690.

† Commons' Journals, Sept. 4. 1660, March 1. 168⅖; Chamberlayne, 1684; Davenant on the Public Revenue, Discourse IV.

‡ I have left the text as it stood in 1848. In the year 1856 the gross receipt of the Post Office was more than 2,800,000l.; and the net receipt was about 1,200,000l. The number of letters conveyed by post was 478,000,000. (1857.)

§ London Gazette, May 5. and 17. 1680.

During the great battle of the Exclusion Bill, many news-papers were suffered to appear, the Protestant Intelligence, the Current Intelligence, the Domestic Intelligence, the True News, the London Mercury.* None of these was published oftener than twice a week. None exceeded in size a single small leaf. The quantity of matter which one of them con-tained in a year was not more than is often found in two numbers of the Times. After the defeat of the Whigs it was no longer necessary for the King to be sparing in the use of that which all his Judges had pronounced to be his undoubted prerogative. At the close of his reign no newspaper was suffered to appear without his allowance: and his allowance was given exclusively to the London Gazette. The London Gazette came out only on Mondays and Thursdays. The contents generally were a royal proclamation, two or three Tory addresses, notices of two or three promotions, an account of a skirmish between the imperial troops and the Janissaries on the Danube, a description of a highwayman, an announce-ment of a grand cockfight between two persons of honour, and an advertisement offering a reward for a strayed dog. The whole made up two pages of moderate size. Whatever was communicated respecting matters of the highest moment was communicated in the most meagre and formal style. Sometimes, indeed, when the government was disposed to gratify the public curiosity respecting an important trans-action, a broadside was put forth giving fuller details than could be found in the Gazette: but neither the Gazette nor any supplementary broadside printed by authority ever con-tained any intelligence which it did not suit the purposes of the Court to publish. The most important parliamentary debates, the most important state trials, recorded in our history, were passed over in profound silence.† In the capital the coffee houses supplied in some measure the place of a journal. Thither the Londoners flocked, as the Athenians of old flocked to the market place, to hear whether there was any news. There men might learn how brutally a Whig had been treated the day before in Westminster Hall, what hor-rible accounts the letters from Edinburgh gave of the tor-turing of Covenanters, how grossly the Navy Board had cheated the crown in the victualling of the fleet, and what

---

* There is a very curious, and, I should think, unique collection of these papers in the British Museum.

† For example, there is not a word in the Gazette about the important parlia-mentary proceedings of November 1685, or about the trial and acquittal of the seven Bishops.

grave charges the Lord Privy Seal had brought against the Treasury in the matter of the hearth money. But people who lived at a distance from the great theatre of political contention could be kept regularly informed of what was passing there only by means of newsletters. To prepare such letters became a calling in London, as it now is among the natives of India. The newswriter rambled from coffee room to coffee room, collecting reports, squeezed himself into the Sessions House at the Old Bailey if there was an interesting trial, nay, perhaps obtained admission to the gallery of White-hall, and noticed how the King and Duke looked. In this way he gathered materials for weekly epistles destined to enlighten some county town or some bench of rustic magis-trates. Such were the sources from which the inhabitants of the largest provincial cities, and the great body of the gentry and clergy, learned almost all that they knew of the history of their own time. We must suppose that at Cam-bridge there were as many persons curious to know what was passing in the world as at almost any place in the kingdom, out of London. Yet at Cambridge, during a great part of the reign of Charles the Second, the Doctors of Laws and the Masters of Arts had no regular supply of news except through the London Gazette. At length the services of one of the col-lectors of intelligence in the capital were employed. That was a memorable day on which the first newsletter from London was laid on the table of the only coffee room in Cambridge.* At the seat of a man of fortune in the country the newsletter was impatiently expected. Within a week after it had arrived it had been thumbed by twenty families. It furnished the neighbouring squires with matter for talk over their October, and the neighbouring rectors with topics for sharp sermons against Whiggery or Popery. Many of these curious journals might doubtless still be detected by a diligent search in the archives of old families. Some are to be found in our public libraries ; and one series, which is not the least valuable part of the literary treasures collected by Sir James Mackintosh, will be occasionally quoted in the course of this work.†

---

* Roger North's Life of Dr. John North. On the subject of newsletters, see the Examen, 133.

† I take this opportunity of express-ing my warm gratitude to the family of my dear and honoured friend Sir James Mackintosh for confiding to me the ma-terials collected by him at a time when he meditated a work similar to that which I have undertaken. I have never seen, and I do not believe that there anywhere exists, within the same com-pass, so noble a collection of extracts from public and private archives. The judgment with which Sir James, in great masses of the rudest ore of history,

It is scarcely necessary to say that there were then no provincial newspapers. Indeed, except in the capital and at the two Universities, there was scarcely a printer in the kingdom. The only press in England north of Trent appears to have been at York.*

The Observator.

It was not only by means of the London Gazette that the government undertook to furnish political instruction to the people. That journal contained a scanty supply of news without comment. Another journal, published under the patronage of the court, consisted of comment without news. This paper, called the Observator, was edited by an old Tory pamphleteer named Roger Lestrange. Lestrange was by no means deficient in readiness and shrewdness; and his diction, though coarse, and disfigured by a mean and flippant jargon which then passed for wit in the green room and the tavern, was not without keenness and vigour. But his nature, at once ferocious and ignoble, showed itself in every line that he penned. When the first Observators appeared there was some excuse for his acrimony. For the Whigs were then powerful; and he had to contend against numerous adversaries, whose unscrupulous violence might seem to justify unsparing retaliation. But in 1685 all opposition had been crushed. A generous spirit would have disdained to insult a party which could not reply, and to aggravate the misery of prisoners, of exiles, of bereaved families : but from the malice of Lestrange the grave was no hiding place, and the house of mourning no sanctuary. In the last month of the reign of Charles the Second, William Jenkyn, an aged dissenting pastor of great note, who had been cruelly persecuted for no crime but that of worshipping God according to the fashion generally followed throughout Protestant Europe, died of hardships and privations in Newgate. The outbreak of popular sympathy could not be repressed. The corpse was followed to the grave by a train of a hundred and fifty coaches. Even courtiers looked sad. Even the unthinking King showed some signs of concern. Lestrange alone set up a howl of savage exultation, laughed at the weak compassion

selected what was valuable, and rejected what was worthless, can be fully appreciated only by one who has toiled after him in the same mine.

* Life of Thomas Gent. A complete list of all printing houses in 1724 will be found in Nichols's Literary Anecdotes

of the eighteenth century. There had then been a great increase within a few years in the number of presses ; and yet there were thirty-four counties in which there was no printer, one of those counties being Lancashire.

of the Trimmers, proclaimed that the blasphemous old impostor had met with a most righteous punishment, and
vowed to wage war, not only to the death, but after death,
with all the mock saints and martyrs.* Such was the spirit
of the paper which was at this time the oracle of the Tory
party, and especially of the parochial clergy.

Literature which could be carried by the post bag then
formed the greater part of the intellectual nutriment rumi-
nated by the country divines and country justices. The
difficulty and expense of conveying large packets from place
to place was so great, that an extensive work was longer in
making its way from Paternoster Row to Devonshire or
Lancashire than it now is in reaching Kentucky. How
scantily a rural parsonage was then furnished, even with
books the most necessary to a theologian, has already been
remarked. The houses of the gentry were not more plentifully supplied. Few knights of the shire had libraries so
good as may now perpetually be found in a servants' hall, or
in the back parlour of a small shopkeeper. An esquire passed
among his neighbours for a great scholar, if Hudibras and
Baker's Chronicle, Tarlton's Jests and the Seven Champions
of Christendom, lay in his hall window among the fishing
rods and fowling pieces. No circulating library, no book
society, then existed even in the capital: but in the capital
those students who could not afford to purchase largely had
a resource. The shops of the great booksellers, near Saint
Paul's Churchyard, were crowded every day and all day long
with readers; and a known customer was often permitted to
carry a volume home. In the country there was no such accommodation; and every man was under the necessity of
buying whatever he wished to read.†

As to the lady of the manor and her daughters, their
literary stores generally consisted of a prayer book and a receipt book. But in truth they lost little by living in rural
seclusion. For, even in the highest ranks, and in those
situations which afforded the greatest facilities for mental
improvement, the English women of that generation were
decidedly worse educated than they have been at any other

Scarcity of books in country places.

Female education.

---

* Observator, Jan. 29. and 31. 1685;
Calamy's Life of Baxter; Nonconformist Memorial.

† Cotton seems, from his Angler, to
have found room for his whole library
in his hall window; and Cotton was a
man of letters. Even when Franklin
first visited London in 1724, circulating
libraries were unknown there. The
crowd at the booksellers' shops in Little
Britain is mentioned by Roger North in
his life of his brother John.

time since the revival of learning.   At an earlier period they
had studied the masterpieces of ancient genius.   In the present day they seldom bestow much attention on the dead
languages; but they are familiar with the tongue of Pascal
and Moliere, with the tongue of Dante and Tasso, with the
tongue of Goethe and Schiller; nor is there any purer or
more graceful English than that which accomplished women
now speak and write.   But, during the latter part of the
seventeenth century, the culture of the female mind seems to
have been almost entirely neglected.   If a damsel had the
least smattering of literature she was regarded as a prodigy.
Ladies highly born, highly bred, and naturally quick witted,
were unable to write a line in their mother tongue without
solecisms and faults of spelling such as a charity girl would
now be ashamed to commit.*

The explanation may easily be found.   Extravagant licentiousness, the natural effect of extravagant austerity, was now
the mode; and licentiousness had produced its ordinary effect,
the moral and intellectual degradation of women.   To their
personal beauty, it was the fashion to pay rude and impudent
homage.   But the admiration and desire which they inspired
were seldom mingled with respect, with affection, or with any
chivalrous sentiment.   The qualities which fit them to be
companions, advisers, confidential friends, rather repelled
than attracted the libertines of Whitehall.   In that court a
maid of honour, who dressed in such a manner as to do full
justice to a white bosom, who ogled significantly, who danced
voluptuously, who excelled in pert repartee, who was not
ashamed to romp with Lords of the Bedchamber and Captains
of the Guards, to sing sly verses with sly expression, or to
put on a page's dress for a frolic, was more likely to be followed and admired, more likely to be honoured with royal
attentions, more likely to win a rich and noble husband than
Jane Grey or Lucy Hutchinson would have been.   In such
circumstances the standard of female attainments was necessarily low; and it was more dangerous to be above that
standard than to be beneath it.   Extreme ignorance and

* One instance will suffice.   Queen
Mary, the daughter of James, had excellent natural abilities, had been educated by a Bishop, was fond of history
and poetry, and was regarded by very
eminent men as a superior woman.
There is, in the library at the Hague, a
superb English Bible which was delivered to her when she was crowned in
Westminster Abbey.   In the titlepage
are these words in her own hand, " This
book was given the King and I, at our
crownation.   Marie R."

frivolity were thought less unbecoming in a lady than the slightest tincture of pedantry. Of the too celebrated women whose faces we still admire on the walls of Hampton Court, few indeed were in the habit of reading anything more valuable than acrostics, lampoons, and translations of the Clelia and the Grand Cyrus.

The literary acquirements, even of the accomplished gentlemen of that generation, seem to have been somewhat less solid and profound than at an earlier or a later period. Greek learning, at least, did not flourish among us in the days of Charles the Second, as it had flourished before the civil war, or as it again flourished long after the Revolution. There were undoubtedly scholars to whom the whole Greek literature, from Homer to Photius, was familiar : but such scholars were to be found almost exclusively among the clergy resident at the Universities, and even at the Universities were few, and were not fully appreciated. At Cambridge it was not thought by any means necessary that a divine should be able to read the Gospels in the original.* Nor was the standard at Oxford higher. When, in the reign of William the Third, Christ Church rose up as one man to defend the genuineness of the Epistles of Phalaris, that great college, then considered as the first seat of philology in the kingdom, could not muster such a stock of Attic learning as is now possessed by several youths at every great public school. It may easily be supposed that a dead language, neglected at the Universities, was not much studied by men of the world. In a former age the poetry and eloquence of Greece had been the delight of Raleigh and Falkland. In a later age the poetry and eloquence of Greece were the delight of Pitt and Fox, of Windham and Grenville. But during the latter part of the seventeenth century there was in England scarcely one eminent statesman who could read with enjoyment a page of Sophocles or Plato.

Good Latin scholars were numerous. The language of Rome, indeed, had not altogether lost its imperial prerogatives, and was still, in many parts of Europe, almost indispensable to a traveller or a negotiator. To speak it well was therefore a much more common accomplishment than in our time ; and neither Oxford nor Cambridge wanted poets who,

Literary attainments of gentlemen

---

* Roger North tells us that his brother John, who was Greek professor at Cambridge, complained bitterly of the general neglect of the Greek tongue among the academical clergy.

on a great occasion, could lay at the foot of the throne happy imitations of the verses in which Virgil and Ovid had cele-brated the greatness of Augustus.

Influence of French literature. Yet even the Latin was giving way to a younger rival. France united at that time almost every species of ascendency. Her military glory was at the height. She had vanquished mighty coalitions. She had dictated treaties. She had subjugated great cities and provinces. She had forced the Castilian pride to yield her the precedence. She had summoned Italian princes to prostrate themselves at her footstool. Her authority was supreme in all matters of good breeding, from a duel to a minuet. She determined how a gentleman's coat must be cut, how long his peruke must be, whether his heels must be high or low, and whether the lace on his hat must be broad or narrow. In literature she gave law to the world. The fame of her great writers filled Europe. No other country could produce a tragic poet equal to Racine, a comic poet equal to Moliere, a trifler so agreeable as La Fontaine, a rhetorician so skilful as Bossuet. The literary glory of Italy and of Spain had set; that of Germany had not yet dawned. The genius, therefore, of the eminent men who adorned Paris shone forth with a splendour which was set off to full advantage by contrast. France, indeed, had at that time an empire over mankind, such as even the Roman Republic never attained. For, when Rome was politically dominant, she was in arts and letters the humble pupil of Greece. France had, over the surrounding countries, at once the ascendency which Rome had over Greece, and the ascendency which Greece had over Rome. French was fast becoming the universal language, the language of fashionable society, the language of diplomacy. At several courts princes and nobles spoke it more accurately and politely than their mother tongue. In our island there was less of this servility than on the Continent. Neither our good nor our bad qualities were those of imitators. Yet even here homage was paid, awkwardly indeed and sullenly, to the literary supremacy of our neighbours. The melodious Tuscan, so familiar to the gallants and ladies of the court of Elizabeth, sank into contempt. A gentleman who quoted Horace or Terence was considered in good company as a pompous pedant. But to garnish his conversation with scraps of French was the best proof which he could give of his parts and attainments.* New canons of criticism, new models of style came into fashion. The quaint ingenuity which had deformed the verses of Donne, and had been a blemish on those of Cowley, disappeared from our poetry. Our prose became less majestic, less artfully involved, less variously musical than that of an earlier age, but more lucid, more easy, and better fitted for controversy and narrative. In these changes it is impossible not to recognise the influence of French precept and of French example. Great masters of our language, in their most dignified compositions, affected to use French words, when English words, quite as expressive and sonorous, were at hand †: and from France was imported the tragedy in rhyme, an exotic which, in our soil, drooped, and speedily died.

It would have been well if our writers had also copied the decorum which their great French contemporaries, with few exceptions, preserved; for the profligacy of the English plays, satires, songs, and novels of that age is a deep blot on our national fame. The evil may easily be traced to its source. The wits and the Puritans had never been on friendly terms. There was no sympathy between the two classes. They looked on the whole system of human life from different points and in different lights. The earnest of each was the jest of the other. The pleasures of each were the torments of the other. To the stern precisian even the innocent sport of the fancy seemed a crime. To light and festive natures the solemnity of the zealous brethren furnished copious matter of ridicule. From the Reformation to the civil war, almost every writer, gifted with a fine sense of the ludicrous, had taken some opportunity of assailing the straighthaired, snuffling, whining saints, who christened their children out of the Book of Nehemiah, who groaned in spirit at the sight of Jack in the Green, and who thought it impious to taste plum porridge on Christmas day. At length a time came when the laughers began to look grave in their turn. The rigid, ungainly zealots, after having furnished much good sport during two generations, rose up in arms, conquered, ruled, and, grimly smiling, trod down under their feet the whole

Marginal note: Immorality of the polite literature of England.

---

* Butler, in a satire of great asperity, says,

"For, though to smatter words of Greek
And Latin be the rhetorique
Of pedants counted, and vainglorious,
To smatter French is meritorious."

† The most offensive instance which I remember is in a poem on the coronation of Charles the Second by Dryden, who certainly could not plead poverty as an excuse for borrowing words from any foreign tongue:—

"Hither in summer evenings you repair
To taste the fraicheur of the cooler air."

crowd of mockers. The wounds inflicted by gay and petu-
lant malice were retaliated with the gloomy and implacable
malice peculiar to bigots who mistake their own rancour for
virtue. The theatres were closed. The players were flogged.
The press was put under the guardianship of austere licensers.
The Muses were banished from their own favourite haunts,
Cambridge and Oxford. Cowley, Crashaw, and Cleveland
were ejected from their fellowships. The young candidate
for academical honours was no longer required to write
Ovidian epistles or Virgilian pastorals, but was strictly interrogated by a synod of lowering Supralapsarians as to the day
and hour when he experienced the new birth. Such a system
was of course fruitful of hypocrites. Under sober clothing
and under visages composed to the expression of austerity lay
hid during several years the intense desire of license and of
revenge. At length that desire was gratified. The Restoration emancipated thousands of minds from a yoke which
had become insupportable. The old fight recommenced, but
with an animosity altogether new. It was now not a sportive
combat, but a war to the death. The Roundhead had no
better quarter to expect from those whom he had persecuted
than a cruel slavedriver can expect from insurgent slaves still
bearing the marks of his collars and his scourges.

The war between wit and Puritanism soon became a war
between wit and morality. The hostility excited by a grotesque caricature of virtue did not spare virtue herself.
Whatever the canting Roundhead had regarded with reverence was insulted. Whatever he had proscribed was favoured.
Because he had been scrupulous about trifles, all scruples
were treated with derision. Because he had covered his failings with the mask of devotion, men were encouraged to
obtrude with Cynic impudence all their most scandalous vices
on the public eye. Because he had punished illicit love with
barbarous severity, virgin purity and conjugal fidelity were
made a jest. To that sanctimonious jargon which was his
Shibboleth, was opposed another jargon not less absurd and
much more odious. As he never opened his mouth except in
scriptural phrase, the new breed of wits and fine gentlemen
never opened their mouths without uttering ribaldry of which
a porter would now be ashamed, and without calling on their
Maker to curse them, sink them, confound them, blast them,
and damn them.

It is not strange, therefore, that our polite literature, when it revived with the revival of the old civil and ecclesiastical polity, should have been profoundly immoral. A few eminent men, who belonged to an earlier and better age, were exempt from the general contagion. The verse of Waller still breathed the sentiments which had animated a more chivalrous generation. Cowley, distinguished as a loyalist and as a man of letters, raised his voice courageously against the immorality which disgraced both letters and loyalty. A mightier poet, tried at once by pain, danger, poverty, obloquy, and blindness, meditated, undisturbed by the obscene tumult which raged all around him, a song so sublime and so holy that it would not have misbecome the lips of those ethereal Virtues whom he saw, with that inner eye which no calamity could darken, flinging down on the jasper pavement their crowns of amaranth and gold. The vigorous and fertile genius of Butler, if it did not altogether escape the prevailing infection, took the disease in a mild form. But these were men whose minds had been trained in a world which had passed away. They gave place in no long time to a younger generation of wits; and of that generation, from Dryden down to Durfey, the common characteristic was hardhearted, shameless, swaggering licentiousness, at once inelegant and inhuman. The influence of these writers was doubtless noxious, yet less noxious than it would have been had they been less depraved. The poison which they administered was so strong that it was, in no long time, rejected with nausea. None of them understood the dangerous art of associating images of unlawful pleasure with all that is endearing and ennobling. None of them was aware that a certain decorum is essential even to voluptuousness, that drapery may be more alluring than exposure, and that the imagination may be far more powerfully moved by delicate hints which impel it to exert itself, than by gross descriptions which it takes in passively.

The spirit of the Antipuritan reaction pervades almost the whole polite literature of the reign of Charles the Second. But the very quintessence of that spirit will be found in the comic drama. The playhouses, shut by the meddling fanatic in the day of his power, were again crowded. To their old attractions new and more powerful attractions had been added. Scenery, dresses, and decorations, such as would now be thought mean or absurd, but such as would have been esteemed incredibly magnificent by those who, early in the seventeenth century, sate on the filthy benches of the Hope, or under the thatched roof of the Rose, dazzled the eyes of the multitude. The fascination of sex was called in to aid the fascination of art : and the young spectator saw, with emotions unknown to the contemporaries of Shakspeare and Johnson, tender and sprightly heroines personated by lovely women. From the day on which the theatres were reopened they became seminaries of vice ; and the evil propagated itself. The profligacy of the representations soon drove away sober people. The frivolous and dissolute who remained required every year stronger and stronger stimulants. Thus the artists corrupted the spectators, and the spectators the artists, till the turpitude of the drama became such as must astonish all who are not aware that extreme relaxation is the natural effect of extreme restraint, and that an age of hypocrisy is, in the regular course of things, followed by an age of impudence.

Nothing is more characteristic of the times than the care with which the poets contrived to put all their loosest verses into the mouths of women. The compositions in which the greatest license was taken were the epilogues. They were almost always recited by favourite actresses ; and nothing charmed the depraved audience so much as to hear lines grossly indecent repeated by a beautiful girl, who was supposed to have not yet lost her innocence.*

Our theatre was indebted in that age for many plots and characters to Spain, to France, and to the old English masters : but whatever our dramatists touched they tainted. In their imitations the houses of Calderon's stately and highspirited Castilian gentlemen became sties of vice, Shakspeare's Viola a procuress, Moliere's Misanthrope a ravisher, Moliere's Agnes an adulteress. Nothing could be so pure or so heroic but that it became foul and ignoble by transfusion through those foul and ignoble minds.

Such was the state of the drama; and the drama was the department of polite literature in which a poet had the best chance of obtaining a subsistence by his pen. The sale of books was so small that a man of the greatest name could hardly expect more than a pittance for the copyright of the best performance. There cannot be a stronger instance than the fate of Dryden's last production, the Fables. That volume was published when he was universally admitted to

* Jeremy Collier has censured this odious practice with his usual force and keenness.

be the chief of living English poets. It contains about twelve thousand lines. The versification is admirable, the narratives and descriptions full of life. To this day Palamon and Arcite, Cymon and Iphigenia, Theodore and Honoria, are the delight both of critics and of schoolboys. The collection includes Alexander's Feast, the noblest ode in our language. For the copyright Dryden received two hundred and fifty pounds, less than in our days has sometimes been paid for two articles in a review.* Nor does the bargain seem to have been a hard one. For the book went off slowly; and the second edition was not required till the author had been ten years in his grave. By writing for the theatre it was possible to earn a much larger sum with much less trouble. Southern made seven hundred pounds by one play.† Otway was raised from beggary to temporary affluence by the success of his Don Carlos.‡ Shadwell cleared a hundred and thirty pounds by a single representation of the Squire of Alsatia.§ The consequence was that every man who had to live by his wit wrote plays, whether he had any internal vocation to write plays or not. It was thus with Dryden. As a satirist he has rivalled Juvenal. As a didactic poet he perhaps might, with care and meditation, have rivalled Lucretius. Of lyric poets he is, if not the most sublime, the most brilliant and spiritstirring. But nature, profuse to him of many rare gifts, had withheld from him the dramatic faculty. Nevertheless all the energies of his best years were wasted on dramatic composition. He had too much judgment not to be aware that in the power of exhibiting character by means of dialogue he was deficient. That deficiency he did his best to conceal, sometimes by surprising and amusing incidents, sometimes by stately declamation, sometimes by harmonious numbers, sometimes by ribaldry but too well suited to the taste of a profane and licentious pit. Yet he never obtained any theatrical success equal to that which rewarded the exertions of some men far inferior to him in general powers. He thought himself fortunate if he cleared a hundred guineas by a play; a scanty remuneration, yet apparently larger than he could have earned in any other way by the same quantity of labour.‖

The recompense which the wits of that age could obtain

---

* The contract will be found in Sir Walter Scott's edition of Dryden.
† See the Life of Southern, by Shiels.
‡ See Rochester's Trial of the Poets.
§ Some Account of the English Stage
‖ Life of Southern, by Shiels.

from the public was so small, that they were under the necessity of eking out their incomes by levying contributions on the great.   Every rich and goodnatured lord was pestered by authors with a mendicancy so importunate, and a flattery so abject, as may in our time seem incredible.   The patron to whom a work was inscribed was expected to reward the writer with a purse of gold.   The fee paid for the dedication of a book was often much larger than the sum which any publisher would give for the copyright.   Books were therefore frequently printed merely that they might be dedicated. This traffic in praise produced the effect which might have been expected.   Adulation pushed to the verge, sometimes of nonsense, and sometimes of impiety, was not thought to disgrace a poet.   Independence, veracity, selfrespect, were things not required by the world from him.   In truth, he was in morals something between a pandar and a beggar.

To the other vices which degraded the literary character was added, towards the close of the reign of Charles the Second, the most savage intemperance of party spirit.   The wits, as a class, had been impelled by their old hatred of Puritanism to take the side of the court, and had been found useful allies.   Dryden, in particular, had done good service to the government.   His Absalom and Achitophel, the greatest satire of modern times, had amazed the town, had made its way with unprecedented rapidity even into rural districts, and had, wherever it appeared, bitterly annoyed the Exclusionists, and raised the courage of the Tories.   But we must not, in the admiration which we naturally feel for noble diction and versification, forget the great distinctions of good and evil.   The spirit by which Dryden and several of his compeers were at this time animated against the Whigs deserves to be called fiendish.   The servile Judges and Sheriffs of those evil days could not shed blood as fast as the poets cried out for it. Calls for more victims, hideous jests on hanging, bitter taunts on those who, having stood by the King in the hour of danger, now advised him to deal mercifully and generously by his vanquished enemies, were publicly recited on the stage, and, that nothing might be wanting to the guilt and the shame, were recited by women, who, having long been taught to discard all modesty, were now taught to discard all compassion.*

---

* If any reader thinks my expressions too severe, I would advise him to read Dryden's Epilogue to the Duke of Guise, and to observe that it was spoken by a woman.

It is a remarkable fact that, while the lighter literature of England was thus becoming a nuisance and a national disgrace, the English genius was effecting in science a revolution which will, to the end of time, be reckoned among the highest achievements of the human intellect. Bacon had sown the good seed in a sluggish soil and an ungenial season. He had not expected an early crop, and in his last testament had solemnly bequeathed his fame to the next age. During a whole generation his philosophy had, amidst tumults, wars, and proscriptions, been slowly ripening in a few well constituted minds. While factions were struggling for dominion over each other, a small body of sages had turned away with benevolent disdain from the conflict, and had devoted themselves to the nobler work of extending the dominion of man over matter. As soon as tranquillity was restored, these teachers easily found attentive audience. For the discipline through which the nation had passed had brought the public mind to a temper well fitted for the reception of the Verulamian doctrine. The civil troubles had stimulated the faculties of the educated classes, and had called forth a restless activity and an insatiable curiosity, such as had not before been known among us. Yet the effect of those troubles was that schemes of political and religious reform were generally regarded with suspicion and contempt. During twenty years the chief employment of busy and ingenious men had been to frame constitutions with first magistrates, without first magistrates, with hereditary senates, with senates appointed by lot, with annual senates, with perpetual senates.   In these plans nothing was omitted. All the detail, all the nomenclature, all the ceremonial of the imaginary government was fully set forth, Polemarchs and Phylarchs, Tribes and Galaxies, the Lord Archon and the Lord Strategus. Which ballot boxes were to be green and which red, which balls were to be of gold and which of silver, which magistrates were to wear hats and which black velvet caps with peaks, how the mace was to be carried and when the heralds were to uncover, these, and a hundred more such trifles, were gravely considered and arranged by men of no common capacity and learning.* But the time for these visions had gone by; and, if any steadfast republican still continued to amuse himself with them, fear of public derision and of a criminal information generally induced him to keep his fancies to himself. It was

* See particularly Harrington's Oceana.

now unpopular and unsafe to mutter a word against the fundamental laws of the monarchy : but daring and ingenious men might indemnify themselves by treating with disdain what had lately been considered as the fundamental laws of nature.   The torrent which had been dammed up in one channel rushed violently into another.   The revolutionary spirit, ceasing to operate in politics, began to exert itself with unprecedented vigour and hardihood in every department of physics.   The year 1660, the era of the restoration of the old constitution, is also the era from which dates the ascendency of the new philosophy.   In that year the Royal Society, destined to be a chief agent in a long series of glorious and salutary reforms, began to exist.*   In a few months experimental science became all the mode.   The transfusion of blood, the ponderation of air, the fixation of mercury, succeeded to that place in the public mind which had been lately occupied by the controversies of the Rota.   Dreams of perfect forms of government made way for dreams of wings with which men were to fly from the Tower to the Abbey, and of doublekeeled ships which were never to founder in the fiercest storm.   All classes were hurried along by the prevailing sentiment.   Cavalier and Roundhead, Churchman and Puritan, were for once allied.   Divines, jurists, statesmen, nobles, princes, swelled the triumph of the Baconian philosophy. Poets sang with emulous fervour the approach of the golden age.   Cowley, in lines weighty with thought and resplendent with wit, urged the chosen seed to take possession of the promised land flowing with milk and honey, that land which their great deliverer and lawgiver had seen, as from the summit of Pisgah, but had not been permitted to enter.†   Dryden, with more zeal than knowledge, joined his voice to the general acclamation, and foretold things which neither he nor anybody else understood.   The Royal Society, he predicted, would soon lead us to the extreme verge of the globe, and there delight us with a better view of the moon.‡   Two able and aspiring prelates, Ward, Bishop of Salisbury, and Wilkins, Bishop of Chester, were conspicuous among the leaders of the movement.   Its history was eloquently written by a younger divine, who was rising to high distinction in his profession,

---

* See Sprat's History of the Royal Society.

† Cowley's Ode to the Royal Society.

‡ " Then we upon the globe's last verge shall go,

And view the ocean leaning on the sky ;
From thence our rolling neighbours we shall know,
And on the lunar world securely pry."
                        Annus Mirabilis, 164.

Thomas Sprat, afterwards Bishop of Rochester. Both Chief Justice Hale and Lord Keeper Guildford stole some hours from the business of their courts to write on hydrostatics. Indeed it was under the immediate direction of Guildford that the first barometers ever exposed to sale in London were constructed.* Chemistry divided, for a time, with wine and love, with the stage and the gaming table, with the intrigues of a courtier and the intrigues of a demagogue, the attention of the fickle Buckingham. Rupert has the credit of having invented mezzotinto; and from him is named that curious bubble of glass which has long amused children and puzzled philosophers. Charles himself had a laboratory at Whitehall, and was far more active and attentive there than at the council board. It was almost necessary to the character of a fine gentleman to have something to say about airpumps and telescopes; and even fine ladies, now and then, thought it becoming to affect a taste for science, went in coaches and six to visit the Gresham curiosities, and broke forth into cries of delight at finding that a magnet really attracted a needle, and that a microscope really made a fly look as large as a sparrow.†

In this, as in every great stir of the human mind, there was doubtless something which might well move a smile. It is the universal law that whatever pursuit, whatever doctrine, becomes fashionable, shall lose a portion of that dignity which it had possessed while it was confined to a small but earnest minority, and was loved for its own sake alone. It is true that the follies of some persons who, without any real aptitude for science, professed a passion for it, furnished matter of contemptuous mirth to a few malignant satirists who belonged to the preceding generation, and were not disposed to unlearn the lore of their youth.‡ But it is not less true that the great work of interpreting nature was performed by the English of that age as it had never before been performed in any age by any nation. The spirit of Francis Bacon was abroad, a spirit admirably compounded of audacity and sobriety. There was a strong persuasion that the whole world was full of secrets of high moment to the happiness of man, and that man had, by his Maker, been entrusted with the key

* North's Life of Guildford.
† Pepys's Diary, May 30. 1667.
‡ Butler was, I think, the only man of real genius who, between the Restoration and the Revolution, showed a bitter enmity to the new philosophy, as it was then called. See the Satire on the Royal Society, and the Elephant in the Moon..

which, rightly used, would give access to them. There was at the same time a conviction that in physics it was impossible to arrive at the knowledge of general laws except by the careful observation of particular facts. Deeply impressed with these great truths, the professors of the new philosophy applied themselves to their task, and, before a quarter of a century had expired, they had given ample earnest of what has since been achieved. Already a reform of agriculture had been commenced. New vegetables were cultivated. New implements of husbandry were employed. New manures were applied to the soil.* Evelyn had, under the formal sanction of the Royal Society, given instruction to his countrymen in planting. Temple, in his intervals of leisure, had tried many experiments in horticulture, and had proved that many delicate fruits, the natives of more favoured climates, might, with the help of art, be grown on English ground. Medicine, which in France was still in abject bondage, and afforded an inexhaustible subject of just ridicule to Moliere, had in England become an experimental and progressive science, and every day made some new advance, in defiance of Hippocrates and Galen. The attention of speculative men had been, for the first time, directed to the important subject of sanitary police. The great plague of 1665 induced them to consider with care the defective architecture, draining, and ventilation of the capital. The great fire of 1666 afforded an opportunity for effecting extensive improvements. The whole matter was diligently examined by the Royal Society; and to the suggestions of that body must be partly attributed the changes which, though far short of what the public welfare required, yet made a wide difference between the new and the old London, and probably put a final close to the ravages of pestilence in our country.† At the same time one of the founders of the Society, Sir William Petty, created the science of political arithmetic, the humble but indispensable handmaid of political philosophy. No kingdom of nature was left unexplored. To that period belong the chemical discoveries of Boyle, and the earliest botanical researches of Sloane. It was then that Ray made a new classification of birds and fishes, and that the attention of Woodward was first drawn towards fossils and shells. One after another phantoms which had haunted the world

---

* The eagerness with which the agriculturists of that age tried experiments and introduced improvements is well described by Aubrey. See the Natural History of Wiltshire, 1685.

† Sprat's History of the Royal Society.

through ages of darkness fled before the light. Astrology and alchymy became jests. Soon there was scarcely a county in which some of the Quorum did not smile contemptuously when an old woman was brought before them for riding on broomsticks or giving cattle the murrain. But it was in those noblest and most arduous departments of knowledge in which induction and mathematical demonstration cooperate for the discovery of truth, that the English genius won in that age the most memorable triumphs. John Wallis placed the whole system of statics on a new foundation. Edmund Halley investigated the properties of the atmosphere, the ebb and flow of the sea, the laws of magnetism, and the course of the comets; nor did he shrink from toil, peril, and exile in the cause of science. While he, on the rock of Saint Helena, mapped the constellations of the southern hemisphere, our national observatory was rising at Greenwich; and John Flamsteed, the first Astronomer Royal, was commencing that long series of observations which is never mentioned without respect and gratitude in any part of the globe. But the glory of these men, eminent as they were, is cast into the shade by the transcendent lustre of one immortal name. In Isaac Newton two kinds of intellectual power, which have little in common, and which are not often found together in a very high degree of vigour, but which nevertheless are equally necessary in the most sublime departments of physics, were united as they have never been united before or since. There may have been minds as happily constituted as his for the cultivation of pure mathematical science: there may have been minds as happily constituted for the cultivation of science purely experimental: but in no other mind have the demonstrative faculty and the inductive faculty coexisted in such supreme excellence and perfect harmony. Perhaps in the days of Scotists and Thomists even his intellect might have run to waste, as many intellects ran to waste which were inferior only to his. Happily the spirit of the age on which his lot was cast, gave the right direction to his mind; and his mind reacted with tenfold force on the spirit of the age. In the year 1685 his fame, though splendid, was only dawning; but his genius was in the meridian. His great work, that work which effected a revolution in the most important provinces of natural philosophy, had been completed, but was not yet published, and was just about to be submitted to the consideration of the Royal Society.

It is not very easy to explain why the nation which was so

far before its neighbours in science should in art have been far
behind them.   Yet such was the fact.   It is true that in architecture, an art which is half a science, an art in which none
but a geometrician can excel, an art which has no standard of
grace but what is directly or indirectly dependent on utility,
an art of which the creations derive a part, at least, of their
majesty from mere bulk, our country could boast of one truly
great man, Christopher Wren; and the fire which laid London in ruins had given him an opportunity, unprecedented in
modern history, of displaying his powers.   The austere beauty
of the Athenian portico, the gloomy sublimity of the Gothic
arcade, he was like almost all his contemporaries, incapable
of emulating, and perhaps incapable of appreciating; but no
man born on our side of the Alps, has imitated with so much
success the magnificence of the palacelike churches of Italy.
Even the superb Lewis has left to posterity no work which can
bear a comparison with Saint Paul's.   But at the close of the
reign of Charles the Second there was not a single English
painter or statuary whose name is now remembered.   This
sterility is somewhat mysterious; for painters and statuaries
were by no means a despised or an ill paid class.   Their social
position was at least as high as at present.   Their gains, when
compared with the wealth of the nation and with the remuneration of other descriptions of intellectual labour, were even
larger than at present.   Indeed the munificent patronage
which was extended to artists drew them to our shores in multitudes.   Lely, who has preserved to us the rich curls, the full
lips, and the languishing eyes of the frail beauties celebrated
by Hamilton, was a Westphalian.   He had died in 1680,
having long lived splendidly, having received the honour of
knighthood, and having accumulated a good estate out of the
fruits of his skill.   His noble collection of drawings and pictures was, after his decease, exhibited by the royal permission in the Banqueting House at Whitehall, and was sold by
auction for the almost incredible sum of twenty-six thousand
pounds, a sum which bore a greater proportion to the fortunes
of the rich men of that day than a hundred thousand pounds
would bear to the fortunes of the rich men of our time.*   Lely
was succeeded by his countryman Godfrey Kneller, who was
made first a knight and then a baronet, and who, after keeping up a sumptuous establishment, and after losing much

* Walpole's Anecdotes of Painting; London Gazette, May 31. 1683; North's
Life of Guildford.

money by unlucky speculations, was still able to bequeath a large fortune to his family. The two Vandeveldes, natives of Holland, had been tempted by English liberality to settle here, and had produced for the King and his nobles some of the finest sea pieces in the world. Another Dutchman, Simon Varelst, painted glorious sunflowers and tulips for prices such as had never before been known. Verrio, a Neapolitan, covered ceilings and staircases with Gorgons and Muses, Nymphs and Satyrs, Virtues and Vices, Gods quaffing nectar, and laurelled princes riding in triumph. The income which he derived from his performances enabled him to keep one of the most expensive tables in England. For his pieces at Windsor alone he received seven thousand pounds, a sum then sufficient to make a gentleman of moderate wishes perfectly easy for life, a sum greatly exceeding all that Dryden, during a literary life of forty years, obtained from the booksellers.* Verrio's assistant and successor, Lewis Laguerre, came from France. The two most celebrated sculptors of that day were also foreigners. Cibber, whose pathetic emblems of Fury and Melancholy still adorn Bedlam, was a Dane. Gibbons, to whose graceful fancy and delicate touch many of our palaces, colleges, and churches owe their finest decorations, was a Dutchman. Even the designs for the coin were made by French artists. Indeed, it was not till the reign of George the Second that our country could glory in a great painter; and George the Third was on the throne before she had reason to be proud of any of her sculptors.

It is time that this description of the England which Charles the Second governed should draw to a close. Yet one subject of the highest moment still remains untouched. Nothing has yet been said of the great body of the people, of those who held the ploughs, who tended the oxen, who toiled at the looms of Norwich, and squared the Portland stone for Saint Paul's. Nor can very much be said. The most numerous class is precisely the class respecting which we have the most meagre information. In those times philanthropists did not yet regard it as a sacred duty, nor had demagogues yet found it a lucrative trade, to talk and write about the distress of the labourer. History was too much occupied with courts and camps to spare a line for the hut of the peasant or the garret of the mechanic. The press now often sends forth in

* The great prices paid to Varelst and Verrio are mentioned in Walpole's Anecdotes of Painting.

a day a greater quantity of discussion and declamation about the condition of the working man than was published during the twenty-eight years which elapsed between the Restoration and the Revolution. But it would be a great error to infer from the increase of complaint that there has been any increase of misery.

State of the common people.

The great criterion of the state of the common people is the amount of their wages; and as four fifths of the common people were, in the seventeenth century, employed in agriculture, it is especially important to ascertain what were then the wages of agricultural industry. On this subject we have the means of arriving at conclusions sufficiently exact for our purpose.

Agricultural wages.

Sir William Petty, whose mere assertion carries great weight, informs us that a labourer was by no means in the lowest state who received for a day's work fourpence with food, or eightpence without food. Four shillings a week therefore were, according to Petty's calculation, fair agricultural wages.*

That this calculation was not remote from the truth we have abundant proof. About the beginning of the year 1685 the justices of Warwickshire, in the exercise of a power entrusted to them by an Act of Elizabeth, fixed, at their quarter sessions, a scale of wages for the county, and notified that every employer who gave more than the authorised sum, and every working man who received more, would be liable to punishment. The wages of the common agricultural labourer, from March to September, were fixed at the precise amount mentioned by Petty, namely four shillings a week without food. From September to March the wages were to be only three and sixpence a week.†

But in that age, as in ours, the earnings of the peasant were very different in different parts of the kingdom. The wages of Warwickshire were probably about the average, and those of the counties near the Scottish border below it: but there were more favoured districts. In the same year, 1685, a gentleman of Devonshire, named Richard Dunning, published a small tract, in which he described the condition of the poor of that county. That he understood his subject well it is impossible to doubt; for a few months later his work was reprinted, and was, by the magistrates assembled in

* Petty's Political Arithmetic.
† Stat. 5 Eliz. c. 4.; Archæologia, vol. xi.

quarter sessions at Exeter, strongly recommended to the attention of all parochial officers. According to him, the wages of the Devonshire peasant were, without food, about five shillings a week.*

Still better was the condition of the labourer in the neighbourhood of Bury Saint Edmund's. The magistrates of Suffolk met there in the spring of 1682 to fix a rate of wages, and resolved that, where the labourer was not boarded, he should have five shillings a week in winter, and six in summer.†

In 1661 the justices at Chelmsford had fixed the wages of the Essex labourer, who was not boarded, at six shillings in winter and seven in summer. This seems to have been the highest remuneration given in the kingdom for agricultural labour between the Restoration and the Revolution; and it is to be observed that, in the year in which this order was made, the necessaries of life were immoderately dear. Wheat was at seventy shillings the quarter, which would even now be considered as almost a famine price.‡

These facts are in perfect accordance with another fact which seems to deserve consideration. It is evident that, in a country where no man can be compelled to become a soldier, the ranks of an army cannot be filled if the government offers much less than the wages of common rustic labour. At present the pay and beer money of a private in a regiment of the line amount to seven shillings and sevenpence a week. This stipend, coupled with the hope of a pension, does not attract the English youth in sufficient numbers; and it is found necessary to supply the deficiency by enlisting largely from among the poorer population of Munster and Connaught. The pay of the private foot soldier in 1685 was only four shillings and eightpence a week; yet it is certain that the government in that year found no difficulty in obtaining many thousands of English recruits at very short notice. The pay of the private foot soldier in the army of the Commonwealth had been seven shillings a week, that is to say, as much as a corporal received under Charles the Second§; and seven shillings a week had been found sufficient to fill the ranks with men decidedly superior to the generality of the people. On

---

* Plain and easy Method shewing how the office of Overseer of the Poor may be managed, by Richard Dunning; 1st edition, 1685; 2d edition, 1686.

† Cullum's History of Hawsted.

‡ Ruggles on the Poor.

§ See, in Thurloe's State Papers, the memorandum of the Dutch Deputies, dated August $\frac{2}{12}$. 1653.

the whole, therefore, it seems reasonable to conclude that, in the reign of Charles the Second, the ordinary wages of the peasant did not exceed four shillings a week; but that, in some parts of the kingdom, five shillings, six shillings, and, during the summer months, even seven shillings were paid. At present a district where a labouring man earns only seven shillings a week is thought to be in a state shocking to humanity. The average is very much higher; and, in prosperous counties, the weekly wages of husbandmen amount to twelve, fourteen, and even sixteen shillings.

Wages of manufacturers.

The remuneration of workmen employed in manufactures has always been higher than that of the tillers of the soil. In the year 1680, a member of the House of Commons remarked that the high wages paid in this country made it impossible for our textures to maintain a competition with the produce of the Indian looms. An English mechanic, he said, instead of slaving like a native of Bengal for a piece of copper, exacted a shilling a day.* Other evidence is extant, which proves that a shilling a day was the pay to which the English manufacturer then thought himself entitled, but that he was often forced to work for less. The common people of that age were not in the habit of meeting for public discussion, of haranguing, or of petitioning Parliament. No newspaper pleaded their cause. It was in rude rhyme that their love and hatred, their exultation and their distress found utterance. A great part of their history is to be learned only from their ballads. One of the most remarkable of the popular lays chaunted about the streets of Norwich and Leeds in the time of Charles the Second may still be read on the original broadside. It is the vehement and bitter cry of labour against capital. It describes the good old times when every artisan employed in the woollen manufacture lived as well as a farmer. But those times were past. Sixpence a day was now all that could be earned by hard labour at the loom. If the poor complained that they could not live on such a pittance, they were told that they were free to take it or leave it. For so miserable a recompense were the producers of wealth compelled to toil, rising early and lying down late, while the master clothier, eating, sleeping, and idling, became rich by their exertions. A shilling a day, the poet declares, is what the weaver would have, if justice were done.† We may there-

---

* The orator was Mr. John Basset, member for Barnstaple. See Smith's Memoirs of Wool. chapter lxviii.

† This ballad is in the British Museum. The precise year is not given; but the Imprimatur of Roger Lestrange

fore conclude that, in the generation which preceded the Revolution, a workman employed in the great staple manufacture of England thought himself fairly paid if he gained six shillings a week.

It may here be noticed that the practice of setting children prematurely to work, a practice which the state, the legitimate protector of those who cannot protect themselves, has, in our time, wisely and humanely interdicted, prevailed in the seventeenth century to an extent which, when compared with the extent of the manufacturing system, seems almost incredible. At Norwich, the chief seat of the clothing trade, a little creature of six years old was thought fit for labour. Several writers of that time, and among them some who were considered as eminently benevolent, mention, with exultation, the fact that, in that single city, boys and girls of very tender age created wealth exceeding what was necessary for their own subsistence by twelve thousand pounds a year.* The more carefully we examine the history of the past, the more reason shall we find to dissent from those who imagine that our age has been fruitful of new social evils. The truth is that the evils are, with scarcely an exception, old. That which is new is the intelligence which discerns and the humanity which remedies them.

[margin: Labour of children in factories.]

When we pass from the weavers of cloth to a different class of artisans, our enquiries will still lead us to nearly the same conclusions. During several generations, the Commissioners of Greenwich Hospital have kept a register of the wages paid to different classes of workmen who have been employed in the repairs of the building. From this valuable record it appears that, in the course of a hundred and twenty years, the daily earnings of the bricklayer have risen from half a crown to four and tenpence, those of the mason from half a

[margin: Wages of different classes of artisans.]

---

fixes the date sufficiently for my purpose. I will quote some of the lines. The master clothier is introduced speaking as follows :—

" In former ages we used to give,
 So that our workfolks like farmers did live ;
 But the times are changed, we will make
 them know.

*   *   *   *   *   *   *

" We will make them to work hard for sixpence a day,
 Though a shilling they deserve if they had
  their just pay ;
 If at all they murmur and say 'tis too small,
 We bid them choose whether they'll work
  at all.

And thus we do gain all our wealth and estate,
By many poor men that work early and late.
Then hey for the clothing trade ! It goes on
  brave ;
We scorn for to toyl and moyl, nor yet to
  slave.
Our workmen do work hard, but we live at
  ease,
We go when we will, and we come when we
  please."

* Chamberlayne's State of England;
Petty's Political Arithmetic, chapter viii.; Dunning's Plain and Easy Method; Firmin's Proposition for the Employing of the Poor. It ought to be observed that Firmin was an eminent philanthropist.

crown to five and threepence, those of the carpenter from half a crown to five and fivepence, and those of the plumber from three shillings to five and sixpence.

It seems clear, therefore, that the wages of labour, estimated in money, were, in 1685, not more than half of what they now are; and there were few articles important to the working man of which the price was not, in 1685, more than half of what it now is. Beer was undoubtedly much cheaper in that age than at present. Meat was also cheaper, but was still so dear that hundreds of thousands of families scarcely knew the taste of it.* In the cost of wheat there has been very little change. The average price of the quarter, during the last twelve years of Charles the Second, was fifty shillings. Bread, therefore, such as is now given to the inmates of a workhouse, was then seldom seen, even on the trencher of a yeoman or of a shopkeeper. The great majority of the nation lived almost entirely on rye, barley, and oats.

The produce of tropical countries, the produce of the mines, the produce of machinery, was positively dearer than at present. Among the commodities for which the labourer would have had to pay higher in 1685 than his posterity now pay were sugar, salt, coals, candles, soap, shoes, stockings, and generally all articles of clothing and all articles of bedding. It may be added, that the old coats and blankets would have been, not only more costly, but less serviceable than the modern fabrics.

Number of paupers.

It must be remembered that those labourers who were able to maintain themselves and their families by means of wages were not the most necessitous members of the community. Beneath them lay a large class which could not subsist without some aid from the parish. There can hardly be a more important test of the condition of the common people than the ratio which this class bears to the whole society. At present the men, women, and children who receive relief appear from the official returns to be, in bad years, one tenth of the inhabitants of England, and, in good years, one thirteenth. Gregory King estimated them in his time at about a fourth; and this estimate, which all our respect for his authority will scarcely prevent us from calling extravagant, was pronounced by Davenant eminently judicious.

* King in his Natural and Political Conclusions roughly estimated the common people of England at 880,000 families. Of these families 440,000, according to him, ate animal food twice a week. The remaining 440,000 ate it not at all, or at most not oftener than once a week.

We are not quite without the means of forming an estimate for ourselves. The poor rate was undoubtedly the heaviest tax borne by our ancestors in those days. It was computed, in the reign of Charles the Second, at near seven hundred thousand pounds a year, much more than the produce either of the excise or of the customs, and little less than half the entire revenue of the crown. The poor rate went on increasing rapidly, and appears to have risen in a short time to between eight and nine hundred thousand a year, that is to say, to one sixth of what it now is. The population was then less than a third of what it now is. The minimum of wages, estimated in money, was half of what it now is; and we can therefore hardly suppose that the average allowance made to a pauper can have been more than half of what it now is. It seems to follow that the proportion of the English people which received parochial relief then must have been larger than the proportion which receives relief now. It is good to speak on such questions with diffidence: but it has certainly never yet been proved that pauperism was a less heavy burden or a less serious social evil during the last quarter of the seventeeth century than it is in our own time.*

In one respect it must be admitted that the progress of civilisation has diminished the physical comforts of a portion of the poorest class. It has already been mentioned that, before the Revolution, many thousands of square miles, now enclosed and cultivated, were marsh, forest, and heath. Of this wild land much was, by law, common, and much of what was not common by law was worth so little that the proprietors suffered it to be common in fact. In such a tract, squatters and trespassers were tolerated to an extent now unknown. The peasant who dwelt there could, at little or no charge, procure occasionally some palatable addition to his hard fare,

* Fourteenth Report of the Poor Law Commissioners, Appendix B. No. 2. Appendix C. No. 1. 1848. Of the two estimates of the poor rate mentioned in the text one was formed by Arthur Moore, the other, some years later, by Richard Dunning. Moore's estimate will be found in Davenant's Essay on Ways and Means; Dunning's in Sir Frederic Eden's valuable work on the poor. King and Davenant estimate the paupers and beggars in 1696, at the incredible number of 1,330,000 out of a population of 5,500,000. In 1846 the number of persons who received relief appears from the official returns to have been only 1,332,089 out of a population of about 17,000,000. It ought also to be observed that, in those returns, a pauper must very often be reckoned more than once.

I would advise the reader to consult De Foe's pamphlet entitled "Giving Alms no Charity," and the Greenwich tables which will be found in Mr. M'Culloch's Commercial Dictionary under the head Prices.

and provide himself with fuel for the winter. He kept a flock of geese on what is now an orchard rich with apple blossoms. He snared wild fowl on the fen which has long since been drained and divided into corn fields and turnip fields. He cut turf among the furze bushes on the moor which is now a meadow bright with clover and renowned for butter and cheese. The progress of agriculture and the increase of population necessarily deprived him of these privileges. But against this disadvantage a long list of advantages is to be set off. Of the blessings which civilisation and philosophy bring with them a large proportion is common to all ranks, and would, if withdrawn, be missed as painfully by the labourer as by the peer. The market-place which the rustic can now reach with his cart in an hour was, a hundred and sixty years ago, a day's journey from him. The street which now affords to the artisan, during the whole night, a secure, a convenient, and a brilliantly lighted walk was, a hundred and sixty years ago, so dark after sunset that he would not have been able to see his hand, so ill paved that he would have run constant risk of breaking his neck, and so ill watched that he would have been in imminent danger of being knocked down and plundered of his small earnings. Every bricklayer who falls from a scaffold, every sweeper of a crossing who is run over by a carriage, may now have his wounds dressed and his limbs set with a skill such as, a hundred and sixty years ago, all the wealth of a great lord like Ormond, or of a merchant prince like Clayton, could not have purchased. Some frightful diseases have been extirpated by science; and some have been banished by police. The term of human life has been lengthened over the whole kingdom, and especially in the towns. The year 1685 was not accounted sickly; yet in the year 1685 more than one in twenty-three of the inhabitants of the capital died.* At present only one inhabitant of the capital in forty dies annually. The difference in salubrity between the London of the nineteenth century and the London of the seventeenth century is very far greater than the difference between London in an ordinary year and London in a year of cholera.

Still more important is the benefit which all orders of society, and especially the lower orders, have derived from the mollifying influence of civilisation on the national character. The groundwork of that character has indeed been the same

Marginal note: Benefits derived by the common people from the progress of civilisation.

* The deaths were 23,222.   Petty's Political Arithmetic.

through many generations, in the sense in which the ground-work of the character of an individual may be said to be the same when he is a rude and thoughtless schoolboy and when he is a refined and accomplished man. It is pleasing to reflect that the public mind of England has softened while it has ripened, and that we have, in the course of ages, become, not only a wiser, but also a kinder people. There is scarcely a page of the history or lighter literature of the seventeenth century which does not contain some proof that our ancestors were less humane than their posterity. The discipline of workshops, of schools, of private families, though not more efficient than at present, was infinitely harsher. Masters, well born and bred, were in the habit of beating their servants. Pedagogues knew no way of imparting knowledge but by beating their pupils. Husbands, of decent station, were not ashamed to beat their wives. The implacability of hostile factions was such as we can scarcely conceive. Whigs were disposed to murmur because Stafford was suffered to die without seeing his bowels burned before his face. Tories reviled and insulted Russell as his coach passed from the Tower to the scaffold in Lincoln's Inn Fields.* As little mercy was shown by the populace to sufferers of a humbler rank. If an offender was put into the pillory, it was well if he escaped with life from the shower of brickbats and paving stones.† If he was tied to the cart's tail, the crowd pressed round him, imploring the hangman to give it the fellow well, and make him howl.‡ Gentlemen arranged parties of pleasure to Bridewell on court days for the purpose of seeing the wretched women who beat hemp there whipped.§ A man pressed to death for refusing to plead, a woman burned for coining, excited less sympathy than is now felt for a galled horse or an overdriven ox. Fights compared with which a boxing match is a refined and humane spectacle were among the favourite diversions of a large part of the town. Multitudes assembled to see gladiators hack each other to pieces with deadly weapons, and shouted with delight when one of the combatants lost a finger or an eye. The prisons were hells on earth, seminaries of every crime and of every disease. At the assizes the lean and yellow culprits brought with them from their cells to the dock an atmosphere of stench and pes-

* Burnet, i. 560.
† Muggleton's Acts of the Witnesses of the Spirit.
‡ Tom Brown describes such a scene in lines which I do not venture to quote.
§ Ward's London Spy.

tilence which sometimes avenged them signally on bench, bar, and jury. But on all this misery society looked with profound indifference. Nowhere could be found that sensitive and restless compassion which has, in our time, extended a powerful protection to the factory child, to the Hindoo widow, to the negro slave, which pries into the stores and watercasks of every emigrant ship, which winces at every lash laid on the back of a drunken soldier, which will not suffer the thief in the hulks to be ill fed or overworked, and which has repeatedly endeavoured to save the life even of the murderer. It is true that compassion ought, like all other feelings, to be under the government of reason, and has, for want of such government, produced some ridiculous and some deplorable effects. But the more we study the annals of the past, the more shall we rejoice that we live in a merciful age, in an age in which cruelty is abhorred, and in which pain, even when deserved, is inflicted reluctantly and from a sense of duty. Every class doubtless has gained largely by this great moral change : but the class which has gained most is the poorest, the most dependent, and the most defenceless.

Delusion which leads men to overrate the happiness of preceding generations.

The general effect of the evidence which has been submitted to the reader seems hardly to admit of doubt. Yet, in spite of evidence, many will still image to themselves the England of the Stuarts as a more pleasant country than the England in which we live. It may at first sight seem strange that society, while constantly moving forward with eager speed, should be constantly looking backward with tender regret. But these two propensities, inconsistent as they may appear, can easily be resolved into the same principle. Both spring from our impatience of the state in which we actually are. That impatience, while it stimulates us to surpass preceding generations, disposes us to overrate their happiness. It is, in some sense, unreasonable and ungrateful in us to be constantly discontented with a condition which is constantly improving. But, in truth, there is constant improvement precisely because there is constant discontent. If we were perfectly satisfied with the present, we should cease to contrive, to labour, and to save with a view to the future. And it is natural that, being dissatisfied with the present, we should form a too favourable estimate of the past.

In truth we are under a deception similar to that which misleads the traveller in the Arabian desert. Beneath the caravan all is dry and bare : but far in advance, and far in the rear, is the semblance of refreshing waters. The pilgrims hasten forward and find nothing but sand where an hour before they had seen a lake. They turn their eyes and see a lake where, an hour before, they were toiling through sand. A similar illusion seems to haunt nations through every stage of the long progress from poverty and barbarism to the highest degrees of opulence and civilisation. But, if we resolutely chase the mirage backward, we shall find it recede before us into the regions of fabulous antiquity. It is now the fashion to place the golden age of England in times when noblemen were destitute of comforts the want of which would be intolerable to a modern footman, when farmers and shopkeepers breakfasted on loaves the very sight of which would raise a riot in a modern workhouse, when to have a clean shirt once a week was a privilege reserved for the higher class of gentry, when men died faster in the purest country air than they now die in the most pestilential lanes of our towns, and when men died faster in the lanes of our towns than they now die on the coast of Guiana. We too shall, in our turn, be outstripped, and in our turn be envied. It may well be, in the twentieth century, that the peasant of Dorsetshire may think himself miserably paid with twenty shillings a week; that the carpenter at Greenwich may receive ten shillings a day; that labouring men may be as little used to dine without meat as they now are to eat rye bread; that sanitary police and medical discoveries may have added several more years to the average length of human life; that numerous comforts and luxuries which are now unknown, or confined to a few, may be within the reach of every diligent and thrifty working man. And yet it may then be the mode to assert that the increase of wealth and the progress of science have benefited the few at the expense of the many, and to talk of the reign of Queen Victoria as the time when England was truly merry England, when all classes were bound together by brotherly sympathy, when the rich did not grind the faces of the poor, and when the poor did not envy the splendour of the rich.

CHAPTER IV.

1685.
Death of
Charles II.

THE death of King Charles the Second took the nation by surprise. His frame was naturally strong, and did not appear to have suffered from excess. He had always been mindful of his health even in his pleasures; and his habits were such as promise a long life and a robust old age. Indolent as he was on all occasions which required tension of the mind, he was active and persevering in bodily exercise. He had, when young, been renowned as a tennis player *, and was, even in the decline of life, an indefatigable walker. His ordinary pace was such that those who were admitted to the honour of his society found it difficult to keep up with him. He rose early, and generally passed three or four hours a day in the open air. He might be seen, before the dew was off the grass in St. James's Park, striding among the trees, playing with his spaniels, and flinging corn to his ducks; and these exhibitions endeared him to the common people, who always love to see the great unbend.†

At length, towards the close of the year 1684, he was prevented, by a slight attack of what was supposed to be gout, from rambling as usual. He now spent his mornings in his laboratory, where he amused himself with experiments on the properties of mercury. His temper seemed to have suffered from confinement. He had no apparent cause for disquiet. His kingdom was tranquil: he was not in pressing want of money: his power was greater than it had ever been: the party which had long thwarted him had been beaten down; but the cheerfulness which had supported him against adverse fortune had vanished in this season of prosperity. A trifle now sufficed to depress those elastic spirits which had borne up against defeat, exile, and penury. His irritation frequently showed itself by looks and words such as could hardly

* Pepys's Diary, Dec. 28. 1663, Sept. 2. 1667.   Lords' Journals, October 28. 1678.; Cibber's Apology.

† Burnet, i. 606.; Spectator, No. 462.;

Charles II

have been expected from a man so eminently distinguished by good humour and good breeding. It was not supposed however that his constitution was seriously impaired.*

His palace had seldom presented a gayer or a more scandalous appearance than on the evening of Sunday the first of February 1685.† Some grave persons who had gone thither, after the fashion of that age, to pay their duty to their sovereign, and who had expected that, on such a day, his court would wear a decent aspect, were struck with astonishment and horror. The great gallery of Whitehall, an admirable relic of the magnificence of the Tudors, was crowded with revellers and gamblers. The king sate there chatting and toying with three women, whose charms were the boast, and whose vices were the disgrace, of three nations. Barbara Palmer, Duchess of Cleveland, was there, no longer young, but still retaining some traces of that superb and voluptuous loveliness which twenty years before overcame the hearts of all men. There too was the Duchess of Portsmouth, whose soft and infantine features were lighted up with the vivacity of France. Hortensia Mancini, Duchess of Mazarin, and niece of the great Cardinal, completed the group. She had been early removed from her native Italy to the court where her uncle was supreme. His power and her own attractions had drawn a crowd of illustrious suitors round her. Charles himself, during his exile, had sought her hand in vain. No gift of nature or of fortune seemed to be wanting to her. Her face was beautiful with the rich beauty of the South, her understanding quick, her manners graceful, her rank exalted, her possessions immense; but her ungovernable passions had turned all these blessings into curses. She had found the misery of an ill assorted marriage intolerable, had fled from her husband, had abandoned her vast wealth, and, after having astonished Rome and Piedmont by her adventures, had fixed her abode in England. Her house was the favourite resort of men of wit and pleasure, who, for the sake of her smiles and her table, endured her frequent fits of insolence and ill humour. Rochester and Godolphin sometimes forgot the cares of state in her company. Barillon and Saint Evremond found in her drawing room consolation for their long banish-

* Burnet, i. 605, 606.; Welwood; North's Life of Guildford, 251.

† I may take this opportunity of mentioning that whenever I give only one date, I follow the old style, which was, in the seventeenth century, the style of England; but I reckon the year from the first of January.

ment from Paris. The learning of Vossius, the witt of Waller, were daily employed to flatter and amuse her. But her diseased mind required stronger stimulants, and sought them in gallantry, in basset, and in usquebaugh.* While Charles flirted with his three sultanas, Hortensia's French page, a handsome boy, whose vocal performances were the delight of Whitehall, and were rewarded by numerous presents of rich clothes, ponies, and guineas, warbled some amorous verses.† A party of twenty courtiers was seated at cards round a large table on which gold was heaped in mountains.‡ Even then the King had complained that he did not feel quite well. He had no appetite for his supper : his rest that night was broken ; but on the following morning he rose, as usual, early.

To that morning the contending factions in his council had, during some days, looked forward with anxiety. The struggle between Halifax and Rochester seemed to be approaching a decisive crisis. Halifax, not content with having already driven his rival from the Board of Treasury, had undertaken to prove him guilty of such dishonesty or neglect in the con-- duct of the finances as ought to be punished by dismission from the public service. It was even whispered that the Lord President would probably be sent to the Tower. The King had promised to enquire into the matter. The second of February had been fixed for the investigation ; and several officers of the revenue had been ordered to attend with their books on that day.§ But a great turn of fortune was at hand.

Scarcely had Charles risen from his bed when his attendants perceived that his utterance was indistinct, and that his thoughts seemed to be wandering. Several men of rank had, as usual, assembled to see their sovereign shaved and dressed. He made an effort to converse with them in his usual gay style ; but his ghastly look surprised and alarmed them. Soon his face grew black ; his eyes turned in his head ; he uttered a cry, staggered, and fell into the arms of one of his lords. A physician who had charge of the royal retorts and crucibles happened to be present. He had no lancet ; but he

---

* Saint Evremond, *passim ;* Saint Réal, Mémoires de la Duchesse de Mazarin ; Rochester's Farewell ; Evelyn's Diary, Sept. 6. 1676, June 11. 1699.

† Evelyn's Diary, Jan. 28. 168⅘; Saint Evremond's Letter to Déry.

‡ Evelyn's Diary, February 4. 168⅘.

§ Roger North's Life of Sir Dudley North, 170. ; The true Patriot vindi-- cated, or a Justification of his Excellency the E—— of R——; Burnet, i. 605. The Treasury Books prove that Burnet had good intelligence.

opened a vein with a penknife. The blood flowed freely; but the King was still insensible.

He was laid on his bed, where, during a short time, the Duchess of Portsmouth hung over him with the familiarity of a wife. But the alarm had been given. The Queen and the Duchess of York were hastening to the room. The favourite concubine was forced to retire to her own apartments. Those apartments had been thrice pulled down and thrice rebuilt by her lover to gratify her caprice. The very furniture of the chimney was massy silver. Several fine paintings, which properly belonged to the Queen, had been transferred to the dwelling of the mistress. The sideboards were piled with richly wrought plate. In the niches stood cabinets, the masterpieces of Japanese art. On the hangings, fresh from the looms of Paris, were depicted, in tints which no English tapestry could rival, birds of gorgeous plumage, landscapes, hunting matches, the lordly terrace of Saint Germains, the statues and fountains of Versailles.* In the midst of this splendour, purchased by guilt and shame, the unhappy woman gave herself up to an agony of grief, which, to do her justice, was not wholly selfish.

And now the gates of Whitehall, which ordinarily stood open to all comers, were closed. But persons whose faces were known were still permitted to enter. The antechambers and galleries were soon filled to overflowing; and even the sick room was crowded with peers, privy councillors, and foreign ministers. All the medical men of note in London were summoned. So high did political animosities run that the presence of some Whig physicians was regarded as an extraordinary circumstance.† One Roman Catholic, whose skill was then widely renowned, Doctor Thomas Short, was in attendance. Several of the prescriptions have been preserved. One of them is signed by fourteen Doctors. The patient was bled largely. Hot iron was applied to his head. A loathsome volatile salt, extracted from human skulls, was forced into his mouth. He recovered his senses; but he was evidently in a situation of extreme danger.

The Queen was for a time assiduous in her attendance. The Duke of York scarcely left his brother's bedside. The Primate and four other bishops were then in London. They remained at Whitehall all day, and took it by turns to sit up

* Evelyn's Diary, Jan. 24. 168½, Oct. 4. 1683.
† Dugdale's Correspondence.

at night in the King's room. The news of his illness filled the capital with sorrow and dismay. For his easy temper and affable manners had won the affection of a large part of the nation; and those who most disliked him preferred his unprincipled levity to the stern and earnest bigotry of his brother.

On the morning of Thursday the fifth of February, the London Gazette announced that His Majesty was going on well, and was thought by the physicians to be out of danger. The bells of all the churches rang merrily; and preparations for bonfires were made in the streets. But in the evening it was known that a relapse had taken place, and that the medical attendants had given up all hope. The public mind was greatly disturbed; but there was no disposition to tumult. The Duke of York, who had already taken on himself to give orders, ascertained that the City was perfectly quiet, and that he might without difficulty be proclaimed as soon as his brother should expire.

The King was in great pain, and complained that he felt as if a fire was burning within him. Yet he bore up against his sufferings with a fortitude which did not seem to belong to his soft and luxurious nature. The sight of his misery affected his wife so much that she fainted, and was carried senseless to her chamber. The prelates who were in waiting had from the first exhorted him to prepare for his end. They now thought it their duty to address him in a still more urgent manner. William Sancroft, Archbishop of Canterbury, an honest and pious, though narrowminded, man, used great freedom. "It is time," he said, "to speak out; for, Sir, you are about to appear before a Judge who is no respecter of persons." The King answered not a word.

Thomas Ken, Bishop of Bath and Wells, then tried his powers of persuasion. He was a man of parts and learning, of quick sensibility and stainless virtue. His elaborate works have long been forgotten; but his morning and evening hymns are still repeated daily in thousands of dwellings. Though, like most of his order, zealous for monarchy, he was no sycophant. Before he became a Bishop, he had maintained the honour of his gown by refusing, when the court was at Winchester, to let Eleanor Gwynn lodge in the house which he occupied there as a prebendary.* The King had sense enough to respect so manly a spirit. Of all the

* Hawkins's Life of Ken, 1713.

prelates he liked Ken the best. It was to no purpose, however, that the good Bishop now put forth all his eloquence. His solemn and pathetic exhortation awed and melted the bystanders to such a degree that some among them believed him to be filled with the same spirit which, in the old time, had, by the mouths of Nathan and Elias, called sinful princes to repentance. Charles however was unmoved. He made no objection indeed when the service for the visitation of the sick was read. In reply to the pressing questions of the divines, he said that he was sorry for what he had done amiss; and he suffered the absolution to be pronounced over him according to the forms of the Church of England: but, when he was urged to declare that he died in the communion of that Church, he seemed not to hear what was said; and nothing could induce him to take the Eucharist from the hands of the Bishops. A table with bread and wine was brought to his bedside, but in vain. Sometimes he said that there was no hurry, and sometimes that he was too weak.

Many attributed this apathy to contempt for divine things, and many to the stupor which often precedes death. But there were in the palace a few persons who knew better. Charles had never been a sincere member of the Established Church. His mind had long oscillated between Hobbism and Popery. When his health was good and his spirits high he was a scoffer. In his few serious moments he was a Roman Catholic. The Duke of York was aware of this, but was entirely occupied with the care of his own interests. He had ordered the outports to be closed. He had posted detachments of the Guards in different parts of the City. He had also procured the feeble signature of the dying King to an instrument by which some duties, granted only till the demise of the Crown, were let to farm for a term of three years. These things occupied the attention of James to such a degree that, though, on ordinary occasions, he was indiscreetly and unseasonably eager to bring over proselytes to his Church, he never reflected that his brother was in danger of dying without the last sacraments. This neglect was the more extraordinary because the Duchess of York had, at the request of the Queen, suggested, on the morning on which the King was taken ill, the propriety of procuring spiritual assistance. For such assistance Charles was at last indebted to an agency very different from that of his pious wife and sister in law. A life of frivolity and vice had not extinguished in the Duchess of Portsmouth all sentiments of religion, or all that kindness which is the glory of her sex. The French ambassador Barillon, who had come to the palace to enquire after the King, paid her a visit. He found her in an agony of sorrow. She took him into a secret room, and poured out her whole heart to him. "I have," she said, "a thing of great moment to tell you. If it were known, my head would be in danger. The King is really and truly a Catholic; but he will die without being reconciled to the Church. His bedchamber is full of Protestant clergymen. I cannot enter it without giving scandal. The Duke is thinking only of himself. Speak to him. Remind him that there is a soul at stake. He is master now. He can clear the room. Go this instant, or it will be too late."

Barillon hastened to the bedchamber, took the Duke aside, and delivered the message of the mistress. The conscience of James smote him. He started as if roused from sleep, and declared that nothing should prevent him from discharging the sacred duty which had been too long delayed. Several schemes were discussed and rejected. At last the Duke commanded the crowd to stand aloof, went to the bed, stooped down, and whispered something which none of the spectators could hear, but which they supposed to be some question about affairs of state. Charles answered in an audible voice, "Yes, yes, with all my heart." None of the bystanders, except the French Ambassador, guessed that the King was declaring his wish to be admitted into the bosom of the Church of Rome.

"Shall I bring a priest?" said the Duke. "Do, brother," replied the sick man. "For God's sake do, and lose no time. But no; you will get into trouble." "If it costs me my life," said the Duke, "I will fetch a priest."

To find a priest, however, for such a purpose, at a moment's notice, was not easy. For, as the law then stood, the person who admitted a proselyte into the Roman Catholic Church was guilty of a capital crime. The Count of Castel Melhor, a Portuguese nobleman, who, driven by political troubles from his native land, had been hospitably received at the English court, undertook to procure a confessor. He had recourse to his countrymen who belonged to the Queen's household; but he found that none of her chaplains knew English or French enough to shrive the King. The Duke and Barillon were about to send to the Venetian Minister for a clergyman when they heard that a Benedictine monk, named John Huddleston, happened to be at Whitehall. This man had, with great risk to himself, saved the King's life after the battle of Worcester, and had, on that account, been, ever since the Restoration, a privileged person. In the sharpest proclamations which had been put forth against Popish priests, when false witnesses had inflamed the nation to fury, Huddleston had been excepted by name.* He readily consented to put his life a second time in peril for his prince; but there was still a difficulty. The honest monk was so illiterate that he did not know what he ought to say on an occasion of such importance. He however obtained some hints, through the intervention of Castel Melhor, from a Portuguese ecclesiastic, and, thus instructed, was brought up the back stairs by Chiffinch, a confidential servant, who, if the satires of that age are to be credited, had often introduced visitors of a very different description by the same entrance. The Duke then, in the King's name, commanded all who were present to quit the room, except Lewis Duras, Earl of Feversham, and John Granville, Earl of Bath. Both these Lords professed the Protestant religion; but James conceived that he could count on their fidelity. Feversham, a Frenchman of noble birth, and nephew of the great Turenne, held high rank in the English army, and was Chamberlain to the Queen. Bath was Groom of the Stole.

The Duke's orders were obeyed; and even the physicians withdrew. The back door was then opened; and Father Huddleston entered. A cloak had been thrown over his sacred vestments; and his shaven crown was concealed by a flowing wig. "Sir," said the Duke, "this good man once saved your life. He now comes to save your soul." Charles faintly answered, "He is welcome." Huddleston went through his part better than had been expected. He knelt by the bed, listened to the confession, pronounced the absolution, and administered extreme unction. He asked if the King wished to receive the Lord's supper. "Surely," said Charles, "if I am not unworthy." The host was brought in. Charles feebly strove to rise and kneel before it. The priest bade him lie still, and assured him that God would accept the humiliation of the soul, and would not require the humi-

* See the London Gazette of Nov. 21. 1678. Barillon and Burnet say that Huddleston was excepted out of all the Acts of Parliament made against priests; but this is a mistake.

liation of the body. The King found so much difficulty in swallowing the bread that it was necessary to open the door and to procure a glass of water. This rite ended, the monk held up a crucifix before the penitent, charged him to fix his last thoughts on the sufferings of the Redeemer, and withdrew. The whole ceremony had occupied about three quarters of an hour; and, during that time, the courtiers who filled the outer room had communicated their suspicions to each other by whispers and significant glances. The door was at length thrown open, and the crowd again filled the chamber of death.

It was now late in the evening. The King seemed much relieved by what had passed. His natural children were brought to his bedside, the Dukes of Grafton, Southampton, and Northumberland, sons of the Duchess of Cleveland, the Duke of Saint Albans, son of Eleanor Gwynn, and the Duke of Richmond, son of the Duchess of Portsmouth. Charles blessed them all, but spoke with peculiar tenderness to Richmond. One face which should have been there was wanting. The eldest and best beloved child was an exile and a wanderer. His name was not once mentioned by his father.

During the night Charles earnestly recommended the Duchess of Portsmouth and her boy to the care of James; "And do not," he goodnaturedly added, "let poor Nelly starve." The Queen sent excuses for her absence by Halifax. She said that she was too much disordered to resume her post by the couch, and implored pardon for any offence which she might unwittingly have given. "She ask my pardon, poor woman!" cried Charles; "I ask hers with all my heart."

The morning light began to peep through the windows of Whitehall; and Charles desired the attendants to pull aside the curtains, that he might have one more look at the day. He remarked that it was time to wind up a clock which stood near his bed. These little circumstances were long remembered, because they proved beyond dispute that, when he declared himself a Roman Catholic, he was in full possession of his faculties. He apologised to those who had stood round him all night for the trouble which he had caused. He had been, he said, a most unconscionable time dying; but he hoped that they would excuse it. This was the last glimpse of that exquisite urbanity, so often found potent to charm away the resentment of a justly incensed nation. Soon after dawn the speech of the dying man failed.

Before ten his senses were gone. Great numbers had repaired to the churches at the hour of morning service. When the prayer for the King was read, loud groans and sobs showed how deeply his people felt for him. At noon on Friday, the sixth of February, he passed away without a struggle.*

* Clarke's Life of James the Second, i. 746. Orig. Mem.; Barillon's Despatch of Feb. $\frac{8}{18}$. 1685; Van Citters's Despatches of Feb. $\frac{3}{13}$ and Feb. $\frac{6}{16}$. Huddleston's Narrative; Letters of Philip, second Earl of Chesterfield, 277.; Sir H. Ellis's Original Letters, First Series, iii. 333.; Second Series, iv. 74.; Chaillot MS.; Burnet, i. 606.; Evelyn's Diary, Feb. 4. 168$\frac{4}{5}$; Welwood's Memoirs, 140.; North's Life of Guildford, 252.; Examen, 648.; Hawkins's Life of Ken; Dryden's Threnodia Augustalis; Sir H. Halford's Essay on Deaths of Eminent Persons. See also a fragment of a letter written by the Earl of Ailesbury, which is printed in the European Magazine for April 1795. Ailesbury calls Burnet an impostor. Yet his own narrative and Burnet's will not, to any candid and sensible reader, appear to contradict each other. I have seen in the British Museum, and also in the Library of the Royal Institution, a curious broadside containing an account of the death of Charles. It will be found in the Somers Collection. The author was evidently a zealous Roman Catholic, and must have had access to good sources of information. I strongly suspect that he had been in communication, directly or indirectly, with James himself. No name is given at length; but the initials are perfectly intelligible, except in one place. It is said that the D. of Y. was reminded of the duty which he owed to his brother by P. M. A. C. F. I must own myself quite unable to decipher the last five letters. It is some consolation that Sir Walter Scott was equally unsuccessful. (1848.) Since the first edition of this work was published, several very ingenious conjectures touching these mysterious letters have been communicated to me; but I am convinced that the true solution has not yet been suggested. (1850.) I still greatly doubt whether the riddle has been solved. But the most plausible interpretation is one which, with some variations, occurred, almost at the same time, to myself and to several other persons; I am inclined to read "Père Mansuete A Cordelier Friar." Mansuete, a Cordelier, was then James's confessor. To

Mansuete therefore it peculiarly belonged to remind James of a sacred duty which had been culpably neglected. The writer of the broadside must have been unwilling to inform the world that a soul which many devout Roman Catholics had left to perish had been snatched from destruction by the courageous charity of a woman of loose character. It is therefore not unlikely that he would prefer a fiction, at once probable and edifying, to a truth which could not fail to give scandal. (1856.)

It should seem that no transactions in history ought to be more accurately known to us than those which took place round the deathbed of Charles the Second. We have several relations written by persons who were actually in his room. We have several relations written by persons who, though not themselves eyewitnesses, had the best opportunity of obtaining information from eyewitnesses. Yet whoever attempts to digest this vast mass of materials into a consistent narrative will find the task a difficult one. Indeed James and his wife, when they told the story to the nuns of Chaillot, could not agree as to some circumstances. The Queen said that, after Charles had received the last sacraments, the Protestant Bishops renewed their exhortations. The King said that nothing of the kind took place. "Surely," said the Queen, "you told me so yourself." "It is impossible that I could have told you so," said the King; "for nothing of the sort happened."

It is much to be regretted that Sir Henry Halford should have taken so little trouble to ascertain the facts on which he pronounced judgment. He does not seem to have been aware of the existence of the narratives of James, Barillon, and Huddleston.

As this is the first occasion on which I cite the correspondence of the Dutch ministers at the English court, I ought here to mention that a series of their despatches, from the accession of James the Second to his flight, forms one of the most valuable parts of the Mackintosh collection. The subsequent despatches, down to the settlement of the government in February 1689, I pro-

Suspicions of poison.

At that time the common people throughout Europe, and nowhere more than in England, were in the habit of attributing the deaths of princes, especially when the prince was popular and the death unexpected, to the foulest and darkest kind of assassination. Thus James the First had been accused of poisoning Prince Henry. Thus Charles the First had been accused of poisoning James the First. Thus when, in the time of the Commonwealth, the Princess Elizabeth died at Carisbrook, it was loudly asserted that Cromwell had stooped to the senseless and dastardly wickedness of mixing noxious drugs with the food of a young girl whom he had no conceivable motive to injure.* A few years later, the rapid decomposition of Cromwell's own corpse was ascribed by many to a deadly potion administered in his medicine. The death of Charles the Second could scarcely fail to occasion similar rumours. The public ear had been repeatedly abused by stories of Popish plots against his life. There was, therefore, in many minds, a strong predisposition to suspicion; and there were some unlucky circumstances which, to minds so predisposed, might seem to indicate that a crime had been perpetrated. The fourteen Doctors who deliberated on the King's case contradicted each other and themselves. Some of them thought that his fit was epileptic, and that he should be suffered to have his doze out. The majority pronounced him apoplectic, and tortured him during some hours like an Indian at a stake. Then it was determined to call his complaint a fever, and to administer doses of bark. One physician, however, protested against this course, and assured the Queen that his brethren would kill the King among them. Nothing better than dissension and vacillation could be expected from such a multitude of advisers. But many of the vulgar not unnaturally concluded, from the perplexity of the great masters of the healing art, that the malady had some extraordinary origin. There is reason to believe that a horrible suspicion did actually cross the mind of Short, who, though

---

cured from the Hague. The Dutch archives have been far too little explored. They abound with information interesting in the highest degree to every Englishman. They are admirably arranged; and they are in the charge of gentlemen whose courtesy, liberality, and zeal for the interests of literature, cannot be too highly praised. I wish to acknowledge, in the strongest manner, my own obliga-

tions to Mr. De Jonge and to Mr. Van Zwanne.

* Clarendon mentions this calumny with just scorn. "According to the charity of the time towards Cromwell, very many would have it believed to be by poison, of which there was no appearance, nor any proof ever after made."— Book xiv.

skilful in his profession, seems to have been a nervous and fanciful man, and whose perceptions were probably confused by dread of the odious imputations to which he, as a Roman Catholic, was peculiarly exposed. We cannot, therefore, wonder that wild stories without number were repeated and believed by the common people. His Majesty's tongue had swelled to the size of a neat's tongue. A cake of deleterious powder had been found in his brain. There were blue spots on his breast. There were black spots on his shoulder. Something had been put into his snuffbox. Something had been put into his broth. Something had been put into his favourite dish of eggs and ambergrease. The Duchess of Portsmouth had poisoned him in a cup of chocolate. The Queen had poisoned him in a jar of dried pears. Such tales ought to be preserved; for they furnish us with a measure of the intelligence and virtue of the generation which eagerly devoured them. That no rumour of the same kind has ever, in the present age, found credit among us, even when lives on which great interests depended have been terminated by unforeseen attacks of disease, is to be attributed partly to the progress of medical and chemical science, but partly also, it may be hoped, to the progress which the nation has made in good sense, justice, and humanity.*

When all was over, James retired from the bedside to his closet, where, during a quarter of an hour, he remained alone. Meanwhile the Privy Councillors who were in the palace assembled. The new King came forth, and took his place at the head of the board. He commenced his administration, according to usage, by a speech to the Council. He expressed his regret for the loss which he had just sustained, and he promised to imitate the singular lenity which had distinguished the late reign. He was aware, he said, that he had been accused of a fondness for arbitrary power. But that was not the only falsehood which had been told of him. He was resolved to maintain the established government both in Church and State. The Church of England he knew to be eminently loyal. It should therefore always be his care to

Speech of James II. to the Privy Council..

---

* Welwood, 139.; Burnet, i. 609.; Sheffield's Character of Charles the Second; North's Life of Guildford, 252.; Examen, 648.; Revolution Politics; Higgons on Burnet. What North says of the embarrassment and vacillation of the physicians is confirmed by the despatches of Van Citters. I have been much perplexed by the strange story about Short's suspicions. I was, at one time, inclined to adopt North's solution. But, though I attach little weight to the authority of Welwood and Burnet in such a case, I cannot reject the testimony of so well informed and so unwilling a witness as Sheffield.

support and defend her.   The laws of England, he also knew, were sufficient to make him as great a King as he could wish to be.   He would not relinquish his own rights; but he would respect the rights of others.   He had formerly risked his life in defence of his country; and he would still go as far as any man in support of her just liberties.

This speech was not, like modern speeches on similar occasions, carefully prepared by the advisers of the sovereign. It was the extemporaneous expression of the new King's feelings at a moment of great excitement.   The members of the Council broke forth into clamours of delight and gratitude. The Lord President, Rochester, in the name of his brethren, expressed a hope that His Majesty's most welcome declaration would be made public.   The Solicitor General, Heneage Finch, offered to act as clerk.   He was a zealous churchman, and, as such, was naturally desirous that there should be some permanent record of the gracious promises which had just been uttered.   " Those promises," he said, " have made so deep an impression on me that I can repeat them word for word." He soon produced his report.   James read it, approved of it, and ordered it to be published.   At a later period he said that he had taken this step without due consideration, that his unpremeditated expressions touching the Church of England were too strong, and that Finch had, with a dexterity which at the time escaped notice, made them still stronger.*

James proclaimed.

The King had been exhausted by long watching and by many violent emotions.   He now retired to rest.   The Privy Councillors, having respectfully accompanied him to his bedchamber, returned to their seats, and issued orders for the ceremony of proclamation.   The Guards were under arms; the heralds appeared in their gorgeous coats; and the pageant proceeded without any obstruction.   Casks of wine were broken up in the streets, and all who passed were invited to drink to the health of the new sovereign.   But, though an occasional shout was raised, the people were not in a joyous mood.   Tears were seen in many eyes; and it was remarked that there was scarcely a housemaid in London who had not contrived to procure some fragment of black crape in honour of King Charles.†

The funeral called forth much censure.   It would, indeed,

* London Gazette, Feb. 9. 168⅘;   † See the authorities cited in the last
Clarke's Life of James the Second, ii. 3.;   note. See also the Examen, 647.; Bur-
Barillon, Feb. 9/19.; Evelyn's Diary, Feb. 6.   net, i. 620.; Higgons on Burnet.

hardly have been accounted worthy of a noble and opulent subject. The Tories gently blamed the new King's parsimony : the Whigs sneered at his want of natural affection; and the fiery Covenanters of Scotland exultingly proclaimed that the curse denounced of old against wicked princes had been signally fulfilled, and that the departed tyrant had been buried with the burial of an ass.* Yet James commenced his administration with a large measure of public good will. His speech to the Council appeared in print, and the impression which it produced was highly favourable to him. This, then, was the prince whom a faction had driven into exile and had tried to rob of his birthright, on the ground that he was a deadly enemy to the religion and laws of England. He had triumphed: he was on the throne; and his first act was to declare that he would defend the Church, and would strictly respect the rights of his people. The estimate which all parties had formed of his character, added weight to every word that fell from him. The Whigs called him haughty, implacable, obstinate, regardless of public opinion. The Tories, while they extolled his princely virtues, had often lamented his neglect of the arts which conciliate popularity. Satire itself had never represented him as a man likely to court public favour by professing what he did not feel, and by promising what he had no intention of performing. On the Sunday which followed his accession, his speech was quoted in many pulpits. "We have now for our Church," cried one loyal preacher, "the word of a King, and of a King who was never worse than his word." This pointed sentence was fast circulated through town and country, and was soon the watchword of the whole Tory party.†

The great offices of state had become vacant by the demise of the crown; and it was necessary for James to determine how they should be filled. Few of the members of the late cabinet had any reason to expect his favour. Sunderland, who was Secretary of State, and Godolphin, who was First Lord of the Treasury, had supported the Exclusion Bill. Halifax, who held the Privy Seal, had opposed that bill with unrivalled powers of argument and eloquence. But Halifax was the mortal enemy of despotism and of Popery. He saw with dread the progress of the French arms on the Continent,

State of the administration.

---

* London Gazette, Feb. 14. 168⅘; Evelyn's Diary of the same day; Burnet, i. 610.; The Hind let loose.   † Burnet, i. 628.; Lestrange, Observator, Feb. 11. 1684.

and the influence of French gold in the counsels of England. Had his advice been followed, the laws would have been strictly observed : clemency would have been extended to the vanquished Whigs : the Parliament would have been convoked in due season : an attempt would have been made to reconcile our domestic factions ; and the principles of the Triple Alliance would again have guided our foreign policy. He had therefore incurred the bitter animosity of James. The Lord Keeper Guildford could hardly be said to belong to either of the parties into which the court was divided. He could by no means be called a friend of liberty ; and yet he had so great a reverence for the letter of the law that he was not a serviceable tool of arbitrary power. He was accordingly designated by the vehement Tories as a Trimmer, and was to James an object of aversion with which contempt was largely mingled. Ormond, who was Lord Steward of the Household and Viceroy of Ireland, then resided at Dublin. His claims on the royal gratitude were superior to those of any other subject. He had fought bravely for Charles the First : he had shared the exile of Charles the Second ; and, since the Restoration, he had, in spite of many provocations, kept his loyalty unstained. Though he had been disgraced during the predominance of the Cabal, he had never gone into factious opposition, and had, in the days of the Popish Plot and the Exclusion Bill, been foremost among the supporters of the throne. He was now old, and had been recently tried by the most cruel of all calamities. He had followed to the grave a son who should have been his own chief mourner, the gallant Ossory. The eminent services, the venerable age, and the domestic misfortunes of Ormond made him an object of general interest to the nation. The Cavaliers regarded him as, both by right of seniority and by right of merit, their head ; and the Whigs knew that, faithful as he had always been to the cause of monarchy, he was no friend either to Popery or to arbitrary power. But, high as he stood in the public estimation, he had little favour to expect from his new master. James, indeed, while still a subject, had urged his brother to make a complete change in the Irish administration. Charles had assented ; and it had been arranged that, in a few months, there should be a new Lord Lieutenant.[*]

Rochester was the only member of the cabinet who stood

[*] The letters which passed between Rochester and Ormond on this subject will be found in the Clarendon Correspondence.

high in the favour of the King. The general expectation was that he would be immediately placed at the head of affairs, and that all the other great officers of state would be changed. This expectation proved to be well founded in part only. Rochester was declared Lord Treasurer, and thus became prime minister. Neither a Lord High Admiral nor a Board of Admiralty was appointed. The new King, who loved the details of naval business, and would have made a respectable clerk in the dockyard at Chatham, determined to be his own minister of marine. Under him the management of that important department was confided to Samuel Pepys, whose library and diary have kept his name fresh to our time. No servant of the late sovereign was publicly disgraced. Sunderland exerted so much art and address, employed so many intercessors, and was in possession of so many secrets, that he was suffered to retain his seals. Godolphin's obsequiousness, industry, experience, and taciturnity, could ill be spared. As he was no longer wanted at the Treasury, he was made Chamberlain to the Queen. With these three Lords the King took counsel on all important questions. As to Halifax, Ormond, and Guildford, he determined not yet to dismiss them, but merely to humble and annoy them.

Halifax was told that he must give up the Privy Seal and accept the Presidency of the Council. He submitted with extreme reluctance. For, though the President of the Council had always taken precedence of the Lord Privy Seal, the Lord Privy Seal was, in that age, a much more important officer than the Lord President. Rochester had not forgotten the jest which had been made a few months before on his own removal from the Treasury, and enjoyed in his turn the pleasure of kicking his rival up stairs. The Privy Seal was delivered to Rochester's elder brother, Henry Earl of Clarendon.

To Barillon James expressed the strongest dislike of Halifax. " I know him well, I never can trust him. He shall have no share in the management of public business. As to the place which I have given him, it will just serve to show how little influence he has." But to Halifax it was thought convenient to hold a very different language. "All the past is forgotten," said the King, " except the service which you did me in the debate on the Exclusion Bill." This speech has often been cited to prove that James was not so vindictive as he had been called by his enemies. It seems rather to prove that he by no means deserved the praises which have been bestowed on his sincerity by his friends.*

Ormond was politely informed that his services were no longer needed in Ireland, and was invited to repair to Whitehall, and to perform the functions of Lord Steward. He dutifully submitted, but did not affect to deny that the new arrangement wounded his feelings deeply. On the eve of his departure he gave a magnificent banquet at Kilmainham Hospital, then just completed, to the officers of the garrison of Dublin. After dinner he rose, filled a goblet to the brim with wine, and, holding it up, asked whether he had spilt one drop. " No, gentlemen : whatever the courtiers may say, I am not yet sunk into dotage. My hand does not fail me yet : and my hand is not steadier than my heart. To the health of King James !" Such was the last farewell of Ormond to Ireland. He left the administration in the hands of Lords Justices, and repaired to London, where he was received with unusual marks of public respect. Many persons of rank went forth to meet him on the road. A long train of equipages followed him into Saint James's Square, where his mansion stood ; and the Square was thronged by a multitude which greeted him with loud acclamations.†

Sir George
Jeffreys.
The Great Seal was left in Guildford's custody ; but a marked indignity was at the same time offered to him. It was determined that another lawyer of more vigour and audacity should be called to assist in the administration. The person selected was Sir George Jeffreys, Chief Justice of the Court of King's Bench. The depravity of this man has passed into a proverb. Both the great English parties have attacked his memory with emulous violence : for the Whigs considered him as their most barbarous enemy ; and the Tories found it convenient to throw on him the blame of all the crimes which had sullied their triumph. A diligent and candid enquiry will show that some frightful stories which have been told concerning him are false or exaggerated. Yet the dispassionate historian will be able to make very little deduction from the vast mass of infamy with which the memory of the wicked judge has been loaded.

He was a man of quick and vigorous parts, but constitu-

---

* The ministerial changes are announced in the London Gazette, Feb. 19. 168$\frac{4}{5}$. See Burnet, i. 621.; Barillon, Feb. $\frac{9}{15}$, $\frac{16}{26}$; and $\frac{Feb. 19.}{Mar. 1.}$

† Carte's Life of Ormond; Secret Consults of the Romish Party in Ireland, 1690; Memoirs of Ireland, 1716.

tionally prone to insolence and to the angry passions. When just emerging from boyhood he had risen into practice at the Old Bailey bar, a bar where advocates have always used a license of tongue unknown in Westminster Hall. Here, during many years, his chief business was to examine and crossexamine the most hardened miscreants of a great capital. Daily conflicts with prostitutes and thieves called out and exercised his powers so effectually that he became the most consummate bully ever known in his profession. Tenderness for others and respect for himself were feelings alike unknown to him. He acquired a boundless command of the rhetoric in which the vulgar express hatred and contempt. The profusion of maledictions and vituperative epithets which composed his vocabulary could hardly have been rivalled in the fishmarket or the beargarden. His countenance and his voice must always have been unamiable. But these natural advantages,—for such he seems to have thought them,—he had improved to such a degree that there were few who, in his paroxysms of rage, could see or hear him without emotion. Impudence and ferocity sate upon his brow. The glare of his eyes had a fascination for the unhappy victim on whom they were fixed. Yet his brow and his eye were less terrible than the savage lines of his mouth. His yell of fury, as was said by one who had often heard it, sounded like the thunder of the judgment day. These qualifications he carried, while still a young man, from the bar to the bench. He early became Common Serjeant, and then Recorder of London. As a judge at the City sessions he exhibited the same propensities which afterwards, in a higher post, gained for him an unenviable immortality. Already might be remarked in him the most odious vice which is incident to human nature, a delight in misery merely as misery. There was a fiendish exultation in the way in which he pronounced sentence on offenders. Their weeping and imploring seemed to titillate him voluptuously ; and he loved to scare them into fits by dilating with luxuriant amplification on all the details of what they were to suffer. Thus, when he had an opportunity of ordering an unlucky adventuress to be whipped at the cart's tail, " Hangman," he would exclaim, " I charge you to pay particular attention to this lady ! Scourge her soundly, man ! Scourge her till the blood runs down ! It is Christmas, a cold time for Madam to strip in ! See that you warm her shoulders thoroughly !"*

* Christmas Sessions Paper of 1678.

He was hardly less facetious when he passed judgment on poor Lodowick Muggleton, the drunken tailor who fancied himself a prophet. "Impudent rogue!" roared Jeffreys "thou shalt have an easy, easy, easy punishment!" One part of this easy punishment was the pillory, in which the wretched fanatic was almost killed with brickbats.*

By this time the heart of Jeffreys had been hardened to that temper which tyrants require in their worst implements. He had hitherto looked for professional advancement to the corporation of London. He had therefore professed himself a Roundhead, and had always appeared to be in a higher state of exhilaration when he explained to Popish priests that they were to be cut down alive, and were to see their own bowels burned, than when he passed ordinary sentences of death. But, as soon as he had got all that the City could give, he made haste to sell his forehead of brass and his tongue of venom to the Court. Chiffinch, who was accustomed to act as broker in infamous contracts of more than one kind, lent his aid. He had conducted many amorous and many political intrigues; but he assuredly never rendered a more scandalous service to his masters than when he introduced Jeffreys to Whitehall. The renegade soon found a patron in the obdurate and revengeful James, but was always regarded with scorn and disgust by Charles, whose faults, great as they were, had no affinity with insolence and cruelty. "That man," said the King, "has no learning, no sense, no manners, and more impudence than ten carted street-walkers."† Work was to be done, however, which could be trusted to no man who reverenced law or was sensible of shame; and thus Jeffreys, at an age at which a barrister thinks himself fortunate if he is employed to conduct an important cause, was made Chief Justice of the King's Bench.

His enemies could not deny that he possessed some of the qualities of a great judge. His legal knowledge, indeed, was merely such as he had picked up in practice of no very high kind. But he had one of those happily constituted intellects which, across labyrinths of sophistry, and through masses of immaterial facts, go straight to the true point. Of his intel-

---

* The Acts of the Witnesses of the Spirit, part v. chapter v. In this work Lodowick, after his fashion, revenges himself on the "bawling devil," as he calls Jeffreys, by a string of curses which Ernulphus, or Jeffreys himself, might have envied. The trial was in January 1677.

† This saying is to be found in many contemporary pamphlets. Titus Oates was never tired of quoting it. See his Εἰκὼν Βασιλική.

lect, however, he seldom had the full use. Even in civil causes his malevolent and despotic temper perpetually disordered his judgment. To enter his court was to enter the den of a wild beast, which none could tame, and which was as likely to be roused to rage by caresses as by attacks. He frequently poured forth on plaintiffs and defendants, barristers and attorneys, witnesses and jurymen, torrents of frantic abuse, intermixed with oaths and curses. His looks and tones had inspired terror when he was merely a young advocate struggling into practice. Now that he was at the head of the most formidable tribunal in the realm, there were few indeed who did not tremble before him. Even when he was sober, his violence was sufficiently frightful. But in general his reason was overclouded and his evil passions stimulated by the fumes of intoxication. His evenings were ordinarily given to revelry. People who saw him only over his bottle would have supposed him to be a man gross indeed, sottish, and addicted to low company and low merriment, but social and goodhumoured. He was constantly surrounded on such occasions by buffoons selected, for the most part, from among the vilest pettifoggers who practised before him. These men bantered and abused each other for his entertainment. He joined in their ribald talk, sang catches with them, and, when his head grew hot, hugged and kissed them in an ecstasy of drunken fondness. But though wine at first seemed to soften his heart, the effect a few hours later was very different. He often came to the judgment seat, having kept the court waiting long, and yet having but half slept off his debauch, his cheeks on fire, his eyes staring like those of a maniac. When he was in this state, his boon companions of the preceding night, if they were wise, kept out of his way : for the recollection of the familiarity to which he had admitted them inflamed his malignity ; and he was sure to take every opportunity of overwhelming them with execration and invective. Not the least odious of his many odious peculiarities was the pleasure which he took in publicly browbeating and mortifying those whom, in his fits of maudlin tenderness, he had encouraged to presume on his favour.

The services which the government had expected from him were performed, not merely without flinching, but eagerly and triumphantly. His first exploit was the judicial murder of Algernon Sidney. What followed was in perfect harmony with this beginning. Respectable Tories lamented the disgrace which the barbarity and indecency of so great a functionary brought upon the administration of justice. But the excesses which filled such men with horror were titles to the esteem of James. Jeffreys, therefore, very soon after the death of Charles, obtained a seat in the cabinet and a peerage. This last honour was a signal mark of royal approbation. For, since the judicial system of the realm had been remodelled in the thirteenth century, no Chief Justice had been a Lord of Parliament.*

Guildford now found himself superseded in all his political functions, and restricted to his business as a judge in equity. At Council he was treated by Jeffreys with marked incivility. The whole legal patronage was in the hands of the Chief Justice ; and it was well known by the bar that the surest way to propitiate the Chief Justice was to treat the Lord Keeper with disrespect.

The revenue collected without an Act of Parliament.

James had not been many hours King when a dispute arose between the two heads of the law. The customs had been settled on Charles for life only, and could not therefore be legally exacted by the new sovereign. Some weeks must elapse before a House of Commons could be chosen. If, in the meantime, the duties were suspended, the revenue would suffer ; the regular course of trade would be interrupted ; the consumer would derive no benefit ; and the only gainers would be those fortunate speculators whose cargoes might happen to arrive during the interval between the demise of the crown and the meeting of the Parliament. The Treasury was besieged by merchants whose warehouses were filled with goods on which duty had been paid, and who were in grievous apprehension of being undersold and ruined. Impartial men must admit that this was one of those cases in which a government may be justified in deviating from the strictly constitutional course. But when it is necessary to deviate from the strictly constitutional course, the deviation clearly ought to be no greater than the necessity requires. Guildford felt this, and gave advice which did him honour. He proposed that the duties should be levied, but should be kept in the

* The chief sources of information concerning Jeffreys are the State Trials and North's Life of Lord Guildford. Some touches of minor importance I owe to contemporary pamphlets in verse and prose. Such are the Bloody Assizes, the Life and Death of George Lord Jeffreys, the Panegyric on the late Lord Jeffreys, the Letter to the Lord Chancellor, Jeffreys's Elegy. See also Evelyn's Diary, Dec. 5. 1683, Oct. 31. 1685. I scarcely need advise every reader to consult Lord Campbell's excellent Life of Jeffreys.

Exchequer apart from other sums till the Parliament should meet. In this way the King, while violating the letter of the laws, would show that he wished to conform to their spirit. Jeffreys gave very different counsel. He advised James to put forth an edict declaring it to be His Majesty's will and pleasure that the customs should continue to be paid. This advice was well suited to the King's temper. The judicious proposition of the Lord Keeper was rejected as worthy only of a Whig, or of what was still worse, a Trimmer. A proclamation, such as the Chief Justice had suggested, appeared. Some people expected that a violent outbreak of public indignation would be the consequence: but they were deceived. The spirit of opposition had not yet revived; and the court might safely venture to take steps which, five years before, would have produced a rebellion. In the City of London, lately so turbulent, scarcely a murmur was heard.*

The proclamation, which announced that the customs would still be levied, announced also that a Parliament would shortly meet. It was not without many misgivings that James had determined to call the Estates of his realm together. The moment was, indeed, most auspicious for a general election. Never since the accession of the House of Stuart had the constituent bodies been so favourably disposed towards the Court. But the new sovereign's mind was haunted by an apprehension not to be mentioned, even at this distance of time, without shame and indignation. He was afraid that by summoning his Parliament he might incur the displeasure of the King of France. *A Parliament called.*

To the King of France it mattered little which of the two English factions triumphed at the elections: for all the Parliaments which had met since the Restoration, whatever might have been their temper as to domestic politics, had been jealous of the growing power of the House of Bourbon. On this subject there was little difference between the Whigs and the sturdy country gentlemen who formed the main strength of the Tory party. Lewis had therefore spared neither bribes nor menaces to prevent Charles from convoking the Houses; and James, who had from the first been in the secret of his brother's foreign politics, had, in becoming King of England, become also a hireling and vassal of France. *Transactions between James and the French King.*

Rochester, Godolphin, and Sunderland, who now formed

* London Gazette, Feb. 12. 168⅘. North's Life of Guildford, 254.

the interior cabinet, were perfectly aware that their late master had been in the habit of receiving money from the court of Versailles. They were consulted by James as to the expediency of convoking the legislature. They acknowledged the importance of keeping Lewis in good humour: but it seemed to them that the calling of a Parliament was not a matter of choice. Patient as the nation appeared to be, there were limits to its patience. The principle, that the money of the subject could not be lawfully taken by the King without the assent of the Commons, was firmly rooted in the public mind; and though, on an extraordinary emergency, even Whigs might be willing to pay, during a few weeks, duties not imposed by statute, it was certain that even Tories would become refractory if such irregular taxation should continue longer than the special circumstances which alone justified it. The Houses then must meet; and, since it was so, the sooner they were summoned the better. Even the short delay which would be occasioned by a reference to Versailles might produce irreparable mischief. Discontent and suspicion would spread fast through society. Halifax would complain that the fundamental principles of the constitution were violated. The Lord Keeper, like a cowardly pedantic special pleader as he was, would take the same side. What might have been done with a good grace would at last be done with a bad grace. Those very ministers whom His Majesty most wished to lower in the public estimation would gain popularity at his expense. The ill temper of the nation might seriously affect the result of the elections. These arguments were unanswerable. The King therefore notified to the country nis intention of holding a Parliament. But he was painfully anxious to exculpate himself from the guilt of having acted undutifully and disrespectfully towards France. He led Barillon into a private room, and there apologised for having dared to take so important a step without the previous sanction of Lewis. "Assure your master," said James, " of my gratitude and attachment. I know that without his protection I can do nothing. I know what troubles my brother brought on himself by not adhering steadily to France. I will take good care not to let the Houses meddle with foreign affairs. If I see in them any disposition to make mischief, I will send them about their business. Explain this to my good brother. I hope that he will not take it amiss that I have acted without consulting him. He has a right to be consulted; and it is my wish to consult him about everything. But in this case the delay even of a week might have produced serious consequences."

These ignominious excuses were, on the following morning, repeated by Rochester. Barillon received them civilly. Rochester, grown bolder, proceeded to ask for money. "It will be well laid out," he said : "your master cannot employ his revenues better. Represent to him strongly how important it is that the King of England should be dependent, not on his own people, but on the friendship of France alone."*

Barillon hastened to communicate to Lewis the wishes of the English government; but Lewis had already anticipated them. His first act, after he was apprised of the death of Charles, was to collect bills of exchange on England to the amount of five hundred thousand livres, a sum equivalent to about thirty-seven thousand five hundred pounds sterling. Such bills were not then to be easily procured in Paris at a day's notice. In a few hours, however, the purchase was effected, and a courier started for London.† As soon as Barillon received the remittance, he flew to Whitehall, and communicated the welcome news. James was not ashamed to shed, or pretend to shed, tears of delight and gratitude. "Nobody but your King," he said, "does such kind, such noble things. I never can be grateful enough. Assure him that my attachment will last to the end of my days." Rochester, Sunderland, and Godolphin came, one after another, to embrace the ambassador, and to whisper to him that he had given new life to their royal master.‡

But though James and his three advisers were pleased with the promptitude which Lewis had shown, they were by no means satisfied with the amount of the donation. As they were afraid, however, that they might give offence by importunate mendicancy, they merely hinted their wishes. They declared that they had no intention of haggling with so generous a benefactor as the French King, and that they were willing to trust entirely to his munificence. They, at the same time, attempted to propitiate him by a large sacri-

---

* The chief authority for these transactions is Barillon's despatch of February ⁹⁄₁₃. 1685. It will be found in the Appendix to Mr. Fox's History. See also Preston's letter to James, dated April ¹³⁄₂₃. 1685, in Dalrymple.

† Lewis to Barillon, Feb. ¹⁶⁄₂₆. 1685.

‡ Barillon, Feb, ¹⁶⁄₂₆. 1685.

fice of national honour. It was well known that one chief end of his politics was to add the Belgian provinces to his dominions. England was bound by a treaty which had been concluded with Spain when Danby was Lord Treasurer, to resist any attempt which France might make on those provinces. The three ministers informed Barillon that their master considered that treaty as no longer obligatory. It had been made, they said, by Charles: it might, perhaps, have been binding on him; but his brother did not think himself bound by it. The most Christian King might, therefore, without any fear of opposition from England, proceed to annex Brabant and Hainault to his empire.*

Churchill sent ambassador to France.

It was at the same time resolved that an extraordinary embassy should be sent to assure Lewis of the gratitude and affection of James. For this mission was selected a man who did not as yet occupy a very eminent position, but whose renown, strangely made up of infamy and glory, filled at a later period the whole civilised world.

His history.

Soon after the Restoration, in the gay and dissolute times which have been celebrated by the lively pen of Hamilton, James, young and ardent in the pursuit of pleasure, had been attracted by Arabella Churchill, one of the maids of honour who waited on his first wife. The young lady was plain: but the taste of James was not nice: and she became his avowed mistress. She was the daughter of a poor Cavalier knight who haunted Whitehall, and made himself ridiculous by publishing a dull and affected folio, long forgotten, in praise of monarchy and monarchs. The necessities of the Churchills were pressing: their loyalty was ardent; and their only feeling about Arabella's seduction seems to have been joyful surprise that so homely a girl should have attained such high preferment.

Her interest was indeed of great use to her relations: but none of them was so fortunate as her eldest brother John, a fine youth, who carried a pair of colours in the foot guards. He rose fast in the court and in the army, and was early distinguished as a man of fashion and of pleasure. His stature was commanding, his face handsome, his address singularly winning, yet of such dignity that the most impertinent fops never ventured to take any liberty with him; his temper, even in the most vexatious and irritating circumstances, always under perfect command. His education had been so

* Barillon, Feb. $\frac{18}{28}$. 1685.

much neglected that he could not spell the most common words of his own language: but his acute and vigorous understanding amply supplied the place of book learning. He was not talkative: but, when he was forced to speak in public, his natural eloquence moved the envy of practised rhetoricians.* His courage was singularly cool and imperturbable. During many years of anxiety and peril, he never, in any emergency, lost, even for a moment, the perfect use of his admirable judgment.

In his twenty-third year he was sent with his regiment to join the French forces, then engaged in operations against Holland. His serene intrepidity distinguished him among thousands of brave soldiers. His professional skill commanded the respect of veteran officers. He was publicly thanked at the head of the army, and received many marks of esteem and confidence from Turenne, who was then at the height of military glory.

Unhappily the splendid qualities of John Churchill were mingled with alloy of the most sordid kind. Some propensities, which in youth are singularly ungraceful, began very early to show themselves in him. He was thrifty in his very vices, and levied ample contributions on ladies enriched by the spoils of more liberal lovers. He was, during a short time, the object of the violent but fickle fondness of the Duchess of Cleveland. On one occasion he was caught with her by the King, and was forced to leap out of the window. She rewarded this hazardous feat of gallantry with a present of five thousand pounds. With this sum the prudent young hero instantly bought an annuity of five hundred a year, well secured on landed property.† Already his private drawer contained a hoard of broad pieces which, fifty years later, when he was a Duke, a Prince of the Empire, and the richest subject in Europe, remained untouched.‡

After the close of the war he was attached to the household of the Duke of York, accompanied his patron to the Low Countries and to Edinburgh, and was rewarded for his

---

* Swift who hated Marlborough, and who was little disposed to allow any merit to those whom he hated, says, in the famous letter to Crassus, " You are no ill orator in the Senate."

† Dartmouth's note on Burnet, i. 264. Chesterfield's Letters, Nov. 18. 1748. Chesterfield is an unexceptionable witness; for the annuity was a charge on the estate of his grandfather, Halifax. I believe that there is no foundation for a disgraceful addition to the story which may be found in Pope:

" The gallant, too, to whom she paid it down,
Lived to refuse his mistress half a crown."

Curll calls this a piece of travelling scandal.

‡ Pope in Spence's Anecdotes.

services with a Scotch peerage and with the command of the only regiment of dragoons which was then on the English establishment.* His wife had a post in the family of James's younger daughter, the Princess of Denmark.

Lord Churchill was now sent as ambassador extraordinary to Versailles. He had it in charge to express the warm gratitude of the English government for the money which had been so generously bestowed. It had been originally intended that he should, at the same time, ask Lewis for a much larger sum; but, on full consideration, it was apprehended that such indelicate greediness might disgust the benefactor whose spontaneous liberality had been so signally displayed. Churchill was therefore directed to confine himself to thanks for what was past, and to say nothing about the future.†

But James and his ministers, even while protesting that they did not mean to be importunate, contrived to hint, very intelligibly, what they wished and expected. In the French ambassador they had a dexterous, a zealous, and, perhaps, not a disinterested intercessor. Lewis made some difficulties, probably with the design of enhancing the value of his gifts. In a very few weeks, however, Barillon received from Versailles fifteen hundred thousand livres more. This sum, equivalent to about a hundred and twelve thousand pounds sterling, he was instructed to dole out cautiously. He was authorised to furnish the English government with thirty thousand pounds, for the purpose of corrupting members of the New House of Commons. The rest he was directed to keep in reserve for some extraordinary emergency, such as a dissolution or an insurrection.‡

The turpitude of these transactions is universally acknowledged: but their real nature seems to be often misunderstood: for though the foreign policy of the last two Kings of the House of Stuart has never, since the correspondence of Barillon was exposed to the public eye, found an apologist among us, there is still a party which labours to excuse their domestic policy. Yet it is certain that between their domestic

---

* See the Historical Records of the First or Royal Dragoons. The appointment of Churchill to the command of this regiment was ridiculed as an instance of absurd partiality. One lampoon of that time, which I do not remember to have seen in print, but of which a manuscript copy is in the British Museum, contains these lines:

"Let's cut our meat with spoons:
	The sense is as good
	As that Churchill should
Be put to command the dragoons."

† Barillon, Feb. $\frac{16}{26}$. 1685.
‡ Barillon, April $\frac{6}{16}$.; Lewis to Barillon, April $\frac{14}{24}$.

policy and their foreign policy there was a necessary and indissoluble connection. If they had upheld, during a single year, the honour of the country abroad, they would have been compelled to change the whole system of their administration at home. To praise them for refusing to govern in conformity with the sense of Parliament, and yet to blame them for submitting to the dictation of Lewis, is inconsistent. For they had only one choice, to be dependent on Lewis, or to be dependent on Parliament.

James, to do him justice, would gladly have found out a third way : but there was none. He became the slave of France : but it would be incorrect to represent him as a contented slave. He had spirit enough to be at times angry with himself for submitting to such thraldom, and impatient to break loose from it; and this disposition was studiously encouraged by the agents of many foreign powers.

His accession had excited hopes and fears in every Continental court : and the commencement of his administration was watched by strangers with interest scarcely less deep than that which was felt by his own subjects. One government alone wished that the troubles which had, during three generations, distracted England, might be eternal. All other governments, whether republican or monarchical, whether Protestant or Roman Catholic, wished to see those troubles happily terminated.

Feelings of the Continental governments towards England.

The nature of the long contest between the Stuarts and their Parliaments was indeed very imperfectly apprehended by foreign statesmen : but no statesman could fail to perceive the effect which that contest had produced on the balance of power in Europe. In ordinary circumstances, the sympathies of the courts of Vienna and Madrid would doubtless have been with a prince struggling against subjects, and especially with a Roman Catholic prince struggling against heretical subjects : but all such sympathies were now overpowered by a stronger feeling. The fear and hatred inspired by the greatness, the injustice, and the arrogance of the French King were at the height. His neighbours might well doubt whether it were more dangerous to be at war or at peace with him. For in peace he continued to plunder and to outrage them ; and they had tried the chances of war against him in vain. In this perplexity they looked with intense anxiety towards England. Would she act on the principles of the Triple Alliance or on the principles of the treaty of Dover? On that issue depended the fate of all her neighbours. With her help Lewis might yet be withstood: but no help could be expected from her till she was at unity with herself. Before the strife between the throne and the Parliament began, she had been a power of the first rank: on the day on which that strife terminated she became a power of the first rank again: but while the dispute remained undecided, she was condemned to inaction and to vassalage. She had been great under the Plantagenets and Tudors: she was again great under the princes who reigned after the Revolution: but, under the Kings of the House of Stuart, she was a blank in the map of Europe. She had lost one class of energies, and had not yet acquired another. That species of force, which, in the fourteenth century, had enabled her to humble France and Spain, had ceased to exist. That species of force, which, in the eighteenth century, humbled France and Spain once more, had not yet been called into action. The government was no longer a limited monarchy after the fashion of the middle ages. It had not yet become a limited monarchy after the modern fashion. With the vices of two different systems it had the strength of neither. The elements of our polity, instead of combining in harmony, counteracted and neutralised each other. All was transition, conflict, and disorder. The chief business of the sovereign was to infringe the privileges of the legislature. The chief business of the legislature was to encroach on the prerogatives of the sovereign. The King readily accepted foreign aid, which relieved him from the misery of being dependent on a mutinous Parliament. The Parliament refused to the King the means of supporting the national honour abroad, from an apprehension, too well founded, that those means might be employed in order to establish despotism at home. The effect of these jealousies was that our country, with all her vast resources, was of as little weight in Christendom as the duchy of Savoy or the duchy of Lorraine, and certainly of far less weight than the small province of Holland.

France was deeply interested in prolonging this state of things.* All other powers were deeply interested in bringing

---

* I might transcribe half Barillon's correspondence in proof of this proposition: but I will quote only one passage, in which the policy of the French government towards England is exhibited concisely and with perfect clearness.

"On peut tenir pour un maxime indubitable que l'accord du Roy d'Angleterre avec son parlement, en quelque manière qu'il se fasse, n'est pas conforme aux intérêts de V. M. Je me contente de penser cela sans m'en ouvrir it to a close. The general wish of Europe was that James would govern in conformity with law and with public opinion. From the Escurial itself came letters, expressing an earnest hope that the new King of England would be on good terms with his Parliament and his people.* From the Vatican itself came cautions against immoderate zeal for the Roman Catholic faith. Benedict Odescalchi, who filled the papal chair under the name of Innocent the Eleventh, felt, in his character of temporal sovereign, all those apprehensions with which other princes watched the progress of the French power. He had also grounds of uneasiness which were peculiar to himself. It was a happy circumstance for the Protestant religion that, at the moment when the last Roman Catholic King of England mounted the throne, the Roman Catholic Church was torn by dissension, and threatened with a new schism. A quarrel similar to that which had raged in the eleventh century between the Emperors and the Supreme Pontiffs had arisen between Lewis and Innocent. Lewis, zealous even to bigotry for the doctrines of the Church of Rome, but tenacious of his regal authority, accused the Pope of encroaching on the secular rights of the French Crown, and was in turn accused by the Pope of encroaching on the spiritual power of the keys. The King, haughty as he was, encountered a spirit even more determined than his own. Innocent was, in all private relations, the meekest and gentlest of men: but, when he spoke officially from the chair of St. Peter, he spoke in the tones of Gregory the Seventh and of Sixtus the Fifth. The dispute became serious. Agents of the King were excommunicated. Adherents of the Pope were banished. The King made the champions of his authority Bishops. The Pope refused them institution. They took possession of the episcopal palaces and revenues : but they were incompetent to perform the episcopal functions. Before

Policy of the court of Rome.

a personne, et je cache avec soin mes sentimens à cet égard."— Barillon to Lewis, $\frac{Feb. 28.}{Mar. 10.}$ 1687. That this was the real secret of the whole policy of Lewis towards our country was perfectly understood at Vienna. The Emperor Leopold wrote thus to James, $\frac{March 30.}{April 9.}$ 1689 : " Galli id unum agebant, ut, perpetuas inter Serenitatem vestram et ejusdem populos fovendo simultates, reliquæ Christianæ Europæ tanto securius insultarent."

* " Que sea unido con su reyno, y en todo buena intelligencia con el parlamento."— Despatch from the King of Spain to Don Pedro Ronquillo, March $\frac{18}{28}$. 1685. This despatch is in the archives of Samancas, which contain a great mass of papers relating to English affairs. Copies of the most interesting of those papers are in the possession of M. Guizot, and were by him lent to me. It is with peculiar pleasure that, at this time, i acknowledge this mark of the friendship of so great a man. (1848.)

the struggle terminated, there were in France thirty prelates who could not confirm or ordain.*

Had any prince then living, except Lewis, been engaged in such a dispute with the Vatican, he would have had all Protestant governments on his side. But the fear and resentment which the ambition and insolence of the French King had inspired were such that whoever had the courage manfully to oppose him was sure of public sympathy. Even Lutherans and Calvinists, who had always detested the Pope, could not refrain from wishing him success against a tyrant who aimed at universal monarchy. It was thus that, in the present century, many who regarded Pius the Seventh as Antichrist were well pleased to see Antichrist confront the gigantic power of Napoleon.

The resentment which Innocent felt towards France disposed him to take a mild and liberal view of the affairs of England. The return of the English people to the fold of which he was the shepherd would undoubtedly have rejoiced his soul. But he was too wise a man to believe that a nation, so bold and stubborn, could be brought back to the Church of Rome by the violent and unconstitutional exercise of royal authority. It was not difficult to foresee that, if James attempted to promote the interests of his religion by illegal and unpopular means, the attempt would fail; the hatred with which the heretical islanders regarded the true faith would become fiercer and stronger than ever; and an indissoluble association would be created in their minds between Protestantism and civil freedom, between Popery and arbitrary power. In the meantime the King would be an object of aversion and suspicion to his people. England would still be, as she had been under James the First, under Charles the First, and under Charles the Second, a power of the third rank; and France would domineer unchecked beyond the Alps and the Rhine. On the other hand, it was probable that James, by acting with prudence and moderation, by strictly observing the laws, and by exerting himself to win the confidence of his Parliament, might be able to obtain, for the professors of his religion, a large measure of relief. Penal statutes would go first. Statutes imposing civil incapacities would soon follow. In the meantime, the English

* Few English readers will be desirous to go deep into the history of this quarrel. Summaries will be found in Cardinal Bausset's Life of Bossuet, and in Voltaire's Age of Lewis XIV.

King and the English nation united might head the European coalition, and might oppose an insuperable barrier to the cupidity of Lewis.

Innocent was confirmed in his judgment by the principal Englishmen who resided at his court. Of these the most illustrious was Philip Howard, sprung from the noblest houses of Britain, grandson, on one side, of an Earl of Arundel, on the other, of a Duke of Lennox. Philip had long been a member of the sacred college : he was commonly designated as the Cardinal of England ; and he was the chief counsellor of the Holy See in matters relating to his country. He had been driven into exile by the outcry of Protestant bigots ; and a member of his family, the unfortunate Stafford, had fallen a victim to their rage. But neither the Cardinal's own wrongs, nor those of his house, had so heated his mind as to make him a rash adviser. Every letter, therefore, which went from the Vatican to Whitehall, recommended patience, moderation, and respect for the prejudices of the English people.*

In the mind of James there was a great conflict. We should do him injustice if we supposed that a state of vassalage was agreeable to his temper. He loved authority and business. He had a high sense of his own personal dignity. Nay, he was not altogether destitute of a sentiment which bore some affinity to patriotism. It galled his soul to think that the kingdom which he ruled was of far less account in the world than many states which possessed smaller natural advantages ; and he listened eagerly to foreign ministers when they urged him to assert the dignity of his rank, to place himself at the head of a great confederacy, to become the protector of injured nations, and to tame the pride of that power which held the Continent in awe. Such exhortations made his heart swell with emotions unknown to his careless and effeminate brother. But those emotions were soon subdued by a stronger feeling. A vigorous foreign policy necessarily implied a conciliatory domestic policy. It was impossible at once to confront the might of France and to trample on the liberties of England. The executive government could undertake nothing great without the support of the Commons, and could obtain their support only by acting in conformity with their opinion. Thus James found that the two things which he most desired could not be enjoyed

Struggle in the mind of James.

Fluctuations of his policy.

* Burnet, i. 661., and Letter from Rome ; Dodd's Church History, part viii. book i. art. 1.

together. His second wish was to be feared and respected abroad. But his first wish was to be absolute master at home. Between the incompatible objects on which his heart was set, he, for a time, went irresolutely to and fro. The conflict in his own breast gave to his public acts a strange appearance of indecision and insincerity. Those who, without the clue, attempted to explore the maze of his politics were unable to understand how the same man could be, in the same week, so haughty and so mean. Even Lewis was perplexed by the vagaries of an ally who passed, in a few hours, from homage to defiance, and from defiance to homage. Yet, now that the whole conduct of James is before us, this inconsistency seems to admit of a simple explanation.

At the moment of his accession he was in doubt whether the kingdom would peaceably submit to his authority. The Exclusionists, lately so powerful, might rise in arms against him. He might be in great need of French money and French troops. He was therefore, during some days, content to be a sycophant and a mendicant. He humbly apologised for daring to call his Parliament together without the consent of the French government. He begged hard for a French subsidy. He wept with joy over the French bills of exchange. He sent to Versailles a special embassy charged with assurances of his gratitude, attachment, and submission. But scarcely had the embassy departed when his feelings underwent a change. He had been everywhere proclaimed without one riot, without one seditious outcry. From all corners of the island he received intelligence that his subjects were tranquil and obedient. His spirit rose. The degrading relation in which he stood to a foreign power seemed intolerable. He became proud, punctilious, boastful, quarrelsome. He held such high language about the dignity of his crown and the balance of power that his whole court fully expected a complete revolution in the foreign politics of the realm. He commanded Churchill to send home a minute report of the ceremonial of Versailles, in order that the honours with which the English embassy was received there might be repaid, and not more than repaid, to the representative of France at Whitehall. The news of this change was received with delight at Madrid, Vienna, and the Hague.* Lewis was at first merely diverted. " My good ally talks big," he said ; " but

* Consultations of the Spanish Council of State on April $\frac{2}{12}$. and April $\frac{16}{26}$. 1685, in the archives of Simancas.

he is as fond of my pistoles as ever his brother was." Soon, however, the altered demeanour of James, and the hopes with which that demeanour inspired both the branches of the House of Austria, began to call for more serious notice. A remarkable letter is still extant, in which the French King intimated a strong suspicion that he had been duped, and that the very money which he had sent to Westminster would be employed against him.*

By this time England had recovered from the sadness and anxiety caused by the death of the goodnatured Charles. The Tories were loud in professions of attachment to their new master. The hatred of the Whigs was kept down by fear. That great mass which is not steadily Whig or Tory, but which inclines alternately to Whiggism and to Toryism, was still on the Tory side. The reaction which had followed the dissolution of the Oxford parliament had not yet spent its force.

The King early put the loyalty of his Protestant friends to the proof. While he was a subject, he had been in the habit of hearing mass with closed doors in a small oratory which had been fitted up for his wife. He now ordered the doors to be thrown open, in order that all who came to pay their duty to him might see the ceremony. When the host was elevated there was a strange confusion in the antechamber. The Roman Catholics fell on their knees: the Protestants hurried out of the room. Soon a new pulpit was erected in the palace; and, during Lent, a series of sermons was preached there by Popish divines, to the great discomposure of zealous churchmen.† *Public celebration of the Roman Catholic rites in the palace.*

A more serious innovation followed. Passion week came; and the King determined to hear mass with the same pomp with which his predecessors had been surrounded when they repaired to the temples of the established religion. He announced his intention to the three members of the interior cabinet, and requested them to attend him. Sunderland, to whom all religions were the same, readily consented. Godolphin, as Chamberlain of the Queen, had already been in the habit of giving her his hand when she repaired to her oratory, and felt no scruple about bowing himself officially in the house of Rimmon. But Rochester was greatly disturbed. His influence in the country arose chiefly from the opinion

---

* Lewis to Barillon, $\frac{\text{May 22.}}{\text{June 1.}}$ 1685 ; Barillon, $\frac{\text{Feb. 19.}}{\text{Mar. 1.}}$ 1685 ; Evelyn's Diary,
Burnet, i. 623.   March 5, 168$\frac{4}{5}$
  † Life of James the Second, i. 5.

entertained by the clergy and by the Tory gentry, that he was a zealous and uncompromising friend of the Church. His orthodoxy had been considered as fully atoning for faults which would otherwise have made him the most unpopular man in the kingdom, for boundless arrogance, for extreme violence of temper, and for manners almost brutal.* He feared that, by complying with the royal wishes, he should greatly lower himself in the estimation of his party. After some altercation he obtained permission to pass the holidays out of town. All the other great civil dignitaries were ordered to be at their posts on Easter Sunday. The rites of the Church of Rome were once more, after an interval of a hundred and twenty seven years, performed at Westminster with regal splendour. The Guards were drawn out. The Knights of the Garter wore their collars. The Duke of Somerset, second in rank among the temporal nobles of the realm, carried the sword of state. A long train of great lords accompanied the King to his seat. But it was remarked that Ormond and Halifax remained in the antechamber. A few years before they had gallantly defended the cause of James against some of those who now pressed past them. Ormond had borne no share in the slaughter of Roman Catholics. Halifax had courageously pronounced Stafford not guilty. As the timeservers who had pretended to shudder at the thought of a Popish king, and who had shed without pity the innocent blood of a Popish peer, now elbowed each other to get near a Popish altar, the accomplished Trimmer might, with some justice, indulge his solitary pride in that unpopular nickname.*

His coronation. Within a week after this ceremony James made a far greater sacrifice of his own religious prejudices than he had yet called on any of his Protestant subjects to make. He was crowned on the twenty-third of April, the feast of the patron saint of the realm. The Abbey and the Hall were splendidly decorated. The presence of the Queen and of the peeresses gave to the solemnity a charm which had been wanting to the magnificent inauguration of the late King. Yet those who remembered that inauguration pronounced that there was a great falling off. The ancient usage was that, before a coronation, the sovereign, with all his heralds, judges, councillors, lords, and great dignitaries, should ride in state from the

---

*   " To those that ask boons
           He swears by God's oons,
And chides them as if they came there to steal spoons."
                    Lamentable Lory, a ballad, 1684.

† Barillon, April $\frac{20}{30}$. 1685.

Tower to Westminster. Of these cavalcades the last and the most glorious was that which passed through the capital while the feelings excited by the Restoration were still in full vigour. Arches of triumph overhung the road. All Cornhill, Cheapside, Saint Paul's Church Yard, Fleet Street, and the Strand, were lined with scaffolding. The whole city had thus been admitted to gaze on royalty in the most splendid and solemn form that royalty could wear. James ordered an estimate to be made of the cost of such a procession, and found that it would amount to about half as much as he proposed to expend in covering his wife with trinkets. He accordingly determined to be profuse where he ought to have been frugal, and niggardly where he might pardonably have been profuse. More than a hundred thousand pounds were laid out in dressing the Queen, and the procession from the Tower was omitted. The folly of this course is obvious. If pageantry be of any use in politics, it is of use as a means of striking the imagination of the multitude. It is surely the height of absurdity to shut out the populace from a show of which the main object is to make an impression on the populace. James would have shown a more judicious munificence and a more judicious parsimony, if he had traversed London from east to west with the accustomed pomp, and had ordered the robes of his wife to be somewhat less thickly set with pearls and diamonds. His example was, however, long followed by his successors; and sums, which, well employed, would have afforded exquisite gratification to a large part of the nation, were squandered on an exhibition to which only three or four thousand privileged persons were admitted. At length the old practice was partially revived. On the day of the coronation of Queen Victoria there was a procession in which many deficiencies might be noted, but which was seen with interest and delight by half a million of her subjects, and which undoubtedly gave far greater pleasure, and called forth far greater enthusiasm, than the more costly display which was witnessed by a select circle within the Abbey.

James had ordered Sancroft to abridge the ritual. The reason publicly assigned was that the day was too short for all that was to be done. But whoever examines the changes which were made will see that the real object was to remove some things highly offensive to the religious feelings of a zealous Roman Catholic. The Communion Service was not read. The ceremony of presenting the sovereign with a richly bound copy of the English Bible, and of exhorting him to prize above all earthly treasures a volume which he had been taught to regard as adulterated with false doctrine, was omitted. What remained, however, after all this curtailment, might well have raised scruples in the mind of a man who sincerely believed the Church of England to be a heretical society, within the pale of which salvation was not to be found. The King made an oblation on the altar. He appeared to join in the petitions of the Litany which was chaunted by the Bishops. He received from those false prophets the unction typical of a divine influence, and knelt with the semblance of devotion, while they called down upon him that Holy Spirit of which they were, in his estimation, the malignant and obdurate foes. Such are the inconsistencies of human nature that this man, who, from a fanatical zeal for his religion, threw away three kingdoms, yet chose to commit what was little short of an act of apostasy, rather than forego the childish pleasure of being invested with the gewgaws symbolical of kingly power.*

Francis Turner, Bishop of Ely, preached. He was one of those writers who still affected the obsolete style of Archbishop Williams and Bishop Andrews. The sermon was made up of quaint conceits, such as seventy years earlier might have been admired, but such as moved the scorn of a generation accustomed to the purer eloquence of Sprat, of South, and of Tillotson. King Solomon was King James. Adonijah was Monmouth. Joab was a Rye House conspirator; Shimei, a Whig libeller; Abiathar, an honest but misguided old Cavalier. One phrase in the Book of Chronicles was construed to mean that the King was above the Parliament; and another was cited to prove that he alone ought to command the militia. Towards the close of the discourse the orator very timidly alluded to the new and embarrassing position in which the Church stood with reference to the sovereign, and reminded his hearers that the Emperor Constantius Chlorus, though not himself a Christian, had held in honour those Christians who remained true to their religion, and had treated with scorn those who sought to earn his favour by apostasy. The service in the Abbey was followed by a stately

---

* From Adda's despatch of $\frac{\text{Jan. 22.}}{\text{Feb. 1.}}$ 1686, and from the expressions of the Père d'Orléans (Histoire des Révolutions d'Angleterre, liv. xi.), it is clear that rigid Catholics thought the King's conduct indefensible.

banquet in the Hall, the banquet by brilliant fireworks, and the fireworks by much bad poetry.*

This may be fixed upon as the moment at which the enthu-siasm of the Tory party reached the zenith. Ever since the accession of the new King, addresses had been pouring in which expressed profound veneration for his person and office, and bitter detestation of the vanquished Whigs. The magis-trates of Middlesex thanked God for having confounded the designs of those regicides and exclusionists who, not content with having murdered one blessed monarch, were bent on destroying the foundations of monarchy. The city of Glou-cester execrated the bloodthirsty villains who had tried to deprive His Majesty of his just inheritance. The burgesses of Wigan assured their sovereign that they would defend him against all plotting Achitophels and rebellious Absaloms. The grand jury of Suffolk expressed a hope that the Parliament would proscribe all the exclusionists. Many corporations pledged themselves never to return to the House of Commons any person who had voted for taking away the birthright of James. Even the capital was profoundly obsequious. The lawyers and the traders vied with each other in servility. Inns of Court and Inns of Chancery sent up fervent profes-sions of attachment and submission. All the great commercial societies, the East India Company, the African Company, the Turkey Company, the Muscovy Company, the Hudson's Bay Company, the Maryland Merchants, the Jamaica Merchants, the Merchant Adventurers, declared that they most cheerfully complied with the royal edict which required them still to pay custom. Bristol, the second city of the island, echoed the voice of London. But nowhere was the spirit of loyalty stronger than in the two Universities. Oxford dec'ared that she would never swerve from those religious principles which bound her to obey the King without any restrictions or limit-ations. Cambridge condemned, in severe terms, the violence and treachery of those turbulent men who had maliciously

Enthusi-asm of the Tories.
Addresses.

---

* London Gazette; Gazette de France; Life of James the Second, ii. 10.; His-tory of the Coronation of King James the Second and Queen Mary, by Francis Sandford, Lancaster Herald, fol. 1687; Evelyn's Diary, May 21. 1685; Despatch of the Dutch Ambassadors, April $\frac{10}{20}$. 1685; Burnet, i. 628.; Eachard, iii. 734.; A sermon preached before their Majes-ties King James the Second and Queen Mary at their Coronation in Westminster Abbey, April 23. 1685, by Francis, Lord Bishop of Ely, and Lord Almoner. I have seen an Italian account of the Co-ronation which was published at Modena, and which is chiefly remarkable for the skill with which the writer sinks the fact that the prayers and psalms were in English, and that the Bishops were here-tics.

endeavoured to turn the stream of succession out of the ancient channel.*

Such addresses as these filled, during a considerable time, every number of the London Gazette. But it was not only by addressing that the Tories showed their zeal. The writs for the new Parliament had gone forth, and the country was agitated by the tumult of a general election. No election had ever taken place under circumstances so favourable to the Court. Hundreds of thousands whom the Popish plot had scared into Whiggism had been scared back by the Rye House plot into Toryism. In the counties the government could depend on an overwhelming majority of the gentlemen of three hundred a year and upwards, and on the clergy almost to a man. Those boroughs which had once been the citadels of Whiggism had recently been deprived of their charters by legal sentence, or had prevented the sentence by voluntary surrender. They had now been reconstituted in such a manner that they were certain to return members devoted to the crown. Where the townsmen could not be trusted, the freedom had been bestowed on the neighbouring squires. In some of the small western corporations, the constituent bodies were in great part composed of Captains and Lieutenants of the Guards. The returning officers were almost everywhere in the interest of the court. In every shire the Lord Lieutenant and his deputies formed a powerful, active, and vigilant committee, for the purpose of cajoling and intimidating the freeholders. The people were solemnly warned from thousands of pulpits not to vote for any Whig candidate, as they should answer it to Him who had ordained the powers that be, and who had pronounced rebellion a sin not less deadly than witchcraft. All these advantages the predominant party not only used to the utmost, but abused in so shameless a manner that grave and reflecting men, who had been true to the monarchy in peril, and who bore no love to republicans and schismatics, stood aghast, and augured from such beginnings the approach of evil times.†

Yet the Whigs, though suffering the just punishment of

---

* See the London Gazette during the months of February, March, and April, 1685.

† It would be easy to fill a volume with what Whig historians and pamphleteers have written on this subject. I will cite only one witness, a churchman and a Tory. "Elections," says Evelyn,

"were thought to be very indecently carried on in most places. God give a better issue of it than some expect!" May 10. 1685. Again he says, "The truth is there were many of the new members whose elections and returns were universally condemned." May 22.

their errors, though defeated, disheartened, and disorganised, did not yield without an effort. They were still numerous among the traders and artisans of the towns, and among the yeomanry and peasantry of the open country. In some districts, in Dorsetshire for example, and in Somersetshire, they were the great majority of the population. In the remodelled boroughs they could do nothing : but, in every county where they had a chance, they struggled desperately. In Bedfordshire, which had lately been represented by the virtuous and unfortunate Russell, they were victorious on the show of hands, but were beaten at the poll.* In Essex they polled thirteen hundred votes to eighteen hundred.† At the election for Northamptonshire the common people were so violent in their hostility to the court candidate that a body of troops was drawn out in the marketplace of the county town, and was ordered to load with ball.‡ The history of the contest for Buckinghamshire is still more remarkable. The Whig candidate, Thomas Wharton, eldest son of Philip Lord Wharton, was a man distinguished alike by dexterity and by audacity, and destined to play a conspicuous, though not always a respectable, part in the politics of several reigns. He had been one of those members of the House of Commons who had carried up the Exclusion Bill to the bar of the Lords. The court was therefore bent on throwing him out by fair or foul means. The Lord Chief Justice Jeffreys himself came down into Buckinghamshire, for the purpose of assisting a gentleman named Hacket, who stood on the high Tory interest. A stratagem was devised which, it was thought, could not fail of success. It was given out that the polling would take place at Ailesbury ; and Wharton, whose skill in all the arts of electioneering was unrivalled, made his arrangements on that supposition. At a moment's warning the Sheriff adjourned the poll to Newport Pagnell. Wharton and his friends hurried thither, and found that Hacket, who was in the secret, had already secured every inn and lodging. The Whig freeholders were compelled to tie their horses to the hedges, and to sleep under the open sky in the meadows which surround the little town. It was with the greatest difficulty that refreshments could be procured at

---

* This fact I learned from a newsletter in the library of the Royal Institution. Van Citters mentions the strength of the Whig party in Bedfordshire.

† Bramston's Memoirs.

‡ Reflections on a Remonstrance and Protestation of all the good Protestants of this Kingdom, 1689; Dialogue between Two Friends, 1689.

such short notice for so large a number of men and beasts,
though Wharton, who was utterly regardless of money when
his ambition and party spirit were roused, disbursed fifteen
hundred pounds in one day, an immense outlay for those
times. Injustice seems, however, to have animated the
courage of the stouthearted yeomen of Bucks, the sons of the
constituents of John Hampden. Not only was Wharton at
the head of the poll; but he was able to spare his second
votes to a man of moderate opinions, and to throw out the
Chief Justice's candidate.*

In Cheshire the contest lasted six days. The Whigs
polled about seventeen hundred votes, the Tories about two
thousand. The common people were vehement on the Whig
side, raised the cry of "Down with the Bishops," insulted
the clergy in the streets of Chester, knocked down one gentleman of the Tory party, broke the windows and beat the
constables. The militia was called out to quell the riot, and
was kept assembled, in order to protect the festivities of the
conquerors. When the poll closed, a salute of five great
guns from the castle proclaimed the triumph of the Church
and the Crown to the surrounding country. The bells rang.
The newly elected members went in state to the City Cross,
accompanied by a band of music, and by a long train of
knights and squires. The procession, as it marched, sang
"Joy to Great Cæsar," a loyal ode, which had lately been
written by Durfey, and which, though like all Durfey's
writings, utterly contemptible, was, at that time, almost as
popular as Lillibullero became a few years later.† Round the
Cross the trainbands were drawn up in order: a bonfire was
lighted: the Exclusion Bill was burned: and the health of
King James was drunk with loud acclamations. The following day was Sunday. In the morning the militia lined
the streets leading to the Cathedral. The two knights of the
shire were escorted with great pomp to their choir by the
magistracy of the city, heard the Dean preach a sermon, probably on the duty of passive obedience, and were afterwards
feasted by the Mayor.‡

In Northumberland the triumph of Sir John Fenwick, a
courtier whose name afterwards obtained a melancholy cele-

* Memoirs of the Life of Thomas
Marquess of Wharton, 1715.

† See the Guardian, No. 67.; an exquisite specimen of Addison's peculiar
manner. It would be difficult to find in

the works of any other writer such an
instance of benevolence delicately flavoured with contempt.

‡ The Observator, April 4. 1685.

brity, was attended by circumstances which excited interest in London, and which were thought not unworthy of being mentioned in the despatches of foreign ministers. Newcastle was lighted up with great piles of coal. The steeples sent forth a joyous peal. A copy of the Exclusion Bill, and a black box, resembling that which, according to the popular fable, contained the contract between Charles the Second and Lucy Walters, were publicly committed to the flames, with loud acclamations.*

The general result of the elections exceeded the most sanguine expectations of the court. James found with delight that it would be unnecessary for him to expend a farthing in buying votes. He said that, with the exception of about forty members, the House of Commons was just such as he should himself have named.† And this House of Commons it was in his power, as the law then stood, to keep to the end of his reign.

Secure of parliamentary support, he might now indulge in the luxury of revenge. His nature was not placable; and, while still a subject, he had suffered some injuries and indignities which might move even a placable nature to fierce and lasting resentment. One set of men in particular had, with a baseness and cruelty beyond all example and all description, attacked his honour and his life, the witnesses of the plot. He may well be excused for hating them; since, even at this day, the mention of their names excites the disgust and horror of all sects and parties.

Some of these wretches were already beyond the reach of human justice. Bedloe had died in his wickedness, without one sign of remorse or shame.‡ Dugdale had followed, driven mad, men said, by the Furies of an evil conscience, and with loud shrieks imploring those who stood round his bed to take away Lord Stafford.§ Carstairs, too, was gone. His end had been all horror and despair; and, with his last breath, he had told his attendants to throw him into a ditch like a dog, for that he was not fit to sleep in a Christian burial ground.‖ But Oates and Dangerfield were still within the reach of the stern prince whom they had wronged. James, a short time before his accession, had instituted a civil suit against Oates

* Despatch of the Dutch Ambassadors, April $\frac{10}{20}$. 1685.
† Burnet, i. 626.
‡ A faithful account of the Sickness, Death, and Burial of Captain Bedlow, 1680; Narrative of Lord Chief Justice North.
§ Smith's Intrigues of the Popish Plot, 1685.
‖ Burnet, i. 439.

for defamatory words ; and a jury had given damages to the
enormous amount of a hundred thousand pounds.* The defendant had been taken in execution, and was lying in prison
as a debtor, without hope of release. Two bills of indictment
against him for perjury had been found by the grand jury of
Middlesex, a few weeks before the death of Charles. Soon
after the close of the elections the trial came on.

Proceed-
ings
against
Oates.

Among the upper and middle classes Oates had few friends
left. The most respectable Whigs were now convinced that,
even if his narrative had some foundation in fact, he had
erected on that foundation a vast superstructure of romance.
A considerable number of low fanatics, however, still regarded
him as a public benefactor. These people well knew that, if
he were convicted, his sentence would be one of extreme
severity, and were therefore indefatigable in their endeavours
to manage an escape. Though he was as yet in confinement
only for debt, he was put into irons by the authorities of the
King's Bench prison ; and even so he was with difficulty kept
in safe custody. The mastiff that guarded his door was
poisoned ; and, on the very night preceding the trial, a
ladder of ropes was introduced into the cell.

On the day in which Titus was brought to the bar, Westminster Hall was crowded with spectators, among whom were
many Roman Catholics, eager to see the misery and humiliation of their persecutor.† A few years earlier his short neck,
his legs uneven, the vulgar said, as those of a badger, his
forehead low as that of a baboon, his purple cheeks, and his
monstrous length of chin, had been familiar to all who frequented the courts of law. He had then been the idol of the
nation. Wherever he had appeared, men had uncovered their
heads to him. The lives and estates of the magnates of the
realm had been at his mercy. Times had now changed ; and
many, who had formerly regarded him as the deliverer of his
country, shuddered at the sight of those hideous features on
which villany seemed to be written by the hand of God.‡

It was proved, beyond all possibility of doubt, that this
man had, by false testimony, deliberately murdered several
guiltless persons. He called in vain on the most eminent
members of the Parliaments which had rewarded and extolled

---

* See the proceedings in the Collection of State Trials.

† Evelyn's Diary, May 7. 1685.

‡ There remain many pictures of
Oates. The most striking descriptions

of his person are in North's Examen,
225., in Dryden's Absalom and Achitophel, and in a broadside entitled, A Hue
and Cry after T. O.

him to give evidence in his favour. Some of those whom he had summoned absented themselves. None of them said anything tending to his vindication. One of them, the Earl of Huntingdon, bitterly reproached him with having deceived the Houses and drawn on them the guilt of shedding innocent blood. The Judges browbeat and reviled the prisoner with an intemperance which, even in the most atrocious cases, ill becomes the judicial character. He betrayed, however, no sign of fear or of shame, and faced the storm of invective which burst upon him from bar, bench, and witness box, with the insolence of despair. He was convicted on both indictments. His offence, though, in a moral light, murder of the most aggravated kind, was, in the eye of the law, merely a misdemeanour. The tribunal, however, was desirous to make his punishment more severe than that of felons or traitors, and not merely to put him to death, but to put him to death by frightful torments. He was sentenced to be stripped of his clerical habit, to be pilloried in Palace Yard, to be led round Westminster Hall with an inscription declaring his infamy over his head, to be pilloried again in front of the Royal Exchange, to be whipped from Aldgate to Newgate, and, after an interval of two days, to be whipped from Newgate to Tyburn. If, against all probability, he should happen to survive this horrible infliction, he was to be kept close prisoner during life. Five times every year he was to be brought forth from his dungeon and exposed on the pillory in different parts of the capital.* This rigorous sentence was rigorously executed. On the day on which Oates was pilloried in Palace Yard he was mercilessly pelted and ran some risk of being pulled in pieces.† But in the City his partisans mustered in great force, raised a riot, and upset the pillory.‡ They were, however, unable to rescue their favourite. It was supposed that he would try to escape the horrible doom which awaited him by swallowing poison. All that he ate and drank was therefore carefully inspected. On the following morning he was brought forth to undergo his first flogging. At an early hour an innumerable multitude filled all the streets from Aldgate to the Old Bailey. The hangman laid on the lash with such unusual severity as showed that he had received special instructions. The blood ran down in rivulets.

* The proceedings will be found at length in the Collection of State Trials.
† Gazette de France, $\frac{May\ 29.}{June\ 9.}$ 1685.
‡ Despatch of the Dutch Ambassadors, May $\frac{19.}{29.}$ 1685.

For a time the criminal showed a strange constancy : but at last his stubborn fortitude gave way. His bellowings were frightful to hear. He swooned several times ; but the scourge still continued to descend. When he was unbound, it seemed that he had borne as much as the human frame can bear without dissolution. James was entreated to remit the second flogging. His answer was short and clear : " He shall go through with it, if he has breath in his body." An attempt was made to obtain the Queen's intercession ; but she indignantly refused to say a word in favour of such a wretch. After an interval of only forty-eight hours, Oates was again brought out of his dungeon. He was unable to stand, and it was necessary to drag him to Tyburn on a sledge. He seemed quite insensible ; and the Tories reported that he had stupified himself with strong drink. A person who counted the stripes on the second day said that they were seventeen hundred. The bad man escaped with life, but so narrowly that his ignorant and bigoted admirers thought his recovery miraculous, and appealed to it as a proof of his innocence. The doors of the prison closed upon him. During many months he remained ironed in the darkest hole of Newgate. It was said that in his cell he gave himself up to melancholy, and sate whole days uttering deep groans, his arms folded, and his hat pulled over his eyes. It was not in England alone that these events excited strong interest. Millions of Roman Catholics, who knew nothing of our institutions or of our factions, had heard that a persecution of singular barbarity had raged in our island against the professors of the true faith, that many pious men had suffered martyrdom, and that Titus Oates had been the chief murderer. There was, therefore, great joy in distant countries when it was known that the divine justice had overtaken him. Engravings of him, looking out from the pillory, and writhing at the cart's tail, were circulated all over Europe; and epigrammatists, in many languages, made merry with the doctoral title which he pretended to have received from the University of Salamanca, and remarked that, since his forehead could not be made to blush, it was but reasonable that his back should do so.*

* Evelyn's Diary, May 22. 1685 ; Eachard, iii. 741. ; Burnet, i. 637. ; Observator, May 27. 1685 ; Oates's Eἰκών, 89. ; Εἰκὼν βροτολοιγοῦ, 1697 ; Commons' Journals of May, June, and July, 1689 ; Tom Brown's Advice to Dr. Oates. Some interesting circumstances are mentioned in a broadside, printed for A. Brooks, Charing Cross, 1685. I have seen contemporary French and Italian

Horrible as were the sufferings of Oates, they did not equal his crimes. The old law of England, which had been suffered to become obsolete, treated the false witness, who had caused death by means of perjury, as a murderer.* This was wise and righteous; for such a witness is, in truth, the worst of murderers. To the guilt of shedding innocent blood he has added the guilt of violating the most solemn engagement into which man can enter with his fellow men, and of making institutions, to which it is desirable that the public should look with respect and confidence, instruments of frightful wrong and objects of general distrust. The pain produced by ordinary murder bears no proportion to the pain produced by murder of which the courts of justice are made the agents. The mere extinction of life is a very small part of what makes an execution horrible. The prolonged mental agony of the sufferer, the shame and misery of all connected with him, the stain abiding even to the third and fourth generation, are things far more dreadful than death itself. In general it may be safely affirmed that the father of a large family would rather be bereaved of all his children by accident or by disease than lose one of them by the hands of the hangman. Murder by false testimony is therefore the most aggravated species of murder; and Oates had been guilty of many such murders. Nevertheless the punishment which was inflicted upon him cannot be justified. In sentencing him to be stripped of his ecclesiastical habit and imprisoned for life, the judges exceeded their legal power. They were undoubtedly competent to inflict whipping; nor had the law assigned a limit to the number of stripes. But the spirit of the law clearly was that no misdemeanour should be punished more severely than the most atrocious felonies. The worst felon could only be hanged. The judges, as they believed, sentenced Oates to be scourged to death. That the law was defective is not a sufficient excuse: for defective laws should be altered by the legislature, and not strained by the tribunals; and

pamphlets containing the history of the trial and execution. A print of Titus in the pillory was published at Milan, with the following curious inscription: "Questo è il naturale ritratto di Tito Otcz, o vero Oatz, Inglese, posto in berlina, uno de' principali professori della religion protestante, acerrimo persecutore de' Cattolici, e gran spergiuro." I have also seen a Dutch engraving of his punishment, with some Latin verses, of which the following are a specimen:

"At Doctor fictus non fictos pertulit ictus,
A tortore datos haud molli in corpore gratos,
Disceret ut vere scelera ob commissa rubere."

The anagram of his name, " Testis Ovat," may be found on many prints published in different countries.

* Blackstone's Commentaries, Chapter of Homicide.

least of all should the law be strained for the purpose of inflicting torture and destroying life. That Oates was a bad man is not a sufficient excuse; for the guilty are almost always the first to suffer those hardships which are afterwards used as precedents against the innocent. Thus it was in the present case. Merciless flogging soon became an ordinary punishment for political misdemeanours of no very aggravated kind. Men were sentenced, for words spoken against the government, to pain so excruciating that they, with unfeigned earnestness, begged to be brought to trial on capital charges, and sent to the gallows. Happily the progress of this great evil was speedily stopped by the Revolution, and by that article of the Bill of Rights which condemns all cruel and unusual punishments.

Proceedings against Danger-field.

The villany of Dangerfield had not, like that of Oates, destroyed many innocent victims; for Dangerfield had not taken up the trade of a witness till the plot had been blown upon and till juries had become incredulous.* He was brought to trial, not for perjury, but for the less heinous offence of libel. He had, during the agitation caused by the Exclusion Bill, put forth a narrative containing some false and odious imputations on the late and on the present King. For this publication he was now, after the lapse of five years, suddenly taken up, brought before the Privy Council, committed, tried, convicted, and sentenced to be whipped from Aldgate to Newgate and from Newgate to Tyburn. The wretched man behaved with great effrontery during the trial; but, when he heard his doom, he went into agonies of despair, gave himself up for dead, and chose a text for his funeral sermon. His forebodings were just. He was not, indeed, scourged quite so severely as Oates had been; but he had not Oates's iron strength of body and mind. After the execution Dangerfield was put into a hackney coach and was taken back to prison. As he passed the corner of Hatton Garden, a Tory gentleman of Gray's Inn, named Francis, stopped the carriage, and cried out with brutal levity, "Well, friend, have you had your heat this morning?" The bleed-

* According to Roger North the judges decided that Dangerfield, having been previously convicted of perjury, was incompetent to be a witness of the plot. But this is one among many instances of Roger's inaccuracy. It appears, from the report of the trial of Lord Castlemaine in June 1680, that, after much altercation between counsel, and much consultation among the judges of the different courts in Westminster Hall, Dangerfield was sworn and suffered to tell his story: but the jury very properly gave no credit to his testimony.

ing prisoner, maddened by this insult, answered with a curse. Francis instantly struck him in the face with a cane which injured the eye. Dangerfield was carried dying into Newgate. This dastardly outrage roused the indignation of the bystanders. They seized Francis, and were with difficulty restrained from tearing him to pieces. The appearance of Dangerfield's body, which had been frightfully lacerated by the whip, inclined many to believe that his death was chiefly, if not wholly, caused by the stripes which he had received. The government and the Chief Justice thought it convenient to lay the whole blame on Francis, who, though he seems to have been at worst guilty only of aggravated manslaughter, was tried and executed for murder. His dying speech is one of the most curious monuments of that age. The savage spirit which had brought him to the gallows remained with him to the last. Boasts of his loyalty and abuse of the Whigs were mingled with the parting ejaculations in which he commended his soul to the divine mercy. An idle rumour had been circulated that his wife was in love with Dangerfield, who was eminently handsome and renowned for gallantry. The fatal blow, it was said, had been prompted by jealousy. The dying husband, with an earnestness, half ridiculous, half pathetic, vindicated the lady's character. She was, he said, a virtuous woman : she came of a loyal stock, and, if she had been inclined to break her marriage vow, would at least have selected a Tory and a churchman for her paramour.*

About the same time a culprit, who bore very little resemblance to Oates or Dangerfield, appeared on the floor of the Court of King's Bench. No eminent chief of a party has ever passed through many years of civil and religious dissension with more innocence than Richard Baxter. He belonged to the mildest and most temperate section of the Puritan body. He was a young man when the civil war broke out. He thought that the right was on the side of the Houses ;

Proceedings against Baxter.

* Dangerfield's trial was not reported; but I have seen a concise account of it in a contemporary broadside. An abstract of the evidence against Francis, and his dying speech, will be found in the Collection of State Trials. See Eachard, iii. 741. Burnet's narrative contains more mistakes than lines. See also North's Examen, 256., the sketch of Dangerfield's life in the Bloody Assizes, the Observator of July 29. 1685, and the poem entitled " Dangerfield's Ghost to Jeffreys." In the very rare volume entitled " Succinct Genealogies, by Robert Halstead," Lord Peterborough says that Dangerfield, with whom he had had some intercourse, was "a young man who appeared under a decent figure, a serious behaviour, and with words that did not seem to proceed from a common understanding."

and he had no scruple about acting as chaplain to a regiment in the parliamentary army: but his clear and somewhat sceptical understanding, and his strong sense of justice, preserved him from all excesses. He exerted himself to check the fanatical violence of the soldiery. He condemned the proceedings of the High Court of Justice. In the days of the Commonwealth he had the boldness to express, on many occasions, and once even in Cromwell's presence, love and reverence for the ancient institutions of the country. While the royal family was in exile, Baxter's life was chiefly passed at Kidderminster in the assiduous discharge of parochial duties. He heartily concurred in the Restoration, and was sincerely desirous to bring about an union between Episcopalians and Presbyterians. For, with a liberality rare in his time, he considered questions of ecclesiastical polity as of small account when compared with the great principles of Christianity, and had never, even when prelacy was most odious to the ruling powers, joined in the outcry against Bishops. The attempt to reconcile the contending factions failed. Baxter cast in his lot with his proscribed friends, refused the mitre of Hereford, quitted the parsonage of Kidderminster, and gave himself up almost wholly to study. His theological writings, though too moderate to be pleasing to the bigots of any party, had an immense reputation. Zealous Churchmen called him a Roundhead; and many Nonconformists accused him of Erastianism and Arminianism. But the integrity of his heart, the purity of his life, the vigour of his faculties, and the extent of his attainments were acknowledged by the best and wisest men of every persuasion. His political opinions, in spite of the oppression which he and his brethren had suffered, were moderate. He was friendly to that small party which was hated by both Whigs and Tories. He could not, he said, join in cursing the Trimmers, when he remembered who it was that had blessed the peacemakers.*

In a Commentary on the New Testament he had complained, with some bitterness, of the persecution which the Dissenters suffered. That men who, for not using the Prayer Book, had been driven from their homes, stripped of their property, and locked up in dungeons, should dare to utter a murmur, was then thought a high crime against the State

* Baxter's preface to Sir Matthew Hale's Judgment of the Nature of True Religion, 1684.

and the Church. Roger Lestrange, the champion of the government and the oracle of the clergy, sounded the note of war in the Observator. An information was filed. Baxter begged that he might be allowed some time to prepare for his defence. It was on the day on which Oates was pilloried in Palace Yard that the illustrious chief of the Puritans, oppressed by age and infirmities, came to Westminster Hall to make this request. Jeffreys burst into a storm of rage. "Not a minute," he cried, "to save his life. I can deal with saints as well as with sinners. There stands Oates on one side of the pillory; and, if Baxter stood on the other, the two greatest rogues in the kingdom would stand together."

When the trial came on at Guildhall, a crowd of those who loved and honoured Baxter filled the court. At his side stood Doctor William Bates, one of the most eminent of the Nonconformist divines. Two Whig barristers of great note, Pollexfen and Wallop, appeared for the defendant. Pollexfen had scarcely begun his address to the jury, when the Chief Justice broke forth: "Pollexfen, I know you well. I will set a mark on you. You are the patron of the faction. This is an old rogue, a schismatical knave, a hypocritical villain. He hates the Liturgy. He would have nothing but long-winded cant without book:" and then his Lordship turned up his eyes, clasped his hands, and began to sing through his nose, in imitation of what he supposed to be Baxter's style of praying "Lord, we are thy people, thy peculiar people, thy dear people." Pollexfen gently reminded the court that his late Majesty had thought Baxter deserving of a bishopric. "And what ailed the old blockhead then," cried Jeffreys, "that he did not take it?" His fury now rose almost to madness. He called Baxter a dog, and swore that it would be no more than justice to whip such a villain through the whole City.

Wallop interposed, but fared no better than his leader. "You are in all these dirty causes, Mr. Wallop," said the Judge. "Gentlemen of the long robe ought to be ashamed to assist such factious knaves." The advocate made another attempt to obtain a hearing, but to no purpose. "If you do not know your duty," said Jeffreys, "I will teach it you."

Wallop sate down; and Baxter himself attempted to put in a word. But the Chief Justice drowned all expostulation in a torrent of ribaldry and invective, mingled with scraps of Hudibras. "My Lord," said the old man, "I have been much blamed by Dissenters for speaking respectfully of Bishops." "Baxter for Bishops!" cried the Judge, "that's a merry conceit indeed. I know what you mean by Bishops, rascals like yourself, Kidderminster Bishops, factious snivelling Presbyterians!" Again Baxter essayed to speak, and again Jeffreys bellowed, "Richard, Richard, dost thou think we will let thee poison the court? Richard, thou art an old knave. Thou hast written books enough to load a cart, and every book as full of sedition as an egg is full of meat. By the grace of God, I'll look after thee. I see a great many of your brotherhood waiting to know what will befall their mighty Don. And there," he continued, fixing his savage eye on Bates, "there is a Doctor of the party at your elbow. But, by the grace of God Almighty, I will crush you all."

Baxter held his peace. But one of the junior counsel for the defence made a last effort, and undertook to show that the words of which complaint was made would not bear the construction put on them by the information. With this view he began to read the context. In a moment he was roared down. "You sha'n't turn the court into a conventicle." The noise of weeping was heard from some of those who surrounded Baxter. "Snivelling calves!" said the Judge.

Witnesses to character were in attendance, and among them were several clergymen of the Established Church. But the Chief Justice would hear nothing. "Does your Lordship think," said Baxter, "that any jury will convict a man on such a trial as this?" "I warrant you, Mr. Baxter," said Jeffreys: "don't trouble yourself about that." Jeffreys was right. The Sheriffs were the tools of the government. The jurymen, selected by the Sheriffs from among the fiercest zealots of the Tory party, conferred for a moment, and returned a verdict of Guilty. "My Lord," said Baxter, as he left the court, "there was once a Chief Justice who would have treated me very differently." He alluded to his learned and virtuous friend Sir Matthew Hale. "There is not an honest man in England," answered Jeffreys, "but looks on thee as a knave."*

The sentence was, for those times, a lenient one. What passed in conference among the judges cannot be certainly known. It was believed among the Nonconformists, and is

* See the Observator of February 25. 1685, the information in the Collection of State Trials, the account of what passed in court given by Calamy, Life of Baxter, chap. xiv., and the very curious extracts from the Baxter MSS. in the Life, by Orme, published in 1830.

highly probable, that the Chief Justice was overruled by his three brethren. He proposed, it is said, that Baxter should be whipped through London at the cart's tail. The majority thought that an eminent divine, who, a quarter of a century before, had been offered a mitre, and who was now in his seventieth year, would be sufficiently punished for a few sharp words by fine and imprisonment.*

The manner in which Baxter was treated by a judge, who was a member of the cabinet and a favourite of the Sovereign, indicated, in a manner not to be mistaken, the feeling with which the government at this time regarded the Protestant Nonconformists. But already that feeling had been indicated by still stronger and more terrible signs. The Parliament of Scotland had met. James had purposely hastened the session of this body, and had postponed the session of the English Houses, in the hope that the example set at Edinburgh would produce a good effect at Westminster. For the legislature of his northern kingdom was as obsequious as those provincial Estates which Lewis the Fourteenth still suffered to play at some of their ancient functions in Britanny and Burgundy. None but an Episcopalian could sit in the Scottish Parliament, or could even vote for a member, and in Scotland an Episcopalian was always a Tory or a timeserver. From an assembly thus constituted little opposition to the royal wishes was to be apprehended; and even the assembly thus constituted could pass no law which had not been previously approved by a committee of courtiers.

Marginal note: Meeting of the Parliament of Scotland.

All that the government asked was readily granted. In a financial point of view, indeed, the liberality of the Scottish Estates was of little consequence. They gave, however, what their scanty means permitted. They annexed in perpetuity to the crown the duties which had been granted to the late King, and which in his time had been estimated at forty thousand pounds sterling a year. They also settled on James for life an additional annual income of two hundred and sixteen thousand pounds Scots, equivalent to eighteen thousand pounds sterling. The whole sum which they were able to bestow was about sixty thousand a year, little more than what was poured into the English Exchequer every fortnight.†

Having little money to give, the Estates supplied the

---

* Baxter MS. cited by Orme.   Jac. VII. April 28. 1685, and May 13.
† Act. Parl. Car. II. March 29. 1661 ;   1685.

defect by loyal professions and barbarous statutes. The
King, in a letter which was read to them at the opening of
their session, called on them in vehement language to provide new penal laws against the refractory Presbyterians, and
expressed his regret that business made it impossible for him
to propose such laws in person from the throne. His commands were obeyed. A statute framed by his ministers was
promptly passed, a statute which stands forth, even among
the statutes of that unhappy country at that unhappy period,
preeminent in atrocity. It was enacted, in few but emphatic
words, that whoever should preach in a conventicle under a
roof, or should attend, either as preacher or as hearer, a conventicle in the open air, should be punished with death and
confiscation of property.*

Feeling of
James
towards
the Puri-
tans.

This law, passed at the King's instance by an assembly
devoted to his will, deserves especial notice. For he has
been frequently represented by ignorant writers as a prince
rash, indeed, and injudicious in his choice of means, but intent on one of the noblest ends which a ruler can pursue,
the establishment of entire religious liberty. Nor can it be
denied that some portions of his life, when detached from
the rest and superficially considered, seem to warrant this
favourable view of his character.

While a subject he had been, during many years, a persecuted man; and persecution had produced its usual effect on
him. His mind, dull and narrow as it was, had profited
under that sharp discipline. While he was excluded from
the Court, from the Admiralty, and from the Council, and
was in danger of being also excluded from the throne, only
because he could not help believing in transubstantiation and
in the authority of the see of Rome, he made such rapid progress in the doctrines of toleration that he left Milton and
Locke behind. What, he often said, could be more unjust,
than to visit speculations with penalties which ought to be
reserved for acts? What more impolitic than to reject the
services of good soldiers, seamen, lawyers, diplomatists,
financiers, because they hold unsound opinions about the
number of the sacraments or the pluripresence of saints?
He learned by rote those commonplaces which all sects repeat so fluently when they are enduring oppression, and
forget so easily when they are able to retaliate it. Indeed

* Act. Parl. Jac. VII. May 8. 1685;   evidently wished to see the precedent
Observator, June 20. 1685. Lestrange   followed in England.

he rehearsed his lesson so well, that those who chanced to hear him on this subject gave him credit for much more sense and much readier elocution than he really possessed. His professions imposed on some charitable persons, and perhaps imposed on himself. But his zeal for the rights of conscience ended with the predominance of the Whig party. When fortune changed, when he was no longer afraid that others would persecute him, when he had it in his power to persecute others, his real propensities began to show themselves. He hated the Puritan sects with a manifold hatred, theological and political, hereditary and personal. He regarded them as the foes of Heaven, as the foes of all legitimate authority in Church and State, as his greatgrandmother's foes and his grandfather's, his father's and his mother's, his brother's and his own. He, who had complained so loudly of the laws against Papists, now declared himself unable to conceive how men could have the impudence to propose the repeal of the laws againt Puritans.* He, whose favourite theme had been the injustice of requiring civil functionaries to take religious tests, established in Scotland, when he resided there as Viceroy, the most rigorous religious test that has ever been known in the empire.† He, who had expressed just indignation when the priests of his own faith were hanged and quartered, amused himself with hearing Covenanters shriek and seeing them writhe while their knees were beaten flat in the boots.‡ In this mood he became King; and he immediately demanded and obtained from the obsequious Estates of Scotland, as the surest pledge of their loyalty, the most sanguinary law that has ever in our island been enacted against Protestant Nonconformists.

With this law the whole spirit of his administration was in perfect harmony. The fiery persecution, which had raged when he ruled Scotland as vicegerent, waxed hotter than ever from the day on which he became sovereign. Those shires in which the Covenanters were most numerous were given up to the license of the army. With the army was

Cruel treatment of the Scotch Covenanters.

---

* His own words reported by himself. Life of James the Second, i. 656. Orig. Mem.

† Act. Parl. Car. II. August 31. 1681.
‡ Burnet, i. 583.; Wodrow, III. v. 2. Unfortunately the Acta of the Scottish Privy Council during almost the whole administration of the Duke of York are wanting. (1848.) This assertion has been met by a direct contradiction. But the fact is exactly as I have stated it. There is in the Acta of the Scottish Privy Council a hiatus extending from August 1678 to August 1682. The Duke of York began to reside in Scotland in December 1679. He left Scotland, never to return, in May 1682. (1857.)

mingled a militia, composed of the most violent and profligate of those who called themselves Episcopalians.   Preeminent among the bands which oppressed and wasted these unhappy districts were the dragoons commanded by John Graham of Claverhouse.   The story ran that these wicked men used in their revels to play at the torments of hell, and to call each other by the names of devils and damned souls.* The chief of this Tophet, a soldier of distinguished courage and professional skill, but rapacious and profane, of violent temper and of obdurate heart, has left a name which, wherever the Scottish race is settled on the face of the globe, is mentioned with a peculiar energy of hatred.   To recapitulate all the crimes, by which this man, and men like him, goaded the peasantry of the Western Lowlands into madness, would be an endless task.   A few instances must suffice; and all those instances shall be taken from the history of a single fortnight, that very fortnight in which the Scottish Parliament, at the urgent request of James, enacted a new law of unprecedented severity against Dissenters.

John Brown, a poor carrier of Lanarkshire, was, for his singular piety, commonly called the Christian carrier.   Many years later, when Scotland enjoyed rest, prosperity, and religious freedom, old men who remembered the evil days described him as one versed in divine things, blameless in life, and so peaceable that the tyrants could find no offence in him except that he absented himself from the public worship of the Episcopalians.   On the first of May he was cutting turf, when he was seized by Claverhouse's dragoons, rapidly examined, convicted of nonconformity, and sentenced to death.   It is said that, even among the soldiers, it was not easy to find an executioner.   For the wife of the poor man was present: she led one little child by the hand: it was easy to see that she was about to give birth to another; and even those wild and hardhearted men, who nicknamed one another Beelzebub and Apollyon, shrank from the great wickedness of butchering her husband before her face.   The prisoner, meanwhile, raised above himself by the near prospect of eternity, prayed loud and fervently as one inspired, till Claverhouse, in a fury, shot him dead.   It was reported by credible witnesses that the widow cried out in her agony, ' Well, sir, well; the day of reckoning will come; " and that the murderer replied, " To man I can answer for what I have

* Wodrow III. ix. 6.

done; and as for God, I will take him into mine own hand."
Yet it was rumoured that even on his seared conscience and
adamantine heart the dying ejaculations of his victim made
an impression which was never effaced.*

On the fifth of May two artisans, Peter Gillies and John
Bryce, were tried in Ayrshire by a military tribunal consisting of fifteen soldiers. The indictment is still extant. The
prisoners were charged, not with any act of rebellion, but
with holding the same pernicious doctrines which had impelled others to rebel, and with wanting only opportunity to
act upon those doctrines. The proceeding was summary.
In a few hours the two culprits were convicted, hanged, and
flung together into a hole under the gallows.†

The eleventh of May was made remarkable by more than
one great crime. Some rigid Calvinists had from the doctrine of reprobation drawn the consequence that to pray for
any person who had been predestined to perdition was an act
of mutiny against the eternal decrees of the Supreme Being.
Three poor labouring men, deeply imbued with this unamiable
divinity, were stopped by an officer in the neighbourhood
of Glasgow. They were asked whether they would pray for
King James the Seventh. They refused to do so except
under the condition that he was one of the elect. A file of
musketeers was drawn out. The prisoners knelt down: they
were blindfolded; and within an hour after they had been
arrested, their blood was lapped up by the dogs.‡

---

* Wodrow, III. ix. 6. The editor of
the Oxford edition of Burnet attempts
to excuse this act by alleging that Claverhouse was then employed to intercept
all communication between Argyle and
Monmouth, and by supposing that John
Brown may have been detected in conveying intelligence between the rebel
camps. Unfortunately for this hypothesis John Brown was shot on the first
of May, when both Argyle and Monmouth were in Holland, and when there
was no insurrection in any part of our
island.

† Wodrow, III. ix. 6.

‡ Ibid. It has been confidently asserted, by persons who have not taken
the trouble to look at the authority to
which I have referred, that I have
grossly calumniated these unfortunate
men; that I do not understand the Calvinistic theology; and that it is impossible that members of the Church of
Scotland can have refused to pray for

any man, on the ground that he was
not one of the elect.

I can only refer to the narrative
which Wodrow has inserted in his History, and which he justly calls plain
and natural. That narrative is signed
by two eyewitnesses, and Wodrow, before he published it, submitted it to a
third eyewitness, who pronounced it
strictly accurate. From that narrative
I will extract the only words which
bear on the point in question: "When
all the three were taken, the officers
consulted among themselves, and, with-
drawing to the west side of the town,
questioned the prisoners, particularly if
they would pray for King James VII.
They answered, they would pray for all
within the election of grace. Balfour
said, Do you question the King's election? They answered, sometimes they
questioned their own. Upon which he
swore dreadfully, and said they should
die presently, because they would not

While this was done in Clydesdale, an act not less horrible was perpetrated in Eskdale. One of the proscribed Covenanters, overcome by sickness, had found shelter in the house of a respectable widow, and had died there. The corpse was discovered by the Laird of Westerhall, a petty tyrant who had, in the days of the Covenant, professed inordinate zeal for the Presbyterian Church, who had, since the Restoration, purchased the favour of the government by apostasy, and who felt towards the party which he had deserted the implacable hatred of an apostate. This man pulled down the house of the poor woman, carried away her furniture, and, leaving her and her younger children to wander in the fields, dragged her son Andrew, who was still a lad, before Claverhouse, who happened to be marching through that part of the country. Claverhouse was just then strangely lenient. Some thought that he had not been quite himself since the death of the Christian carrier, ten days before. But Westerhall was eager to signalise his loyalty, and extorted a sullen consent. The guns were loaded, and the youth was told to pull his bonnet over his face. He refused, and stood confronting his murderers with the Bible in his hand. " I can look you in the face," he said ; " I have done nothing of which I need be ashamed. But how will you look in that day when you shall be judged by what is written in this book ? " He fell dead, and was buried in the moor.*

On the same day two women, Margaret Maclachlan and Margaret Wilson, the former an aged widow, the latter a maiden of eighteen, suffered death for their religion in Wigtonshire. They were offered their lives if they would consent to adjure the cause of the insurgent Covenanters, and to attend the Episcopal worship. They refused ; and they were sentenced to be drowned. They were carried to a spot which the Solway overflows twice a day, and were fastened to stakes fixed in the sand, between high and low water mark. The elder sufferer was placed near to the advancing flood, in the hope that her last agonies might terrify the younger into submission. The sight was dreadful. But the courage of the survivor was sustained by an enthusiasm as lofty as any that is recorded in martyrology. She saw the sea draw

pray for Christ's vicegerent, and so without one word more, commanded Thomas Cook to go to his prayers, for he should die.

In this narrative Wodrow saw nothing improbable ; and I shall not easily be convinced that any writer now living understands the feelings and opinions of the Covenanters better than Wodrow did. (1857.)

* Wodrow, III. ix. 6. Cloud of Witnesses.

nearer and nearer, but gave no sign of alarm. She prayed and sang verses of psalms till the waves choked her voice. After she had tasted the bitterness of death, she was, by a cruel mercy unbound and restored to life. When she came to herself, pitying friends and neighbours implored her to yield. "Dear Margaret, only say, God save the King!" The poor girl, true to her stern theology, gasped out, "May God save him, if it be God's will!" Her friends crowded round the presiding officer. "She has said it; indeed, sir, she has said it." "Will she take the abjuration?" he demanded. "Never!" she exclaimed. "I am Christ's: let me go!" And the waters closed over her for the last time.*

Thus was Scotland governed by that prince whom ignorant men have represented as a friend of religious liberty, whose misfortune it was to be too wise and too good for the age in which he lived. Nay, even those laws which authorised him to govern thus were in his judgment reprehensibly lenient. While his officers were committing the murders which have just been related, he was urging the Scottish Parliament to pass a new Act compared with which all former Acts might be called merciful.

In England his authority, though great, was circumscribed by ancient and noble laws which even the Tories would not patiently have seen him infringe. Here he could not hurry Dissenters before military tribunals, or enjoy at Council the luxury of seeing them swoon in the boots. Here he could not drown young girls for refusing to take the abjuration, or shoot poor countrymen for doubting whether he was one of the elect. Yet even in England he continued to persecute the Puritans as far as his power extended, till events which will hereafter be related induced him to form the design of uniting Puritans and Papists in a coalition for the humiliation and spoliation of the established Church.

One sect of Protestant Dissenters indeed he, even at this early period of his reign, regarded with some tenderness, the Society of Friends. His partiality for that singular fraternity cannot be attributed to religious sympathy; for, of all who acknowledge the divine mission of Jesus, the Roman Catholic and the Quaker differ most widely. It may seem paradoxical to say that this very circumstance constituted a tie

Feeling of James towards the Quakers.

* Wodrow, III. ix. 6. The epitaph of Margaret Wilson, in the churchyard at Wigton, is printed in the Appendix to the Cloud of Witnesses:

"Murdered for owning Christ supreme Head of his Church, and no more crime, But her not owning Prelacy, And not abjuring Presbytery, Within the sea, tied to a stake, She suffered for Christ Jesus' sake."

between the Roman Catholic and the Quaker; yet such was
really the case.   For they deviated in opposite directions so
far from what the great body of the nation regarded as right,
that even liberal men generally considered them both as lying
beyond the pale of the largest toleration.   Thus the two
extreme sects, precisely because they were extreme sects,
had a common interest distinct from the interest of the
intermediate sects.   The Quakers were also guiltless of all
offence against James and his House.   They had not been
in existence as a community till the war between his father
and the Long Parliament was drawing towards a close.   They
had been cruelly persecuted by some of the revolutionary
governments.   They had, since the Restoration, in spite of
much ill usage, submitted themselves meekly to the royal authority.   For they had, though reasoning on premises which
the Anglican divines regarded as heterodox, arrived, like the
Anglican divines, at the conclusion, that no excess of tyranny
on the part of a prince can justify active resistance on the
part of a subject.   No libel on the government had ever been
traced to a Quaker.*   In no conspiracy against the government had a Quaker been implicated.   The society had not
joined in the clamour for the Exclusion Bill, and had solemnly condemned the Rye House plot as a hellish design
and a work of the devil.†   Indeed, the friends then took very
little part in civil contentions; for they were not, as now,
congregated in large towns, but were generally engaged in
agriculture, a pursuit from which they have been gradually
driven by the vexations consequent on their strange scruple
about paying tithe.   They were, therefore, far removed from
the scene of political strife.   They also, even in domestic privacy, avoided on principle all political conversation.   For
such conversation was, in their opinion, unfavourable to their
spirituality of mind, and tended to disturb the austere composure of their deportment.   The yearly meetings of that age
repeatedly admonished the brethren not to hold discourse
touching affairs of state.‡   Even within the memory of persons now living those grave elders who retained the habits of
an earlier generation systematically discouraged such worldly
talk.§   It was natural that James should make a wide distinction between these harmless people and those fierce and

---

* See the letter to King Charles II.
prefixed to Barclay's Apology.
    † Sewel's History of the Quakers,
book x.

‡ Minutes of Yearly Meetings, 1689,
1690.
    § Clarkson on Quakerism; Peculiar
Customs, chapter v.

reckless sects which considered resistance to tyranny as a Christian duty, which had, in Germany, France, and Holland, made war on legitimate princes, and which had, during four generations, borne peculiar enmity to the House of Stuart.

It happened, moreover, that it was possible to grant large relief to the Roman Catholic and to the Quaker without mitigating the sufferings of the Puritan sects. A law was in force which imposed severe penalties on every person who refused to take the oath of supremacy when required to do so. This law did not affect Presbyterians, Independents, or Baptists; for they were all ready to call God to witness that they renounced all spiritual connection with foreign prelates and potentates. But the Roman Catholic would not swear that the Pope had no jurisdiction in England, and the Quaker would not swear to anything. On the other hand, neither the Roman Catholic nor the Quaker was touched by the Five Mile Act, which, of all the laws in the Statute Book, was perhaps the most annoying to the Puritan Nonconformists.*

The Quakers had a powerful and zealous advocate at court. William Though, as a class, they mixed little with the world, and Penn. shunned politics as a pursuit dangerous to their spiritual interests, one of them, widely distinguished from the rest by station and fortune, lived in the highest circles, and had constant access to the royal ear. This was the celebrated William Penn. His father had held great naval commands, had been a Commissioner of the Admiralty, had sate in Parliament, had received the honour of knighthood, and had been encouraged to expect a peerage. The son had been liberally educated, and had been designed for the profession of arms, but had, while still young, injured his prospects and disgusted his friends by joining what was then generally considered as a gang of crazy heretics. He had been sent sometimes to the Tower, and sometimes to Newgate. He had been tried at the Old Bailey for preaching in defiance of the law. After a time, however, he had been reconciled to his family, and had succeeded in obtaining such powerful protection that, while all the gaols of England were filled with his brethren, he was

---

* After this passage was written, I found, in the British Museum, a manuscript (Harl. MS. 7506.) entitled, "An Account of the Seizures, Sequestrations, great Spoil and Havock made upon the Estates of the several Protestant Dissenters called Quakers, upon Prosecution of Old Statutes made against Papist and Popish Recusants." The manuscript is marked as having belonged to James, and appears to have been given by his confidential servant, Colonel Graham, to Lord Oxford. This circumstance appears to me to confirm the view which I have taken of the King's conduct towards the Quakers.

permitted, during many years, to profess his opinions without molestation. Towards the close of the late reign he had obtained, in satisfaction of an old debt due to him from the crown, the grant of an immense region in North America. In this tract, then peopled only by Indian hunters, he had invited his persecuted friends to settle. His colony was still in its infancy when James mounted the throne.

Between James and Penn there had long been a familiar acquaintance. The Quaker now became a courtier, and almost a favourite. He was every day summoned from the gallery into the closet, and sometimes had long audiences while peers were kept waiting in the antechambers. It was noised abroad that he had more real power to help and hurt than many nobles who filled high offices. He was soon surrounded by flatterers and suppliants. His house at Kensington was sometimes thronged, at his hour of rising, by more than two hundred suitors.* He paid dear, however, for this seeming prosperity. Even his own sect looked coldly on him, and requited his services with obloquy. He was loudly accused of being a Papist, nay, a Jesuit. Some affirmed that he had been educated at St. Omers, and others that he had been ordained at Rome. These calumnies, indeed, could find credit only with the undiscerning multitude; but with these calumnies were mingled accusations much better founded.

To speak the whole truth concerning Penn is a task which requires some courage; for he is rather a mythical than a historical person. Rival nations and hostile sects have agreed in canonising him. England is proud of his name. A great commonwealth beyond the Atlantic regards him with a reverence similar to that which the Athenians felt for Theseus, and the Romans for Quirinus. The respectable society of which he was a member honours him as an apostle. By pious men of other persuasions he is generally regarded as a bright pattern of Christian virtue. Meanwhile admirers of a very different sort have sounded his praises. The French philosophers of the eighteenth century pardoned what they regarded as his superstitious fancies in consideration of his contempt

* Penn's visits to Whitehall, and levees at Kensington, are described with great vivacity, though in very bad Latin, by Gerard Croese. "Sumebat," he says, "rex sæpe secretum, non horarium, vero horarum plurium, in quo de variis rebus cum Penno serio sermonem conferebat, et interim differebat audire præcipuorum nobilium ordinem, qui hoc interim spatio in procœtone, in proximo, regem conventum præsto erant." Of the crowd of suitors at Penn's house, Croese says, "Visi quandoque de hoc genere hominum non minus bis centum."—Historia Quakeriana, lib. ii. 1695.

for priests, and of his cosmopolitan benevolence, impartially extended to all races and to all creeds. His name has thus become, throughout all civilised countries, a synonyme for probity and philanthropy.

Nor is this high reputation altogether unmerited. Penn was without doubt a man of eminent virtues. He had a strong sense of religious duty and a fervent desire to promote the happiness of mankind. On one or two points of high importance, he had notions more correct than were, in his day, common even among men of enlarged minds ; and as the proprietor and legislator of a province which, being almost uninhabited when it came into his possession, afforded a clear field for moral experiments, he had the rare good fortune of being able to carry his theories into practice without any compromise, and yet without any shock to existing institutions. He will always be mentioned with honour as a founder of a colony, who did not, in his dealings with a savage people, abuse the strength derived from civilisation, and as a lawgiver who, in an age of persecution, made religious liberty the corner stone of a polity. But his writings and his life furnish abundant proofs that he was not a man of strong sense. He had no skill in reading the characters of others. His confidence in persons less virtuous than himself led him into great errors and misfortunes. His enthusiasm for one great principle sometimes impelled him to violate other great principles which he ought to have held sacred. Nor was his rectitude altogether proof against the temptations to which it was exposed in that splendid and polite, but deeply corrupted society, with which he now mingled. The whole court was in a ferment with intrigues of gallantry and intrigues of ambition. The traffic in honours, places, and pardons was incessant. It was natural that a man who was daily seen at the palace, and who was known to have free access to majesty, should be frequently importuned to use his influence for purposes which a rigid morality must condemn. The integrity of Penn had stood firm against obloquy and persecution. But now, attacked by royal smiles, by female blandishments, by the insinuating eloquence and delicate flattery of veteran diplomatists and courtiers, his resolution began to give way. Titles and phrases against which he had often borne his testimony dropped occasionally from his lips and his pen. It would be well if he had been guilty of nothing worse than such compliances with the fashions of the world. Unhappily it cannot be concealed that he bore a chief part in some transactions condemned, not merely by the rigid code of the society to which he belonged, but by the general sense of all honest men. He afterwards solemnly protested that his hands were pure from illicit gain, and that he had never received any gratuity from those whom he had obliged, though he might easily, while his influence at court·lasted, have made a hundred and twenty thousand pounds.* To this assertion full credit is due. But bribes may be offered to vanity as well as to cupidity; and it is impossible to deny that Penn was cajoled into bearing a part in some unjustifiable transactions of which others enjoyed the profits.

Peculiar favour shown to Roman Catholics and Quakers.

The first use which he made of his credit was highly commendable. He strongly represented the sufferings of his brethren to the new King, who saw with pleasure that it was possible to grant indulgence to these quiet sectaries and to the Roman Catholics, without showing similar favour to other classes which were then under persecution. A list was framed of prisoners against whom proceedings had been instituted for not taking the oaths, or for not going to church, and of whose loyalty certificates had been produced to the government. These persons were discharged, and orders were given that no similar proceeding should be instituted till the royal pleasure should be further signified. In this way about fifteen hundred Quakers, and a still greater number of Roman Catholics, regained their liberty.†

And now the time had arrived when the English Parliament was to meet. The members of the House of Commons who had repaired to the capital were so numerous that there was much doubt whether their chamber, as it was then fitted up, would afford sufficient accommodation for them. They employed the days which immediately preceded the opening of the session in talking over public affairs with each other and with the agents of the government. A great meeting of the loyal party was held at the Fountain Tavern in the Strand; and Roger Lestrange, who had recently been knighted

---

* " Twenty thousand into my pocket; and a hundred thousand into my province."—Penn's Letter to Popple."

† These orders, signed by Sunderland, will be found in Sewel's History. They bear date April 18. 1685. They are written in a style singularly obscure and intricate: but I think that I have exhibited the meaning correctly. I have not been able to find any proof that any person, not a Roman Catholic or a Quaker, regained his freedom under these orders. See Neal's History of the Puritans, vol. ii. chap. ii.; Gerard Croese, lib. ii. Croese estimates the number of Quakers liberated at fourteen hundred and sixty.

by the King, and returned to Parliament by the city of Winchester, took a leading part in their consultations.*

It soon appeared that a large portion of the Commons had views which did not altogether agree with those of the Court. The Tory country gentlemen were, with scarcely one exception, desirous to maintain the Test Act and the Habeas Corpus Act; and some among them talked of voting the revenue only for a term of years. But they were perfectly ready to enact severe laws against the Whigs, and would gladly have seen all the supporters of the Exclusion Bill made incapable of holding office. The King, on the other hand, desired to obtain from the Parliament a revenue for life, the admission of Roman Catholics to office, and the repeal of the Habeas Corpus Act. On these three objects his heart was set; and he was by no means disposed to accept as a substitute for them a penal law against Exclusionists. Such a law, indeed, would have been positively unpleasing to him; for one class of Exclusionists stood high in his favour, that class of which Sunderland was the representative, that class which had joined the Whigs in the days of the plot, merely because the Whigs were predominant, and which had changed with the change of fortune. James justly regarded these renegades as the most serviceable tools that he could employ. It was not from the stouthearted Cavaliers, who had been true to him in his adversity, that he could expect abject and unscrupulous obedience in his prosperity. The men who, impelled, not by zeal for liberty or for religion, but merely by selfish cupidity and selfish fear, had assisted to oppress him when he was weak, were the very men who, impelled by the same cupidity and the same fear, would assist him to oppress his people now that he was strong.† Though vindictive, he was not indiscriminately vindictive. Not a single instance can be mentioned in which he showed a generous compassion to those who had opposed him honestly and on public grounds. But he frequently spared and promoted those whom some vile motive had induced to injure him. For that meanness which marked them out as fit implements of tyranny was so precious in his estimation that he regarded it with some indulgence even when it was exhibited at his own expense.

* Barillon, $\frac{May\ 28.}{June\ 7.}$ 1685. Observator, May 27. 1685; Sir J. Reresby's Memoirs.

† Lewis wrote to Barillon about this class of Exclusionists as follows: "L'intérêt qu'ils auront à effacer cette tâche par des services considérables les portera, selons toutes les apparences, à le servir plus utilement que ne pourroient faire ceux qui ont toujours été les plus attachés à sa personne." May $\frac{15}{25}$. 1685.

The King's wishes were communicated through several channels to the Tory members of the Lower House. The majority was easily persuaded to forego all thoughts of a penal law against the Exclusionists, and to consent that His Majesty should have the revenue for life. But about the Test Act and the Habeas Corpus Act the emissaries of the Court could obtain no satisfactory assurances.*

Meeting of the English Parliament.

On the nineteenth of May the session was opened. The benches of the Commons presented a singular spectacle. That great party, which, in the last three Parliaments, had been predominant, had now dwindled to a pitiable minority, and was indeed little more than a fifteenth part of the House. Of the five hundred and thirteen knights and burgesses only a hundred and thirty-five had ever sate in that place before. It is evident that a body of men so raw and inexperienced must have been, in some important qualities, far below the average of our representative assemblies.†

The management of the House was confided by James to two peers of the kingdom of Scotland. One of them, Charles Middleton, Earl of Middleton, after holding high office at Edinburgh, had, shortly before the death of the late King, been sworn of the English Privy Council, and appointed one of the Secretaries of State. With him was joined Richard Graham, Viscount Preston, who had long held the post of Envoy at Versailles.

Trevor chosen speaker.

The first business of the Commons was to elect a Speaker. Who should be the man, was a question which had been much debated in the cabinet. Guildford had recommended Sir Thomas Meres, who, like himself, ranked among the Trimmers. Jeffreys, who missed no opportunity of crossing the Lord Keeper, had pressed the claims of Sir John Trevor. Trevor had been bred half a pettifogger and half a gambler, had brought to political life sentiments and principles worthy of both his callings, had become a parasite of the Chief Justice, and could, on occasion, imitate, not unsuccessfully, the vituperative style of his patron. The minion of Jeffreys was, as might have been expected, preferred by James, was proposed by Middleton, and was chosen without opposition.‡

Character of Seymour.

Thus far all went smoothly. But an adversary of no common prowess was watching his time. This was Edward

---

* Barillon, May $\frac{4}{14}$. 1685; Sir John   May 22. 1685.
Reresby's Memoirs.   ‡ Roger North's Life of Guildford,
† Burnet, i. 626.; Evelyn's Diary,   218.; Bramston's Memoirs.

Seymour of Berry Pomeroy Castle, member for the city of Exeter. Seymour's birth put him on a level with the noblest subjects in Europe. He was the right heir male of the body of that Duke of Somerset who had been brother in law of King Henry the Eighth, and Protector of the realm of England. In the limitation of the dukedom of Somerset, the elder son of the Protector had been postponed to the younger son. From the younger son the Dukes of Somerset were descended. From the elder son was descended the family which dwelt at Berry Pomeroy. Seymour's fortune was large, and his influence in the West of England extensive. Nor was the importance derived from descent and wealth the only importance which belonged to him. He was one of the most skilful debaters and men of business in the kingdom. He had sate many years in the House of Commons, had studied all its rules and usages, and thoroughly understood its peculiar temper. He had been elected speaker in the late reign under circumstances which made that distinction peculiarly honourable. During several generations none but lawyers had been called to the chair; and he was the first country gentleman whose abilities and acquirements enabled him to break that long prescription. He had subsequently held high political office, and had sate in the Cabinet. But his haughty and unaccommodating temper had given so much disgust that he had been forced to retire. He was a Tory and a Churchman: he had strenuously opposed the Exclusion Bill: he had been persecuted by the Whigs in the day of their prosperity; and he could therefore safely venture to hold language for which any person suspected of republicanism would have been sent to the Tower. He had long been at the head of a strong parliamentary connection, which was called the Western Alliance, and which included many gentlemen of Devonshire, Somersetshire, and Cornwall.*

In every House of Commons, a member who unites eloquence, knowledge, and habits of business, to opulence and illustrious descent, must be highly considered. But in a House of Commons from which many of the most eminent orators and parliamentary tacticians of the age were excluded, and which was crowded with people who had never heard a debate, the influence of such a man was peculiarly formidable. Weight of moral character was indeed wanting to Edward Seymour. He was licentious, profane, corrupt, too proud to

* North's Life of Guildford, 228.; News from Westminster.

behave with common politeness, yet not too proud to pocket illicit gain. But he was so useful an ally, and so mischievous an enemy, that he was frequently courted even by those who most detested him.*

He was now in bad humour with the government. His interest had been weakened in some places by the remodelling of the western boroughs: his pride had been wounded by the elevation of Trevor to the chair; and he took an early opportunity of revenging himself.

The King's speech to the Parliament.

On the twenty-second of May the Commons were summoned to the bar of the Lords; and the King, seated on his throne, made a speech to both Houses. He declared himself resolved to maintain the established government in Church and State. But he weakened the effect of this declaration by addressing an extraordinary admonition to the Commons. He was apprehensive, he said, that they might be inclined to dole out money to him, from time to time, in the hope that they should thus force him to call them frequently together. But he must warn them that he was not to be so dealt with, and that, if they wished him to meet them often, they must use him well. As it was evident that without money the government could not be carried on, these expressions plainly implied that, if they did not give him as much money as he wished, he would take it. Strange to say, this harangue was received with loud cheers by the Tory gentlemen at the bar. Such acclamations were then usual. It has now been, during many years, the grave and decorous usage of Parliaments to hear, in respectful silence, all expressions, acceptable or unacceptable, which are uttered from the throne.†

It was then the custom that, after the King had concisely explained his reasons for calling Parliament together, the minister who held the Great Seal should, at more length, explain to the Houses the state of public affairs. Guildford, in imitation of his predecessors, Clarendon, Bridgeman, Shaftesbury, and Nottingham, had prepared an elaborate oration, but found, to his great mortification, that his services were not wanted.‡

Debate in the Commons.

As soon as the Commons had returned to their own chamber, it was proposed that they should resolve them-

* Burnet, i. 382.; Letter from Lord Conway to Sir George Rawdon, Dec. 28. 1677, in the Rawdon Papers.

† London Gazette, May 25. 1685; Evelyn's Diary, May 22. 1685.
‡ North's Life of Guildford, 256.

selves into a Committee, for the purpose of settling a revenue on the King.

Then Seymour stood up. How he stood, looking like what he was, the chief of a dissolute and high spirited gentry, with the artifical ringlets clustering in fashionable profusion round his shoulders, and a mingled expression of voluptuousness and disdain in his eye and on his lip, the likenesses of him which still remain enable us to imagine. It was not, the haughty Cavalier said, his wish that the Parliament should withhold from the Crown the means of carrying on the government. But was there indeed a Parliament? Were there not on the benches many men who had, as all the world knew, no right to sit there, many men whose elections were tainted by corruption, many men forced by intimidation on reluctant voters, and many men returned by corporations which had no legal existence? Had not constituent bodies been remodelled, in defiance of royal charters and of immemorial prescription? Had not returning officers been everywhere the unscrupulous agents of the Court? Seeing that the very principle of representation had been thus systematically attacked, he knew not how to call the throng of gentlemen which he saw around him by the honourable name of a House of Commons. Yet never was there a time when it more concerned the public weal that the character of Parliament should stand high. Great dangers impended over the ecclesiastical and civil constitution of the realm. It was matter of vulgar notoriety, it was matter which required no proof, that the Test Act, the rampart of religion, and the Habeas Corpus Act, the rampart of liberty, were marked out for destruction. "Before we proceed to legislate on questions so momentous, let us at least ascertain whether we really are a legislature. Let our first proceeding be to enquire into the manner in which the elections have been conducted. And let us look to it that the enquiry be impartial. For, if the nation shall find that no redress is to be obtained by peaceful methods, we may perhaps ere long suffer the justice which we refuse to do." He concluded by moving that, before any supply was granted, the House would take into consideration petitions against returns, and that no member whose right to sit was disputed should be allowed to vote.

Not a cheer was heard. Not a member ventured to second the motion. Indeed, Seymour had said much that no other man could have said with impunity. The proposition fell to

Speech of Seymour.

the ground, and was not even entered on the journals. But a mighty effect had been produced. Barillon informed his master that many who had not dared to applaud that remarkable speech had cordially approved of it, that it was the universal subject of conversation throughout London, and that the impression made on the public mind seemed likely to be durable.*

The revenue voted.

The Commons went into committee without delay, and voted to the King, for life, the whole revenue enjoyed by his brother.†

Proceedings of the Commons concerning religion.

The zealous churchmen who formed the majority of the House seem to have been of opinion that the promptitude with which they had met the wish of James, touching the revenue, entitled them to expect some concession on his part. They said that much had been done to gratify him, and that they must now do something to gratify the nation. The House, therefore, resolved itself into a Grand Committee of Religion, in order to consider the best means of providing for the security of the ecclesiastical establishment. In that Committee two resolutions were unanimously adopted. The first expressed fervent attachment to the Church of England. The second called on the King to put in execution the penal laws against all persons who were not members of that Church.‡

The Whigs would doubtless have wished to see the Protestant dissenters tolerated, and the Roman Catholics alone persecuted. But the Whigs were a small and a disheartened minority. They therefore kept themselves as much as possible out of sight, dropped their party name, abstained from obtruding their peculiar opinions on a hostile audience, and steadily supported every proposition tending to disturb the harmony which as yet subsisted between the Parliament and the Court.

When the proceedings of the Committee of Religion were known at Whitehall, the King's anger was great. Nor can we justly blame him for resenting the conduct of the Tories. If they were disposed to require the rigorous execution of the penal code, they clearly ought to have supported the Exclusion

---

* Burnet, i. 639.; Evelyn's Diary, May 22. 1685; Barillon, $\frac{May\ 25.}{June\ 2.}$ and $\frac{May\ 25.}{June\ 4.}$ 1685. The silence of the journals perplexed Mr. Fox: but it is explained by the circumstance that Seymour's motion was not seconded.

† Journals, May 22. Stat. Jac. II. i. 1.

‡ Journals, May 26, 27. Sir J. Reresby's Memoirs.

Bill. For to place a Papist on the throne, and then to insist on his persecuting to the death the teachers of that faith in which alone, on his principles, salvation could be found, was monstrous. In mitigating by a lenient administration the severity of the bloody laws of Elizabeth, the King violated no constitutional principle. He only exerted a power which has always belonged to the crown. Nay, he only did what was afterwards done by a succession of sovereigns zealous for Protestantism, by William, by Anne, and by the princes of the House of Brunswick. Had he suffered Roman Catholic priests, whose lives he could save without infringing any law, to be hanged, drawn, and quartered, for discharging what he considered as their first duty, he would have drawn on himself the hatred and contempt even of those to whose prejudices he had made so shameful a concession; and, had he contented himself with granting to the members of his own Church a practical toleration by a large exercise of his unquestioned prerogative of mercy, posterity would have unanimously applauded him.

The Commons probably felt on reflection that they had acted absurdly. They were also disturbed by learning that the King, to whom they looked up with superstitious reverence, was greatly provoked. They made haste, therefore, to atone for their offence. In the House, they unanimously reversed the decision which, in the Committee, they had unanimously adopted, and passed a resolution importing that they relied with entire confidence on His Majesty's gracious promise to protect that religion which was dearer to them than life itself.*

Three days later the King informed the House that his brother had left some debts, and that the stores of the navy and ordnance were nearly exhausted. It was promptly resolved that new taxes should be imposed. The person on whom devolved the task of devising ways and means was Sir Dudley North, younger brother of the Lord Keeper. Dudley North was one of the ablest men of his time. He had early in life been sent to the Levant, and had there been long engaged in mercantile pursuits. Most men would, in such a situation, have allowed their faculties to rust. For at Smyrna and Constantinople there were few books and few intelligent companions. But the young factor had one of those vigorous understandings which are independent of ex-

Additional taxes voted.

Sir Dudley North.

* Commons' Journals, May 27. 1685.

ternal aids. In his solitude he meditated deeply on the philosophy of trade, and thought out by degrees a complete and admirable theory, substantially the same with that which, a century later, was expounded by Adam Smith. After an exile of many years, Dudley North returned to England with a large fortune, and commenced business as a Turkey merchant in the City of London. His profound knowledge, both speculative and practical, of commercial matters, and the perspicuity and liveliness with which he explained his views, speedily introduced him to the notice of statesmen. The government found in him at once an enlightened adviser and an unscrupulous slave. For with his rare mental endowments were joined lax principles and an unfeeling heart. When the Tory reaction was in full progress, he had consented to be made Sheriff for the express purpose of assisting the vengeance of the court. His juries had never failed to find verdicts of Guilty; and, on a day of judicial butchery, carts, loaded with the legs and arms of quartered Whigs, were, to the great discomposure of his lady, driven to his fine house in Basinghall Street for orders. His services had been rewarded with the honour of knighthood, with an Alderman's gown, and with the office of Commissioner of the Customs. He had been brought into Parliament for Banbury, and, though a new member, was the person on whom the Lord Treasurer chiefly relied for the conduct of financial business in the Lower House.*

Though the Commons were unanimous in their resolution to grant a further supply to the crown, they were by no means agreed as to the sources from which that supply should be drawn. It was speedily determined that part of the sum which was required should be raised by laying an additional impost, for a term of eight years, on wine and vinegar: but something more than this was needed. Several absurd schemes were suggested. Many country gentlemen were disposed to put a heavy tax on all new buildings in the capital. Such a tax, it was hoped, would check the growth of a city which had long been regarded with jealousy and aversion by the rural aristocracy. Dudley North's plan was that additional duties should be imposed, for a term of eight years, on sugar and tobacco. A great clamour was raised. Colonial merchants, grocers, sugar bakers and tobacconists,

* Roger North's Life of Sir Dudley   Mr. M'Culloch's Literature of Political
North; Life of Lord Guildford, 166.;   Economy.

petitioned the House and besieged the public offices. The people of Bristol, who were deeply interested in the trade with Virginia and Jamaica, sent up a deputation which was heard at the bar of the Commons. Rochester was for a moment staggered; but North's ready wit and perfect knowledge of trade prevailed, both in the Treasury and in the Parliament, against all opposition. The old members were amazed at seeing a man who had not been a fortnight in the House, and whose life had been chiefly passed in foreign countries, assume with confidence, and discharge with ability, all the functions of a Chancellor of the Exchequer.*

His plan was adopted; and thus the Crown was in possession of a clear income of about nineteen hundred thousand pounds, derived from England alone. Such an income was then more than sufficient for the support of the government in time of peace.†

The Lords had, in the meantime, discussed several important questions. The Tory party had always been strong among the peers. It included the whole bench of Bishops, and had been reinforced during the four years which had elapsed since the last dissolution, by several fresh creations. Of the new nobles, the most conspicuous were the Lord Treasurer Rochester, the Lord Keeper Guildford, the Lord Chief Justice Jeffreys, the Lord Godolphin, and the Lord Churchill, who, after his return from Versailles, had been made a Baron of England.

Proceedings of the Lords.

The peers early took into consideration the case of four members of their body who had been impeached in the late reign, but had never been brought to trial, and had, after a long confinement, been admitted to bail by the Court of King's Bench. Three of the noblemen who were thus under recognisances were Roman Catholics. The fourth was a Protestant of great note and influence, the Earl of Danby. Since he had fallen from power and had been accused of treason by the Commons, four Parliaments had been dissolved; but he had been neither acquitted nor condemned. In 1679 the Lords had considered, with reference to his situation, the question whether an impeachment was or was not terminated by a dissolution. They had resolved, after long debate and full examination of precedents, that the impeachment was still pending. That resolution they now rescinded. A few Whig

---

* Life of Dudley North, 176.; Lonsdale's Memoirs; Van Citters, June. $\frac{12}{22}$. 1685.
† Commons' Journals, March 1. 1689.

nobles protested against this step, but to little purpose. The Commons silently acquiesced in the decision of the Upper House. Danby again took his seat among his peers, and became an active and powerful member of the Tory party.*

The constitutional question on which the Lords thus, in the short space of six years, pronounced two diametrically opposite decisions, slept during more than a century, and was at length revived by the dissolution which took place during the long trial of Warren Hastings. It was then necessary to determine whether the rule laid down in 1679, or the opposite rule laid down in 1685, was to be accounted the law of the land. The point was long debated in both houses; and the best legal and parliamentary abilities which an age preeminently fertile both in legal and in parliamentary ability could supply were employed in the discussion. The lawyers were not unequally divided. Thurlow, Kenyon, Scott, and Erskine maintained that the dissolution had put an end to the impeachment. The contrary doctrine was held by Mansfield, Camden, Loughborough, and Grant. But among those statesmen who grounded their arguments, not on precedents and technical analogies, but on deep and broad constitutional principles, there was little difference of opinion. Pitt and Grenville, as well as Burke and Fox, held that the impeachment was still pending. Both Houses by great majorities set aside the decision of 1685, and pronounced the decision of 1679 to be in conformity with the law of Parliament.

Bill for reversing the attainder of Stafford. Of the national crimes which had been committed during the panic excited by the fictions of Oates, the most signal had been the judicial murder of Stafford. The sentence of that unhappy nobleman was now regarded by all impartial persons as unjust. The principal witness for the prosecution had been convicted of a series of foul perjuries. It was the duty of the legislature, in such circumstances, to do justice to the memory of a guiltless sufferer, and to efface an unmerited stain from a name long illustrious in our annals. A bill for reversing the attainder of Stafford was passed by the Upper House, in spite of the murmurs of a few peers who were unwilling to admit that they had shed innocent blood. The Commons read the bill twice without a division, and ordered it to be committed. But, on the day appointed for the committee, arrived news that a formidable rebellion had broken out in the West of England. It was consequently necessary

---

* Lords' Journals, March 18, 19. 1679, May 22, 1685.

to postpone much important business. The amends due to the memory of Stafford were deferred, as was supposed, only for a short time. But the misgovernment of James in a few months completely turned the tide of public feeling. During several generations the Roman Catholics were in no condition to demand reparation for injustice, and accounted themselves happy if they were permitted to live unmolested in obscurity and silence. At length, in the reign of King George the Fourth, more than a hundred and forty years after the day on which the blood of Stafford was shed on Tower Hill, the tardy expiation was accomplished. A law annulling the attainder and restoring the injured family to its ancient dignities was presented to Parliament by the ministers of the crown, was eagerly welcomed by public men of all parties, and was passed without one dissentient voice.*

It is now necessary that I should trace the origin and progress of that rebellion by which the deliberations of the Houses were suddenly interrupted.

* Stat. 5 Geo. IV. c. 46.

CHAPTER V.

TOWARDS the close of the reign of Charles the Second, some Whigs who had been deeply implicated in the plot so fatal to their party, and who knew themselves to be marked out for destruction, had sought an asylum in the Low Countries.

These refugees were in general men of fiery temper and weak judgment. They were also under the influence of that peculiar illusion which seems to belong to their situation. A politician driven into banishment by a hostile faction generally sees the society which he has quitted through a false medium. Every object is distorted and discoloured by his regrets, his longings, and his resentments. Every little discontent appears to him to portend a revolution. Every riot is a rebellion. He cannot be convinced that his country does not pine for him as much as he pines for his country. He imagines that all his old associates, who still dwell at their homes and enjoy their estates, are tormented by the same feelings which make life a burden to himself. The longer his expatriation, the greater does this hallucination become. The lapse of time, which cools the ardour of the friends whom he has left behind, inflames his. Every month his impatience to revisit his native land increases; and every month his native land remembers and misses him less. This delusion becomes almost a madness when many exiles who suffer in the same cause herd together in a foreign country. Their chief employment is to talk of what they once were, and of what they may yet be, to goad each other into animosity against the common enemy, to feed each other with extravagant hopes of victory and revenge. Thus they become ripe for enterprises which would at once be pronounced hopeless by any man whose passions had not deprived him of the power of calculating chances.

In this mood were many of the outlaws who had assembled on the Continent. The correspondence which they kept up with England was, for the most part, such as tended to excite

Whig refugees on the Continent.

Their correspondents in England.

their feelings and to mislead their judgment. Their information concerning the temper of the public mind was chiefly derived from the worst members of the Whig party, from men who were plotters and libellers by profession, who were pursued by the officers of justice, who were forced to skulk in disguise through back streets, and who sometimes lay hid for weeks together in cocklofts and cellars. The statesmen who had formerly been the ornaments of the Country Party, the statesmen who afterwards guided the councils of the Convention, would have given advice very different from that which was given by such men as John Wildman and Henry Danvers.

Wildman had served forty years before in the parliamentary army, but had been more distinguished there as an agitator than as a soldier, and had early quitted the profession of arms for pursuits better suited to his temper. His hatred of monarchy had induced him to engage in a long series of conspiracies, first against the Protector, and then against the Stuarts. But with Wildman's fanaticism was joined a tender care for his own safety. He had a wonderful skill in grazing the edge of treason. No man understood better how to instigate others to desperate enterprises by words which, when repeated to a jury, might seem innocent, or, at worst, ambiguous. Such was his cunning that, though always plotting, though always known to be plotting, and though long malignantly watched by a vindictive government, he eluded every danger, and died in his bed, after having seen two generations of his accomplices die on the gallows.* Danvers was a man of the same class, hotheaded, but fainthearted, constantly urged to the brink of danger by enthusiasm, and constantly stopped on that brink by cowardice. He had considerable influence among a portion of the Baptists, had written largely in defence of their peculiar opinions, and had drawn down on himself the severe censure of the most respectable Puritans by attempting to palliate the crimes of Matthias and John of Leyden. It is probable that, had he possessed a little courage, he would have trodden in the footsteps of the wretches whom he defended. He was, at this time, concealing himself from the officers of justice; for warrants were out against him on

* Clarendon's History of the Rebellion, book xiv.; Burnet's Own Times, i. 546. 625.; Wade's and Ireton's Narratives, Lansdowne MS. 1152.; West's information in the Appendix to Sprat's True Account.

account of a grossly calumnious paper of which the government had discovered him to be the author.*

Characters of the leading refugees.

It is easy to imagine what kind of intelligence and counsel men, such as have been described, were likely to send to the outlaws in the Netherlands. Of the general character of those outlaws an estimate may be formed from a few samples.

Ayloffe.

One of the most conspicuous among them was John Ayloffe, a lawyer connected by affinity with the Hydes, and through the Hydes, with James. Ayloffe had early made himself remarkable by offering a whimsical insult to the government. At a time when the ascendency of the court of Versailles had excited general uneasiness, he had contrived to put a wooden shoe, the established type, among the English, of French tyranny, into the chair of the House of Commons. He had subsequently been concerned in the Whig plot; but there is no reason to believe that he was a party to the design of assassinating the royal brothers. He was a man of parts and courage; but his moral character did not stand high. The Puritan divines whispered that he was a careless Gallio or something worse, and that, whatever zeal he might profess for civil liberty, the Saints would do well to avoid all connection with him.†

Wade.

Nathaniel Wade was, like Ayloffe, a lawyer. He had long resided at Bristol, and had been celebrated in his own neighbourhood as a vehement republican. At one time he had formed a project of emigrating to New Jersey, where he expected to find institutions better suited to his taste than those of England. His activity in electioneering had introduced him to the notice of some Whig nobles. They had employed him professionally, and had, at length, admitted him to their most secret counsels. He had been deeply concerned in the scheme of insurrection, and had undertaken to head a rising in his own city. He had also been privy to the more odious plot against the lives of Charles and James. But he always declared that, though privy to it, he had abhorred it, and had attempted to dissuade his associates from carrying their de-

---

* London Gazette, January 4. 168⁴⁄₅.; Ferguson MS. in Eachard's History, iii. 764.; Grey's Narrative; Sprat's True Account; Danvers's Treatise on Baptism; Danvers's Innocency and Truth vindicated; Crosby's History of the English Baptists.

† Sprat's True Account; Burnet, i. 634.; Wade's Confession, Harl. MS. 6845

Lord Howard of Escrick accused Ayloffe of proposing to assassinate the Duke of York; but Lord Howard was an abject liar; and this story was not part of his original confession, but was added afterwards by way of supplement, and therefore deserves no credit whatever.

sign into effect. For a man bred to civil pursuits, Wade seems to have had, in an unusual degree, that sort of ability and that sort of nerve which make a good soldier. Unhappily his principles and his courage proved to be not of sufficient force to support him when the fight was over, and when, in a prison, he had to choose between death and infamy.*

Another fugitive was Richard Goodenough, who had for- Good-
merly been Under Sheriff of London. On this man his party enough.
had long relied for services of no honourable kind, and especially for the selection of jurymen not likely to be troubled
with scruples in political cases. He had been deeply concerned in those dark and atrocious parts of the Whig plot
which had been carefully concealed from the most respectable Whigs. Nor is it possible to plead, in extenuation of his
guilt, that he was misled by inordinate zeal for the public
good. For it will be seen that, after having disgraced a
noble cause by his crimes, he betrayed it in order to escape
from his well merited punishment.†

Very different was the character of Richard Rumbold. He had Rumbold.
held a commission in Cromwell's own regiment, had guarded
the scaffold before the Banqueting House on the day of the
great execution, had fought at Dunbar and Worcester, and
had always shown in the highest degree the qualities which
distinguished the invincible army in which he served, courage
of the truest temper, fiery enthusiasm, both political and religious, and with that enthusiasm, all the power of selfgovern-
ment which is characteristic of men trained in well disciplined
camps to command and to obey. When the republican troops
were disbanded, Rumbold became a maltster, and carried on
his trade near Hoddesdon, in that building from which the Rye
House plot derives its name. It had been suggested, though
not absolutely determined, in the conferences of the most
violent and unscrupulous of the malecontents, that armed men
should be stationed in the Rye House to attack the Guards
who were to escort Charles and James from Newmarket to
London. In these conferences Rumbold had borne a part
from which he would have shrunk with horror, if his clear
understanding had not been overclouded, and his manly heart
corrupted, by party spirit.‡

* Wade's Confession, Harl. MS. 6845.; Lansdowne MS. 1152.; Holloway's narrative in the Appendix to Sprat's True Account. Wade owned that Holloway had told nothing but truth.

† Sprat's True Account and Appen-dix, *passim.*

‡ Sprat's True Account and Appendix; Proceedings against Rumbold in the Collection of State Trials; Burnet's Own

A more important exile was Ford Grey, Lord Grey of Wark.
He had been a zealous Exclusionist, had concurred in the de-
Lord Grey. sign of insurrection, and had been committed to the Tower,
but had succeeded in making his keepers drunk, and in effecting his escape to the Continent. His parliamentary abilities
were great, and his manners pleasing : but his life had been
sullied by a great domestic crime. His wife was a daughter
of the noble house of Berkeley. Her sister, the Lady Henrietta Berkeley, was allowed to associate and correspond with
him as with a brother by blood. A fatal attachment sprang
up. The high spirit and strong passions of Lady Henrietta
broke through all restraints of virtue and decorum. A scandalous elopement disclosed to the whole kingdom the shame
of two illustrious families. Grey and some of the agents who
had served him in his amour were brought to trial on a charge
of conspiracy. A scene unparalleled in our legal history was
exhibited in the Court of King's Bench. The seducer appeared
with dauntless front, accompanied by his paramour. Nor
did the great Whig lords flinch from their friend's side even
in that extremity. Those whom he had wronged stood over
against him, and were moved to transports of rage by the sight
of him. The old Earl of Berkeley poured forth reproaches
and curses on the wretched Henrietta. The Countess gave
evidence broken by many sobs, and at length fell down in a
swoon. The jury found a verdict of Guilty. When the court
rose, Lord Berkeley called on all his friends to help him to
seize his daughter. The partisans of Grey rallied round her.
Swords were drawn on both sides : a skirmish took place in
Westminster Hall ; and it was with difficulty that the Judges
and tipstaves parted the combatants. In our time such a
trial would be fatal to the character of a public man ; but in
that age the standard of morality among the great was so low,
and party spirit was so violent, that Grey still continued to
have considerable influence, though the Puritans, who formed
a strong section of the Whig party, looked somewhat coldly
on him.*

One part of the character, or rather, it may be, of the fortune, of Grey deserves notice. It was admitted that everywhere, except on the field of battle, he showed a high degree
of courage. More than once, in embarrassing circumstances,

Times, i. 633.; Appendix to Fox's His-   Collection of State Trials ; Sprat's True
tory, No. IV.   Account.
  * Grey's Narrative; his trial in the

when his life and liberty were at stake, the dignity of his deportment and his perfect command of all his faculties extorted praise from those who neither loved nor esteemed him. But as a soldier he incurred, less perhaps by his fault than by mischance, the degrading imputation of personal cowardice.

In this respect he differed widely from his friend the Duke of Monmouth. Ardent and intrepid on the field of battle, Monmouth was everywhere else effeminate and irresolute. The accident of his birth, his personal courage, and his superficial graces, had placed him in a post for which he was altogether unfitted. After witnessing the ruin of the party of which he had been the nominal head, he had retired to Holland. The Prince and Princess of Orange had now ceased to regard him as a rival. They received him most hospitably; for they hoped that, by treating him with kindness, they should establish a claim to the gratitude of his father. They knew that paternal affection was not yet wearied out, that letters and supplies of money still came secretly from Whitehall to Monmouth's retreat, and that Charles frowned on those who sought to pay their court to him by speaking ill of his banished son. The Duke had been encouraged to expect that, in a very short time, if he gave no new cause of displeasure, he would be recalled to his native land, and restored to all his high honours and commands. Animated by such expectations he had been the life of the Hague during the late winter. He had been the most conspicuous figure at a succession of balls in that splendid Orange Hall, which blazes on every side with the most ostentatious colouring of Jordaens and Hondthorst.* He had taught the English country dance to the Dutch ladies, and had in his turn learned from them to skate on the canals. The Princess had accompanied him in his expeditions on the ice; and the figure which she made there, poised on one leg, and clad in petticoats shorter than are generally worn by ladies so strictly decorous, had caused some wonder and mirth to the foreign ministers. The sullen gravity which had been characteristic of the Stadtholder's court seemed to have vanished before the influence of the fascinating Englishman. Even the stern and pensive William relaxed into good humour when his brilliant guest appeared.†

Monmouth.

---

* In the Pepysian Collection is a print representing one of the balls which about this time William and Mary gave in the Oranje Zaal.

† Avaux Neg. January 25. 1685. Letter from James to the Princess of Orange dated January 168⅘, among Birch's Extracts in the British Museum.

Monmouth meanwhile carefully avoided all that could give offence in the quarter to which he looked for protection. He saw little of any Whigs, and nothing of those violent men who had been concerned in the worse part of the Whig plot. He was therefore loudly accused, by his old associates, of fickleness and ingratitude.*

Ferguson.   By none of the exiles was this accusation urged with more vehemence and bitterness than by Robert Ferguson, the Judas of Dryden's great satire. Ferguson was by birth a Scot; but England had long been his residence. At the time of the Restoration, indeed, he had held a living in Kent. He had been bred a Presbyterian; but the Presbyterians had cast him out, and he had become an Independent. He had been master of an academy which the Dissenters had set up at Islington as a rival to Westminster School and the Charter House; and he had preached to large congregations at a meeting house in Moorfields. He had also published some theological treatises which may still be found in the dusty recesses of a few old libraries; but, though texts of scripture were always on his lips, those who had pecuniary transactions with him soon found him to be a mere swindler.

At length he turned his attention almost entirely from theology to the worst part of politics. He belonged to the class whose office it is to render in troubled times to exasperated parties those services from which honest men shrink in disgust and prudent men in fear, the class of fanatical knaves. Violent, malignant, regardless of truth, insensible to shame, insatiable of notoriety, delighting in intrigue, in tumult, in mischief for its own sake, he toiled during many years in the darkest mines of faction. He lived among libellers and false witnesses. He was the keeper of a secret purse from which agents too vile to be acknowledged received hire, and the director of a secret press whence pamphlets, bearing no name, were daily issued. He boasted that he had contrived to scatter lampoons about the terrace of Windsor, and even to lay them under the royal pillow. In this way of life he was put to many shifts, was forced to assume many names, and at one time had four different lodgings in different corners of London. He was deeply engaged in the Rye House plot. There is, indeed, reason to believe that he was the orignal author of those sanguinary

* Grey's Narrative; Wade's Confession, Lansdowne MS. 1152.

schemes which brought so much discredit on the whole Whig party. When the conspiracy was detected and his associates were in dismay, he bade them farewell with a laugh, and told them that they were novices, that he had been used to flight, concealment, and disguise, and that he should never leave off plotting while he lived. He escaped to the Continent. But it seemed that even on the Continent he was not secure. The English envoys at foreign courts were directed to be on the watch for him. The French government offered a reward of five hundred pistoles to any who would seize him. Nor was it easy for him to escape notice; for his broad Scotch accent, his tall and lean figure, his lantern jaws, the gleam of his sharp eyes which were always overhung by his wig, his cheeks inflamed by an eruption, his shoulders deformed by a stoop, and his gait distinguished from that of other men by a peculiar shuffle, made him remarkable wherever he appeared. But, though he was, as it seemed, pursued with peculiar animosity, it was whispered that this animosity was feigned, and that the officers of justice had secret orders not to see him. That he was really a bitter malecontent can scarcely be doubted. But there is strong reason to believe that he provided for his own safety by pretending at Whitehall to be a spy on the Whigs, and by furnishing the government with just so much information as sufficed to keep up his credit. This hypothesis furnishes a simple explanation of what seemed to his associates to be his unnatural recklessness and audacity. Being himself out of danger, he always gave his vote for the most violent and perilous course, and sneered very complacently at the pusillanimity of men who, not having taken the infamous precautions on which he relied, were disposed to think twice before they placed life, and objects dearer than life, on a single hazard.*

As soon as he was in the Low Countries he began to form new projects against the English government, and found among his fellow emigrants men ready to listen to his evil counsels. Monmouth, however, stood obstinately aloof; and, without the help of Monmouth's immense popularity, it was impossible to effect anything. Yet such was the impatience and rashness of the exiles that they tried to find another

* Burnet, i. 542.; Wood, Ath. Ox. 697.; Sprat's True Account, *passim*; under the name of Owen; Absalom and Lond. Gaz. Aug. 6. 1683; Nonconformist's Memorial; North's Examen, 399.

leader. They sent an embassy to that solitary retreat on the shores of Lake Leman where Edmund Ludlow, once conspicuous among the chiefs of the parliamentary army and among the members of the High Court of Justice, had, during many years, hidden himself from the vengeance of the restored Stuarts. The stern old regicide, however, refused to quit his hermitage. His work, he said, was done. If England was still to be saved, she must be saved by younger men.*

The unexpected demise of the crown changed the whole aspect of affairs. Any hope which the proscribed Whigs might have cherished of returning peaceably to their native land was extinguished by the death of a careless and good-natured prince, and by the accession of a prince obstinate in all things, and especially obstinate in revenge. Ferguson was in his element. Destitute of the talents both of a writer and of a statesman, he had in a high degree the unenviable qualifications of a tempter; and now, with the malevolent activity and dexterity of an evil spirit, he ran from outlaw to outlaw, chattered in every ear, and stirred up in every bosom savage animosities and wild desires.

He no longer despaired of being able to seduce Monmouth. The situation of that unhappy young man was completely changed. While he was dancing and skating at the Hague, and expecting every day a summons to London, he was overwhelmed with misery by the tidings of his father's death and of his uncle's accession. During the night which followed the arrival of the news, those who lodged near him could distinctly hear his sobs and his piercing cries. He quitted the Hague the next day, having solemnly pledged his word, both to the Prince and to the Princess of Orange, not to attempt anything against the government of England, and having been supplied by them with money to meet immediate demands.†

The prospect which lay before Monmouth was not a bright one. There was now no probability that he would be recalled from banishment. On the Continent his life could no longer be passed amidst the splendour and festivity of a court. His cousins at the Hague seem to have really regarded him with kindness; but they could no longer countenance him openly without serious risk of producing a rupture between England and Holland. William offered a kind and judicious suggestion.

* Wade's Confession, Harl. MS. 6845.   Monmouth's letter to James from Ring-
† Avaux Neg. Feb. 20. 22. 1685;   wood.

The war which was then raging in Hungary, between the Emperor and the Turks, was watched by all Europe with interest almost as great as that which the Crusades had excited five hundred years earlier. Many gallant gentlemen, both Protestant and Catholic, were fighting as volunteers in the common cause of Christendom. The Prince advised Monmouth to repair to the Imperial camp, and assured him that, if he would do so, he should not want the means of making an appearance befitting an English nobleman.* This counsel was excellent: but the Duke could not make up his mind. He retired to Brussels accompanied by Henrietta Wentworth, Baroness Wentworth of Nettlestede, a damsel of high rank and ample fortune, who loved him passionately, who had sacrificed for his sake her maiden honour and the hope of a splendid alliance, who had followed him into exile, and whom he believed to be his wife in the sight of heaven. Under the soothing influence of female friendship, his lacerated mind healed fast. He seemed to have found happiness in obscurity and repose, and to have forgotten that he had been the ornament of a splendid court and the head of a great party, that he had commanded armies, and that he had aspired to a throne.

But he was not suffered to remain quiet. Ferguson employed all his powers of temptation. Grey, who knew not where to turn for a pistole, and was ready for any undertaking, however desperate, lent his aid. No art was spared which could draw Monmouth from retreat. To the first invitations which he received from his old associates he returned unfavourable answers. He pronounced the difficulties of a descent on England insuperable, protested that he was sick of public life, and begged to be left in the enjoyment of his newly found happiness. But he was little in the habit of resisting skilful and urgent importunity. It is said, too, that he was induced to quit his retirement by the same powerful influence which had made that retirement delightful. Lady Wentworth wished to see him a King. Her rents, her diamonds, her credit were put at his disposal. Monmouth's judgment was not convinced; but he had not firmness to resist such solicitations.†

<hr />

* Boyer's History of King William the Third, 2d edition, 1703, vol. i. 160.

† Welwood's Memoirs, App. xv.; Burnet, i. 630. Grey told a somewhat different story: but he told it to save his life. The Spanish ambassador at the English court, Don Pedro de Ronquillo, in a letter to the governor of the Low Countries written about this time, sneers at Monmouth for living on the

Scotch
refugees.

By the English exiles he was joyfully welcomed, and unanimously acknowledged as their head. But there was another class of emigrants who were not disposed to recognise his supremacy. Misgovernment, such as had never been known in the southern part of our island, had driven from Scotland to the Continent many fugitives, the intemperance of whose political and religious zeal was proportioned to the oppression which they had undergone. These men were not willing to follow an English leader. Even in destitution and exile they retained their punctilious national pride, and would not consent that their country should be, in their persons, degraded into a province. They had a captain of their own, Archibald,

Earl of
Argyle

ninth Earl of Argyle, who, as chief of the great tribe of Campbell, was known among the population of the Highlands by the proud name of Mac Callum More. His father, the Marquess of Argyle, had been the head of the Scotch Covenanters, had greatly contributed to the ruin of Charles the First, and was not thought by the Royalists to have atoned for this offence by consenting to bestow the empty title of King, and a state prison in a palace, on Charles the Second. After the return of the royal family the Marquess was put to death. His marquisate became extinct; but his son was permitted to inherit the ancient earldom, and was still among the greatest, if not the greatest, of the nobles of Scotland. The Earl's conduct during the twenty years which followed the Restoration had been, as he afterwards thought, criminally moderate. He had, on some occasions, opposed the administration which afflicted his country : but his opposition had been languid and cautious. His compliances in ecclesiastical matters had given scandal to rigid Presbyterians : and so far had he been from showing any inclination to resistance that, when the Covenanters had been persecuted into insurrection, he had brought into the field a large body of his dependents to support the government.

Such had been his political course until the Duke of York came down to Edinburgh armed with the whole regal authority. The despotic viceroy soon found that he could not expect entire support from Argyle. Since the most powerful chief in the kingdom could not be gained, it was thought

bounty of a fond woman, and hints a very unfounded suspicion that the Duke's passion was altogether interested. " Hallandose hoy tan falto de medios que ha menester trasformarse en Amor con Miledi en vista de la necesidad de poder subsistir."—Ronquillo to Grana, $\frac{\text{March 30}}{\text{April 9.}}$ 1685.

necessary that he should be destroyed. On grounds so frivolous that even the spirit of party and the spirit of chicane were ashamed of them, he was brought to trial for treason, convicted, and sentenced to death. The partisans of the Stuarts afterwards asserted that it was never meant to carry this sentence into effect, and that the only object of the prosecution was to frighten him into ceding his extensive jurisdiction in the Highlands. Whether James designed, as his enemies suspected, to commit murder, or only, as his friends affirmed, to commit extortion by threatening to commit murder, cannot now be ascertained. " I know nothing of the Scotch law," said Halifax to King Charles; "but this I know, that we should not hang a dog here on the grounds on which my Lord Argyle has been sentenced."*

Argyle escaped in disguise to England, and thence passed over to Friesland. In that secluded province his father had bought a small estate, as a place of refuge for the family in civil troubles. It was said, among the Scots, that this purchase had been made in consequence of the predictions of a Celtic seer, to whom it had been revealed that Mac Callum More would one day be driven forth from the ancient mansion of his race at Inverary.† But it is probable that the politic Marquess had been warned rather by the signs of the times than by the visions of any prophet. In Friesland Earl Archibald resided during some time so quietly that it was not generally known whither he had fled. From his retreat he carried on a correspondence with his friends in Great Britain, was a party to the Whig conspiracy, and concerted with the chiefs of that conspiracy a plan for invading Scotland.‡ This plan had been dropped upon the detection of the Rye House plot, but became again the subject of his thoughts after the demise of the crown.

He had, during his residence on the Continent, reflected much more deeply on religious questions than in the preceding years of his life. In one respect the effect of these reflections on his mind had been pernicious. His partiality for the synodical form of church government now amounted to bigotry. When he remembered how long he had conformed

* Proceedings against Argyle in the Collection of State Trials; Burnet, i. 521.; A True and Plain Account of the Discoveries made in Scotland, 1684; The Scotch Mist Cleared; Sir George Mackenzie's Vindication; Lord Fountainhall's Chronological Notes.

† Information of Robert Smith in the Appendix to Sprat's True Account.

‡ True and Plain Account of the Discoveries made in Scotland.

to the established worship, he was overwhelmed with shame
and remorse, and showed too many signs of a disposition to
atone for his defection by violence and intolerance. He had
however, in no long time, an opportunity of proving that the
fear and love of a higher Power had nerved him for the most
formidable conflicts by which human nature can be tried.

To his companions in adversity his assistance was of the
highest moment. Though proscribed and a fugitive, he was
still, in some sense, the most powerful subject in the British
dominions. In wealth, even before his attainder, he was
probably inferior, not only to the great English nobles, but
to some of the opulent esquires of Kent and Norfolk. But
his patriarchal authority, an authority which no wealth could
give, and which no attainder could take away, made him, as
a leader of an insurrection, truly formidable. No southern
lord could feel any confidence that, if he ventured to resist
the government, even his own gamekeepers and huntsmen
would stand by him. An Earl of Bedford, an Earl of Devonshire, could not engage to bring ten men into the field.
Mac Callum More, penniless and deprived of his earldom,
might, at any moment, raise a serious civil war. He had
only to show himself on the coast of Lorn ; and an army
would, in a few days, gather round him. The force, which,
in favourable circumstances, he could bring into the field,
amounted to five thousand fighting men, devoted to his service,
accustomed to the use of target and broadsword, not afraid
to encounter regular troops even in the open plain, and perhaps
superior to regular troops in the qualifications requisite for
the defence of wild mountain passes, hidden in mist, and torn
by headlong torrents. What such a force, well directed,
could effect, even against veteran regiments and skilful commanders, was proved, a few years later, at Killiecrankie.

Sir Patrick
Hume.

But, strong as was the claim of Argyle to the confidence of
the exiled Scots, there was a faction among them which
regarded him with no friendly feeling, and which wished to
make use of his name and influence, without entrusting to
him any real power. The chief of this faction was a lowland
gentleman, who had been implicated in the Whig plot, and
had with difficulty eluded the vengeance of the court, Sir
Patrick Hume, of Polwarth, in Berwickshire. Great doubt
has been thrown on his integrity, but without sufficient
reason. It must, however, be admitted that he injured his
cause by perverseness as much as he could have done by

treachery. He was a man incapable alike of leading and of following, conceited, captious, and wrongheaded, an endless talker, a sluggard in action against the enemy, and active only against his own allies. With Hume was closely connected another Scottish exile of great note, who had many of the same faults, Sir John Cochrane, second son of the Earl of Dundonald. Sir John Cochrane.

A far higher character belonged to Andrew Fletcher of Saltoun, a man distinguished by learning and eloquence, distinguished also by courage, disinterestedness, and public spirit, but of an irritable and impracticable temper. Like many of his most illustrious contemporaries, Milton for example, Harrington, Marvel, and Sidney, Fletcher had, from the misgovernment of several successive princes, conceived a strong aversion to hereditary monarchy. Yet he was no democrat. He was the head of an ancient Norman house, and was proud of his descent. He was a fine speaker and a fine writer, and was proud of his intellectual superiority. Both in his character of gentleman, and in his character of scholar, he looked down with disdain on the common people, and was so little disposed to entrust them with political power that he thought them unfit even to enjoy personal freedom. It is a curious circumstance that this man, the most honest, fearless, and uncompromising republican of his time, should have been the author of a plan for reducing a large part of the working classes of Scotland to slavery. He bore, in truth, a lively resemblance to those Roman Senators who, while they hated the name of King, guarded the privileges of their order with inflexible pride against the encroachments of the multitude, and governed their bondmen and bondwomen by means of the stocks and the scourge. Fletcher of Saltoun.

Amsterdam was the place where the leading emigrants, Scotch and English, assembled. Argyle repaired thither from Friesland, Monmouth from Brabant. It soon appeared that the fugitives had scarcely anything in common except hatred of James and impatience to return from banishment. The Scots were jealous of the English, the English of the Scots. Monmouth's high pretensions were offensive to Argyle, who, proud of ancient nobility and of a legitimate descent from kings, was by no means inclined to do homage to the offspring of a vagrant and ignoble love. But of all the dissensions by which the little band of outlaws was distracted the most serious was that which arose between Argyle and a

portion of his own followers. Some of the Scottish exiles
had, in a long course of opposition to tyranny, been excited

Unreason-
able con-
duct of the
Scotch
refugees.
into a morbid state of understanding and temper, which made
the most just and necessary restraint insupportable to them.
They knew that without Argyle they could do nothing.
They ought to have known that, unless they wished to run
headlong to ruin, they must either repose full confidence in
their leader, or relinquish all thoughts of military enterprise.
Experience has fully proved that in war every operation, from
the greatest to the smallest, ought to be under the absolute
direction of one mind, and that every subordinate agent, in
his degree, ought to obey implicitly, strenuously, and with
the show of cheerfulness, orders which he disapproves, or of
which the reasons are kept secret from him. Representative
assemblies, public discussions, and all the other checks by
which, in civil affairs, rulers are restrained from abusing
power, are out of place in a camp. Machiavel justly imputed
many of the disasters of Venice and Florence to the jealousy
which led those republics to interfere with every act of their
generals.* The Dutch practice of sending to an army deputies, without whose consent no great blow could be struck,
was almost equally pernicious. It is undoubtedly by no means
certain that a captain, who has been entrusted with dictatorial
power in the hour of peril, will quietly surrender that power
in the hour of triumph; and this is one of the many considerations which ought to make men hesitate long before they
resolve to vindicate public liberty by the sword. But, if they
determine to try the chance of war, they will, if they are
wise, entrust to their chief that plenary authority without
which war cannot be well conducted. It is possible that, if
they give him that authority, he may turn out a Cromwell or
a Napoleon. But it is almost certain that, if they withhold
from him that authority, their enterprises will end like the
enterprise of Argyle.

Some of the Scottish emigrants, heated with republican
enthusiasm, and utterly destitute of the skill necessary to the
conduct of great affairs, employed all their industry and ingenuity, not in collecting means for the attack which they
were about to make on a formidable enemy, but in devising
restraints on their leader's power and securities against his
ambition. The selfcomplacent stupidity with which they
insisted on organising an army as if they had been organising

* Discorsi sopra la prima Deca di Tito Livio, lib. ii. cap. 33.

a commonwealth would be incredible if it had not been frankly and even boastfully recorded by one of themselves.*

At length all differences were compromised. It was deter- Arrange-ment for an attempt on Eng-land and Scotland. mined that an attempt should be forthwith made on the western coast of Scotland, and that it should be promptly followed by a descent on England.

Argyle was to hold the nominal command in Scotland: but he was placed under the control of a Committee which reserved to itself all the most important parts of the military administration. This Committee was empowered to determine where the expedition should land, to appoint officers, to superintend the levying of troops, to dole out provisions and ammunition. All that was left to the general was to direct the evolutions of the army in the field, and he was forced to promise that even in the field, except in the case of a surprise, he would do nothing without the assent of a council of war.

Monmouth was to command in England. His soft mind had, as usual, taken an impress from the society which surrounded him. Ambitious hopes, which had seemed to be extinguished, revived in his bosom. He remembered the affection with which he had been constantly greeted by the common people in town and country, and expected that they would now rise by hundreds of thousands to welcome him. He remembered the good will which the soldiers had always borne him, and flattered himself that they would come over to him by regiments. Encouraging messages reached him in quick succession from London. He was assured that the violence and injustice with which the elections had been carried on had driven the nation mad, that the prudence of the leading Whigs had with difficulty prevented a sanguinary outbreak on the day of the coronation, and that all the great Lords who had supported the Exclusion Bill were impatient to rally round him. Wildman, who loved to talk treason in parables, sent to say that the Earl of Richmond, just two hundred years before, had landed in England with a handful of men, and had a few days later been crowned, on the field of Bosworth, with the diadem taken from the head of Richard. Danvers undertook to raise the City. The Duke was deceived into the belief that, as soon as he set up his standard, Bedfordshire, Buckinghamshire, Hampshire, Cheshire would rise in arms.† He consequently became eager for the enterprise

---

* See Sir Patrick Hume's Narrative, *passim.* † Grey's Narrative; Wade's Confession, Harl. MS. 6845.

from which a few weeks before he had shrunk. His country-men did not impose on him restrictions so elaborately absurd as those which the Scotch emigrants had devised. All that was required of him was to promise that he would not assume the regal title till his pretensions had been submitted to the judgment of a free Parliament.

It was determined that two Englishmen, Ayloffe and Rumbold, should accompany Argyle to Scotland, and that Fletcher should go with Monmouth to England. Fletcher, from the beginning, had augured ill of the enterprise : but his chivalrous spirit would not suffer him to decline a risk which his friends seemed eager to encounter. When Grey repeated with approbation what Wildman had said about Richmond and Richard, the well read and thoughtful Scot justly remarked that there was a great difference between the fifteenth century and the seventeenth. Richmond was assured of the support of barons, each of whom could bring an army of feudal retainers into the field ; and Richard had not one regiment of regular soldiers.*

The exiles were able to raise, partly from their own resources and partly from the contributions of well wishers in Holland, a sum sufficient for the two expeditions. Very little was obtained from London. Six thousand pounds had been expected thence. But instead of the money came excuses from Wildman, which ought to have opened the eyes of all who were not wilfully blind. The Duke made up the deficiency by pawning his own jewels and those of Lady Wentworth. Arms, ammunition, and provisions were bought, and several ships which lay at Amsterdam were freighted.†

John Locke.

It is remarkable that the most illustrious and the most grossly injured man among the British exiles stood far aloof from these rash counsels. John Locke hated tyranny and persecution as a philosopher; but his intellect and his temper preserved him from the violence of a partisan. He had lived on confidential terms with Shaftesbury, and had thus incurred the displeasure of the court. Locke's prudence had, however, been such that it would have been to little purpose to bring him even before the corrupt and partial tribunals of that age. In one point, however, he was vulnerable. He was a student of Christ Church in the University of Oxford. It was determined to drive from that celebrated college the greatest man of whom it could ever boast. But this was not easy. Locke had, at Oxford, abstained from expressing any opinion on the

* Burnet, i. 631.   † Grey's Narrative.

politics of the day. Spies had been set about him. Doctors of Divinity and Masters of Arts had not been ashamed to perform the vilest of all offices, that of watching the lips of a companion in order to report his words to his ruin. The conversation in the hall had been purposely turned to irritating topics, to the Exclusion Bill, and to the character of the Earl of Shaftesbury, but in vain. Locke neither broke out nor dissembled, but maintained such steady silence and composure as forced the tools of power to own with vexation that never man was so complete a master of his tongue and of his passions. When it was found that treachery could do nothing, arbitrary power was used. After vainly trying to inveigle Locke into a fault, the government resolved to punish him without one. Orders came from Whitehall that he should be ejected; and those orders the Dean and Canons made haste to obey.

Locke was travelling on the Continent for his health when he learned that he had been deprived of his home and of his bread without a trial or even a notice. The injustice with which he had been treated would have excused him if he had resorted to violent methods of redress. But he was not to be blinded by personal resentment: he augured no good from the schemes of those who had assembled at Amsterdam; and he quietly repaired to Utrecht, where, while his partners in misfortune were planning their own destruction, he employed himself in writing his celebrated letter on Toleration.*

The English government was early apprised that something was in agitation among the outlaws. An invasion of England seems not to have been at first expected; but it was apprehended that Argyle would shortly appear in arms among his clansmen. A proclamation was accordingly issued directing that Scotland should be put into a state of defence. The militia was ordered to be in readiness. All the clans hostile to the name of Campbell were set in motion. John Murray, Marquess of Athol, was appointed Lord Lieutenant of Argyleshire, and, at the head of a great body of his followers, occu-

Preparations made by government for the defence of Scotland.

---

* Le Clerc's Life of Locke; Lord King's Life of Locke; Lord Grenville's Oxford and Locke. Locke must not be confounded with the Anabaptist Nicholas Look, whose name is spelt Locke in Grey's Confession, and who is mentioned in the Lansdowne MS. 1152., and in the Buccleuch narrative appended to Mr. Rose's dissertation. I should hardly think it necessary to make this remark, but that the similarity of the two names appears to have misled a man so well acquainted with the history of those times as Speaker Onslow. See his note on Burnet, i. 629.

pied the castle of Inverary. Some suspected persons were arrested. Others were compelled to give hostages. Ships of war were sent to cruise near the isle of Bute; and part of the army of Ireland was moved to the coast of Ulster.*

Conversation of James with the Dutch ambassadors.

While these preparations were making in Scotland, James called into his closet Arnold Van Citters, who had long resided in England as Ambassador from the United Provinces, and Everard Van Dykvelt, who, after the death of Charles, had been sent by the States General on a special mission of condolence and congratulation. The King said that he had received from unquestionable sources intelligence of designs which were forming against his throne by his banished subjects in Holland. Some of the exiles were cutthroats, whom nothing but the special providence of God had prevented from committing a foul murder; and among them was the owner of the spot which had been fixed for the butchery. " Of all men living," said the King, " Argyle has the greatest means of annoying me; and of all places Holland is that whence a blow may be best aimed against me." The Dutch envoys assured his Majesty that what he had said should instantly be communicated to the government which they represented, and expressed their full confidence that every exertion would be made to satisfy him.†

Ineffectual attempts to prevent Argyle from sailing.

They were justified in expressing this confidence. Both the Prince of Orange and the States General were, at this time, most desirous that the hospitality of their country should not be abused for purposes of which the English government could justly complain. James had lately held language which encouraged the hope that he would not patiently submit to the ascendency of France. It seemed probable that he would consent to form a close alliance with the United Provinces and the House of Austria. There was, therefore, at the Hague, an extreme anxiety to avoid all that could give him offence. The personal interest of William was also on this occasion identical with the interest of his father in law.

But the case was one which required rapid and vigorous action; and the nature of the Batavian institutions made such action almost impossible. The Union of Utrecht, rudely formed, amidst the agonies of a revolution, for the purpose of meeting immediate exigencies, had never been deliberately

---

* Wodrow, book iii. chap. ix.; London Gazette, May 11. 1685; Barillon, May $\frac{11}{21}$.   † Register of the Proceedings of the States General, May $\frac{5}{15}$. 1685.

revised and perfected in a time of tranquillity. Every one of the seven commonwealths which that Union had bound together retained almost all the rights of sovereignty, and asserted those rights punctiliously against the central government. As the federal authorities had not the means of exacting prompt obedience from the provincial authorities, so the provincial authorities had not the means of exacting prompt obedience from the municipal authorities. Holland alone contained eighteen cities, each of which was, for many purposes, an independent state, jealous of all interference from without. If the rulers of such a city received from the Hague an order which was unpleasing to them, they either neglected it altogether, or executed it languidly and tardily. In some town councils, indeed, the influence of the Prince of Orange was all powerful. But unfortunately the place where the British exiles had congregated, and where their ships had been fitted out, was the rich and populous Amsterdam; and the magistrates of Amsterdam were the heads of the faction hostile to the federal government and to the House of Nassau. The naval administration of the United Provinces was conducted by five distinct boards of Admiralty. One of those boards sate at Amsterdam, was partly nominated by the authorities of that city, and seems to have been entirely animated by their spirit.

All the endeavours of the federal government to effect what James desired were frustrated by the evasions of the functionaries of Amsterdam, and by the blunders of Colonel Bevil Skelton, who had just arrived at the Hague as envoy from England. Skelton had been born in Holland during the English troubles, and was therefore supposed to be peculiarly qualified for his post[*]; but he was, in truth, unfit for that and for every other diplomatic situation. Excellent judges of character pronounced him to be the most shallow, fickle, passionate, presumptuous, and garrulous of men.[†] He took no serious notice of the proceedings of the refugees till three vessels which had been equipped for the expedition to Scotland were safe out of the Zuyder Zee, till the arms, ammunition, and provisions were on board, and till the passengers had embarked. Then, instead of applying, as he should have done, to the States General, who sate close to his own door, he sent a messenger to the magistrates of Amsterdam, with

---

[*] This is mentioned in his credentials dated on the 16th of March, $163\frac{5}{6}$.

[†] Bonrepaux to Seignelay, February $\frac{4}{14}$. 1686.

a request that the suspected ships might be detained. The magistrates of Amsterdam answered that the entrance of the Zuyder Zee was out of their jurisdiction, and referred him to the federal government. It was notorious that this was a mere excuse, and that, if there had been any real wish at the Stadthouse of Amsterdam to prevent Argyle from sailing, no difficulties would have been made. Skelton now addressed himself to the States General. They showed every disposition to comply with his demand, and, as the case was urgent, departed from the course which they ordinarily observed in the transaction of business. On the same day on which he made his application to them, an order, drawn in exact conformity with his request, was despatched to the Admiralty of Amsterdam. But this order, in consequence of some misinformation, did not correctly describe the situation of the ships. They were said to be in the Texel. They were in the Vlie. The Admiralty of Amsterdam made this error a plea for doing nothing; and, before the error could be rectified, the three ships had sailed.[*]

Departure of Argyle from Holland.   The last hours which Argyle passed on the coast of Holland were hours of great anxiety. Near him lay a Dutch man of war whose broadside would in a moment have put an end to his expedition. Round his little fleet a boat was rowing, in which were some persons with telescopes whom he suspected to be spies. But no effectual step was taken for the purpose of detaining him; and on the afternoon of the second of May he stood out to sea before a favourable breeze.

The voyage was prosperous. On the sixth the Orkneys were in sight. Argyle very unwisely anchored off Kirkwall, and allowed two of his followers to go on shore there. The Bishop ordered them to be arrested. The refugees proceeded to hold a long and animated debate on this misadventure; for, from the beginning to the end of their expedition, however languid and irresolute their conduct might be, they never in debate wanted spirit or perseverance. Some were for an attack on Kirkwall. Some were for proceeding without delay to Argyleshire. At last the Earl seized some gentlemen who lived near the coast of the island, and proposed to the Bishop an exchange of prisoners. The Bishop re-

---

* Avaux Neg. $\frac{April\ 30.}{May\ 10.}$, May $\frac{1}{11}$., May $\frac{5}{15}$. 1685; Sir Patrick Hume's Narrative; Letter from the Admiralty of Amsterdam to the States General, dated June 20. 1685; Memorial of Skelton, delivered to the States General, May 10. 1685.

turned no answer; and the fleet, after losing three days, sailed away.

This delay was full of danger. It was speedily known at Edinburgh that the rebel squadron had touched at the Orkneys. Troops were instantly put in motion. When the Earl reached his own province, he found that preparations had been made to repel him. At Dunstaffnage he sent his second son Charles on shore to call the Campbells to arms. But Charles returned with gloomy tidings. The herdsmen and fishermen were indeed ready to rally round Mac Callum More; but, of the heads of the clan, some were in confinement, and others had fled. Those gentlemen who remained at their homes were either well affected to the government or afraid of moving, and refused even to see the son of their chief. From Dunstaffnage the small armament proceeded to Campbelltown, near the southern extremity of the peninsula of Kintyre. Here the Earl published a manifesto, drawn up in Holland, under the direction of the Committee, by James Stewart, a Scotch advocate, whose pen was, a few months later, employed in a very different way. In this paper were set forth, with a strength of language sometimes approaching to scurrility, many real and some imaginary grievances. It was hinted that the late King had died by poison. A chief object of the expedition was declared to be the entire suppression, not only of Popery, but of Prelacy, which was termed the most bitter root and offspring of Popery; and all good Scotchmen were exhorted to do valiantly for the cause of their country and of their God.

Zealous as Argyle was for what he considered as pure religion, he did not scruple to practise one rite half Popish and half Pagan. The mysterious cross of yew, first set on fire, and then quenched in the blood of a goat, was sent forth to summon all the Campbells, from sixteen to sixty. The isthmus of Tarbet was appointed for the place of gathering. The muster, though small indeed when compared with what it would have been if the spirit and strength of the clan had been unbroken, was still formidable. The whole force assembled amounted to about eighteen hundred men. Argyle divided his mountaineers into three regiments, and proceeded to appoint officers.

The bickerings which had begun in Holland had never been intermitted during the whole course of the expedition: but at Tarbet they became more violent than ever. The Com-

He lands in Scotland.

His disputes with his followers.

mittee wished to interfere even with the patriarchal dominion of the Earl over the Campbells, and would not allow him to settle the military rank of his kinsmen by his own authority. While these disputatious meddlers tried to wrest from him his power over the Highlands, they carried on their own correspondence with the Lowlands, and received and sent letters which were never communicated to the nominal General. Hume and his confederates had reserved to themselves the superintendence of the stores, and conducted this important part of the administration of war with a laxity hardly to be distinguished from dishonesty, suffered the arms to be spoiled, wasted the provisions, and lived riotously at a time when they ought to have set to all beneath them an example of abstemiousness.

The great question was whether the Highlands or the Lowlands should be the seat of war. The Earl's first object was to establish his authority over his own domains, to drive out the invading clans which had been poured from Perthshire into Argyleshire, and to take possession of the ancient seat of his family at Inverary. He might then hope to have four or five thousand claymores at his command. With such a force he would be able to defend that wild country against the whole power of the kingdom of Scotland, and would also have secured an excellent base for offensive operations. This seems to have been the wisest course open to him. Rumbold, who had been trained in an excellent military school, and who, as an Englishman, might be supposed to be an impartial umpire between the Scottish factions, did all in his power to strengthen the Earl's hands. But Hume and Cochrane were utterly impracticable. Their jealousy of Argyle was, in truth, stronger than their wish for the success of the expedition. They saw that, among his own mountains and lakes, and at the head of an army chiefly composed of his own tribe, he would be able to bear down their opposition, and to exercise the full authority of a General. They muttered that the only men who had the good cause at heart were the Lowlanders, and that the Campbells took up arms neither for liberty nor for the Church of God, but for Mac Callum More alone. Cochrane declared that he would go to Ayrshire if he went by himself, and with nothing but a pitchfork in his hand. Argyle, after long resistance, consented, against his better judgment, to divide his little army. He remained with Rumbold in the Highlands.

Cochrane and Hume were at the head of the force which sailed to invade the Lowlands.

Ayrshire was Cochrane's object: but the coast of Ayrshire was guarded by English frigates; and the adventurers were under the necessity of running up the estuary of the Clyde to Greenock, then a small fishing village consisting of a single row of thatched hovels, now a great and flourishing port, of which the customs amount to more than five times the whole revenue which the Stuarts derived from the kingdom of Scotland. A party of militia lay at Greenock: but Cochrane, who wanted provisions, was determined to land. Hume objected. Cochrane was peremptory, and ordered an officer, named Elphinstone, to take twenty men in a boat to the shore. But the wrangling spirit of the leaders had infected all ranks. Elphinstone answered that he was bound to obey only reasonable commands, that he considered this command as unreasonable, and, in short, that he would not go. Major Fullarton, a brave man, esteemed by all parties, but peculiarly attached to Argyle, undertook to land with only twelve men, and did so in spite of a fire from the coast. A slight skirmish followed. The militia fell back. Cochrane entered Greenock and procured a supply of meal, but found no disposition to insurrection among the people.

In fact, the state of public feeling in Scotland was not such as the exiles, misled by the infatuation common in all ages to exiles, had supposed it to be. The government was, indeed, hateful and hated. But the malecontents were divided into parties which were almost as hostile to one another as to their rulers; nor was any of those parties eager to join the invaders. Many thought that the insurrection had no chance of success. The spirit of many had been effectually broken by long and cruel oppression. There was, indeed, a class of enthusiasts who were little in the habit of calculating chances, and whom oppression **had** not tamed but maddened. But these men saw little difference between Argyle and James. Their wrath had been heated to such a temperature that what every body else would have called boiling zeal seemed to them Laodicean lukewarmness. The Earl's past life had been stained by what they regarded as the vilest apostasy. The very Highlanders whom he now summoned to extirpate Prelacy he had a few years before summoned to defend it. And were slaves who knew nothing and cared nothing about religion, who were ready to fight for synodical government, for Episcopacy, for

Temper of the Scotch nation.

Popery, just as Mac Callum More might be pleased to command, fit allies for the people of God? The manifesto, indecent and intolerant as was its tone, was, in the view of these fanatics, a cowardly and worldly performance. A settlement such as Argyle would have made, such as was afterwards made by a mightier and happier deliverer, seemed to them not worth a struggle. They wanted not only freedom of conscience for themselves, but absolute dominion over the consciences of others; not only the Presbyterian doctrine, polity, and worship, but the Covenant in its utmost rigour. Nothing would content them but that every end for which civil society exists should be sacrificed to the ascendency of a theological system. One who believed no form of church government to be worth a breach of Christian charity, and who recommended comprehension and toleration, was, in their phrase, halting between Jehovah and Baal. One who condemned such acts as the murder of Cardinal Beatoun and Archbishop Sharpe fell into the same sin for which Saul had been rejected from being King over Israel. All the rules, by which, among civilised and Christian men, the horrors of war are mitigated, were abominations in the sight of the Lord. Quarter was to be neither taken nor given. A Malay running a muck, a mad dog pursued by a crowd, were the models to be imitated by warriors fighting in just selfdefence. To reasons such as guide the conduct of statesmen and generals the minds of these zealots were absolutely impervious. That a man should venture to urge such reasons was sufficient evidence that he was not one of the faithful. If the divine blessing were withheld, little would be effected by crafty politicians, by veteran captains, by cases of arms from Holland, or by regiments of unregenerate Celts from the mountains of Lorn. If, on the other hand, the Lord's time were indeed come, he could still, as of old, cause the foolish things of the world to confound the wise, and could save alike by many and by few. The broadswords of Athol and the bayonets of Claverhouse would be put to rout by weapons as insignificant as the sling of David or the pitcher of Gideon.*

Cochrane, having found it impossible to raise the population on the south of the Clyde, rejoined Argyle, who was in the

* If any person is inclined to suspect that I have exaggerated the absurdity and ferocity of these men, I would advise him to read two books, which will convince him that I have rather softened than overcharged the portrait, the Hind Let Loose, and Faithful Contendings Displayed.

island of Bute. The Earl now again proposed to make an attempt upon Inverary. Again he encountered a pertinacious opposition. The seamen sided with Hume and Cochrane. The Highlanders were absolutely at the command of their chieftain. There was reason to fear that the two parties would come to blows; and the dread of such a disaster induced the Committee to make some concession. The castle of Ealan Ghierig, situated at the mouth of Loch Riddan, was selected to be the chief place of arms. The military stores were disembarked there. The squadron was moored close to the walls in a place where it was protected by rocks and shallows such as, it was thought, no frigate could pass. Outworks were thrown up. A battery was planted with some small guns taken from the ships. The command of the fort was most unwisely given to Elphinstone, who had already proved himself much more disposed to argue with his commanders than to fight the enemy.

And now, during a few hours, there was some show of vigour. Rumbold took the castle of Ardkinglass. The Earl skirmished successfully with Athol's troops, and was about to advance on Inverary, when alarming news from the ships and factions in the Committee forced him to turn back. The King's frigates had come nearer to Ealan Ghierig than had been thought possible. The Lowland gentlemen positively refused to advance further into the Highlands. Argyle hastened back to Ealan Ghierig. There he proposed to make an attack on the frigates. His ships, indeed, were ill fitted for such an encounter. But they would have been supported by a flotilla of thirty large fishing boats, each well manned with armed Highlanders. The Committee, however, refused to listen to this plan, and effectually counteracted it by raising a mutiny among the sailors.

All was now confusion and despondency. The provisions had been so ill managed by the Committee that there was no longer food for the troops. The Highlanders consequently deserted by hundreds; and the Earl, brokenhearted by his misfortunes, yielded to the urgency of those who still pertinaciously insisted that he should march into the Lowlands.

The little army therefore hastened to the shore of Loch Long, passed that inlet by night in boats, and landed in Dumbartonshire. Hither, on the following morning, came news that the frigates had forced a passage, that all the Earl's ships had been taken, and that Elphinstone had fled from Ealan

Ghierig without a blow, leaving the castle and stores to the enemy.

All that remained was to invade the Lowlands under every disadvantage. Argyle resolved to make a bold push for Glasgow. But, as soon as this resolution was announced, the very men, who had, up to that moment, been urging him to hasten into the low country, took fright, argued, remonstrated, and when argument and remonstrance proved vain, laid a scheme for seizing the boats, making their own escape, and leaving their General and his clansmen to conquer or perish unaided. This scheme failed; and the poltroons who had formed it were compelled to share with braver men the risks of the last venture.

During the march through the country which lies between Loch Long and Loch Lomond, the insurgents were constantly infested by parties of militia. Some skirmishes took place, in which the Earl had the advantage; but the bands which he repelled, falling back before him, spread the tidings of his approach, and, soon after he had crossed the river Leven, he found a strong body of regular and irregular troops prepared to encounter him.

He was for giving battle. Ayloffe was of the same opinion. Hume, on the other hand, declared that to fight would be madness. He saw one regiment in scarlet. More might be behind. To attack such a force was to rush on certain death. The best course was to remain quiet till night, and then to give the enemy the slip.

A sharp altercation followed, which was with difficulty quieted by the mediation of Rumbold. It was now evening. The hostile armies encamped at no great distance from each other. The Earl ventured to propose a night attack, and was again overruled.

Argyle's forces dispersed.

Since it was determined not to fight, nothing was left but to take the step which Hume had recommended. There was a chance that, by decamping secretly, and hastening all night across heaths and morasses, the Earl might gain many miles on the enemy, and might reach Glasgow without further obstruction. The watch fires were left burning; and the march began. And now disaster followed disaster fast. The guides mistook the track across the moors, and led the army into boggy ground. Military order could not be preserved by undisciplined and disheartened soldiers under a dark sky, and on a treacherous and uneven soil. Panic after panic spread through the broken ranks. Every sight and sound was thought to indicate the approach of pursuers. Some of the officers contributed to spread the terror which it was their duty to calm. The army had become a mob; and the mob melted fast away. Great numbers fled under cover of the night. Rumbold and a few other brave men whom no danger could have scared lost their way, and were unable to rejoin the main body. When the day broke, only five hundred fugitives, wearied and dispirited, assembled at Kilpatrick.

All thought of prosecuting the war was at an end: and it was plain that the chiefs of the expedition would have sufficient difficulty in escaping with their lives. They fled in different directions. Hume reached the Continent in safety. Cochrane was taken and sent up to London. Argyle hoped to find a secure asylum under the roof of one of his old servants who lived near Kilpatrick. But this hope was disappointed; and he was forced to cross the Clyde. He assumed the dress of a peasant and pretended to be the guide of Major Fullarton, whose courageous fidelity was proof to all danger. The friends journeyed together through Renfrewshire as far as Inchinnan. At that place the Black Cart and the White Cart, two streams which now flow through prosperous towns, and turn the wheels of many factories, but which then held their quiet course through moors and sheepwalks, mingle before they join the Clyde. The only ford by which the travellers could cross was guarded by a party of militia. Some questions were asked. Fullarton tried to draw suspicion on himself, in order that his companion might escape unnoticed. But the minds of the questioners misgave them that the guide was not the rude clown that he seemed. They laid hands on him. He broke loose and sprang into the water, but was instantly chased. He stood at bay for a short time against five assailants. But he had no arms except his pocket pistols, and they were so wet, in consequence of his plunge, that they would not go off. He was struck to the ground with a broadsword, and secured.

He owned himself to be the Earl of Argyle, probably in the hope that his great name would excite the awe and pity of those who had seized him. And indeed they were much moved. For they were plain Scotchmen of humble rank, and, though in arms for the crown, probably cherished a preference for the Calvinistic church government and worship, and had been accustomed to reverence their captive as the

Argyle a prisoner.

head of an illustrious house and as a champion of the Protestant religion. But, though they were evidently touched, and though some of them even wept, they were not disposed to relinquish a large reward and to incur the vengeance of an implacable government. They therefore conveyed their prisoner to Renfrew. The man who bore the chief part in the arrest was named Riddell. On this account the whole race of Riddells was, during more than a century, held in abhorrence by the great tribe of Campbell. Within living memory, when a Riddell visited a fair in Argyleshire, he found it necessary to assume a false name.

And now commenced the brightest part of Argyle's career. His enterprise had hitherto brought on him nothing but reproach and derision. His great error was that he did not resolutely refuse to accept the name without the power of a general. Had he remained quietly at his retreat in Friesland, he would in a few years have been recalled with honour to his country, and would have been conspicuous among the ornaments and the props of constitutional monarchy. Had he conducted his expedition according to his own views, and carried with him no followers but such as were prepared implicitly to obey all his orders, he might possibly have effected something great. For what he wanted as a captain seems to have been, not courage, nor activity, nor skill, but simply authority. He should have known that of all wants this is the most fatal. Armies have triumphed under leaders who possessed no very eminent qualifications. But what army commanded by a debating club ever escaped discomfiture and disgrace?

The great calamity which had fallen on Argyle had this advantage, that it enabled him to show, by proofs not to be mistaken, what manner of man he was. From the day when he quitted Friesland to the day when his followers separated at Kilpatrick, he had never been a free agent. He had borne the responsibility of a long series of measures which his judgment disapproved. Now at length he stood alone. Captivity had restored to him the noblest kind of liberty, the liberty of governing himself in all his words and actions according to his own sense of the right and of the becoming. From that moment he became as one inspired with new wisdom and virtue. His intellect seemed to be strengthened and concentrated, his moral character to be at once elevated and softened. The insolence of the conquerors spared nothing that could try the temper of a man proud of ancient nobility and of patriarchal dominion. The prisoner was dragged through Edinburgh in triumph. He walked on foot, bareheaded, up the whole length of that stately street which, overshadowed by dark and gigantic piles of stone, leads from Holyrood House to the Castle. Before him marched the hangman, bearing the ghastly instrument which was to be used at the quartering block. The victorious party had not forgotten that, thirty-five years before this time, the father of Argyle had been at the head of the faction which put Montrose to death. Before that event the houses of Graham and Campbell had borne no love to each other; and they had ever since been at deadly feud. Care was taken that the prisoner should pass through the same gate and the same streets through which Montrose had been led to the same doom.* When the Earl reached the Castle his legs were put in irons, and he was informed that he had but a few days to live. It had been determined not to bring him to trial for his recent offence, but to put him to death under the sentence pronounced against him several years before, a sentence so flagitiously unjust that the most servile and obdurate lawyers of that bad age could not speak of it without shame.

But neither the ignominious procession up the High Street, nor the near view of death, had power to disturb the gentle and majestic patience of Argyle. His fortitude was tried by a still more severe test. A paper of interrogatories was laid before him by order of the Privy Council. He replied to those questions to which he could reply without danger to any of his friends, and refused to say more. He was told that unless he returned fuller answers he should be put to the torture. James, who was doubtless sorry that he could not feast his own eyes with the sight of Argyle in the boots, sent down to Edinburgh positive orders that nothing should be omitted which could wring out of the traitor information against all who had been concerned in the treason. But menaces were vain. With torments and death in immediate prospect Mac Callum More thought far less of himself than of his poor clansmen. "I was busy this day," he wrote from his cell, "treating for them, and in some hopes. But this evening orders came that I must die upon Monday or Tues-

---

* A few words which were in the first five editions have been omitted in this place. Here and in another passage I had, as Mr. Aytoun has observed, mistaken the City Guards, which were commanded by an officer named Graham, for the Dragoons of Graham of Claverhouse.

day ; and I am to be put to the torture if I answer not all questions upon oath. Yet I hope God shall support me."

The torture was not inflicted. Perhaps the magnanimity of the victim had moved the conquerors to unwonted compassion. He himself remarked that at first they had been very harsh to him, but that they soon began to treat him with respect and kindness. God, he said, had melted their hearts. It is certain that he did not, to save himself from the utmost cruelty of his enemies, betray any of his friends. On the last morning of his life he wrote these words : " I have named none to their disadvantage. I thank God he hath supported me wonderfully."

He composed his own epitaph, a short poem, full of meaning and spirit, simple and forcible in style, and not contemptible in versification. In this little piece he complained that, though his enemies had repeatedly decreed his death, his friends had been still more cruel. A comment on these expressions is to be found in a letter which he addressed to a lady residing in Holland. She had furnished him with a large sum of money for his expedition, and he thought her entitled to a full explanation of the causes which had led to his failure. He acquitted his coadjutors of treachery, but described their folly, their ignorance, and their factious perverseness, in terms which their own testimony has since proved to have been richly deserved. He afterwards doubted whether he had not used language too severe to become a dying Christian, and, in a separate paper, begged his friend to suppress what he had said of these men. " Only this I must acknowledge," he mildly added ; " they were not governable."

Most of his few remaining hours were passed in devotion, and in affectionate intercourse with some members of his family. He professed no repentance on account of his last enterprise, but bewailed, with great emotion, his former compliance in spiritual things with the pleasure of the government. He had, he said, been justly punished. One who had so long been guilty of cowardice and dissimulation was not worthy to be the instrument of salvation to the State and Church. Yet the cause, he frequently repeated, was the cause of God, and would assuredly triumph. " I do not," he said, " take on myself to be a prophet. But I have a strong impression on my spirit, that deliverance will come very suddenly." It is not strange that some zealous Presbyterians should have laid up his saying in their hearts, and should, at a later period, have attributed it to divine inspiration.

So effectually had religious faith and hope, co-operating with natural courage and equanimity, composed his spirits, that, on the very day on which he was to die, he dined with appetite, conversed with gaiety at table, and, after his last meal, lay down, as he was wont, to take a short slumber, in order that his body and mind might be in full vigour when he should mount the scaffold. At this time one of the Lords of the Council, who had probably been bred a Presbyterian, and had been seduced by interest to join in oppressing the Church of which he had once been a member, came to the Castle with a message from his brethren, and demanded admittance to the Earl. It was answered that the Earl was asleep. The Privy Councillor thought that this was a subterfuge, and insisted on entering. The door of the cell was softly opened; and there lay Argyle on the bed, sleeping, in his irons, the placid sleep of infancy. The conscience of the renegade smote him. He turned away sick at heart, ran out of the Castle, and took refuge in the dwelling of a lady of his family who lived hard by. There he flung himself on a couch, and gave himself up to an agony of remorse and shame. His kinswoman, alarmed by his looks and groans, thought that he had been taken with sudden illness, and begged him to drink a cup of sack. "No, no," he said; "that will do me no good." She prayed him to tell her what had disturbed him. "I have been," he said, "in Argyle's prison. I have seen him within an hour of eternity, sleeping as sweetly as ever man did. But as for me ——."

And now the Earl had risen from his bed, and had prepared himself for what was yet to be endured. He was first brought down the High Street to the Council House, where he was to remain during the short interval which was still to elapse before the execution. During that interval he asked for pen and ink, and wrote to his wife: "Dear heart, God is unchangeable: He hath always been good and gracious to me; and no place alters it. Forgive me all my faults; and now comfort thyself in Him, in whom only true comfort is to be found. The Lord be with thee, bless and comfort thee, my dearest. Adieu."

It was now time to leave the Council House. The divines who attended the prisoner were not of his own persuasion; His execution.

but he listened to them with civility, and exhorted them to caution their flocks against those doctrines which all Protestant churches unite in condemning. He mounted the scaffold, where the rude old guillotine of Scotland, called the Maiden, awaited him, and addressed the people in a speech, tinctured with the peculiar phraseology of his sect, but breathing the spirit of serene piety. His enemies, he said, he forgave, as he hoped to be forgiven. Only a single acrimonious expression escaped him. One of the episcopal clergymen who attended him went to the edge of the scaffold, and called out in a loud voice, "My Lord dies a Protestant." "Yes," said the Earl, stepping forward, "and not only a Protestant, but with a heart hatred of Popery, of Prelacy, and of all superstition." He then embraced his friends, put into their hands some tokens of remembrance for his wife and children, kneeled down, laid his head on the block, prayed during a few minutes, and gave the signal to the executioner. His head was fixed on the top of the Tolbooth, where the head of Montrose had formerly decayed.*

Execution of Rumbold.

The head of the brave and sincere, though not blameless Rumbold, was already on the West Port of Edinburgh. Surrounded by factious and cowardly associates, he had, through the whole campaign, behaved himself like a soldier trained in the school of the great Protector, had in council strenuously supported the authority of Argyle, and had in the field been distinguished by tranquil intrepidity. After the dispersion of the army he was set upon by a party of militia. He defended himself desperately, and would have cut his way through them, had they not hamstringed his horse. He was brought to Edinburgh mortally wounded. The wish of the government was that he should be executed in England. But he was so near death that, if he was not hanged in Scotland, he could not be hanged at all; and the pleasure of hanging him was one which the conquerors could not bear to forego. It was indeed not to be expected that they would

---

* The authors from whom I have taken the history of Argyle's expedition are Sir Patrick Hume, who was an eye-witness of what he related, and Wodrow, who had access to materials of the greatest value, among which were the Earl's own papers. Wherever there is a question of veracity between Argyle and Hume, I have no doubt that Argyle's narrative ought to be followed.

See also Burnet, i. 631. and the life of Bresson, published by Dr. Mac Crie. The account of the Scotch rebellion in the Life of James the Second, is a ridiculous romance, not written by the King himself, nor derived from his papers, but composed by a Jacobite who did not even take the trouble to look at a map of the seat of war.

show much lenity to one who was regarded as the chief of the Rye House plot, and who was the owner of the building from which that plot took its name : but the insolence with which they treated the dying man seems to our more humane age almost incredible. One of the Scotch Privy Councillors told him that he was a confounded villain. " I am at peace with God," answered Rumbold, calmly ; " how then can I be confounded ? "

He was hastily tried, convicted, and sentenced to be hanged and quartered within a few hours, near the City Cross in the High Street. Though unable to stand without the support of two men, he maintained his fortitude to the last, and under the gibbet raised his feeble voice against Popery and tyranny with such vehemence that the officers ordered the drums to strike up, lest the people should hear him. He was a friend, he said, to limited monarchy. But he never would believe that Providence had sent a few men into the world ready booted and spurred to ride, and millions ready saddled and bridled to be ridden. " I desire," he cried, " to bless and magnify God's holy name for this, that I stand here, not for any wrong that I have done, but for adhering to his cause in an evil day. If every hair of my head were a man, in this quarrel I would venture them all."

Both at his trial and at his execution he spoke of assassination with the abhorrence which became a good Christian and a brave soldier. He had never, he protested, on the faith of a dying man, harboured the thought of committing such villany. But he frankly owned that, in conversation with his fellow conspirators, he had mentioned his own house as a place where Charles and James might with advantage be attacked, and that much had been said on the subject, though nothing had been determined. It may at first sight seem that this acknowledgment is inconsistent with his declaration that he had always regarded assassination with horror. But the truth appears to be that he was imposed upon by a distinction which deluded many of his contemporaries. Nothing would have induced him to put poison into the food of the two princes, or to poniard them in their sleep. But to make an unexpected onset on the troop of Life Guards which surrounded the royal coach, to exchange sword cuts and pistol shots, and to take the chance of slaying or of being slain, was, in his view, a lawful military operation. Ambuscades and surprises were among the ordinary incidents of war. Every old soldier, Cavalier or Roundhead, had been engaged in such enterprises. If in the skirmish the King should fall, he would fall by fair fighting and not by murder. Precisely the same reasoning was employed, after the Revolution, by James himself and by some of his most devoted followers, to justify a wicked attempt on the life of William the Third. A band of Jacobites was commissioned to attack the Prince of Orange in his winter quarters. The meaning latent under this specious phrase was that the Prince's throat was to be cut as he went in his coach from Richmond to Kensington. It may seem strange that such fallacies, the dregs of the Jesuitical casuistry, should have had power to seduce men of heroic spirit, both Whigs and Tories, into a crime on which divine and human laws have justly set a peculiar note of infamy. But no sophism is too gross to delude minds distempered by party spirit.*

Argyle, who survived Rumbold a few hours, left a dying testimony to the virtues of the gallant Englishman. "Poor Rumbold was a great support to me, and a brave man, and died Christianly."†

Death of
Ayloffe. Ayloffe showed as much contempt of death as either Argyle or Rumbold: but his end did not, like theirs, edify pious minds. Though political sympathy had drawn him towards the Puritans, he had no religious sympathy with them, and was indeed regarded by them as little better than an atheist. He belonged to that section of the Whigs which sought for models rather among the patriots of Greece and Rome than among the prophets and judges of Israel. He was taken prisoner, and carried to Glasgow. There he attempted to destroy himself with a small penknife: but though he gave himself several wounds, none of them proved mortal, and he had strength enough left to bear a journey to London. He was brought before the Privy Council, and interrogated by

---

* Wodrow, III. ix. 10.; Western Martyrology; Burnet, i. 633.; Fox's History, Appendix iv. I can find no way, except that indicated in the text, of reconciling Rumbold's denial that he had ever admitted into his mind the thought of assassination with his confession that he had himself mentioned his own house as a convenient place for an attack on the royal brothers. The distinction which I suppose him to have taken was certainly taken by another Rye House conspirator, who was, like

him, an old soldier of the Commonwealth, Captain Walcot. On Walcot's trial, West, the witness for the crown, said, "Captain, you did agree to be one of those that were to fight the Guards." "What, then, was the reason," asked Chief Justice Pemberton, "that he would not kill the King?" "He said," answered West, "that it was a base thing to kill a naked man, and he would not do it."

† Wodrow, III. ix. 9.

the King, but had too much elevation of mind to save himself by informing against others. A story was current among the Whigs that the King said, "You had better be frank with me, Mr. Ayloffe. You know that it is in my power to pardon you." Then, it was rumoured, the captive broke his sullen silence, and answered, "It may be in your power; but it is not in your nature." He was executed under his old outlawry before the gate of the Temple, and died with stoical composure.*

In the meantime the vengeance of the conquerors was mercilessly wreaked on the people of Argyleshire. Many of the Campbells were hanged by Athol without a trial; and he was with difficulty restrained by the Privy Council from taking more lives. The country to the extent of thirty miles round Inverary was wasted. Houses were burned: the stones of mills were broken to pieces: fruit trees were cut down, and the very roots seared with fire. The nets and fishing boats, the sole means by which many inhabitants of the coast subsisted, were destroyed. More than three hundred rebels and malecontents were transported to the colonies. Many of them were also sentenced to mutilation. On a single day the hangman of Edinburgh cut off the ears of thirty-five prisoners. Several women were sent across the Atlantic after being first branded in the cheek with a hot iron. It was even in contemplation to obtain an act of Parliament proscribing the name of Campbell, as the name of Macgregor had been proscribed eighty years before.†

Argyle's expedition appears to have produced little sensation in the south of the island. The tidings of his landing reached London just before the English Parliament met. The King mentioned the news from the throne; and the Houses assured him that they would stand by him against every enemy. Nothing more was required of them. Over Scotland they had no authority; and a war of which the theatre was so distant, and of which the event might, almost from the first, be easily foreseen, excited only a languid interest in London.

But, a week before the final dispersion of Argyle's army, England was agitated by the news that a more formidable

Marginal notes: Devasta- tion of Argyle- shire.

Ineffectual attempts to prevent

* Wade's narrative, Harl. MS. 6845.; Burnet, i. 634.; Van Citters' Despatch of Oct. 30. / Nov. 9. 1685; Luttrell's Diary of the same date.

† Wodrow, III. ix. 4. and III. ix. 10. Wodrow gives from the Acts of Council the names of all the prisoners who were transported, mutilated, or branded.

invader had landed on her own shores.   It had been agreed
among the refugees that Monmouth should sail from Holland
six days after the departure of the Scots.   He had deferred
his expedition a short time, probably in the hope that most
of the troops in the south of the island would be moved to
the north as soon as war broke out in the Highlands, and
that he should find no force ready to oppose him.   When at
length he was desirous to proceed, the wind had become adverse and violent.

Monmouth
from
leaving
Holland.

While his small fleet lay tossing in the Texel, a contest was
going on among the Dutch authorities.   The States General
and the Prince of Orange were on one side, the Town Council
and Admiralty of Amsterdam on the other.

Skelton had delivered to the States General a list of the
refugees whose residence in the United Provinces caused uneasiness to his master.   The States General, anxious to grant
every reasonable request which James could make, sent copies
of the list to the provincial authorities.   The provincial authorities sent copies to the municipal authorities.   The magistrates of all the towns were directed to take such measures
as might prevent the proscribed Whigs from molesting the
English government.   In general those directions were obeyed.
At Rotterdam in particular, where the influence of William
was all powerful, such activity was shown as called forth warm
acknowledgments from James.   But Amsterdam was the
chief seat of the emigrants ; and the governing body of Amsterdam would see nothing, hear nothing, know of nothing.
The High Bailiff of the city, who was himself in daily communication with Ferguson, reported to the Hague that he did
not know where to find a single one of the refugees ; and with
this excuse the federal government was forced to be content.
The truth was that the English exiles were as well known at
Amsterdam, and as much stared at in the streets, as if they
had been Chinese.*

* Skelton's letter is dated the $\frac{7}{17}$th of
May 1686.   It will be found, together
with a letter of the Schout or High
Bailiff of Amsterdam, in a little volume
published a few months later, and entitled, "Histoire des Evènemens Tragiques d'Angleterre."   The documents
inserted in that work are, as far as I
have examined them, given exactly from
the Dutch archives, except that Skelton's French, which was not the purest,
is slightly corrected.   See also Grey's
Narrative.

Goodenough, on his examination after
the battle of Sedgemoor, said, "The
Schout of Amsterdam was a particular
friend to this last design."   Lansdowne
MS. 1152.

It is not worth while to refute those
writers who represent the Prince of
Orange as an accomplice in Monmouth's
enterprise.   The circumstance on which

A few days later, Skelton received orders from his Court to request that, in consequence of the dangers which threatened his master's throne, the three Scotch regiments in the service of the United Provinces might be sent to Great Britain without delay. He applied to the Prince of Orange; and the prince undertook to manage the matter, but predicted that Amsterdam would raise some difficulty. The prediction proved correct. The deputies of Amsterdam refused to consent, and succeeded in causing some delay. But the question was not one of those on which, by the constitution of the republic, a single city could prevent the wish of the majority from being carried into effect. The influence of William prevailed; and the troops were embarked with great expedition.*

Skelton was at the same time exerting himself, not indeed very judiciously or temperately, to stop the ships which the English refugees had fitted out. He expostulated in warm terms with the Admiralty of Amsterdam. The negligence of that board, he said, had already enabled one band of rebels to invade Britain. For a second error of the same kind there could be no excuse. He peremptorily demanded that a large vessel, named the Helderenbergh, might be detained. It was pretended that this vessel was bound for the Canaries. But, in truth, she had been freighted by Monmouth, carried twenty-six guns, and was loaded with arms and ammunition. The Admiralty of Amsterdam replied that the liberty of trade and navigation was not to be restrained for light reasons, and that the Helderenbergh could not be stopped without an order from the States General. Skelton, whose uniform practice seems to have been to begin at the wrong end, now had recourse to the States General. The States General gave the necessary orders. Then the Admiralty of Amsterdam pretended that there was not a sufficient naval force in the Texel to seize so large a ship as the Helderenbergh, and suffered Monmouth to sail unmolested.†

The weather was bad: the voyage was long; and several

they chiefly rely is that the authorities of Amsterdam took no effectual steps for preventing the expedition from sailing. This circumstance is in truth the strongest proof that the expedition was not favoured by William. No person, not profoundly ignorant of the institutions and politics of Holland, would hold the Stadtholder answerable for the proceedings of the heads of the Loevestein party.

* Avaux Neg. June $\frac{7}{17}$. $\frac{8}{18}$. $\frac{14}{24}$. 1685; Letter of the Prince of Orange to Lord Rochester, June 9. 1685.

† Van Citters, June $\frac{9}{19}$., June $\frac{12}{22}$. 1685. The correspondence of Skelton with the States General and with the Admiralty of Amsterdam is in the archives at the Hague. Some pieces will be found in the Evènemens Tragiques d'Angleterre. See also Burnet, i. 640.

English men of war were cruising in the Channel. But
Monmouth escaped both the sea and the enemy. As he
passed by the cliffs of Dorsetshire, it was thought desirable to
send a boat to the beach with one of the refugees named
Thomas Dare. This man, though of low mind and manners,
had great influence at Taunton. He was directed to hasten
thither across the country, and to apprise his friends that
Monmouth would soon be on English ground.*

His arrival
at Lyme.

On the morning of the eleventh of June the Helderenbergh,
accompanied by two smaller vessels, appeared off the port of
Lyme. That town is a small knot of steep and narrow alleys,
lying on a coast wild, rocky, and beaten by a stormy sea.
The place was then chiefly remarkable for a pier which, in
the days of the Plantagenets, had been constructed of stones,
unhewn and uncemented. This ancient work, known by the
name of the Cob, enclosed the only haven where, in a space
of many miles, the fishermen could take refuge from the tem-
pests of the Channel.

The appearance of the three ships, foreign built and without colours, perplexed the inhabitants of Lyme ; and the
uneasiness increased when it was found that the Customhouse
officers, who had gone on board according to usage, did not
return. The town's people repaired to the cliffs, and gazed
long and anxiously, but could find no solution of the mystery.
At length seven boats put off from the largest of the strange
vessels, and rowed to the shore. From these boats landed
about eighty men, well armed and appointed. Among them
were Monmouth, Grey, Fletcher, Ferguson, Wade, and
Anthony Buyse, an officer who had been in the service of the
Elector of Brandenburg.†

Monmouth commanded silence, kneeled down on the shore,
thanked God for having preserved the friends of liberty and
pure religion from the perils of the sea, and implored the
divine blessing on what was yet to be done by land. He then
drew his sword, and led his men over the cliffs into the town.

As soon as it was known under what leader and for what
purpose the expedition came, the enthusiasm of the populace
burst through all restraints. The little town was in an
uproar with men running to and fro, and shouting " A Monmouth ! a Monmouth ! the Protestant religion !"   Mean-

---

* Wade's Confession in the Hard-   mouth and Fletcher in the Collection of
wicke Papers ; Harl. MS. 6845.   State Trials.
† See Buyse's evidence against Mon-

while the ensign of the adventurers, a blue flag, was set up in the marketplace. The military stores were deposited in the town hall; and a Declaration setting forth the objects of the expedition was read from the Cross.*

This Declaration, the masterpiece of Ferguson's genius, *His Declaration.* was not a grave manifesto such as ought to be put forth by a leader drawing the sword for a great public cause, but a libel of the lowest class, both in sentiment and language.† It contained undoubtedly many just charges against the government. But these charges were set forth in the prolix and inflated style of a bad pamphlet; and the paper contained other charges of which the whole disgrace falls on those who made them. The Duke of York, it was positively affirmed, had burned down London, had strangled Godfrey, had cut the throat of Essex, and had poisoned the late King. On account of those villanous and unnatural crimes, but chiefly of that execrable fact, the late horrible and barbarous parricide,— such was the copiousness and such the felicity of Ferguson's diction,—James was declared a mortal and bloody enemy, a tyrant, a murderer, and an usurper. No treaty should be made with him. The sword should not be sheathed till he had been brought to condign punishment as a traitor. The government should be settled on principles favourable to liberty. All Protestant sects should be tolerated. The forfeited charters should be restored. Parliament should be held annually, and should no longer be prorogued or dissolved by royal caprice. The only standing force should be the militia: the militia should be commanded by the Sheriffs; and the Sheriffs should be chosen by the freeholders. Finally Monmouth declared that he could prove himself to have been born in lawful wedlock, and to be, by right of blood, King of England, but that, for the present, he waived his claims, that he would leave them to the judgment of a free Parliament, and that, in the meantime, he desired to be considered only as the Captain General of the English Protestants, who were in arms against tyranny and Popery.

Disgraceful as this manifesto was to those who put it forth, *His popularity in the West of England.* it was not unskilfully framed for the purpose of stimulating the passions of the vulgar. In the West the effect was great. The gentry and clergy of that part of England were indeed,

* Journals of the House of Commons, June 13. 1685; Harl. MS. 6845.; Lansdowne MS. 1152.

† Burnet, i. 641.; Goodenough's confession in the Lansdowne MS. 1152. Copies of the Declaration, as originally printed, are very rare; but there is one in the British Museum.

with few exceptions, Tories. But the yeomen, the traders of
the towns, the peasants, and the artisans were generally
animated by the old Roundhead spirit. Many of them were
Dissenters, and had been goaded by petty persecution into a
temper fit for desperate enterprise. The great mass of the
population abhorred Popery and adored Monmouth. He was
no stranger to them. His progress through Somersetshire and
Devonshire in the summer of 1680 was still fresh in the
memory of all men. He was on that occasion sumptuously
entertained by Thomas Thynne at Longleat Hall, then, and
perhaps still, the most magnificent country house in England.
From Longleat to Exeter the hedges were lined with shouting
spectators. The roads were strewn with boughs and flowers.
The multitude, in their eagerness to see and touch their
favourite, broke down the palings of parks, and besieged the
mansions where he was feasted. When he reached Chard his
escort consisted of five thousand horsemen. At Exeter all
Devonshire had been gathered together to welcome him.
One striking part of the show was a company of nine hundred young men who, clad in a white uniform, marched
before him into the city.* The turn of fortune which had
alienated the gentry from his cause had produced no effect
on the common people. To them he was still the good Duke,
the Protestant Duke, the rightful heir whom a vile conspiracy kept out of his own. They came to his standard in
crowds. All the clerks whom he could employ were too few
to take down the names of the recruits. Before he had been
twenty-four hours on English ground he was at the head of
fifteen hundred men. Dare arrived from Taunton with forty
horsemen of no very martial appearance, and brought encouraging intelligence as to the state of public feeling in
Somersetshire. As yet all seemed to promise well.†

But a force was collecting at Bridport to oppose the insurgents. On the thirteenth of June the red regiment of
Dorsetshire militia came pouring into that town. The
Somersetshire, or yellow regiment, of which Sir William
Portman, a Tory gentleman of great note, was Colonel, was
expected to arrive on the following day.‡ The Duke determined to strike an immediate blow. A detachment of his

---

* Historical Account of the Life and
magnanimous Actions of the most illustrious Protestant Prince James, Duke of
Monmouth, 1683.

† Wade's Confession, Hardwicke Papers; Axe Papers; Harl. MS. 6845.
‡ Harl. MS. 6845.

troops was preparing to march to Bridport when a disastrous event threw the whole camp into confusion.

Fletcher of Saltoun had been appointed to command the cavalry under Grey. Fletcher was ill mounted; and indeed there were few chargers in the camp which had not been taken from the plough. When he was ordered to Bridport, he thought that the exigency of the case warranted him in borrowing, without asking permission, a fine horse belonging to Dare. Dare resented this liberty, and assailed Fletcher with gross abuse. Fletcher kept his temper better than any one who knew him expected. At last Dare, presuming on the patience with which his insolence had been endured, ventured to shake a switch at the high born and high spirited Scot. Fletcher's blood boiled. He drew a pistol and shot Dare dead. Such sudden and violent revenge would not have been thought strange in Scotland, where the law had always been weak, where he who did not right himself by the strong hand was not likely to be righted at all, and where, consequently, human life was held almost as cheap as in the worst governed provinces of Italy. But the people of the southern part of the island were not accustomed to see deadly weapons used and blood spilled on account of a rude word or gesture, except in duel between gentlemen with equal arms. There was a general cry for vengeance on the foreigner who had murdered an Englishman. Monmouth could not resist the clamour. Fletcher, who, when his first burst of rage had spent itself, was overwhelmed with remorse and sorrow, took refuge on board of the Helderenbergh, escaped to the Continent, and repaired to Hungary, where he fought bravely against the common enemy of Christendom.*

Situated as the insurgents were, the loss of a man of parts and energy was not easily to be repaired. Early on the morning of the following day, the fourteenth of June, Grey, accompanied by Wade, marched with about five hundred men to attack Bridport. A confused and indecisive action took place, such as was to be expected when two bands of ploughmen, officered by country gentlemen and barristers, were opposed to each other. For a time Monmouth's men drove the militia before them. Then the militia made a stand, and Monmouth's men retreated in some confusion. Grey and his cavalry never stopped till they were safe at Lyme again: but

Encounter of the rebels with the militia at Bridport.

* Buyse's evidence in the Collection of State Trials; Burnet, i. 642 : Ferguson's MS. quoted by Eachard.

Wade rallied the infantry and brought them off in good order.*

There was a violent outcry against Grey; and some of the adventurers pressed Monmouth to take a severe course. Monmouth, however, would not listen to this advice. His lenity has been attributed by some writers to his good nature, which undoubtedly often amounted to weakness. Others have supposed that he was unwilling to deal harshly with the only peer who served in his army. It is probable, however, that the Duke, who, though not a general of the highest order, understood war very much better than the preachers and lawyers who were always obtruding their advice on him, made allowances which people altogether inexpert in military affairs never thought of making. In justice to a man who has had few defenders, it must be observed that the task, which, throughout this campaign, was assigned to Grey, was one which, if he had been the boldest and most skilful of soldiers, he could scarcely have performed in such a manner as to gain credit. He was at the head of the cavalry. It is notorious that a horse soldier requires a longer training than a foot soldier, and that the war horse requires a longer training than his rider. Something may be done with a raw infantry which has enthusiasm and animal courage : but nothing can be more helpless than a raw cavalry, consisting of yeomen and tradesmen mounted on cart horses and post horses; and such was the cavalry which Grey commanded. The wonder is, not that his men did not stand fire with resolution, not that they did not use their weapons with vigour, but that they were able to keep their seats.

Still recruits came in by hundreds. Arming and drilling went on all day. Meantime the news of the insurrection had spread fast and wide. On the evening on which the Duke landed, Gregory Alford, Mayor of Lyme, a zealous Tory, and a bitter persecutor of Nonconformists, sent off his servants to give the alarm to the gentry of Somersetshire and Dorsetshire, and himself took horse for the West. Late at night he stopped at Honiton, and thence despatched a few hurried lines to London with the ill tidings.† He then pushed on to Exeter, where he found Christopher Monk, Duke of Albemarle. This nobleman, the son and heir of George

---

* London Gazette, June 18. 1685 ; Wade's Confession, Hardwicke Papers.
† Lords' Journals, June 13. 1685.

Monk, the restorer of the Stuarts, was Lord Lieutenant of Devonshire, and was then holding a muster of militia. Four thousand men of the trainbands were actually assembled under his command. He seems to have thought that, with this force, he should be able at once to crush the rebellion. He therefore marched towards Lyme.

But when, on the afternoon of Monday the fifteenth of June, he reached Axminster, he found the insurgents drawn up there to encounter him. They presented a resolute front. Four field pieces were pointed against the royal troops. The thick hedges, which on each side overhung the narrow lanes, were lined with musketeers. Albemarle, however, was less alarmed by the preparations of the enemy than by the spirit which appeared in his own ranks. Such was Monmouth's popularity among the common people of Devonshire that, if once the trainbands had caught sight of his well known face and figure, they would probably have gone over to him in a body. *Encounter of the rebels with the militia at Axminster.*

Albemarle, therefore, though he had a great superiority of force, thought it advisable to retreat. The retreat soon became a rout. The whole country was strewn with the arms and uniforms which the fugitives had thrown away; and, had Monmouth urged the pursuit with vigour, he would probably have taken Exeter without a blow. But he was satisfied with the advantage which he had gained, and thought it desirable that his recruits should be better trained before they were employed in any hazardous service. He therefore marched towards Taunton, where he arrived on the eighteenth of June, exactly a week after his landing.*

The Court and the Parliament had been greatly moved by the news from the West. At five in the morning of Saturday the thirteenth of June, the King had received the letter which the Mayor of Lyme had despatched from Honiton. The Privy Council was instantly called together. Orders were given that the strength of every company of infantry and of every troop of cavalry should be increased. Commissions were issued for the levying of new regiments. Alford's communication was laid before the Lords; and its substance was communicated to the Commons by a message. The Commons examined the couriers who had arrived from the West, and instantly ordered a bill to be brought in for attainting Monmouth of *News of the rebellion carried to London.* *Loyalty of the Parliament.*

---

* Wade's Confession; Ferguson MS.; Axe Papers, Harl. MS. 6845.; Oldmixon, 701, 702. Oldmixon, who was then a boy, lived very near the scene of these events.

high treason.   Addresses were voted assuring the King that
both his peers and his people were determined to stand by
him with life and fortune against all his enemies.   At the
next meeting of the Houses they ordered the Declaration of
the rebels to be burned by the hangman, and passed the bill
of attainder through all its stages.   That bill received the
royal assent on the same day; and a reward of five thousand
pounds was promised for the apprehension of Monmouth.*

The fact that Monmouth was in arms against the government was so notorious that the bill of attainder became a law
with only a faint show of opposition from one or two peers, and
has seldom been severely censured even by Whig historians.
Yet, when we consider how important it is that legislative and
judicial functions should be kept distinct, how important it is
that common fame, however strong and general, should not
be received as a legal proof of guilt, how important it is to
maintain the rule that no man shall be condemned to death
without an opportunity of defending himself, and how easily
and speedily breaches in great principles, when once made,
are widened, we shall probably be disposed to think that the
course taken by the Parliament was open to some objection.
Neither House had before it anything which even so corrupt
a judge as Jeffreys could have directed a jury to consider as
proof of Monmouth's crime.   The messengers examined by
the Commons were not on oath, and might therefore have related mere fictions without incurring the penalties of perjury.
The Lords, who might have administered an oath, appear
not to have examined any witness, and to have had no evidence before them except the letter of the Mayor of Lyme,
which, in the eye of the law, was no evidence at all.   Extreme
danger, it is true, justifies extreme remedies.   But the Act of
Attainder was a remedy which could not operate till all danger was over, and which would become superfluous at the very
moment at which it ceased to be null.   While Monmouth was
in arms it was impossible to execute him.   If he should be
vanquished and taken, there would be no hazard and no difficulty in trying him.   It was afterwards remembered as a
curious circumstance that, among the zealous Tories who went
up with the bill from the House of Commons to the bar of the
Lords, was Sir John Fenwick, member for Northumberland.
This gentleman, a few years later, had occasion to reconsider

* London Gazette, June 18. 1685; Lords' and Commons' Journals, June 13. and
15.; Dutch Despatch, June $\frac{16}{24}$.

the whole subject, and then came to the conclusion that acts of attainder are altogether unjustifiable.*

The Parliament gave other proofs of loyalty in this hour of peril. The Commons authorised the King to raise an extraordinary sum of four hundred thousand pounds for his present necessities, and, that he might have no difficulty in finding the money, proceeded to devise new imposts. The scheme of taxing houses lately built in the capital was revived and strenuously supported by the country gentlemen. It was resolved not only that such houses should be taxed, but that a bill should be brought in prohibiting the laying of any new foundations within the bills of mortality. The resolution, however, was not carried into effect. Powerful men who had land in the suburbs, and who hoped to see new streets and squares rise on their estates, exerted all their influence against the project. It was found that to adjust the details would be a work of time; and the King's wants were so pressing that he thought it necessary to quicken the movements of the House by a gentle exhortation to speed. The plan of taxing buildings was therefore relinquished; and new duties were imposed for a term of five years on foreign silks, linens, and spirits.†

The Tories of the Lower House proceeded to introduce what they called a bill for the preservation of the King's person and government. They proposed that it should be high treason to say that Monmouth was legitimate, to utter any words tending to bring the person or government of the sovereign into hatred or contempt, or to make any motion in Parliament for changing the order of succession. Some of these provisions excited general disgust and alarm. The Whigs, few and weak as they were, attempted to rally, and found themselves reinforced by a considerable number of moderate and sensible Cavaliers. Words, it was said, may easily be misunderstood by a dull man. They may easily be misconstrued by a knave. What was spoken metaphorically may be apprehended literally. What was spoken ludicrously may be apprehended seriously. A particle, a tense, a mood, an emphasis, may make the whole difference between guilt and innocence. The Saviour of mankind himself, in whose blameless life malice could find no act to impeach, had been called

---

* Oldmixon is wrong in saying that Fenwick carried up the bill. It was carried up, as appears from the Journals, by Lord Ancram. See Delamere's Observations on the Attainder of the late Duke of Monmouth.

† Commons' Journals of June 17, 18, and 19. 1685; Reresby's Memoirs.

in question for words spoken. False witnesses had suppressed a syllable which would have made it clear that those words were figurative, and had thus furnished the Sanhedrim with a pretext under which the foulest of all judicial murders had been perpetrated. With such an example on record, who could affirm that, if mere talk were made a substantive treason, the most loyal subject would be safe? These arguments produced so great an effect that in the committee amendments were introduced which greatly mitigated the severity of the bill. But the clause which made it high treason in a member of Parliament to propose the exclusion of a prince of the blood seems to have raised no debate, and was retained. That clause was indeed altogether unimportant, except as a proof of the ignorance and inexperience of the hotheaded Royalists who thronged the House of Commons. Had they learned the first rudiments of legislation, they would have known that the enactment to which they attached so much value would be superfluous while the Parliament was disposed to maintain the order of succession, and would be repealed as soon as there was a Parliament bent on changing the order of succession.*

The bill, as amended, was passed and carried up to the Lords, but did not become law. The King had obtained from the Parliament all the pecuniary assistance that he could expect; and he conceived that, while rebellion was actually raging, the loyal nobility and gentry would be of more use in their counties than at Westminster. He therefore hurried their deliberations to a close, and, on the second of July, dismissed them. On the same day the royal assent was given to a law reviving that censorship of the press which had terminated in 1679. This object was effected by a few words at the end of a miscellaneous statute which continued several expiring acts. The courtiers did not think that they had gained a triumph. The Whigs did not utter a murmur. Neither in the Lords nor in the Commons was there any division, or even, as far as can now be learned, any debate on a question which would, in our age, convulse the whole frame of society. In truth, the change was slight and almost imperceptible; for, since the detection of the Rye House

* Commons' Journals, June 19, 29. 1685; Lord Lonsdale's Memoirs, 8, 9.; Burnet, i. 639. The bill, as amended by the committee, will be found in Mr. Fox's historical work, Appendix iii. If Burnet's account be correct, the offences, which, by the amended bill, were made punishable only with civil incapacities, were, by the original bill, made capital.

plot, the liberty of unlicensed printing had existed only in name. During many months scarcely one Whig pamphlet had been published except by stealth; and by stealth such pamphlets might be published still.*

The Houses then rose. They were not prorogued, but only adjourned, in order that, when they should reassemble, they might take up their business in the exact state in which they had left it.†

While the Parliament was devising sharp laws against Monmouth and his partisans, he found at Taunton a reception which might well encourage him to hope that his enterprise would have a prosperous issue. Taunton, like most other towns in the south of England, was, in that age, more important than at present. Those towns have not indeed declined. On the contrary, they are, with very few exceptions, larger and richer, better built and better peopled, than in the seventeenth century. But, though they have positively advanced, they have relatively gone back. They have been far outstripped in wealth and population by the great manufacturing and commercial cities of the north, cities which, in the time of the Stuarts, were but beginning to be known as seats of industry. When Monmouth marched into Taunton it was an eminently prosperous place. Its markets were plentifully supplied. It was a celebrated seat of the woollen manufacture. The people boasted that they lived in a land flowing with milk and honey. Nor was this language held only by partial natives; for every stranger who climbed the graceful tower of St. Mary Magdalene owned that he saw beneath him the most fertile of English valleys. It was a country rich with orchards and green pastures, among which were scattered, in gay abundance, manor houses, cottages, and village spires. The townsmen had long leaned towards Presbyterian divinity and Whig politics. In the great civil war Taunton had, through all vicissitudes, adhered to the Parliament, had been twice closely besieged by Goring, and had been twice defended with heroic valour by Robert Blake, afterwards the renowned Admiral of the Commonwealth. Whole streets had been burned down by the mortars and grenades of the Cavaliers. Food had been so scarce that the resolute governor had announced his intention of putting the

Reception of Monmouth at Taunton.

---

* 1 Jac. II. c. 17.; Lords' Journals, July 2. 1685.   † Lords' and Commons' Journals, July 2. 1685.

garrison on rations of horse flesh. But the spirit of the town had never been subdued either by fire or by hunger.*

The Restoration had produced no effect on the temper of the Taunton men. They had still continued to celebrate the anniversary of the happy day on which the siege laid to their town by the royal army had been raised; and their stubborn attachment to the old cause had excited so much fear and resentment at Whitehall that, by a royal order, their moat had been filled up, and their wall demolished to the foundation.† The puritanical spirit had been kept up to the height among them by the precepts and example of one of the most celebrated of the dissenting clergy, Joseph Alleine. Alleine was the author of a tract, entitled, An Alarm to the Unconverted, which is still popular both in England and in America. From the gaol to which he was consigned by the victorious Cavaliers, he addressed to his loving friends at Taunton many epistles breathing the spirit of a truly heroic piety. His frame soon sank under the effects of study, toil, and persecution: but his memory was long cherished with exceeding love and reverence by those whom he had exhorted and catechised.‡

The children of the men who, forty years before, had manned the ramparts of Taunton against the Royalists, now welcomed Monmouth with transports of joy and affection. Every door and window was adorned with wreaths of flowers. No man appeared in the streets without wearing in his hat a green bough, the badge of the popular cause. Damsels of the best families in the town wove colours for the insurgents. One flag in particular was embroidered gorgeously with emblems of royal dignity, and was offered to Monmouth by a train of young girls. He received the gift with the winning courtesy which distinguished him. The lady who headed the procession presented him also with a small Bible of great price. He took it with a show of reverence. " I come," he said, " to defend the truths contained in this book, and to seal them, if it must be so, with my blood." §

But, while Monmouth enjoyed the applause of the multitude, he could not but perceive, with concern and apprehension, that the higher classes were, with scarcely an exception, hostile to his undertaking, and that no rising had

---

* Savage's edition of Toulmin's History of Taunton.
† Sprat's True Account; Toulmin's History of Taunton.

‡ Life and Death of Joseph Alleine, 1672; Nonconformists' Memorial.
§ Harl. MS. 7006.; Oldmixon, 702.; Eachard, iii. 763.

taken place except in the counties where he had himself appeared. He had been assured by agents, who professed to have derived their information from Wildman, that the whole Whig aristocracy was eager to take arms. Nevertheless more than a week had now elapsed since the blue standard had been set up at Lyme. Day labourers, small farmers, shopkeepers, apprentices, dissenting preachers, had flocked to the rebel camp : but not a single peer, baronet, or knight, not a single member of the House of Commons, and scarcely any esquire of sufficient note to have ever been in the commission of the peace, had joined the invaders. Ferguson, who, ever since the death of Charles, had been Monmouth's evil angel, had a suggestion ready. The Duke had put himself into a false position by declining the royal title. Had he declared himself sovereign of England, his cause would have worn a show of legality. At present it was impossible to reconcile his Declaration with the principles of the constitution. It was clear that either Monmouth or his uncle was rightful King. Monmouth did not venture to pronounce himself the rightful King, and yet denied that his uncle was so. Those who fought for James fought for the only person who ventured to claim the throne, and were therefore clearly in their duty, according to the laws of the realm. Those who fought for Monmouth fought for some unknown polity, which was to be set up by a convention not yet in existence. None could wonder that men of high rank and ample fortune stood aloof from an enterprise which threatened with destruction that system in the permanence of which they were deeply interested. If the Duke would assert his legitimacy and assume the crown, he would at once remove this objection. The question would cease to be a question between the old constitution and a new constitution. It would be merely a question of hereditary right between two princes.

On such grounds as these Ferguson, almost immediately after the landing, had earnestly pressed the Duke to proclaim himself King ; and Grey had seconded Ferguson. Monmouth had been very willing to take this advice ; but Wade and other republicans had been refractory ; and their chief, with his usual pliability, had yielded to their arguments. At Taunton the subject was revived. Monmouth talked in private with the dissentients, assured them that he saw no other way of obtaining the support of any portion of the

He takes the title of King

aristocracy, and succeeded in extorting their reluctant consent. On the morning of the twentieth of June he was proclaimed in the market place of Taunton. His followers repeated his new title with affectionate delight. But, as some confusion might have arisen if he had been called King James the Second, they commonly used the strange appellation of King Monmouth: and by this name their unhappy favourite was often mentioned in the western counties, within the memory of persons still living.*

Within twenty-four hours after he had assumed the regal title, he put forth several proclamations headed with his sign manual. By one of these he set a price on the head of his rival. Another declared the Parliament then sitting at Westminster an unlawful assembly, and commanded the members to disperse. A third forbade the people to pay taxes to the usurper. A fourth pronounced Albemarle a traitor.†

Albemarle transmitted these proclamations to London merely as specimens of folly and impertinence. They produced no effect, except wonder and contempt; nor had Monmouth any reason to think that the assumption of royalty had improved his position. Only a week had elapsed since he had solemnly bound himself not to take the crown till a free Parliament should have acknowledged his rights. By breaking that engagement he had incurred the imputation of levity, if not of perfidy. The class which he had hoped to conciliate still stood aloof. The reasons which prevented the great Whig lords and gentlemen from recognising him as their King were at least as strong as those which had prevented them from rallying round him as their Captain General. They disliked indeed the person, the religion, and the politics of James. But James was no longer young. His eldest daughter was justly popular. She was attached to the reformed faith. She was married to a prince who was the hereditary chief of the Protestants of the Continent, to a prince who had been bred in a republic, and whose sentiments were supposed to be such as became a constitutional King. Was it wise to incur the horrors of civil war, for the mere chance of being able to effect immediately what nature would,

---

* Wade's Confession; Goodenough's Confession, Harl, MS. 1152.; Oldmixon, 702. Ferguson's denial is quite undeserving of credit. A copy of the proclamation is in the Harl. MS 7006.

† Copies of the last three proclamations are in the British Museum; Harl. MS. 7006. The first I have never seen; but it is mentioned by Wade.

without bloodshed, without any violation of law, effect, in all probability, before many years should have expired? Perhaps there might be reasons for pulling down James. But what reason could be given for setting up Monmouth? To exclude a prince from the throne on account of unfitness was a course agreeable to Whig principles. But on no principle could it be proper to exclude rightful heirs, who were admitted to be, not only blameless, but eminently qualified for the highest public trust. That Monmouth was legitimate, nay, that he thought himself legitimate, intelligent men could not believe. He was therefore not merely an usurper, but an usurper of the worst sort, an impostor. If he made out any semblance of a case, he could do so only by means of forgery and perjury. All honest and sensible persons were unwilling to see a fraud which, if practised to obtain an estate, would have been punished with the scourge and the pillory, rewarded with the English crown. To the old nobility of the realm it seemed insupportable that the bastard of Lucy Walters should be set up high above the lawful descendants of the Fitzalans and De Veres. Those who were capable of looking forward must have seen that, if Monmouth should succeed in overpowering the existing government, there would still remain a war between him and the House of Orange, a war which might last longer and produce more misery than the war of the Roses, a war which might probably break up the Protestants of Europe into hostile parties, might arm England and Holland against each other, and might make both those countries an easy prey to France. The opinion, therefore, of almost all the leading Whigs seems to have been that Monmouth's enterprise could not fail to end in some great disaster to the nation, but that, on the whole, his defeat would be a less disaster than his victory.

It was not only by the inaction of the Whig aristocracy that the invaders were disappointed. The wealth and power of London had sufficed in the preceding generation, and might again suffice, to turn the scale in a civil conflict. The Londoners had formerly given many proofs of their hatred of Popery and of their affection for the Protestant Duke. He had too readily believed that, as soon as he landed, there would be a rising in the capital. But, though advices came down to him that many thousands of the citizens had been enrolled as volunteers for the good cause, nothing was done. The plain truth was that the agitators who had urged him to invade England, who had promised to rise on the first signal, and who had perhaps imagined, while the danger was remote, that they should have the courage to keep their promise, lost heart when the critical time drew near. Wildman's fright was such that he seemed to have lost his understanding. The craven Danvers at first excused his inaction by saying that he would not take up arms till Monmouth was proclaimed King, and, when Monmouth had been proclaimed King, turned round and declared that good republicans were absolved from all engagements to a leader who had so shamefully broken faith. In every age the vilest specimens of human nature are to be found among demagogues.*

On the day following that on which Monmouth had assumed the regal title he marched from Taunton to Bridgewater. His own spirits, it was remarked, were not high. The acclamations of the devoted thousands who surrounded him wherever he turned could not dispel the gloom which sate on his brow. Those who had seen him during his progress through Somersetshire five years before could not now observe without pity the traces of distress and anxiety on those soft and pleasing features which had won so many hearts.†

Ferguson was in a very different temper. With this man's knavery was strangely mingled an eccentric vanity which resembled madness. The thought that he had raised a rebellion and bestowed a crown had turned his head. He swaggered about, brandishing his naked sword, and crying to the crowd of spectators who had assembled to see the army march out of Taunton, " Look at me ! You have heard of me. I am Ferguson, the famous Ferguson, the Ferguson for whose head so many hundred pounds have been offered." And this man, at once unprincipled and brainsick, had in his keeping the understanding and the conscience of the unhappy Monmouth.‡

His reception at Bridgewater.

Bridgewater was one of the few towns which still had some Whig magistrates. The Mayor and Aldermen came in their robes to welcome the Duke, walked before him in procession to the high cross, and there proclaimed him King. His troops found excellent quarters, and were furnished with necessaries at little or no cost by the people of the town and neighbourhood. He took up his residence in the Castle, a building

* Grey's Narrative ; Ferguson's MS.,   † Persecution   Exposed,   by   John
Eachard, iii. 754.   Whiting.   ‡ Harl. MS. 6845.

which had been honoured by several royal visits. In the Castle Field his army was encamped. It now consisted of about six thousand men, and might easily have been increased to double the number, but for the want of arms. The Duke had brought with him from the Continent but a scanty supply of pikes and muskets. Many of his followers had, therefore, no other weapons than such as could be fashioned out of the tools which they had used in husbandry or mining. Of these rude implements of war the most formidable was made by fastening the blade of a scythe erect on a strong pole.* The tithing men of the country round Taunton and Bridgewater received orders to search everywhere for scythes and to bring all that could be found to the camp. It was impossible, however, even with the help of these contrivances, to supply the demand; and great numbers who were desirous to enlist were sent away.†

The foot were divided into six regiments. Many of the men had been in the militia, and still wore their uniforms, red and yellow. The cavalry were about a thousand in number; but most of them had only large colts, such as were then bred in great herds on the marshes of Somersetshire for the purpose of supplying London with coach horses and cart horses. These animals were so far from being fit for any military purpose that they had not yet learned to obey the bridle, and became ungovernable as soon as they heard a gun fired or a drum beaten. A small body guard of forty young men, well armed, and mounted at their own charge, attended Monmouth. The people of Bridgewater, who were enriched by a thriving coast trade, furnished him with a small sum of money.‡

All this time the forces of the government were fast assembling. On the west of the rebel army, Albemarle still kept together a large body of Devonshire militia. On the east, the trainbands of Wiltshire had mustered under the command of Thomas Herbert, Earl of Pembroke. On the north east, Henry Somerset, Duke of Beaufort, was in arms. The power of Beaufort bore some faint resemblance to that of the great barons of the fifteenth century. He was President of Wales and Lord Lieutenant of four English counties. His official tours through the extensive region in which he repre-

Preparations of the government to oppose him.

* One of these weapons may still be seen in the Tower.
† Grey's Narrative; Paschall's Narrative in the Appendix to Heywood's Vindication.
‡ Oldmixon, 702.

sented the majesty of the throne were scarcely inferior in pomp to royal progresses. His household at Badminton was regulated after the fashion of an earlier generation. The land to a great extent round his pleasure grounds was in his own hands ; and the labourers who cultivated it formed part of his family. Nine tables were every day spread under his roof for two hundred persons. A crowd of gentlemen and pages were under the orders of the steward. A whole troop of cavalry obeyed the master of the horse. The fame of the kitchen, the cellar, the kennel, and the stables was spread over all England. The gentry, many miles round, were proud of the magnificence of their great neighbour, and were at the same time charmed by his affability and good nature. He was a zealous Cavalier of the old school. At this crisis, therefore, he used his whole influence and authority in support of the crown, and occupied Bristol with the trainbands of Gloucestershire, who seem to have been better disciplined than most other troops of that description.*

In the counties more remote from Somersetshire the supporters of the throne were on the alert. The militia of Sussex began to march westward, under the command of Richard, Lord Lumley, who, though he had lately been converted from the Roman Catholic religion, was still firm in his allegiance to a Roman Catholic King. James Bertie, Earl of Abingdon, called out the array of Oxfordshire. John Fell, Bishop of Oxford, who was also Dean of Christchurch, summoned the undergraduates of his University to take arms for the crown. The gownsmen crowded to give in their names. Christchurch alone furnished near a hundred pikemen and musketeers. Young noblemen and gentlemen commoners acted as officers ; and the eldest son of the Lord Lieutenant was Colonel.†

But it was chiefly on the regular troops that the King relied. Churchill had been sent westward with the Blues ; and Feversham was following with all the forces that could be spared from the neighbourhood of London. A courier had started for Holland with a letter directing Skelton instantly to request that the three English regiments in the Dutch service might be sent to the Thames. When the request was made, the party hostile to the House of Orange, headed by

* North's Life of Guildford, 132. Accounts of Beaufort's progress through Wales and the neighbouring counties are in the London Gazettes of July 1684. Letter of Beaufort to Clarendon, June 19. 1685.

† Bishop Fell to Clarendon, June 20. ; Abingdon to Clarendon, June 20. 25, 26. 1685 ; Lansdowne MS. 846.

the deputies of Amsterdam, again tried to cause delay. But the energy of William, who had almost as much at stake as James, and who saw Monmouth's progress with serious uneasiness, bore down opposition; and in a few days the troops sailed.* The three Scotch regiments were already in England. They had arrived at Gravesend in excellent condition, and James had reviewed them on Blackheath. He repeatedly declared to the Dutch Ambassador that he had never in his life seen finer or better disciplined soldiers, and expressed the warmest gratitude to the Prince of Orange and the States for so valuable and seasonable a reinforcement. This satisfaction, however, was not unmixed. Excellently as the men went through their drill, they were not untainted with Dutch politics and Dutch divinity. One of them was shot and another flogged for drinking the Duke of Monmouth's health, It was therefore not thought advisable to place them in the post of danger. They were kept in the neighbourhood of London till the end of the campaign. But their arrival enabled the King to send to the West some infantry which would otherwise have been wanted in the capital.†

While the government was thus preparing for a conflict with the rebels in the field, precautions of a different kind were not neglected. In London alone two hundred of those persons who were thought most likely to be at the head of a Whig movement were arrested. Among the prisoners were some merchants of great note. Every man who was obnoxious to the Court went in fear. A general gloom overhung the capital. Business languished on the Exchange; and the theatres were so generally deserted that a new opera, written by Dryden, and set off by decorations of unprecedented magnificence, was withdrawn, because the receipts would not cover the expenses of the performance.‡ The magistrates and clergy were everywhere active. The Dissenters were everywhere closely observed. In Cheshire and Shropshire a fierce persecution raged; in Northamptonshire arrests were numerous; and the gaol of Oxford was crowded with prisoners. No Puritan divine, however moderate his opinions, however guarded his conduct, could feel any confidence that he should not be torn from his family and flung into a dungeon.§

* Avaux, July $\frac{5}{15}$, $\frac{6}{16}$. 1685.

† Van Citters, $\frac{June\ 30}{July\ 10}$, July $\frac{8}{18}$. $\frac{21}{31}$. 1685; Avaux Neg. July $\frac{5}{15}$.; London Gazette, July 6.

‡ Barillon, July $\frac{6}{16}$. 1685; Scott's preface to Albion and Albanius.

§ Abingdon to Clarendon, June 29. 1685; Life of Philip Henry, by Bates.

Meanwhile Monmouth advanced from Bridgewater harassed through the whole march by Churchill, who appears to have done all that, with a handful of men, it was possible for a brave and skilful officer to effect. The rebel army, much annoyed, both by the enemy and by a heavy fall of rain, halted in the evening of the twenty-second of June at Glastonbury. The houses of the little town did not afford shelter for so large a force. Some of the troops were therefore quartered in the churches, and others lighted their fires among the venerable ruins of the Abbey, once the wealthiest religious house in our island. From Glastonbury the Duke marched to Wells, and from Wells to Shepton Mallet.*

His design on Bristol.

Hitherto he seems to have wandered from place to place with no other object than that of collecting troops. It was now necessary for him to form some plan of military operations. His first scheme was to seize Bristol. Many of the chief inhabitants of that important place were Whigs. One of the ramifications of the Whig plot had extended thither. The garrison consisted only of the Gloucestershire trainbands. If Beaufort and his rustic followers could be overpowered before the regular troops arrived, the rebels would at once find themselves possessed of ample pecuniary resources; the credit of Monmouth's arms would be raised; and his friends throughout the kingdom would be encouraged to declare themselves. Bristol had fortifications which, on the north of the Avon towards Gloucestershire, were weak, but on the south towards Somersetshire were much stronger. It was therefore determined that the attack should be made on the Gloucestershire side. But for this purpose it was necessary to take a circuitous route, and to cross the Avon at Keynsham. The bridge at Keynsham had been partly demolished by the militia, and was at present impassable. A detachment was therefore sent forward to make the necessary repairs. The other troops followed more slowly, and on the evening of the twenty-fourth of June halted for repose at Pensford. At Pensford they were only five miles from the Somersetshire side of Bristol; but the Gloucestershire side, which could be reached only by going round through Keynsham, was distant a long day's march.†

That night was one of great tumult and expectation in Bristol. The partisans of Monmouth knew that he was

* London Gazette, June 22. and June 25. 1685; Wade's Confession; Oldmixon, 703.; Harl. MS. 6845.   † Wade's Confession.

almost within sight of their city, and imagined that he would be among them before daybreak. About an hour after sunset a merchantman lying at the quay took fire. Such an occurrence, in a port crowded with shipping, could not but excite great alarm. The whole river was in commotion. The streets were crowded. Seditious cries were heard amidst the darkness and confusion. It was afterwards asserted, both by Whigs and by Tories, that the fire had been kindled by the friends of Monmouth, in the hope that the trainbands would be busied in preventing the conflagration from spreading, and that in the meantime the rebel army would make a bold push, and would enter the city on the Somersetshire side. If such was the design of the incendiaries, it completely failed. Beaufort, instead of sending his men to the quay, kept them all night drawn up under arms round the beautiful church of Saint Mary Redcliff, on the south of the Avon. He would see Bristol burnt down, he said, nay, he would burn it down himself, rather than that it should be occupied by traitors. He was able, with the help of some regular cavalry which had joined him from Chippenham a few hours before, to prevent an insurrection. It might perhaps have been beyond his power at once to overawe the malecontents within the walls and to repel an attack from without : but no such attack was made. The fire, which caused so much commotion at Bristol, was distinctly seen at Pensford. Monmouth, however, did not think it expedient to change his plan. He remained quiet till sunrise, and then marched to Keynsham. There he found the bridge repaired. He determined to let his army rest during the afternoon, and, as soon as night came, to proceed to Bristol.*

But it was too late. The King's forces were now near at hand. Colonel Oglethorpe, at the head of about a hundred men of the Life Guards, dashed into Keynsham, scattered two troops of rebel horse which ventured to oppose him, and retired after inflicting much injury and suffering little. In these circumstances it was thought necessary to relinquish the design on Bristol.† He relinquishes that design.

But what was to be done? Several schemes were proposed and discussed. It was suggested that Monmouth might hasten to Gloucester, might cross the Severn there, might

* Wade's Confession; Oldmixon, 703.; Harl. MS. 6845.; Charge of Jeffreys to the grand jury of Bristol, Sept. 21. 1685   † London Gazette, June 29. 1685; Wade's Confession.

break down the bridge behind him, and, with his right flank protected by the river, might march through Worcestershire into Shropshire and Cheshire. He had formerly made a progress through those counties, and had been received there with as much enthusiasm as in Somersetshire and Devonshire. His presence might revive the zeal of his old friends; and his army might in a few days be swollen to double its present numbers.

On full consideration, however, it appeared that this plan, though specious, was impracticable. The rebels were ill shod for such work as they had lately undergone, and were exhausted by toiling, day after day, through deep mud under heavy rain. Harassed and impeded as they would be at every stage by the enemy's cavalry, they could not hope to reach Gloucester without being overtaken by the main body of the royal troops, and forced to a general action under every disadvantage.

Then it was proposed to enter Wiltshire. Persons who professed to know that county well assured the Duke that he would be joined there by such strong reinforcements as would make it safe for him to give battle.*

He took this advice, and turned towards Wiltshire. He first summoned Bath. But Bath was strongly garrisoned for the King; and Feversham was fast approaching. The rebels, therefore, made no attempt on the walls, but hastened to Philip's Norton, where they halted on the evening of the twenty-sixth of June.

Feversham followed them thither. Early on the morning of the twenty-seventh they were alarmed by tidings that he was close at hand. They got into order, and lined the hedges leading to the town.

The advanced guard of the royal army soon appeared. It consisted of about five hundred men, commanded by the Duke of Grafton, a youth of bold spirit and rough manners, who was probably eager to show that he had no share in the disloyal schemes of his half brother. Grafton soon found himself in a deep lane with fences on both sides of him, from which a galling fire of musketry was kept up. Still he pushed boldly on till he came to the entrance of Philip's Norton. There his way was crossed by a barricade, from which a third fire met him full in front. His men now lost heart, and made the best of their way back. Before they got out of the lane

Skirmish at Philip's Norton.

* Wade's Confession.

more than a hundred of them had been killed or wounded. Grafton's retreat was intercepted by some of the rebel cavalry : but he cut his way gallantly through them, and came off safe.*

The advanced guard, thus repulsed, fell back on the main body of the royal forces. The two armies were now face to face ; and a few shots were exchanged that did little or no execution. Neither side was impatient to come to action. Feversham did not wish to fight till his artillery came up, and fell back to Bradford. Monmouth, as soon as the night closed in, quitted his position, marched southward, and by daybreak arrived at Frome, where he hoped to find reinforcements.

Frome was as zealous in his cause as either Taunton or Bridgewater, but could do nothing to serve him. There had been a rising a few days before ; and Monmouth's declaration had been posted up in the market place. But the news of this movement had been carried to the Earl of Pembroke, who lay at no great distance with the Wiltshire militia. He had instantly marched to Frome, had routed a mob of rustics who, with scythes and pitchforks, attempted to oppose him, had entered the town and had disarmed the inhabitants. No weapons, therefore, were left there ; nor was Monmouth able to furnish any.†

The rebel army was in evil case. The march of the preceding night had been wearisome. The rain had fallen in torrents ; and the roads had become mere quagmires. Nothing was heard of the promised succours from Wiltshire. One messenger brought news that Argyle's forces had been dispersed in Scotland. Another reported that Feversham, having been joined by his artillery, was about to advance. Monmouth understood war too well not to know that his followers, with all their courage and all their zeal, were no match for regular soldiers. He had till lately flattered himself with the hope that some of those regiments which he had formerly commanded would pass over to his standard : but that hope he was now compelled to relinquish. His heart failed him. He could scarcely muster firmness enough to give orders. In his misery he complained bitterly of the evil counsellors who had induced him to quit his happy retreat in Brabant. Against Wildman in particular he broke forth into

Despond-
ence of
Mon-
mouth.

---

* London Gazette, July 2. 1685 ; Barillon, July $\frac{6}{16}$. ; Wade's Confession. † London Gazette, June 29. 1685 ; Van Citters, $\frac{June\ 30.}{July\ 10.}$

violent imprecations.* And now an ignominious thought rose in his weak and agitated mind. He would leave to the mercy of the government the thousands who had, at his call and for his sake, abandoned their quiet fields and dwellings. He would steal away with his chief officers, would gain some seaport before his flight was suspected, would escape to the Continent, and would forget his ambition and his shame in the arms of Lady Wentworth. He seriously discussed this scheme with his leading advisers. Some of them, trembling for their necks, listened to it with approbation : but Grey, who, by the admission of his detractors, was intrepid everywhere except where swords were clashing and guns going off around him, opposed the dastardly proposition with great ardour, and implored the Duke to face every danger rather than requite with ingratitude and treachery the devoted attachment of the Western peasantry.†

The scheme of flight was abandoned : but it was not now easy to form any plan for a campaign. To advance towards London would have been madness ; for the road lay right across Salisbury Plain ; and on that vast open space regular troops, and above all regular cavalry, would have acted with every advantage against undisciplined men. At this juncture a report reached the camp that the rustics of the marshes near Axbridge had risen in defence of the Protestant religion, had armed themselves with flails, bludgeons, and pitchforks, and were assembling by thousands at Bridgewater. Monmouth determined to return thither, and to strengthen himself with these new allies.‡

The rebels accordingly proceeded to Wells, and arrived there in no amiable temper. They were, with few exceptions, hostile to Prelacy ; and they showed their hostility in a way very little to their honour. They not only tore the lead from the roof of the magnificent Cathedral to make bullets, an act for which they might fairly plead the necessities of war, but wantonly defaced the ornaments of the building. Grey with difficulty preserved the altar from the insults of some ruffians who wished to carouse round it, by taking his stand before it with his sword drawn.§

He returns to Bridgewater. On Thursday, the second of July, Monmouth again entered Bridgewater, in circumstances far less cheering than those in

* Harl. MS. 6845.; Wade's Confession. § London Gazette, July 6. 1685 ; Van
† Wade's Confession ; Eachard, iii. 766. Citters, July ³⁄₁₃. ; Oldmixon, 703.
‡ Wade's Confession,

which he had marched thence ten days before. The reinforcement which he found there was inconsiderable. The royal army was close upon him. At one moment he thought of fortifying the town; and hundreds of labourers were summoned to dig trenches and throw up mounds. Then his mind recurred to the plan of marching into Cheshire, a plan which he had rejected as impracticable when he was at Keynsham, and which assuredly was not more practicable now that he was at Bridgewater.*

While he was thus wavering between projects equally hopeless, the King's forces came in sight. They consisted of about two thousand five hundred regular troops, and of about fifteen hundred of the Wiltshire militia. Early on the morning of Sunday, the fifth of July, they left Somerton, and pitched their tents that day about three miles from Bridgewater, on the plain of Sedgemoor. *(The royal army encamps at Sedgemoor.)*

Dr. Peter Mew, Bishop of Winchester, accompanied them. This prelate had in his youth borne arms for Charles the First against the Parliament. Neither his years nor his profession had wholly extinguished his martial ardour; and he probably thought that the appearance of a father of the Protestant Church in the King's camp might confirm the loyalty of some honest men who were wavering between their horror of Popery and their horror of rebellion.

The steeple of the parish church of Bridgewater is said to be the loftiest in Somersetshire, and commands a wide view over the surrounding country. Monmouth, accompanied by some of his officers, went up to the top of the square tower from which the spire ascends, and observed through a telescope the position of the enemy. Beneath him lay a flat expanse, now rich with cornfields and apple trees, but then, as its name imports, for the most part a dreary morass. When the rains were heavy, and the Parret and its tributary streams rose above their banks, this tract was often flooded. It was indeed anciently part of that great swamp which is renowned in our early chronicles as having arrested the progress of two successive races of invaders, which long protected the Celts against the aggressions of the kings of Wessex, and which sheltered Alfred from the pursuit of the Danes. In those remote times this region could be traversed only in boats. It was a vast pool, wherein were scattered many islets of shifting and treacherous soil, overhung with rank jungle, and

* Wade's Confession.

swarming with deer and wild swine. Even in the days of the Tudors, the traveller whose journey lay from Ilchester to Bridgewater was forced to make a circuit of several miles in order to avoid the waters. When Monmouth looked upon Sedgemoor, it had been partially reclaimed by art, and was intersected by many deep and wide trenches which, in that country, are called rhines. In the midst of the moor rose, clustering round the towers of churches, a few villages, of which the names seem to indicate that they once were surrounded by waves. In one of these villages, called Weston Zoyland, the royal cavalry lay; and Feversham had fixed his head quarters there. Many persons still living have seen the daughter of the servant girl who waited on him that day at table; and a large dish of Persian ware, which was set before him, is still carefully preserved in the neighbourhood. It is to be observed that the population of Somersetshire does not, like that of the manufacturing districts, consist of emigrants from distant places. It is by no means unusual to find farmers who cultivate the same land which their ancestors cultivated when the Plantagenets reigned in England. The Somersetshire traditions are, therefore, of no small value to a historian.*

At a greater distance from Bridgewater lies the village of Middlezoy. In that village and its neighbourhood, the Wiltshire militia were quartered, under the command of Pembroke.

On the open moor, not far from Chedzoy, were encamped several battalions of regular infantry. Monmouth looked gloomily on them. He could not but remember how, a few years before, he had, at the head of a column composed of some of those very men, driven before him in confusion the fierce enthusiasts who defended Bothwell Bridge. He could distinguish among the hostile ranks that gallant band which was then called from the name of its Colonel, Dumbarton's regiment, but which has long been known as the first of the line, and which, in all the four quarters of the world, has nobly supported its early reputation. "I know those men," said Monmouth; "they will fight. If I had but them, all would go well."†

---

* Matt. West. Flor. Hist., A.D. 788; MS. Chronicle quoted by Mr. Sharon Turner in the History of the Anglo-Saxons, book IV. chap. xix.; Drayton's Polyolbion, iii.; Leland's Itinerary; Oldmixon, 703. Oldmixon was then at Bridgewater, and probably saw the Duke on the church tower. The dish mentioned in the text is the property of Mr. Stradling, who has taken laudable pains to preserve the relics and traditions of the Western insurrection.

† Oldmixon, 703.

Yet the aspect of the enemy was not altogether discouraging. The three divisions of the royal army lay far apart from one another. There was an appearance of negligence and of relaxed discipline in all their movements. It was reported that they were drinking themselves drunk with the Zoyland cider. The incapacity of Feversham, who commanded in chief, was notorious. Even at this momentous crisis he thought only of eating and sleeping. Churchill was indeed a captain equal to tasks far more arduous than that of scattering a crowd of ill armed and ill trained peasants. But the genius, which, at a later period, humbled six Marshals of France, was not now in its proper place. Feversham told Churchill little, and gave him no encouragement to offer any suggestion. The lieutenant, conscious of superior abilities and science, impatient of the control of a chief whom he despised, and trembling for the fate of the army, nevertheless preserved his characteristic self-command, and dissembled his feelings so well that Feversham praised his submissive alacrity, and promised to report it to the King.*

Monmouth, having observed the disposition of the royal forces, and having been apprised of the state in which they were, conceived that a night attack might be attended with success. He resolved to run the hazard; and preparations were instantly made.

It was Sunday; and his followers, who had, for the most part, been brought up after the Puritan fashion, passed a great part of the day in religious exercises. The Castle Field, in which the army was encamped, presented a spectacle such as, since the disbanding of Cromwell's soldiers, England had never seen. The dissenting preachers who had taken arms against Popery, and some of whom had probably fought in the great civil war, prayed and preached in red coats and huge jackboots, with swords by their sides. Ferguson was one of those who harangued. He took for his text the awful imprecation by which the Israelites who dwelt beyond Jordan cleared themselves from the charge ignorantly brought against them by their brethren on the other side of the river. "The Lord God of Gods, the Lord God of Gods, he knoweth; and Israel he shall know. If it be in rebellion, or if in transgression against the Lord, save us not this day."†

That an attack was to be made under cover of the night

---

* Churchill to Clarendon, July 4.   † Oldmixon, 703.; Observator, Aug.
1685.   1. 1685.

was no secret in Bridgewater. The town was full of women, who had repaired thither by hundreds from the surrounding region, to see their husbands, sons, lovers, and brothers once more. There were many sad partings that day; and many parted never to meet again.* The report of the intended attack came to the ears of a young girl who was zealous for the King. Though of modest character, she had the courage to resolve that she would herself bear the intelligence to Feversham. She stole out of Bridgewater, and made her way to the royal camp. But that camp was not a place where female innocence could be safe. Even the officers, despising alike the irregular force to which they were opposed, and the negligent general who commanded them, had indulged largely in wine, and were ready for any excess of licentiousness and cruelty. One of them seized the unhappy maiden, refused to listen to her errand, and brutally outraged her. She fled in agonies of rage and shame, leaving the wicked army to its doom.†

And now the time for the great hazard drew near. The night was not ill suited for such an enterprise. The moon was indeed at the full, and the northern streamers were shining brilliantly. But the marsh fog lay so thick on Sedgemoor that no object could be discerned there at the distance of fifty paces.‡

Battle of
Sedge-
moor.

The clock struck eleven; and the Duke with his body guard rode out of the Castle. He was not in the frame of mind which befits one who is about to strike a decisive blow. The very children who pressed to see him pass observed, and long remembered, that his look was sad and full of evil augury. His army marched by a circuitous path, near six miles in length, towards the royal encampment on Sedgemoor. Part of the route is to this day called War Lane. The foot were led by Monmouth himself. The horse were confided to

---

* Paschall's Narrative in Heywood's Appendix.

† Kennet, ed. 1719, iii. 432. I am forced to believe that this lamentable story is true. The Bishop declares that it was communicated to him in the year 1718 by a brave officer of the Blues, who had fought at Sedgemoor, and who had himself seen the poor girl depart in an agony of distress.

‡ Narrative of an officer of the Horse Guards in Kennet, ed. 1719, iii. 432.; MS. Journal of the Western Rebellion,

kept by Mr. Edward Dummer; Dryden's Hind and Panther, part II. The lines of Dryden are remarkable:—

"Such were the pleasing triumphs of the sky
For James's late nocturnal victory,
The pledge of his almighty patron's love,
The fireworks which his angels made above.
I saw myself the lambent easy light
Gild the brown horror and dispel the night.
The messenger with speed the tidings bore,
News which three labouring nations did restore;
But heaven's own Nuntius was arrived before."

Grey, in spite of the remonstrances of some who remembered the mishap at Bridport. Orders were given that strict silence should be preserved, that no drum should be beaten, and no shot fired. The word by which the insurgents were to recognise one another in the darkness was Soho. It had doubtless been selected in allusion to Soho Fields in London, where their leader's palace stood.*

At about one in the morning of Monday the sixth of July, the rebels were on the open moor. But between them and the enemy lay three broad rhines filled with water and soft mud. Two of these, called the Black Ditch and the Langmoor Rhine, Monmouth knew that he must pass. But, strange to say, the existence of a trench, called the Bussex Rhine, which immediately covered the royal encampment, had not been mentioned to him by any of his scouts.

The wains which carried the ammunition remained at the entrance of the moor. The horse and foot, in a long narrow column, passed the Black Ditch by a causeway. There was a similar causeway across the Langmoor Rhine: but the guide, in the fog, missed his way. There was some delay and some tumult before the error could be rectified. At length the passage was effected: but, in the confusion, a pistol went off. Some men of the Horse Guards, who were on watch, heard the report, and perceived that a great multitude was advancing through the mist. They fired their carbines, and galloped off in different directions to give the alarm. Some hastened to Weston Zoyland, where the cavalry lay. One trooper spurred to the encampment of the infantry, and cried out vehemently that the enemy was at hand. The drums of Dumbarton's regiment beat to arms; and the men got fast into their ranks. It was time; for Monmouth was already drawing up his army for action. He ordered Grey to lead the way with the cavalry, and followed himself at the head of the infantry. Grey pushed on till his progress was unexpectedly arrested by the Bussex Rhine. On the opposite side of the ditch the King's foot were hastily forming in order of battle.

"For whom are you?" called out an officer of the Foot Guards. "For the King," replied a voice from the ranks

* It has been said by several writers, and among them by Pennant, that the district in London called Soho derived its name from the watchword of Monmouth's army at Sedgemoor. Mention of Soho Fields will be found in many books printed before the Western insurrection; for example, in Chamberlayne's State of England, 1684.

of the rebel cavalry. "For which King?" was then demanded. The answer was a shout of "King Monmouth," mingled with the war cry, which forty years before had been inscribed on the colours of the parliamentary regiments, "God with us." The royal troops instantly fired such a volley of musketry as sent the rebel horse flying in all directions. The world agreed to ascribe this ignominious rout to Grey's pusillanimity. Yet it is by no means clear that Churchill would have succeeded better at the head of men who had never before handled arms on horseback, and whose horses were unused, not only to stand fire, but to obey the rein.

A few minutes after the Duke's horse had dispersed themselves over the moor, his infantry came up running fast, and guided through the gloom by the lighted matches of Dumbarton's regiment.

Monmouth was startled by finding that a broad and profound trench lay between him and the camp which he had hoped to surprise. The insurgents halted on the edge of the rhine, and fired. Part of the royal infantry on the opposite bank returned the fire. During three quarters of an hour the roar of the musketry was incessant. The Somersetshire peasants behaved themselves as if they had been veteran soldiers, save only that they levelled their pieces too high.

But now the other divisions of the royal army were in motion. The Life Guards and Blues came pricking fast from Weston Zoyland, and scattered in an instant some of Grey's horse, who had attempted to rally. The fugitives spread a panic among their comrades in the rear, who had charge of the ammunition. The waggoners drove off at full speed, and never stopped till they were many miles from the field of battle. Monmouth had hitherto done his part like a stout and able warrior. He had been seen on foot, pike in hand, encouraging his infantry by voice and by example. But he was too well acquainted with military affairs not to know that all was over. His men had lost the advantage which surprise and darkness had given them. They were deserted by the horse and by the ammunition waggons. The King's forces were now united and in good order. Feversham had been awakened by the firing, had got out of bed, had adjusted his cravat, had looked at himself well in the glass, and had come to see what his men were doing. Meanwhile, what was of much more importance, Churchill had rapidly made an entirely new disposition of the royal infantry. The day was about to break. The event of a conflict on an open plain, by broad sunlight, could not be doubtful. Yet Monmouth should have felt that it was not for him to fly, while thousands whom affection for him had hurried to destruction were still fighting manfully in his cause. But vain hopes and the intense love of life prevailed. He saw that if he tarried the royal cavalry would soon intercept his retreat. He mounted and rode from the field.

Yet his foot, though deserted, made a gallant stand. The Life Guards attacked them on the right, the Blues on the left: but the Somersetshire clowns, with their scythes and the butt ends of their muskets, faced the royal horse like old soldiers. Oglethorpe made a vigorous attempt to break them and was manfully repulsed. Sarsfield, a brave Irish officer, whose name afterwards obtained a melancholy celebrity, charged on the other flank. His men were beaten back. He was himself struck to the ground, and lay for a time as one dead. But the struggle of the hardy rustics could not last. Their powder and ball were spent. Cries were heard of "Ammunition! For God's sake ammunition!" But no ammunition was at hand. And now the King's artillery came up. It had been posted half a mile off, on the high road from Weston Zoyland to Bridgewater. So defective were then the appointments of an English army that there would have been much difficulty in dragging the great guns to the place where the battle was raging, had not the Bishop of Winchester offered his coach horses and traces for the purpose. This interference of a Christian prelate in a matter of blood has, with strange inconsistency, been condemned by some Whig writers who can see nothing criminal in the conduct of the numerous Puritan ministers then in arms against the government. Even when the guns had arrived, there was such a want of gunners that a sergeant of Dumbarton's regiment was forced to take on himself the management of several pieces.* The cannon, however, though ill served, brought the engagement to a speedy close. The pikes of the rebel battalions began to shake: the ranks broke; the King's cavalry charged again, and bore down everything before them; the King's infantry came pouring across the ditch. Even in that extremity the Mendip miners stood bravely to their arms, and sold their

---

* There is a warrant of James directing that forty pounds should be paid to Sergeant Weems, of Dumbarton's regiment, " for good service in the action at Sedgemoor in firing the great guns against the rebels."—Historical Record of the First or Royal Regiment of Foot.

lives dearly. But the rout was in a few minutes complete. Three hundred of the soldiers had been killed or wounded. Of the rebels more than a thousand lay dead on the moor.*

So ended the last fight deserving the name of battle, that has been fought on English ground. The impression left on the simple inhabitants of the neighbourhood was deep and lasting. That impression, indeed, has been frequently renewed. For even in our own time the plough and the spade have not seldom turned up ghastly memorials of the slaugh-

---

* James the Second's account of the battle of Sedgemoor in Lord Hardwicke's State Papers; Wade's Confession; Ferguson's MS. Narrative in Eachard, iii. 768.; Narrative of an Officer of the Horse Guards in Kennet, ed. 1719, iii. 432.; London Gazette, July 9. 1685; Oldmixon, 703.; Paschall's Narrative; Burnet, i. 643.; Evelyn's Diary, July 8.; Van Citters, July $\frac{7}{17}$.; Barillon, July $\frac{9}{19}$.; Reresby's Memoirs; the Duke of Buckingham's Battle of Sedgemoor, a Farce; MS. Journal of the Western Rebellion, kept by Mr. Edward Dummer, then serving in the train of artillery employed by His Majesty for the suppression of the same. The last mentioned manuscript is in the Pepysian library, and is of the greatest value, not on account of the narrative, which contains little that is remarkable, but on account of the plans, which exhibit the battle in four or five different stages.

"The history of a battle," says the greatest of living generals, "is not unlike the history of a ball. Some individuals may recollect all the little events of which the great result is the battle won or lost; but no individual can recollect the order in which, or the exact moment at which, they occurred, which makes all the difference as to their value or importance. . . . Just to show you how little reliance can be placed even on what are supposed the best accounts of a battle, I mention that there are some circumstances mentioned in General ——'s account which did not occur as he relates them. It is impossible to say when each important occurrence took place, or in what order."—Wellington Papers, Aug. 8. and 17. 1815.

The battle concerning which the Duke of Wellington wrote thus was that of Waterloo, fought only a few weeks before, by broad day, under his own vigilant and experienced eye. What then must be the difficulty of compiling from twelve or thirteen narratives an account of a battle fought more than a hundred and sixty years ago in such darkness that not a man of those engaged could see fifty paces before him? The difficulty is aggravated by the circumstance that those witnesses who had the best opportunity of knowing the truth were by no means inclined to tell it. The paper which I have placed at the head of my list of authorities was evidently drawn up with extreme partiality to Feversham. Wade was writing under the dread of the halter. Ferguson, who was seldom scrupulous about the truth of his assertions, lied on this occasion like Bobadil or Parolles. Oldmixon, who was a boy at Bridgewater when the battle was fought, and passed a great part of his subsequent life there, was so much under the influence of local passions that his local information was useless to him. His desire to magnify the valour of the Somersetshire peasants, a valour which their enemies acknowledged, and which did not need to be set off by exaggeration and fiction, led him to compose an absurd romance. The eulogy which Barillon, a Frenchman accustomed to despise raw levies, pronounced on the vanquished army, is of much more value, "Son infanterie fit fort bien. On eut de la peine à les rompre, et les soldats combattoient avec les crosses de mousquet et les scies qu'ils avoient au bout de grands bastons au lieu de picques."

Little is now to be learned by visiting the field of battle; for the face of the country has been greatly changed; and the old Bussex Rhine, on the banks of which the great struggle took place, has long disappeared. The rhine now called by that name is of later date, and takes a different course.

I have derived much assistance from Mr. Roberts's account of the battle. Life of Monmouth, chap. xxii. His narrative is in the main confirmed by Dummer's plans.

ter, skulls, and thighbones, and strange weapons made out of implements of husbandry. Old peasants related very recently that, in their childhood, they were accustomed to play on the moor at the fight between King James's men and King Monmouth's men, and that King Monmouth's men always raised the cry of Soho.*

What seems most extraordinary in the battle of Sedgemoor is that the event should have been for a moment doubtful, and that the rebels should have resisted so long. That five or six thousand colliers and ploughmen should contend during an hour with half that number of regular cavalry and infantry would now be thought a miracle. Our wonder will, perhaps, be diminished when we remember that, in the time of James the Second, the discipline of the regular army was extremely lax, and that, on the other hand, the peasantry were accustomed to serve in the militia. The difference, therefore, between a regiment of the Foot Guards and a regiment of clowns just enrolled, though doubtless considerable, was by no means what it now is. Monmouth did not lead a mere mob to attack good soldiers. For his followers were not altogether without a tincture of soldiership; and Feversham's troops, when compared with English troops of our time, might almost be called a mob.

It was four o'clock: the sun was rising; and the routed army came pouring into the streets of Bridgewater. The uproar, the blood, the gashes, the ghastly figures which sank down and never rose again, spread horror and dismay through the town. The pursuers, too, were close behind. Those inhabitants who had favoured the insurrection expected sack and massacre, and implored the protection of their neighbours who professed the Roman Catholic religion, or had made themselves conspicuous by Tory politics; and it is acknowledged by the bitterest of Whig historians that this protection was kindly and generously given.†

During that day the conquerors continued to chase the fugitives. The neighbouring villagers long remembered with what a clatter of horsehoofs and what a storm of curses the whirlwind of cavalry swept by. Before evening five hundred prisoners had been crowded into the parish church of Weston Zoyland. Eighty of them were wounded ; and five expired within the consecrated walls. Great numbers of labourers

Pursuit of the rebels.

---

* I learned these things from persons living close to Sedgemoor.
† Oldmixon, 704.

were impressed for the purpose of burying the slain. A few, who were notoriously partial to the vanquished side, were set apart for the hideous office of quartering the captives. The tithing men of the neighbouring parishes were busied in setting up gibbets and providing chains. All this while the bells of Weston Zoyland and Chedzoy rang joyously; and the soldiers sang and rioted on the moor amidst the corpses. For the farmers of the neighbourhood had made haste, as soon as the event of the fight was known, to send hogsheads of their best cider as peace offerings to the victors.*

Military executions.

Feversham passed for a goodnatured man: but he was a foreigner, ignorant of the laws and careless of the feelings of the English. He was accustomed to the military license of France, and had learned from his great kinsman, the conqueror and devastator of the Palatinate, not indeed how to conquer, but how to devastate. A considerable number of prisoners were immediately selected for execution. Among them was a youth famous for his speed. Hopes were held out to him that his life would be spared if he could run a race with one of the colts of the marsh. The space through which the man kept up with the horse is still marked by well known bounds on the moor, and is about three quarters of a mile. Feversham was not ashamed, after seeing the performance, to send the wretched performer to the gallows. The next day a long line of gibbets appeared on the road leading from Bridgewater to Weston Zoyland. On each gibbet a prisoner was suspended. Four of the sufferers were left to rot in irons.†

Flight of Monmouth.

Meanwhile Monmouth, accompanied by Grey, by Buyse, and by a few other friends, was flying from the field of battle. At Chedzoy he stopped a moment to mount a fresh horse and to hide his blue riband and his George. He then hastened towards the Bristol Channel. From the rising ground on the north of the field of battle he saw the flash and the smoke of the last volley fired by his deserted followers. Before six o'clock he was twenty miles from Sedgemoor. Some of his companions advised him to cross the water, and to seek refuge in Wales; and this would undoubtedly have been his wisest course. He would have been in Wales many hours before the news of his defeat was known there; and, in a country so wild and so remote from the seat of government, he might have remained long undiscovered. He determined, however,

* Locke's Western Rebellion; Stradling's Chilton Priory.

† Locke's Western Rebellion; Stradling's Chilton Priory; Oldmixon, 704.

to push for Hampshire, in the hope that he might lurk in the cabins of deerstealers among the oaks of the New Forest, till means of conveyance to the Continent could be procured. He therefore, with Grey and the German, turned to the south east. But the way was beset with dangers. The three fugitives had to traverse a country in which every one already knew the event of the battle, and in which no traveller of suspicious appearance could escape a close scrutiny. They rode on all day, shunning towns and villages. Nor was this so difficult as it may now appear. For men then living could remember the time when the wild deer ranged freely through a succession of forests from the banks of the Avon in Wiltshire to the southern coast of Hampshire.* At length, on Cranbourne Chase, the strength of the horses failed. They were therefore turned loose. The bridles and saddles were concealed. Monmouth and his friends procured rustic attire, disguised themselves, and proceeded on foot towards the New Forest. They passed the night in the open air : but before morning they were surrounded on every side by toils. Lord Lumley, who lay at Ringwood with a strong body of the Sussex militia, had sent forth parties in every direction. Sir William Portman, with the Somerset militia, had formed a chain of posts from the sea to the northern extremity of Dorset. At five in the morning of the seventh, Grey, who had wandered from his friends, was seized by two of the Sussex scouts. He submitted to his fate with the calmness of one to whom suspense was more intolerable than despair. " Since we landed," he said, " I have not had one comfortable meal or one quiet night." It could hardly be doubted that the chief rebel was not far off. The pursuers redoubled their vigilance and activity. The cottages scattered over the heathy country on the boundaries of Dorsetshire and Hampshire were strictly examined by Lumley ; and the clown with whom Monmouth had changed clothes was discovered. Portman came with a strong body of horse and foot to assist in the search. Attention was soon drawn to a place well fitted to shelter fugitives. It was an extensive tract of land separated by an enclosure from the open country, and divided by numerous hedges into small fields. In some of these fields the rye, the pease, and the oats were high enough to conceal a man. Others were overgrown with fern and brambles. A poor woman reported that she had seen two strangers lurking in this covert. The

---

* Aubrey's Natural History of Wiltshire, 1691.

near prospect of reward animated the zeal of the troops. It was agreed that every man who did his duty in the search should have a share of the promised five thousand pounds. The outer fence was strictly guarded: the space within was examined with indefatigable diligence; and several dogs of quick scent were turned out among the bushes. The day closed before the work could be completed: but careful watch was kept all night. Thirty times the fugitives ventured to look through the outer hedge: but everywhere they found a sentinel on the alert: once they were seen and fired at; they then separated and concealed themselves in different hiding places.

His capture.

At sunrise the next morning the search recommenced, and Buyse was found. He owned that he had parted from the Duke only a few hours before. The corn and copsewood were now beaten with more care than ever. At length a gaunt figure was discovered hidden in a ditch. The pursuers sprang on their prey. Some of them were about to fire: but Portman forbade all violence. The prisoner's dress was that of a shepherd; his beard, prematurely grey, was of several days' growth. He trembled greatly, and was unable to speak. Even those who had often seen him were at first in doubt whether this were truly the brilliant and graceful Monmouth. His pockets were searched by Portman, and in them were found, among some raw pease gathered in the rage of hunger, a watch a purse of gold, a small treatise on fortification, an album filled with songs, receipts, prayers, and charms, and the George with which, many years before, King Charles the Second had decorated his favourite son. Messengers were instantly despatched to Whitehall with the good news, and with the George as a token that the news was true. The prisoner was conveyed under a strong guard to Ringwood.*

And all was lost; and nothing remained but that he should prepare to meet death as became one who had thought himself not unworthy to wear the crown of William the Conqueror and of Richard the Lionhearted, of the hero of Cressy and of the hero of Agincourt. The captive might easily have called to mind other domestic examples, still better suited to his condition. Within a hundred years, two sovereigns whose blood ran in his veins, one of them a delicate woman, had

---

* Account of the manner of taking the late Duke of Monmouth, published by His Majesty's command; Gazette de France, July $\frac{18}{28}$. 1685; Eachard, iii. 770.; Burnet, i. 664., and Dartmouth's note; Van Citters, July $\frac{10}{20}$. 1685.

been placed in the same situation in which he now stood. They had shown, in the prison and on the scaffold, virtue of which, in the season of prosperity, they had seemed incapable, and had half redeemed great crimes and errors by enduring with Christian meekness and princely dignity all that victorious enemies could inflict. Of cowardice Monmouth had never been accused; and, even had he been wanting in constitutional courage, it might have been expected that the defect would be supplied by pride and by despair. The eyes of the whole world were upon him. The latest generations would know how, in that extremity, he had borne himself. To the brave peasants of the West he owed it to show that they had not poured forth their blood for a leader unworthy of their attachment. To her who had sacrificed everything for his sake he owed it so to bear himself that, though she might weep for him, she should not blush for him. It was not for him to lament and supplicate. His reason, too, should have told him that lamentation and supplication would be unavailing. He had done that which could never be forgiven. He was in the grasp of one who never forgave.

But the fortitude of Monmouth was not that highest sort of fortitude which is derived from reflection and from selfrespect; nor had nature given him one of those stout hearts from which neither adversity nor peril can extort any sign of weakness. His courage rose and fell with his animal spirits. It was sustained on the field of battle by the excitement of action, by the hope of victory, by the strange influence of sympathy. All such aids were now taken away. The spoiled darling of the court and of the populace, accustomed to be loved and worshipped wherever he appeared, was now surrounded by stern gaolers in whose eyes he read his doom. Yet a few hours of gloomy seclusion, and he must die a violent and shameful death. His heart sank within him. Life seemed worth purchasing by any humiliation; nor could his mind, always feeble, and now distracted by terror, perceive that humiliation must degrade, but could not save him.

As soon as he reached Ringwood he wrote to the King. The letter was that of a man whom a craven fear had made insensible to shame. He professed in vehement terms his remorse for his treason. He affirmed that, when he promised his cousins at the Hague not to raise troubles in England, he had fully meant to keep his word. Unhappily he had afterwards been seduced from his allegiance by some horrid people *His letter to the King.*

who had heated his mind by calumnies and misled him by sophistry : but now he abhorred them : he abhorred himself. He begged in piteous terms that he might be admitted to the royal presence. There was a secret which he could not trust to paper, a secret which lay in a single word, and which, if he spoke that word, would secure the throne against all danger. On the following day he despatched letters, imploring the Queen Dowager and the Lord Treasurer to intercede in his behalf.*

When it was known in London how he had abased himself the general surprise was great; and no man was more amazed than Barillon, who had resided in England during two bloody proscriptions, and had seen numerous victims, both of the Opposition and of the Court, submit to their fate without womanish entreaties and lamentations.†

He is
carried to
London. Monmouth and Grey remained at Ringwood two days. They were then carried up to London, under the guard of a large body of regular troops and militia. In the coach with the Duke was an officer whose orders were to stab the prisoner if a rescue were attempted. At every town along the road the trainbands of the neighbourhood had been mustered under the command of the principal gentry. The march lasted three days, and terminated at Vauxhall, where a regiment, commanded by George Legge, Lord Dartmouth, was in readiness to receive the prisoners. They were put on board of a state barge, and carried down the river to Whitehall Stairs. Lumley and Portman had alternately watched the Duke day and night till they had brought him within the walls of the palace.‡

Both the demeanour of Monmouth and that of Grey, during the journey, filled all observers with surprise. Monmouth was altogether unnerved. Grey was not only calm but cheerful, talked pleasantly of horses, dogs, and field sports, and even made jocose allusions to the perilous situation in which he stood.

The King cannot be blamed for determining that Monmouth should suffer death. Every man who heads a rebellion against an established government stakes his life on the event; and

* The letter to the King was printed at the time by authority; that to the Queen Dowager will be found in Sir H. Ellis's Original Letters; that to Rochester in the Clarendon Correspondence.
† "On trouve," he wrote, "fort à

redire icy qu'il ayt fait une chose si peu ordinaire aux Anglois." July ⅓. 1685.
‡ Account of the manner of taking the Duke of Monmouth; Gazette, July 16. 1685; Van Citters, July ⁴⁄₂₄.

rebellion was the smallest part of Monmouth's crime. He had declared against his uncle a war without quarter. In the manifesto put forth at Lyme, James had been held up to execration as an incendiary, as an assassin who had strangled one innocent man and cut the throat of another, and, lastly, as the poisoner of his own brother. To spare an enemy who had not scrupled to resort to such extremities would have been an act of rare, perhaps of blamable generosity. But to see him and not to spare him was an outrage on humanity and decency.* This outrage the King resolved to commit. The arms of the prisoner were bound behind him with a silken cord; and, thus secured, he was ushered into the presence of the implacable kinsman whom he had wronged.

Then Monmouth threw himself on the ground, and crawled to the King's feet. He wept. He tried to embrace his uncle's knees with his pinioned arms. He begged for life, only life, life at any price. He owned that he had been guilty of a great crime, but tried to throw the blame on others, particularly on Argyle, who would rather have put his legs into the boots than have saved his own life by such baseness. By the ties of kindred, by the memory of the late King, who had been the best and truest of brothers, the unhappy man adjured James to show some mercy. James gravely replied that this repentance was of the latest, that he was sorry for the misery which the prisoner had brought on himself, but that the case was not one for lenity. A Declaration, filled with atrocious calumnies, had been put forth. The regal title had been assumed. For treasons so aggravated there could be no pardon on this side of the grave. The poor terrified Duke vowed that he had never wished to take the crown, but had been led into that fatal error by others. As to the Declaration, he had not written it: he had not read it: he had signed it without looking at it: it was all the work of Ferguson, that bloody villain Ferguson. "Do you expect me to believe," said James, with contempt but too well merited, "that you set your hand to a paper of such moment without knowing what it contained?" One depth of infamy only remained; and even to that the prisoner descended. He was preeminently the champion of the Protestant religion. The interest of that religion had been his plea for conspiring against the govern-

His interview with the King.

---

* Barillon was evidently much shocked. 'Il se vient," he says, " de passer icy. une chose bien extraordinaire et fort opposée à l'usage ordinaire des autres nations." July $\frac{13}{23}$. 1685.

ment of his father, and for bringing on his country the miseries of civil war: yet he was not ashamed to hint that he was inclined to be reconciled to the Church of Rome. The King eagerly offered him spiritual assistance, but said nothing of pardon or respite. "Is there then no hope?" asked Monmouth. James turned away in silence. Then Monmouth strove to rally his courage, rose from his knees, and retired with a firmness which he had not shown since his overthrow.*

Grey was introduced next. He behaved with a propriety and fortitude which moved even the stern and resentful King, frankly owned himself guilty, made no excuses, and did not once stoop to ask his life. Both the prisoners were sent to the Tower by water. There was no tumult; but many thousands of people, with anxiety and sorrow in their faces, tried to catch a glimpse of the captives. The Duke's resolution failed as soon as he had left the royal presence. On his way to his prison he bemoaned himself, accused his followers, and abjectly implored the intercession of Dartmouth. "I know, my Lord, that you loved my father. For his sake, for God's sake, try if there be any room for mercy." Dartmouth replied that the King had spoken the truth, and that a subject who assumed the regal title excluded himself from all hope of pardon.†

Soon after Monmouth had been lodged in the Tower, he was informed that his wife had, by the royal command, been sent to see him. She was accompanied by the Earl of Clarendon, Keeper of the Privy Seal. Her husband received her very coldly, and addressed almost all his discourse to Clarendon, whose intercession he earnestly implored. Clarendon held out no hopes; and that same evening two prelates, Turner, Bishop of Ely, and Ken, Bishop of Bath and Wells, arrived at the Tower with a solemn message from the King. It was Monday night. On Wednesday morning Monmouth was to die.

He was greatly agitated. The blood left his cheeks; and

---

* Burnet, i. 644.; Evelyn's Diary, July 15.; Sir J. Bramston's Memoirs; Reresby's Memoirs; James to the Prince of Orange, July 14. 1685; Barillon, July $\frac{16}{26}$.; Buccleuch MS.

† James to the Prince of Orange, July 14. 1685; Dutch Despatch of the same date; Dartmouth's note on Burnet, i. 646.; Narcissus Luttrell's Diary. (1848.) A copy of this Diary, from July 1685 to Sept. 1690, is among the Mackintosh papers. To the rest I was allowed access by the kindness of the Warden of All Souls' College, where the original MS. is deposited. The Delegates of the Press of the University of Oxford have since published the whole, in six substantial volumes, which will, I am afraid, find little favour with readers who seek only for amusement, but which will always be useful as materials for history. (1857.)

it was some time before he could speak. Most of the short time which remained to him he wasted in vain attempts to obtain, if not a pardon, at least a respite. He wrote piteous letters to the King and to several courtiers, but in vain. Some Roman Catholic divines were sent to him from Whitehall. But they soon discovered that, though he would gladly have purchased his life by renouncing the religion of which he had professed himself in an especial manner the defender, yet, if he was to die, he would as soon die without their absolution as with it.*

Nor were Ken and Turner much better pleased with his frame of mind. The doctrine of nonresistance was, in their view, as in the view of most of their brethren, the distinguishing badge of the Anglican Church. The two Bishops insisted on Monmouth's owning that, in drawing the sword against the government, he had committed a great sin; and, on this point, they found him obstinately heterodox. Nor was this his only heresy. He maintained that his connection with Lady Wentworth was blameless in the sight of God. He had been married, he said, when a child. He had never cared for his Duchess. The happiness which he had not found at home he had sought in a round of loose amours, condemned by religion and morality. Henrietta had reclaimed him from a life of vice. To her he had been strictly constant. They had, by common consent, offered up fervent prayers for the divine guidance. After those prayers they had found their affection for each other strengthened; and they could then no longer doubt that, in the sight of God, they were a wedded pair. The Bishops were so much scandalised by this view of the conjugal relation that they refused to administer the sacrament to the prisoner. All that they could obtain from him was a promise that, during the single night which still remained to him, he would pray to be enlightened if he were in error.

On the Wednesday morning, at his particular request, Doctor Thomas Tenison, who then held the vicarage of Saint Martin's, and, in that important cure, had obtained the high esteem of the public, came to the Tower. From Tenison, whose opinions were known to be moderate, the Duke expected more indulgence than Ken and Turner were disposed to show. But Tenison, whatever might be his sentiments

* Buccleuch MS.; Life of James the Second, ii. 37. Orig. Mem.; Van Citters. July $\frac{14}{24}$. 1685; Gazette de France August $\frac{3}{11}$.

concerning nonresistance in the abstract, thought the late
rebellion rash and wicked, and considered Monmouth's notion
respecting marriage as a most dangerous delusion.   Monmouth was obstinate.   He had prayed, he said, for the divine
direction.   His sentiments remained unchanged; and he
could not doubt that they were correct.   Tenison's exhortations were in a milder tone than those of the Bishops.   But
he, like them, thought that he should not be justified in ad-
ministering the Eucharist to one whose penitence was of so
unsatisfactory a nature.*

The hour drew near: all hope was over; and Monmouth
had passed from pusillanimous fear to the apathy of despair.
His children were brought to his room that he might take
leave of them, and were followed by his wife.   He spoke to
her kindly, but without emotion.   Though she was a woman
of great strength of mind, and had little cause to love him,
her misery was such that none of the bystanders could refrain
from weeping.   He alone was unmoved.†

His execu-
tion.

It was ten o'clock.   The coach of the Lieutenant of the
Tower was ready.   Monmouth requested his spiritual advisers to accompany him to the place of execution; and they
consented: but they told him that, in their judgment, he
was about to die in a perilous state of mind, and that, if they
attended him, it would be their duty to exhort him to the
last.   As he passed along the ranks of the guards he saluted
them with a smile; and he mounted the scaffold with a firm
tread.   Tower Hill was covered up to the chimney tops with
an innumerable multitude of gazers, who, in awful silence,
broken only by sighs and the noise of weeping, listened for
the last accents of the darling of the people.   "I shall say
little," he began.   "I come here, not to speak, but to die.
I die a Protestant of the Church of England."   The Bishops
interrupted him, and told him that, unless he acknowledged
resistance to be sinful, he was no member of their church.
He went on to speak of his Henrietta.   She was, he said, a
young lady of virtue and honour.   He loved her to the last,
and he could not die without giving utterance to his feelings.
The Bishops again interfered, and begged him not to use such
language.   Some altercation followed.   The divines have been
accused of dealing harshly with the dying man.   But they

* Buccleuch MS.; Life of James the   i. 645.; Tenison's account in Kennet, iii.
Second, ii. 37, 38. Orig. Mem.; Burnet   432. ed. 1719.   † Buccleuch MS.

appear to have only discharged what, in their view, was a sacred duty. Monmouth knew their principles, and, if he wished to avoid their importunity, should have dispensed with their attendance. Their general arguments against resistance had no effect on him. But when they reminded him of the ruin which he had brought on his brave and loving followers, of the blood which had been shed, of the souls which had been sent unprepared to the great account, he was touched, and said, in a softened voice, "I do own that. I am sorry that it ever happened." They prayed with him long and fervently; and he joined in their petitions till they invoked a blessing on the King. He remained silent. "Sir," said one of the Bishops, "do you not pray for the King with us?" Monmouth paused some time, and, after an internal struggle, exclaimed "Amen." But it was in vain that the prelates implored him to address to the soldiers and to the people a few words on the duty of obedience to the government. "I will make no speeches," he exclaimed. "Only ten words, my Lord." He turned away, called his servant, and put into the man's hand a toothpick case, the last token of ill starred love. "Give it," he said, "to that person." He then accosted John Ketch the executioner, a wretch who had butchered many brave and noble victims, and whose name has, during a century and a half, been vulgarly given to all who have succeeded him in his odious office.* "Here," said the Duke, "are six guineas for you. Do not hack me as you did my Lord Russell. I have heard that you struck him three or four times. My servant will give you some more gold if you do the work well." He then undressed, felt the edge of the axe, expressed some fear that it was not sharp enough, and laid his head on the block. The divines in the meantime continued to ejaculate with great energy: "God accept your repentance! God accept your imperfect repentance!"

The hangman addressed himself to his office. But he had been disconcerted by what the Duke had said. The first blow inflicted only a slight wound. The Duke struggled, rose

---

* The name of Ketch was often associated with that of Jeffreys in the lampoons of those days.

"While Jeffreys on the bench, Ketch on the gibbet sits,"

says one poet. In the year which followed Monmouth's execution Ketch was turned out of his office for insulting one of the Sheriffs, and was succeeded by a butcher named Rose. But in four months Rose himself was hanged at Tyburn, and Ketch was reinstated. Luttrell's Diary, January 20. and May 28. 1686. See a curious note by Dr. Grey, on Hudibras, part iii. canto ii. line 1534.

from the block, and looked reproachfully at the executioner. The head sank down once more. The stroke was repeated again and again; but still the neck was not severed, and the body continued to move. Yells of rage and horror rose from the crowd. Ketch flung down the axe with a curse. " I cannot do it," he said; " my heart fails me." " Take up the axe, man," cried the sheriff. " Fling him over the rails," roared the mob. At length the axe was taken up. Two more blows extinguished the last remains of life; but a knife was used to separate the head from the shoulders. The crowd was wrought up to such an ecstasy of rage that the executioner was in danger of being torn in pieces, and was conveyed away under a strong guard.*

In the meantime many handkerchiefs were dipped in the Duke's blood; for by a large part of the multitude he was regarded as a martyr who had died for the Protestant religion. The head and body were placed in a coffin covered with black velvet, and were laid privately under the communion table of Saint Peter's Chapel in the Tower. Within four years the pavement of the chancel was again disturbed, and hard by the remains of Monmouth were laid the remains of Jeffreys. In truth there is no sadder spot on the earth than that little cemetery. Death is there associated, not, as in Westminster Abbey and St. Paul's, with genius and virtue, with public veneration and imperishable renown; not, as in our humblest churches and churchyards, with everything that is most endearing in social and domestic charities; but with whatever is darkest in human nature and in human destiny, with the savage triumph of implacable enemies, with the inconstancy, the ingratitude, the cowardice of friends, with all the miseries of fallen greatness and of blighted fame. Thither have been carried, through successive ages, by the rude hands of gaolers, without one mourner following, the bleeding relics of men who had been the captains of armies, the leaders of parties, the oracles of senates, and the ornaments of courts. Thither was borne, before the window where Jane Grey was praying, the mangled corpse of Guilford Dudley. Edward Seymour, Duke of Somerset, and Protector of the realm, reposes there by the brother whom he murdered. There has mouldered away the

---

* Account of the execution of Monmouth, signed by the divines who attended him; Buccleuch MS.; Burnet, i. 646.; Van Citters, July $\frac{17}{27}$. 1685; Luttrell's Diary; Evelyn's Diary, July 15.; Barillon, July $\frac{19}{29}$.

headless trunk of John Fisher, Bishop of Rochester and Cardinal of Saint Vitalis, a man worthy to have lived in a better age, and to have died in a better cause. There are laid John Dudley, Duke of Northumberland, Lord High Admiral, and Thomas Cromwell, Earl of Essex, Lord High Treasurer. There, too, is another Essex, on whom nature and fortune had lavished all their bounties in vain, and whom valour, grace, genius, royal favour, popular applause, conducted to an early and ignominious doom. Not far off sleep two chiefs of the great house of Howard, Thomas, fourth Duke of Norfolk, and Philip, eleventh Earl of Arundel. Here and there, among the thick graves of unquiet and aspiring statesmen, lie more delicate sufferers; Margaret of Salisbury, the last of the proud name of Plantagenet, and those two fair Queens who perished by the jealous rage of Henry. Such was the dust with which the dust of Monmouth mingled.*

Yet a few months, and the quiet village of Toddington, in Bedfordshire, witnessed a still sadder funeral. Near that village stood an ancient and stately hall, the seat of the Wentworths. The transept of the parish church had long been their burial place. To that burial place, in the spring which followed the death of Monmouth, was borne the coffin of the young Baroness Wentworth of Nettlestede. Her family reared a sumptuous mausoleum over her remains: but a less costly memorial of her was long contemplated with far deeper interest. Her name, carved by the hand of him whom she loved too well, was, a few years ago, still discernible on a tree in the adjoining park.

It was not by Lady Wentworth alone that the memory of Monmouth was cherished with idolatrous fondness. His hold on the hearts of the people lasted till the generation which had seen him had passed away. Ribands, buckles, and other trifling articles of apparel which he had worn, were treasured up as precious relics by those who had fought under him at Sedgemoor. Old men who long survived him desired, when they were dying, that these trinkets might be buried with them. One button of gold thread which narrowly escaped this fate may still be seen at a house which overlooks the field of battle. Nay, such was the devotion of the people to

His memory cherished by the common people.

* I cannot refrain from expressing my disgust at the barbarous stupidity which has transformed this most inter-esting little church into the likeness of a meetinghouse in a manufacturing town.

their unhappy favourite that, in the face of the strongest evidence by which the fact of a death was ever verified, many continued to cherish a hope that he was still living, and that he would again appear in arms. A person, it was said, who was remarkably like Monmouth, had sacrificed himself to save the Protestant hero. The vulgar long continued, at every important crisis, to whisper that the time was at hand, and that King Monmouth would soon show himself. In 1686, a knave who had pretended to be the Duke, and had levied contributions in several villages of Wiltshire, was apprehended, and whipped from Newgate to Tyburn. In 1698. when England had long enjoyed constitutional freedom under a new dynasty, the son of an innkeeper passed himself on the yeomanry of Sussex as their beloved Monmouth, and defrauded many who were by no means of the lowest class. Five hundred pounds were collected for him. The farmers provided him with a horse. Their wives sent him baskets of chickens and ducks, and were lavish, it was said, of favours of a more tender kind; for, in gallantry at least, the counterfeit was a not unworthy representative of the original. When this impostor was thrown into prison for his fraud, his followers maintained him in luxury. Several of them appeared at the bar to countenance him when he was tried at the Horsham assizes. So long did this delusion last that, when George the Third had been some years on the English throne, Voltaire thought it necessary gravely to confute the hypothesis that the man in the iron mask was the Duke of Monmouth.*

It is, perhaps, a fact scarcely less remarkable that, to this day, the inhabitants of some parts of the West of England, when any bill affecting their interest is before the House of Lords, think themselves entitled to claim the help of the Duke of Buccleuch, the descendant of the unfortunate leader for whom their ancestors bled.

The history of Monmouth would alone suffice to refute the imputation of inconstancy which is so frequently thrown on

---

* Observator, August 1. 1685; Gazette de France, Nov. 2. 1686; Letter from Humphrey Wanley, dated Aug. 25. 1698, in the Aubrey Collection; Voltaire, Dict. Phil. There are, in the Pepysian Collection, several ballads written after Monmouth's death which represent him as living, and predict his speedy return. I will give two specimens:

"Though this is a dismal story
    Of the fall of my design,

Yet I'll come again in glory,
    If I live till eighty-nine.

"For I'll have a stronger army,
    And of ammunition store."

Again ;

"Then shall Monmouth in his glories
    Unto his English friends appear,
And will stifle all such stories
    As are vended everywhere.

"They'll see I was not so degraded.
    To be taken gathering pease,
Or in a cock of hay up braided.
    What strange stories now are these ! "

the common people. The common people are some times
inconstant; for they are human beings. But that they are
inconstant as compared with the educated classes, with aristocracies, or with princes, may be confidently denied. It would
be easy to name demagogues whose popularity has remained
undiminished while sovereigns and parliaments have withdrawn their confidence from a long succession of statesmen.
When Swift had survived his faculties many years, the Irish
populace still continued to light bonfires on his birthday, in
commemoration of the services which they fancied that he
had rendered to his country when his mind was in full vigour.
While seven administrations were raised to power and hurled
from it in consequence of court intrigues or of changes in the
sentiments of the higher classes of society, the profligate
Wilkes retained his hold on the affections of a rabble whom
he pillaged and ridiculed. Politicians, who, in 1807, had
sought to curry favour with George the Third by defending
Caroline of Brunswick, were not ashamed, in 1820, to curry
favour with George the Fourth by persecuting her. But in
1820, as in 1807, the whole body of working men was fanati-
cally devoted to her cause. So it was with Monmouth. In
1680, he had been adored alike by the gentry and by the
peasantry of the West. In 1685 he came again. To the
gentry he had become an object of aversion: but by the
peasantry he was still loved with a love strong as death, with
a love not to be extinguished by misfortunes or faults, by the
flight from Sedgemoor, by the letter from Ringwood, or by
the tears and abject supplications at Whitehall. The charge
which may with justice be brought against the common people
is, not that they are inconstant, but that they almost invariably choose their favourite so ill that their constancy is a vice
and not a virtue.

While the execution of Monmouth occupied the thoughts
of the Londoners, the counties which had risen against the
government were enduring all that a ferocious soldiery could
inflict. Feversham had been summoned to the court, where
honours and rewards which he little deserved awaited him.
He was made a Knight of the Garter and Captain of the first
and most lucrative troop of Life Guards: but Court and City
laughed at his military exploits; and the wit of Buckingham
gave forth its last feeble flash at the expense of the general
who had won a battle in bed.* Feversham left in command

Cruelties
of the
soldiers in
the West.

* London Gazette, August 3. 1685; the Battle of Sedgemore, a Farce.

at Bridgewater Colonel Percy Kirke, a military adventurer whose vices had been developed by the worst of all schools, Tangier. Kirke had during some years commanded the garrison of that town, and had been constantly employed in hostilities against tribes of foreign barbarians, ignorant of the laws which regulate the warfare of civilised and Christian nations. Within the ramparts of his fortress he was a despotic prince. The only check on his tyranny was the fear of being called to account by a distant and a careless government. He might therefore safely proceed to the most audacious excesses of rapacity, licentiousness, and cruelty. He lived with boundless dissoluteness, and procured by extortion the means of indulgence. No goods could be sold till Kirke had had the refusal of them. No question of right could be decided till Kirke had been bribed. Once, merely from a malignant whim, he staved all the wine in a vintner's cellar. On another occasion he drove all the Jews from Tangier. Two of them he sent to the Spanish Inquisition, which forthwith burned them. Under this iron domination scarce a complaint was heard ; for hatred was effectually kept down by terror. Two persons who had been refractory were found murdered ; and it was universally believed that they had been slain by Kirke's order. When his soldiers displeased him he flogged them with merciless severity : but he indemnified them by permitting them to sleep on watch, to reel drunk about the streets, to rob, beat, and insult the merchants and the labourers.

When Tangier was abandoned, Kirke returned to England. He still continued to command his old soldiers, who were designated sometimes as the First Tangier Regiment, and sometimes as Queen Catharine's Regiment. As they had been levied for the purpose of waging war on an infidel nation, they bore on their flag a Christian emblem, the Paschal Lamb. In allusion to this device, and with a bitterly ironical meaning, these men, the rudest and most ferocious in the English army, were called Kirke's Lambs. The regiment, now the second of the line, still retains this ancient badge, which is however thrown into the shade by decorations honourably earned in Egypt, in Spain, and in the heart of Asia.*

Such was the captain and such the soldiers who were now let loose on the people of Somersetshire. From Bridgewater

* Pepys's Diary, kept at Tangier ; Historical Records of the Second or Queen's Royal Regiment of Foot.

Kirke marched to Taunton. He was accompanied by two carts filled with wounded rebels whose gashes had not been dressed, and by a long drove of prisoners on foot, who were chained two and two. Several of these he hanged as soon as he reached Taunton, without the form of a trial. They were not suffered even to take leave of their nearest relations. The signpost of the White Hart Inn served for a gallows. It is said that the work of death went on in sight of the windows where the officers of the Tangier regiment were carousing, and that at every health a wretch was turned off. When the legs of the dying man quivered in the last agony, the colonel ordered the drums to strike up. He would give the rebels, he said, music to their dancing. The tradition runs that one of the captives was not even allowed the indulgence of a speedy death. Twice he was suspended from the signpost, and twice cut down. Twice he was asked if he repented of his treason; and twice he replied that, if the thing were to do again, he would do it. Then he was tied up for the last time. So many dead bodies were quartered that the executioner stood ankle deep in blood. He was assisted by a poor man whose loyalty was suspected, and who was compelled to ransom his own life by seething the remains of his friends in pitch. The peasant who had consented to perform this hideous office afterwards returned to his plough. But a mark like that of Cain was upon him. He was known through his village by the horrible name of Tom Boilman. The rustics long continued to relate that, though he had, by his sinful and shameful deed, saved himself from the vengeance of the Lambs, he had not escaped the vengeance of a higher power. In a great storm he fled for shelter under an oak, and was there struck dead by lightning.*

The number of those who were thus butchered cannot now be ascertained. Nine were entered in the parish registers of Taunton : but those registers contained the names of such only as had Christian burial. Those who were hanged in chains, and those whose heads and limbs were sent to the neighbouring villages, must have been much more numerous. It was believed in London, at the time, that Kirke put a hundred captives to death during the week which followed the battle.†

* Bloody Assizes; Burnet, i. 647.; Luttrell's Diary, July 15. 1685; Locke's Western Rebellion; Toulmin's History of Taunton, edited by Savage.

† Luttrell's Diary, July 15. 1685; Toulmin's Hist. of Taunton.

Cruelty, however, was not this man's only passion. He loved money; and was no novice in the arts of extortion. A safe conduct might be bought of him for thirty or forty pounds; and such a safe conduct, though of no value in law, enabled the purchaser to pass the post of the Lambs without molestation, to reach a seaport, and to fly to a foreign country. The ships which were bound for New England were crowded at this juncture with so many fugitives from Sedgemoor that there was great danger lest the water and provisions should fail.†

Kirke was also, in his own coarse and ferocious way, a man of pleasure; and nothing is more probable than that he employed his power for the purpose of gratifying his licentious appetites. It was reported that he conquered the virtue of a beautiful woman by promising to spare the life of one to whom she was strongly attached, and that, after she had yielded, he showed her suspended on the gallows the lifeless remains of him for whose sake she had sacrificed her honour. This tale an impartial judge must reject. It is unsupported by proof. The earliest authority for it is a poem written by Pomfret. The respectable historians of that age, while they speak with just severity of the crimes of Kirke, either omit all mention of this most atrocious crime, or mention it as a thing rumoured but not proved. Those who tell the story tell it with such variations as deprive it of all title to credit. Some lay the scene at Taunton, some at Exeter. Some make the heroine of the tale a maiden, some a married woman. The relation for whom the shameful ransom was paid is described by some as her father, by some as her brother, and by some as her husband. Lastly the story is one which, long before Kirke was born, had been told of many other oppressors, and had become a favourite theme of novelists and dramatists. Two politicans of the fifteenth century, Rhynsault, the favourite of Charles the Bold of Burgundy, and Oliver le Dain, the favourite of Lewis the Eleventh of France, had been accused of the same crime. Cintio had taken it for the subject of a romance. Whetstone had made out of Cintio's narrative the rude play of Promos and Cassandra; and Shakspeare had borrowed from Whetstone the plot of the noble tragicomedy of Measure for Measure. As Kirke was not the first, so he was not the last,

† Oldmixon, 705.; Life and Errors of John Dunton, chap. vii.

to whom this excess of wickedness was popularly imputed. During the reaction which followed the Jacobin tyranny in France, a very similar charge was brought against Joseph Lebon, one of the most odious agents of the Committee of Public Safety, and, after enquiry, was admitted even by his prosecutors to be unfounded.*

The government was dissatisfied with Kirke, not on account of the barbarity with which he had treated his needy prisoners, but on account of the interested lenity which he had shown to rich delinquents.† He was soon recalled from the West. A less irregular and more cruel massacre was about to be perpetrated. The vengeance was deferred during some weeks. It was thought desirable that the Western Circuit should not begin till the other circuits had terminated. In the meantime the gaols of Somersetshire and Dorsetshire were filled with thousands of captives. The chief friend and protector of these unhappy men in their extremity was one who abhorred their religious and political opinions, one whose order they hated, and to whom they had done unprovoked wrong, Bishop Ken. That good prelate used all his influence to soften the gaolers, and retrenched from his own episcopal state that he might be able to make some addition to the coarse and scanty fare of those who had defaced his beloved Cathedral. His conduct on this occasion was of a piece with his whole life. His intellect was indeed darkened by many superstitions and prejudices : but his moral character, when impartially reviewed, sustains a comparison with any in ecclesiastical history, and seems to approach, as near as human infirmity permits, to the ideal perfection of Christian virtue.‡

---

* The silence of Whig writers so credulous and so malevolent as Oldmixon and the compilers of the Western Martyrology would alone seem to me to settle the question. It also deserves to be remarked that the story of Rhynsault is told by Steele in the Spectator, No. 491. Surely it is hardly possible to believe that, if a crime exactly resembling that of Rhynsault had been committed within living memory in England by an officer of James the Second, Steele, who was indiscreetly and unseasonably forward to display his Whiggism, would have made no allusion to that fact. For the case of Lebon, see the Moniteur, 4 Messidor, l'an 3.

† Sunderland to Kirke, July 14. and 28 1685. "His Majesty," says Sun-

derland, "commands me to signify to you his dislike of these proceedings, and desires you to take care that no person concerned in the rebellion be at large." It is but just to add that, in the same letter, Kirke is blamed for allowing his soldiers to live at free quarter.

‡ I should be very glad if I could give credit to the popular story that Ken, immediately after the battle of Sedgemoor, represented to the chiefs of the royal army the illegality of military executions. He would, I doubt not, have exerted all his influence on the side of law and of mercy, if he had been present. But there is no trustworthy evidence that he was then in the West at all. Indeed what we know about his proceedings at this time amounts very

Jeffreys
sets out
on the
Western
Circuit.
His labour of love was of no long duration. A rapid and
effectual gaol delivery was at hand. Early in September,
Jeffreys, accompanied by four other judges, set out on that
circuit of which the memory will last as long as our race and
language. The officers who commanded the troops in the districts through which his course lay had orders to furnish him
with whatever military aid he might require. His ferocious
temper needed no spur; yet a spur was applied. The health
and spirits of the Lord Keeper had given way. He had been
deeply mortified by the coldness of the King and by the insolence of the Chief Justice, and could find little consolation
in looking back on a life, not indeed blackened by any atrocious crime, but sullied by cowardice, selfishness, and servility.
So deeply was the unhappy man humbled that, when he appeared for the last time in Westminster Hall, he took with
him a nosegay to hide his face, because, as he afterwards
owned, he could not bear the eyes of the bar and of the
audience. The prospect of his approaching end seems to
have inspired him with unwonted courage. He determined to
discharge his conscience, requested an audience of the King,
spoke earnestly of the dangers inseparable from violent and
arbitrary counsels, and condemned the lawless cruelties which
the soldiers had committed in Somersetshire. He soon after
retired from London to die. He breathed his last a few days
after the Judges set out for the West. It was immediately
notified to Jeffreys that he might expect the Great Seal as the
reward of faithful and vigorous service.*

Trial of
Alice
Lisle.
At Winchester the Chief Justice first opened his commission. Hampshire had not been the theatre of war; but many
of the vanquished rebels had, like their leader, fled thither.
Two of them, John Hicks, a Nonconformist divine, and Richard
Nelthorpe, a lawyer who had been outlawed for taking part in
the Rye House plot, had sought refuge at the house of Alice,
widow of John Lisle. John Lisle had sate in the Long Parliament and in the High Court of Justice, had been a Commissioner of the Great Seal in the days of the Commonwealth,
and had been created a Lord by Cromwell. The titles given
by the Protector had not been recognised by any government

---

nearly to proof of an *alibi*. It is certain
from the Journals of the House of Lords
that, on the Thursday before the battle,
he was at Westminster; it is equally
certain that, on the Monday after the
battle, he was with Monmouth in the
Tower; and, in that age, a journey from
London to Bridgewater and back again
was no light thing.

* North's Life of Guildford, 260. 263.
273.; Mackintosh's View of the Reign
of James the Second, page 16. note;
Letter of Jeffreys to Sunderland, Sept.
5. 1685.

Judge Jeffreys

which had ruled England since the downfall of his house; but they appear to have been often used in conversation even by Royalists. John Lisle's widow was therefore commonly known as the Lady Alice. She was related to many respectable, and to some noble, families; and she was generally esteemed even by the Tory gentlemen of her country. For it was well known to them that she had deeply regretted some violent acts in which her husband had borne a part, that she had shèd bitter tears for Charles the First, and that she had protected and relieved many Cavaliers in their distress. The same womanly kindness, which had led her to befriend the Royalists in their time of trouble, would not suffer her to refuse a meal and a hiding place to the wretched men who now entreated her to protect them. She took them into her house, set meat and drink before them, and showed them where they might take rest. The next morning her dwelling was surrounded by soldiers. Strict search was made. Hickes was found concealed in the malthouse, and Nelthorpe in the chimney. If Lady Alice knew her guests to have been concerned in the insurrection, she was undoubtedly guilty of what in strictness was a capital crime. For the law of principal and accessory, as respects high treason, then was, and is to this day, in a state disgraceful to English jurisprudence. In cases of felony, a distinction, founded on justice and reason, is made between the principal and the accessory after the fact. He who conceals from justice one whom he knows to be a murderer is liable to punishment, but not to the punishment of murder. He, on the other hand, who shelters one whom he knows to be a traitor is, according to all our jurists, guilty of high treason. It is unnecessary to point out the absurdity and cruelty of a law which includes under the same definition, and visits with the same penalty, offences lying at the opposite extremes of the scale of guilt. The feeling which makes the most loyal subject shrink from the thought of giving up to a shameful death the rebel who, vanquished, hunted down, and in mortal agony, begs for a morsel of bread and a cup of water, may be a weakness; but it is surely a weakness very nearly allied to virtue, a weakness which, constituted as human beings are, we can hardly eradicate from the mind without eradicating many noble and benevolent sentiments. A wise and good ruler may not think it right to sanction this weakness; but he will generally connive at it, or punish it very tenderly. In no case will he treat it as a crime of the blackest

dye.   Whether Flora Macdonald was justified in concealing
the attainted heir of the Stuarts, whether a brave soldier of
our own time was justified in assisting the escape of Lavalette,
are questions on which casuists may differ : but to class such
actions with the crimes of Guy Faux and Fieschi is an outrage
to humanity and common sense. Such, however, is the classification of our law.   It is evident that nothing but a lenient
administration could make such a state of the law endurable.
And it is just to say that, during many generations, no English
government, save one, has treated with rigour persons guilty
merely of harbouring defeated and flying insurgents.   To
women especially has been granted, by a kind of tacit prescription, the right of indulging, in the midst of havoc and
vengeance, that compassion which is the most endearing of
all their charms.   Since the beginning of the great civil war,
numerous rebels, some of them far more important than
Hickes or Nelthorpe, have been protected from the severity
of victorious governments by female adroitness and generosity.
But no English ruler who has been thus baffled, the savage
and implacable James alone excepted, has had the barbarity
even to think of putting a lady to a cruel and shameful death
for so venial and amiable a transgression.

    Odious as the law was, it was strained for the purpose of
destroying Alice Lisle. She could not, according to the doctrine laid down by the highest authority, be convicted till after
the conviction of the rebels whom she had harboured.*   She
was, however, set to the bar before either Hickes or Nelthorpe
had been tried.   It was no easy matter in such a case to
obtain a verdict for the crown.   The witnesses prevaricated.
The jury, consisting of the principal gentlemen of Hampshire,
shrank from the thought of sending a fellow creature to the
stake for conduct which seemed deserving rather of praise
than of blame.   Jeffreys was beside himself with fury.   This
was the first case of treason on the circuit ; and there seemed
to be a strong probability that his prey would escape him.
He stormed, cursed, and swore in language which no wellbred
man would have used at a race or a cockfight.   One witness
named Dunne, partly from concern for Lady Alice, and partly
from fright at the threats and maledictions of the Chief Justice,
entirely lost his head, and at last stood silent.   " Oh how hard
the truth is," said Jeffreys, " to come out of a lying Presby-

* See the preamble of the Act of Parliament reversing her attainder.

terian knave." The witness, after a pause of some minutes, stammered a few unmeaning words. "Was there ever," exclaimed the judge, with an oath, "was there ever such a villain on the face of the earth? Dost thou believe that there is a God? Dost thou believe in hell fire? Of all the witnesses that I ever met with I never saw thy fellow." Still the poor man, scared out of his senses, remained mute; and again Jeffreys burst forth. "I hope, gentlemen of the jury, that you take notice of the horrible carriage of this fellow. How can one help abhorring both these men and their religion? A Turk is a saint to such a fellow as this. A Pagan would be ashamed of such villany. Oh blessed Jesus! What a generation of vipers do we live among!" "I cannot tell what to say, my Lord," faltered Dunne. The judge again broke forth into a volley of oaths. "Was there ever," he cried, "such an impudent rascal? Hold the candle to him that we may see his brazen face. You, gentlemen, that are of counsel for the crown, see that an information for perjury be preferred against this fellow." After the witnesses had been thus handled, the Lady Alice was called on for her defence. She began by saying, what may possibly have been true, that though she knew Hickes to be in trouble when she took him in, she did not know or suspect that he had been concerned in the rebellion. He was a divine, a man of peace. It had, therefore, never occurred to her that he could have borne arms against the government; and she had supposed that he wished to conceal himself because warrants were out against him for field preaching. The Chief Justice began to storm. "But I will tell you. There is not one of those lying, snivelling, canting Presbyterians but, one way or another, had a hand in the rebellion. Presbytery has all manner of villany in it. Nothing but Presbytery could have made Dunne such a rogue. Show me a Presbyterian; and I'll show thee a lying knave." He summed up in the same style, declaimed during an hour against Whigs and Dissenters, and reminded the jury that the prisoner's husband had borne a part in the death of Charles the First, a fact which had not been proved by any testimony, and which, if it had been proved, would have been utterly irrelevant to the issue. The jury retired, and remained long in consultation. The judge grew impatient. He could not conceive, he said, how, in so plain a case, they should even have left the box. He sent a messenger to tell them that, if they did not instantly

return, he would adjourn the court and lock them up all
night.   Thus put to the torture, they came, but came to say
that they doubted whether the charge had been made out.
Jeffreys expostulated with them vehemently, and, after another
consultation, they gave a reluctant verdict of Guilty.

On the following morning sentence was pronounced.   Jeffreys gave directions that Alice Lisle should be burned alive
that very afternoon.   This excess of barbarity moved the pity
and indignation even of the class which was most devoted to
the crown.   The clergy of Winchester Cathedral remonstrated
with the Chief Justice, who, brutal as he was, was not mad
enough to risk a quarrel on such a subject with a body so
much respected by the Tory party.   He consented to put off
the execution five days.   During that time the friends of the
prisoner besought James to be merciful.   Ladies of high rank
interceded for her.   Feversham, whose recent victory had increased his influence at court, and who, it is said, had been
bribed to take the compassionate side, spoke in her favour.
Clarendon, the King's brother in law, pleaded her cause.   But
all was vain.   The utmost that could be obtained was that
her sentence should be commuted from burning to beheading.
She was put to death on a scaffold in the marketplace of
Winchester, and underwent her fate with serene courage.*

The
Bloody
Assizes

In Hampshire Alice Lisle was the only victim : but, on the
day following her execution, Jeffreys reached Dorchester, the
principal town of the county in which Monmouth had landed ;
and the judicial massacre began.   The court was hung, by
order of the Chief Justice, with scarlet ; and this innovation
seemed to the multitude to indicate a bloody purpose.   It was
also rumoured that, when the clergyman who preached the
assize sermon enforced the duty of mercy, the ferocious mouth
of the Judge was distorted by an ominous grin.   These things
made men augur ill of what was to follow.†

More than three hundred prisoners were to be tried.   The
work seemed heavy ; but Jeffreys had a contrivance for making
it light.   He let it be understood that the only chance of obtaining pardon or respite was to plead guilty.   Twenty-nine
persons, who put themselves on their country and were convicted, were ordered to be tied up without delay.   The remaining prisoners pleaded guilty by scores.   Two hundred and

* Trial of Alice Lisle in the Collection of State Trials ; Act of the First of
William and Mary for annulling and
making void the Attainder of Alice

Lisle, widow ; Burnet, i. 649. ; Caveat
against the Whigs.
    † Bloody Assizes.

ninety-two received sentence of death. The whole number hanged in Dorsetshire amounted to seventy-four.

From Dorchester Jeffreys proceeded to Exeter. The civil war had barely grazed the frontier of Devonshire. Here, therefore, comparatively few persons were capitally punished. Somersetshire, the chief seat of the rebellion, had been reserved for the last and most fearful vengeance. In this county two hundred and thirty-three prisoners were in a few days hanged, drawn, and quartered. At every spot where two roads met, on every marketplace, on the green of every large village which had furnished Monmouth with soldiers, ironed corpses clattering in the wind, or heads and quarters stuck on poles, poisoned the air, and made the traveller sick with horror. In many parishes the peasantry could not assemble in the house of God without seeing the ghastly face of a neighbour grinning at them over the porch. The Chief Justice was all himself. His spirits rose higher and higher as the work went on. He laughed, shouted, joked, and swore in such a way that many thought him drunk from morning to night. But in him it was not easy to distinguish the madness produced by evil passions from the madness produced by brandy. A prisoner affirmed that the witnesses who appeared against him were not entitled to credit. One of them, he said, was a Papist, and another a prostitute. "Thou impudent rebel," exclaimed the Judge, " to reflect on the King's evidence ! I see thee, villain, I see thee already with the halter round thy neck." Another produced testimony that he was a good Protestant. "Protestant ! " said Jeffreys ; " you mean Presbyterian. I'll hold you a wager of it. I can smell a Presbyterian forty miles." One wretched man moved the pity even of bitter Tories. "My Lord," they said, " this poor creature is on the parish." " Do not trouble yourselves," said the Judge, " I will ease the parish of the burden." It was not only against the prisoners that his fury broke forth. Gentlemen and noblemen of high consideration and stainless loyalty, who ventured to bring to his notice any extenuating circumstance, were almost sure to receive what he called, in the coarse dialect which he had learned in the pothouses of Whitechapel, a lick with the rough side of his tongue. Lord Stawell, a Tory peer, who could not conceal his horror at the remorseless manner in which his poor neighbours were butchered, was punished by having a corpse suspended in

chains at his park gate.* In such spectacles originated
many tales of terror, which were long told over the cider by
the Christmas fires of the farmers of Somersetshire. Within
the last forty years, peasants, in some districts, well knew the
accursed spots, and passed them unwillingly after sunset.†

Jeffreys boasted that he had hanged more traitors than all
his predecessors together since the Conquest. It is certain
that the number of persons whom he put to death in one month,
and in one shire, very much exceeded the number of all the
political offenders who have been put to death in our island
since the Revolution. The rebellions of 1715 and 1745 were
of longer duration, of wider extent, and of more formidable
aspect than that which was put down at Sedgemoor. It has
not been generally thought that, either after the rebellion of
1715, or after the rebellion of 1745, the House of Hanover
erred on the side of clemency. Yet all the executions of
1715 and 1745 added together will appear to have been few
indeed when compared with those which disgraced the Bloody
Assizes. The number of the rebels whom Jeffreys hanged on
this circuit was three hundred and twenty. ‡

Such havoc must have excited disgust even if the sufferers
had been generally odious. But they were, for the most part,
men of blameless life, and of high religious profession. They
were regarded by themselves, and by a large proportion of
their neighbours, not as wrongdoers, but as martyrs who
sealed with blood the truth of the Protestant religion. Very
few of the convicts professed any repentance for what they
had done. Many, animated by the old Puritan spirit, met
death, not merely with fortitude, but with exultation. It
was in vain that the ministers of the Established Church
lectured them on the guilt of rebellion and on the importance
of priestly absolution. The claim of the King to unbounded
authority in things temporal, and the claim of the clergy to
the spiritual power of binding and loosing, moved the bitter
scorn of the intrepid sectaries. Some of them composed
hymns in the dungeon, and chaunted them on the fatal sledge.
Christ, they sang while they were undressing for the butchery,
would soon come to rescue Zion and to make war on Babylon,

---

* Locke's Western Rebellion.

† This I can attest from my own
childish recollections.

‡ Lord Lonsdale says seven hundred;
Burnet six hundred. I have followed
the list which the Judges sent to the

Treasury, and which may still be seen
there in the letter book of 1685. See
the Bloody Assizes; Locke's Western
Rebellion; the Panegyric on Lord Jeffreys; Burnet, i. 648.; Eachard, iii.
775.; Oldmixon, 705.

would set up his standard, would blow his trumpet, and would requite his foes tenfold for all the evil which had been inflicted on his servants. The dying words of these men were noted down: their farewell letters were kept as treasures; and, in this way, with the help of some invention and exaggeration, was formed a copious supplement to the Marian martyrology.*

A few cases deserve special mention. Abraham Holmes, a retired officer of the parliamentary army, and one of those zealots who would own no king but King Jesus, had been taken at Sedgemoor. His arm had been frightfully mangled and shattered in the battle; and, as no surgeon was at hand, the stout old soldier amputated it himself. He was carried up to London, and examined by the King in Council, but would make no submission. "I am an aged man," he said; "and what remains to me of life is not worth a falsehood or a baseness. I have always been a republican; and I am so still." He was sent back to the West and hanged. The people remarked with awe and wonder that the beasts which were to drag him to the gallows became restive and went back. Holmes himself doubted not that the Angel of the Lord, as in the old time, stood in the way sword in hand, invisible to human eyes, but visible to the inferior animals. "Stop, gentlemen," he cried: "let me go on foot. There is more in this than you think. Remember how the ass saw him whom the prophet could not see." He walked manfully to the gallows, harangued the people with a smile, prayed fervently that God would hasten the downfall of Antichrist and the deliverance of England, and went up the ladder with an apology for mounting so awkwardly. "You see," he said, "I have but one arm."†

Not less courageously died Christopher Battiscombe, a young Templar of good family and fortune, who, at Dorchester, an agreeable provincial town proud of its taste and refinement, was regarded by all as the model of a fine gentleman. Great interest was made to save him. It was believed through the West of England that he was engaged to a young lady of gentle blood, the sister of the Sheriff, that she threw herself at the feet of Jeffreys to beg for mercy, and that Jeffreys drove her from him with a jest so hideous that to repeat it

Marginal notes: Abraham Holmes. / Christopher Battiscombe.

---

* Some of the prayers, exhortations, and hymns of the sufferers will be found in the Bloody Assizes.

† Bloody Assizes; Locke's Western Rebellion; Lord Lonsdale's Memoirs;

Account of the Battle of Sedgemoor in the Hardwicke Papers. The story in the Life of James the Second, ii. 43., is not taken from the King's manuscripts, and sufficiently refutes itself.

would be an offence against decency and humanity. Her lover suffered at Lyme piously and courageously.*

The Hew-
lings. A still deeper interest was excited by the fate of two gallant brothers, William and Benjamin Hewling. They were young, handsome, accomplished, and well connected. Their maternal grandfather was named Kiffin. He was one of the first merchants in London, and was generally considered as the head of the Baptists. The Chief Justice behaved to William Hewling on the trial with characteristic brutality. "You have a grandfather," he said, "who deserves to be hanged as richly as you." The poor lad, who was only nineteen, suffered death with so much meekness and fortitude, that an officer of the army who attended the execution, and who had made himself remarkable by rudeness and severity, was strangely melted, and said, " I do not believe that my Lord Chief Justice himself could be proof against this." Hopes were entertained that Benjamin would be pardoned. One victim of tender years was surely enough for one house to furnish. Even Jeffreys was, or pretended to be, inclined to lenity. The truth was that one of his kinsmen, from whom he had large expectations, and whom, therefore, he could not treat as he generally treated intercessors, pleaded strongly for the afflicted family. Time was allowed for a reference to London. The sister of the prisoner went to Whitehall with a petition. Many courtiers wished her success ; and Churchill, among whose numerous faults cruelty had no place, obtained admittance for her. "I wish well to your suit with all my heart," he said, as they stood together in the antechamber ; " but do not flatter yourself with hopes. This marble,"—and he laid his hand on the chimneypiece,—" is not harder than the King." The prediction proved true. James was inexorable. Benjamin Hewling died with dauntless courage, amidst lamentations in which the soldiers who kept guard round the gallows could not refrain from joining.†

Yet those rebels who were doomed to death were less to be pitied than some of the survivors. Several prisoners to whom Jeffreys was unable to bring home the charge of high treason

---

* Bloody Assizes ; Locke's Western Rebellion ; Humble Petition of Widows and Fatherless Children in the West of England ; Panegyric on Lord Jeffreys.

† As to the Hewlings, I have followed Kiffin's Memoirs, and Mr. Hewling Luson's narrative, which will be found in the second edition of the Hughes Correspondence, vol. ii. Appendix. The accounts in Locke's Western Rebellion and in the Panegyric on Jeffreys are full of errors. Great part of the account in the Bloody Assizes was written by Kiffin, and agrees word for word with his Memoirs.

were convicted of misdemeanours, and were sentenced to scourging not less terrible than that which Oates had undergone. A woman for some idle words, such as had been uttered by half the women in the districts where the war had raged, was condemned to be whipped through all the market towns in the county of Dorset. She suffered part of her punishment before Jeffreys returned to London; but, when he was no longer in the West, the gaolers, with the humane connivance of the magistrates, took on themselves the responsibility of sparing her any further torture. A still more frightful sentence was passed on a lad named Tutchin, who was tried for seditious words. He was, as usual, interrupted in his defence by ribaldry and scurrility from the judgment seat. "You are a rebel; and all your family have been rebels since Adam. They tell me that you are a poet. I'll cap verses with you." The sentence was that the boy should be imprisoned seven years, and should, during that period, be flogged through every market town in Dorsetshire every year. The women in the galleries burst into tears. The clerk of the arraigns stood up in great disorder. "My Lord," said he, "the prisoner is very young. There are many market towns in our county. The sentence amounts to whipping once a fortnight for seven years." "If he is a young man," said Jeffreys, "he is an old rogue. Ladies, you do not know the villain as well as I do. The punishment is not half bad enough for him. All the interest in England shall not alter it." Tutchin in his despair petitioned, and probably with sincerity, that he might be hanged. Fortunately for him he was, just at this conjuncture, taken ill of the smallpox and given over. As it seemed highly improbable that the sentence would ever be executed, the Chief Justice consented to remit it, in return for a bribe which reduced the prisoner to poverty. The temper of Tutchin, not originally very mild, was exasperated to madness by what he had undergone. He lived to be known as one of the most acrimonious and pertinacious enemies of the House of Stuart and of the Tory party.[*]

The number of prisoners whom Jeffreys transported was eight hundred and forty-one. These men, more wretched than their associates who suffered death, were distributed into gangs, and bestowed on persons who enjoyed favour at court. The conditions of the gift were that the convicts should be

Punishment of Tutchin.

Rebels transported.

[*] See Tutchin's account of his own case in the Bloody Assizes.

carried beyond sea as slaves, that they should not be emancipated for ten years, and that the place of their banishment
should be some West Indian island. This last article was
studiously framed for the purpose of aggravating the misery
of the exiles. In New England or New Jersey they would
have found a population kindly disposed to them and a climate
not unfavourable to their health and vigour. It was therefore
determined that they should be sent to colonies where a
Puritan could hope to inspire little sympathy, and where a
labourer born in the temperate zone could hope to enjoy little
health. Such was the state of the slave market that these
bondmen, long as was the passage, and sickly as they were
likely to prove, were still very valuable. It was estimated by
Jeffreys that, on an average, each of them, after all charges
were paid, would be worth from ten to fifteen pounds. There
was therefore much angry competition for grants. Some
Tories in the West conceived that they had, by their exertions
and sufferings during the insurrection, earned a right to
share in the profits which had been eagerly snatched up by
the sycophants of Whitehall. The courtiers, however, were
victorious. *

The misery of the exiles fully equalled that of the negroes
who are now carried from Congo to Brazil. It appears from
the best information which is at present accessible that more
than one fifth of those who were shipped were flung to the
sharks before the end of the voyage. The human cargoes
were stowed close in the holds of small vessels. So little
space was allowed that the wretches, many of whom were still
tormented by unhealed wounds, could not all lie down at once
without lying on one another. They were never suffered to
go on deck. The hatchway was constantly watched by sentinels armed with hangers and blunderbusses. In the dungeon
below all was darkness, stench, lamentation, disease and
death. Of ninety-nine convicts who were carried out in one
vessel, twenty-two died before they reached Jamaica, although
the voyage was performed with unusual speed. The survivors
when they arrived at their house of bondage were mere skele-
tons. During some weeks coarse biscuit and fetid water had
been doled out to them in such scanty measure that any one
of them could easily have consumed the ration which was assigned to five. They were, therefore, in such a state that the

* Sunderland to Jeffreys, Sept. 14. 1685; Jeffreys to the King, Sept. 19. 1685,
in the State Paper Office.

merchant to whom they had been consigned found it expedient to fatten them before selling them.*

Meanwhile the property both of the rebels who had suffered death, and of those more unfortunate men who were withering under the tropical sun, was fought for and torn in pieces by a crowd of greedy informers. By law a subject attainted of treason forfeits all his substance; and this law was enforced after the Bloody Assizes with a rigour at once cruel and ludicrous. The brokenhearted widows and destitute orphans of the labouring men whose corpses hung at the cross roads were called upon by the agents of the Treasury to explain what had become of a basket, of a goose, of a flitch of bacon, of a keg of cider, of a sack of beans, of a truss of hay.† While the humbler retainers of the government were pillaging the families of the slaughtered peasants, the Chief Justice was fast accumulating a fortune out of the plunder of a higher class of Whigs. He traded largely in pardons. His most lucrative transaction of this kind was with a gentleman named Edmund Prideaux. It is certain that Prideaux had not been in arms against the government; and it is probable that his only crime was the wealth which he had inherited from his father, an eminent lawyer who had been high in office under the Protector. No exertions were spared to make out a case for the crown. Mercy was offered to some prisoners on condition that they would bear evidence against Prideaux. The unfortunate man lay long in gaol, and at length, overcome by fear of the gallows, consented to pay fifteen thousand pounds for his liberation. This great sum was received by Jeffreys. He bought with it an estate, to which the people gave the name of Aceldama, from that accursed field which was purchased with the price of innocent blood.‡

He was ably assisted in the work of extortion by the crew of parasites who were in the habit of drinking and laughing with him. The office of these men was to drive hard bargains with convicts under the strong terrors of death, and with parents trembling for the lives of children. A portion of the

*Confisca-
tion and
extortion.*

---

* The best account of the sufferings of those rebels who were sentenced to transportation is to be found in a very curious narrative written by John Coad, an honest, Godfearing carpenter who joined Monmouth, was badly wounded at Philip's Norton, was tried by Jeffreys, and was sent to Jamaica. The original manuscript was kindly lent to me by Mr. Phippard, to whom it belongs.

† In the Treasury records of the autumn of 1685 are several letters directing search to be made for trifles of this sort.

‡ Commons' Journals, Oct. 9., Nov 10., Dec. 26. 1690; Oldmixon, 706. Panegyric on Jeffreys.

spoil was abandoned by Jeffreys to his agents. To one of his boon companions, it is said, he tossed a pardon for a rich traitor across the table during a revel. It was not safe to have recourse to any intercession except that of his creatures ; for he guarded his profitable monopoly of mercy with jealous care. It was even suspected that he sent some persons to the gibbet solely because they had applied for the royal clemency through channels independent of him.*

Rapacity of the Queen and of her ladies.

Some courtiers nevertheless contrived to obtain a small share of this traffic. The ladies of the Queen's household distinguished themselves preeminently by rapacity and hardheartedness. Part of the disgrace which they incurred falls on their mistress : for it was solely on account of the relation in which they stood to her that they were able to enrich themselves by so odious a trade ; and there can be no question that she might with a word or a look have restrained them. But in truth she encouraged them by her evil example, if not by her express approbation. She seems to have been one of that large class of persons who bear adversity better than prosperity. While her husband was a subject and an exile, shut out from public employment, and in imminent danger of being deprived of his birthright, the suavity and humility of her manners conciliated the kindness even of those who most abhorred her religion. But when her good fortune came her good nature disappeared. The meek and affable Duchess turned out an ungracious and haughty Queen.† The misfortunes which she subsequently endured have made her an object of some interest ; but that interest would be not a little heightened if it could be shown that, in the season of her greatness, she saved, or even tried to save, one single victim from the most frightful proscription that England has ever seen. Unhappily the only request that she is known to have preferred touching the rebels was that a hundred of those who were sentenced to transportation might be given to her.‡ The profit which she cleared on the cargo, after making large allowance for those who died of hunger and fever during the passage, cannot be estimated at less then a thousand guineas. We cannot wonder that her attendants should have imitated her unprincely greediness and her unwomanly cruelty. They

---

* Life and Death of Lord Jeffreys ; Panegyric on Jeffreys ; Kiffin's Memoirs.

† Burnet, i. 368.; Evelyn's Diary, Feb. 4. 168⅘, July 13. 1686. In one of the satires of that time are these lines :

"When Duchess, she was gentle, mild, and civil ;
When Queen, she proved a raging furious devil."

‡ Sunderland to Jeffreys, Sept. 14. 1685.

exacted a thousand pounds from Roger Hoare, a merchant of Bridgewater, who had contributed to the military chest of the rebel army. But the prey on which they pounced most eagerly was one which it might have been thought that even the most ungentle natures would have spared. Already some of the girls who had presented the standard to Monmouth at Taunton had cruelly expiated their offence. One of them had been thrown into a prison where an infectious malady was raging. She had sickened and died there. Another had presented herself at the bar before Jeffreys to beg for mercy. "Take her, gaoler," vociferated the Judge, with one of those frowns which had often struck terror into stouter hearts than hers. She burst into tears, drew her hood over her face, followed the gaoler out of court, fell ill of fright, and in a few hours was a corpse. Most of the young ladies, however, who had walked in the procession, were still alive. Some of them were under ten years of age. All had acted under the orders of their schoolmistress, without knowing that they were committing a crime. The Queen's maids of honour asked the royal permission to wring money out of the parents of the poor children; and the permission was granted. An order was sent down to Taunton that all these little girls should be seized and imprisoned. Sir Francis Warre of Hestercombe, the Tory member for Bridgewater, was requested to undertake the office of exacting the ransom. He was charged to declare in strong language that the maids of honour would not endure delay, that they were determined to prosecute to outlawry, unless a reasonable sum were forthcoming, and that by a reasonable sum was meant seven thousand pounds. Warre excused himself from taking any part in a transaction so scandalous. The maids of honour then requested William Penn to act for them; and Penn accepted the commission. Yet it should seem that a little of the pertinacious scrupulosity which he had often shown about taking off his hat would not have been altogether out of place on this occasion. He probably silenced the remonstrances of his conscience by repeating to himself that none of the money which he extorted would go into his own pocket; that if he refused to be the agent of the ladies they would find agents less humane; that by complying he should increase his influence at the court, and that his influence at the court had already enabled him, and might still enable him, to render great services to his oppressed brethren. The maids of honour were at last forced to content themselves with less than a third part of what they had demanded.*

* Locke's Western Rebellion; Toulmin's History of Taunton, edited by Savage; Letter of the Duke of Somerset to Sir F. Warre; Letter of Sunderland to Penn, Feb. 13. 168⅖, from the State Paper Office, in the Mackintosh Collection. (1848.)

The letter of Sunderland is as follows:—

"Whitehall, Feb. 13. 1685-6.

"Mr. Penne,

"Her Majesty's Maids of Honour having acquainted me that they designe to employ you and Mr. Walden in making a composition with the Relations of the Maids of Taunton for the high Misdemeanour they have been guilty of, I do at their request hereby let you know that His Majesty has been pleased to give their Fines to the said Maids of Honour, and therefore recommend it to Mr. Walden and you to make the most advantageous composition you can in their behalfe.

"I am, Sir,
"Your humble servant,
"SUNDERLAND."

That the person to whom this letter was addressed was William Penn the Quaker was not doubted by Sir James Mackintosh who first brought it to light, or, as far as I am aware, by any other person, till after the publication of the first part of this History. It has since been confidently asserted that the letter was addressed to a certain George Penn, who appears from an old account book lately discovered to have been concerned in a negotiation for the ransom of one of Monmouth's followers, named Azariah Pinney.

If I thought that I had committed an error, I should, I hope, have the honesty to acknowledge it. But, after full consideration, I am satisfied that Sunderland's letter was addressed to William Penn.

Much has been said about the way in which the name is spelt. The Quaker, we are told, was not Mr. Penne, but Mr. Penn. I feel assured that no person conversant with the books and manuscripts of the seventeenth century will attach any importance to this argument. It is notorious that a proper name was then thought to be well spelt if the sound were preserved. To go no further than the persons who, in Penn's time, held

the Great Seal, one of them is sometimes Hyde and sometimes Hide: another is Jefferies, Jeffries, Jeffereys, and Jeffreys: a third is Somers, Sommers, and Summers: a fourth is Wright and Wrighte; and a fifth is Cowper and Cooper. The Quaker's name was spelt in three ways. He, and his father the Admiral before him, invariably, as far as I have observed, spelt it Penn: but most people spelt it Pen; and there were some who adhered to the ancient form, Penne. For example, William the father is Penne in a letter from Disbrowe to Thurloe, dated on the 7th of December 1654; and William the son is Penne in a newsletter of the 22nd of September 1688, printed in the Ellis Correspondence. In Richard Ward's Life and Letters of Henry More, printed in 1710, the name of the Quaker will be found spelt in all the three ways, Penn in the index, Pen in page 197., and Penne in page 311. The name is Penne in the Commission which the Admiral carried out with him on his expedition to the West Indies. Burchett, who became Secretary to the Admiralty soon after the Revolution, and remained in office long after the accession of the House of Hanover, always, in his Naval History, wrote the name Penne. Surely it cannot be thought strange that an old-fashioned spelling, in which the Secretary of the Admiralty persisted so late as 1720, should have been used at the office of the Secretary of State in 1686. I am quite confident that, if the letter which we are considering had been of a different kind, if Mr. Penne had been informed that, in consequence of his earnest intercession, the King had been graciously pleased to grant a free pardon to the Taunton girls, and if I had attempted to deprive the Quaker of the credit of that intercession on the ground that his name was not Penne, the very persons who now complain so bitterly that I am unjust to his memory would have complained quite as bitterly, and, I must say, with much more reason.

I think myself, therefore, perfectly justified in considering the names, Penn and Penne, as the same. To which, then, of the two persons who bore that name, George or William, is it probable that the letter of the Secretary of State was addressed?

George was evidently an adventurer of

No English sovereign has ever given stronger proofs of a cruel nature than James the Second. Yet his cruelty was a very low class. All that we learn about him from the papers of the Pinney family is that he was employed in the purchase of a pardon for the younger son of a dissenting minister. The whole sum which appears to have passed through George's hands on this occasion was sixty-five pounds. His commission on the transaction must therefore have been small. The only other information which we have about him, is that he, some time later, applied to the government for a favour which was very far from being an honour. In England the Groom Porter of the Palace had a jurisdiction over games of chance, and made some very dirty gain by issuing lottery tickets and licensing hazard tables. George appears to have petitioned for a similar privilege in the American colonies.

William Penn was, during the reign of James the Second, the most active and powerful solicitor about the Court. I will quote the words of his admirer Croese. " Quum autem Pennus tanta gratia plurimum apud regem valeret, et per id perplures sibi amicos acquireret, illum omnes, etiam qui modo aliqua notitia erant conjuncti, quoties aliquid a rege postulandum agendumve apud regem esset, adire, ambire, orare, ut eos apud regem adjuvaret." He was overwhelmed by business of this kind, " obrutus negotiationibus curationibusque." His house and the approaches to it were every day blocked up by crowds of persons who came to request his good offices; "domus ac vestibula quotidie referta clientium et supplicantium." From the Fountainhall papers it appears that his influence was felt even in the highlands of Scotland. We learn from himself that, at this time, he was always toiling for others, that he was a daily suitor at Whitehall, and that, if he had chosen to sell his influence, he could, in little more than three years, have put twenty thousand pounds into his pocket, and obtained a hundred thousand more for the improvement of the colony of which he was proprietor.

Such was the position of these two men. Which of them, then, was the more likely to be employed in the matter to which Sunderland's letter related? Was it George or William, an agent of the lowest or of the highest class? The persons interested were ladies of rank and fashion, resident at the palace, where George would hardly have been admitted into an outer room, but where William was every day in the presence chamber and was frequently called into the closet. The greatest nobles in the kingdom were zealous and active in the cause of their fair friends, nobles with whom William lived in habits of familiar intercourse, but who would hardly have thought George fit company for their grooms. The sum in question was seven thousand pounds, a sum not large when compared with the masses of wealth with which William had constantly to deal, but more than a hundred times as large as the only ransom which is known to have passed through the hands of George. These considerations would suffice to raise a strong presumption that Sunderland's letter was addressed to William, and not to George: but there is a still stronger argument behind.

It is most important to observe that the person to whom this letter was addressed was not the first person whom the Maids of Honour had requested to act for them. They applied to him because another person to whom they had previously applied, had, after some correspondence, declined the office. From their first application we learn with certainty what sort of person they wished to employ. If their first application had been made to some obscure pettifogger or needy gambler, we should be warranted in believing that the Penne to whom their second application was made was George. If, on the other hand, their first application was made to a gentleman of the highest consideration, we can hardly be wrong in saying that the Penne to whom their second application was made must have been William. To whom, then, was their first application made? It was to Sir Francis Warre of Hestercombe, a Baronet and a Member of Parliament. The letters are still extant in which the Duke of Somerset, the proud Duke, not a man very likely to have corresponded with George Penne, pressed Sir Francis to undertake the commission. The latest of those letters is dated about three weeks before Sunderland's letter to Mr. Penne. Somerset tells Sir Francis that the town clerk of Bridgewater, whose name, I may remark in passing, is spelt sometimes Bird and sometimes Birde, had offered his services, but that not more odious than his mercy. Or perhaps it may be more correct to say that his mercy and his cruelty were such that each reflects infamy on the other. Our horror at the fate of the simple clowns, the young lads, the delicate women, to whom he was inexorably severe, is increased when we find to whom and for what considerations he granted his pardon.

The rule by which a prince ought, after a rebellion, to be guided in selecting rebels for punishment is perfectly obvious. The ringleaders, the men of rank, fortune and education,

those services had been declined. It is clear, therefore, that the Maids of Honour were desirous to have an agent of high station and character. And they were right. For the sum which they demanded was so large that no ordinary jobber could safely be entrusted with the care of their interests.

As Sir Francis Warre excused himself from undertaking the negotiation, it became necessary for the Maids of Honour and their advisers to choose somebody who might supply his place; and they chose Penne. Which of the two Pennes, then, must have been their choice, George, a petty broker to whom a percentage on sixty-five pounds was an object, and whose highest ambition was to derive an infamous livelihood from cards and dice, or William, not inferior in social position to any commoner in the kingdom? Is it possible to believe that the ladies who, in January, employed the Duke of Somerset to procure for them an agent in the first rank of the English gentry, and who did not think an attorney, though occupying a respectable post in a respectable corporation, good enough for their purpose, would, in February, have resolved to trust everything to a fellow who was as much below Bird as Bird was below Warre?

But, it is said, Sunderland's letter is dry and distant; and he never would have written in such a style to William Penn with whom he was on friendly terms. Can it be necessary for me to reply that the official communications which a Minister of State makes to his dearest friends and nearest relations are as cold and formal as those which he makes to strangers? Will it be contended that the General Wellesley, to whom the Marquis Wellesley, when Governor of India, addressed so many letters beginning with "Sir," and ending with "I have the honour to be your obedient servant," cannot possibly have been his Lordship's brother Arthur?

But, it is said, Oldmixon tells a different story. According to him, a Popish lawyer named Brent, and a subordinate jobber, named Crane, were the agents in the matter of the Taunton girls. Now it is notorious that of all our historians Oldmixon is the least trustworthy. His most positive assertion would be of no value when opposed to such evidence as is furnished by Sunderland's letter. But Oldmixon asserts nothing positively. Not only does he not assert positively that Brent and Crane acted for the Maids of Honour; but he does not even assert positively that the Maids of Honour were at all concerned. He goes no further than "It was said," and "It was reported." It is plain, therefore, that he was very imperfectly informed. I do not think it impossible, however, that there may have been some foundation for the rumour which he mentions. We have seen that one busy lawyer, named Bird, volunteered to look after the interest of the Maids of Honour, and that they were forced to tell him that they did not want his services. Other persons, and among them the two whom Oldmixon names, may have tried to thrust themselves into so lucrative a job, and may, by pretending to interest at Court, have succeeded in obtaining a little money from terrified families. But nothing can be more clear than that the authorised agent of the Maids of Honour was the Mr. Penne, to whom the Secretary of State wrote; and I firmly believe that Mr. Penne to have been William the Quaker.

If it be said that it is incredible that so good a man would have been concerned in so bad an affair, I can only answer that this affair was very far indeed from being the worst in which he was concerned.

For these reasons I leave the text, and shall leave it exactly as it originally stood. (1857.)

whose power and whose artifices have led the multitude into error, are the proper objects of severity. The deluded populace, when once the slaughter on the field of battle is over, can scarcely be treated too leniently. This rule, so evidently agreeable to justice and humanity, was not only not observed: it was inverted. While those who ought to have been spared were slaughtered by hundreds, the few who might with propriety have been left to the utmost rigour of the law were spared. This eccentric clemency has perplexed some writers, and has drawn forth ludicrous eulogies from others. It was neither at all mysterious, nor at all praiseworthy. It may be distinctly traced in every case either to a sordid or to a malignant motive, either to thirst for money or to thirst for blood.

In the case of Grey there was no mitigating circumstance. Grey.
His parts and knowledge, the rank which he had inherited in the state, and the high command which he had borne in the rebel army, would have pointed him out to a just government as a much fitter object of punishment than Alice Lisle, than William Hewling, than any of the hundreds of ignorant peasants whose skulls and quarters were exposed in Somersetshire. But Grey's estate was large and was strictly entailed. He had only a life interest in his property; and he could forfeit no more interest than he had. If he died, his lands at once devolved on the next heir. If he were pardoned, he would be able to pay a large ransom. He was therefore suffered to redeem himself by giving a bond for forty thousand pounds to the Lord Treasurer, and smaller sums to other courtiers.*

Sir John Cochrane had held among the Scotch rebels the Cochrane.
same rank which had been held by Grey in the West of England. That Cochrane should be forgiven by a prince vindictive beyond all example, seemed incredible. But Cochrane was the younger son of a rich family; it was therefore only by sparing him that money could be made out of him. His father, Lord Dundonald, offered a bribe of five thousand pounds to the priests of the royal household; and a pardon was granted.†

Samuel Storey, a noted sower of sedition, who had been Storey.
Commissary to the rebel army, and who had inflamed the ignorant populace of Somersetshire by vehement harangues in which James had been described as an incendiary and a

* Burnet, i. 646., and Speaker Onslow's note; Clarendon to Rochester, May 8. 1686. † Burnet i. 634.

poisoner, was admitted to mercy. For Storey was able to give important assistance to Jeffreys in wringing fifteen thousand pounds out of Prideaux.*

None of the traitors had less right to expect favour than Wade, Goodenough, and Ferguson. These three chiefs of the rebellion had fled together from the field of Sedgemoor, and had reached the coast in safety. But they had found a frigate cruising near the spot where they had hoped to embark. They had then separated. Wade and Goodenough were soon discovered and brought up to London. Deeply as they had been implicated in the Rye House plot, conspicuous as they had been among the chiefs of the Western insurrection, they were suffered to live, because they had it in their power to give information which enabled the King to slaughter and plunder some persons whom he hated, but to whom he had never yet been able to bring home any crime.†

How Ferguson escaped was, and still is, a mystery. Of all the enemies of the government he was, without doubt, the most deeply criminal. He was the original author of the plot for assassinating the royal brothers. He had written that Declaration which, for insolence, malignity, and mendacity, stands unrivalled even among the libels of those stormy times. He had instigated Monmouth first to invade the kingdom, and then to usurp the crown. It was reasonable to expect that a strict search would be made for the archtraitor, as he was often called; and such a search a man of so singular an aspect and dialect could scarcely have eluded. It was confidently reported in the coffee houses of London that Ferguson was taken; and this report found credit with men who had excellent opportunities of knowing the truth. The next thing that was heard of him was that he was safe on the Continent. It was strongly suspected that he had been in constant communication with the government against which he was constantly plotting, that he had, while urging his associates to every excess of rashness, sent to Whitehall just so much information about their proceedings as might suffice to save his own neck, and that therefore orders had been given to let him escape.†

* Calamy's Memoirs; Commons' Journals, December 26. 1690; Sunderland to Jeffreys, September 14. 1685; Privy Council Book, February 26. 168⅚.

† Lansdowne MS. 1152.; Harl. MS. 6845.; London Gazette, July 20. 1685.

‡ Many writers have asserted, without the slightest foundation, that a pardon was granted to Ferguson by James. Some have been so absurd as to cite this imaginary pardon, which, if it were real, would prove only that Fer-

And now Jeffreys had done his work, and returned to claim his reward. He arrived at Windsor from the West, leaving carnage, mourning, and terror behind him. The hatred with which he was regarded by the people of Somersetshire has no parallel in our history. It was not to be quenched by time or by political changes, was long transmitted from generation to generation, and raged fiercely against his innocent progeny. When he had been many years dead, when his name and title were extinct, his granddaughter, the Countess of Pomfret, travelling along the western road, was insulted by the populace, and found that she could not safely venture herself among the descendants of those who had witnessed the Bloody Assizes.*

But at the Court Jeffreys was cordially welcomed. He was a judge after his master's own heart. James had watched the circuit with interest and delight. In his drawingroom and at his table he had frequently talked of the havoc which was making among his disaffected subjects with a glee at which the foreign ministers stood aghast. With his own hand he had penned accounts of what he facetiously called his Lord Chief Justice's campaign in the West. Some hundreds of rebels, His Majesty wrote to the Hague, had been condemned. Some of them had been hanged: more should be hanged: and the rest should be sent to the plantations. It was to no purpose that Ken wrote to implore mercy for the misguided people, and described with pathetic eloquence the frightful state of his diocese. He complained that it was impossible to walk along the highways without seeing some terrible spectacle, and that the whole air of Somersetshire was tainted with death. The King read, and remained, according to the saying of Churchill, hard as the marble chimneypieces of Whitehall. At Windsor the great seal of England

guson was a court spy, in proof of the magnanimity and benignity of the prince who beheaded Alice Lisle and burned Elizabeth Gaunt. Ferguson was not only not specially pardoned, but was excluded by name from the general pardon published in the following spring. (London Gazette, March 15. 168⅘.) If, as the public suspected, and as seems probable, indulgence was shown to him, it was indulgence of which James was, not without reason, ashamed, and which was, as far as possible, kept secret. The reports which were current in London at the time are mentioned in

the Observator, Aug. 1. 1685.

Sir John Reresby, who ought to have been well informed, positively affirms that Ferguson was taken three days after the battle of Sedgemoor. But Sir John was certainly wrong as to the date, and may therefore have been wrong as to the whole story. From the London Gazette, and from Goodenough's confession (Lansdowne MS. 1152.), it is clear that, a fortnight after the battle, Ferguson had not been caught, and was supposed to be still lurking in England.

* Granger's Biographical History.

was put into the hands of Jeffreys, and in the next London Gazette it was solemnly notified that this honour was the re-
Jeffreys made Lord Chancellor. ward of the many eminent and faithful services which he had rendered to the crown.*

At a later period, when all men of all parties spoke with horror of the Bloody Assizes, the wicked Judge and the wicked King attempted to vindicate themselves by throwing the blame on each other. Jeffreys, in the Tower, protested that, in his utmost cruelty, he had not gone beyond his mas- ter's express orders, nay, that he had fallen short of them. James, at Saint Germain's, would willingly have had it be- lieved that his own inclinations had been on the side of cle- mency, and that unmerited obloquy had been brought on him by the violence of his minister. But neither of these hard- hearted men must be absolved at the expense of the other. The plea set up for James can be proved under his own hand to be false in fact. The plea of Jeffreys, even if it be true in fact, is utterly worthless.

Trial and execution of Cornish. The slaughter in the West was over. The slaughter in London was about to begin. The government was peculiarly desirous to find victims among the great Whig merchants of the City. They had, in the last reign, been a formidable part of the strength of the opposition. They were wealthy; and their wealth was not, like that of many noblemen and country gentlemen, protected by entail against forfeiture. In the case of Grey, and of men situated like him, it was im- possible to gratify cruelty and rapacity at once: but a rich trader might be both hanged and plundered. The com- mercial grandees, however, though in general hostile to Popery and to arbitrary power, had yet been too scrupulous or too timid to incur the guilt of high treason. One of the most considerable among them was Henry Cornish. He had been an Alderman under the old charter of the City, and had filled the office of Sheriff when the question of the Exclusion Bill occupied the public mind. In politics he was a Whig: his religious opinions leaned towards Presbyterianism: but his temper was cautious and moderate. It is not proved by trustworthy evidence that he ever approached the verge of treason. He had, indeed, when Sheriff, been very unwilling to employ as his deputy a man so violent and unprincipled as Goodenough. When the Rye House plot was discovered,

* Burnet, i. 648.; James to the Prince   Lonsdale's Memoirs; London Gazette, of Orange, Sept. 10. and 24. 1685; Lord   Oct. 1. 1685.

great hopes were entertained at Whitehall that Cornish would appear to have been concerned: but these hopes were disappointed. One of the conspirators, indeed, John Rumsey, was ready to swear anything: but a single witness was not sufficient; and no second witness could be found. More than two years had since elapsed. Cornish thought himself safe; but the eye of the tyrant was upon him. Goodenough, terrified by the near prospect of death, and still harbouring malice on account of the unfavourable opinion which had always been entertained of him by his old master, consented to supply the testimony which had hitherto been wanting. Cornish was arrested while transacting business on the Exchange, was hurried to gaol, was kept there some days in solitary confinement, and was brought altogether unprepared to the bar of the Old Bailey. The case against him rested wholly on the evidence of Rumsey and Goodenough. Both were, by their own confession, accomplices in the plot with which they charged the prisoner. Both were impelled by the strongest pressure of hope and fear to criminate him. Evidence was produced which proved that Goodenough was also under the influence of personal enmity. Rumsey's story was inconsistent with the story which he had told when he appeared as a witness against Lord Russell. But these things were urged in vain. On the bench sate three judges who had been with Jeffreys in the West; and it was remarked by those who watched their deportment that they had come back from the carnage of Taunton in a fierce and excited state. It is indeed but too true that the taste for blood is a taste which even men not naturally cruel may, by habit, speedily acquire. The bar and the bench united to browbeat the unfortunate Whig. The jury, named by a courtly Sheriff, readily found a verdict of Guilty; and, in spite of the indignant murmurs of the public, Cornish suffered death within ten days after he had been arrested. That no circumstance of degradation might be wanting, the gibbet was set up where King Street meets Cheapside, in sight of the house where he had long lived in general respect, of the Exchange where his credit had always stood high, and of the Guildhall where he had distinguished himself as a popular leader. He died with courage and with many pious expressions, but showed, by look and gesture, such strong resentment at the barbarity and injustice with which he had been treated, that his enemies spread a calumnious report concerning him. He was drunk, they said, or out of his mind, when he was turned off. William Penn, however, who stood near the gallows, and whose prejudices were all on the side of the government, afterwards said that he could see in Cornish's deportment nothing but the natural indignation of an innocent man slain under the forms of law. The head of the murdered magistrate was placed over the Guildhall.*

Trials and executions of Fernley and Elizabeth Gaunt. Black as this case was, it was not the blackest which disgraced the sessions of that autumn at the Old Bailey. Among the persons concerned in the Rye House plot was a man named James Burton. By his own confession he had been present when the design of assassination was discussed by his accomplices. When the conspiracy was detected, a reward was offered for his apprehension. He was saved from death by an ancient matron of the Baptist persuasion, named Elizabeth Gaunt. This woman, with the peculiar manners and phraseology which then distinguished her sect, had a large charity. Her life was passed in relieving the unhappy of all religious denominations, and she was well known as a constant visitor of the gaols. Her political and theological opinions, as well as her compassionate disposition, led her to do everything in her power for Burton. She procured a boat which took him to Gravesend, where he got on board of a ship bound for Amsterdam. At the moment of parting she put into his hand a sum of money which, for her means, was very large. Burton, after living some time in exile, returned to England with Monmouth, fought at Sedgemoor, fled to London, and took refuge in the house of John Fernley, a barber in Whitechapel. Fernley was very poor. He was besieged by creditors. He knew that a reward of a hundred pounds had been offered by the government for the apprehension of Burton. But the honest man was incapable of betraying one who, in extreme peril, had come under the shadow of his roof. Unhappily it was soon noised abroad that the anger of James was more strongly excited against those who harboured rebels than against the rebels themselves. He had publicly declared that of all forms of treason the hiding of traitors from his vengeance was the most unpardonable. Burton knew this. He delivered himself up to the government; and he gave information against Fernley and Elizabeth Gaunt. They were brought to trial. The villain

---

* Trial of Cornish in the Collection of State Trials; Sir J. Hawles's Remarks on Mr. Cornish's Trial; Burnet, i. 651.; Bloody Assizes; Stat. 1 Gul. and Mar.

whose life they had preserved had the heart and the forehead to appear as the principal witness against them. They were convicted. Fernley was sentenced to the gallows, Elizabeth Gaunt to the stake. Even after all the horrors of that year, many thought it impossible that these judgments should be carried into execution. But the King was without pity. Fernley was hanged. Elizabeth Gaunt was burned alive at Tyburn on the same day on which Cornish suffered death in Cheapside. She left a paper written, indeed, in no graceful style, yet such as was read by many thousands with compassion and horror. "My fault," she said, "was one which a prince might well have forgiven. I did but relieve a poor family; and lo! I must die for it." She complained of the insolence of the judges, of the ferocity of the gaoler, and of the tyranny of him, the great one of all, to whose pleasure she and so many other victims had been sacrificed. In so far as they had injured herself, she forgave them: but, in that they were implacable enemies of that good cause which would yet revive and flourish, she left them to the judgment of the King of Kings. To the last she preserved a tranquil courage, which reminded the spectators of the most heroic deaths of which they had read in Fox. William Penn, for whom exhibitions which humane men generally avoid seem to have had a strong attraction, hastened from Cheapside, where he had seen Cornish hanged, to Tyburn, in order to see Elizabeth Gaunt burned. He afterwards related that, when she calmly disposed the straw about her in such a manner as to shorten her sufferings, all the bystanders burst into tears. It was much noticed that, while the foulest judicial murder which had disgraced even those times was perpetrating, a tempest burst forth, such as had not been known since that great hurricane which had raged round the deathbed of Oliver. The oppressed Puritans reckoned up, not without a gloomy satisfaction, the houses which had been blown down, and the ships which had been cast away, and derived some consolation from thinking that heaven was bearing awful testimony against the iniquity which afflicted the earth. Since that terrible day no woman has suffered death in England for any political offence.*

It was not thought that Goodenough had yet earned his

* Trials of Fernley and Elizabeth Gaunt, in the Collection of State Trials; Burnet, i. 649.; Bloody Assizes; Sir J. Bramston's Memoirs; Luttrell's Diary, Oct. 23. 1685.

pardon. The government was bent on destroying a victim of no high rank, a surgeon in the City, named Bateman. He

had attended Shaftesbury professionally, and had been a zealous Exclusionist. He may possibly have been privy to the Whig plot; but it is certain that he had not been one of the leading conspirators; for, in the great mass of depositions published by the government, his name occurs only once, and then not in connection with any crime bordering on high treason. From his indictment, and from the scanty account which remains of his trial, it seems clear that he was not even accused of participating in the design of murdering the royal brothers. The malignity with which so obscure a man, guilty of so slight an offence, was hunted down, while traitors far more criminal and far more eminent were allowed to ransom themselves by giving evidence against him, seemed to require explanation; and a disgraceful explanation was found. When Oates, after his scourging, was carried into Newgate insensible, and, as all thought, in the last agony, he had been bled and his wounds had been dressed by Bateman. This was an offence not to be forgiven. Bateman was arrested and indicted. The witnesses against him were men of infamous character, men, too, who were swearing for their own lives. None of them had yet got his pardon; and it was a popular saying, that they fished for prey, like tame cormorants, with ropes round their necks. The prisoner, stupefied by illness, was unable to articulate, or to understand what passed. His son and daughter stood by him at the bar. They read as well as they could some notes which he had set down, and examined his witnesses. It was to little purpose. He was convicted, hanged, and quartered.*

Never, not even under the tyranny of Laud, had the condition of the Puritans been so deplorable as at that time. Never had spies been so actively employed in detecting congregations. Never had magistrates, grand jurors, rectors and churchwardens been so much on the alert. Many Dissenters were cited before the ecclesiastical courts. Others found it necessary to purchase the connivance of the agents of the government by presents of hogsheads of wine, and of gloves stuffed with guineas. It was impossible for the separatists to pray together without precautions such as are em-

---

* Bateman's Trial in the Collection of State Trials; Sir John Hawles's Remarks. It is worth while to compare Thomas Lee's evidence on this occasion with his confession previously published by authority.

ployed by coiners and receivers of stolen goods. The places of meeting were frequently changed. Worship was performed sometimes just before break of day and sometimes at dead of night. Round the building where the little flock was gathered sentinels were posted to give the alarm if a stranger drew near. The minister in disguise was introduced through the garden and the back yard. In some houses there were trap doors through which, in case of danger, he might descend. Where Nonconformists lived next door to each other, the walls were often broken open, and secret passages were made from dwelling to dwelling. No psalm was sung; and many contrivances were used to prevent the voice of the preacher, in his moments of fervour, from being heard beyond the walls. Yet, with all this care, it was often found impossible to elude the vigilance of informers. In the suburbs of London, especially, the law was enforced with the utmost rigour. Several opulent gentlemen were accused of holding conventicles. Their houses were strictly searched, and distresses were levied to the amount of many thousands of pounds. The fiercer and bolder sectaries, thus driven from the shelter of roofs, met in the open air, and determined to repel force by force. A Middlesex justice, who had learned that a nightly prayer meeting was held in a gravel pit about two miles from London, took with him a strong body of constables, broke in upon the assembly, and seized the preacher. But the congregation, which consisted of about two hundred men, soon rescued their pastor, and put the magistrate and his officers to flight.* This, however, was no ordinary occurrence. In general the Puritan spirit seemed to be more effectually cowed at this conjuncture than at any moment before or since. The Tory pamphleteers boasted that not one fanatic dared to move tongue or pen in defence of his religious opinions. Dissenting ministers, however blameless in life, however eminent for learning and abilities, could not venture to walk the streets for fear of outrages, which were not only not repressed, but encouraged, by those whose duty it was to preserve the peace. Some divines of great fame were in prison. Among these was Richard Baxter. Others, who had, during a quarter of a century, borne up against oppression, now lost heart, and quitted the kingdom. Among these was John Howe. Great numbers of persons who had been accustomed to frequent

* Van Citters, Oct. $\frac{13}{23}$. 1685.

conventicles repaired to the parish churches. It was remarked that the schismatics who had been terrified into this
show of conformity might easily be distinguished by the
difficulty which they had in finding out the collect, and by
the awkward manner in which they bowed at the name of
Jesus.*

Through many years the autumn of 1685 was remembered
by the Nonconformists as a time of misery and terror. Yet
in that autumn might be discerned the first faint indications
of a great turn of fortune; and before eighteen months had
elapsed, the intolerant King and the intolerant Church were
eagerly bidding against each other for the support of the
party which both had so deeply injured.

* Neal's History of the Puritans,
Calamy's Account of the ejected Ministers, and the Nonconformists' Memorial, contain abundant proofs of the
severity of this persecution. Howe's
farewell letter to his flock will be found
in the interesting life of that great man,
by Mr. Rogers. Howe complains that
he could not venture to show himself in
the streets of London, and that his
health had suffered from want of air
and exercise. But the most vivid picture of the distress of the Nonconformists
is furnished by their deadly enemy, Lestrange, in the Observators of September
and October, 1685.

CHAPTER VI.

JAMES was now at the height of power and prosperity. Both in England and in Scotland he had vanquished his enemies, and had punished them with a severity which had indeed excited their bitterest hatred, but had, at the same time, effectually quelled their courage. The Whig party seemed extinct. The name of Whig was never used except as a term of reproach. The Parliament was devoted to the King; and it was in his power to keep that Parliament to the end of his reign. The Church was louder than ever in professions of attachment to him, and had, during the late insurrection, acted up to those professions. The Judges were his tools; and, if they ceased to be so, it was in his power to remove them. The corporations were filled with his creatures. His revenues far exceeded those of his predecessors. His pride rose high. He was not the same man who, a few months before, in doubt whether his throne might not be overturned in an hour, had implored foreign help with unkingly supplications, and had accepted it with tears of gratitude. Visions of dominion and glory rose before him. He already saw himself, in imagination, the umpire of Europe, the champion of many states oppressed by one too powerful monarchy. So early as the month of June he had assured the United Provinces that, as soon as the affairs of England were settled, he would show the world how little he feared France. In conformity with these assurances, he, within a month after the battle of Sedgemoor, concluded with the States General a defensive treaty, framed in the very spirit of the Triple League. It was regarded, both at the Hague and at Versailles, as a most significant circumstance that Halifax, who was the constant and mortal enemy of French ascendency, and who had scarcely ever before been consulted on any grave affair since the beginning of the reign, took the lead on this occasion, and seemed to have the royal ear. It was a circumstance not less significant that no previous communication

The power of James at the height.

was made to Barillon. Both he and his master were taken by surprise. Lewis was much troubled, and expressed great, and not unreasonable, anxiety as to the ulterior designs of the prince who had lately been his pensioner and vassal. There were strong rumours that William of Orange was busied in organising a great confederacy, which was to include both branches of the House of Austria, the United Provinces, the kingdom of Sweden, and the electorate of Brandenburg. It now seemed that this confederacy would have at its head the King and Parliament of England.*

His foreign policy.

In fact, negotiations tending to such a result were actually opened. Spain proposed to form a close alliance with James; and he listened to the proposition with favour, though it was evident that such an alliance would be little less than a declaration of war against France. But he postponed his final decision till after the Parliament should have reassembled. The fate of Christendom depended on the temper in which he might then find the Commons. If they were disposed to acquiesce in his plans of domestic government, there would be nothing to prevent him from interfering with vigour and authority in the great dispute which must soon be brought to an issue on the Continent. If they were refractory, he must relinquish all thought of arbitrating between contending nations, must again implore French assistance, must again submit to French dictation, must sink into a potentate of the third or fourth class, and must indemnify himself for the contempt with which he would be regarded abroad by triumphs over law and public opinion at home.

His plans of domestic government.

It seemed, indeed, that it would not be easy for him to demand more than the Commons were disposed to give. Already they had abundantly proved that they were desirous to maintain his prerogatives unimpaired, and that they were by no means extreme to mark his encroachments on the rights of the people. Indeed eleven twelfths of the members were either dependents of the court, or zealous Cavaliers from the country. There were few things which such an assembly could pertinaciously refuse to the Sovereign; but, happily for the nation, those few things were the very things on which James had set his heart.

The Habeas Corpus Act.

One of his objects was to obtain a repeal of the Habeas Corpus Act, which he hated, as it was natural that a tyrant

* Avaux Neg., Aug. $\frac{6}{16}$. 1685; Despatch of Van Citters and his colleagues, enclosing the treaty, August $\frac{14}{24}$.; Lewis to Barillon, August $\frac{14}{24}$. $\frac{20}{30}$.

James II

should hate the most stringent curb that ever legislation imposed on tyranny. This feeling remained deeply fixed in his mind to the last, and appears in the instructions which he drew up, in exile, for the guidance of his son.* But the Habeas Corpus Act, though passed during the ascendency of the Whigs, was not more dear to the Whigs than to the Tories. It is indeed not wonderful that this great law should be highly prized by all Englishmen without distinction of party: for it is a law which, not by circuitous, but by direct operation, adds to the security and happiness of every inhabitant of the realm.†

James had yet another design, odious to the party which had set him on the throne and which had upheld him there. He wished to form a great standing army. He had taken advantage of the late insurrection to make large additions to the military force which his brother had left. The bodies now designated as the first six regiments of dragoon guards, the third and fourth regiments of dragoons, and the nine regiments of infantry of the line, from the seventh to the fifteenth inclusive, had just been raised.‡ The effect of these augmentations, and of the recall of the garrison of Tangier, was that the number of regular troops in England had, in a few months, been increased from six thousand to near twenty thousand. No English King had ever, in time of peace, had such a force at his command. Yet even with this force James was not content. He often repeated that no confidence could be placed in the fidelity of the trainbands, that they sympathised with all the passions of the class to which they belonged, that, at Sedgemoor, there had been more militiamen in the rebel army than in the royal encampment, and that, if the throne had been defended only by the array of the counties, Monmouth would have marched in triumph from Lyme to London.

The revenue, large as it was when compared with that of former Kings, barely sufficed to meet this new charge. A great part of the produce of the new taxes was absorbed by the naval expenditure. At the close of the late reign the whole cost of the army, the Tangier regiments included, had been under three hundred thousand pounds a year. Six hun-

The standing army.

---

* Instructions headed, "For my son the Prince of Wales, 1692," among the Stuart Papers.

† "The Habeas Corpus," said Johnson, the most bigoted of Tories, to Boswell, "is the single advantage which our government has over that of other countries."

‡ See the Historical Records of Regiments, published under the supervision of the Adjutant General.

dred thousand pounds a year would not now suffice.* If any further augmentation were made, it would be necessary to demand a supply from Parliament; and it was not likely that Parliament would be in a complying mood. The very name of standing army was hateful to the whole nation, and to no part of the nation more hateful than to the Cavalier gentlemen who filled the Lower House. In their minds a standing army was inseparably associated with the Rump, with the Protector, with the spoliation of the Church, with the purgation of the Universities, with the abolition of the peerage, with the murder of the King, with the sullen reign of the Saints, with cant and asceticism, with fines and sequestrations, with the insults which Major Generals, sprung from the dregs of the people, had offered to the oldest and most honourable families of the kingdom. There was, moreover, scarcely a baronet or a squire in the Parliament who did not owe part of his importance in his own county to his rank in the militia. If that national force were set aside, the gentry of England must lose much of their dignity and influence. It was therefore probable that the King would find it more difficult to obtain funds for the support of his army than even to obtain the repeal of the Habeas Corpus Act.

Designs in favour of the Roman Catholic religion.

But both the designs which have been mentioned were subordinate to one great design on which the King's whole soul was bent, but which was abhorred by those Tory gentlemen who were ready to shed their blood for his rights, abhorred by that Church which had never, during three generations of civil discord, wavered in fidelity to his house, abhorred even by that army on which, in the last extremity, he must rely.

His religion was still under proscription. Many rigorous laws against Roman Catholics appeared on the Statute Book, and had, within no long time, been rigorously executed. The Test Act excluded from civil and military office all who dissented from the Church of England; and, by a subsequent Act, passed when the fictions of Oates had driven the nation wild, it had been provided that no person should sit in either House of Parliament without solemnly abjuring the doctrine of transubstantiation. That the King should wish to obtain for the Church to which he belonged a complete toleration was natural and right; nor is there any reason to doubt that, by

* Barillon, Dec. $\frac{3}{13}$. 1685. He had studied the subject much. "C'est un détail," he says, "dont j'ai connoissance." It appears from the Treasury Warrant Book that the charge of the army for the year 1687 was fixed on the first of January at 623,104*l.* 9*s.* 11*d.*

a little patience, prudence, and justice, such a toleration might have been obtained.

The extreme antipathy and dread with which the English people regarded his religion was not to be ascribed solely or chiefly to theological animosity. That salvation might be found in the Church of Rome, nay, that some members of that Church had been among the brightest examples of Christian virtue, was admitted by all divines of the Anglican communion and by the most illustrious Nonconformists. It is notorious that the penal laws against Popery were strenuously defended by many who thought Arianism, Quakerism, and Judaism more dangerous, in a spiritual point of view, than Popery, and who yet showed no disposition to enact similar laws against Arians, Quakers, or Jews.

It is easy to explain why the Roman Catholic was treated with less indulgence than was shown to men who renounced the doctrine of the Nicene fathers, and even to men who had not been admitted by baptism within the Christian pale. There was among the English a strong conviction that the Roman Catholic, where the interests of his religion were concerned, thought himself free from all the ordinary rules of morality, nay, that he thought it meritorious to violate those rules if, by so doing, he could avert injury or reproach from the Church of which he was a member.

Nor was this opinion destitute of a show of reason. It was impossible to deny that Roman Catholic casuists of great eminence had written in defence of equivocation, of mental reservation, of perjury, and even of assassination. Nor, it was said, had the speculations of this odious school of sophists been barren of results. The massacre of Saint Bartholomew, the murder of the first William of Orange, the murder of Henry the Third of France, the numerous conspiracies which had been formed against the life of Elizabeth, and, above all, the gunpowder treason, were constantly cited as instances of the close connection between vicious theory and vicious practice. It was alleged that every one of those crimes had been prompted or applauded by Roman Catholic divines. The letters which Everard Digby wrote in lemon juice from the Tower to his wife had recently been published, and were often quoted. He was a scholar and a gentleman, upright in all ordinary dealings, and strongly impressed with a sense of duty to God. Yet he had been deeply concerned in the plot for blowing up King, Lords, and Commons, and had, on the

brink of eternity, declared that it was incomprehensible to
him how any Roman Catholic should think such a design sinful. The inference popularly drawn from these things was that,
however fair the general character of a Papist might be, there
was no excess of fraud or cruelty of which he was not capable
when the safety and honour of his Church were at stake.

The extraordinary success of the fables of Oates is to be
chiefly ascribed to the prevalence of this opinion. It was to
no purpose that the accused Roman Catholic appealed to the
integrity, humanity, and loyalty which he had shown through
the whole course of his life. It was to no purpose that he
called crowds of respectable witnesses, of his own persuasion,
to contradict monstrous romances invented by the most infamous of mankind. It was to no purpose that, with the
halter round his neck, he invoked on himself the whole vengeance of the God before whom, in a few moments, he must
appear, if he had been guilty of meditating any ill to his
prince or to his Protestant fellow countrymen. The evidence
which he produced in his favour proved only how little Popish
oaths were worth. His very virtues raised a presumption of
his guilt. That he had before him death and judgment in
immediate prospect only made it more likely that he would
deny what, without injury to the holiest of causes, he could
not confess. Among the unhappy men who were convicted
of the murder of Godfrey was one Protestant of no high character, Henry Berry. It is a remarkable and well attested
circumstance, that Berry's last words did more to shake the
credit of the plot than the dying declarations of pious and
honourable Roman Catholics who underwent the same fate.*

It was not only by the ignorant populace, it was not only
by zealots in whom fanaticism had extinguished all reason
and charity, that the Roman Catholic was regarded as a man
the very tenderness of whose conscience might make him a
false witness, an incendiary, or a murderer, as a man who,
where his Church was concerned, shrank from no atrocity
and could be bound by no oath. If there were in that age
two persons inclined by their judgment and by their temper
to toleration, those persons were Tillotson and Locke. Yet
Tillotson, whose indulgence for various kinds of schismatics
and heretics brought on him the reproach of heterodoxy, told
the House of Commons from the pulpit that it was their duty
to make effectual provision against the propagation of a

* Burnet, i. 447.

religion more mischievous than irreligion itself, of a religion which demanded from its followers services directly opposed to the first principles of morality. His temper, he truly said, was prone to lenity; but his duty to the community forced him to be, in this one instance, severe. He declared that, in his judgment, Pagans who had never heard the name of Christ, and who were guided only by the light of nature, were more trustworthy members of civil society than men who had been formed in the schools of the Popish casuists.* Locke, in the celebrated treatise in which he laboured to show that even the grossest forms of idolatry ought not to be prohibited under penal sanctions, contended that the Church which taught men not to keep faith with heretics had no claim to toleration.†

It is evident that, in such circumstances, the greatest service which an English Roman Catholic could render to his brethren in the faith was to convince the public that, whatever some too subtle theorists might have written, whatever some rash men might, in times of violent excitement, have done, his Church did not hold that any end could sanctify means inconsistent with morality. And this great service it was in the power of James to render. He was King. He was more powerful than any English King had been within the memory of the oldest man. It depended on him whether the reproach which lay on his religion should be taken away or should be made permanent.

Had he conformed to the laws, had he kept his promises, had he abstained from employing any unrighteous methods for the propagation of his own theological tenets, had he suspended the operation of the penal statutes by a large exercise of his unquestionable prerogative of mercy, but, at the same time, carefully abstained from violating the civil or ecclesiastical constitution of the realm, the feeling of his people must have undergone a rapid change. So conspicuous an example of good faith punctiliously observed by a Popish prince towards a Protestant nation would have quieted the public apprehensions. Men who saw that a Roman Catholic might safely be suffered to direct the whole executive administration, to command the army and navy, to convoke and dissolve the legislature, to appoint the Bishops and Deans of the Church of England, would soon have ceased to fear that any

* Tillotson's Sermon, preached before the House of Commons, Nov. 5. 1678.
† Locke, First Letter on Toleration.

great evil would arise from allowing a Roman Catholic to be captain of a company or alderman of a borough. It is probable that, in a few years, the sect so long detested by the nation would, with general applause, have been admitted to office and to Parliament.

If, on the other hand, James should attempt to promote the interest of his Church by violating the fundamental laws of his kingdom and the solemn promises which he had repeatedly made in the face of the whole world, it could hardly be doubted that the charges which it had been the fashion to bring against the Roman Catholic religion would be considered by all Protestants as fully established. For, if ever a Roman Catholic could be expected to keep faith with heretics, James might have been expected to keep faith with the Anglican clergy. To them he owed his crown. But for their strenuous opposition to the Exclusion Bill he would have been a banished man. He had repeatedly and emphatically acknowledged the debt which he owed to them, and had vowed to maintain them in all their legal rights. If he could not be bound by ties like these, it must be evident that, where his superstition was concerned, no tie of gratitude or of honour could bind him. To trust him would thenceforth be impossible ; and, if his people could not trust him, what member of his Church could they trust ? He was not supposed to be constitutionally or habitually treacherous. To his blunt manner, and to his want of consideration for the feelings of others, he owed a much higher reputation for sincerity than he at all deserved. His eulogists affected to call him James the Just. If then it should appear that, in turning Papist, he had also turned dissembler and promisebreaker, what conclusion was likely to be drawn by a nation already disposed to believe that Popery had a pernicious influence on the moral character ?

For these reasons many of the most eminent Roman Catholics of that age, and among them the Supreme Pontiff, were of opinion that the interest of their Church in our island would be most effectually promoted by a moderate and constitutional policy. But such considerations had no effect on the slow understanding and imperious temper of James. In his eagerness to remove the disabilities under which the professors of his religion lay, he took a course which convinced the most enlightened and tolerant Protestants of his time that those disabilities were essential to the safety of the state.

To his policy the English Roman Catholics owed three years of lawless and insolent triumph, and a hundred and forty years of subjection and degradation.

Many members of his Church held commissions in the newly raised regiments. This breach of the law for a time passed uncensured: for men were not disposed to note every irregularity which was committed by a King suddenly called upon to defend his crown and his life against rebels. But the danger was now over. The insurgents had been vanquished and punished. Their unsuccessful attempt had strengthened the government which they had hoped to overthrow. Yet still James continued to grant commissions to unqualified persons; and speedily it was announced that he was determined to be no longer bound by the Test Act, that he hoped to induce the Parliament to repeal that Act, but that, if the Parliament proved refractory, he would not the less have his own way. *Violation of the Test Act.*

As soon as this was known, a deep murmur, the forerunner of a tempest, gave him warning that the spirit before which his grandfather, his father, and his brother had been compelled to recede, though dormant, was not extinct. Opposition appeared first in the cabinet. Halifax did not attempt to conceal his disgust and alarm. At the Council board he courageously gave utterance to those feelings which, as it soon appeared, pervaded the whole nation. None of his colleagues seconded him; and the subject dropped. He was summoned to the royal closet, and had two long conferences with his master. James tried the effect of compliments and blandishments, but to no purpose. Halifax positively refused to promise that he would give his vote in the House of Lords for the repeal either of the Test Act or of the Habeas Corpus Act. *Disgrace of Halifax*

Some of those who were about the King advised him not, on the eve of the meeting of Parliament, to drive the most eloquent and accomplished statesman of the age into opposition. They represented that Halifax loved the dignity of office, that, while he continued to be Lord President, it would be hardly possible for him to put forth his whole strength against the government, and that to dismiss him from his high post was to emancipate him from all restraint. The King was peremptory. Halifax was informed that his services were no longer needed, and his name was struck out of the Council Book.*

His dismission produced a great sensation not only in

* Council Book. The erasure is dated Oct. 21. 1685. Barillon, Oct. $\frac{18}{28}$.

England, but also at Paris, at Vienna, and at the Hague:
for it was well known that he had always laboured to coun-

General
discontent.
teract the influence exercised by the court of Versailles on
English affairs. Lewis expressed much pleasure at the news.
The ministers of the United Provinces and of the House of
Austria, on the other hand, extolled the wisdom and virtue of
the discarded statesman in a manner which gave serious
offence at Whitehall. James was particularly angry with the
secretary of the imperial legation, who did not scruple to say
that the eminent service which Halifax had performed in the
debate on the Exclusion Bill had been requited with gross
ingratitude.*

It soon became clear that Halifax would have many followers. A portion of the Tories, with their old leader,
Danby, at their head, began to hold Whiggish language.
Even the prelates hinted that there was a point at which
the loyalty due to the prince must yield to higher considerations. The discontent of the chiefs of the army was still
more extraordinary and still more formidable. Already
began to appear the first symptoms of that feeling which,
three years later, impelled so many officers of high rank te
desert the royal standard. Men who had never before had a
scruple had on a sudden become strangely scrupulous.
Churchill gently whispered that the King was going too far.
Kirke, just returned from his Western butchery, swore to
stand by the Protestant religion. Even if he abjured the
faith in which he had been bred, he would never, he said,
become a Papist. He was already bespoken. If ever he did
apostatise, he was bound by a solemn promise to the Emperor
of Morocco to turn Mussulman.†

Persecu-
tion of the
French
Huguenots.
While the nation, agitated by many strong emotions, looked
anxiously forward to the reassembling of the Houses, tidings,
which increased the prevailing excitement, arrived from
France.

The long and heroic struggle which the Huguenots had
maintained against the French government had been brought
to a final close by the ability and vigour of Richelieu. That
great statesman vanquished them; but he confirmed to them
the liberty of conscience which had been bestowed on them

---

* Barillon, $\frac{Oct. 26.}{Nov. 5.}$ 1685; Lewis to
Barillon, $\frac{Oct. 27.}{Nov. 6.}$; Nov. $\frac{6}{16}$.

† There is a remarkable account of

the first appearance of the symptoms of
discontent among the Tories in a letter
of Halifax to Chesterfield, written in
October, 1685. Burnet, i. 684.

by the edict of Nantes. They were suffered, under some restraints of no galling kind, to worship God according to their own ritual, and to write in defence of their own doctrine. They were admissible to political and military employment; nor did their heresy, during a considerable time, practically impede their rise in the world. Some of them commanded the armies of the state; and others presided over important departments of the civil administration. At length a change took place. Lewis the Fourteenth had, from an early age, regarded the Calvinists with an aversion at once religious and political. As a zealous Roman Catholic, he detested their theological dogmas. As a prince fond of arbitrary power, he detested those republican theories which were intermingled with the Genevese divinity. He gradually retrenched all the privileges which the schismatics enjoyed. He interfered with the education of Protestant children, confiscated property bequeathed to Protestant consistories, and on frivolous pretexts shut up Protestant Churches. The Protestant ministers were harassed by the taxgatherers. The Protestant magistrates were deprived of the honour of nobility. The Protestant officers of the royal household were informed that His Majesty dispensed with their services. Orders were given that no Protestant should be admitted into the legal profession. The oppressed sect showed some faint signs of that spirit which in the preceding century had bidden defiance to the whole power of the House of Valois. Massacres and executions followed. Dragoons were quartered in the towns where the heretics were numerous, and in the country seats of the heretic gentry; and the cruelty and licentiousness of these rude missionaries was sanctioned or leniently censured by the government. Still, however, the edict of Nantes, though practically violated in its most essential provisions, had not been formally rescinded; and the King repeatedly declared in solemn public acts that he was resolved to maintain it. But the bigots and flatterers who had his ear gave him advice which he was but too willing to take. They represented to him that his rigorous policy had been eminently successful, that little or no resistance had been made to his will, that thousands of Huguenots had already been converted, that, if he would take the one decisive step which yet remained, those who were still obstinate would speedily submit, France would be purged from the taint of heresy and her prince would have earned a heavenly crown not less glorious than that of Saint Lewis. These arguments prevailed. The final blow was struck. The edict of Nantes was revoked; and a crowd of decrees against the sectaries appeared in rapid succession. Boys and girls were torn from their parents and sent to be educated in convents. All Calvinistic ministers were commanded either to abjure their religion or to quit their country within a fortnight. The other professors of the reformed faith were forbidden to leave the kingdom; and, in order to prevent them from making their escape, the outports and frontiers were strictly guarded. It was thought that the flocks, thus separated from the evil shepherds, would soon return to the true fold. But in spite of all the vigilance of the military police there was a vast emigration. It was calculated that, in a few months, fifty thousand families quitted France for ever. Nor were the refugees such as a country can well spare. They were generally persons of intelligent minds, of industrious habits, and of austere morals. In the list are to be found names eminent in war, in science, in literature, and in art. Some of the exiles offered their swords to William of Orange, and distinguished themselves by the fury with which they fought against their persecutor. Others avenged themselves with weapons still more formidable, and, by means of the presses of Holland, England, and Germany, inflamed, during thirty years, the public mind of Europe against the French government. A more peaceful class erected silk manufactories in the eastern suburb of London. One detachment of emigrants taught the Saxons to make the stuffs and hats of which France had hitherto enjoyed a monopoly. Another planted the first vines in the neighbourhood of the Cape of Good Hope.*

In ordinary circumstances the courts of Spain and of Rome would have eagerly applauded a prince who had made vigorous war on heresy. But such was the hatred inspired by the injustice and haughtiness of Lewis that, when he became a persecutor, the courts of Spain and Rome took the side of religious liberty, and loudly reprobated the cruelty of turning a savage and licentious soldiery loose on an unoffending people.† One cry of grief and rage rose from the

---

* The contemporary tracts in various languages on the subject of this persecution are innumerable. An eminently clear, terse, and spirited summary will be found in Voltaire's Siècle de Louis XIV.

† "Misionarios embotados," says Ronquillo. "Apostoli armati," says

whole of Protestant Europe. The tidings of the revocation of the edict of Nantes reached England about a week before the day to which the Parliament stood adjourned. It was clear then that the spirit of Gardiner and of Alva was still the spirit of the Roman Catholic Church. Lewis was not inferior to James in generosity and humanity, and was certainly far superior to James in all the abilities and acquirements of a statesman. Lewis had, like James, repeatedly promised to respect the privileges of his Protestant subjects. Yet Lewis was now avowedly a persecutor of the reformed religion. What reason was there, then, to doubt that James waited only for an opportunity to follow the example? He was already forming, in defiance of the law, a military force officered to a great extent by Roman Catholics. Was there anything unreasonable in the apprehension that this force might be employed to do what the French dragoons had done?

James was almost as much disturbed as his subjects by the conduct of the court of Versailles. In truth, that court had acted as if it had meant to embarrass and annoy him. He was about to ask from a Protestant legislature a full toleration for Roman Catholics. Nothing, therefore, could be more unwelcome to him than the intelligence that, in a neighbouring country, toleration had just been withdrawn by a Roman Catholic government from Protestants. His vexation was increased by a speech which the Bishop of Valence, in the name of the Gallican clergy, addressed at this time to Lewis the Fourteenth. The pious Sovereign of England, the orator said, looked to the most Christian King for support against a heretical nation. It was remarked that the members of the House of Commons showed particular anxiety to procure copies of this harangue, and that it was read by all Englishmen with indignation and alarm.* James was desirous to counteract the impression which these things had made, and was also at that moment by no means unwilling to let all Europe see that he was not the slave of France. He therefore declared publicly that he disapproved of the manner in which the Huguenots had been treated, granted to the exiles

Effect of that persecution in England.

Innocent. There is, in the Mackintosh Collection, a remarkable letter on this subject from Ronquillo, dated $\frac{\text{March 26.}}{\text{April 5.}}$ 1686. See Venier, Relatione di Francia, 1689, quoted by Professor Ranke in his Römischen Päpste, book viii.

* "Mi dicono che tutti questi parlamentarii ne hanno voluto copia, il che assolutamente avrà causate pessime impressioni."—Adda, Nov. $\frac{9}{19}$. 1685. See Evelyn's Diary, Nov. 3.

some relief from his privy purse, and, by letters under his great seal, invited his subjects to imitate his liberality. In a very few months it became clear that all this compassion was feigned for the purpose of cajoling his Parliament, that he regarded the refugees with mortal hatred, and that he regretted nothing so much as his own inability to do what Lewis had done.

Meeting of Parliament; speech of the King.

On the ninth of November the Houses met. The Commons were summoned to the bar of the Lords; and the King spoke from the throne. His speech had been composed by himself. He congratulated his loving subjects on the suppression of the rebellion in the West: but he added that the speed with which that rebellion had risen to a formidable height, and the length of time during which it had continued to rage, must convince all men how little dependence could be placed on the militia. He had, therefore, made additions to the regular army. The charge of that army would henceforth be more than double of what it had been; and he trusted that the Commons would grant him the means of defraying the increased expense. He then informed his hearers that he had employed some officers who had not taken the test; but he knew those officers to be fit for public trust. He feared that artful men might avail themselves of this irregularity to disturb the harmony which existed between himself and his Parliament. But he would speak out. He was determined not to part with servants on whose fidelity he could rely, and whose help he might perhaps soon need.[*]

An opposition formed in the House of Commons.

This explicit declaration that he had broken the laws which were regarded by the nation as the chief safeguards of the established religion, and that he was resolved to persist in breaking those laws, was not likely to soothe the excited feelings of his subjects. The Lords, seldom disposed to take the lead in opposition to a government, consented to vote him formal thanks for what he had said. But the Commons were in a less complying mood. When they had returned to their own House there was a long silence; and the faces of many of the most respectable members expressed deep concern. At length Middleton rose and moved the House to go instantly into committee on the King's speech: but Sir Edmund Jennings, a zealous Tory from Yorkshire, who was supposed to speak the sentiments of Danby, protested against this

[*] Lords' Journals, Nov. 9. 1685. S. M. stessa abbia composto il discorso." " Vengo assicurato," says Adda, " che —Despatch of Nov. $\frac{14}{26}$. 1685.

course, and demanded time for consideration. Sir Thomas Clarges, maternal uncle of the Duke of Albemarle, and long distinguished in Parliament as a man of business and a vigilant steward of the public money, took the same side. The feeling of the House could not be mistaken. Sir John Ernley, Chancellor of the Exchequer, insisted that the delay should not exceed forty-eight hours : but he was overruled ; and it was resolved that the discussion should be postponed for three days.*

The interval was well employed by those who took the lead against the Court. They had indeed no light work to perform. In three days a country party was to be organised. The difficulty of the task is in our age not easily to be appreciated; for in our age all the nation assists at every deliberation of the Lords and Commons. What is said by the leaders of the ministry and of the opposition after midnight is read by the whole metropolis at dawn, by the inhabitants of Northumberland and Cornwall in the afternoon, and in Ireland and the Highlands of Scotland on the morrow. In our age, therefore, the stages of legislation, the rules of debate, the tactics of faction, the opinions, temper, and style of every active member of either house, are familiar to hundreds of thousands. Every man who now enters Parliament possesses what, in the seventeeth century, would have been called a great stock of parliamentary knowledge. Such knowledge was then to be obtained only by actual parliamentary service. The difference between an old and a new member was as great as the difference between a veteran soldier and a recruit just taken from the plough ; and James's Parliament contained a most unusual proportion of new members, who had brought from their country seats to Westminster no political knowledge and many violent prejudices. These gentlemen hated the Papists, but hated the Whigs not less intensely, and regarded the King with superstitious veneration. To form an opposition out of such materials was a feat which required the most skilful and delicate management. Some men of great weight, however, undertook the work, and performed it with success. Several experienced Whig politicians who had not seats in that Parliament, gave

* Commons' Journals; Bramston's Memoirs; James Van Leeuwen to the States General, Nov. $\frac{10}{20}$. 1685. Van Leeuwen was secretary of the Dutch embassy, and conducted the correspondence in the absence of Van Citters. As to Clarges, see Burnet, i. 98.

useful advice and information.   On the day preceding that which had been fixed for the debate, many meetings were held at which the leaders instructed the novices; and it soon appeared that these exertions had not been thrown away.*

Sentiments of foreign governments.

The foreign embassies were all in a ferment.   It was well understood that a few days would now decide the great question, whether the King of England was or was not to be the vassal of the King of France.   The ministers of the House of Austria were most anxious that James should give satisfaction to his Parliament.   Innocent had sent to London two persons charged to inculcate moderation, both by admonition and by example.   One of them was John Leyburn, an English Dominican, who had been secretary to Cardinal Howard, and who, with some learning and a rich vein of natural humour, was the most cautious, dexterous, and taciturn of men. He had recently been consecrated Bishop of Adrumetum, and named Vicar Apostolic in Great Britain.   Ferdinand, Count of Adda, an Italian of no eminent abilities, but of mild temper and courtly manners, had been appointed Nuncio.   These functionaries were eagerly welcomed by James.   No Roman Catholic Bishop had exercised spiritual functions in the island during more than half a century.   No Nuncio had been received here during the hundred and twenty-seven years which had elapsed since the death of Mary.   Leyburn was lodged in Whitehall, and received a pension of a thousand pounds a year.   Adda did not yet assume a public character.   He passed for a foreigner of rank whom curiosity had brought to London, appeared daily at court, and was treated with high consideration.   Both the Papal emissaries did their best to diminish, as much as possible, the odium inseparable from the offices which they filled, and to restrain the rash zeal of James.   The Nuncio, in particular, declared that nothing could be more injurious to the interests of the Church of Rome than a rupture between the King and the Parliament.†

Barillon was active on the other side.   The instructions which he received from Versailles on this occasion well deserve to be studied; for they furnish a key to the policy systema-

* Barillon, Nov. $\frac{16}{26}$. 1685.

† Dodd's Church History; Van Leeuwen, Nov. $\frac{17}{27}$. 1685; Barillon, Dec. 24. 1685. Barillon says of Adda, "On l'avoit fait prévenir que la sureté et l'avantage des Catholiques consistoient dans une réunion entière de sa Majesté Britannique et de son parlement." Letters of Innocent to James, dated $\frac{July\ 27.}{Aug.\ 6.}$ and $\frac{Sept.\ 25.}{Oct.\ 5.}$ 1685; Despatches of Adda, Nov. $\frac{9}{19}$. and Nov. $\frac{16}{26}$. 1685. The very interesting correspondence of Adda, copied from the Papal archives, is in the British Museum.

tically pursued by his master towards England during the twenty years which preceded our revolution. The advices from Madrid, Lewis wrote, were alarming. Strong hopes were entertained there that James would ally himself closely with the House of Austria, as soon as he should be assured that his Parliament would give him no trouble. In these circumstances, it was evidently the interest of France that the Parliament should prove refractory. Barillon was therefore directed to act, with all possible precautions against detection, the part of a makebait. At court he was to omit no opportunity of stimulating the religious zeal and the kingly pride of James ; but at the same time it might be desirable to have some secret communication with the malecontents. Such communication would indeed be hazardous, and would require the utmost adroitness : yet it might perhaps be in the power of the Ambassador, without committing himself or his government, to animate the zeal of the opposition for the laws and liberties of England, and to let it be understood that those laws and liberties were not regarded by his master with an unfriendly eye.*

Lewis, when he dictated these instructions, did not foresee how speedily and how completely his uneasiness would be removed by the obstinacy and stupidity of James. On the twelfth of November the House of Commons resolved itself into a committee on the royal speech. The Solicitor General, Heneage Finch, was in the chair. The debate was conducted by the chiefs of the new country party with rare tact and address. No expression indicating disrespect to the Sovereign or sympathy for rebels was suffered to escape. The Western insurrection was always mentioned with abhorrence. Nothing was said of the barbarities of Kirke and Jeffreys. It was admitted that the heavy expenditure which had been occasioned by the late troubles justified the King in asking some further supply : but strong objections were made to the augmentation of the army and to the infraction of the Test Act.

Committee of the Commons on the King's Speech.

The subject of the Test Act the courtiers appear to have carefully avoided. They harangued, however, with some force on the great superiority of a regular army to a militia. One of them tauntingly asked whether the defence of the kingdom was to be entrusted to the beefeaters. Another said that he should be glad to know how the Devonshire trainbands, who

* This most remarkable despatch and will be found in the Appendix to bears date the $\frac{9}{15}$th of November 1685, Mr. Fox's History.

had fled in confusion before Monmouth's scythemen, would have faced the household troops of Lewis. But these arguments had little effect on Cavaliers who still remembered with bitterness the stern rule of the Protector. The general feeling was forcibly expressed by the first of the Tory country gentlemen of England, Edward Seymour. He admitted that the militia was not in a satisfactory state, but maintained that it might be remodelled. The remodelling might require money; but, for his own part, he would rather give a million to keep up a force from which he had nothing to fear, than half a million to keep up a force of which he must ever be afraid. Let the trainbands be disciplined; let the navy be strengthened; and the country would be secure. A standing army was at best a mere drain on the public resources. The soldier was withdrawn from all useful labour. He produced nothing: he consumed the fruits of the industry of other men; and he domineered over those by whom he was supported. But the nation was now threatened, not only with a standing army, but with a Popish standing army, with a standing army officered by men who might be very amiable and honourable, but who were on principle enemies to the constitution of the realm. Sir William Twisden, member for the county of Kent, spoke on the same side with great keenness and loud applause. Sir Richard Temple, one of the few Whigs who had a seat in that Parliament, dexterously accommodating his speech to the temper of his audience, reminded the House that a standing army had been found, by experience, to be as dangerous to the just authority of princes as to the liberty of nations. Sir John Maynard, the most learned lawyer of his time, took part in the debate. He was now more than eighty years old, and could well remember the political contests of the reign of James the First. He had sate in the Long Parliament, and had taken part with the Roundheads, but had always been for lenient counsels, and had laboured to bring about a general reconciliation. His abilities, which age had not impaired, and his professional knowledge, which had long overawed all Westminster Hall, commanded the ear of the House of Commons. He, too, declared himself against the augmentation of the regular forces.

After much debate it was resolved that a supply should be granted to the Crown; but it was also resolved that a bill should be brought in for making the militia more efficient. This last resolution was tantamount to a declaration against the standing army. The King was greatly displeased; and it was whispered that, if things went on thus, the session would not be of long duration.*

On the morrow the contention was renewed. The language of the country party was perceptibly bolder and sharper than on the preceding day. That paragraph of the King's speech which related to supply preceded the paragraph which related to the test. On this ground Middleton proposed that the paragraph relating to supply should be first considered in committee. The opposition moved the previous question. They contended that the reasonable and constitutional practice was to grant no money till grievances had been redressed, and that there would be an end of this practice if the House thought itself bound servilely to follow the order in which matters were mentioned by the King from the throne.

The division was taken on the question whether Middleton's motion should be put. The Noes were ordered by the Speaker to go forth into the lobby. They resented this much, and complained loudly of his servility and partiality: for they conceived that, according to the intricate and subtle rule which was then in force, and which, in our time, was superseded by a more rational and convenient practice, they were entitled to keep their seats; and it was held by all the parliamentary tacticians of that age that the party which stayed in the House had an advantage over the party which went out; for the accommodation on the benches was then so deficient that no person who had been fortunate enough to get a good seat was willing to lose it. Nevertheless, to the dismay of the ministers, many persons on whose votes the Court had absolutely depended were seen moving towards the door. Among them was Charles Fox, Paymaster of the Forces, and son of Sir Stephen Fox, Clerk of the Green Cloth. The Paymaster had been induced by his friends to absent himself during part

* Commons' Journals, Nov. 12. 1685; Van Leeuwen, Nov. $\frac{13}{23}$.; Barillon, Nov. $\frac{16}{26}$.; Sir John Bramston's Memoirs. The best report of the debates of the Commons in November 1685, is one of which the history is somewhat curious. There are two manuscript copies of it in the British Museum, Harl. 7187.; Lans. 253. In these copies the names of the speakers are given at length. The author of the Life of James published in 1702 transcribed this report, but gave only the initials of the speakers. The editors of Chandler's Debates and of the Parliamentary History guessed from these initials at the names, and sometimes guessed wrong. They ascribe to Waller a very remarkable speech, which will hereafter be mentioned, and which was really made by Windham, member for Salisbury. It was with some concern that I found myself forced to give up the belief that the last words uttered in public by Waller were so honourable to him.

of the discussion. But his anxiety had become insupportable. He came down to the Speaker's chamber, heard part of the debate, withdrew, and, after hesitating for an hour or two between conscience and five thousand pounds a year, took a manly resolution and rushed into the House just in time to vote. Two officers of the army, Colonel John Darcy, son of the Lord Conyers, and Captain James Kendall, withdrew to the lobby. Middleton went down to the bar and expostulated warmly with them. He particularly addressed himself to Kendall, a needy retainer of the Court, who had, in obedience to the royal mandate, been sent to Parliament by a packed corporation in Cornwall, and who had recently obtained a grant of a hundred head of rebels sentenced to transportation. " Sir," said Middleton, " have not you a troop of horse in His Majesty's service?" " Yes, my Lord," answered Kendall : " but my elder brother is just dead, and has left me seven hundred a year."

Defeat of the government.

When the tellers had done their office it appeared that the Ayes were one hundred and eighty-two, and the Noes one hundred and eighty-three. In that House of Commons which had been brought together by the unscrupulous use of chicanery, of corruption, and of violence, in that House of Commons of which James had said that more than eleven twelfths of the members were such as he would himself have nominated, the Court had sustained a defeat on a vital question.*

In consequence of this vote the expressions which the King had used respecting the test were taken into consideration. It was resolved, after much discussion, that an address should be presented to him, reminding him that he could not legally continue to employ officers who refused to qualify, and pressing him to give such directions as might quiet the apprehensions and jealousies of his people.†

A motion was then made that the Lords should be requested to join in the address. Whether this motion was honestly made by the opposition, in the hope that the concurrence of the peers would add weight to the remonstrance, or artfully made by the courtiers, in the hope that a breach be-

---

* Commons' Journals, Nov. 13. 1685; Bramston's Memoirs; Reresby's Memoirs; Barillon, Nov. $\frac{16}{26}$.; Van Leeuwen, Nov. $\frac{13}{23}$.; Memoirs of Sir Stephen Fox, 1717; The Case of the Church of Eng-

land fairly stated; Burnet, i. 666. and Speaker Onslow's note.

† Commons' Journals, Nov. 13. 1685; Harl. MS. 7187.; Lansdowne MS. 253.

tween the Houses might be the consequence, it is now impossible to discover. The proposition was rejected.*

The House then resolved itself into a committee, for the purpose of considering the amount of supply to be granted. The King wanted fourteen hundred thousand pounds : but the ministers saw that it would be vain to ask for so large a sum. The Chancellor of the Exchequer mentioned twelve hundred thousand pounds. The chiefs of the opposition replied that to vote for such a grant would be to vote for the permanence of the present military establishment : they were disposed to give only so much as might suffice to keep the regular troops on foot till the militia could be remodelled ; and they therefore proposed four hundred thousand pounds. The courtiers exclaimed against this motion as unworthy of the House and disrespectful to the King : but they were manfully encountered. One of the Western members, John Windham, who sate for Salisbury, especially distinguished himself. He had always, he said, looked with dread and aversion on standing armies ; and recent experience had strengthened those feelings. He then ventured to touch on a theme which had hitherto been studiously avoided. He described the desolation of the Western counties. The people, he said, were weary of the oppression of the troops, weary of free quarters, of depredations, of still fouler crimes which the law called felonies, but for which, when perpetrated by this class of felons, no redress could be obtained. The King's servants had indeed told the House that excellent rules had been laid down for the government of the army ; but none could venture to say that these rules had been observed. What, then, was the inevitable inference ? Did not the contrast between the paternal injunctions issued from the throne and the insupportable tyranny of the soldiers prove that the

* The conflict of testimony on this subject is most extraordinary ; and, after long consideration, I must own that the balance seems to me to be exactly poised. In the Life of James (1702), the motion is represented as a court motion. This account is confirmed by a remarkable passage in the Stuart Papers, which was corrected by the Pretender himself. (Life of James the Second, ii. 55.) On the other hand, Reresby, who was present, and Barillon, who ought to have been well informed, represent the motion as an opposition motion. The Harleian and Lansdowne manuscripts differ in the single word on which the whole depends. Unfortunately Bramston was not at the House that day. James Van Leeuwen mentions the motion and the division, but does not add a word which can throw the smallest light on the state of parties. I must own myself unable to draw with confidence any inference from the names of the tellers, Sir Joseph Williamson and Sir Francis Russell for the majority, and Lord Ancram and Sir Henry Goodricke for the minority. I should have thought Lord Ancram likely to go with the court, and Sir Henry Goodricke likely to go with the opposition.

army was even now too strong for the prince as well as for the people ? The Commons might surely, with perfect consistency, while they reposed entire confidence in the intentions of His Majesty, refuse to make any addition to a force which it was clear that His Majesty could not manage.

Second defeat of the government.

The motion that the sum to be granted should not exceed four hundred thousand pounds, was lost by twelve votes. This victory of the ministers was little better than a defeat. The leaders of the country party, nothing disheartened, retreated a little, made another stand, and proposed the sum of seven hundred thousand pounds. The committee divided again, and the courtiers were beaten by two hundred and twelve votes to one hundred and seventy.*

The King reprimands the Commons.

On the following day the Commons went in procession to Whitehall with their address on the subject of the test. The King received them on his throne. The address was drawn up in respectful and affectionate language; for the great majority of those who had voted for it were zealously and even superstitiously loyal, and had readily agreed to insert some complimentary phrases, and to omit every word which the courtiers thought offensive. The answer of James was a cold and sullen reprimand. He declared himself greatly displeased and amazed that the Commons should have profited so little by the admonition which he had given them. " But," said he, " however you may proceed on your part, I will be very steady in all the promises which I have made to you."†

The Commons reassembled in their chamber, discontented, yet somewhat overawed. To most of them the King was still an object of filial reverence. Three more years filled with bitter injuries, and with not less bitter insults, were scarcely sufficient to dissolve the ties which bound the Cavalier gentry to the throne.

The Speaker repeated the substance of the King's reply. There was, for some time, a solemn stillness : then the order of the day was read in regular course ; and the House went into committee on the bill for remodelling the militia.

Coke committed by the Commons for disrespect to the King.

In a few hours, however, the spirit of the opposition revived. When, at the close of the day, the Speaker resumed the chair, Wharton, the boldest and most active of the Whigs, proposed that a time should be appointed for taking His Majesty's answer into consideration. John Coke, member for Derby,

* Commons' Journals, Nov. 16. 1685;   † Commons' Journals, Nov. 17, 18. Harl. MS. 7187. ; Lansdowne MS. 235.   1685.

though a noted Tory, seconded Wharton. " I hope," he said, " that we are all Englishmen, and that we shall not be frightened from our duty by a few high words."

It was manfully, but not wisely, spoken. The whole House was in a tempest. " Take down his words," " To the bar," " To the Tower," resounded from every side. Those who were most lenient proposed that the offender should be reprimanded : but the ministers vehemently insisted that he should be sent to prison. The House might pardon, they said, offences committed against itself, but had no right to pardon an insult offered to the Crown. Coke was sent to the Tower. The indiscretion of one man had deranged the whole system of tactics which had been so ably concerted by the chiefs of the opposition. It was in vain that, at that moment, Edward Seymour attempted to rally his followers, exhorted them to fix a day for discussing the King's answer, and expressed his confidence that the discussion would be conducted with the respect due from subjects to the sovereign. The members were so much cowed by the royal displeasure, and so much incensed by the rudeness of Coke, that it would not have been safe to divide.*

The House adjourned ; and the ministers flattered themselves that the spirit of opposition was quelled. But on the morrow, the nineteenth of November, new and alarming symptoms appeared. The time had arrived for taking into consideration the petitions which had been presented from all parts of England against the late elections. When, on the first meeting of the Parliament, Seymour had complained of the force and fraud by which the government had prevented the sense of constituent bodies from being fairly taken, he had found no seconder. But many who had then flinched from his side had subsequently taken heart, and, with Sir John Lowther, member for Cumberland, at their head, had, before the recess, suggested that there ought to be an enquiry into the abuses which had so much excited the public mind. The House was now in a much more angry temper ; and many voices were boldly raised in menace and accusation. The ministers were told that the nation expected, and should have, signal redress. Meanwhile it was dexterously intimated that the best atonement which a gentleman who had been brought into the House by irregular means could make to the public

* Commons' Journals, Nov. 18. 1685 ; Harl. MS. 7187. ; Lansdowne MS. 253 ; Burnet, i. 667.

was to use his ill acquired power in defence of the religion and liberties of his country. No member, who, in that crisis, did his duty, had anything to fear. It might be necessary to unseat him; but the whole influence of the opposition should be employed to procure his re-election.*

Opposition to the government in the Lords. The Earl of Devonshire.

On the same day it became clear that the spirit of opposition had spread from the Commons to the Lords, and even to the episcopal bench. William Cavendish, Earl of Devonshire, took the lead in the Upper House; and he was well qualified to do so. In wealth and influence he was second to none of the English nobles; and the general voice designated him as the finest gentleman of his time. His magnificence, his taste, his talents, his classical learning, his high spirit, the grace and urbanity of his manners, were admitted by his enemies. His eulogists, unhappily, could not pretend that his morals had escaped untainted from the widespread contagion of that age. Though an enemy of Popery and of arbitrary power, he had been averse to extreme courses, had been willing, when the Exclusion Bill was lost, to agree to a compromise, and had never been concerned in the illegal and imprudent schemes which had brought discredit on the Whig party. But, while blaming part of the conduct of his friends, he had not failed to perform zealously the most arduous and perilous duties of friendship. He had stood near Russell at the bar, had parted from him on the sad morning of the execution with close embraces and with many bitter tears, nay, had offered to manage an escape at the hazard of his own life.† This great nobleman now proposed that a day should be fixed for considering the royal speech. It was contended, on the other side, that the Lords, by voting thanks for the speech, had precluded themselves from complaining of it. But this objection was treated with contempt by Halifax. "Such thanks," he said with the sarcastic pleasantry in which he excelled, "imply no approbation. We are thankful whenever our gracious Sovereign deigns to speak to us. Especially thankful

---

* Lonsdale's Memoirs. Burnet tells us (i. 667.) that a sharp debate about elections took place in the House of Commons after Coke's committal. It must therefore have been on the 19th of November; for Coke was committed late on the 18th, and the Parliament was prorogued on the 20th. Burnet's narrative is confirmed by the Journals, from which it appears that several elections were under discussion on the 19th.

† Burnet, i. 560.; Funeral Sermon of the Duke of Devonshire. preached by Kennet, 1708; Travels of Cosmo III. in England; The Hazard of a Death-bed Repentance argued from the Remorse of Conscience of W——, late D—— of D——, when dying, a most absurd pamphlet by John Dunton which reached a tenth edition.

are we when, as on the present occasion, he speaks out, and gives us fair warning of what we are to suffer."[*]   Doctor Henry Compton, Bishop of London, spoke strongly for the motion. Though not gifted with eminent abilities, nor deeply versed in the learning of his profession, he was always heard by the House with respect; for he was one of the few clergymen who could, in that age, boast of noble blood. His own loyalty, and the loyalty of his family, had been signally proved. His father, the second Earl of Northampton, had fought bravely for King Charles the First, and, surrounded by the parliamentary soldiers, had fallen, sword in hand, refusing to give or take quarter. The Bishop himself, before he was ordained, had borne arms in the Guards; and, though he generally did his best to preserve the gravity and sobriety befitting a prelate, some flashes of his military spirit would, to the last, occasionally break forth. He had been entrusted with the religious education of the two Princesses, and had acquitted himself of that important duty in a manner which had satisfied all good Protestants, and had secured to him considerable influence over the minds of his pupils, especially of the Lady Anne.[†] He now declared that he was empowered to speak the sense of his brethren, and that, in their opinion and in his own, the whole civil and ecclesiastical constitution of the realm was in danger.

The Bishop of London.

One of the most remarkable speeches of that day was made by a young man, whose eccentric career was destined to amaze Europe. This was Charles Mordaunt, Viscount Mordaunt, widely renowned, many years later, as Earl of Peterborough. Already he had given abundant proofs of his courage, of his capacity, and of that strange unsoundness of mind which made his courage and capacity almost useless to his country. Already he had distinguished himself as a wit and a scholar, as a soldier and a sailor. He had even set his heart on rivalling Bourdaloue and Bossuet. Though an avowed freethinker, he had sate up all night at sea to compose sermons, and had with great difficulty been prevented from edifying the crew of a man of war with his pious oratory.[‡] He now addressed the House of Peers, for the first time, with characteristic eloquence, sprightliness, and audacity. He blamed the Com-

Viscount Mordaunt.

---

* Bramston's Memoirs. Burnet is incorrect both as to the time when the remark was made and as to the person who made it. In Halifax's Letter to a Dissenter will be found a remarkable allusion to this discussion.

† Wood, Ath. Ox.; Gooch's Funeral Sermon on Bishop Compton.

‡ Teonge's Diary.

mons for not having taken a bolder line. " They have been afraid," he said, " to speak out. They have talked of apprehensions and jealousies. What have apprehension and jealousy to do here? Apprehension and jealousy are the feelings with which we regard future and uncertain evils. The evil which we are considering is neither future nor uncertain. A standing army exists. It is officered by Papists. We have no foreign enemy. There is no rebellion in the land. For what, then, is this force maintained, except for the purpose of subverting our laws, and establishing that arbitrary power which is so justly abhorred by Englishmen?"*

Jeffreys spoke against the motion in the coarse and savage style of which he was a master; but he soon found that it was not quite so easy to browbeat the proud and powerful barons of England in their own hall as to intimidate advocates whose bread depended on his favour or prisoners whose necks were at his mercy. A man whose life has been passed in attacking and domineering, whatever may be his talents and courage, generally makes a poor figure when he is vigorously assailed: for, being unaccustomed to stand on the defensive, he becomes confused; and the knowledge that all those whom he has insulted are enjoying his confusion confuses him still more. Jeffreys was now, for the first time since he had become a great man, encountered on equal terms by adversaries who did not fear him. To the general delight, he passed at once from the extreme of insolence to the extreme of meanness, and could not refrain from weeping with rage and vexation.† Nothing indeed was wanting to his humiliation; for the House was crowded by about a hundred peers, a larger number than had voted even on the great day of the Exclusion Bill. The King, too, was present. His

---

* Barillon has given the best account of this debate. I will extract his report of Mordaunt's speech. " Milord Mordaunt, quoique jeune, parla avec éloquence et force. Il dit que la question n'étoit pas réduite, comme la Chambre des Communes le prétendoit, à guérir des jalousies et défiances, qui avoient lieu dans les choses incertaines; mais que ce qui se passoit ne l'étoit pas, qu'il y avoit une armée sur pied qui subsistoit, et qui étoit remplie d'officiers Catholiques, qui ne pouvoit être conservée que pour le renversement des loix, et que la subsistance de l'armée, quand il n'y a

aucune guerre ni au dedans ni au dehors, étoit l'établissement du gouvernement arbitraire, pour lequel les Anglois ont une aversion si bien fondée."

† He was very easily moved to tears. " He could not," says the author of the Panegyric, "refrain from weeping on bold affronts." And again: " They talk of his hectoring and proud carriage; what could be more humble than for a man in his great post to cry and sob?" In the Answer to the Panegyric it is said that " his having no command of his tears spoiled him for a hypocrite."

brother had been in the habit of attending the sittings of the Lords for amusement, and used often to say that a debate was as entertaining as a comedy. James came, not to be diverted, but in the hope that his presence might impose some restraint on the discussion. He was disappointed. The sense of the House was so strongly manifested that, after a closing speech, of great keenness, from Halifax, the courtiers did not venture to divide. An early day was fixed for taking the royal speech into consideration; and it was ordered that every peer who was in or near the capital should be in his place.*

On the following morning the King came down, in his robes, to the House of Lords. The Usher of the Black Rod summoned the Commons to the bar; and the Chancellor announced that the Parliament was prorogued to the tenth of February.† The members who had voted against the Court were dismissed from the public service. Charles Fox quitted the Pay Office: the Bishop of London ceased to be Dean of the Chapel Royal; and his name was struck out of the list of Privy Councillors.

Proroga-tion.

The effect of the prorogation was to put an end to a legal proceeding of the highest importance. Thomas Grey, Earl of Stamford, sprung from one of the most illustrious houses of England, had been recently arrested and committed close prisoner to the Tower on a charge of high treason. He was accused of having been concerned in the Rye House plot. A true bill had been found against him by the grand jury of the City of London, and had been removed into the House of Lords, the only court before which a temporal peer can, during a session of Parliament, be arraigned for any offence higher than a misdemeanour. The first of December had been fixed for the trial; and orders had been given that Westminster Hall should be fitted up with seats and hangings. In consequence of the prorogation, the hearing of the cause was postponed for an indefinite period; and Stamford soon regained his liberty.‡

Three other Whigs of great eminence were in confinement

* Lords' Journals, Nov. 19. 1685 Barillon, Nov. 23/Dec. 3.; Dutch Despatch, Nov. 20/30.; Luttrell's Diary, Nov. 19.; Burnet, i. 665. The closing speech of Halifax is mentioned by the Nuncio in his despatch of Nov. 16/26. Adda, about a month later, bears strong testimony to Halifax's powers. " Da questo uomo che ha gran credito nel parlamento, e grande

eloquenza, non si possono attendere che fiere contradizioni, e nel partito Regio non vi è un uomo da contrapporsi." Dec. 21/31.

† Lords' and Commons' Journals, Nov. 20. 1685.

‡ Lords' Journals, Nov. 11. 17. 18. 1685.

when the session closed, Charles Gerard, Lord Gerard of Brandon, eldest son of the Earl of Macclesfield, John Hampden, grandson of the renowned leader of the Long Parliament, and Henry Booth, Lord Delamere. Gerard and Hampden were accused of having taken part in the Rye House plot, Delamere of having abetted the Western insurrection.

Trials of Lord Gerard and of Hampden. It was not the intention of the government to put either Gerard or Hampden to death. Grey had stipulated for their lives before he consented to become a witness against them.* But there was a still stronger reason for sparing them. They were heirs to large property: but their fathers were still living. The Court could therefore get little in the way of forfeiture, and might get much in the way of ransom. Gerard was tried, and, from the very scanty accounts which have come down to us, seems to have defended himself with great spirit and force. He boasted of the exertions and sacrifices made by his family in the cause of Charles the First, and proved Rumsey, the witness who had murdered Russell by telling one story and Cornish by telling another, to be utterly undeserving of credit. The jury, with some hesitation, found a verdict of Guilty. After long imprisonment, Gerard was suffered to redeem himself.† Hampden had inherited the political opinions and a large share of the abilities of his grandfather, but had degenerated from the uprightness and the courage by which his grandfather had been distinguished. It appears that the prisoner was, with cruel cunning, long kept in an agony of suspense, in order that his family might be induced to pay largely for mercy. His spirit sank under the terrors of death. When brought to the bar of the Old Bailey, he not only pleaded guilty, but disgraced the illustrious name which he bore by abject submissions and entreaties. He protested that he had not been privy to the design of assassination; but he owned that he had meditated rebellion, professed deep repentance for his offence, implored the intercession of the Judges, and vowed that, if the royal clemency were extended to him his whole life should be passed in evincing his gratitude for such goodness. The Whigs were furious at his pusillanimity, and loudly declared him to be far more deserving of blame than Grey, who, even in turning King's evidence, had preserved a certain decorum. Hampden's life was spared; but his family paid several thousand

---

* Burnet, i. 646.   † Bramston's Memoirs; Luttrell's Diary.

pounds to the Chancellor. Some courtiers of less note succeeded in extorting smaller sums. The unhappy man had spirit enough to feel keenly the degradation to which he had stooped. He survived the day of his ignominy several years. He lived to see his party triumphant, to be once more an important member of it, and to make his persecutors tremble in their turn. But his prosperity was embittered by one insupportable recollection. He never regained his cheerfulness, and at length died by his own hand.*

That Delamere, if he had needed the royal mercy, would have found it, is not very probable. It is certain that every advantage which the letter of the law gave to the government was used against him without scruple or shame. He was in a different situation from that in which Stamford stood. The indictment against Stamford had been removed into the House of Lords during the session of Parliament, and therefore could not be prosecuted till the Parliament should reassemble. All the peers would then have voices, and would be judges as well of law as of fact. But the bill against Delamere was not found till after the prorogation.† He was therefore within the jurisdiction of the Court to which belongs, during a recess of Parliament, the cognisance of treasons and felonies committed by temporal peers; and this Court was then so constituted that no prisoner charged with a political offence could expect an impartial trial. The King named a Lord High Steward. The Lord High Steward named, at his discretion, certain peers to sit on their accused brother. The number to be summoned was indefinite. No challenge was allowed. A simple majority, provided that it consisted of twelve, was sufficient to convict. The High Steward was sole judge of the law; and the Lords Triers formed merely a jury to pronounce on the question of fact. Jeffreys was appointed High Steward. He selected thirty Triers; and the selection was characteristic of the man and of the times. All the thirty were in politics vehemently opposed to the prisoner. Fifteen of them were colonels of regiments, and might be removed from their lucrative commands at the pleasure of the King. Among the remaining fifteen were the Lord Treasurer, the principal Secretary of State, the Steward of the Household, the Comptroller of the Household, the Captain of the Band of Gentlemen Pensioners,

Trial of Delamere.

* See the trial in the Collection of State Trials; Bramston's Memoirs; Burnet, i. 647.; Lords' Journ. Dec. 20, 1689.
† Lords' Journals, Nov. 9, 10. 16. 1685.

the Queen's Chamberlain, and other persons who were bound
by strong ties of interest to the government. Nevertheless,
Delamere had some great advantages over the humbler culprits
who had been arraigned at the Old Bailey. There the jurymen, violent partisans, taken for a single day by courtly
Sheriffs from the mass of society and speedily sent back to
mingle with that mass, were under no restraint of shame, and
being little accustomed to weigh evidence, followed without
scruple the directions of the bench. But in the High Steward's Court every Trier was a man of some experience in grave
affairs. Every Trier filled a considerable space in the public
eye. Every Trier, beginning from the lowest, had to rise
separately and to give in his verdict, on his honour, before a
great concourse. That verdict, accompanied with his name,
would go to every part of the world, and would live in history.
Moreover, though the selected nobles were all Tories, and
almost all placemen, many of them had begun to look with
uneasiness on the King's proceedings, and to doubt whether
the case of Delamere might not soon be their own.

Jeffreys conducted himself, as was his wont, insolently and
unjustly. He had indeed an old grudge to stimulate his zeal.
He had been Chief Justice of Chester when Delamere, then
Mr. Booth, represented that county in Parliament. Booth
had bitterly complained to the Commons that the dearest
interests of his constituents were intrusted to a drunken jack-
pudding.* The revengeful judge was now not ashamed to
resort to artifices which even in an advocate would have been
culpable. He reminded the Lords Triers, in very significant
language, that Delamere had, in Parliament, objected to the
bill for attainting Monmouth, a fact which was not, and could
not be, in evidence. But it was not in the power of Jeffreys
to overawe a synod of peers as he had been in the habit of
overawing common juries. The evidence for the crown would
probably have been thought amply sufficient on the Western
Circuit, or at the City Sessions, but could not for a moment
impose on such men as Rochester, Godolphin, and Churchill;
nor were they, with all their faults, depraved enough to condemn a fellow creature to death against the plainest rules of
justice. Grey, Wade, and Goodenough were produced, but
could only repeat what they had heard said by Monmouth
and by Wildman's emissaries. The principal witness for the
prosecution, a miscreant named Saxton, who had been con-

---

* Speech on the Corruption of the Judges in Lord Delamere's works, 1694.

cerned in the rebellion, and who was now labouring to earn his pardon by swearing against all who were obnoxious to the government, was proved by overwhelming evidence to have told a series of falsehoods. All the Triers, from Churchill, who, as junior baron, spoke first, up to the Treasurer, pronounced, on their honour, that Delamere was not guilty. The gravity and pomp of the whole proceeding made a deep impression even on the Nuncio, accustomed as he was to the ceremonies of Rome, ceremonies which, in solemnity and splendour, exceed all that the rest of the world can show.* The King, who was present, and was unable to complain of a decision evidently just, went into a rage with Saxton, and vowed that the wretch should first be pilloried before Westminster Hall for perjury, and then sent down to the West to be hanged, drawn, and quartered for treason.†

The public joy at the acquittal of Delamere was great. The reign of terror was over. The innocent began to breathe freely, and false accusers to tremble. One letter written on this occasion is scarcely to be read without tears. The widow of Russell, in her retirement, learned the good news with mingled feelings. "I do bless God," she wrote, "that he has caused some stop to be put to the shedding of blood in this poor land. Yet, when I should rejoice with them that do rejoice, I seek a corner to weep in. I find I am capable of no more gladness; but every new circumstance, the very comparing my night of sorrow, after such a day, with theirs of joy, does, from a reflection of one kind or another, rack my uneasy mind. Though I am far from wishing the close of theirs like mine, yet I cannot refrain giving some time to lament mine was not like theirs."‡

And now the tide was on the turn. The death of Stafford, witnessed with signs of tenderness and remorse by the populace to whose rage he was sacrificed, marks the close of one proscription. The acquittal of Delamere marks the close of another. The crimes which had disgraced the stormy tribuneship of Shaftesbury had been fearfully expiated. The blood of innocent Papists had been avenged more than tenfold by the blood of zealous Protestants. Another great reaction had commenced. Factions were fast taking new forms.

Effect of his acquittal.

---

* " Fu una funzione piena di gravità, di ordine, e di gran speciosità."—Adda, Jan. $\frac{15}{25}$. 1686.

† The Trial is in the Collection of

State Trials. Van Leeuwen, Jan. $\frac{15}{25}$. $\frac{19}{29}$. 1686.

‡ Lady Russell to Dr. Fitzwilliam, Jan. 1686.

Old allies were separating.   Old enemies were uniting.   Discontent was spreading fast through all the ranks of the party lately dominant.   A hope, still indeed faint and indefinite, of victory and revenge, animated the party which had lately seemed to be extinct.   With such omens the eventful and troubled year 1685 terminated, and the year 1686 began.

Parties in the court.

The prorogation had relieved the King from the gentle remonstrances of the Houses : but he had still to listen to remonstrances, similar in substance, though uttered in a tone even more cautious and subdued.   Some men, who had hitherto served him but too strenuously for their own fame and for the public welfare, had begun to feel painful misgivings, and occasionally ventured to hint a small part of what they felt.

Feeling of the Protestant Tories.

During many years the zeal of the English Tory for hereditary monarchy and his zeal for the established religion had grown up together and had strengthened each other.   It had never occurred to him that the two sentiments, which seemed inseparable and even identical, might one day be found to be not only distinct but incompatible.   From the commencement of the strife between the Stuarts and the Commons, the cause of the Crown and the cause of the hierarchy had, to all appearance, been one.   Charles the First was regarded by the Church as her own martyr.   If Charles the Second had plotted against her, he had plotted in secret.   In public he had ever professed himself her grateful and devoted son, had knelt at her altars, and in spite of his loose morals, had succeeded in persuading the great body of her adherents that he felt a sincere preference for her.   Whatever conflicts, therefore, the honest Cavalier might have had to maintain against Whigs and Roundheads, he had at least been hitherto undisturbed by conflict in his own mind.   He had seen the path of duty plain before him.   Through good and evil he was to be true to Church and King.   But, if those two august and venerable powers, which had hitherto seemed to be so closely connected that those who were true to one could not be false to the other, should be divided by a deadly enmity, what course was the orthodox Royalist to take ?   What situation could be more trying than that of a man distracted between two duties equally sacred, between two affections equally ardent ?   How would it be possible to give to Cæsar all that was Cæsar's, and yet to withhold from God no part of what was God's ?   None who felt thus could have watched, without deep concern and gloomy forebodings, the dispute between the King and the Parliament on the subject of the test. If James could even now be induced to reconsider his course, to let the Houses reassemble, and to comply with their wishes, all might yet be well.

Such were the sentiments of the King's two kinsmen, the Earls of Clarendon and Rochester. The power and favour of these noblemen seemed to be great indeed. The younger brother was Lord Treasurer and prime minister; and the elder, after holding the Privy Seal during some months, had been appointed Lord Lieutenant of Ireland. The venerable Ormond took the same side. Middleton and Preston, who, as managers of the House of Commons, had recently learned by proof how dear the established religion was to the loyal gentry of England, were also for moderate counsels.

At the very beginning of the new year these statesmen and the great party which they represented had to suffer a cruel mortification. That the late King had been at heart a Roman Catholic had been, during some months, suspected and whispered, but not formally announced. The disclosure indeed, could not be made without great scandal. Charles had, times without number, declared himself a Protestant, and had been in the habit of receiving the Eucharist from the Bishops. Those Churchmen who had stood by him in his difficulties, and who still cherished an affectionate remembrance of him, must be filled with shame and indignation by learning that his whole life had been a lie, that, while he professed to belong to their communion, he had really regarded them as heretics, and that the demagogues who had represented him as a concealed Papist had been the only people who had formed a correct judgment of his character. Even Lewis understood enough of the state of public feeling in England to be aware that the divulging of the truth might do harm, and had, of his own accord, promised to keep the conversion of Charles strictly secret.* James, while his power was still new, had thought that on this point it was advisable to be cautious, and had not ventured to inter his brother with the rites of the Church of Rome. For a time, therefore, every man was at liberty to believe what he wished. The Papists claimed the deceased prince as their proselyte. The Whigs execrated him as a hypocrite and a renegade. The Tories regarded the report of his apostasy as a calumny

* Lewis to Barillon, Feb. $\frac{19}{20}$. 168$\frac{5}{6}$.

Publica-
tion of
papers
found in
the strong
box of
Charles II.
which Papists and Whigs had, for very different reasons, a
common interest in circulating. James now took a step
which greatly disconcerted the whole Anglican party. Two
papers, in which were set forth very concisely the arguments
ordinarily used by Roman Catholics against Protestants, had
been found in Charles's strong box, and appeared to be in his
handwriting. These papers James showed triumphantly to
several Protestants, and declared that, to his knowledge, his
brother had lived and died a Roman Catholic.* One of the
persons to whom the manuscripts were exhibited was Archbishop Sancroft. He read them with much emotion, and
remained silent. Such silence was only the natural effect of a
struggle between respect and vexation. But James supposed
that the Primate was struck dumb by the irresistible force of
reason, and eagerly challenged His Grace to produce, with the
help of the whole episcopal bench, a satisfactory reply. " Let
me have a solid answer, and in a gentlemanlike style ; and it
may have the effect which you so much desire of bringing me
over to your Church." The Archbishop mildly said that, in
his opinion, such an answer might, without much difficulty,
be written, but declined the controversy on the plea of
reverence for the memory of his deceased master. This plea
the King considered as the subterfuge of a vanquished dis-
putant.† Had His Majesty been well acquainted with the
polemical literature of the preceding century and a half, he
would have known that the documents to which he attached
so much value might have been composed by any lad of
fifteen in the college of Douay, and contained nothing which
had not, in the opinion of all Protestant divines, been ten
thousand times refuted. In his ignorant exultation, he
ordered these tracts to be printed with the utmost pomp of
typography, and appended to them a declaration attested by
his sign manual, and certifying that the originals were in his
brother's own hand. James himself distributed the whole
edition among his courtiers and among the people of humbler
rank who crowded round his coach. He gave one copy to a
young woman of mean condition whom he supposed to be of
his own religious persuasion, and assured her that she would
be greatly edified and comforted by the perusal. In requital
of his kindness, she delivered to him, a few days later, an

* Evelyn's Diary, October 2. 1685.
† Life of James the Second, ii. 9. Orig. Mem.

epistle adjuring him to come out of the mystical Babylon and to dash from his lips the cup of fornications.*

These things gave great uneasiness to Tory churchmen. Nor were the most respectable Roman Catholic noblemen much better pleased. They might indeed have been excused if passion had, at this conjuncture, made them deaf to the voice of prudence and justice; for they had suffered much. Protestant jealousy had degraded them from the rank to which they were born, had closed the doors of the Parliament House on the heirs of barons who had signed the Charter, had pronounced the command of a company of foot too high a trust for the descendants of the generals who had conquered at Flodden and Saint Quentin. There was scarcely one eminent peer attached to the old faith whose honour, whose estate, whose life had not been in jeopardy, who had not passed months in the Tower, who had not often anticipated for himself the fate of Stafford. Men who had been so long and cruelly oppressed might have been pardoned if they had eagerly seized the first opportunity of obtaining at once greatness and revenge. But neither fanaticism nor ambition, neither resentment for past wrongs nor the intoxication produced by sudden good fortune, could prevent the most distinguished Roman Catholics from perceiving that the prosperity which they at length enjoyed was only temporary, and, unless wisely used, might be fatal to them. They had been taught, by a cruel experience, that the antipathy of the nation to their religion was not a fancy which would yield to the mandate of a prince, but a profound sentiment, the growth of five generations, diffused through all ranks and parties, and intertwined not less closely with the principles of the Tory than with the principles of the Whig. It was indeed in the power of the King, by the exercise of his prerogative of mercy, to suspend the operation of the penal laws. It might hereafter be in his power, by discreet management, to obtain from the Parliament a repeal of the acts which imposed civil disabilities on those who professed his religion. But if he attempted to subdue the Protestant feeling of England by rude means, it was easy to see that the violent compression of so powerful and elastic a spring would be followed by as violent a recoil. The Roman Catholic peers,

Feeling of the respectable Roman Catholics.

---

* Van Leeuwen, Jan $\frac{1}{11}$ and $\frac{12}{22}$. 1686. Her letter, though very long and very absurd, was thought worth sending to the States General as a sign of the times.

by prematurely attempting to force their way into the Privy Council and the House of Lords, might lose their mansions and their ample estates, and might end their lives as traitors on Tower Hill, or as beggars at the porches of Italian convents.

Such was the feeling of William Herbert, Earl of Powis, who was generally regarded as the chief of the Roman Catholic aristocracy, and who, according to Oates, was to have been prime minister if the Popish plot had succeeded. John Lord Bellasyse took the same view of the state of affairs. In his youth he had fought gallantly for Charles the First, had been rewarded after the restoration with high honours and commands, and had quitted them when the Test Act was passed. With these distinguished leaders all the noblest and most opulent members of their church concurred, except Lord Arundell of Wardour, an old man fast sinking into second childhood.

Cabal of violent Roman Catholics.

But there was at the court a small knot of Roman Catholics whose hearts had been ulcerated by old injuries, whose heads had been turned by recent elevation, who were impatient to climb to the highest honours of the state, and who, having little to lose, were not troubled by thoughts of the day of reckoning. One of these was Roger Palmer, Earl of Castelmaine in Ireland, and husband of the Duchess of Cleveland. His title had notoriously been purchased by his wife's dishonour and his own. His fortune was small. His temper, naturally ungentle, had been exasperated by his domestic vexations, by the public reproaches, and by what he had undergone in the days of the Popish plot. He had been long a prisoner, and had at length been tried for his life. Happily for him, he was not put to the bar till the first burst of popular rage had spent itself, and till the credit of the false witnesses had been blown upon. He had therefore escaped, though very narrowly.* With Castelmaine was allied one of the most favoured of his wife's hundred lovers, Henry Jermyn, whom James had lately created a peer by the title of Lord Dover. Jermyn had been distinguished more than twenty years before by his vagrant amours and his desperate duels. He was now ruined by play, and was eager to retrieve his fallen fortunes by means of lucrative posts from which the laws excluded him.† To the same party belonged an intri-

Castelmaine.

Jermyn.

---

* See his trial in the Collection of State Trials, and his curious manifesto, printed in 1681.

† Mémoires de Grammont; Pepys's Diary, Aug. 19. 1662.; Bonrepaux to Seignelay, Feb. $\frac{1}{11}$. 1686.

guing pushing Irishman named White, who had been much abroad, who had served the House of Austria as something between an envoy and a spy, and who had been rewarded by that House for his services with the title of Marquess of Albeville.*

Soon after the prorogation this reckless faction was strengthened by an important reinforcement. Richard Talbot, Earl of Tyrconnel, the fiercest and most uncompromising of all those who hated the liberties and religion of England, arrived at court from Dublin.

Talbot was descended from an old Norman family which had been long settled in Leinster, which had there sunk into degeneracy, which had adopted the manners of the Celts, which had, like the Celts, adhered to the old religion, and which had taken part with the Celts in the rebellion of 1641. In his youth he had been one of the most noted sharpers and bullies of London. He had been introduced to Charles and James when they were exiles in Flanders, as a man fit and ready for the infamous service of assassinating the Protector. Soon after the Restoration, Talbot attempted to obtain the favour of the royal family by a service more infamous still. A plea was wanted which might justify the Duke of York in breaking that promise of marriage by which he had obtained from Anne Hyde the last proof of female affection. Such a plea Talbot, in concert with some of his dissolute companions, undertook to furnish. They agreed to describe the poor young lady as a creature without virtue, shame, or delicacy, and made up long romances about tender interviews and stolen favours. Talbot in particular related how, in one of his secret visits to her, he had unluckily overturned the Chancellor's inkstand upon a pile of papers, and how cleverly she had averted a discovery by laying the blame of the accident on her monkey. These stories, which, if they had been true, would never have passed the lips of any but the basest of mankind, were pure inventions. Talbot was soon forced to own that they were so; and he owned it without a blush. The injured lady became Duchess of York. Had her husband been a man really upright and honourable, he would have driven from his presence with indignation and contempt the wretches who had slandered her. But one of the peculiarities of James's character was that no act, however wicked and shameful, which had been prompted by

Marginal note: Tyrconnel

---

* Bonrepaux to Seignelay, Feb. $\frac{1}{11}$. 1686.

a desire to gain his favour, ever seemed to him deserving of disapprobation. Talbot continued to frequent the court, appeared daily with brazen front before the princess whose ruin he had plotted, and was installed into the lucrative post of chief pandar to her husband. In no long time Whitehall was thrown into confusion by the news that Dick Talbot, as he was commonly called, had laid a plan to murder the Duke of Ormond. The bravo was sent to the Tower: but in a few days he was again swaggering about the galleries, and carrying billets backward and forward between his patron and the ugliest maids of honour. It was in vain that old and discreet councillors implored the royal brothers not to countenance this bad man, who had nothing to recommend him except his fine person and his taste in dress. Talbot was not only welcome at the palace when the bottle or the dicebox was going round, but was heard with attention on matters of business. He affected the character of an Irish patriot, and pleaded, with great audacity, and sometimes with success, the cause of his countrymen whose estates had been confiscated. He took care, however, to be well paid for his services, and succeeded in acquiring, partly by the sale of his influence, partly by gambling, and partly by pimping, an estate of three thousand pounds a year. For under an outward show of levity, profusion, improvidence, and eccentric impudence, he was in truth one of the most mercenary and crafty of mankind. He was now no longer young, and was expiating by severe sufferings the dissoluteness of his youth: but age and disease had made no essential change in his character and manners. He still, whenever he opened his mouth, ranted, cursed, and swore with such frantic violence that superficial observers set him down for the wildest of libertines. The multitude was unable to conceive that a man who, even when sober, was more furious and boastful than others when they were drunk, and who seemed utterly incapable of disguising any emotion or keeping any secret, could really be a coldhearted, farsighted, scheming sycophant. Yet such a man was Talbot. In truth his hypocrisy was of a far higher and rarer sort than the hypocrisy which had flourished in Barebone's Parliament. For the consummate hypocrite is not he who conceals vice behind the semblance of virtue, but he who makes the vice which he has no objection to show a stalking horse to cover darker and more profitable vice which it is for his interest to hide.

Talbot, raised by James to the earldom of Tyrconnel, had commanded the troops in Ireland during the nine months which elapsed between the termination of the viceroyalty of Ormond and the commencement of the viceroyalty of Clarendon. When the new Lord Lieutenant was about to leave London for Dublin, the General was summoned from Dublin to London. Dick Talbot had long been well known on the road which he had now to travel. Between Chester and the capital there was not an inn where he had not been in a brawl. He was now more insolent and turbulent than ever. He pressed horses in defiance of law, swore at the cooks and postilions, and almost raised mobs by his insolent rodomontades. The Reformation, he told the people, had ruined everything. But fine times were coming. The Catholics would soon be uppermost. The heretics should pay for all. Raving and blaspheming incessantly, like a demoniac, he came to the Court.* As soon as he was there, he allied himself closely with Castelmaine, Dover, and Albeville. These men called with one voice for war on the constitution of the Church and the State. They told their master that he owed it to his religion and to the dignity of his crown to stand firm against the outcry of heretical demagogues, and exhorted him to let the Parliament see from the first that he would be master in spite of opposition, and that the only effect of opposition would be to make him a hard master.

Each of the two parties into which the Court was divided had zealous foreign allies. The ministers of Spain, of the Empire, and of the States General were now as anxious to support Rochester as they had formerly been to support Halifax. All the influence of Barillon was employed on the other side; and Barillon was assisted by another French agent, inferior to him in station, but superior in abilities, Bonrepaux. Barillon was not without parts, and possessed in large measure the graces and accomplishments which then distinguished the French gentry. But his capacity was scarcely equal to what his great place required. He had become sluggish and selfindulgent, liked the pleasures of society and of the table better than business, and on great emergencies generally waited for admonitions and even for reprimands from Ver-

Feeling of the ministers of foreign governments.

---

* Mémoires de Grammont; Life of Edward, Earl of Clarendon; Correspondence of Henry, Earl of Clarendon, *passim*, particularly the letter dated Dec. 29. 1685; Sheridan MS. among the the Stuart Papers; Ellis Correspondence, Jan. 12. 1686.

sailles before he showed much activity.* Bonrepaux had
raised himself from obscurity by the intelligence and industry
which he had exhibited as a clerk in the department of the
marine, and was esteemed an adept in the mystery of mercantile politics. At the close of the year 1685, he was sent to
London charged with several special commissions of high importance. He was to lay the ground for a treaty of commerce;
he was to ascertain and report the state of the English fleets
and dockyards; and he was to make some overtures to the
Huguenot refugees, who, it was supposed, had been so effectually tamed by penury and exile, that they would thankfully
accept almost any terms of reconciliation. The new Envoy's
origin was plebeian: his stature was dwarfish: his countenance was ludicrously ugly; and his accent was that of his
native Gascony: but his strong sense, his keen penetration,
and his lively wit eminently qualified him for his post. In
spite of every disadvantage of birth and figure, he was soon
known as a pleasing companion and as a skilful diplomatist.
He contrived, while flirting with the Duchess of Mazarin,
discussing literary questions with Waller and Saint Evremond,
and corresponding with La Fontaine, to acquire a considerable
knowledge of English politics. His skill in maritime affairs
recommended him to James, who had, during many years,
paid close attention to the business of the Admiralty, and
understood that business as well as he was capable of understanding anything. They conversed every day long and freely
about the state of the shipping and the dockyards. The result
of this intimacy was, as might have been expected, that the
keen and vigilant Frenchman conceived a great contempt for
the King's abilities and character. The world, he said, had
much overrated his Britannic Majesty, who had less capacity
than Charles, and not more virtue.†

The two envoys of Lewis, though pursuing one object, very
judiciously took different paths. They made a partition of
the court. Bonrepaux lived chiefly with Rochester and
Rochester's adherents. Barillon's connections were chiefly
with the opposite faction. The consequence was that they
sometimes saw the same event in different points of view.

* See his later correspondence, *passim;*
Saint Evremond, *passim;* and Madame
de Sévigné's Letters in the beginning of
1689. See also the instructions to Tal-
lard after the peace of Ryswick, in the
French archives.

† Saint Simon, Mémoires, 1697, 1719;
Saint Evremond; La Fontaine; Bonre-
paux to Seignelay, $\frac{\text{Jan. 28.}}{\text{Feb. 7.}}$, Feb. $\frac{8}{18}$. 1686

The best account now extant of the contest which at this time agitated Whitehall is to be found in their despatches.

As each of the two parties at the court of James had the support of foreign princes, so each had also the support of an ecclesiastical authority to which the King paid great deference. The Supreme Pontiff was for legal and moderate courses; and his sentiments were expressed by the Nuncio and by the Vicar Apostolic.* On the other side was a body of which the weight balanced even the weight of the Papacy, the mighty Order of Jesus.

The Pope and the Order of Jesus opposed to each other

That at this conjuncture these two great spiritual powers, once, as it seemed, inseparably allied, should have been opposed to each other, is a most important and remarkable circumstance. During a period of little less than a thousand years the regular clergy had been the chief support of the Holy See. By that See they had been protected from episcopal interference; and the protection which they had received had been amply repaid. But for their exertions it is probable that the Bishop of Rome would have been merely the honorary president of a vast aristocracy of prelates. It was by the aid of the Benedictines that Gregory the Seventh was enabled to contend at once against the Franconian Cæsars and against the secular priesthood. It was by the aid of the Dominicans and Franciscans that Innocent the Third crushed the Albigensian sectaries. Three centuries later the Pontificate, exposed to new dangers more formidable than had ever before threatened it, was saved by a new religious order, which was animated by intense enthusiasm and organised with exquisite skill. When the Jesuits came to the rescue, they found the Papacy in extreme peril: but from that moment the tide of battle turned. Protestantism, which had, during a whole generation, carried all before it, was stopped in its progress, and rapidly beaten back from the foot of the Alps to the shores of the Baltic. Before the Order had existed a hundred years, it had filled the whole world with memorials of great things done and suffered for the faith. No religious community could produce a list of men so variously distinguished: none had extended its operations over so vast a space: yet in none

The Order of Jesus.

* Adda, Nov. 16/26., Dec. 7/17., and Dec. 21/31. 1685. In these despatches Adda gives strong reasons for compromising matters by abolishing the penal laws and leaving the test. He calls the quarrel with the Parliament a "gran disgrazia." He repeatedly hints that the King might, by a constitutional policy, have obtained much for the Roman Catholics, and that the attempt to relieve them illegally is likely to bring great calamities on them.

had there ever been such perfect unity of feeling and action. There was no region of the globe, no walk of speculative or of active life, in which Jesuits were not to be found. They guided the counsels of Kings. They deciphered Latin inscriptions. They observed the motions of Jupiter's satellites. They published whole libraries, controversy, casuistry, history, treatises on optics, Alcaic odes, editions of the fathers, madrigals, catechisms, and lampoons. The liberal education of youth passed almost entirely into their hands, and was conducted by them with conspicuous ability. They appear to have discovered the precise point to which intellectual culture can be carried without risk of intellectual emancipation. Enmity itself was compelled to own that, in the art of managing and forming the tender mind, they had no equals. Meanwhile they assiduously and successfully cultivated the eloquence of the pulpit. With still greater assiduity and still greater success they applied themselves to the ministry of the confessional. Throughout Roman Catholic Europe the secrets of every government and of almost every family of note were in their keeping. They glided from one Protestant country to another under innumerable disguises, as gay Cavaliers, as simple rustics, as Puritan preachers. They wandered to countries which neither mercantile avidity nor liberal curiosity had ever impelled any stranger to explore. They were to be found in the garb of Mandarins, superintending the observatory at Pekin. They were to be found, spade in hand, teaching the rudiments of agriculture to the savages of Paraguay. Yet, whatever might be their residence, whatever might be their employment, their spirit was the same, entire devotion to the common cause, unreasoning obedience to the central authority. None of them had chosen his dwelling-place or his vocation for himself. Whether the Jesuit should live under the arctic circle or under the equator, whether he should pass his life in arranging gems and collating manuscripts at the Vatican or in persuading naked barbarians under the Southern Cross not to eat each other, were matters which he left with profound submission to the decision of others. If he was wanted at Lima, he was on the Atlantic in the next fleet. If he was wanted at Bagdad, he was toiling through the desert with the next caravan. If his ministry was needed in some country where his life was more insecure than that of a wolf, where it was a crime to harbour him, where the heads and quarters of his brethren, fixed in the public places, showed him what he had to expect, he went without remonstrance or hesitation to his doom. Nor is this heroic spirit yet extinct. When, in our own time, a new and terrible pestilence passed round the globe, when, in some great cities, fear had dissolved all the ties which hold society together, when the secular clergy had forsaken their flocks, when medical succour was not to be purchased by gold, when the strongest natural affections had yielded to the love of life, even then the Jesuit was found by the pallet which bishop and curate, physician and nurse, father and mother, had deserted, bending over infected lips to catch the faint accents of confession, and holding up to the last, before the expiring penitent, the image of the expiring Redeemer.

But with the admirable energy, disinterestedness, and self-devotion which were characteristic of the Society, great vices were mingled. It was alleged, and not without foundation, that the ardent public spirit which made the Jesuit regardless of his ease, of his liberty, and of his life, made him also regardless of truth and of mercy ; that no means which could promote the interest of his religion seemed to him unlawful, and that by the interest of his religion he too often meant the interest of his Society. It was alleged that, in the most atrocious plots recorded in history, his agency could be distinctly traced ; that, constant only in attachment to the fraternity to which he belonged, he was in some countries the most dangerous enemy of freedom, and in others the most dangerous enemy of order. The mighty victories which he boasted that he had achieved in the cause of the Church were, in the judgment of many illustrious members of that Church, rather apparent than real. He had indeed laboured with a wonderful show of success to reduce the world under her laws; but he had done so by relaxing her laws to suit the temper of the world. Instead of toiling to elevate human nature to the noble standard fixed by divine precept and example, he had lowered the standard till it was beneath the average level of human nature. He gloried in multitudes of converts who had been baptised in the remote regions of the East : but it was reported that from some of those converts the facts on which the whole theology of the Gospel depends had been cunningly concealed, and that others were permitted to avoid persecution by bowing down before the images of false gods, while internally repeating Paters and Aves. Nor was it only in heathen countries that such arts were said to be practised. It was not

strange that people of all ranks, and especially of the highest
ranks, crowded to the confessionals in the Jesuit temples;
for from those confessionals none went discontented away.
There the priest was all things to all men. He showed just so
much rigour as might not drive those who knelt at his spiritual tribunal to the Dominican or the Franciscan church.
If he had to deal with a mind truly devout, he spoke in the
saintly tones of the primitive fathers : but with that large part
of mankind who have religion enough to make them uneasy
when they do wrong, and not religion enough to keep them
from doing wrong, he followed a different system. Since he
could not reclaim them from vice, it was his business to save
them from remorse. He had at his command an immense dis-
pensary of anodynes for wounded consciences. In the books of
casuistry which had been written by his brethren, and printed
with the approbation of his superiors, were to be found doctrines consolatory to transgressors of every class. There the
bankrupt was taught how he might, without sin, secrete his
goods from his creditors. The servant was taught how he
might, without sin, run off with his master's plate. The pandar was assured that a Christian man might innocently earn
his living by carrying letters and messages between married
women and their gallants. The high spirited and punctilious
gentlemen of France were gratified by a decision in favour of
duelling. The Italians, accustomed to darker and baser
modes of vengeance, were glad to learn that they might, without any crime, shoot at their enemies from behind hedges. To
deceit was given a license sufficient to destroy the whole value
of human contracts and of human testimony. In truth, if
society continued to hold together, if life and property enjoyed
any security, it was because common sense and common humanity restrained men from doing what the Order of Jesus
assured them that they might with a safe conscience do.

So strangely were good and evil intermixed in the character
of these celebrated brethren ; and the intermixture was the
secret of their gigantic power. That power could never have
belonged to mere hypocrites. It could never have belonged
to rigid moralists. It was to be attained only by men sincerely
enthusiastic in the pursuit of a great end, and at the same time
unscrupulous as to the choice of means.

From the first the Jesuits had been bound by a peculiar
allegiance to the Pope. Their mission had been not less to
quell all mutiny within the Church than to repel the hostility

of her avowed enemies. Their doctrine was in the highest degree what has been called on our side of the Alps Ultramontane, and differed almost as much from the doctrine of Bossuet as from that of Luther. They condemned the Gallican liberties, the claim of œcumenical councils to control the Holy See, and the claim of Bishops to an independent commission from heaven. Lainez, in the name of the whole fraternity, proclaimed at Trent, amidst the applause of the creatures of Pius the Fourth, and the murmurs of French and Spanish prelates, that the government of the faithful had been committed by Christ to the Pope alone, that in the Pope alone all sacerdotal authority was concentrated, and that through the Pope alone priests and bishops derived whatever power they possessed.* During many years the union between the Supreme Pontiffs and the Order had continued unbroken. Had that union been still unbroken when James the Second ascended the English throne, had the influence of the Jesuits as well as the influence of the Pope been exerted in favour of a moderate and constitutional policy, it is probable that the great revolution which in a short time changed the whole state of European affairs would never have taken place. But even, before the middle of the seventeenth century, the Society, proud of its services and confident in its strength, had become impatient of the yoke. A generation of Jesuits sprang up, who looked for protection and guidance rather to the court of France than to the court of Rome ; and this disposition was not a little strengthened when Innocent the Eleventh was raised to the papal throne.

The Jesuits were, at that time, engaged in a war to the death against an enemy whom they had at first disdained, but whom they had at length been forced to regard with respect and fear. Just when their prosperity was at the height, they were braved by a handful of opponents, who had indeed no influence with the rulers of this world, but who were strong in religious faith and intellectual energy. Then followed a long, a strange, a glorious conflict of genius against power. The Jesuit called cabinets, tribunals, universities to his aid; and they responded to the call. Port Royal appealed, not in vain, to the hearts and to the understandings of millions. The dictators of Christendom found themselves, on a sudden, in the position of culprits. They were arraigned on the charge of having systematically debased the standard

* Fra Paolo, lib. vii. ; Pallavicino, lib. xviii. cap. 15.

of evangelical morality, for the purpose of increasing their own influence; and the charge was enforced in a manner which at once arrested the attention of the whole world: for the chief accuser was Blaise Pascal. His powers of mind were such as have rarely been bestowed on any of the children of men; and the vehemence of the zeal which animated him was but too well proved by the cruel penances and vigils under which his macerated frame sank into an early grave. His spirit was the spirit of Saint Bernard: but the delicacy of his wit, the purity, the energy, the simplicity of his rhetoric, had never been equalled, except by the great masters of Attic eloquence. All Europe read and admired, laughed and wept. The Jesuits attempted to reply: but their feeble answers were received by the public with shouts of mockery. They wanted, it is true, no talent or accomplishment into which men can be drilled by elaborate discipline; but such discipline, though it may bring out the powers of ordinary minds, has a tendency to suffocate, rather than to develope, original genius. It was universally acknowledged that, in the literary contest, the Jansenists were completely victorious. To the Jesuits nothing was left but to oppress the sect which they could not confute. Lewis the Fourteenth was now their chief support. His conscience had, from boyhood, been in their keeping; and he had learned from them to abhor Jansenism quite as much as he abhorred Protestantism, and very much more than he abhorred Atheism. Innocent the Eleventh, on the other hand, leaned to the Jansenist opinions. The consequence was that the Society found itself in a situation never contemplated by its founder. The Jesuits were estranged from the Supreme Pontiff; and they were closely allied with a prince who proclaimed himself the champion of the Gallican liberties and the enemy of Ultramontane pretensions. The Order therefore became in England an instrument of the designs of Lewis, and laboured, with a success which the Roman Catholics afterwards long and bitterly deplored, to widen the breach between the King and the Parliament, to thwart the Nuncio, to undermine the power of the Lord Treasurer, and to support the most desperate schemes of Tyrconnel.

Thus on one side were the Hydes and the whole body of Tory churchmen, Powis and all the most respectable noblemen and gentlemen of the King's own faith, the States General, the House of Austria, and the Pope. On the other side were a few Roman Catholic adventurers, of broken fortune and tainted reputation, backed by France and by the Jesuits.

The chief representative of the Jesuits at Whitehall was an English brother of the Order, who had, during some time, acted as Viceprovincial, who had been long regarded by James with peculiar favour, and who had lately been made Clerk of the Closet. This man, named Edward Petre, was descended from an honourable family: his manners were courtly: his speech was flowing and plausible: but he was weak and vain, covetous and ambitious. Of all the evil counsellors who had access to the royal ear, he bore, perhaps, the largest part in the ruin of the House of Stuart.

The obstinate and imperious nature of the King gave great advantages to those who advised him to be firm, to yield nothing, and to make himself feared. One state maxim had taken possession of his small understanding, and was not to be dislodged by reason. To reason, indeed, he was not in the habit of attending. His mode of arguing, if it is to be so called, was one not uncommon among dull and stubborn persons, who are accustomed to be surrounded by their inferiors. He asserted a proposition; and, as often as wiser people ventured respectfully to show that it was erroneous, he asserted it again, in exactly the same words, and conceived that, by doing so, he at once disposed of all objections.* "I will make no concession," he often repeated; "my father made concessions, and he was beheaded."† Even if it had been true that concession had been fatal to Charles the First, a man of sense would have remembered that a single experiment is not sufficient to establish a general rule even in sciences much less complicated than the science of government; that, since the beginning of the world, no two political experiments were ever made of which all the conditions were exactly alike; and that the only way to learn civil prudence from history is to examine and compare an immense number of cases. But, if the single instance on which the King relied proved anything, it proved that he was in the wrong. There can be little doubt that, if Charles had frankly

Father Petre.

The King's temper and opinions

* This was the practice of his daughter Anne; and Marlborough said that she had learned it from her father. See the Vindication of the Duchess of Marlborough.

† Down to the time of the trial of the Bishops, James went on telling Adda that all the calamities of Charles the First were "per la troppa indulgenza." Despatch of $\frac{\text{June 29.}}{\text{July 9.}}$ 1688

made to the Short Parliament, which met in the spring of
1640, but one half of the concessions which he made, a few
months later, to the Long Parliament, he would have lived
and died a powerful King.　On the other hand, there can be
no doubt whatever that, if he had refused to make any concession to the Long Parliament, and had resorted to arms in
defence of the Shipmoney and of the Star Chamber, he would
have seen, in the hostile ranks, Hyde and Falkland side by
side with Hollis and Hampden.　It would indeed be more
correct to say that, if he had refused to make any concession,
he would not have been able to resort to arms; for not
twenty Cavaliers would have joined his standard.　It was to
his large concessions alone that he owed the support of that
great body of noblemen and gentlemen who fought so long
and so gallantly in his cause.　But it would have been useless to represent these things to James.

Another fatal delusion had taken possession of his mind,
and was never dispelled till it had ruined him.　He firmly
believed that, do what he might, the members of the Church
of England would act up to their principles.　It had, he
knew, been proclaimed from ten thousand pulpits, it had
been solemnly declared by the University of Oxford, that
even tyranny as frightful as that of the most depraved of the
Cæsars did not justify subjects in resisting the royal authority; and hence he was weak enough to conclude that the
whole body of Tory gentlemen and clergymen would let him
plunder, oppress, and insult them, without lifting an arm
against him.　It seems strange that any man should have
passed his fiftieth year without discovering that people sometimes do what they think wrong: and James had only to
look into his own heart for abundant proof that even a strong
sense of religious duty will not always prevent frail human
beings from indulging their passions in defiance of divine
laws, and at the risk of awful penalties.　He must have been
conscious that, though he thought adultery sinful, he was an
adulterer: but nothing could convince him that any man
who professed to think rebellion sinful would ever, in any
extremity, be a rebel.　The Church of England was, in his
view, a passive victim, which he might, without danger, outrage and torture at his pleasure; nor did he ever see his
error till the Universities were preparing to coin their plate
for the purpose of supplying the military chest of his enemies, and till a Bishop, long renowned for loyalty, had thrown

aside the cassock, put on jackboots, and taken the command of a regiment of insurgents.

In these fatal follies the King was artfully encouraged by a minister who had been an Exclusionist, and who still called himself a Protestant, the Earl of Sunderland. The motives and conduct of this unprincipled politician have often been misrepresented. He was, in his own lifetime, accused by the Jacobites of having, even before the beginning of the reign of James, determined to bring about a revolution in favour of the Prince of Orange, and of having, with that view, recommended a succession of outrages on the civil and ecclesiastical constitution of the realm. This idle story has been repeated down to our own days by ignorant writers. But no well informed historian, whatever might be his prejudices, has condescended to adopt it: for it rests on no evidence whatever; and scarcely any evidence would convince reasonable men that Sunderland deliberately incurred guilt and infamy in order to bring about a change by which it was clear that he could not possibly be a gainer, and by which, in fact, he lost immense wealth and influence. Nor is there the smallest reason for resorting to so strange a hypothesis. For the truth lies on the surface. Crooked as this man's course was, the law which determined it was simple. His conduct is to be ascribed to the alternate influence of cupidity and fear on a mind highly susceptible of both those passions, and quicksighted rather than farsighted. He wanted more power and more money. More power he could obtain only at Rochester's expense; and the obvious way to obtain power at Rochester's expense was to encourage the dislike which the King felt for Rochester's moderate counsels. Money could be most easily and most largely obtained from the court of Versailles; and Sunderland was eager to sell himself to that court. He had no jovial generous vices. He cared little for wine or for beauty: but he desired riches with an ungovernable and insatiable desire. The passion for play raged in him without measure, and had not been tamed by ruinous losses. His hereditary fortune was ample. He had long filled lucrative posts, and had neglected no art which could make them more lucrative: but his ill luck at the hazard table was such that his estates were daily becoming more and more encumbered. In the hope of extricating himself from his embarrassments, he betrayed to Barillon all the schemes adverse to France which had been meditated in the English cabinet, and hinted

The King encouraged in his errors by Sunderland.

that a Secretary of State could in such times render services
for which it might be wise in Lewis to pay largely. The
Ambassador told his master that six thousand guineas was
the smallest gratification that could be offered to so important a minister. Lewis consented to go as high as twenty-
five thousand crowns, equivalent to about five thousand six
hundred pounds sterling. It was agreed that Sunderland
should receive this sum yearly, and that he should, in return,
exert all his influence to prevent the reassembling of the
Parliament.*

He joined himself therefore to the Jesuitical cabal, and
made so dexterous an use of the influence of that cabal that
he was appointed to succeed Halifax in the high dignity of
Lord President without being required to resign the far more
active and lucrative post of Secretary.† He felt, however,
that he could never hope to obtain paramount influence in
the Court while he was supposed to belong to the Established
Church. All religions were the same to him. In private
circles, indeed, he was in the habit of talking with profane
contempt of the most sacred things. He therefore determined to let the King have the delight and glory of effecting
a conversion. Some management, however, was necessary.
No man is utterly without regard for the opinion of his
fellow creatures : and even Sunderland, though not very sensible to shame, flinched from the infamy of public apostasy.
He played his part with rare adroitness. To the world he
showed himself as a Protestant. In the Royal Closet he
assumed the character of an earnest enquirer after truth, who
was almost persuaded to declare himself a Roman Catholic,
and who, while waiting for fuller illumination, was disposed
to render every service in his power to the professors of the
old faith. James, who was never very discerning, and who
in religious matters was absolutely blind, suffered himself,
notwithstanding all that he had seen of human knavery, of
the knavery of courtiers as a class, and of the knavery of
Sunderland in particular, to be duped into the belief that
divine grace had touched the most false and callous of human
hearts. During many months the wily minister continued

---

* Barillon, Nov. $\frac{16}{26}$. 1685 ; Lewis to
Barillon, $\frac{\text{Nov. 26.}}{\text{Dec. 6.}}$ In a highly curious
paper which was written in 1687, almost
certainly by Bonrepaux, and which is
now in the French archives, Sunderland
is described thus :—"La passion qu'il

a pour le jeu, et les pertes considerables
qu'il y fait, incommodent fort ses affaires.
Il n'aime pas le vin ; et il haït les femmes."

† It appears from the Council Book
that he took his place as President on
the 4th of December, 1685.

to be regarded at court as a promising catechumen, without exhibiting himself to the public in the character of a renegade.*

He early suggested to the King the expediency of appointing a secret committee of Roman Catholics to advise on all matters affecting the interests of their religion. This committee met sometimes at Chiffinch's lodgings, and sometimes at the official apartments of Sunderland, who, though still nominally a Protestant, was admitted to all its deliberations, and soon obtained a decided ascendency over the other members. Every Friday the Jesuitical cabal dined with the Secretary. The conversation at table was free; and the weaknesses of the prince whom the confederates hoped to manage were not spared. To Petre Sunderland promised a Cardinal's hat; to Castelmaine a splendid embassy to Rome; to Dover a lucrative command in the Guards; and to Tyrconnel high employment in Ireland. Thus bound together by the strongest ties of interest, these men addressed themselves to the task of subverting the Treasurer's power.†

There were two Protestant members of the cabinet who took no decided part in the struggle. Jeffreys was at this time tortured by a cruel internal malady which had been aggravated by intemperance. At a dinner which a wealthy Alderman gave to some of the leading members of the government, the Lord Treasurer and the Lord Chancellor were so drunk that they stripped themselves almost stark naked, and were with difficulty prevented from climbing up a signpost to drink His Majesty's health. The pious Treasurer escaped with nothing but the scandal of the debauch: but the Chancellor brought on a violent fit of his complaint. His life was for some time thought to be in serious danger. James expressed great uneasiness at the thought of losing a minister who suited him so well, and said, with some truth, that the loss of such a man could not be easily repaired. Jeffreys, when he became convalescent, promised his support to both the contending parties, and waited to see which of them would prove victorious. Some curious proofs of his duplicity are still extant. It has been already said that the

Perfidy of Jeffreys.

* Bonrepaux was not so easily deceived as James. "En son particulier il (Sunderland) n'en professe aucune (religion), et en parle fort librement. Ces sortes de discours seroient en exécration en France. Ici ils sont ordinaires parmi un certain nombre de gens du pais."—Bonrepaux to Seignelay, $\frac{\text{May 25.}}{\text{June 4.}}$ 1687.

† Life of James the Second, ii. 74. 77. Orig. Mem.; Sheridan MS.; Barillon, March $\frac{12}{22}$. 1686.

two French agents who were then resident in London had divided the English court between them. Bonrepaux was constantly with Rochester; and Barillon lived with Sunderland. Lewis was informed in the same week by Bonrepaux that the Chancellor was entirely with the Treasurer, and by Barillon that the Chancellor was in league with the Secretary.*

Godolphin.

Godolphin, cautious and taciturn, did his best to preserve neutrality. His opinions and wishes were undoubtedly with Rochester: but his office made it necessary for him to be in

The Queen. constant attendance on the Queen; and he was naturally unwilling to be on bad terms with her. There is indeed some reason to believe that he regarded her with an attachment more romantic than often finds place in the hearts of veteran statesmen; and circumstances, which it is now necessary to relate, had thrown her entirely into the hands of the Jesuitical cabal.†

Amours of the King.

The King, stern as was his temper and grave as was his deportment, was scarcely less under the influence of female attractions than his more lively and amiable brother had been. The beauty, indeed, which distinguished the favourite ladies of Charles was not necessary to James. Barbara Palmer, Eleanor Gwynn, and Louisa de Querouaille were among the finest women of their time. James, when young, had surrendered his liberty, descended below his rank, and incurred the displeasure of his family, for the coarse features of Anne Hyde. He had soon, to the great diversion of the whole court, been drawn away from his plain consort by a plainer mistress, Arabella Churchill. His second wife, though twenty years younger than himself, and of no unpleasing face or figure, had frequent reason to complain of his inconstancy. But of

Catharine Sedley.

all his illicit attachments the strongest was that which bound him to Catharine Sedley.

This woman was the daughter of Sir Charles Sedley, one of the most brilliant and profligate wits of the Restoration. The licentiousness of his writings is not redeemed by much grace or vivacity; but the charms of his conversation were acknowledged even by sober men who had no esteem for his character. To sit near him at the theatre, and to hear his criticisms on

---

* Reresby's Memoirs; Luttrell's Diary, Feb. 2. 168$\frac{5}{6}$; Barillon, Feb. $\frac{4}{14}$. $\frac{\text{Jan. 28.}}{\text{Feb. 7.}}$ Bonrepaux, $\frac{\text{Jan. 25}}{\text{Feb. 4.}}$

† Dartmouth's note on Burnet, i. 621.

In a contemporary satire it is remarked that Godolphin

" Beats time with politic head, and all approves, Pleased with the charge of the Queen's muff and gloves."

a new play, was regarded as an intellectual treat.* Dryden had done him the honour to make him a principal interlocutor in the Dialogue on Dramatic Poesy. The morals of Sedley were such as, even in that age, gave great scandal. He on one occasion, after a wild revel, exhibited himself without a shred of clothing in the balcony of a tavern near Covent Garden, and harangued the people who were passing in language so indecent and profane that he was driven in by a shower of brickbats, was prosecuted for a misdemeanour, was sentenced to a heavy fine, and was reprimanded by the Court of King's Bench in the most cutting terms.† His daughter had inherited his abilities and his impudence. Personal charms she had none, with the exception of two brilliant eyes, the lustre of which, to men of delicate taste, seemed fierce and unfeminine. Her form was lean, her countenance haggard. Charles, though he liked her conversation, laughed at her ugliness, and said that the priests must have recommended her to his brother by way of penance. She well knew that she was not handsome, and jested freely on her own homeliness. Yet, with strange inconsistency she loved to adorn herself magnificently, and drew on herself much keen ridicule by appearing in the theatre and the ring plastered, painted, clad in Brussels lace, glittering with diamonds, and affecting all the graces of eighteen.‡

The nature of her influence over James is not easily to be explained. He was no longer young. He was a religious man : at least he was willing to make for his religion exertions and sacrifices from which the great majority of those who are called religious men would shrink. It seems strange that any attraction should have drawn him into a course of life which he must have regarded as highly criminal ; and in this case none could understand where the attraction lay. Catharine herself was astonished by the violence of his passion. " It cannot be my beauty," she said ; " for he must see that I have none ; and it cannot be my wit ; for he has not enough to know that I have any."

At the moment of the King's accession, a sense of the new responsibility which lay on him made his mind for a time peculiarly open to religious impressions. He formed and announced many good resolutions, spoke in public with great severity of the impious and licentious manners of the age, and

<hr />

* Pepys, Oct 4. 1664.
† Ibid. July 1. 1663.

‡ See Dorset's satirical lines on her.

in private assured his Queen and his confessor that he would
see Catharine Sedley no more. He wrote to his mistress
entreating her to quit the apartments which she occupied at
Whitehall, and to go to a house in St. James's Square which
had been splendidly furnished for her at his expense. He at
the same time promised to allow her a large pension from his
privy purse. Catharine, clever, strongminded, intrepid, and
conscious of her power, refused to stir. In a few months it
began to be whispered that the services of Chiffinch were
again employed, and that the mistress frequently passed and
repassed through that private door through which Father
Huddleston had borne the host to the bedside of Charles.
The King's Protestant ministers had, it seems, conceived a
hope that their master's infatuation for this woman might
cure him of the more pernicious infatuation which impelled
him to attack their religion. She had all the talents which
could qualify her to play on his feelings, to make game of his
scruples, to set before him in a strong light the difficulties
and dangers into which he was running headlong. Rochester, the champion of the Church, exerted himself to strengthen
her influence. Ormond, who is popularly regarded as the
personification of all that is pure and highminded in the
English Cavalier, encouraged the design. Even Lady Rochester was not ashamed to cooperate, and to cooperate in the very
worst way. Her office was to direct the jealousy of the injured wife towards a young lady who was perfectly innocent.
The whole court took notice of the coldness and rudeness
with which the Queen treated the poor girl on whom suspicion had been thrown: but the cause of Her Majesty's ill
humour was a mystery. For a time the intrigue went on
prosperously and secretly. Catharine often told the King
plainly what the Protestant Lords of the Council only dared
to hint in the most delicate phrases. His crown, she said,
was at stake: the old dotard Arundell and the blustering
Tyrconnel would lead him to his ruin. It is possible that her
caresses might have done what the united exhortations of the
Lords and the Commons, of the House of Austria and the
Holy See, had failed to do, but for a strange mishap which
changed the whole face of affairs. James, in a fit of fondness, determined to make his mistress Countess of Dorchester
in her own right. Catharine saw all the peril of such a step,
and declined the invidious honour. Her lover was obstinate,
and himself forced the patent into her hands. She at last

Intrigues
of Roch-
ester in
favour of
Catharine
Sedley.

accepted it on one condition, which shows her confidence in her own power and in his weakness. She made him give her a solemn promise, not that he would never quit her, but that, if he did so, he would himself announce his resolution to her, and grant her one parting interview.

As soon as the news of her elevation got abroad, the whole palace was in an uproar. The warm blood of Italy boiled in the veins of the Queen. Proud of her youth and of her charms, of her high rank and of her stainless chastity, she could not without agonies of grief and rage see herself deserted and insulted for such a rival. Rochester, perhaps remembering how patiently, after a short struggle, Catharine of Braganza had consented to treat the mistresses of Charles with politeness, had expected that, after a little complaining and pouting, Mary of Modena would be equally submissive. It was not so. She did not even attempt to conceal from the eyes of the world the violence of her emotions. Day after day the courtiers who came to see her dine observed that the dishes were removed untasted from the table. She suffered the tears to stream down her cheeks unconcealed in the presence of the whole circle of ministers and envoys. To the King she spoke with wild vehemence. " Let me go," she cried. " You have made your woman a Countess : make her a Queen. Put my crown on her head. Only let me hide myself in some convent, where I may never see her more." Then, more soberly, she asked him how he reconciled his conduct to his religious professions. " You are ready," she said, " to put your kingdom to hazard for the sake of your soul ; and yet you are throwing away your soul for the sake of that creature." Father Petre, on bended knees, seconded these remonstrances. It was his duty to do so ; and his duty was not the less strenuously performed because it coincided with his interest. The King went on for a time sinning and repenting. In his hours of remorse his penances were severe. Mary treasured up to the end of her life, and at her death bequeathed to the convent of Chaillot, the scourge with which he had vigorously avenged her wrongs upon his own shoulders. Nothing but Catharine's absence could put an end to this struggle between an ignoble love and an ignoble superstition. James wrote, imploring and commanding her to depart. He owned that he had promised to bid her farewell in person. " But I know too well," he added, " the power which you have over me. I have not strength of mind enough to keep my resolution if I see you." He offered her a yacht to convey her with all dignity and comfort to Flanders, and threatened that if she did not go quietly she should be sent away by force. She at one time worked on his feelings by pretending to be ill. Then she assumed the airs of a martyr, and impudently proclaimed herself a sufferer for the Protestant religion. Then again she adopted the style of John Hampden. She defied the King to remove her. She would try the right with him. While the Great Charter and the Habeas Corpus Act were the law of the land, she would live where she pleased. "And Flanders!" she cried; "never! I have learned one thing from my friend the Duchess of Mazarin; and that is never to trust myself in a country where there are convents." At length she selected Ireland as the place of her exile, probably because the brother of her patron Rochester was viceroy there. After many delays she departed, leaving the victory to the Queen.*

The history of this extraordinary intrigue would be imperfect, if it were not added that there is still extant a religious meditation, written by the Treasurer, with his own hand, on the very same day on which the intelligence of his attempt to govern his master by means of a concubine was despatched by Bonrepaux to Versailles. No composition of Ken or Leighton breathes a spirit of more fervent and exalted piety than this effusion. Hypocrisy cannot be suspected: for the paper was evidently meant only for the writer's own eye, and was not published till he had been more than a century in his grave. So much is history stranger than fiction; and so true is it that nature has caprices which art dares not imitate. A dramatist would scarcely venture to bring on the stage a grave prince, in the decline of life, ready to sacrifice his crown in order to serve the interests of his religion, indefatigable in making proselytes, and yet deserting and insulting a virtuous wife who had youth and beauty for the sake of a profligate paramour who had neither. Still less, if possible, would a dramatist venture to introduce a statesman stooping to the wicked and shameful part of a procurer, and calling in his

* The chief materials for the history of this intrigue are the despatches of Barillon and Bonrepaux at the beginning of the year 1686. See Barillon, $\frac{Jan. 25}{Feb. 4}$, $\frac{Jan. 28}{Feb. 7}$, Feb. $\frac{1}{11}$, Feb. $\frac{8}{18}$, Feb. $\frac{19}{29}$, and Bonrepaux under the first four dates; Evelyn's Diary, January 19.; Reresby's Memoirs; Burnet, i. 682.; Sheridan MS; Chaillot MS.; Adda's Despatches, $\frac{Jan. 22}{Feb. 1}$ and $\frac{Jan. 29}{Feb. 8}$ 1686. Adda writes like a pious, but weak and ignorant man. He appears to have known nothing of James's past life.

wife to aid him in that dishonourable office, yet, in his moments of leisure, retiring to his closet, and there secretly pouring out his soul to his God in penitent tears and devout ejaculations.*

The Treasurer soon found that, in using scandalous means for the purpose of obtaining a laudable end, he had committed, not only a crime, but a folly. The Queen was now his enemy. She affected, indeed, to listen with civility while the Hydes excused their recent conduct as well as they could; and she occasionally pretended to use her influence in their favour: but she must have been more or less than woman if she had really forgiven the conspiracy which had been formed against her dignity and her domestic happiness by the family of her husband's first wife. The Jesuits strongly represented to the King the danger which he had so narrowly escaped. His reputation, they said, his peace, his soul, had been put in peril by the machinations of his prime minister. The Nuncio, who would gladly have counteracted the influence of the violent party, and cooperated with the moderate members of the cabinet, could not honestly or decently separate himself on this occasion from Father Petre. James himself, when parted by the sea from the charms which had so strongly fascinated him, could not but regard with resentment and contempt those who had sought to govern him by means of his vices. What had passed must have had the effect of raising his own Church in his esteem, and of lowering the Church of England. The Jesuits, whom it was the fashion to represent as the most unsafe of spiritual guides, as sophists who refined away the whole system of evangelical morality, as sycophants who owed their influence chiefly to the indulgence with which they treated the sins of the great, had reclaimed him from a life of guilt by rebukes as sharp and bold as those which David had heard from Nathan and Herod from the Baptist. On the other hand,

Decline of Rochester's influence.

---

* The meditation bears date $\frac{\text{Jan. 25.}}{\text{Feb. 4.}}$ 168$\frac{5}{6}$. Bonrepaux, in his despatch of the same day, says, "L'intrigue avoit été conduite par Milord Rochester et sa femme. . . . Leur projet étoit de faire gouverner le Roy d'Angleterre par la nouvelle comtesse. Ils s'étoient assurés d'elle." While Bonrepaux was writing thus, Rochester was writing as follows; "Oh God, teach me so to number my days that I may apply my heart unto wisdom. Teach me to number the days that I have spent in vanity and idleness, and teach me to number those that I have spent in sin and wickedness. Oh God, teach me to number the days of my affliction too, and to give thanks for all that is come to me from thy hand. Teach me likewise to number the days of this world's greatness of which I have so great a share; and teach me to look upon them as vanity and vexation of spirit."

zealous Protestants, whose favourite theme was the laxity of Popish casuists and the wickedness of doing evil that good might come, had attempted to obtain advantages for their own Church in a way which all Christians regarded as highly criminal. The victory of the cabal of evil counsellors was therefore complete. The King looked coldly on Rochester. The courtiers and foreign ministers soon perceived that the Lord Treasurer was prime minister only in name. He continued to offer his advice daily, and had the mortification to find it daily rejected. Yet he could not prevail on himself to relinquish the outward show of power, and the emoluments which he directly and indirectly derived from his great place. He did his best, therefore, to conceal his vexations from the public eye. But his violent passions and his intemperate habits disqualified him for the part of a dissembler. His gloomy looks, when he came out of the council chamber, showed how little he was pleased with what had passed at the board; and, when the bottle had gone round freely, words escaped him which betrayed his uneasiness.*

He might, indeed, well be uneasy. Indiscreet and unpopular measures followed one another in rapid succession. All thought of returning to the policy of the Triple Alliance was abandoned. The King explicitly avowed to the ministers of those Continental powers with which he had lately intended to ally himself, that all his views had undergone a change, and that England was still to be, as she had been under his grandfather, his father, and his brother, of no account in Europe. "I am in no condition," he said to the Spanish Ambassador, "to trouble myself about what passes abroad. It is my resolution to let foreign affairs take their course, to establish my authority at home, and to do something for my religion." A few days later he announced the same intentions to the States General.† From that time to the close of his ignominious reign, he made no serious effort to escape from vassalage, though, to the last, he could never hear, without transports of rage, that men called him a vassal.

The two events which proved to the public that Sunderland and Sunderland's party were victorious were the prorogation of the Parliament from February to May, and the departure

---

* " Je vis Milord Rochester comme il sortoit du conseil fort chagrin; et, sur la fin du souper, il lui en échappa quelque chose."—Bonrepaux, Feb. $\frac{18}{28}$. 1686. See also Barillon, March $\frac{1}{11}$, $\frac{4}{14}$.

† Barillon, $\frac{\text{March } 22.}{\text{April 1.}}$ April $\frac{12}{22}$. 1686.

of Castelmaine for Rome with the appointments of an Ambassador of the highest rank.*

Hitherto all the business of the English government at the papal court had been transacted by John Caryl. This gentleman was known to his contemporaries as a man of fortune and fashion, and as the author of two successful plays, a tragedy in rhyme which had been made popular by the action and recitation of Betterton, and a comedy which owes all its value to scenes borrowed from Molière. These pieces have long been forgotten; but what Caryl could not do for himself has been done for him by a more powerful genius. Half a line in the Rape of the Lock has made his name immortal.

Caryl, who was, like all the other respectable Roman Catholics, an enemy to violent courses, had acquitted himself of his delicate errand at Rome with good sense and good feeling. The business confided to him was well done; but he assumed no public character, and carefully avoided all display. His mission, therefore, put the government to scarcely any charge, and excited scarcely any murmurs. His place was now most unwisely supplied by a costly and ostentatious embassy, offensive in the highest degree to the people of England, and by no means welcome to the court of Rome. Castelmaine had it in charge to demand a Cardinal's hat for his confederate Petre.

Castelmaine sent to Rome.

About the same time the King began to show, in an unequivocal manner, the feeling which he really entertained towards the banished Huguenots. While he had still hoped to cajole his Parliament into submission, and to become the head of an European coalition against France, he had affected to blame the revocation of the Edict of Nantes, and to pity the unhappy men whom persecution had driven from their country. He had caused it to be announced that, at every church in the kingdom, a collection would be made under his sanction for their benefit. A proclamation on this subject had been drawn up in terms which might have wounded the pride of a sovereign less sensitive and vainglorious than Lewis. But all was now changed. The principles of the treaty of Dover were again the principles of the foreign policy of England. Ample apologies were therefore made for the discourtesy with which the English government had acted towards France in showing favour to exiled Frenchmen. The

The Huguenots ill-treated by James.

* London Gazette, Feb. 11. 168⅚.; Feb. ⁹⁄₁₉.; Life of James, ii. 75. Orig. Luttrell's Diary, Feb. 8.; Van Leeuwen, Mem.

proclamation which had displeased Lewis was recalled.* The
Huguenot ministers were admonished to speak with reverence
of their oppressor in their public discourses, as they would
answer it at their peril. James not only ceased to express
commiseration for the sufferers, but declared that he believed
them to harbour the worst designs, and owned that he had
been guilty of an error in countenancing them. One of the
most eminent of the refugees, John Claude, had published on
the Continent a small volume in which he described with
great force the sufferings of his brethren. Barillon demanded
that some opprobrious mark should be put on this book.
James complied, and in full council declared it to be his
pleasure that Claude's libel should be burned by the hangman
before the Royal Exchange. Even Jeffreys was startled, and
ventured to represent that such a proceeding was without
example, that the book was written in a foreign tongue, that
it had been printed at a foreign press, that it related entirely
to transactions which had taken place in a foreign country,
and that no English government had ever animadverted on
such works. James would not suffer the question to be discussed. " My resolution," he said, " is taken. It has become
the fashion to treat Kings disrespectfully; and they must
stand by each other. One King should always take another's
part; and I have particular reasons for showing this respect
to the King of France." There was silence at the board :
the order was forthwith issued ; and Claude's pamphlet was
committed to the flames, not without the deep murmurs of
many who had always been reputed steady loyalists.†

The promised collection was long put off under various
pretexts. The King would gladly have broken his word : but
it was pledged so solemnly that he could not for very shame
retract.‡ Nothing, however, which could cool the zeal of
congregations was omitted. It had been expected that,
according to the practice usual on such occasions, the people
would be exhorted to liberality from the pulpits. But James
was determined not to tolerate declamations against his religion and his ally. The Archbishop of Canterbury was therefore commanded to inform the clergy that they must merely

---

* Van Leeuwen, $\frac{\text{Feb. 23.}}{\text{Mar. 5.}}$ 1686.

† Barillon, $\frac{\text{April 26.}}{\text{May 6.}}$, May $\frac{3}{13}$. 1686 ; Van
Citters, May $\frac{7}{17}$.; Evelyn's Diary, May
5.; Luttrell's Diary of the same date;
Privy Council Book, May 2.

‡ Lady Russell to Dr. Fitzwilliam,

Jan. 22. 1686; Barillon, Feb. $\frac{15}{25}$. $\frac{\text{Feb. 22.}}{\text{Mar. 4.}}$
1686. " Ce prince témoigne," says Ba-
rillon, " une grande aversion pour eux,
et aurait bien voulu se dispenser de la
collecte, qui est ordonnée en leur faveur:
mais il n'a pas cru que cela fût possible."

read the brief, and must not presume to preach on the sufferings of the French Protestants.* Nevertheless the contributions were so large that, after all deductions, the sum of forty thousand pounds was paid into the Chamber of London. Perhaps none of the munificent subscriptions of our own age has borne so great a proportion to the means of the nation.†

The King was bitterly mortified by the large amount of the collection which had been made in obedience to his own call. He knew, he said, what all this liberality meant. It was mere Whiggish spite to himself and his religion.‡ He had already resolved that the money should be of no use to those whom the donors wished to benefit. He had been, during some weeks, in close communication with the French embassy on this subject, and had, with the approbation of the court of Versailles, determined on a course which it is not very easy to reconcile with those principles of toleration to which he afterwards pretended to be attached. The refugees were zealous for the Calvinistic discipline and worship. James therefore gave orders that none should receive a crust of bread or a basket of coals who did not first take the sacrament according to the Anglican ritual.§ It is strange that this inhospitable rule should have been devised by a prince who affected to consider the Test Act as an outrage on the rights of conscience: for, however unjustifiable it may be to establish a sacramental test for the purpose of ascertaining whether men are fit for civil and military office, it is surely much more unjustifiable to establish a sacramental test for the purpose of ascertaining whether, in their extreme distress, they are fit objects of charity. Nor had James the plea which may be urged in extenuation of the guilt of almost all other persecutors: for the religion which he commanded the refugees to profess, on pain of being left to starve, was not his own religion. His conduct towards them was therefore less excusable than that of Lewis: for Lewis oppressed them in the hope of bringing them over from a damnable heresy to the true Church: James oppressed them only for

* Barillon, $\frac{\text{Feb. 22.}}{\text{Mar. 4.}}$ 1686.

† Account of the Commissioners, dated March 15. 1688.

‡ "Le Roi d'Angleterre connoit bien que les gens mal intentionnés pour lui sont les plus prompts et les plus disposés à donner considérablement. . . . . Sa Majesté Britannique connoit bien qu'il auroit été à propos de ne point ordonner de collecte, et que les gens mal intentionnés contre la réligion Catholique et contre lui se servent de cette occasion pour témoigner leur zèle."—Barillon, April $\frac{19}{29}$. 1686.

§ Barillon, Feb. $\frac{15}{25}$., $\frac{\text{Feb. 22.}}{\text{Mar. 4.}}$, April $\frac{19}{29}$. 1686; Lewis to Barillon, Mar. $\frac{5}{15}$.

the purpose of forcing them to apostatise from one damnable heresy to another.

Several Commissioners, of whom the Chancellor was one, had been appointed to dispense the public alms. When they met, for the first time, Jeffreys announced the royal pleasure. The refugees, he said, were too generally enemies of monarchy and episcopacy. If they wished for relief, they must become members of the Church of England, and must take the sacrament from the hands of his chaplain. Many exiles, who had come full of gratitude and hope to apply for succour, heard their sentence, and went brokenhearted away.*

The dispensing power.

May was now approaching; and that month had been fixed for the meeting of the Houses: but they were again prorogued to November.† It was not strange that the King did not wish to meet them: for he had determined to adopt a policy which he knew to be, in the highest degree, odious to them. From his predecessors he had inherited two prerogatives, of which the limits had never been defined with strict accuracy, and which, if exerted without any limit, would of themselves have sufficed to overturn the whole polity of the State and of the Church. These were the dispensing power and the ecclesiastical supremacy. By means of the dispensing power, the King purposed to admit Roman Catholics, not merely to civil and military, but to spiritual, offices. By means of the ecclesiastical supremacy, he hoped to make the Anglican clergy his instruments for the destruction of their own religion.

This scheme developed itself by degrees. It was not thought safe to begin by granting to the whole Roman Catholic body a dispensation from all statutes imposing penalties and tests. For nothing was more fully established than that such a dispensation was illegal. The Cabal had, in 1672, put forth a general Declaration of Indulgence. The Commons, as soon as they met, had protested against it. Charles the Second had ordered it to be cancelled in his presence, and had, both by his own mouth and by a written message, assured the Houses that the step which had caused so much complaint, should never be drawn into precedent. It would have been difficult to find in all the Inns of Court a barrister of reputation to argue in defence of a prerogative

* Barillon, April $\frac{19}{29}$. 1686; Lady   sad hearts."
Russell to Dr. Fitzwilliam, April 14.   † London Gazette of May 13. 1686.
"He sent away many," she says, "with

which the Sovereign, seated on his throne in full Parliament, had solemnly renounced a few years before. But it was not quite so clear that the King might not, on special grounds, grant exemptions to individuals by name. The first object of James, therefore, was to obtain from the courts of common law an acknowledgment that, to this extent, at least, he possessed the dispensing power.

But, though his pretensions were moderate when compared with those which he put forth a few months later, he soon found that he had against him almost the whole sense of Westminster Hall. Four of the Judges gave him to understand that they could not, on this occasion, serve his purpose; and it is remarkable that all the four were violent Tories, and that among them were men who had accompanied Jeffreys on the Bloody Circuit, and who had been consenting to the death of Cornish and of Elizabeth Gaunt. Jones, the Chief Justice of the Common Pleas, a man who had never before shrunk from any drudgery, however cruel or servile, now held in the royal closet language which might have become the lips of the purest magistrates in our history. He was plainly told that he must either give up his opinion or his place. "For my place," he answered, "I care little. I am old and worn out in the service of the Crown : but I am mortified to find that Your Majesty thinks me capable of giving a judgment which none but an ignorant or a dishonest man could give." "I am determined," said the King, "to have twelve judges who will be all of my mind as to this matter." "Your Majesty," answered Jones, "may find twelve Judges of your mind, but hardly twelve lawyers."[*] He was dismissed, together with Montague, Chief Baron of the Exchequer, and two puisne Judges, Neville and Charlton. One of the new Judges was Christopher Milton, younger brother of the great poet. Of Christopher little is known, except that, in the time of the civil war, he had been a Royalist, and that he now, in his old age, leaned towards Popery. It does not appear that he was ever formally reconciled to the Church of Rome : but he certainly had scruples about communicating with the Church of England, and had therefore a strong interest in supporting the dispensing power.[†]

The King found his counsel as refractory as his Judges.

Dismission of refractory Judges.

---

* Reresby's Memoirs; Eachard, iii. 797.; Kennet, iii. 451.
† London Gazette, April 22. and 29.

1686; Barillon, April $\frac{19}{29}$.; Evelyn's Diary, June 2.; Luttrell's Diary, June 8.; Dodd's Church History.

The first barrister who learned that he was expected to defend the dispensing power was the Solicitor General, Heneage Finch. He peremptorily refused, and was turned out of office on the following day.* The Attorney General, Sawyer, was ordered to draw warrants authorising members of the Church of Rome to hold benefices belonging to the Church of England. Sawyer had been deeply concerned in some of the harshest and most unjustifiable prosecutions of that age; and the Whigs abhorred him as a man stained with the blood of Russell and Sidney: but on this occasion he showed no want of honesty or of resolution. "Sir," said he, "this is not merely to dispense with a statute: it is to annul the whole statute law from the accession of Elizabeth to the present day. I dare not do it; and I implore Your Majesty to consider whether such an attack upon the rights of the Church be in accordance with your late gracious promises." † Sawyer would have been instantly dismissed, as Finch had been, if the government could have found a successor: but this was no easy matter. It was necessary, for the protection of the rights of the Crown, that one at least of the Crown lawyers should be a man of learning, ability, and experience; and no such man was willing to defend the dispensing power. The Attorney General was therefore permitted to retain his place during some months. Thomas Powis, an obscure barrister, who had no qualification for high employment except servility, was appointed Solicitor.

Case of Sir Edward Hales.

The preliminary arrangements were now complete. There was a Solicitor General to argue for the dispensing power, and a bench of Judges to decide in favour of it. The question was therefore speedily brought to a hearing. Sir Edward Hales, a gentleman of Kent, had been converted to Popery in days when it was not safe for any man of note openly to declare himself a Papist. He had kept his secret, and, when questioned, had affirmed that he was a Protestant with a solemnity which did little credit to his principles. When James had ascended the throne, disguise was no longer necessary. Sir Edward publicly apostatised, and was rewarded with the command of a regiment of foot. He had held his commission more than three months without taking the sacrament. He was therefore liable to a penalty of five hundred pounds, which an informer might recover by action of debt. A menial servant was employed to bring a suit for

---

* North's Life of Guildford, 288.   † Reresby's Memoirs.

this sum in the Court of King's Bench. Sir Edward did not dispute the facts alleged against him, but pleaded that he had letters patent authorising him to hold his commission notwithstanding the Test Act. The plaintiff demurred, that is to say, admitted Sir Edward's plea to be true in fact, but denied that it was a sufficient answer. Thus was raised a simple issue of law to be decided by the court. A barrister, who was notoriously a tool of the government, appeared for the mock plaintiff, and made some feeble objections to the defendant's plea. The new Solicitor General replied. The Attorney General took no part in the proceedings. Judgment was given by the Lord Chief Justice, Sir Edward Herbert. He announced that he had submitted the question to all the twelve Judges, and that, in the opinion of eleven of them, the King might lawfully dispense with penal statutes in particular cases, and for special reasons of grave importance. The single dissentient, Baron Street, was not removed from his place. He was a man of morals so bad that his own relations shrank from him, and that the Prince of Orange, at the time of the Revolution, was advised not to see him. The character of Street makes it impossible to believe that he would have been more scrupulous than his brethren. The character of James makes it impossible to believe that a refractory Baron of the Exchequer would have been permitted to retain his post. There can, therefore, be no reasonable doubt that the dissenting Judge was, like the plaintiff and the plaintiff's counsel, acting collusively. It was important that there should be a great preponderance of authority in favour of the dispensing power; yet it was important that the bench, which had been carefully packed for the occasion, should appear to be independent. One Judge, therefore, the least respectable of the twelve, was permitted, or more probably commanded, to give his voice against the prerogative.*

The power which the courts of law had thus recognised was not suffered to lie idle. Within a month after the decision of the King's Bench had been pronounced, four Roman Catholic Lords were sworn of the Privy Council. Two of them, Powis and Bellasyse, were of the moderate party, and probably took their seats with reluctance and with many sad fore-

* See the account of the case in the Collection of State Trials; Van Citters, May $\frac{4}{14}$., $\frac{June 22.}{July 2.}$ 1686; Evelyn's Diary, June 27.; Luttrell's Diary, June 21. As to Street, see Clarendon's Diary, Dec. 27. 1688.

bodings. The other two, Arundell and Dover, had no such misgivings.*

Roman Catholics authorised to hold ecclesiastical benefices.

The dispensing power was, at the same time, employed for the purpose of enabling Roman Catholics to hold ecclesiastical preferment. The new Solicitor readily drew the warrants in which Sawyer had refused to be concerned. One of these warrants was in favour of a wretch named Edward

Sclater.

Sclater, who had two livings which he was determined to keep through all changes. He administered the sacrament to his parishioners according to the rites of the Church of England on Palm Sunday 1686. On Easter Sunday, only seven days later, he was at mass. The royal dispensation authorised him to retain the emoluments of his benefices. To the remonstrances of the patrons from whom he had received his preferment he replied in terms of insolent defiance, and, while the Roman Catholic cause prospered, put forth an absurd treatise in defence of his apostasy. But, a very few weeks after the Revolution, a great congregation assembled at St. Mary's in the Savoy, to see him received again into the bosom of the Church which he had deserted. He read his recantation with tears flowing from his eyes, and pronounced a bitter invective against the Popish priests whose arts had seduced him.†

Walker.

Scarcely less infamous was the conduct of Obadiah Walker. He was an aged priest of the Church of England, and was well known in the University of Oxford as a man of learning. He had in the late reign been suspected of leaning towards Popery, but had outwardly conformed to the established religion, and had at length been chosen Master of University College. Soon after the accession of James, Walker determined to throw off the disguise which he had hitherto worn. He absented himself from the public worship of the Church of England, and, with some fellows and undergraduates whom he had perverted, heard mass daily in his own apartments. One of the first acts performed by the new Solicitor General was to draw up an instrument which authorised Walker and his proselytes to hold their benefices, notwithstanding their apostasy. Builders were immediately employed to turn two sets of rooms into an oratory. In a few weeks

---

* London Gazette, July 19. 1686.

† The letters patent are in Gutch's Collectanea Curiosa. The date is the 3d of May, 1686. See Sclater's Consensus Veterum; Gee's reply, entitled Veteres Vindicati; Dr. Anthony Horneck's account of Mr. Sclater's recantation of the errors of Popery on the 5th of May, 1689; Dodd's Church History, part viii. book ii. art. 3.

the Roman Catholic rites were publicly performed in University College. A Jesuit was quartered there as chaplain. A press was established there under royal license for the printing of Roman Catholic tracts. During two years and a half, Walker continued to make war on Protestantism with all the rancour of a renegade : but when fortune turned he showed that he wanted the courage of a martyr. He was brought to the bar of the House of Commons to answer for his conduct, and was base enough to protest that he had never changed his religion, that he had never cordially approved of the doctrines of the Church of Rome, and that he had never tried to bring any other person within the pale of that Church. It was hardly worth while to violate the most sacred obligations of law and of plighted faith, for the purpose of making such converts as these.*

In a short time the King went a step further. Sclater and Walker had only been permitted to keep, after they became Papists, the preferment which had been bestowed on them while they passed for Protestants. To confer a high office in the Established Church on an avowed enemy of that Church was a far bolder violation of the laws and of the royal word. But no course was too bold for James. The Deanery of Christchurch became vacant. That office was, both in dignity and in emolument, one of the highest in the University of Oxford. The Dean was charged with the government of a greater number of youths of high connections and of great hopes than could be found in any other college. He was also the head of a Cathedral. In both characters it was necessary that he should be a member of the Church of England. Nevertheless John Massey, who was notoriously a member of the Church of Rome, and who had not one single recommendation, except that he was a member of the Church of Rome, was appointed by virtue of the dispensing power; and soon, within the walls of Christchurch, an altar was decked, at which mass was daily celebrated.† To the Nuncio the King said that what had been done at Oxford should very soon be done at Cambridge.‡

The Dean ery of Christchurch given to a Roman Catholic

Yet even this was a small evil compared with that which Protestants had good ground to apprehend. It seemed but

Disposal of bishoprics.

* Gutch's Collectanea Curiosa ; Dodd, viii. ii. 3.; Wood, Ath. Ox.; Ellis Correspondence, Feb. 27. 1686; Commons' Journals, Oct. 26. 1689.

† Gutch's Collectanea Curiosa; Wood's Athenæ Oxonienses ; Dialogue between a Churchman and a Dissenter, 1689.
‡ Adda, July $\frac{9}{19}$. 1686.

too probable that the whole government of the Anglican Church would shortly pass into the hands of her deadliest enemies. Three important sees had lately become vacant, that of York, that of Chester, and that of Oxford. The Bishopric of Oxford was given to Samuel Parker, a parasite, whose religion, if he had any religion, was that of Rome, and who called himself a Protestant only because he was encumbered with a wife. "I wished," the King said to Adda, "to appoint an avowed Catholic: but the time is not come. Parker is well inclined to us: he is one of us in feeling; and by degrees he will bring round his clergy."* The Bishopric of Chester, vacant by the death of John Pearson, a great name both in philology and in divinity, was bestowed on Thomas Cartwright, a still viler sycophant than Parker. The Archbishopric of York remained several years vacant. As no good reason could be found for leaving so important a place unfilled, men suspected that the nomination was delayed only till the King could venture to place the mitre on the head of an avowed Papist. It is indeed highly probable that the Church of England was saved from this outrage solely by the good sense and good feeling of the Pope. Without a special dispensation from Rome no Jesuit could be a Bishop; and Innocent could not be induced to grant such a dispensation to Petre.

Resolution of James to use his ecclesiastical supremacy against the Church.

James did not even make any secret of his intention to exert vigorously and systematically for the destruction of the Established Church all the powers which he possessed as her head. He plainly said that, by a wise dispensation of Providence, the Act of Supremacy would be the means of healing the fatal breach which it had caused. Henry and Elizabeth had usurped a dominion which rightfully belonged to the Holy See. That dominion had, in the course of succession, descended to an orthodox prince, and would be held by him in trust for the Holy See. He was authorised by law to repress spiritual abuses; and the first spiritual abuse which he would repress should be the liberty which the Anglican clergy assumed of defending their own religion and of attacking the doctrines of Rome.†

* Adda, $\frac{\text{July 30.}}{\text{Aug. 9.}}$ 1686.

† "Ce prince m'a dit que Dieu avoit permis que toutes les loix qui ont été faites pour établir la réligion Protestante, et détruire la réligion Catholique, servent présentement de fondement à ce qu'il veut faire pour l'établissement de la vraie réligion, et le mettent en droit d'exercer un pouvoir encore plus grand que celui qu'ont les rois Catholiques sur les affaires ecclésiastiques dans les autres pays."— Barillon, July $\frac{12}{22}$. 1686. To Adda His

But he was met by a great difficulty. The ecclesiastical supremacy which had devolved on him was by no means the same great and terrible prerogative which Elizabeth, James the First, and Charles the First had possessed. The enactment which annexed to the crown an almost boundless visitatorial authority over the Church, though it had never been formally repealed, had really lost a great part of its force. The substantive law remained; but it remained unaccompanied by any formidable sanction or by any efficient system of procedure, and was therefore little more than a dead letter.

The statute, which restored to Elizabeth the spiritual dominion assumed by her father and resigned by her sister, contained a clause authorising the sovereign to constitute a tribunal which might investigate, reform, and punish all ecclesiastical delinquencies. Under the authority given by this clause the Court of High Commission was created. That court was, during many years, the terror of Nonconformists, and, under the harsh administration of Laud, became an object of fear and hatred even to those who most loved the Established Church. When the Long Parliament met, the High Commission was generally regarded as the most grievous of the many grievances under which the nation laboured. An Act was therefore somewhat hastily passed, which not only took away from the Crown the power of appointing visitors to superintend the Church, but abolished all ecclesiastical courts without distinction.

After the Restoration, the Cavaliers who filled the House of Commons, zealous as they were for the prerogative, still remembered with bitterness the tyranny of the High Commission, and were by no means disposed to revive an institution so odious. They at the same time thought, and with reason, that the statute which had swept away all the courts Christian of the realm, without providing any substitute, was open to grave objection. They accordingly repealed that statute, with the exception of the part which related to the High Commission. Thus, the Archidiaconal Courts, the Consistory Courts, the Court of Arches, the Court of Peculiars, and the Court of Delegates were revived: but the enactment by which Elizabeth and her successors had been empowered to appoint Commissioners with visitatorial autho-

---

Majesty said, a few days later, "Che l'autorità concessale dal parlamento sopra l'Ecclesiastico senza alcun limite con fine contrario fosse adesso per servire al vantaggio de' medesimi Cattolici." ^{July 23.} ^{Aug. 2}

rity over the Church was not only not revived, but was
declared, with the utmost strength of language, to be completely abrogated.   It is therefore as clear as any point of
constitutional law can be that James the Second was not
competent to appoint a Commission with power to visit and
govern the Church of England.*   But, if this were so, it
was to little purpose that the Act of Supremacy, in high
sounding words, empowered him to amend what was amiss
in that Church.   Nothing but a machinery as stringent as
that which the Long Parliament had destroyed could force
the Anglican clergy to become his agents for the destruction of the Anglican doctrine and discipline.   He therefore,
as early as the month of April 1686, determined to revive
the Court of High Commission.   This design was not immediately executed.   It encountered the opposition of every
minister who was not devoted to France and to the Jesuits.
It was regarded by lawyers as an outrageous violation of the
law, and by Churchmen as a direct attack upon the Church.
Perhaps the contest might have lasted longer, but for an
event which wounded the pride and inflamed the rage of the
King.   He had, as supreme ordinary, put forth directions,
charging the clergy of the establishment to abstain from
touching in their discourses on controverted points of
doctrine.   Thus, while sermons in defence of the Roman
Catholic religion were preached on every Sunday and holiday
within the precincts of the royal palaces, the Church of the
state, the Church of the great majority of the nation, was
forbidden to explain and vindicate her own principles.   The
spirit of the whole clerical order rose against this injustice.
William Sherlock, a divine of distinguished abilities, who
had written with sharpness against Whigs and Dissenters,
and had been rewarded by the government with the Master-
ship of the Temple and with a pension, was one of the first
who incurred the royal displeasure.   His pension was stopped ;
and he was severely reprimanded.†   John Sharp, Dean of
Norwich and Rector of Saint Giles's in the Fields, soon gave
still greater offence.   He was a man of learning and fervent
piety, a preacher of great fame, and an exemplary parish
priest.   In politics he was, like most of his brethren, a Tory,

---

* The whole question is lucidly and
unanswerably argued in a little contemporary tract, entitled " The King's Power
in Matters Ecclesiastical fairly stated."
See also a concise but forcible argument

by Archbishop Sancroft, Doyly's Life of
Sancroft, i. 92.

† Letter from James to Clarendon,
Feb. 18. 168⅚.

and had just been appointed one of the royal chaplains. He received an anonymous letter which purported to come from one of his parishioners, who had been staggered by the arguments of Roman Catholic theologians, and who was anxious to be satisfied that the Church of England was a branch of the true Church of Christ. No divine, not utterly lost to all sense of religious duty and of professional honour, could refuse to answer such a call. On the following Sunday Sharp delivered an animated discourse against the high pretensions of the see of Rome. Some of his expressions were exaggerated, distorted, and carried by talebearers to Whitehall. It was falsely said that he had spoken with contumely of the theological disquisitions which had been found in the strong box of the late King, and which the present King had published. Compton, the Bishop of London, received orders from Sunderland to suspend Sharp till the royal pleasure should be further known. The Bishop was in great perplexity. His recent conduct in the House of Lords had given deep offence to the Court. Already his name had been struck out of the list of Privy Councillors. Already he had been dismissed from his office in the royal chapel. He was unwilling to give fresh provocation : but the act which he was directed to perform was a judicial act. He felt that it was unjust, and he was assured by the best advisers that it was also illegal, to inflict punishment without giving any opportunity for defence. He accordingly, in the humblest terms, represented his difficulties to the King, and privately requested Sharp not to appear in the pulpit for the present. Reasonable as were Compton's scruples, obsequious as were his apologies, James was greatly incensed. What insolence to plead either natural justice or positive law in opposition to an express command of the Sovereign ! Sharp was forgotten. The Bishop became a mark for the whole vengeance of the government.* The King felt more painfully than ever the want of that tremendous engine which had once coerced refractory ecclesiastics. He probably knew that, for a few angry words uttered against his father's government, Bishop Williams had been suspended by the High Commission from all ecclesiastical dignities and functions. The design of reviving that formidable tribunal was pushed on more eagerly than ever. In July, London was alarmed by the news that

He creates a new Court of High Commission.

* The best account of these transactions is in the Life of Sharp, by his son. Van Citters, $\frac{June 29.}{July 9.}$ 1686.

the King had, in direct defiance of two Acts of Parliament drawn in the strongest terms, entrusted the whole government of the Church to seven Commissioners.* The words in which the jurisdiction of these officers was described were loose, and might be stretched to almost any extent. All colleges and grammar schools, even those which had been founded by the liberality of private benefactors, were placed under the authority of the new board. All who depended for bread on situations in the Church or in academical institutions, from the Primate down to the youngest curate, from the Vicechancellors of Oxford and Cambridge down to the humblest pedagogue who taught Corderius, were subjected to this despotic tribunal. If any one of those many thousands was suspected of doing or saying anything distasteful to the government, the Commissioners might cite him before them. In their mode of dealing with him they were fettered by no rule. They were themselves at once prosecutors and judges. The accused party was to be furnished with no copy of the charge. He was to be examined and crossexamined. If his answers did not give satisfaction, he was liable to be suspended from his office, to be ejected from it, to be pronounced incapable of holding any preferment in future. If he were contumacious, he might be excommunicated, or, in other words, be deprived of all civil rights and imprisoned for life. He might also, at the discretion of the court, be loaded with all the costs of the proceeding by which he had been reduced to beggary. No appeal was given. The Commissioners were directed to execute their office notwithstanding any law which might be, or might seem to be, inconsistent with these regulations. Lastly, lest any person should doubt that it was intended to revive that terrible court from which the Long Parliament had freed the nation, the new Visitors were directed to use a seal bearing exactly the same device and the same superscription with the seal of the old High Commission.†

The chief Commissioner was the Chancellor. His presence and assent were declared necessary to every proceeding. All men knew how unjustly, insolently, and barbarously he had acted in courts where he had been, to a certain extent, re-

---

* Barillon, $\frac{\text{July 21.}}{\text{Aug. 1.}}$, 1686. Van Citters, July $\frac{16}{26}$.; Privy Council Book, July 17.; Ellis Correspondence, July 17.; Evelyn's Diary, July 14.; Luttrell's Diary, August 5, 6.

† The device was a rose and crown.

Before the device was the initial letter of the Sovereign's name; after it the letter R. Round the seal was this inscription, " Sigillum commissariorum regiæ majestatis ad causas ecclesiasticas."

strained by the known laws of England. It was, therefore, not difficult to foresee how he would conduct himself in a situation in which he was at entire liberty to make forms of procedure and rules of evidence for himself.

Of the other six Commissioners three were prelates and three laymen. The name of Archbishop Sancroft stood first. But he was fully convinced that the court was illegal, that all its judgments would be null, and that by sitting in it he should incur a serious responsibility. He therefore determined not to comply with the royal mandate. He did not, however, act on this occasion with that courage and sincerity which he showed when driven to extremity two years later. He begged to be excused on the plea of business and ill health. The other members of the board, he added, were men of too much ability to need his assistance. These disingenuous apologies ill became the Primate of all England at such a crisis; nor did they avert the royal displeasure. Sancroft's name was not indeed struck out of the list of Privy Councillors: but, to the bitter mortification of the friends of the Church, he was no longer summoned on Council days. "If," said the King, "he is too sick or too busy to go to the Commission, it is a kindness to relieve him from attendance at Council." *

The government found no similar difficulty with Nathaniel Crewe, Bishop of the great and opulent see of Durham, a man nobly born, and raised so high in his profession that he could scarcely wish to rise higher, but mean, vain, and cowardly. He had been made Dean of the Chapel Royal when the Bishop of London was banished from the palace. The honour of being an Ecclesiastical Commissioner turned Crewe's head. It was to no purpose that some of his friends represented to him the risk which he ran by sitting in an illegal tribunal. He was not ashamed to answer that he could not live out of the royal smile, and exultingly expressed his hope that his name would appear in history, a hope which has not been altogether disappointed.†

Thomas Sprat, Bishop of Rochester, was the third clerical Commissioner. He was a man to whose talents posterity has scarcely done justice. Unhappily for his fame, it has been usual to print his verses in collections of the British poets; and those who judge of him by his verses must consider him

* Append to Clarendon's Diary; Van Citters, Oct. $\frac{8}{18}$. 1686; Barillon, Oct. $\frac{11}{21}$.; Doyly's Life of Sancroft. † Burnet, i. 676.

as a servile imitator, who, without one spark of Cowley's admirable genius, mimicked whatever was least commendable in Cowley's manner: but those who are acquainted with Sprat's prose writings will form a very different estimate of his powers. He was indeed a great master of our language, and possessed at once the eloquence of the preacher, of the controversialist, and of the historian. His moral character might have passed with little censure had he belonged to a less sacred profession; for the worst that can be said of him is that he was indolent, luxurious, and worldly: but such failings, though not commonly regarded as very heinous in men of secular callings, are scandalous in a prelate. The Archbishopric of York was vacant: Sprat hoped to obtain it, and therefore accepted a seat at the ecclesiastical board: but he was too good-natured a man to behave harshly; and he was too sensible a man not to know that he might at some future time be called to a serious account by a Parliament. He therefore, though he consented to act, tried to do as little mischief, and to make as few enemies, as possible.*

The three remaining Commissioners were the Lord Treasurer, the Lord President, and the Chief Justice of the King's Bench. Rochester, disapproving and murmuring, consented to serve. Much as he had to endure at the Court, he could not bear to quit it. Much as he loved the Church, he could not bring himself to sacrifice for her sake his white staff, his patronage, his salary of eight thousand pounds a year, and the far larger indirect emoluments of his office. He excused his conduct to others, and perhaps to himself, by pleading that, as a Commissioner, he might be able to prevent much evil, and that, if he refused to act, some person less attached to the Protestant religion would be found to fill the vacant place. Sunderland was the representative of the Jesuitical cabal. Herbert's recent decision on the question of the dispensing power seemed to prove that he would not flinch from any service which the King might require.

Proceedings against the Bishop of London. As soon as the Commission had been opened, the Bishop of London was cited before the new tribunal. He appeared. "I demand of you," said Jeffreys, "a direct and positive answer. Why did not you suspend Dr. Sharp?"

The Bishop requested a copy of the Commission in order that he might know by what authority he was thus interrogated. "If you mean," said Jeffreys, "to dispute our

* Burnet. i. 675. ii. 629.; Sprat's Letters to Dorset.

authority, I shall take another course with you. As to the Commission, I do not doubt that you have seen it. At all events you may see it in any coffeehouse for a penny." The insolence of the Chancellor's reply appears to have shocked the other Commissioners; and he was forced to make some awkward apologies. He then returned to the point from which he had started. "This," he said, "is not a court in which written charges are exhibited. Our proceedings are summary, and by word of mouth. The question is a plain one. Why did you not obey the King?" With some difficulty Compton obtained a brief delay, and the assistance of counsel. When the case had been heard, it was evident to all men that the Bishop had done only what he was bound to do. The Treasurer, the Chief Justice, and Sprat were for acquittal. The King's wrath was moved. It seemed that his Ecclesiastical Commission would fail him as his Tory Parliament had failed him. He offered Rochester a simple choice, to pronounce the Bishop guilty, or to quit the Treasury. Rochester was base enough to yield. Compton was suspended from all spiritual functions; and the charge of his great diocese was committed to his judges, Sprat and Crewe. He continued, however, to reside in his palace and to receive his revenues; for it was known that, had any attempt been made to deprive him of his temporalities, he would have put himself under the protection of the common law; and Herbert himself declared that, at common law, judgment must be given against the crown. This consideration induced the King to pause. Only a few weeks had elapsed since he had packed the courts of Westminster Hall in order to obtain a decision in favour of his dispensing power. He now found that, unless he packed them again, he should not be able to obtain a decision in favour of the proceedings of his Ecclesiastical Commission. He determined, therefore, to postpone for a short time the confiscation of the freehold property of refractory clergymen.*

The temper of the nation was indeed such as might well make him hesitate. During some months discontent had been steadily and rapidly increasing. The celebration of the Roman Catholic worship had long been prohibited by Act of Parliament. During several generations no Roman Catholic clergyman had dared to exhibit himself in any public place

Discontent excited by the public display of Roman Catholic rites and vestments.

---

* Burnet, i. 677.; Barillon, Sept. $\frac{6}{16}$. 1686. The public proceedings are in the Collection of State Trials.

with the badges of his office. Against the regular clergy, and against the restless and subtle Jesuits by name, had been enacted a succession of rigorous statutes. Every Jesuit who set foot in this country was liable to be hanged, drawn, and quartered. A reward was offered for his detection. He was not allowed to take advantage of the general rule, that men are not bound to accuse themselves. Whoever was suspected of being a Jesuit might be interrogated, and, if he refused to answer, might be sent to prison for life.* These laws, though they had not, except when there was supposed to be some peculiar danger, been strictly executed, and though they had never prevented Jesuits from resorting to England, had made disguise necessary. But all disguise was now thrown off. Injudicious members of the King's Church, encouraged by him, took a pride in defying statutes which were still of undoubted validity, and feelings which had a stronger hold of the national mind than at any former period. Roman Catholic chapels rose all over the country. Cowls, girdles of ropes, and strings of beads constantly appeared in the streets, and astonished a population, the oldest of whom had never seen a conventual garb except on the stage. A convent rose at Clerkenwell, on the site of the ancient cloister of Saint John. The Franciscans occupied a mansion in Lincoln's Inn Fields. The Carmelites were quartered in the City. A society of Benedictine monks was lodged in Saint James's Palace. In the Savoy a spacious house, including a church and a school, was built for the Jesuits.† The skill and care with which those fathers had, during several generations, conducted the education of youth, had drawn forth reluctant praises from the wisest Protestants. Bacon had pronounced the mode of instruction followed in the Jesuit colleges to be the best yet known in the world, and had warmly expressed his regret that so admirable a system of intellectual and moral discipline should be employed on the side of error.‡ It was not improbable that the new academy in the Savoy might, under royal patronage, prove a formidable rival to the great foundations of Eton, Westminster, and Winchester. Indeed, soon after the school was opened, the classes consisted of four hundred boys, about one half of whom were Protestants. The Protestant pupils were not required to attend mass: but there could

* 27 Eliz. c. 2.; 2 Jac. I. c. 34.; Jac.   † Life of James the Second, ii. 79,80.
I. c. 5.   Orig. Mem.   ‡ De Augmentis, i. vi. 4.

be no doubt that the influence of able preceptors, devoted to the Roman Catholic Church, and versed in all the arts which win the confidence and affection of youth, would make many converts.

These things produced great excitement among the popu- Riots. lace, which is always more moved by what impresses the senses than by what is addressed to the reason.   Thousands of rude and ignorant men, to whom the dispensing power and the Ecclesiastical Commission were words without a meaning, saw with dismay and indignation a Jesuit college rising on the banks of the Thames, friars in hoods and gowns walking in the Strand, and crowds of devotees pressing in at the doors of temples where homage was paid to graven images.   Riots broke out in several parts of the country.   At Coventry and Worcester the Roman Catholic worship was violently interrupted.*   At Bristol the rabble, countenanced, it was said, by the magistrates, exhibited a profane and indecent pageant, in which the Virgin Mary was represented by a buffoon, and in which a mock host was carried in procession.   Soldiers were called out to disperse the mob.   The mob, then and ever since one of the fiercest in the kingdom, resisted.   Blows were exchanged, and serious hurts inflicted.†   The agitation was great in the capital, and greater in the City, properly so called, than at Westminster.   For the people of Westminster had been accustomed to see among them the private chapels of Roman Catholic Ambassadors : but the City had not, within living memory, been polluted by any idolatrous exhibition.   Now, however, the resident of the Elector Palatine, encouraged by the King, fitted up a chapel in Lime Street. The heads of the corporation, though men selected for office on account of their known Toryism, protested against this proceeding, which, as they said, the ablest gentlemen of the long robe regarded as illegal.   The Lord Mayor was ordered to appear before the Privy Council.   " Take heed what you do," said the King.   " Obey me ; and do not trouble yourself either about gentlemen of the long robe or gentlemen of the short robe."   The Chancellor took up the word, and reprimanded the unfortunate magistrate with the genuine eloquence of the Old Bailey bar.   The chapel was opened.   All the neighbourhood was soon in commotion.   Great crowds assembled in Cheapside to attack the new mass house.   The

* Van Citters, May $\frac{14}{24}$. 1686.
† Van Citters, May $\frac{18}{28}$. 1686 ; Adda, May $\frac{19}{29}$.

priests were insulted.   A crucifix was taken out of the building and set up on the parish pump.   The Lord Mayor came
to quell the tumult, but was received with cries of " No wooden
gods."   The trainbands were ordered to disperse the crowd :
but the trainbands shared in the popular feeling ; and murmurs were heard from the ranks : " We cannot in conscience
fight for Popery."*

The Elector Palatine was, like James, a sincere and zealous
Catholic, and was, like James, the ruler of a Protestant
people ; but the two princes resembled each other little in
temper and understanding.   The Elector had promised to
respect the rights of the Church which he found established
in his dominions.   He had strictly kept his word, and had not
suffered himself to be provoked to any violence by the indiscretion of preachers who, in their antipathy to his faith,
occasionally forgot the respect which they owed to his person.†
He learned, with concern, that great offence had been given
to the people of London by the injudicious act of his representative, and, much to his honour, declared that he would
forego the privilege to which, as a sovereign prince, he was
entitled, rather than endanger the peace of a great city.   " I,
too," he wrote to James, " have Protestant subjects ; and I
know with how much caution and delicacy it is necessary that
a Catholic prince so situated should act."   James, instead of
expressing gratitude for this humane and considerate conduct,
turned the letter into ridicule before the foreign ministers.
It was determined that the Elector should have a chapel in
the City whether he would or not, and that, if the trainbands
refused to do their duty, their place should be supplied by the
Guards.‡

The effect of these disturbances on trade was serious.   The
Dutch minister informed the States General that the business
of the Exchange was at a stand.   The Commissioners of the
Customs reported to the King that, during the month which
followed the opening of the Lime Street Chapel, the receipt
in the port of the Thames had fallen off by some thousands of
pounds.§   Several Aldermen, who, though zealous royalists
appointed under the new charter, were deeply interested in
the commercial prosperity of their city, and loved neither

* Ellis Correspondence. April 27.   April $\frac{2}{12}$, $\frac{\text{April 23.}}{\text{May 3.}}$
1686 ; Barillon, April $\frac{19}{29}$.; Van Citters,
April $\frac{20}{30}$.; Privy Council Book, March   † Burnet's Travels.
26 ; Luttrell's Diary; Adda, $\frac{\text{Feb. 26.}}{\text{Mar. 8.}}$ $\frac{\text{Mar. 26.}}{\text{April 5.}}$ ‡ Barillon, $\frac{\text{May 27.}}{\text{June 6.}}$ 1686.
                                        § Van Citters, $\frac{\text{May 25.}}{\text{June 4.}}$ 1686.

Popery nor martial law, tendered their resignations. But the King was resolved not to yield. He formed a camp on Hounslow Heath, and collected there, within a circumference of about two miles and a half, fourteen battalions of foot and thirty-two squadrons of horse, amounting to thirteen thousand fighting men. Twenty-six pieces of artillery, and many wains laden with arms and ammunition, were dragged from the Tower through the City to Hounslow.* The Londoners saw this great force assembled in their neighbourhood with a terror which familiarity soon diminished. A visit to Hounslow became their favourite amusement on holidays. The camp presented the appearance of a vast fair. Mingled with the musketeers and dragoons, a multitude of fine gentlemen and ladies from Soho Square, sharpers and painted women from Whitefriars, invalids in sedans, monks in hoods and gowns, lacqueys in rich liveries, pedlars, orange girls, mischievous apprentices, and gaping clowns, was constantly passing and repassing through the long lanes of tents. From some pavilions were heard the noises of drunken revelry, from others the curses of gamblers. In truth the place was merely a gay suburb of the capital. The King, as was amply proved two years later, had greatly miscalculated. He had forgotten that vicinity operates in more ways than one. He had hoped that his army would overawe London: but the result of his policy was that the feelings and opinions of London took complete possession of his army.†

Scarcely indeed had the encampment been formed when there were rumours of quarrels between the Protestant and Popish soldiers.‡ A little tract, entitled A humble and hearty Address to all English Protestants in the Army, had been actively circulated through the ranks. The writer vehemently exhorted the troops to use their arms in defence, not of the mass book, but of the Bible, of the Great Charter, and of the Petition of Right. He was a man already under the frown of power. His character was remarkable, and his history not uninstructive.

His name was Samuel Johnson. He was a priest of the

margin note: A camp formed at Hounslow.

margin note: Samuel Johnson.

---

* Ellis Correspondence, June 26. 1686; Van Citters, July $\frac{2}{12}$.; Luttrell's Diary, July 19.

† See the contemporary poems, entitled Hounslow Heath and Cæsar's Ghost; Evelyn's Diary, June 2. 1686. A ballad in the Pepysian Collection contains the following lines:—

" I liked the place beyond expressing,
I ne'er saw a camp so fine,
Not a maid in a plain dressing,
But might taste a glass of wine."

‡ Luttrell's Diary. June 18. 1686.

Church of England, and had been chaplain to Lord Russell. Johnson was one of those persons who are mortally hated by their opponents, and less loved than respected by their allies. His morals were pure, his religious feelings ardent, his learning and abilities not contemptible, his judgment weak, his temper acrimonious, turbulent, and unconquerably stubborn. His profession made him peculiarly odious to the zealous supporters of monarchy; for a republican in holy orders was a strange and almost an unnatural being. During the late reign Johnson had published a book entitled Julian the Apostate. The object of this work was to show that the Christians of the fourth century did not hold the doctrine of nonresistance. It was easy to produce passages from Chrysostom and Jerome written in a spirit very different from that of the Anglican divines who preached against the Exclusion Bill. Johnson, however, went further. He attempted to revive the odious imputation which had, for very obvious reasons, been thrown by Libanius on the Christian soldiers of Julian, and insinuated that the dart which slew the imperial renegade came, not from the enemy, but from some Rumbold or Ferguson in the Roman ranks. A hot controversy followed. Whig and Tory disputants wrangled fiercely about an obscure passage, in which Gregory of Nazianzus praises a pious Bishop who was going to bastinado somebody. The Whigs maintained that the holy man was going to bastinado the Emperor; the Tories that, at the worst, he was only going to bastinado a captain of the guard. Johnson wrote a reply to his assailants, in which he drew an elaborate parallel between Julian and James, then Duke of York. Julian had, during many years, pretended to abhor idolatry, while in heart an idolater. Julian had, to serve a turn, occasionally affected respect for the rights of conscience. Julian had punished cities which were zealous for the true religion, by taking away their municipal privileges. Julian had, by his flatterers, been called the Just. James was provoked beyond endurance. Johnson was prosecuted for a libel, convicted, and condemned to a fine which he had no means of paying. He was therefore kept in gaol; and it seemed likely that his confinement would end only with his life.*

Hugh
Speke.

Over the room which he occupied in the King's Bench prison lodged another offender whose character well deserves

* See the memoirs of Johnson, prefixed to the folio edition of his life, his Julian, and his answers to his opponents. See also Hickes's Jovian.

to be studied. This was Hugh Speke, a young man of good family, but of a singularly base and depraved nature. His love of mischief and of dark and crooked ways amounted almost to madness. To cause confusion without being found out was his business and his pastime ; and he had a rare skill in using honest enthusiasts as the instruments of his coldblooded malice. He had attempted, by means of one of his puppets, to fasten on Charles and James the crime of murdering Essex in the Tower. On this occasion the agency of Speke had been traced ; and though he succeeded in throwing the greater part of the blame on his dupe, he had not escaped with impunity. He was now a prisoner ; but his fortune enabled him to live with comfort ; and he was under so little restraint that he was able to keep up regular communication with one of his confederates who managed a secret press.

Johnson was the very man for Speke's purposes, zealous and intrepid, a scholar and a practised controversialist, yet as simple as a child. A close intimacy sprang up between the two fellow prisoners. Johnson wrote a succession of bitter and vehement treatises which Speke conveyed to the printer. When the camp was formed at Hounslow, Speke urged Johnson to compose an address which might excite the troops to mutiny. The paper was instantly drawn up. Many thousands of copies were struck off and brought to Speke's room, whence they were distributed over the whole country, and especially among the soldiers. A milder government than that which then ruled England would have been moved to high resentment by such a provocation. Strict search was made. A subordinate agent who had been employed to circulate the address saved himself by giving up Johnson ; and Johnson was not the man to save himself by giving up Speke. An information was filed, and a conviction obtained without difficulty. Julian Johnson, as he was popularly called, was sentenced to stand thrice in the pillory, and to be whipped from Newgate to Tyburn. The Judge, Sir Francis Withins, told the criminal to be thankful for the great lenity of the Attorney General, who might have treated the case as one of high treason. " I owe him no thanks," answered Johnson, dauntlessly. "Am I, whose only crime is that I have defended the Church and the laws, to be grateful for being scourged like a dog, while Popish scribblers are suffered daily to insult the Church and to violate the laws with impunity ? " The energy with which he spoke was such that both the Judges and

Pro-
ceedings
against
Johnson.

the crown lawyers thought it necessary to vindicate themselves, and to protest that they knew of no Popish publications such as those to which the prisoner alluded. He instantly drew from his pocket some Roman Catholic books and trinkets which were then freely exposed for sale under the royal patronage, read aloud the titles of the books, and threw a rosary across the table to the King's counsel. " And now," he cried with a loud voice, " I lay this information before God, before this court, and before the English people. We shall soon see whether Mr. Attorney will do his duty."

It was resolved that, before the punishment was inflicted, Johnson should be degraded from the priesthood. The prelates who had been charged by the Ecclesiastical Commission with the care of the diocese of London cited him before them in the chapter house of St. Paul's Cathedral. The manner in which he went through the ceremony made a deep impression on many minds. When he was stripped of his sacred robe he exclaimed, " You are taking away my gown because I have tried to keep your gowns on your backs." The only part of the formalities which seemed to distress him was the plucking of the Bible out of his hand. He made a faint struggle to retain the sacred book, kissed it, and burst into tears. " You cannot," he said, " deprive me of the hopes which I owe to it." Some attempts were made to obtain a remission of the flogging. A Roman Catholic priest offered to intercede in consideration of a bribe of two hundred pounds. The money was raised; and the priest did his best, but in vain. " Mr. Johnson," said the King, " has the spirit of a martyr; and it is fit that he should be one." William the Third said, a few years later, of one of the most acrimonious and intrepid Jacobites, " He has set his heart on being a martyr; and I have set mine on disappointing him." These two speeches would alone suffice to explain the widely different fates of the two princes.

The day appointed for the flogging came. A whip of nine lashes was used. Three hundred and seventeen stripes were inflicted; but the sufferer never winced. He afterwards said that the pain was cruel, but that, as he was dragged at the tail of the cart, he remembered how patiently the cross had been borne up Mount Calvary, and was so much supported by the thought that, but for the fear of incurring the suspicion of vainglory, he would have sung a psalm with as firm and cheerful a voice as if he had been worshipping God in the congregation. It is impossible not to wish that so much heroism had been less alloyed by intemperance and intolerance.*

Among the clergy of the Church of England Johnson found no sympathy. He had attempted to justify rebellion : he had even hinted approbation of regicide ; and they still, in spite of much provocation, clung to the doctrine of nonresistance. But they saw with alarm and concern the progress of what they considered as a noxious superstition, and, while they abjured all thought of defending their religion by the sword, betook themselves manfully to weapons of a different kind. To preach against the errors of Popery was now regarded by them as a point of duty and a point of honour. The London clergy, who were then in abilities and influence decidedly at the head of their profession, set an example which was bravely followed by their ruder brethren all over the country. Had only a few bold men taken this freedom, they would probably have been at once cited before the Ecclesiastical Commission ; but it was hardly possible to punish an offence which was committed every Sunday by thousands of divines, from Berwick to Penzance. The presses of the capital, of Oxford, and of Cambridge, never rested. The Act which subjected literature to a censorship did not seriously impede the exertions of Protestant controversialists ; for that Act contained a proviso in favour of the two Universities, and authorised the publication of theological works licensed by the Archbishop of Canterbury. It was therefore out of the power of the government to silence the defenders of the established religion. They were a numerous, an intrepid, and a well appointed band of combatants. Among them were eloquent declaimers, expert dialecticians, scholars deeply read in the writings of the fathers and in all parts of ecclesiastical history. Some of them, at a later period, turned against one another the formidable arms which they had wielded against the common enemy, and by their fierce contentions and insolent triumphs brought reproach on the Church which they had saved. But at present they formed an united phalanx. In the van appeared a rank of steady and skilful veterans, Tillotson, Stillingfleet, Sherlock, Prideaux, Whitby, Patrick, Tenison, Wake. The rear was brought up by the most distinguished

Marginal note: Zeal of the Anglican clergy against Popery.

---

* Life of Johnson, prefixed to his works ; Secret History of the happy Revolution, by Hugh Speke ; State Trials ; Van Citters, $\frac{\text{Nov. 23.}}{\text{Dec. 3.}}$ 1686. Van Citters gives the best account of the trial. I have seen a broadside which confirms his narrative.

bachelors of arts who were studying for deacon's orders. Conspicuous amongst the recruits whom Cambridge sent to the field was a distinguished pupil of the great Newton, Henry Wharton, who had, a few months before, been senior wrangler of his year, and whose early death was soon after deplored by men of all parties as an irreparable loss to letters.* Oxford was not less proud of a youth, whose great powers, first essayed in this conflict, afterwards troubled the Church and the State during forty eventful years, Francis Atterbury. By such men as these every question in issue between the Papists and the Protestants was debated, sometimes in a popular style which boys and women could comprehend, sometimes with the utmost subtlety of logic, and sometimes with an immense display of learning. The pretensions of the Holy See, the authority of tradition, purgatory, transubstantiation, the sacrifice of the mass, the adoration of the host, the denial of the cup to the laity, confession, penance, indulgences, extreme unction, the invocation of saints, the adoration of images, the celibacy of the clergy, the monastic vows, the practice of celebrating public worship in a tongue unknown to the multitude, the corruptions of the court of Rome, the history of the Reformation, the characters of the chief Reformers, were copiously discussed. Great numbers of absurd legends about miracles wrought by saints and relics were translated from the Italian, and published as specimens of the priestcraft by which the greater part of Christendom had been fooled. Of the tracts put forth on these subjects by Anglican divines during the short reign of James the Second many have probably perished. Those which may still be found in our great libraries make up a mass of near twenty thousand pages.†

The Roman Catholic divines overmatched.

The Roman Catholics did not yield the victory without a struggle. One of them, named Henry Hills, had been appointed printer to the royal household and chapel, and had been placed by the King at the head of a great office in London from which theological tracts came forth by hundreds. Obadiah Walker's press was not less active at Oxford. But, with the exception of some bad translations of Bossuet's ad-

---

* See the preface to Henry Wharton's Posthumous Sermons.

† This I can attest from my own researches. There is an excellent collection in the British Museum. Birch tells us, in his Life of Tillotson, that Archbishop Wake had not been able to form even a perfect catalogue of all the tracts published in this controversy.

mirable works, these establishments put forth nothing of the smallest value. It was indeed impossible for any intelligent and candid Roman Catholic to deny that the champions of his Church were, in every talent and acquirement, completely overmatched. The ablest of them would not, on the other side, have been considered as of the third rate. Many of them, even when they had something to say, knew not how to say it. They had been excluded by their religion from English schools and universities; nor had they ever, till the accession of James, found England an agreeable, or even a safe, residence. They had therefore passed the greater part of their lives on the Continent, and had almost unlearned their mother tongue. When they preached, their outlandish accent moved the derision of the audience. They spelt like washerwomen. Their diction was disfigured by foreign idioms; and, when they meant to be eloquent, they imitated, as well as they could, what was considered as fine writing in those Italian academies where rhetoric had then reached the last stage of corruption. Disputants labouring under these disadvantages would scarcely, even with truth on their side, have been able to make head against men whose style is eminently distinguished by simple purity and grace.*

The situation of England in the year 1686 cannot be better described than in the words of the French Ambassador.

---

* Cardinal Howard spoke strongly to Burnet at Rome on this subject. Burnet, i. 662. There is a curious passage to the same effect in a despatch of Barillon or Bonrepaux : but I have mislaid the reference.

One of the Roman Catholic divines who engaged in this controversy, a Jesuit named Andrew Pulton, whom Mr. Oliver, in his biography of the Order, pronounces to have been a man of distinguished ability, very frankly owns his deficiencies. " A. P., having been eighteen years out of his own country, pretends not yet to any perfection of the English expression or orthography." His spelling is indeed deplorable. In one of his letters wright is put for write, woed for would. He challenged Tenison to dispute with him in Latin, that they might be on equal terms. In a contemporary satire, entitled the Advice, is the following couplet :—

" Send Pulton to be lashed at Busby's school,
    That he in print no longer play the fool."

Another Roman Catholic, named William Clench, wrote a treatise on the Pope's supremacy, and dedicated it to the Queen in Italian. The following specimen of his style may suffice. " O del sagro marito fortunata consorte ! O dolce alleviamento d'affari alti ! O grato ristoro di pensieri noiosi, nel cui petto latteo, lucente specchio d'illibata matronal pudicizia, nel cui seno odorato, come in porto d'amor, si ritira il Giacomo ! O beata regia coppia ! O felice inserto tra l' invincibil leoni e le candide aquile !"

Clench's English is of a piece with his Tuscan. For example, " Peter signifies an inexpugnable rock, able to evacuate all the plots of hell's divan, and naufragate all the lurid designs of empoisoned heretics."

Another Roman Catholic treatise, entitled " The Church of England truly represented," begins by informing us that " the ignis fatuus of reformation, which had grown to a comet by many acts of spoil and rapine, had been ushered into England, purified of the filth which it had contracted among the lakes of the Alps."

" The discontent," he wrote, " is great and general : but the
fear of incurring still worse evils restrains all who have anything to lose.   The King openly expresses his joy at finding
himself in a situation to strike bold strokes.   He likes to be
complimented on this subject. He has talked to me about it,
and has assured me that he will not flinch."*

State of
Scotland.

Meanwhile in other parts of the empire events of grave importance had taken place.   The situation of the episcopalian
Protestants of Scotland differed widely from that in which
their English brethren stood.   In the south of the island the
religion of the state was the religion of the people, and had a
strength altogether independent of the strength derived from
the support of the government.   The sincere conformists
were far more numerous than the Papists and the Protestant
Dissenters taken together.   The Established Church of Scotland was the Church of a minority.   The lowland population
was generally attached to the Presbyterian discipline.   Prelacy was abhorred by the great body of Scottish Protestants,
both as an unscriptural and as a foreign institution.   It was
regarded by the disciples of Knox as a relic of the abominations of Babylon the Great.   It painfully reminded a people
proud of the memory of Wallace and Bruce that Scotland,
since her sovereigns had succeeded to a fairer inheritance,
had been independent in name only.   The episcopal polity
was also closely associated in the public mind with all the
evils produced by twenty-five years of cruel and corrupt maladministration.   Nevertheless this polity stood, though on a
narrow basis and amidst fearful storms, tottering indeed, yet
upheld by the civil magistrate, and leaning for support, whenever danger became serious, on the power of England.   The
records of the Scottish Parliament were thick set with laws
denouncing vengeance on those who in any direction strayed
from the prescribed pale.   By an Act passed in the time of
Knox, and breathing his spirit, it was a high crime to hear
mass, and the third offence was capital.†   An Act recently
passed, at the instance of James, made it death to preach in
any Presbyterian conventicle whatever, and even to attend
such a conventicle in the open air.‡   The Eucharist was not,
as in England, degraded into a civil test ; but no person
could hold any office, could sit in Parliament, or could even
vote for a member of Parliament, without subscribing, under

---

* Barillon, July $\frac{19}{29}$. 1686.
† Act Parl. Aug. 24. 1560. ; Dec. 15. 1567.   ‡ Act Parl. May 8. 1685.

the sanction of an oath, a declaration which condemned in the strongest terms the principles both of the Papists and of the Covenanters.*

In the Privy Council of Scotland there were two parties corresponding to the two parties which were contending against each other at Whitehall. William Douglas, Duke of Queensberry, was Lord Treasurer, and had, during some years, been considered as first minister. He was nearly connected by affinity, by similarity of opinions, and by similarity of temper, with the Treasurer of England. Both were Tories: both were men of hot temper and strong prejudices: both were ready to support their master in any attack on the civil liberties of his people; but both were sincerely attached to the Established Church. Queensbury had early notified to the court that, if any innovation affecting that Church were contemplated, to such innovation he could be no party. But among his colleagues were several men not less unprincipled than Sunderland. In truth the Council chamber at Edinburgh had been, during a quarter of a century, a seminary of all public and all private vices; and some of the politicians whose character had been formed there had a peculiar hardness of heart and forehead to which Westminster, even in that bad age, could hardly show anything quite equal. The Chancellor, James Drummond, Earl of Perth, and his brother, the Secretary of State, John Lord Melfort, were bent on supplanting Queensberry. The Chancellor had already an unquestionable title to the royal favour. He had brought into use a little steel thumbscrew which gave such exquisite torment that it had wrung confessions even out of men on whom His Majesty's favourite boot had been tried in vain.† But it was well known that even barbarity was not so sure a way to the heart of James as apostasy. To apostasy, therefore, Perth and Melfort resorted with a certain audacious baseness which no English statesman could hope to emulate. They declared that the papers found in the strong box of Charles the Second had converted them both to the true faith; and they began to confess and to hear mass.‡ How little conscience had to do with Perth's change of religion he amply proved by taking to wife, a few weeks later, in direct defiance of the laws of the Church which he had just joined, a lady who was his cousin german, without waiting for a dispensation. When the good Pope learned this, he said, with scorn and indigna-

Margin note: Queensberry.

Margin note: Perth and Melfort.

* Act Parl. Aug. 31. 1681.   † Burnet, i. 584.   ‡ Ibid. i. 652, 653.

tion which well became him, that this was a strange sort of conversion.* But James was more easily satisfied. The apostates presented themselves at Whitehall, and there received such assurances of his favour, that they ventured to bring direct charges against the Treasurer. Those charges, however, were so evidently frivolous that James was forced to acquit the accused minister; and many thought that the Chancellor had ruined himself by his malignant eagerness to ruin his rival. There were a few, however, who judged more correctly. Halifax, to whom Perth expressed some apprehensions, answered with a sneer that there was no danger. "Be of good cheer, my Lord: thy faith hath made thee whole." The prediction was correct. Perth and Melfort went back to Edinburgh, the real heads of the government of their country.† Another member of the Scottish Privy Council, Alexander Stuart, Earl of Murray, the descendant and heir of the Regent, abjured the religion of which his illustrious ancestor had been the foremost champion, and declared himself a member of the Church of Rome. Devoted as Queensberry had always been to the cause of prerogative, he could not stand his ground against competitors who were willing to pay such a price for the favour of the Court. He had to endure a succession of mortifications and humiliations similar to those which, about the same time, began to embitter the life of his friend Rochester. Royal letters came down authorising Papists to hold offices without taking the test. The clergy were strictly charged not to reflect on the Roman Catholic religion in their discourses. The Chancellor took on himself to send the macers of the Privy Council round to the few printers and booksellers who could then be found in Edinburgh, charging them not to publish any work without his license. It was well understood that this order was intended to prevent the circulation of Protestant treatises. One honest stationer told the messengers that he had in his shop a book which reflected in very coarse terms on Popery, and begged to know whether he might sell it. They asked to see it; and he showed them a copy of the Bible.‡ A cargo of copes, images, beads, crosses and censers arrived at Leith directed to Lord Perth. The importation of such articles had long been considered as illegal; but now the officers of the customs allowed the superstitious garments and trinkets

Favour shown to the Roman Catholic religion in Scotland.

---

* Burnet, i. 678.   † Ibid. i. 653.   ‡ Fountainhall, Jan. 28. 1685⅚

to pass.* In a short time it was known that a Popish chapel had been fitted up in the Chancellor's house, and that mass was regularly said there. The mob rose. The mansion where the idolatrous rites were celebrated was fiercely attacked. The iron bars which protected the windows were wrenched off. Lady Perth and some of her female friends were pelted with mud. One rioter was seized, and ordered by the Privy Council to be whipped. His fellows rescued him and beat the hangman. The city was all night in confusion. The students of the University mingled with the crowd and animated the tumult. Zealous burghers drank the health of the college lads and confusion to Papists, and encouraged each other to face the troops. The troops were already under arms. They were received with a shower of stones, which wounded an officer. Orders were given to fire; and several citizens were killed. The disturbance was serious; but the Drummonds, inflamed by resentment and ambition, exaggerated it strangely. Queensberry observed that their reports would lead any person, who had not witnessed what had passed, to believe that a sedition as formidable as that of Masaniello had been raging at Edinburgh. The brothers in return accused the Treasurer, not only of extenuating the crime of the insurgents, but of having himself prompted it, and did all in their power to obtain evidence of his guilt. One of the ringleaders, who had been taken, was offered a pardon if he would own that Queensberry had set him on; but the same religious enthusiasm, which had impelled the unhappy prisoner to criminal violence, prevented him from purchasing his life by a calumny. He and several of his accomplices were hanged. A soldier, who was accused of exclaiming, during the affray, that he should like to run his sword through a Papist, was shot; and Edinburgh was again quiet: but the sufferers were regarded as martyrs; and the Popish Chancellor became an object of mortal hatred, which in no long time was largely gratified.†

The King was much incensed. The news of the tumult reached him when the Queen, assisted by the Jesuits, had just triumphed over Lady Dorchester and her Protestant allies. The malecontents should find, he declared, that the only effect of the resistance offered to his will was to make him

Riots at Edinburgh.

Anger of the King

---

* Fountainhall. Jan. 11. 168⅚.
† Ibid. Jan. 31. and Feb. 1. 168⅚; Barnet, i. 678.; Trials of David Mow- bray and Alexander Keith, in the Collection of State Trials; Bonrepaux, Feb. 11/11.

more and more resolute.* He sent orders to the Scottish
Council to punish the guilty with the utmost severity, and to
make unsparing use of the boot.† He pretended to be fully
convinced of the Treasurer's innocence, and wrote to that
minister in gracious words; but the gracious words were
accompanied by ungracious acts. The Scottish Treasury was
put into commission in spite of the earnest remonstrances of
Rochester, who probably saw his own fate prefigured in that
of his kinsman.‡ Queensberry was, indeed, named First
Commissioner, and was made President of the Privy Council:
but his fall, though thus broken, was still a fall. He was
also removed from the government of the castle of Edinburgh,
and was succeeded in that confidential post by the Duke of
Gordon, a Roman Catholic.§

His plans concerning Scotland.

And now a letter arrived from London, fully explaining to
the Scottish Privy Council the intentions of the King.
What he wanted was that the Roman Catholics should be
exempted from all laws imposing penalties and disabilities on
account of nonconformity, but that the persecution of the
Covenanters should go on without mitigation.‖ This scheme
encountered strenuous opposition in the Council. Some
members were unwilling to see the existing laws relaxed.
Others, who were by no means averse to relaxation, felt that
it would be monstrous to admit Roman Catholics to the
highest honours of the State, and yet to leave unrepealed the
Act which made it death to attend a Presbyterian conventicle. The answer of the board was, therefore, less obse-

Deputation of Scotch Privy Councillors sent to London.

quious than usual. The King in reply sharply reprimanded
his undutiful Councillors, and ordered three of them, the
Duke of Hamilton, Sir George Lockhart, and General Drummond, to attend him at Westminster. Hamilton's abilities
and knowledge, though by no means such as would have
sufficed to raise an obscure man to eminence, appeared highly
respectable in one who was premier peer of Scotland. Lockhart had long been regarded as one of the first jurists, logi-
cians, and orators that his country had produced, and enjoyed
also that sort of consideration which is derived from large
possessions; for his estate was such as at that time very few

---

* Lewis to Barillon, Feb. ⅛/²⁸. 1686.
† Fountainhall, Feb. 16.; Wodrow, book iii. chap. x. sec. 3. "We require," His Majesty graciously wrote, "that you spare no legal trial by torture or

otherwise."
‡ Bonrepaux, Feb. ⅛/²⁸. 1686.
§ Fountainhall, March 11. 1686; Adda, March ⅟₁₁.
‖ This letter is dated March 4. 1686.

Scottish nobles possessed.* He had been lately appointed President of the Court of Session. Drummond, a cousin of Perth and Melfort, was commander of the forces in Scotland. He was a loose and profane man: but a sense of honour which his two kinsmen wanted restrained him from public apostasy. He lived and died, in the significant phrase of one of his countrymen, a bad Christian, but a good Protestant.†

James was pleased by the dutiful language which the three Councillors used when first they appeared before him. He spoke highly of them to Barillon, and particularly extolled Lockhart as the ablest and most eloquent Scotchman living. They soon proved, however, less tractable than had been expected; and it was rumoured at Court that they had been perverted by the company which they had kept in London. Hamilton lived much with zealous churchmen; and it might be feared that Lockhart, who was related to the Wharton family, had fallen into still worse society. In truth it was natural that statesmen, fresh from a country where opposition in any other form than that of insurrection and assassination had long been almost unknown, and where all that was not lawless fury was abject submission, should have been struck by the earnest and stubborn, yet sober, discontent which pervaded England, and should have been emboldened to try the experiment of constitutional resistance to the royal will. They indeed declared themselves willing to grant large relief to the Roman Catholics; but on two conditions; first, that similar indulgence should be extended to the Calvinistic sectaries; and, secondly, that the King should bind himself by a solemn promise not to attempt anything to the prejudice of the Protestant religion.

Both conditions were highly distasteful to James. He reluctantly agreed, however, after a dispute which lasted several days, that some indulgence should be granted to the Presbyterians: but he would by no means consent to allow them the full liberty which he demanded for members of his own communion.‡ To the second condition proposed by the

Their negotiations with the King.

---

* Barillon, April $\frac{19}{29}$. 1686; Burnet, i. 370.

† The words are in a letter of Johnstone of Waristoun.

‡ Some words of Barillon deserve to be transcribed. They would alone suffice to decide a question which ignorance and party spirit have done much to perplex. " Cette liberté accordée aux nonconformistes a faite une grande difficulté, et a été débattue pendant plusieurs jours. Le Roy d'Angleterre avoit fort envie que les Catholiques eussent seuls la liberté de l'exercice de leur religion." April $\frac{19}{29}$. 1686.

three Scottish Councillors he positively refused to listen. The Protestant religion, he said, was false; and he would not give any guarantee that he would not use his power to the prejudice of a false religion. The altercation was long, and was not brought to a conclusion satisfactory to either party.*

Meeting of the Scotch Estates. The time fixed for the meeting of the Scottish Estates drew near; and it was necessary that the three Councillors should leave London to attend their parliamentary duty at Edinburgh. On this occasion another affront was offered to Queensberry. In the late session he had held the office of Lord High Commissioner, and had in that capacity represented the majesty of the absent King. This dignity, the greatest to which a Scottish noble could aspire, was now transferred to the renegade Murray.

They prove refractory. On the twenty-ninth of April the Parliament met at Edinburgh. A letter from the King was read. He exhorted the Estates to give relief to his Roman Catholic subjects, and offered in return a free trade with England and an amnesty for political offences. A committee was appointed to draw up an answer. That committee, though named by Murray, and composed of Privy Councillors and courtiers, framed a reply, full indeed of dutiful and respectful expressions, yet clearly indicating a determination to refuse what the King demanded. The Estates, it was said, would go as far as their consciences would allow to meet His Majesty's wishes respecting his subjects of the Roman Catholic religion. These expressions were far from satisfying the Chancellor; yet, such as they were, he was forced to content himself with them, and even had some difficulty in persuading the Parliament to adopt them. Objection was taken by some zealous Protestants to the mention made of the Roman Catholic religion. There was no such religion. There was an idolatrous apostasy, which the laws punished with the halter, and to which it did not become Christian men to give flattering titles. To call such a superstition Catholic was to give up the whole question which was at issue between Rome and the reformed Churches. The offer of a free trade with England was treated as an insult. "Our fathers," said one orator, "sold their king for southern gold; and we still lie under the reproach of that foul bargain. Let it not be said of us that we have sold our God!" Sir John Lauder of Fountainhall,

* Barillon, April $\frac{19}{29}$. 1686; Citters, April $\frac{13}{23}$. $\frac{20}{30}$., May $\frac{9}{19}$.

one of the Senators of the College of Justice, suggested the words, "the persons commonly called Roman Catholics." "Would you nickname His Majesty?" exclaimed the Chancellor. The answer drawn by the committee was carried; but a large and respectable minority voted against the proposed words as too courtly.* It was remarked that the representatives of the towns were, almost to a man, against the government. Hitherto those members had been of very small account in the Parliament, and had generally been considered as the retainers of powerful noblemen. They now showed, for the first time, an independence, a resolution, and a spirit of combination which alarmed the court.†

The answer was so unpleasing to James that he did not suffer it to be printed in the Gazette. Soon he learned that a law, such as he wished to see passed, would not even be brought in. The Lords of Articles, whose business was to draw up the Acts on which the Estates were afterwards to deliberate, were virtually nominated by himself. Yet even the Lords of Articles proved refractory. When they met, the three Privy Councillors who had lately returned from London took the lead in opposition to the royal will. Hamilton declared plainly that he could not do what was asked. He was a faithful and loyal subject; but there was a limit imposed by conscience. "Conscience!" said the Chancellor: "conscience is a vague word, which signifies anything or nothing." Lockhart, who sate in Parliament as representative of the great county of Lanark, struck in. "If conscience," he said, be a word without meaning, we will change it for another phrase which, I hope, means something. For conscience let us put the fundamental laws of Scotland." These words raised a fierce debate. General Drummond, who represented Perthshire, declared that he agreed with Hamilton and Lockhart. Most of the Bishops present took the same side.‡

---

* Fountainhall, May 6. 1686.

† Ibid. June 15. 1686.

‡ Van Citters, May $\frac{11}{21}$. 1686. Van Citters informed the States that he had his intelligence from a sure hand. I will transcribe part of his narrative. It is an amusing specimen of the pyebald dialect in which the Dutch diplomatists of that age corresponded.

"Des konigs missive, boven en behalven den Hoog Commissaris aensprake, aen het parlement afgesonden, gelyck dat altoos gebruyckelyck is, waerby Syne Majesteyt nu in genere versocht heft de mitigatie der rigoureuse ofte sanglante wetten van het Ryck jegens het Pausdom, in het Generale Comitée des Articles (soo men het daer naemt) na ordre gestelt en gelesen synde, in 't voteren, den Hertog van Hamilton onder anderen klaer uyt seyde dat hy daertoe niet soude verstaen, dat hy anders genegen was den konig in allen voorval getrouw te dienen volgens het dictamen syner conscientie: 't gene reden gaf aen de Lord Cancelier de Grave Ports te seggen dat het woort conscientie niets en beduyde, en alleen een individuum vagum was, waerop der

It was plain that, even in the Committee of Articles, James could not command a majority. He was mortified and irritated by the tidings. He held warm and menacing language, and punished some of his mutinous servants, in the hope that the rest would take warning. Several persons were dismissed from the Council board. Several were deprived of pensions, which formed an important part of their income. Sir George Mackenzie of Rosehaugh was the most distinguished victim. He had long held the office of Lord Advocate, and had taken such a part in the persecution of the Covenanters that to this day he holds, in the estimation of the austere and godly peasantry of Scotland, a place not far removed from the unenviable eminence occupied by Claverhouse. The legal learning of Mackenzie was not profound: but, as a scholar, a wit, and an orator, he stood high in the opinion of his countrymen; and his renown had spread even to the coffeehouses of London and to the cloisters of Oxford. The remains of his forensic speeches prove him to have been a man of parts, but are somewhat disfigured by what he doubtless considered as Ciceronian graces, interjections which show more art than passion, and elaborate amplifications, in which epithet rises above epithet in wearisome climax. He had now, for the first time, been found scrupulous. He was, therefore, in spite of all his claims on the gratitude of the government, deprived of his office. He retired into the country, and soon after went up to London for the purpose of clearing himself, but was refused admission to the royal presence.* While the King was thus trying to terrify the Lords of Articles into submission, the popular voice encouraged them to persist. The utmost exertions of the Chancellor could not prevent the national sentiment from expressing itself through the pulpit and the press. One tract, written with such boldness and acrimony that no printer dared to put it in type, was widely circulated in manuscript. The papers which appeared on the other side of the question had much less effect, though they were disseminated at the public charge, and though the

Chevalier Locquard dan verder gingh; wil man niet verstaen de betyckenis van het woordt conscientie, soo sal ik in fortioribus seggen dat wy meynen volgens de fondamentale wetten van het ryck."

There is, in the Hind Let Loose, a curious passage to which I should have given no credit, but for this despatch of Van Citters. "They cannot endure so much as to hear of the name of conscience. One that was well acquaint with the Council's humour in this point told a gentleman that was going before them, 'I beseech you, whatever you do, speak nothing of conscience before the Lords, for they cannot abide to hear that word.'"

* Fountainhall, May 17. 1686.

Scottish defenders of the government were assisted by an English auxiliary of great note, Lestrange, who had been sent down to Edinburgh, and lodged in Holyrood House.*

At length, after three weeks of debate, the Lords of Articles came to a decision. They proposed merely that Roman Catholics should be permitted to worship God in private houses without incurring any penalty; and it soon appeared that, far as this measure was from coming up to the King's demands and expectations, the Estates either would not pass it at all, or would pass it with great restrictions and modifications.

While the contest lasted the anxiety in London was intense. Every report, every line, from Edinburgh was eagerly devoured. One day the story ran that Hamilton had given way, and that the government would carry every point. Then came intelligence that the opposition had rallied and was more obstinate than ever. At the most critical moment, orders were sent to the postoffice that the bags from Scotland should be transmitted to Whitehall. During a whole week, not a single private letter from beyond the Tweed was delivered in London. In our age, such an interruption of communication would throw the whole island into confusion: but there was then so little trade and correspondence between England and Scotland that the inconvenience was probably much smaller than has often been occasioned in our own time by a short delay in the arrival of the Indian mail. While the ordinary channels of information were thus closed, the crowd in the galleries of Whitehall observed with attention the countenances of the King and his ministers. It was noticed, with great satisfaction, that, after every express from the North, the enemies of the Protestant religion looked more and more gloomy. At length, to the general joy, it was announced that the struggle was over, that the government had been unable to carry its measures, and that the Lord High Commissioner had adjourned the Parliament.† They are adjourned.

If James had not been proof to all warning, these events would have sufficed to warn him. A few months before this time, the most obsequious of English Parliaments had refused to submit to his pleasure. But the most obsequious of English Parliaments might be regarded as an independent and even Arbitrary system of government in Scotland.

* Wodrow, III. x. 3.

† Van Citters. $\frac{\text{May 28.}}{\text{June 7,}}$ June $\frac{1}{11}$. $\frac{4}{14}$. 1686; Fountainhall, June 15.; Luttrell's Diary, June 2. 16.

as a mutinous assembly when compared with any Parliament
that had ever sate in Scotland; and the servile spirit of Scottish
Parliaments was always to be found in the highest perfection,
extracted and condensed, among the Lords of Articles.   Yet
even the Lords of Articles had been refractory. It was plain
that all those classes, all those institutions, which, up to this
year, had been considered as the strongest supports of monarchical power, must, if the King persisted in his insane policy,
be reckoned as parts of the strength of the opposition. All these
signs, however, were lost upon him.   To every expostulation
he had one answer: he would never give way; for concession had
ruined his father; and his unconquerable firmness was loudly
applauded by the French embassy and by the Jesuitical cabal.

He now proclaimed that he had been only too gracious when
he had condescended to ask the assent of the Scottish Estates
to his wishes. His prerogative would enable him, not only to
protect those whom he favoured, but to punish those who had
crossed him.   He was confident that, in Scotland, his dispensing power would not be questioned by any court of law.
There was a Scottish Act of Supremacy which gave to the
sovereign such a control over the Church as might have satisfied Henry the Eighth. Accordingly Papists were admitted
in crowds to offices and honours. The Bishop of Dunkeld,
who, as a Lord of Parliament, had opposed the government,
was arbitrarily ejected from his see, and a successor was appointed.   Queensberry was stripped of all his employments,
and was ordered to remain at Edinburgh till the accounts of
the Treasury during his administration had been examined
and approved.* As the representatives of the towns had been
found the most unmanageable part of the Parliament, it was
determined to make a revolution in every burgh throughout
the kingdom. A similar change had recently been effected in
England by judicial sentences : but in Scotland a simple mandate of the prince was thought sufficient.   All elections of magistrates and of town councils were prohibited ; and the King
assumed to himself the right of filling up the chief municipal
offices.† In a formal letter to the Privy Council he announced
his intention to fit up a Roman Catholic chapel in his palace
of Holyrood ; and he gave orders that the Judges should be
directed to treat all the laws against Papists as null, on pain
of his high displeasure. He however comforted the Protestant Episcopalians by assuring them that, though he was de-

* Fountainhall, June 21. 1686.   † Ibid. Sept. 16. 1686.

termined to protect the Roman Catholic Church against them, he was equally determined to protect them against any encroachment on the part of the fanatics. To this communication Perth proposed an answer couched in the most servile terms. The Council now contained many Papists: the Protestant members who still had seats had been cowed by the King's obstinacy and severity; and only a few faint murmurs were heard. Hamilton threw out against the dispensing power some hints which he made haste to explain away. Lockhart said that he would lose his head rather than sign such a letter as the Chancellor had drawn, but took care to say this in a whisper which was heard only by friends. Perth's words were adopted with inconsiderable modifications; and the royal commands were obeyed; but a sullen discontent spread through that minority of the Scottish nation by the aid of which the government had hitherto held the majority down.*

When the historian of this troubled reign turns to Ireland, his task becomes peculiarly difficult and delicate. His steps, to borrow the fine image used on a similar occasion by a Roman poet, are on the thin crust of ashes, beneath which the lava is still glowing. The seventeenth century has, in that unhappy country, left to the nineteenth a fatal heritage of malignant passions. No amnesty for the mutual wrongs inflicted by the Saxon defenders of Londonderry, and by the Celtic defenders of Limerick, has ever been granted from the heart by either race. To this day a more than Spartan haughtiness alloys the many noble qualities which characterise the children of the victors, while a Helot feeling, compounded of awe and hatred, is but too often discernible in the children of the vanquished. Neither of the hostile castes can justly be absolved from blame; but the chief blame is due to that short-sighted and headstrong prince who, placed in a situation in which he might have reconciled them, employed all his power to inflame their animosity, and at length forced them to close in a grapple for life and death. *Ireland.*

The grievances under which the members of his Church laboured in Ireland differed widely from those which he was attempting to remove in England and Scotland. The Irish Statute Book, afterwards polluted by intolerance as barbarous as that of the dark ages, then contained scarcely a single enactment, and not a single stringent enactment, imposing any penalty on Papists as such. On our side of Saint George's *State of the law on the subject of religion,*

* Fountainhall, Sept. 16.; Wodrow, III. x. 3.

Channel every priest who received a neophyte into the bosom of the Church of Rome was liable to be hanged, drawn, and quartered. On the other side he incurred no such danger. A Jesuit who landed at Dover took his life in his hand; but he walked the streets of Dublin in security. Here no man could hold office, or even earn his livelihood as a barrister or a schoolmaster, without previously taking the oath of supremacy: but in Ireland a public functionary was not held to be under the necessity of taking that oath unless it were formally tendered to him.* It therefore did not exclude from employment any person whom the government wished to promote. The sacramental test and the declaration against transubstantiation were unknown; nor was either House of Parliament closed by law against any religious sect.

Hostility of races.

It might seem, therefore, that the Irish Roman Catholic was in a situation which his English and Scottish brethren in the faith might well envy. In fact, however, his condition was more pitiable and irritating than theirs. For, though not persecuted as a Roman Catholic, he was oppressed as an Irishman. In his country the same line of demarcation which separated religions separated races; and he was of the conquered, the subjugated, the degraded race. On the same soil dwelt two populations, locally intermixed, morally and politically sundered. The difference of religion was by no means the only difference, or even the chief difference, which existed between them. They sprang from different stocks. They spoke different languages. They had different national characters as strongly opposed as any two national characters in Europe. They were in widely different stages of civilisation. Between two such populations there could be little sympathy; and centuries of calamities and wrongs had generated a strong antipathy. The relation in which the minority stood to the majority resembled the relation in which the followers of William the Conqueror stood to the Saxon churls, or the relation in which the followers of Cortes stood to the Indians of Mexico.

The appellation of Irish was then given exclusively to the Celts and to those families which, though not of Celtic origin,

* The provisions of the Irish Act of Supremacy, 2 Eliz. chap. 1., are substantially the same with those of the English Act of Supremacy, 1 Eliz. chap. 1.: but the English Act was soon found to be defective; and the defect was supplied by a more stringent act, 5 Eliz. chap. 1.   No such supplementary law was made in Ireland. That the construction mentioned in the text was put on the Irish Act of Supremacy, we are told by Archbishop King: State of Ireland, chap. ii. sec. 9. He calls this construction Jesuitical; but I cannot see it in that light.

had in the course of ages degenerated into Celtic manners. These people, probably about a million in number, had, with few exceptions, adhered to the Church of Rome. Among them resided about two hundred thousand colonists, proud of their Saxon blood and of their Protestant faith.*

The great preponderance of numbers on one side was more than compensated by a great superiority of intelligence, vigour, and organisation on the other. The English settlers seem to have been, in knowledge, energy, and perseverance, rather above than below the average level of the population of the mother country. The aboriginal peasantry, on the contrary, were in an almost savage state. They never worked till they felt the sting of hunger. They were content with accommodation inferior to that which, in happier countries, was provided for domestic cattle. Already the potato, a root which can be cultivated with scarcely any art, industry, or capital, and which cannot be long stored, had become the food of the common people.† From a people so fed diligence and forethought were not to be expected. Even within a few miles of Dublin, the traveller, on a soil the richest and most verdant in the world, saw with disgust the miserable burrows out of which squalid and half naked barbarians stared wildly at him as he passed.‡

Aboriginal peasantry.

The aboriginal aristocracy retained in no common measure the pride of birth, but had lost the influence which is derived from wealth and power. Their lands had been divided by Cromwell among his followers. A portion, indeed, of the vast territory which he had confiscated had, after the restoration of the House of Stuart, been given back to the ancient proprietors. But much the greater part was still held by English emigrants under the guarantee of an Act of Parliament. This act had been in force a quarter of a century; and under it mortgages, settlements, sales, and leases without number had been made. The old Irish gentry were scattered over the whole world. Descendants of Milesian chieftains swarmed in all the courts and camps of the Continent. Those despoiled proprietors who still remained in their native land, brooded gloomily over their losses, pined for the opulence and dignity of which they had been deprived, and cherished wild hopes of another revolution. A person of this class was described by

Aboriginal aristocracy.

---

* Political Anatomy of Ireland.　　Account of Ireland, 1699.
† Political Anatomy of Ireland, 1672;　‡ Clarendon to Rochester, May 4.
Irish Hudibras, 1689; John Dunton's 1686.

his countrymen as a gentleman who would be rich if justice were done, as a gentleman who had a fine estate if he could only get it.* He seldom betook himself to any peaceful calling. Trade, indeed, he thought a far more disgraceful resource than marauding. Sometimes he turned freebooter. Sometimes he contrived, in defiance of the law, to live by coshering, that is to say, by quartering himself on the old tenants of his family, who, wretched as was their own condition, could not refuse a portion of their pittance to one whom they still regarded as their rightful lord.† The native gentleman who had been so fortunate as to keep or to regain some of his land too often lived like the petty prince of a savage tribe, and indemnified himself for the humiliations which the dominant race made him suffer by governing his vassals despotically, by keeping a rude harem, and by maddening or stupefying himself daily with strong drink.‡ Politically he was insignificant. No statute, indeed, excluded him from the House of Commons; but he had almost as little chance of obtaining a seat there as a man of colour has of being chosen a Senator of the United States. In fact only one Papist had been returned to the Irish Parliament since the Restoration. The whole legislative and executive power was in the hands of the colonists; and the ascendency of the ruling caste was upheld by a standing army of seven thousand men, on whose zeal for what was called the English interest full reliance could be placed.§

On a close scrutiny it would have been found that neither the Irishry nor the Englishry formed a perfectly homogeneous body. The distinction between those Irish who were of Celtic blood, and those Irish who sprang from the followers of Strongbow and De Burgh, was not altogether effaced. The Fitzes sometimes permitted themselves to speak with scorn of the Os and Macs; and the Os and Macs sometimes repaid that scorn with aversion. In the preceding generation one of the most powerful of the O'Neills refused to pay any mark of respect to a Roman Catholic gentleman of old Norman descent. "They say that the family has been here four hundred years. No matter. I hate the clown as if he had come

* Bishop Malony's Letter to Bishop Tyrrel, March 8. 1689.

† Statute 10 & 11 Charles I. chap. 16.; King's State of the Protestants of Ireland, chap. ii. sec. 8.

‡ King, chap. ii. sec. 8. Miss Edgeworth's King Corny belongs to a later

and much more civilised generation; but whoever has studied that admirable portrait can form some notion of what King Corny's greatgrandfather must have been.

§ King, chap. iii. sec. 2.

yesterday."* It seems, however, that such feelings were rare, and that the feud which had long raged between the aboriginal Celts and the degenerate English had nearly given place to the fiercer feud which separated both races from the modern and Protestant colony.

That colony had its own internal disputes, both national and religious. The majority was English; but a large minority came from the south of Scotland. One half of the settlers belonged to the Established Church: the other half were Dissenters. But in Ireland Scot and Southron were strongly bound together by their common Saxon origin. Churchman and Presbyterian were strongly bound together by their common Protestantism. All the colonists had a common language and a common pecuniary interest. They were surrounded by common enemies, and could be safe only by means of common precautions and exertions. The few penal laws, therefore, which had been made in Ireland against Protestant Nonconformists, were a dead letter.† The bigotry of the most sturdy churchman would not bear exportation across Saint George's Channel. As soon as the Cavalier arrived in Ireland, and found that, without the hearty and courageous assistance of his Puritan neighbours, he and all his family would run imminent risk of being murdered by Popish marauders, his hatred of Puritanism, in spite of himself, began to languish and die away. It was remarked by eminent men of both parties that a Protestant who, in Ireland, was called a high Tory would in England have been considered as a moderate Whig.‡

The Protestant Nonconformists, on their side, endured, with more patience than could have been expected, the sight of the most absurd ecclesiastical establishment that the world has ever seen. Four Archbishops and eighteen Bishops were employed in looking after about a fifth part of the number of churchmen who inhabited the single diocese of London. Of

State of the English colony

* Sheridan MS.; Preface to the first volume of the Hibernia Anglicana, 1690; Secret Consults of the Romish party in Ireland, 1689.

† "There was a free liberty of conscience by connivance, though not by the law."—King, chap. iii. sec. 1.

‡ In a letter to James found among Bishop Tyrrel's papers, and dated Aug. 14. 1686, are some remarkable expressions. "There are few or none Protestants in that country but such as are

joined with the Whigs against the common enemy." And again: "Those that passed for Tories here" (that is in England) "publicly espouse the Whig quarrel on the other side the water." Swift said the same thing to King William a few years later: "I remember when I was last in England I told the King that the highest Tories we had with us would make tolerable Whigs there."—Letter concerning the Sacramental Test.

the parochial clergy a large proportion were pluralists, and resided at a distance from their cures. There were some who drew from their benefices incomes of little less than a thousand pounds a year, without ever performing any spiritual function. Yet this monstrous institution was much less disliked by the Puritans settled in Ireland than the Church of England by the English sectaries. For in Ireland religious divisions were subordinate to national divisions; and the Presbyterian, while, as a theologian, he could not but condemn the established hierarchy, yet looked on that hierarchy with a sort of complacency when he considered it as a sumptuous and ostentatious trophy of the victory achieved by the great race from which he sprang.*

Thus the grievances of the Irish Roman Catholic had hardly anything in common with the grievances of the English Roman Catholic. The Roman Catholic of Lancashire or Staffordshire had only to turn Protestant; and he was at once, in all respects, on a level with his neighbours: but, if the Roman Catholics of Munster and Connaught had turned Protestants, they would still have continued to be a subject people. Whatever evils the Roman Catholic suffered in England were the effects of harsh legislation, and might have been remedied by a more liberal legislation. But between the two populations which inhabited Ireland there was an inequality which legislation had not caused and could not remove. The dominion which one of those populations exercised over the other was the dominion of wealth over poverty, of knowledge over ignorance, of civilised over uncivilised man.

Course which James ought to have followed.

James himself seemed, at the commencement of his reign, to be perfectly aware of these truths. The distractions of Ireland, he said, arose, not from the differences between the Catholics and the Protestants, but from the differences between the Irish and the English.† The consequences which he should have drawn from this just proposition were sufficiently obvious; but, unhappily for himself and for Ireland, he failed to perceive them.

If only national animosity could be allayed, there could be little doubt that religious animosity, not being kept alive, as

* The wealth and negligence of the established clergy of Ireland are mentioned in the strongest terms by the Lord Lieutenant Clarendon, a most unexceptionable witness.

† Clarendon reminds the King of this in a letter dated March 14. 168⅚. "It certainly is," Clarendon adds, "a most true notion."

in England, by cruel penal acts and stringent test acts, would of itself fade away. To allay a national animosity such as that which the two races inhabiting Ireland felt for each other could not be the work of a few years. Yet it was a work to which a wise and good prince might have contributed much; and James would have undertaken that work with advantages such as none of his predecessors or successors possessed. At once an Englishman and a Roman Catholic, he belonged half to the ruling and half to the subject caste, and was therefore peculiarly qualified to be a mediator between them. Nor is it difficult to trace the course which he ought to have pursued. He ought to have determined that the existing settlement of landed property should be inviolable; and he ought to have announced that determination in such a manner as effectually to quiet the anxiety of the new proprietors, and to extinguish any wild hopes which the old proprietors might entertain. Whether, in the great transfer of estates, injustice had or had not been committed, was immaterial. That transfer, just or unjust, had taken place so long ago, that to reverse it would be to unfix the foundations of society. There must be a time of limitation to all rights. After thirty-five years of actual possession, after twenty-five years of possession solemnly guaranteed by statute, after innumerable leases and releases, mortgages and devises, it was too late to search for flaws in titles. Nevertheless something might have been done to heal the lacerated feelings and to raise the fallen fortunes of the Irish gentry. The colonists were in a thriving condition. They had greatly improved their property by building, planting, and enclosing. The rents had almost doubled within a few years; trade was brisk; and the revenue, amounting to about three hundred thousand pounds a year, more than defrayed all the charges of the local government, and afforded a surplus which was remitted to England. There was no doubt that the next Parliament which should meet at Dublin, though representing almost exclusively the English interest, would, in return for the King's promise to maintain that interest in all its legal rights, willingly grant to him a very considerable sum for the purpose of indemnifying, at least in part, such native families as had been wrongfully despoiled. It was thus that in our own time the French government put an end to the disputes engendered by the most extensive confiscation that ever took place in Europe. And thus, if James had been guided by the advice of his most loyal Protestant counsellors, he would have at least greatly mitigated one of the chief evils which afflicted Ireland.*

Having done this, he should have laboured to reconcile the hostile races to each other by impartially defending the rights and restraining the excesses of both. He should have punished with equal severity the native who indulged in the license of barbarism, and the colonist who abused the strength of civilisation. As far as the legitimate authority of the crown extended,—and in Ireland it extended far,—no man who was qualified for office by integrity and ability should have been considered as disqualified by extraction or by creed for any public trust. It is probable that a Roman Catholic King, with an ample revenue absolutely at his disposal, would, without much difficulty, have secured the cooperation of the Roman Catholic prelates and priests in the great work of reconciliation. Much, however, must still have been left to the healing influence of time. The native race would still have had to learn from the colorists industry and forethought, the arts of civilised life, and the language of England. There could not be equality between men who lived in houses and men who lived in sties, between men who were fed on bread and men who were fed on potatoes, between men who spoke the noble tongue of great philosophers and poets, and men who, with a perverted pride, boasted that they could not writhe their mouths into chattering such a jargon as that in which the Advancement of Learning and the Paradise Lost were written.† Yet it is not unreasonable to believe that, if the gentle policy which has been described had been steadily followed by the government, all distinctions would gradually have been effaced, and that there would now have been no more trace of the hostility which has been the curse of Ireland than there is of the equally deadly hostility which once raged between the Saxons and the Normans in England.

His errors. Unhappily James, instead of becoming a mediator, became the fiercest and most reckless of partisans. Instead of allaying the animosity of the two populations, he inflamed it to a height before unknown. He determined to reverse their relative position, and to put the Protestant colonists under

---

* Clarendon strongly recommended this course, and was of opinion that the Irish Parliament would do its part. See his letter to Ormond, Aug. 28. 1686.

† It was an O'Neil of great eminence who said that it did not become him to writhe his mouth to chatter English. Preface to the first volume of the Hibernia Anglicana.

the feet of the Popish Celts. To be of the established religion, to be of the English blood, was, in his view, a disqualification for civil and military employment. He meditated the design of again confiscating and again portioning out the soil of half the island, and showed his inclination so clearly that one class was soon agitated by terrors which he afterwards vainly wished to soothe, and the other by cupidity which he afterwards vainly wished to restrain. But this was the smallest part of his guilt and madness. He deliberately resolved, not merely to give to the aboriginal inhabitants of Ireland the entire dominion of their own country, but also to use them as his instruments for setting up arbitrary government in England. The event was such as might have been foreseen. The colonists turned to bay with the stubborn hardihood of their race. The mother country justly regarded their cause as her own. Then came a desperate struggle for a tremendous stake. Everything dear to nations was wagered on both sides : nor can we justly blame either the Irishman or the Englishman for obeying, in that extremity, the law of selfpreservation. The contest was terrible, but short. The weaker went down. His fate was cruel ; and yet for the cruelty with which he was treated there was, not indeed a defence, but an excuse : for, though he suffered all that tyranny could inflict, he suffered nothing that he would not himself have inflicted. The effect of the insane attempt to subjugate England by means of Ireland was that the Irish became hewers of wood and drawers of water to the English. The old proprietors, by their effort to recover what they had lost, lost the greater part of what they had retained. The momentary ascendency of Popery produced such a series of barbarous laws against Popery as made the statute book of Ireland a proverb of infamy throughout Christendom. Such were the bitter fruits of the policy of James.

We have seen that one of his first acts, after he became King, was to recall Ormond from Ireland. Ormond was the head of the English interest in that kingdom : he was firmly attached to the Protestant religion ; and his power far exceeded that of an ordinary Lord Lieutenant, first, because he was in rank and wealth the greatest of the colonists, and secondly, because he was not only the chief of the civil administration, but also commander of the forces. The King was not at that time disposed to commit the government wholly to Irish hands. He had indeed been heard to say that a native viceroy would soon become an independent sovereign.* For the present, therefore, he determined to divide the power which Ormond had possessed, to entrust the civil administration to an English and Protestant Lord Lieutenant, and to give the command of the army to an Irish and Roman Catholic General. The Lord Lieutenant was Clarendon: the General was Tyrconnel.

Tyrconnel sprang, as has already been said, from one of those degenerate families of the Pale which were popularly classed with the aboriginal population of Ireland. He sometimes indeed, in his rants, talked with Norman haughtiness of the Celtic barbarians:† but all his sympathies were really with the natives. The Protestant colonists he hated; and they returned his hatred. Clarendon's inclinations were very different: but he was, from temper, interest, and principle, an obsequious courtier. His spirit was mean: his circumstances were embarrassed; and his mind had been deeply imbued with the political doctrines which the Church of England had in that age too assiduously taught. His abilities, however, were not contemptible; and, under a good King, he would probably have been a respectable viceroy.

Clarendon arrives in Ireland as Lord Lieutenant.

About three quarters of a year elapsed between the recall of Ormond and the arrival of Clarendon at Dublin. During that interval the King was represented by a board of Lords Justices: but the military administration was in Tyrconnel's hands. Already the designs of the court began gradually to unfold themselves. A royal order came from Whitehall for disarming the population. This order Tyrconnel strictly executed as respected the English. Though the country was infested by predatory bands, a Protestant gentleman could scarcely obtain permission to keep a brace of pistols. The native peasantry, on the other hand, were suffered to retain their weapons.‡ The joy of the colonists was therefore great, when at length, in December 1685, Tyrconnel went to London, and Clarendon came to Dublin. But it soon appeared that the government was really directed, not at Dublin, but in London. Every mail that crossed Saint George's Channel

---

* Sheridan MS. among the Stuart Papers. I ought to acknowledge the courtesy with which Mr. Glover assisted me in my search for this valuable manuscript. James appears, from the instructions which he drew up for his son in 1692, to have retained to the last the notion that Ireland could not without danger be entrusted to an Irish Lord Lieutenant.

† Sheridan MS.

‡ Clarendon to Rochester, Jan. 19. 168⅚; Secret Consults of the Romish Party in Ireland, 1690.

brought tidings of the boundless influence which Tyrconnel exercised on Irish affairs. It was said that he was to be a Marquess, that he was to be a Duke, that he was to have the sole command of the forces, that he was to be entrusted with the task of remodelling the army and the courts of justice.* Clarendon was bitterly mortified at finding himself a subordinate member of that administration of which he had expected to be the head. He complained that whatever he did was misrepresented by his detractors, and that the gravest resolutions touching the country which he governed were adopted at Westminster, made known to the public, discussed at coffee houses, communicated in hundreds of private letters, some weeks before one hint had been given to the Lord Lieutenant. His own personal dignity, he said, mattered little : but it was no light thing that the representative of the majesty of the throne should be made an object of contempt to the people.† Panic spread fast among the English, when they found that the viceroy, their fellow countryman and fellow Protestant, was unable to extend to them the protection which they had expected from him. They began to know by bitter experience what it is to be a subject caste. They were harassed by the natives with accusations of treason and sedition. This Protestant had corresponded with Monmouth : that Protestant had said something disrespectful of the King four or five years ago, when the Exclusion Bill was under discussion ; and the evidence of the most infamous of mankind was ready to substantiate every charge. The Lord Lieutenant expressed his apprehension that, if these practices were not stopped, there would soon be at Dublin a reign of terror similar to that which he had seen in London, when every man held his life and honour at the mercy of Oates and Bedloe.‡

His mortifications.

Panic among the colonists.

Clarendon was soon informed, by a concise despatch from Sunderland, that it had been resolved to make without delay a complete change in both the civil and the military government of Ireland, and to bring a large number of Roman Catholics instantly into office. His Majesty, it was most ungraciously added, had taken counsel on these matters with persons more competent to advise him than his inexperienced Lord Lieutenant could possibly be.§

* Clarendon to Rochester, February 27. 168⅖.
† Clarendon to Rochester and Sunderland, March 2. 168⅚ ; and to Rochester, March 14.
‡ Clarendon to Sunderland, February 26. 168⅖.
§ Sunderland to Clarendon, March 11. 168⅖.

Before this letter reached the viceroy the intelligence which it contained had, through many channels, arrived in Ireland. The terror of the colonists was extreme. Outnumbered as they were by the native population, their condition would be pitiable indeed if the native population were to be armed against them with the whole power of the state; and nothing less than this was threatened. The English inhabitants of Dublin passed each other in the streets with dejected looks. On the Exchange business was suspended. Landowners hastened to sell their estates for whatever could be got, and to remit the purchase money to England. Traders began to call in their debts, and to make preparations for retiring from business. The alarm soon affected the revenue.* Clarendon attempted to inspire the dismayed settlers with a confidence which he was himself far from feeling. He assured them that their property would be held sacred, and that, to his certain knowledge, the King was fully determined to maintain the Act of Settlement which guaranteed their right to the soil. But his letters to England were in a very different strain. He ventured even to expostulate with the King, and, without blaming His Majesty's intention of employing Roman Catholics, expressed a strong opinion that the Roman Catholics who might be employed ought to be Englishmen.†

The reply of James was dry and cold. He declared that he had no intention of depriving the English colonists of their land, but that he regarded a large portion of them as his enemies, and that, since he consented to leave so much property in the hands of his enemies, it was the more necessary that the civil and military administration should be in the hands of his friends.‡

Accordingly several Roman Catholics were sworn of the Privy Council; and orders were sent to corporations to admit Roman Catholics to municipal advantages.§ Many officers of the army were arbitrarily deprived of their commissions and of their bread. It was to no purpose that the Lord Lieutenant pleaded the cause of some whom he knew to be good soldiers and loyal subjects. Among them were old Cavaliers, who had fought bravely for monarchy, and who bore the marks of honourable wounds. Their places were

* Clarendon to Rochester, March 14. 168⅚.
† Clarendon to James, March 4. 168⅚.
‡ James to Clarendon, April 6. 1686.
§ Sunderland to Clarendon, May 22. 1686; Clarendon to Ormond, May 30. Clarendon to Sunderland, July 6. 11.

supplied by men who had no recommendation but their
religion.   Of the new Captains and Lieutenants, it was
said, some had been cowherds, some footmen, some noted
marauders; some had been so used to wear brogues that they
stumbled and shuffled about strangely in their military jack
boots.   Not a few of the officers who were discarded took
refuge in the Dutch service, and enjoyed, four years later, the
pleasure of driving their successors before them in ignominious rout from the margin of the Boyne.*

The distress and alarm of Clarendon were increased by
news which reached him through private channels.   Without
his approbation, without his knowledge, preparations were
making for arming and drilling the whole Celtic population
of the country of which he was the nominal governor.   Tyrconnel from London directed the design; and the prelates of
the Roman Catholic Church were his agents.   Every priest
had been instructed to prepare an exact list of all his male
parishioners capable of bearing arms, and to forward it to
his Bishop.†

It had already been rumoured that Tyrconnel would soon
return to Dublin armed with extraordinary and independent
powers; and the rumour gathered strength daily.   The Lord
Lieutenant, whom no insult could drive to resign the pomp
and emoluments of his place, declared that he should submit
cheerfully to the royal pleasure, and approve himself in all
things a faithful and obedient subject.   He had never, he
said, in his life, had any difference with Tyrconnel, and he
trusted that no difference would now arise.‡   Clarendon appears not to have recollected that there had once been a plot
to ruin the fame of his innocent sister, and that in that plot
Tyrconnel had borne a chief part.   This is not exactly one
of the injuries which highspirited men most readily pardon.
But, in the wicked court where the Hydes had long been
pushing their fortunes, such injuries were easily forgiven and
forgotten, not from magnanimity or Christian charity, but
from mere baseness and want of moral sensibility.   In June
1686, Tyrconnel came.   His commission authorised him only   Arrival of
to command the troops: but he brought with him royal   Tyrconnel
instructions touching all parts of the administration, and at as General.

---

* Clarendon to Rochester and Sunder-   the Protestants of Ireland, 1689.
land, June 1. 1686; to Rochester, June   † Clarendon to Rochester, May 15.
12.; King's State of the Protestants of   1686.
Ireland, chap. ii. sec. 6, 7.; Apology for   ‡ Ibid. May 11. 1686.

once took the real government of the island into his own hands. On the day after his arrival he explicitly said that commissions must be largely given to Roman Catholic officers and that room must be made for them by dismissing more Protestants. He pushed on the remodelling of the army eagerly and indefatigably. It was indeed the only part of the functions of a Commander in Chief which he was competent to perform; for, though courageous in brawls and duels, he knew nothing of military duty. At the very first review which he held, it was evident to all who were near him that he did not know how to draw up a regiment.* To turn

His partiality and violence.

Englishmen out and to put Irishmen in was, in his view, the beginning and the end of the administration of war. He had the insolence to cashier the Captain of the Lord Lieutenant's own Body Guard; nor was Clarendon aware of what had happened till he saw a Roman Catholic, whose face was quite unknown to him, escorting the state coach.† The change was not confined to the officers alone. The ranks were completely broken up and recomposed. Four or five hundred soldiers were turned out of a single regiment chiefly on the ground that they were below the proper stature. Yet the most unpractised eye at once perceived that they were taller and better made men than their successors, whose wild and squalid appearance disgusted the beholders.‡ Orders were given to the new officers that no man of the Protestant religion was to be suffered to enlist. The recruiting parties, instead of beating their drums for volunteers at fairs and markets, as had been the old practice, repaired to places to which the Roman Catholics were in the habit of making pilgrimages for purposes of devotion. In a few weeks the General had introduced more than two thousand natives into the ranks; and the people about him confidently affirmed that by Christmas day not a man of English race would be left in the whole army.§

On all questions which arose in the Privy Council, Tyrconnel showed similar violence and partiality. John Keating, Chief Justice of the Common Pleas, a man distinguished by ability, integrity, and loyalty, represented with great mildness that perfect equality was all that the General could reasonably

* Clarendon to Rochester, June 8. 1686.

† Secret Consults of the Romish Party in Ireland.

‡ Clarendon to Rochester, June 26.

and July 4. 1686; Apology for the Protestants of Ireland, 1689.

§ Clarendon to Rochester, July 4. 22. 1686; to Sunderland, July 6.; to the King, August 14.

ask for his own Church. The King, he said, evidently meant that no man fit for public trust should be excluded because he was a Roman Catholic, and that no man unfit for public trust should be admitted because he was a Protestant. Tyrconnel immediately began to curse and swear. " I do not know what to say to that; I would have all Catholics in."[*] The most judicious Irishmen of his own religious persuasion were dismayed at his rashness, and ventured to remonstrate with him; but he drove them from him with imprecations.[†] His brutality was such that many thought him mad. Yet it was less strange than the shameless volubility with which he uttered falsehoods. He had long before earned the nickname of Lying Dick Talbot; and, at Whitehall, any wild fiction was commonly designated as one of Dick Talbot's truths. He now daily proved that he was well entitled to this unenviable reputation. Indeed in him mendacity was almost a disease. He would, after giving orders for the dismission of English officers, take them into his closet, assure them of his confidence and friendship, and implore Heaven to confound him, sink him, blast him, if he did not take good care of their interests. Sometimes those to whom he had thus perjured himself learned, before the day closed, that he had cashiered them.[‡]

On his arrival, though he swore savagely at the Act of Settlement, and called the English interest a foul thing, a roguish thing, and a damned thing, he yet pretended to be convinced that the distribution of property could not, after the lapse of so many years, be altered.[§] But when he had been a few weeks at Dublin, his language changed. He began to harangue vehemently at the Council board on the necessity of giving back the land to the old owners. He had not, however, as yet obtained his master's sanction to this fatal project. National feeling still struggled feebly against superstition in the mind of James. He was an Englishman: he was an English King; and he could not, without some misgivings, consent to the destruction of the greatest colony that England had ever planted. The English Roman Catholics with whom he was in the habit of taking

He is bent on the repeal of the Act of Settlement.

---

[*] Clarendon to Rochester, June 19. 1686.

[†] Ibid. June 22. 1686.

[‡] Sheridan MS.; King's State of the Protestants of Ireland, chap. iii. sec. 3.

sec. 8. There is a most striking instance of Tyrconnel's impudent mendacity in Clarendon's Letter to Rochester, July 22. 1686.

[§] Clarendon to Rochester, June 8. 1686.

counsel were almost unanimous in favour of the Act of Settlement. Not only the honest and moderate Powis, but the dissolute and headstrong Dover, gave judicious and patriotic advice. Tyrconnel could hardly hope to counteract at a distance the effect which such advice must produce on the royal mind. He determined to plead the cause of his caste in person; and accordingly he set out, at the end of August, for England.

He returns to England

His presence and his absence were equally dreaded by the Lord Lieutenant. It was, indeed, painful to be daily browbeaten by an enemy: but it was not less painful to know that an enemy was daily breathing calumny and evil counsel in the royal ear. Clarendon was overwhelmed by manifold vexations. He made a progress through the country, and found that he was everywhere treated by the Irish population with contempt. The Roman Catholic priests exhorted their congregations to withhold from him all marks of honour. The native gentry, instead of coming to pay their respects to him, remained at their houses. The native peasantry everywhere sang Celtic ballads in praise of Tyrconnel, who would, they doubted not, soon reappear to complete the humiliation of their oppressors.* The viceroy had scarcely returned to Dublin, from his unsatisfactory tour, when he received letters which informed him that he had incurred the King's serious displeasure. His Majesty,—so these letters ran,—expected his servants not only to do what he commanded, but to do it from the heart, and with a cheerful countenance. The Lord Lieutenant had not, indeed, refused to cooperate in the reform of the army and of the civil administration: but his cooperation had been reluctant and perfunctory: his looks had betrayed his feelings; and everybody saw that he disapproved of the policy which he was employed to carry into effect.† In great anguish of mind he wrote to defend himself; but he was sternly told that his defence was not satisfactory. He then, in the most abject terms, declared that he would not attempt to justify himself; that he acquiesced in the royal judgment, be it what it might; that he prostrated himself in the dust; that he implored pardon; that of all penitents he was the most sincere; that he should think it glorious to die in his Sovereign's cause, but found it impos-

The King displeased with Clarendon.

* Clarendon to Rochester, Sept. 23.   † Clarendon to Rochester October 6. and October 2. 1686; Secret Consults of   1686. the Romish Party in Ireland, 1690.

sible to live under his Sovereign's displeasure. Nor was this
mere interested hypocrisy, but, at least in part, unaffected
slavishness and poverty of spirit; for in confidential letters,
not meant for the royal eye, he bemoaned himself to his
family in the same strain.   He was miserable: he was
crushed: the wrath of the King was insupportable: if that
wrath could not be mitigated, life would not be worth
having.* The poor man's terror increased when he learned
that it had been determined at Whitehall to recall him, and
to appoint, as his successor, his rival and calumniator, Tyrconnel.† Then for a time the prospect seemed to clear: the
King was in better humour; and during a few days Clarendon
flattered himself that his brother's intercession had prevailed,
and that the crisis was passed.‡

In truth the crisis was only beginning.   While Clarendon
was trying to lean on Rochester, Rochester was unable longer
to support himself.   As in Ireland the elder brother, though
retaining the guard of honour, the sword of state, and the
title of Excellency, had really been superseded by the Commander of the Forces, so in England, the younger brother,
though holding the white staff, and walking, by virtue of his
high office, before the greatest hereditary nobles, was fast
sinking into a mere financial clerk.   The Parliament was
again prorogued to a distant day, in opposition to the
Treasurer's known wishes.   He was not even told that there
was to be another prorogation, but was left to learn the news
from the Gazette.   The real direction of affairs had passed
to the cabal which dined with Sunderland on Fridays.   The
cabinet met only to hear the despatches from foreign courts
read ; nor did those despatches contain anything which was
not known on the Royal Exchange; for all the English
Envoys had received orders to put into the official letters
only the common talk of antechambers, and to reserve important secrets for private communications which were addressed to James himself, to Sunderland, or to Petre.§   Yet
the victorious faction was not content.   The King was
assured by those whom he most trusted that the obstinacy
with which the nation opposed his designs was really to
be imputed to Rochester.   How could the people believe that

Marginal note: Rochester attacked by the Jesuitical cabal.

---

* Clarendon to the King and to Rochester, October 23. 1686.

† Clarendon to Rochester, October 29,
30. 1686.

‡ Clarendon to Rochester, November
27. 1686,

§ Barillon, Sept. $\frac{13}{23}$. 1686; Life of
James the Second, ii. 99.

their Sovereign was unalterably resolved to persevere in the
course on which he had entered, when they saw at his right
hand, ostensibly first in power and trust among his counsellors, a man who notoriously regarded that course with strong
disapprobation? Every step which had been taken with the
object of humbling the Church of England and of elevating
the Church of Rome, had been opposed by the Treasurer.
True it was that, when he had found opposition vain, he had
gloomily submitted, nay, that he had sometimes even assisted
in carrying into effect the very plans against which he had
most earnestly contended. True it was that, though he
disliked the Ecclesiastical Commission, he had consented to
be a Commissioner. True it was that he had, while declaring
that he could see nothing blamable in the conduct of the
Bishop of London, voted sullenly and reluctantly for the
sentence of suspension. But this was not enough. A prince,
engaged in an enterprise so important and arduous as that
on which James was bent, had a right to expect from his
first minister, not unwilling and ungracious acquiescence,
but zealous and strenuous cooperation. While such advice
was daily given to James by those in whom he reposed confidence, he received, by the penny post, many anonymous
letters filled with calumnies against the Lord Treasurer.
This mode of attack had been contrived by Tyrconnel, and
was in perfect harmony with every part of his infamous life.*

The King hesitated. He seems, indeed, to have really
regarded his brother in law with personal kindness, the effect
of near affinity, of long and familiar intercourse, and of
many mutual good offices. It seemed probable that, as long
as Rochester continued to submit himself, though tardily and
with murmurs, to the royal· pleasure, he would continue to
be in name prime minister. Sunderland, therefore, with
exquisite cunning, suggested to his master the propriety of
asking the only proof of obedience which it was quite certain
that Rochester never would give. At present,—such was
the language of the artful Secretary,—it was impossible to
consult with the first of the King's servants respecting the
object nearest to the King's heart. It was lamentable to
think that religious prejudices should, at such a conjuncture,
deprive the government of such valuable assistance. Perhaps those prejudices might not prove insurmountable.
Then the deceiver whispered that, to his knowledge, Ro-

* Sheridan MS.

chester had of late had some misgivings about the points in
dispute between the Protestants and Catholics.* This was
enough. The King eagerly caught at the hint. He began Attempts of James to convert Rochester.
to flatter himself that he might at once escape from the
disagreeable necessity of removing a friend, and secure an
able coadjutor for the great work which was in progress.
He was also elated by the hope that he might have the merit
and the glory of saving a fellow creature from perdition. He
seems, indeed, about this time, to have been seized with an
unusually violent fit of zeal for his religion ; and this is the
more remarkable, because he had just relapsed, after a short
interval of selfrestraint, into debauchery which all Christian
divines condemn as sinful, and which, in an elderly man
married to an agreeable young wife, is regarded even by
people of the world as disreputable. Lady Dorchester had
returned from Dublin, and was again the King's mistress.
Her return was politically of no importance. She had
learned by experience the folly of attempting to save her
lover from the destruction to which he was running headlong.
She therefore suffered the Jesuits to guide his political conduct ; and they, in return, suffered her to wheedle him out
of money. She was, however, only one of several abandoned
women who at this time shared, with his beloved Church,
the dominion over his mind.† He seems to have determined
to make some amends for neglecting the welfare of his own
soul by taking care of the souls of others. He set himself,
therefore, to labour, with real good will, but with the good
will of a coarse, stern, and arbitrary mind, for the conversion
of his kinsman. Every audience which the Treasurer obtained was spent in arguments about the authority of the
Church and the worship of images. Rochester was firmly
resolved not to abjure his religion : but he had no scruple
about employing in selfdefence artifices as discreditable as
those which had been used against him. He affected to
speak like a man whose mind was not made up, professed
himself desirous to be enlightened if he was in error, borrowed Popish books, and listened with civility to Popish
divines. He had several interviews with Leyburn, the Vicar
Apostolic, with Godden, the chaplain and almoner of the
Queen Dowager, and with Bonaventure Giffard, a theologian
trained to polemics in the schools of Douay. It was agreed

* Life of James the Second, ii. 100.
† Barillon, Sept. 13/23. 1686 ; Bonrepaux, June 4. 1687.

that there should be a formal disputation between these doctors and some Protestant clergymen. The King told Rochester to choose any ministers of the Established Church, with two exceptions. The proscribed persons were Tillotson and Stillingfleet. Tillotson, the most popular preacher of that age, and in manners the most inoffensive of men, had been much connected with some leading Whigs; and Stillingfleet, who was renowned as a consummate master of all the weapons of controversy, had given still deeper offence by publishing an answer to the papers which had been found in the strong box of Charles the Second. Rochester took the two royal chaplains who happened to be in waiting. One of them was Simon Patrick, whose commentaries on the Bible still form a part of theological libraries : the other was Jane, a vehement Tory, who had assisted in drawing up that decree by which the University of Oxford had solemnly adopted the worst follies of Filmer. The conference took place at Whitehall on the thirtieth of November. Rochester, who did not wish it to be known that he had even consented to hear the arguments of Popish priests, stipulated for secrecy. No auditor was suffered to be present except the King. The subject discussed was the real presence. The Roman Catholic divines took on themselves the burden of the proof. Patrick and Jane said little ; nor was it necessary that they should say much ; for the Earl himself undertook to defend the doctrine of his Church, and, as was his habit, soon warmed with conflict, lost his temper, and asked with great vehemence whether it was expected that he should change his religion on such frivolous grounds. Then he remembered how much he was risking, began again to dissemble, complimented the disputants on their skill and learning, and asked time to consider what had been said.*

Slow as James was, he could not but see that this was mere trifling. He told Barillon that Rochester's language was not that of a man honestly desirous of arriving at the truth. Still the King did not like to propose directly to his brother in law the simple choice, apostasy or dismissal : but, three days after the conference, Barillon waited on the Treasurer, and, with much circumlocution and many expres-

* Barillon, Dec. ²/₁₂. 1686 ; Burnet, i. 684. ; Life of James the Second, ii. 100. ; Dodd's Church History. I have tried to frame a fair narrative out of these conflicting materials. It seems clear to me, from Rochester's own papers, that he was on this occasion by no means so stubborn as he has been represented by Burnet and by the biographer of James.

sions of friendly concern, broke the unpleasant truth. " Do you mean," said Rochester, bewildered by the involved and ceremonious phrases in which the intimation was made, " that, if I do not turn Catholic, the consequence will be that I shall lose my place ? " " I say nothing about consequences," answered the wary diplomatist. " I only come as a friend to express a hope that you will take care to keep your place." " But surely," said Rochester, " the plain meaning of all this is that I must turn Catholic or go out." He put many questions for the purpose of ascertaining whether the communication was made by authority, but could extort only vague and mysterious replies. At last, affecting a confidence which he was far from feeling, he declared that Barillon must have been imposed upon by idle or malicious reports. " I tell you," he said, " that the King will not dismiss me, and I will not resign. I know him : he knows me ; and I fear nobody." The Frenchman answered that he was charmed, that he was ravished to hear it, and that his only motive for interfering was a sincere anxiety for the prosperity and dignity of his excellent friend the Treasurer. And thus the two statesmen parted, each flattering himself that he had duped the other.*

Meanwhile, in spite of all injunctions of secrecy, the news that the Lord Treasurer had consented to be instructed in the doctrines of Popery had spread fast through London. Patrick and Jane had been seen going in at that mysterious door which led to Chiffinch's apartments. Some Roman Catholics about the Court had, indiscreetly or artfully, told all, and more than all, that they knew. The Tory churchmen waited anxiously for fuller information. They were mortified to think that their leader should even have pretended to waver in his opinion ; but they could not believe that he would stoop to be a renegade. The unfortunate minister, tortured at once by his fierce passions and his low desires, annoyed by the censures of the public, annoyed by the hints which he had received from Barillon, afraid of losing character, afraid of losing office, repaired to the royal closet. He was determined to keep his place, if it could be kept by any villany but one. He would pretend to be shaken in his religious opinions, and to be half a convert : he would promise to give strenuous support to that policy which he had hitherto opposed : but, if he were driven to extremity, he

* From Rochester's Minutes, dated Dec. 3. 1686.

would refuse to change his religion. He began, therefore, by telling the King that the business in which His Majesty took so much interest was not sleeping, that Jane and Giffard were engaged in consulting books on the points in dispute between the Churches, and that, when these researches were over, it would be desirable to have another conference. Then he complained bitterly that all the town was apprised of what ought to have been carefully concealed, and that some persons, who, from their station, might be supposed to be well informed, reported strange things as to the royal intentions. "It is whispered," he said, "that, if I do not do as Your Majesty would have me, I shall not be suffered to continue in my present station." The King said, with some general expressions of kindness, that it was difficult to prevent people from talking, and that loose reports were not to be regarded. These vague phrases were not likely to quiet the perturbed mind of the minister. His agitation became violent, and he began to plead for his place as if he had been pleading for his life. "Your Majesty sees that I do all in my power to obey you. Indeed I will do all that I can to obey you in everything. I will serve you in your own way. Nay," he cried, in an agony of baseness, "I will do what I can to believe as you would have me. But do not let me be told, while I am trying to bring my mind to this, that, if I find it impossible to comply, I must lose all. For I must needs tell Your Majesty that there are other considerations." "Oh, you must needs," exclaimed the King with an oath. For a single word of honest and manly sound, escaping in the midst of all this abject supplication, was sufficient to move his anger. "I hope, sir," said poor Rochester, "that I do not offend you. Surely Your Majesty could not think well of me if I did not say so." The King recollected himself, protested that he was not offended, and advised the Treasurer to disregard idle rumours, and to confer again with Jane and Giffard.*

Dismission of Rochester.

After this conversation a fortnight elapsed before the decisive blow fell. That fortnight Rochester passed in intriguing and imploring. He attempted to interest in his favour those Roman Catholics who had the greatest influence at court. He could not, he said, renounce his own religion : but, with that single reservation, he would do all that they could desire. Indeed, if he might only keep his place, they should find that he could be more useful to them as a Protestant

* From Rochester's Minutes, Dec. 4. 1686.

than as one of their own communion.* His wife, who was
on a sick bed, had already, it was said, solicited the honour
of a visit from the much injured Queen, and had attempted
to work on her Majesty's feelings of compassion.† But the
Hydes abased themselves in vain. Petre regarded them with
peculiar malevolence, and was bent on their ruin.‡ On the
evening of the seventeenth of December the Earl was called
into the royal closet. James was unusually discomposed,
and even shed tears. The occasion, indeed, could not but
call up some recollections which might well soften a hard
heart. He expressed his regret that his duty made it impossible for him to indulge his private partialities. It was
absolutely necessary, he said, that those who had the chief
direction of his affairs should partake his opinions and feelings. He owned that he had very great personal obligations
to Rochester, and that no fault could be found with the way
in which the financial business had lately been done : but the
office of Lord Treasurer was of such high importance that, in
general, it ought not to be entrusted to a single person, and
could not safely be entrusted by a Roman Catholic King to a
person zealous for the Church of England. "Think better
of it, my Lord," he continued. "Read again the papers
from my brother's box. I will give you a little more time
for consideration, if you desire it." Rochester saw that all
was over, and that the wisest course left to him was to make
his retreat with as much money and as much credit as possible. He succeeded in both objects. He obtained a pension
of four thousand pounds a year for two lives on the post
office. He had made great sums out of the estates of traitors,
and carried with him in particular Grey's bond for forty
thousand pounds, and a grant of all the estate which the
crown had in Grey's extensive property.§ No person had
ever quitted office on terms so advantageous. To the applause of the sincere friends of the Established Church
Rochester had, indeed, very slender claims. To save his
place he had sate in that tribunal which had been illegally
created for the purpose of persecuting her. To save his place
he had given a dishonest vote for degrading one of her most
eminent ministers, had affected to doubt her orthodoxy, had

* Barillon, Dec. $\frac{20}{30}$. 1686.

† Burnet, i. 684.

‡ Bonrepaux, $\frac{May\ 25.}{June\ 4.}$ 1687.

§ Rochester's Minutes, Dec. 19. 1686 ;

Barillon, $\frac{Dec.\ 30.}{Jan.\ 9.}$ 168$\frac{6}{7}$; Burnet, i. 685. :
Life of James the Second, ii. 102. ; Trea-
sury Warrant Book, December 29. 1686.

listened with the outward show of docility to teachers who
called her schismatical and heretical, and had offered to cooperate strenuously with her deadliest enemies in their designs against her. The highest praise to which he was
entitled was this, that he had shrunk from the exceeding
wickedness and baseness of publicly abjuring, for lucre, the
religion in which he had been brought up, which he believed
to be true, and of which he had long made an ostentatious
profession. Yet he was extolled by the great body of Churchmen as if he had been the bravest and purest of martyrs.
The Old and New Testaments, the Martyrologies of Eusebius
and of Fox, were ransacked to find parallels for his heroic
piety. He was Daniel in the den of Lions, Shadrach in the
fiery furnace, Peter in the dungeon of Herod, Paul at the bar
of Nero, Ignatius in the amphitheatre, Latimer at the stake.
Among the many facts which prove that the standard of
honour and virtue among the public men of that age was low,
the admiration excited by Rochester's constancy is, perhaps,
the most decisive.

Dismission
of Claren-
don.
In his fall he dragged down Clarendon. On the seventh
of January 1687, the Gazette announced to the people of
London that the Treasury was put into commission. On the
eighth arrived at Dublin a despatch formally signifying that
Tyrconnel
Lord
Deputy.
in a month Tyrconnel would assume the government of Ireland. It was not without great difficulty that this man had
surmounted the numerous impediments which stood in the
way of his ambition. It was well known that the extermina-
tion of the English colony in Ireland was the object on which
his heart was set. He had, therefore, to overcome some
scruples in the royal mind. He had to surmount the opposition, not merely of all the Protestant members of the government, not merely of the moderate and respectable heads of
the Roman Catholic body, but even of several members of
the Jesuitical cabal.* Sunderland shrank from the thought
of an Irish revolution, religious, political, and social. To the
Queen Tyrconnel was personally an object of aversion. Powis
was therefore suggested as the man best qualified for the

---

* Bishop Malony in a letter to Bishop
Tyrrel says, "Never a Catholic or other
English will ever think or make a step,
nor suffer the King to make a step for
your restauration, but leave you as you
were hitherto, and leave your enemies
over your heads ; nor is there any Englishman, Catholic or other, of what quality or degree soever alive, that will stick
to sacrifice all Ireland for to save the
least interest of his own in England, and
would as willingly see all Ireland over
inhabited by English of whatsoever religion as by the Irish."

viceroyalty. He was of illustrious birth: he was a sincere
Roman Catholic; and yet he was generally allowed by candid
Protestants to be an honest man and a good Englishman.
All opposition, however, yielded to Tyrconnel's energy and
cunning. He fawned, bullied, and bribed indefatigably.
Petre's help was secured by flattery. Sunderland was plied
at once with promises and menaces. An immense price was
offered for his support, no less than an annuity of five thousand pounds a year from Ireland, redeemable by payment of
fifty thousand pounds down. If this proposal were rejected,
Tyrconnel threatened to let the King know that the Lord
President had, at the Friday dinners, described His Majesty
as a fool who must be governed either by a woman or by a
priest. Sunderland, pale and trembling, offered to procure
for Tyrconnel supreme military command, enormous appointments, anything but the viceroyalty: but all compromise
was rejected; and it was necessary to yield. Mary of Modena
herself was not free from suspicion of corruption. There was
in London a renowned chain of pearls which was valued at
ten thousand pounds. It had belonged to Prince Rupert;
and by him it had been left to Margaret Hughes, a courtesan
who, towards the close of his life, had exercised a boundless
empire over him. Tyrconnel loudly boasted that with this
chain he had purchased the support of the Queen. There
were those, however, who suspected that this story was one
of Dick Talbot's truths, and that it had no more foundation
than the calumnies which, twenty-six years before, he had
invented to blacken the fame of Anne Hyde. To the Roman
Catholic courtiers generally he spoke of the uncertain tenure
by which they held offices, honours, and emoluments. The
King might die tomorrow, and might leave them at the
mercy of a hostile government and a hostile rabble. But, if
the old faith could be made dominant in Ireland, if the Protestant interest in that country could be destroyed, there
would still be, in the worst event, an asylum at hand to
which they might retreat, and where they might either
negotiate or defend themselves with advantage. A Popish
priest was hired with the promise of the mitre of Waterford
to preach at Saint James's against the Act of Settlement;
and his sermon, though heard with deep disgust by the
English part of the auditory, was not without its effect. The
struggle which patriotism had for a time maintained against

bigotry in the royal mind was at an end. "There is work to be done in Ireland," said James, "which no Englishman will do."*

All obstacles were at length removed; and in February 1687, Tyrconnel began to rule his native country with the power and appointments of Lord Lieutenant, but with the humbler title of Lord Deputy.

Dismay of the English colonists in Ireland. His arrival spread dismay through the whole English population. Clarendon was accompanied, or speedily followed, across Saint George's Channel, by a large proportion of the most respectable inhabitants of Dublin, gentlemen, tradesmen, and artificers. It was said that fifteen hundred families emigrated in a few days. The panic was not unreasonable. The work of putting the colonists down under the feet of the natives went rapidly on. In a short time almost every Privy Councillor, Judge, Sheriff, Mayor, Alderman, and Justice of the Peace was a Celt and a Roman Catholic. It seemed that things would soon be ripe for a general election, and that a House of Commons bent on abrogating the Act of Settlement would easily be assembled.† Those who had lately been the lords of the island now cried out, in the bitterness of their souls, that they had become a prey and a laughing-stock to their own serfs and menials; that houses were burnt and cattle stolen with impunity; that the new soldiers roamed the country, pillaging, insulting, ravishing, maiming, tossing one Protestant in a blanket, tying up another by the hair and scourging him; that to appeal to the law was vain; that Irish Judges, Sheriffs, juries, and witnesses were all in a league to save Irish criminals; and that, even without an Act of Parliament, the whole soil would soon change hands, for that, in every action of ejectment tried under the administration of Tyrconnel, judgment had been given for the native against the Englishman.‡

While Clarendon was at Dublin the Privy Seal had been in the hands of Commissioners. His friends hoped that it would, on his return to London, be again delivered to him. But the King and the Jesuitical cabal had determined that the disgrace of the Hydes should be complete. Lord Arundell of Wardour, a Roman Catholic, obtained the Privy Seal.

---

* The best account of these transactions is in the Sheridan MS.

† Sheridan MS.; Oldmixon's Memoirs of Ireland; King's State of the Protestants of Ireland, particularly chapter iii.;

Apology for the Protestants of Ireland, 1689.

‡ Secret Consults of the Romish Party in Ireland, 1690.

Bellasyse, a Roman Catholic, was made First Lord of the Treasury; and Dover, another Roman Catholic, had a seat at the board. The appointment of a ruined gambler to such a trust would alone have sufficed to disgust the public. The dissolute Etherege, who then resided at Ratisbon as English envoy, could not refrain from expressing, with a sneer, his hope that his old boon companion, Dover, would keep the King's money better than his own. In order that the finances might not be ruined by incapable and inexperienced Papists, the obsequious, diligent and silent Godolphin was named a Commissioner of the Treasury, but continued to be Chamberlain to the Queen.*

The dismission of the two brothers is a great epoch in the reign of James. From that time it was clear that what he really wanted was not liberty of conscience for the members of his own church, but liberty to persecute the members of other churches. Pretending to abhor tests, he had himself imposed a test. He thought it hard, he thought it monstrous, that able and loyal men should be excluded from the public service solely for being Roman Catholics. Yet he had himself turned out of office a Treasurer, whom he admitted to be both loyal and able, solely for being a Protestant. The cry was that a general proscription was at hand, and that every public functionary must make up his mind to lose his soul or to lose his place.† Who indeed could hope to stand where the Hydes had fallen? They were the brothers in law of the King, the uncles and natural guardians of his children, his friends from early youth, his steady adherents in adversity and peril, his obsequious servants since he had been on the throne. Their sole crime was their religion; and for this crime they had been discarded. In great perturbation men began to look round for help; and soon all eyes were fixed on one whom a rare concurrence both of personal qualities and of fortuitous circumstances pointed out as the deliverer.

Effect of the fall of the Hydes.

* London Gazette, Jan. 6. and March 14. 168$\frac{6}{7}$; Evelyn's Diary, March 10. Etherege's letter to Dover is in the British Museum.

† "Pare che gli animi sono inaspriti della voce che corre per il popolo, d'esser cacciato il detto ministro per non essere Cattolico, perciò tirarsi al esterminio de' Protestanti."— Adda, $\frac{Dec. 31.}{Jan. 10.}$ 1687.

This book, designed by
Eric Tschumi,
is a production of
Heron Books, London

Printed in Switzerland